Charlemagne & France

The Laura Shannon Series in French Medieval Studies

CHARLEMAGNE & France

A Thousand Years of Mythology

ROBERT MORRISSEY

translated by
CATHERINE TIHANYI

University of Notre Dame Press
Notre Dame, Indiana

Manufactured in the United States of America

Translated by Catherine Tihanyi from *L'Empereur à la barbe fleurie:
Charlemagne dans la mythologie et l'histoire de France* by Robert Morrissey,
published by Éditions Gallimard, Paris, France.

© Éditions Gallimard, 1997

The publisher is grateful to
THE FRENCH MINISTRY OF CULTURE — CENTRE NATIONAL DU LIVRE
for support of the costs of translation.

Library of Congress Cataloging-in-Publication Data
Morrissey, Robert John, 1947–
[Empereur à la barbe fleurie, English]
Charlemagne and France : a thousand years of mythology / Robert Morrissey ;
translated by Catherine Tihanyi.
p.   cm. — (The Laura Shannon series in French medieval studies)
Includes index.
ISBN 0-268-02277-1
1. Charlemagne, Emperor, 742–814—Influence.   2. Holy Roman
Empire—Kings and rulers—Biography.   3. Civilization, Medieval.
4. Charlemagne, Emperor, 742–814—Legends—History and criticism.
5. Charlemagne, Emperor, 742–814—Romances—History and criticism.
6. Charlemagne, Emperor, 742–814—In literature.   I. Title.   II. Series.
DC73 .M7513   2003
944'.014'092 — dc21

2002013900

To my tribe . . .

CONTENTS

ACKNOWLEDGMENTS

The idea for this book came out of a University of Chicago seminar on culture and politics in modern France that I led with the historian Keith Baker; many of his ideas and comments echo in this work. I am also indebted to the great medievalist Peter Dembowski, with whom I led several seminars and who has always generously shared his remarkable philosophical knowledge. I would also like to acknowledge the important contribution of the historian and publisher Pierre Nora, who was of great assistance in the early stages of the work.

I would like to express my gratitude to those who read all or part of this work and contributed their suggestions, critiques, and valuable information. In the field of medieval studies, I thank Michael Allen, Emmanuèle Baumgartner, Sylvia Huot, and Steven Maddux; in the field of literary studies, Marc Fumaroli, Henri Mitterand, Jacques Neefs, Thomas Pavel, and François Rigolot; and in the fields of history and political science, François Furet, Colin Lucas, Krzysztof Pomian, Jean-Luc Pouthier, Pierre Rosanvallon, and William Sewell.

I also wish to thank the students at the University of Chicago who participated in the many seminars related to different aspects of my research. Among others, I would like to single out Daniel Gordon, Margaret Jewett, Stephane Gerson, and Kent Wright. My assistants, Audra Dianora, James Miller, and John Iverson, have also been of great help.

I express my deepest gratitude for the loyalty and work of Marie-Agnès Crosnier, who has taken the time to carefully read every draft of the manuscript. I thank Henrianne Rouselle, who, through faxes and phone calls seemed to shorten the distance between us in order to prepare the original French manuscript for publication. Thanks are due as well to Teresa Fagan for her work on the translation.

Finally, with all my heart I thank my wife, Marie-Claire, whose constant support, critical intelligence, and smile have enabled me to successfully complete this work.

ILLUSTRATIONS

21 Ary Scheffer, *Charlemagne Presents His First Capitularies to the Assembly of the Franks in 779*, 1827, Musée de Versailles. © Réunion des Musées Nationaux/Art Resource, New York (see p. 272).

22 *The Works of Charlemagne*, engraving by L. Pouzargues from G. Gautherot, *Histoire de France*. Used by permission of the Archives Charmet/Bridgeman Art Library (see p. 299).

23 *Saint Charlemagne, the Patron of Scholars*, 1892. Engraving appeared in the *Petit Journal illustré*. Used by permission of Archives Charmet/Bridgeman Art Library (see p. 299).

24. Louis Rochet (1867–1875), equestrian statue of Charlemagne outside the Cathedral of Notre Dame, Paris. Photograph by Raymond Depardon. Used by permission of Magnum Photos (see pp. 294–5).

INTRODUCTION

"Charlemagne, claimed by the Church as a saint, by the French as their greatest king, by the Germans as their compatriot, by the Italians as their emperor, heads all modern histories in one way or another; he is the creator of a new order of things. . . ."[1] In his *Histoire des Français* (1821), Sismondi indeed grasped the polyvalent nature and symbolic importance of the emperor *à la barbe fleurie*, the emperor with the flowing white beard.[2] Sismondi wrote at a time when France was in search of its roots, of continuity, of an enduring identity. Following the Revolution's radical attempts to banish history, to break away from it, to escape history by denying it, post-Revolutionary France was eagerly restoring it. In fact, it is clear that the passion for remembering is reborn and renewed each time France redefines itself. Now, as a new Europe is being created, such a passion is again manifesting itself in the many studies on French identity that have been published in the last few years.

In this book I examine the way in which the French have adopted as their own a figure who throughout history has been claimed by other countries and institutions. "The emperor with the flowing white beard": every French child learns of him in the earliest days of elementary school. Appearing in every school book, the emperor known as the founder of schools is one of the most popular figures in historical folklore. And yet, the idea of placing Charlemagne at the heart of a French mythology might seem strange, since he is certainly no longer one of the primary points of reference in the collective identity of France today. Things were quite different before the twentieth century. Indeed, looking back, we discover that Charlemagne was a figure with whom the French identified quite strongly. From the time of his reign to the end of the nineteenth century, France was continually defined and redefined with reference to Charlemagne. His symbolic power derived from several sources. The range of activities on which Charlemagne left an enduring mark—military exploits, the writing of laws or "capitularies," his activities in support of a revival of letters and education, his relationship with the Church, his establishment of an empire—have made him a legitimizing point of reference that appears time and again in many different realms of study. As Sismondi rightly says, the great conqueror appears "at the beginning of all modern histories." Evoking the figure of Charlemagne becomes not only a way of imagining and legitimizing one's origins, but is also a way of doing so in relation to the Other. It is a way of examining and determining the limits between self and other and of affirming or contesting different, and at times even contradictory, solidarities and modes of belonging.

Charlemagne is not only a historical figure. His life has inspired a host of epic myths and legends, a "poetical" dimension that has magnified his symbolic power. For the epic provides a dynamic representation of power and its exercise, a visualization that enables us to question the limits of power and the way that it functions. And although *chansons de geste* are no longer written, later interpretations of such legends and poems play a crucial role in defining and redefining the nation. To the French, wrote Gaston Paris in 1865, "the figure of Charlemagne, as conceived in national poetry, forever becomes the most complete symbol of the genius of a people, the sum of its aspirations, the embodiment of its ideal."[3]

Charlemagne's persona thus assumes a foundational or "constitutive/constitutional" value insofar as for more than ten centuries it was deemed useful and important to demonstrate that the national privileges being claimed, the activities being undertaken, indeed the view of France being defended could all be traced back to Charlemagne. His symbolic power derives from his being a privileged locus in whom myth, history, and poetry meet and blend together.

This figure's extraordinary plasticity becomes evident when we trace its manifestations through the course of history. Such plasticity endows the figure with both legitimizing power and subversive potential in that it enables that figure to bring together elements that normally would appear to be mutually exclusive. Because of this, Charlemagne's figure is deployed not only to prove the historical depth of one's roots and to demonstrate conformity to the greatness of an unparalleled moment in history, but also to demand radical social and political changes in the name of the original framing principles guiding the collectivity. This powerful topos of an originary moment thus becomes an ideal site for exploring the difference between what we *should be* and what we *have become*, for measuring the distance between the purity of origins and the decadence brought on by history.

Psychoanalysis has taught us that in order to know ourselves, to know our history (which in a way is the same thing), and to be masters of it insofar as this is possible, we need to be aware not only of that which has triumphed, but also of that which has failed, of that which has been dismissed, or repressed. Hence, studying powerful representations of originary moments with a view to understanding their function within the social body might well lead to greater self-knowledge. There are thus definite benefits to be derived from exploring Charlemagne's "case" at a time when he has ceased to be at the center of France's collective identity. The waning of Charlemagne's legitimating influence provides us with a critical distance that can help us better unveil and understand, simultaneously on several different planes, the mechanisms of reappropriation and redeployment of the past. Through Charlemagne's enduring presence we discover the links that connect successive political forms—monarchy, empire, and republic; constantly evolving fundamental themes—universality, sovereignty, religion, and origins; endlessly reconfiguring and regenerating central entities—Europe, Christendom, Rome, Italy, Spain, France, and Germany; the emerging play of magnetic poles—the North and the South—that are constantly and alternatively exerting their pull in opposite directions; and, finally, the ways in which a social collectivity has focused on an individual who is seen as transcending all others.

Because the present study is located at the juncture of myth, history, and poetics, it provides a "concrete" take on the relations within a set of practices where history, literature, and politics meet: erudition and interpretation, poetry and ideology, solidarity and protest. In the course of this study I move constantly from one level to another, carried by the discursive developments and the most significant productions.

This book is divided into two parts that correspond to what might be characterized as the two fundamental cycles in the history of Charlemagne's representation. The first part or cycle begins shortly after the great emperor's death and continues until the end of the sixteenth century: it goes from an epic and legitimizing vision of his reign to a radical critique of the fabulous aspect of that history, a critique that led to the rejection of Charlemagne as an essential legitimizing referent. But the seeds engendering a remythologizing of Charlemagne were sown in Renaissance and Reformation France in the context of the violence of the wars of religion. I describe this process in Part II. In the face of rising absolutism, the figure of Charlemagne resurfaces as an alternative image, a counterpower imbued with a timeless legitimacy nurtured by representations created during the first cycle. Thus the first historical cycle engenders the second, and we must understand it first in order to grasp the logic and necessity of Charlemagne's return. The enduring quality of the millenarian reference makes it possible to use him to imagine a collective self different from the one arising out of the Capetian monarchy. Transformed into a subject of curiosity, erudition, and study, Charlemagne's time became a key element in the metamorphosis of the Middle Ages into what might be called the antiquity of modernity, a vision challenging the primacy of classical antiquity. The power of this representation was to remain effective until the first years of the Third Republic.

The "myth-history" of the great founding hero underwent moments of flux and reflux in the course of a trajectory starting with the first evocations of the emperor of the West. Thus, as I pursued this history, I was forced to choose from among these representations and their uses throughout time. Yet, in spite of this selectivity, it was important to show the diversity of the fields of representation, the continuity of tradition, the mechanisms and processes of transformation, and the interaction between the different fields. This said, it was not possible to describe in exhaustive detail the many ways the figure of Charlemagne has been used, as this would have required separate full-length studies of each century of the Middle Ages and beyond.

In Part I, I focus on constitutive elements that stand out due to their forcefulness as well as to their importance in relation to later evocations. The first two chapters in particular focus on certain key texts that serve as sources for later reconstructions, variants, and interpretations. These initial analyses are more textual than contextual, as they serve to establish boundaries for later fields of interpretation and to locate the constitutive elements of the topos. My aim in this part is to look at enduring elements rather than explore the details of how they were created. In contrast, I devote more time to contextual circumstances when examining the subsequent uses of these primary sources. In other words, in order to understand the significance of evocations of Charlemagne in modern history, we must begin with some understanding of what the source texts actually say. In the course of this study, I focus increasing attention on the context of production, a movement that corresponds to that of the emergence of a modern critical consciousness of history. From a methodological standpoint, the last two chapters of the first part form the turning point of the book, introducing the dialectic between what is said (*le dire*) and what is meant (*le vouloir-dire*), between the documents and the conditions of their production, between texts and contexts.

Throughout this long history, the entity that is France never ceases to redefine and reinvent itself. As we look at these constantly changing identities, the distance between the kingdom of the Franks and the kingdom of France might make them appear to be two entirely different lands. And yet, the word *Francia* with its constellation of meanings, traditions, and heroes was passed down to a France that retained it as an essential referent. At the heart of this legacy, the figure of Charlemagne stands out. Whether France has assumed the traits of a kingdom, a nation, or an empire, whether it has been a monarchy or a republic, whether its territory has expanded or shrunk, whether it has invaded its neighbors or has retreated behind its "natural boundaries," this entity, which is never quite the same nor entirely different from itself, has acquired a unity conferred by memory. In following representations of Charlemagne throughout the history of France we obtain a better understanding of how the modern nation-state has emerged out of the Ancien Régime, and a better grasp of the extent to which the French Revolution began and ended under the appearance of a return to distant origins.

Today, as nationalism is once again reasserting itself, a study of how history has been reappropriated might enable us to avoid the sort of blind adherence to dogma that has led to so much abuse. Perhaps, as we create a new Europe, a close study of the avatars of that which, in many respects, formed the most powerful discourse on origins might enable us to live *another* history instead of yet again reliving the past.

In the course of this work, I was faced with a number of different French languages. I have occasionally modernized the spelling of quotes so as to make them easier to read. I have sought to remain faithful to the aim of this study and most of the time have used those works that were available to nineteenth-century readers, including Guizot's translations in his *Collection des mémoires relatifs à l'histoire de France*.

In this American edition there are a few changes. I have corrected some mis-typings and some factual errors found in the original French edition. I have added to the notes of the translation some additional works not included in the French original. For reasons of cost and space, there is no bibliography. A complete bibliography on the subject would in itself take several volumes. However, all authors cited in the text or in the notes are listed in the index. I have not attempted to cite all the works I consulted, but only those that were most important to me in the context of this project.

PART ONE

BETWEEN MYTH
AND
HISTORY

ONE

The Magic of Origins

BEGINNINGS REVISITED

We never tire of pondering the question of origins. Sometimes we do so only to reject it, to declare it irrelevant, claiming the issue is outdated, useless to explain the structures that rule the present. At other times we broach the subject in order to explore the past as a source from which everything flows, as a privileged moment of crystallization that has determined, or has at least informed, everything that later followed. The search for roots as well as their rejection are two poles tugging at a dialectical pendulum in perpetual motion, as if a passion for embraces should unavoidably lead to a divorce followed by a new desire for rapprochement. A curiosity about the past as well as a rejection of it are in every case rooted in the present. As Michel de Certeau puts it, the present is the true beginning of any evocation of the past.[1]

I would like to open this study with three descriptions of a similar attempt to revisit an originary moment, three representations of a return to beginnings where the line of demarcation between worship and violation remains unclear. These include two portrayals, one a text and the other an image, as well as a "primary source," all three describing the same scene of a return to the past. I have chosen them for their emblematic value, for the striking way they raise the question at the heart of this book, that is, the representation of an originary figure, its unfolding, and its function throughout time.

In a passage from his *Mémoires d'outre-tombe*, a work that has much to say about a "legitimate" past for future generations, Chateaubriand ponders the dangers incurred by the *Restauration*, the restored reign of the French monarchy after the Revolution, in its obsession with reclaiming the past. Pursued with the acute consciousness of someone who drew his fundamental values from a sense of tradition, Chateaubriand's reflection evokes the richness of a vision of the past but also, and perhaps above all, the past's precarious relation to the present as he takes up the motif of the tomb and weaves it into his memories "from beyond the grave."

> Let us respect the majesty of time; let us contemplate past centuries with reverence, centuries that memory and the vestiges of our fathers made sacred; and yet . . . we should not try to go back to them. They no longer hold any part of our true nature, and if we tried to grasp them they would disappear. It is said that around the year 1450 the Chapter of Our Lady of Aix-la-Chapelle [Aachen] had Charlemagne's tomb opened. The emperor was found seated on a golden chair, his skeleton's hands holding the Gospels written in golden letters; his golden scepter and shield had been placed in front of him; at his side was his sword Joyeuse in its golden sheath. He was dressed in the imperial clothes. His head, held up by a golden chain, was covered with a shroud that hid what had been his face. The shroud was topped by a crown. Someone touched the ghostly remains: they disintegrated into dust.[2]

The iconographic richness overflowing with the symbols of faith and power, along with the seemingly forceful presence of this emperor equipped with all the trappings of his might, proves to be fragile. Nothing remains but a phantom of legitimacy: by attempting to seize it, we only destroy it. Here the meaning of history is grasped in the act of looking at a "real" and present object: Charlemagne's remains. It is sight rather than touch or abstract reason that provides the model for a "common sense" that makes communication with a common past possible. For observing an object involves at once a tangible, substantive presence and a safe distance which enables contemplation while maintaining the integrity of the object. In contrast to the violent proximity of touch, the distance created by observation alone enables conservation. The past is not seized bodily. It is to be contemplated rather than touched or embraced.

But we are not dealing with just any past, and it is no coincidence that, in order to write about the *Restauration*, Chateaubriand goes back to one of the sources of monarchical legitimacy: Charlemagne. Nor is it by chance that he legitimizes his return on the basis of "it is said" (*on dit*), that is, by calling upon popular rumor or what might be called "historical hearsay." In terms of his exemplum, the tale is worth more than history. Freed from the criterion of having to be "truly real," legend proves to be a more universal vehicle for instruction. But the lesson to be learned bears on the attitude one should have toward history. In a way it is in the act of rejecting history (through the simple insertion of "it is said") that Chateaubriand is able to represent the dangers of a past that is all the more seductive in that it is constantly embroidered upon. So, in effect, history continues to be "touched," if only to be held at a distance.

Let us look at another example of what "is said" of this act of penetrating, of breaking into the tomb of a past power so that one might come closer to it, might enter into the very presence of the most illustrious of forefathers. The scene of the contemplation of the emperor's remains was redrawn in 1847 in Aachen itself. The Art Commission of the Rhineland and Westphalia had organized a contest whose winner would be commissioned to paint a series of frescoes in the royal hall of the town hall of Aachen depicting important moments in Charlemagne's life. The form of these paintings was to be both historical and symbolic and was to highlight the universal meaning of the chosen topics. The winner of the contest, the young artist Alfred Rethel, conceived several scenes, the last being Otto III's visit to the tomb of his great predecessor. In fact, Rethel began with this last scene that in itself summed up so fully the spirit and the raison d'être of his enterprise (fig. 1). The topic is a sort of "historical apotheosis." Already under Otto III, German national feeling was seen as seeking to compensate for the pitfalls of the present by contemplating a glorious past.[3] For Rethel, Charlemagne's life assumed its primary meaning as a voice from beyond the grave.

Let us contemplate this work for a moment. Seated on his throne slightly to the left of the center of the painting, Charlemagne, dressed in imperial clothes, dominates majestically. One also sees the scepter, the book, and the globe. On his right are his oversized sword and shield, the symbols of his strength and of the violence inherent in the authority he was able to impose and maintain. Carried over his shoulder and crossing his body sideways, that is, parallel to the line drawn by the scepter in the emperor's right hand and to the sword hanging next to him, is an ivory horn whose shape recalls that of the shield. This horn, an instrument used in hunting as well as in musical performances, is often mentioned in epic poetry. Throughout the centuries, *chansons de geste*, like so many successive echoes, often resonated with the theme of the activities of Charlemagne's sword and scepter. The book lying open on his lap could well be the Gospels, but it might also be a book of laws, Charlemagne's famous capitularies. Next to the horn, writing makes its presence known, and the emperor's left hand rests on the text while holding the globe, a sign of universality. On his head is a modest crown topped by a cross, which makes up for the absence of the cross usually found on the globe as the unambiguous symbol of universal Christendom.

What is most fascinating is the veil covering the emperor's face (fig. 2). This veil hides the emperor's features while allowing us to have a glimpse of them. The emperor's head had always been invested with strong symbolic meaning. It was the uppermost part, the one closest to God. In the Aachen Gospel Book dating from around 975 is an image of Otto III as emperor (fig. 3). His head is crowned twice: once with the imperial aura that surrounds his body and also with the divine aura surrounding his head as well as the hand of God that is touching it, perhaps to place the crown on it. The meaning is clear: the head is the most sacred element, and the shroud that covers it in Rethel's fresco echoes the idea of the veil covering the tabernacle, the metaphorical image of the sky separating the earth from the heavens. "In ipso tabernaculo imperator militavit pro nobis," writes Saint Augustine in an exegesis of the Ninetieth Psalm that was well known in the Middle Ages. In this passage the words "tabernacle" and "emperor" are used metaphorically to refer to the flesh and to Christ.[4] In addition to alluding to the emperor's twin nature—earthly and celestial—the partially transparent shroud in Rethel's fresco reveals the dead emperor's features while hiding the decaying flesh. What remains is a symbolic presence and the shadow of a human face. We are tempted to see this veil as a screen on which various images of Charlemagne can be projected, a canvas upon which the hero's many images can be drawn once again. It is up to the observer to add what he or she cannot see, including perhaps the flowing beard that Charlemagne probably did not have, a beard that grew, so to speak, only after his death.

The visitors occupy the right side of the painting: six men, the last of whom has not yet completely entered the vault. On the ground one can see the stones that have been pulled off to enter the vault. This return in order to contemplate is associated here with an act of violence and includes a destructive element. Surprisingly, no one in this little group is looking at the emperor. This is no doubt a sign of the respect they hold for him, but it also reminds us that our relationship with the past passes through an averted gaze, at best through the indirect view of a veiled figure. In this confrontation of a ruler's power with the past, the living emperor is not ready to touch the dead emperor. Head bent, he holds his hands out toward his predecessor in a gesture of prayer and supplication, his fingers forming a sort of circle mirroring the image of the globe Charlemagne holds in his left hand. It is toward that image that the gaze of the living emperor, a gaze that is invisible to us, seems to be directed.

Where does this story of Charlemagne retaining his majesty and his place on the throne even after his death come from? There is a third evocation of this same scene, one so emblematic of the issue of one's relationship to origins. This time we shall go back to one of the historical "sources" of this tale: the Novalesa Chronicle, written by a monk between 1027 and 1050. The narrative of this event is backed by the authority of an eyewitness, Count Otto of Lomello, who is supposed to have entered the vault with Otto III. Since Charlemagne's death in 814, any trace of where in the basilica his tomb was located had been lost. It was in the year 1000, and not in 1456, that Otto III undertook a search to find the tomb. More than a quarter of a century later, the chronicler of Novalesa gives us a narrative of the event:

> We approached Charles. He was not recumbent like the bodies of other dead, but was seated on a throne as if he were still alive. He wore a golden crown on his head; he held the scepter in his hands that were covered by gloves which his nails had torn as they had grown. Above him was a magnificent slab of limestone and marble, and when we got there, we made a hole in it as we broke it. As we came near him, there was a very strong odor. We bowed down before him and immediately the emperor Otto dressed him in white clothes, cut his nails, and fixed everything around him that required repair. None of his limbs had been destroyed by decay except for his nose, from which a bit was missing and which the emperor had replaced with gold. He pulled a tooth from the mouth of the dead man, then had the slab repaired and left.[5]

Although the peculiarity of the seated position and the presence of the symbols are noted here, there is no mention of a veil. The strangeness of the event is emphasized through "realistic" details. We see and feel clearly. The stench, the nails that had grown so as to rip through the tips of the gloves, the decay that had eaten away the tip of the nose—it is almost as if that feature had destroyed itself so as not to smell its own decomposition: all these details underline the fact that we are dealing with genuine mortal remains. Otto III takes great care with the body even as he violates it. It is no doubt the same spirit of adoration that leads him to break the slab to enter the vault; to extract one of the emperor's teeth and take it away; and to kneel in front of him to pray, to cut his fingernails, to cover him with new clothes, and to repair his nose.

To break and to restore, to see and to hide: these same acts recur in the three representations of this scene that I consider as being emblematic of the relationship to an originary past. We see them constantly at play in the course that we follow. Underlying these acts, in some way motivating them, are the desire and movement of seeking and transmission. We seek the traces and data of history, the documents and the monuments that enable us to see, to get a hold on the past. We then transmit what we have found and what we have done with it, the vision we have constructed out of the remains of the past.

WHY CHARLEMAGNE?

Although the elements I have just mentioned are found in every discourse on history, Charlemagne's case remains a special one, not only in relation to France, but as regards the rest of Europe as well. This study will focus on France, but it will also have a bearing on the rest of Europe as we attempt to uncover similarities and differences within the European arena. As occurs in every community, national identity develops not only following an internal logic but also in relation to the Other, in relation to what a given community is not.[6] Of all the heroes who have played a role in the development and transformation of French national consciousness, Charlemagne, more than anyone else, was endowed with a double significance. On the one hand, as a historical figure, he is often considered the founder of a certain France, a figure situated at the origins of the "nation" at the point where history began. On the other hand, of all the other monarchs he is the figure whose history is most closely related to myth and legend. This dual status exponentially extends the discussion about Charlemagne, turning it into a strategic locus for the construction of a national identity in France, indeed of various national and local identities throughout Europe. Let us emphasize at the outset the extraordinary plasticity of this mythical-historical figure. The shimmering of the legend constantly blends with the historical reflection and constitutes an essential element of Charlemagne's image. Charlemagne is the quintessential representation of a founding father.

But an objection quickly arises: exactly what did he found? After all, the originary myth of the Christian world Charlemagne inherited is found in the Bible. Moreover, the unity Charlemagne forged did not last long; it was irreparably destroyed under the reign of his son and successor, Louis the Pious, who had nonetheless dreamt of even greater glory.[7] And yet, the idea of unity persisted even in the face of fragmentation, an idea so fundamental that it subsumed the oppositions and divisions which it had itself engendered: in this regard let us recall in Rethel's painting the circle Otto III forms with his hands, which seems to absorb his thoughts. The figure of Charlemagne is central to this idea. He becomes the originator of an entire group of political powers and institutions, which, in spite of the discord and conflicts pitting them against each other, nonetheless continued to see Charlemagne as their point of reference. The authorities and regimes who used Charlemagne to legitimize their claims to power were found at the local level—a monastery or a county, at the national level—France and Germany, and even at the supranational level—Christendom, empires, or all of Europe.

Some elements of Charlemagne's "epic" and "biblical" persona appear to have already been sketched and embellished in explicit terms during his lifetime, not only in regard to the Franks (*Rex Francorum*) but also vis-à-vis all of Europe. In "Karolus Magnus et Leo papa," a poem that had long been attributed to Angilbert, a member of the Palace School, the *Rex Karolus* is presented on two occasions as the "beacon of Europe" (vv. 12, 169), as the "venerable apex of Europe" (v. 92), and as the father of Europe (*Rex, pater Europae*, v. 505).[8] Charlemagne's piety is reminiscent of that of King David ("sic denique David / Inlustrat magno pietatis lumine terras," vv. 14–15), and the construction of Aachen is likened to that of Carthage in the *Aeneid*.

The concept of Europe remains vague in this occasional poem, which appears to have been written on the eve of a meeting in Paderborn between Charlemagne and Pope Leo III. The pope had recently fled after having been attacked and mutilated in Rome, where his attackers had attempted to gouge out his eyes and cut out his tongue. But the image of Charlemagne, confronting those who prevent others from seeing (here, literally by gouging out eyes), rises up to shed his light over all the lands of Europe. This image was reinforced with an etymological word play that was to become common in the legend of Charlemagne: "Haec *cara* est populis *lux* et sapientia terris" [this light dear to the people and this wisdom dear to lands]—my emphasis: "Karolus," divided in two, yields *carus* [dear] and *lux* [light].[9] As we will see, Charlemagne's luminous gaze, in some way a relay of the divine gaze, was to become a most forceful image, one linked both to his power and to his wisdom.

His posthumous fame is based on the accomplishments of his forty-seven–year reign. His activities covered all domains of public life. First, he was a great warrior: he continuously battled and subjugated Saxons, Avars, Saracens, Slavs. He was also a man of peace: after 800 his policies were directed less toward territorial expansion than toward the defense and administration of the territories he had already acquired. He was also Defender of the Faith: Charlemagne, and not the emperor in Constantinople as it should have been, protected the papacy against the Lombards and restored Leo III to the papal see. He founded churches and monasteries; he strove to reestablish the liturgy, to reform the customs and practices of the clergy.[10] The spread of the Faith motivated and justified the extraordinary expansion of his empire. King Charlemagne was a maker and keeper of laws, as is seen in his capitularies. He was also an administrator as evidenced by his use of general *plaids*, or assemblies, and particularly of royal envoys (*missi dominici*). A great civilizer, he fostered a renewal in the arts and sciences and had a capital built in Aachen whose architecture and magnificence dazzled his contemporaries. He hosted scholars who came from all over Europe in his famous Palace School where the study of the *trivium* (grammar, rhetoric, dialectic) and of the *quadrivium* (arithmetic, geometry, astronomy, and music) flourished.

Charlemagne was no less admirable in his private life. Einhard, his biographer, describes him as an excellent father and family man, sensitive, understanding, and open to friendship, a moderate and kind individual.

Our purpose here is not to rewrite a history of Charlemagne, as there are a number of excellent ones available.[11] Nor is an attempt made to identify what his accomplishments really were and what has been purposely or mistakenly attributed to him. Instead, we will attempt to discover the vestiges of a figure that encouraged a community at different times in its collective development, one forever in the process of transformation, to recognize itself in him—or sometimes to reject him violently. In other words, this study aims to provide a better understanding of the role Charlemagne played in subsequent attempts to give meaning both to history and to the successive present moments that have occurred over the centuries. In order to do this, we must question not only history but also the myth that has been constructed around the figure. Our purpose lies much more in exploring the many different representations of Charlemagne than in knowing what the man truly did; we are more concerned with examining what has been drawn on the veil than in looking beneath it.

As a methodological point of departure we will begin with the notion of a discourse, a topos on Charlemagne that is located at the juncture of history, myth, and poetry. This is a strategic locus where every genre and ideological viewpoint meet, where one constantly finds a tension between the weight of a tradition and demands of a conjuncture and individual writers. In the complex play of interactions between these different historical perspectives the figure of Charlemagne is constantly reworked according to criteria that may or may not be acknowledged. In the case of France, this process has involved reformulating the discourse of national origins. But the emperor is also a figure who transcends the French experience both in the realms of time and of space. The age of Charlemagne predates national history. It is considered to be something like prehistory: a transition period preceding, so to speak, the existence of France, a period that planted the seeds of nations to come. As regards space, the extent of Charlemagne's empire formed a sort of first draft of Europe. His capital was located outside the confines of France in Aachen. Because he preceded France and because other nations also claimed him, the great emperor has become a liminal figure for France. The discourse on Charlemagne thus proves to be a place of rivalry and confrontation, a vulnerable locus easily penetrable by

Others where French national identity might be challenged, perhaps even threatened, by other identities and loyalties.

CHARLEMAGNE: ELUSIVE AND FUNDAMENTAL

It is a fact that for some time the "birth of the French nation" has been evoked without much reference to Charlemagne.[12] The reasons for this reticence are complex. They stem in part from the dual nature of a figure who is half historical, half mythical: Charlemagne is fragmented between various disciplines—history, literature, philology. But this silence can primarily be explained by the fact that, by and large, any national identification has been conceded to Germany. Worse, in terms of recent history, Charlemagne has turned into the precursor of the invader, an invader who sought to destroy France. In this context, for the French to recognize themselves in Charlemagne is for them to see in their origins the seeds of their own destruction—or for them to reclaim their own past as conquering invaders. Thus this battleground has been deserted: in France the discussion about Charlemagne as a key figure for understanding the national identity has almost been silenced.[13] I wish now to break this silence, a silence that has been overdetermined not only by the development of disciplines and the fragmentation of knowledge but also by the history of a violence and a destruction that might well be overcome with the creation of a new Europe.

The primary aim of this study is to examine Charlemagne's role in the emergence of modern France. It is in this light that we will look at the evolution of an at once elusive and fundamental figure through the study of different genres and disciplines. Rather than focusing this inquiry exclusively on the Middle Ages, which was dominated in so many ways by the shadow of this great king, I will develop my analysis in reference to later periods when France's collective identity was being radically and continually formed and reformed. In this more recent period extending from the seventeenth to the twentieth century, the face of the great emperor has been constantly redrawn and transformed. As an originary figure he had the double advantage of keeping his prestige and his distance and could be evoked as the first instance of a protonational power located at the dawn of a post-Roman era, which was nonetheless not yet our own. As we shall see, for a long time Charlemagne remained the image of authority, of power, of sovereignty, of a certain legitimacy: to speak of Charlemagne became a way to discuss the problematical ties that linked these concepts, a way of going from a series of abstract notions to an embodied vision of their practice. But to evoke Charlemagne involved raising the issues of the relationships between culture and politics, between the public and the private, between individuals and history.

We have been aware for some time that historical representations are not constructed on the basis of a single discipline or a single cultural space. Historians, novelists, artists, and journalists are all participants in the "discussion" that conditions and expresses visions of the past. In this "dialogical" space, the space of "it is said," a place of honor must be granted to the discussion on origins, a discussion located at the juncture of the representation of history and of what may be called the "social imaginary" or the spectrum of collective representations of social reality.[14]

In order to understand the elements that make up Charlemagne's topos, as a key component in the discourse on origins, we will proceed differently from the way we began. We started by looking at modern representations and traveled back in time to one of the sources of the tale. The aim was to evoke three emblematic representations that would convey the implications of this inquiry, to show that the study is indeed situated at a secondary level, that of a perception of origins rather than that of origins themselves. The components of a vision of Charlemagne were developed during the Middle Ages. As has been noted, the fame of the Carolingian renaissance spread to all the major domains of public life: military, law, religion, education, literature. Very quickly—from the ninth century on—the Emperor of the West became supremely important in the construction of monarchical power in France as well as in Germany and Spain. He became a source of legitimacy upon which many charters and diplomas—acts and grants, public treaties, deeds of conveyance, and the like—were based, documents that were often made up as needed long after his death.

The monarchy used him, but so did many others, sometimes to get closer to royal power, other times to protect themselves against its usurpations. In some cases, abbots, for example, turned Charlemagne into a weapon of resistance to assert their privileged status against the authority of the bishops, who closely supported the nobility's avid desire to suppress the privileges and the independence of the monasteries. As the first king to combine priestly consecrations and royal coronations, as in the single ceremony for his son, Louis the Pious, Charlemagne was present as a symbol of sovereignty, grandeur, legitimacy, heroic power, and justice in the coronation ceremonies of the kings of France and of the emperors of the Holy Germanic Empire. His symbolism survived even the changing of dynasties; the Capetians were careful to link themselves to Charlemagne through ties of blood.

Recent studies enable us to understand better the extraordinary wealth of references to Charlemagne in the Middle Ages and to determine how they functioned within specific political contexts.[15] Thus, rather than examining all of the medieval evocations of the great emperor, it seems more worthwhile in this context to look at those that carried the most weight in terms of transmission, to observe the most striking features that people have believed they perceived through the veil, or perhaps that they themselves were drawing on it. For this reason, we shall return to a few powerful representations, to texts we might consider fundamental or even exemplary in the way they formulate elements that are found again and again, surfacing sometimes at a much later date. These initial excavations in a preliminary field of investigation will enable us, on the one hand, to place Charlemagne within a discourse on origins and, on the other, will help us to extract some characteristics that are essential for an understanding of that discourse and of its later transformations. There is a teleological aspect to this first step in that its goal is to study representations that have served as foundations for later representations. The analyses in the present and in the following chapter are more textual than contextual. The goal of these analyses is to set down boundary markers on the field of interpretations to come and to explore certain key documents upon which those interpretations will be based.

In this framework, respect for chronology is less important than the issue of the modes of transmission employed. We will not try to establish a genealogy of representation, a project that would entail following the thread leading from one source to another; rather we will investigate a certain logic among them. There are two aspects to this logic: that of narration and that of accumulation. In both cases, one finds the same desire to provide an increasingly exhaustive explanation of history as the principal source of legitimacy. The logic of narration or of tales unfolds on a horizontal axis that proves to be infinitely extensible: one can always insert another story that develops aspects requiring clarification. A priori, the logic of narration admits no contradictory explanations in the sense that one event cannot occur in two different ways. In contrast, the logic of accumulation—that of collecting and of archives—functions along a vertical axis that does not exclude contradiction; it has no difficulty in collecting divergent, even contradictory, narratives of the same event. These can be told in different registers, both in the sacred and the profane, and in different languages and genres, such as Latin or the vulgate, poetry or prose. Narrative logic can thus also be considered a priori as the logic of identity, and cumulative logic as that of contrasts and difference. We will see both of them at work in the "sources" from which derive later representations of Charlemagne.

Since our aim is to understand the foundations of a modern discourse, I will primarily evoke those texts that have had the greatest influence on that discourse. In principle, every surviving document or piece of information dealing with the great emperor could lend itself to analysis insofar as it is included in what "is said" or at least in what might be said about Charlemagne—for instance, one might analyze his capitularies or Alcuin's letters. But I will confine myself here to establishing the framework of the topos and to sketching some of the broad outlines of it that serve as points of reference in the following study. The texts we will be looking at can be divided into two groups: the first dates from the ninth century; and the second starts in the eleventh century, around the time of the first Crusades, and continues until the fourteenth century. Overall we examine texts that introduced the basic elements of the topos: the conqueror with the flowing white beard; the founder of schools who rewarded poor but hard-working students while reproaching rich youths for their laziness; the emperor who spoke with the people during the meetings of the general assemblies; and the crusading emperor who journeyed to the Holy Land.

Warrior and Protector: The Annales Regni Francorum

"*La geste*"—a collective term inherited from the Latin *gesta* designating the historical record or achievements—is the word often used to refer to a whole range of texts as diverse as the *Annales Regni Francorum*, Einhard's *Vita Karoli Magni* [Life of Charlemagne], the *Gesta Karoli Magni imperatoris* by Notker the Stammerer, *Karolinus* by Gilles of Paris, the *Chanson de Roland*, the *Pseudo-Turpin Chronicle* or *Historia Karoli Magni of Rotholand*, and the *Grandes Chroniques de France*. In these texts, which speak of the *res gestae*, great deeds, one finds little contrast between myth and history, or legend and reality. Similarly, there is little distinction between historical narrative and historical analysis. Written both in Latin, the language of the clerics, a holy language, and in "Romance," the vulgate, a profane language, these "records" of events thus alternate between the prestige and authority of prose and the playfulness of poetry.[16] Though it might have been far removed from the discipline of history, one of the main functions of the *geste* was to give meaning to the past; it provided a way of understanding the world as it had become. I will begin with an attempt to follow a certain logic of narration and focus on the development of an early tale about Charlemagne, because this story gives the monarch an enduring identity; one might even say, paraphrasing Mallarmé, that in a way it is writing that makes him who he is. And it is no coincidence that these texts, which describe him, go to great lengths to reveal how important the glorious monarch considered the written word, an interest that was in itself quite innovative in the kingdom of the Franks.

The *Annales Regni Francorum* or *The Royal Frankish Annals* constitute what might be called ground zero of the narrative. They formulate in a rough-hewn manner the fundamental traits of a figure who represented the source of power, glory, and legitimacy. These annals, which began during Charlemagne's reign and span the years 741 to 829, were written by several authors and were rewritten after the emperor's death. It is possible, though not entirely known, that some of these changes might have been the work of Einhard, who is believed to have had the *Annals* available (for this there is more evidence) while he was writing his *Life of Charlemagne*.[17] In any event, they constitute one of the main official sources of information about the reign of the great monarch. The basic order that regulates the presentation of facts is, by definition, a chronological one. Thus, even though the *Annals* contain in some places hints of continuous narration, each episode always unfolds within the boundary set by a date. And even though, due mainly to subsequent reworking, the figure of Charlemagne forms the center of everything that occurs, it remains just as fragmented as the *Annals*'s recorded story itself.

The *Annals* provide above all the image of an emperor running from one end of his territory to the other dealing with various crises. There are initial attempts at introducing causality and even psychological motivation, but the true emphasis is simply the list of years.[18] And yet, this seemingly meaningless repetition does become significant, as the rhythm of the repetition appears to mirror the constant return of the same events that structure one's existence. These events are the supreme collective moments that served to define normal, everyday relationships with people on the one hand, and, on the other, with God: the assemblies or general *plaids* (*populi generalis conventus, synodus publicus, placitum*) and the holidays of Easter and Christmas. Each year, the *Annals* endlessly recount the convening of the general assembly and the celebration of the two feast days and where they took place:

> (772) Pope Stephen having died in Rome, Adrian succeeded him to the pontificate. King Charles, after having held his assembly at Worms, resolved [*statuit*] to wage war in Saxony, went there promptly, destroyed everything by arms and fire [*ferro et igni cuncta depopulatus*], took the fortified castle of Ehresburg, and overturned the idol the Saxons called Irminsul. During the three days he remained there for this destruction, it happened that, because the sky remained cloudless, all of the rivers and fountains were dry, and nothing could be found to drink. There was fear that the army, tired by thirst, would not be able to continue its work; but one day and, it is believed, through divine providence [*divinitus factum creditur*], while all were resting around noon, an enormous amount of water all of a sudden filled the bed of a torrent near the mountain next to which the camp had been set up, and the entire army was thus able to quench its thirst. The king, having destroyed the idol, continued up to the Weser and there received twelve hostages from the Saxons. Upon his return to France he participated in the ceremonies of Christmas and Easter in his land of Herstall.[19]

Assemblies prior to military campaigns, wars, and feast days: such was the structure of the annual activities, whose center was located wherever King Charles happened to be. This structure appears as essentially circular, as it is repeated year after year. But taken alone, the entry for the year 772, for example, constitutes a whole; it contains what might be called a narrative core, a short story having a beginning, a middle, and an end. As everywhere in the *Annals*, Charles is characterized by his will ("resolved"), his speed, and by implacable violence ("destroyed by arms and fire"). An image of the king and his activities begins to emerge from these narrative cores that are strung together like the beads of a rosary. The unity of Charles has been reinforced through editorial reworking, but paradoxically it is based as well on the extreme paucity of the narrative. For example, we are never told what happens during these assemblies. There seems to be no gap between willing and doing.

And yet, in the entry for the year 772, there is mention of other figures besides Charles, foremost the pope, whose succession is noted without comment. This event has no place in the story of the campaign against the Saxons, but it already prepares the narrative core of the following year. Adrian was to call on Charles, king of the Franks, to come to his aid against King Didier and the Lombards: "The king, having carefully pondered the discord between the Lombards and the Romans, decided to wage war to defend the latter" (A.D. 773).[20] The image of Charles, Defender of the Faith and of the Church, already emerges in the *Annals*, as shown by his destruction of the pagan idol. But the annalist clerks of the court remain very careful and discrete. Here for instance, the king intervenes to defend the Romans, not the Church. Later, when the pope crowns the emperor, the *Annals* note that the new emperor was acclaimed by the Roman people and that he was "adored by the pontiff." Such an account of the events enables the emperor to maintain his independence, indeed his superiority, vis-à-vis the Church; it enables him, in effect, to remain at the center of his own annals.

And what are we to make of the torrent that suddenly emerges to save his troops? The divine presence seems on the verge of declaring itself in favor of the king of the Franks. But here again the writers of the *Annals* exercise prudence: the miracle is only suggested indirectly and in passing by the insertion of "it is said" or rather "it is believed" (*creditur*). This is no doubt yet another way of asserting the king's independence. Charles is on the side of the true Church, of the true religion, but in these *Annals* he never becomes the simple instrument of another being, even of God himself.[21] Such restraint on the part of the annalists can be explained by the arbitrariness of these signs. The wonders that occur over the years could well manifest a hostile nature, even a hostile God. The earthquake that occurred in 801 is such an example. The account of the year 800 tells how Charles intervened to save Pope Leo III and to put him back on the pontifical see, and how the pope "cleansed himself with an oath from the crimes of which he was accused." At the beginning of the year 801 (in fact, on December 25, 800), the annalist tells us, without evoking any causal link with the preceding events, how this same pope, Leo, "put a crown on Charles's head" and how all the Roman people cheered: "To Charles Augustus, crowned by God, great and pacific emperor of the Romans, life and victory!" [cuncto Romanorum populo adclamante: "Karolo augusto, a Deo coronato magno et pacifico imperatori Romanorum, vita et victoria!"].[22] This same year, according to the *Annals* (in fact, it was the following year), while Charles was still in Italy, in Spoleto, "the earth was disturbed on the second hour of the night by a very great motion that strongly shook the whole of Italy; this tremor caused a big portion of the roof of the Basilica of Saint Peter to collapse along with its beams; and in several places mountains and towns collapsed. In the same year several places shook in Gaul and Germany near the Rhine river, and the mild winter that year brought the plague."

It would be rather dangerous to try to develop a semiotics of wondrous events here! While the torrent of water could be interpreted as a sign of divine support for Charlemagne's policy toward the Saxons, what might be said of the relationship between the earthquakes destroying a part of the pontifical basilica right after the restoration of the pope and Charlemagne's coronation? The annals format has the advantage of not subjecting events to the logic of narration, to a coherent order of meaning and explanation. In this case, we remain within the logic of accumulation: these are events whose temporal contiguity in no way implies causal links. They simply belong to different registers of reality. But we must emphasize that such wonders serve to remind us that while Charles remains at the center of the *Annals*, there is nonetheless another order of things that escapes his power and transcends his area of influence.

However, the royal will indeed orchestrates everything pertaining to the human realm of experience: peace and war as well as the laws and the ruling of the kingdom. From this perspective, Charlemagne's famous capitularies—another constitutive role conferred upon the written word during his reign—appear to emanate directly from the monarch's will: these include not only the measures he stipulates to ensure the proper administration of his royal domain, but also involve the sending of the *missi dominici* throughout the kingdom as so many expressions of the royal will as well as oaths of loyalty demanded of "every man throughout the kingdom," oaths that confirmed the concentration of royal power and the suppression of any other will.[23]

In Charlemagne's empire, territorial boundaries are mostly drawn with reference to the constant presence of enemies. Oppositions are strong and simple. Whether they come from the outside (as the Saxons) or, which is rarer, are internal (Tassilo's revolt, for instance), enemies are always "perfidious," and this motivates and justifies Charles's violence. Such opposition determines the king's movements, and it is mainly within this context that the beginnings of a logic of narration emerge. Most of the time (but not always) it is *because* he is attacked, *because* he is threatened that Charles wages war. The king of the Franks responds to the perfidy of others. He forms the center, but he is always found wherever the boundaries of his kingdom are being established; indeed, it is he who draws them. The monarch's travels enable him to affirm his sovereignty wherever he goes, but they also establish his identity as king. This explains the surprising observation in the 790 entry in which Charlemagne appears to be, so to speak, traveling arbitrarily: "The king, however, *so as to not appear to remain idle and waste his time*, embarked on the Main River, arrived at his palace of Seltz, built near the Saale River, and from there returned to Worms the same way by following the river's course."[24] Movement defines not only the range but also the very function of sovereignty.[25] The repetition of community activities (the assemblies) and religious activities (the celebration of holidays) ensures social identity. In effect, sovereignty and social identity only exist through Charlemagne.

Out of the circular, iterative narrative structure (assemblies/war/religious celebrations) there emerges the figure of the king as sovereign and warrior.[26] In fact, the warrior king is defined above all *against* his enemies. But the king is not only the center in motion. Gradually, with the passing of time, he increasingly becomes the center of a whole system of symbolic exchanges. Thus, in the passage cited earlier, he is given hostages. In most cases, the gift of hostages is accompanied by one's word as a sign of good faith. The exchange of hostages as a guarantee had long been a common practice among the Franks. But the annalists reserve an important place for oaths and promises, and this tactic is understandable for, on the one hand, it opens up another field for action and relationships than that of war, and it places Charlemagne, the receiver of the promised word, at the very center of that field. On the other hand, it facilitates his enemies' transgressions, their perfidy, and justifies the emperor's resorting to force. In this regard, one might recall that Charlemagne ordered the killing of forty-five hundred Saxons in 782 to punish them for yet another uprising under the leadership of their chief, Widukind.

But Charlemagne doesn't receive only promises and oaths. He also receives a host of ambassadors through whom a continual exchange of gifts takes place. Recounting symbolic exchanges also serves to demonstrate that Charlemagne's power is recognized. In 796, Pope Leo gives Charlemagne the key to St. Peter's tomb, which stands for the city of Rome. The king of the Franks also receives "the oath of loyalty and obedience of the Roman people" [populum Romanum ad suam fidem atque subiectionem per sacramenta firmaret]. In 799, the Saracen Axan, governor of Huesca, sends him the keys to that city "and promised to give the city to him at the first opportunity." In 800, the Patriarch of Jerusalem offers him the keys to the Holy Sepulchre and Calvary, as well as the keys to the city and Mount Zion, along with a banner. It is no coincidence that these events are mentioned as the coronation of Charlemagne draws near, but the structure of the *Annals* does not permit an explanatory development. And yet, the repetition of the same act in the narrative entries over several years acquires a certain weight. Each year, Charlemagne is the same—and a little bit more.

Symbolic movement extends Charlemagne's power well beyond the areas of actual travel, as it is also a way for other powers to present themselves in relation to him—according to the logic of the "potlatch" studied so well by Mauss.[27] Like war, symbolic exchange proves to be an arena for the struggle to establish one's identity in relation to the Other. Thus, in the entry for the year 798, following the military campaign against the Saxons, those "traitors who had betrayed their faith" [*foedifragos ac desertores*], a campaign during which the king of the Franks "devastated through arms and fire" a part of their country, Charlemagne returned to Aachen where "he received the ambassadors sent from Constantinople by the empress Irene. After he sent them back, there then came those from Alphonso, king of Spain, Basilisk and Froia, bringing presents that their king had carefully chosen for Charles from the booty taken after the siege and seizure of the city of Lisbon. The gift consisted of seven Moors and as many mules and suits of armor. *Even though these objects were sent as gifts, they were rather the symbols of victory* [magis tamen insignia victoriae videbantur]. The king graciously received the ambassadors and sent them back with presents, as well."[28]

The comment added by the annalist in his narrative leaves no doubt that this exchange of gifts involves both a recognition of the Other and an affirmation of oneself. In addition to the importance of military power, the writers of the *Annals* also stress that of the power to give and particularly the power to receive. The importance of the gift heightens the prestige of the recipient. The gifts from the King of Persia are most extraordinary indeed: an elephant (mentioned three times),[29] tents and amazingly colorful tent cloth, silk cloaks, perfumes, ointments, and "a clock of gilded bronze admirably assembled through mechanical art," a description of which bears mention:

> The twelve hours surrounded the face, and there were as many little balls of bronze that fell at the completion of each hour, and their fall caused a cymbal placed beneath to ring. There was also a same number

of horsemen that came out of twelve windows at the end of the hours, and as they emerged their movement caused windows that had previously been open to close. There were other things on this clock too numerous to report here. (807)

The somewhat disproportionate amount of space given to the description of gifts, particularly to that of the clock, implies how important such things were to the court and how fascinated the courtiers were with a technology that far surpassed anything then known in the West. The description emphasizes the greatness of the giver, the King of Persia, and the extravagance of his gesture of recognition toward Charlemagne emphasizes the greatness of the king of the Franks. This circle formed by two great powers that demonstrate mutual recognition widens the emperor's field of influence. It is perhaps no coincidence that the object most fascinating to the annalists in a certain sense fulfills the same functions as the *Annals*: to mark the passing of time and to enhance the greatness of the king. It is time that determines the structure of the clock and of the *Annals*, and the circular nature of the mechanism echoes that of the writing: the regular repetition of the same noises and the same movements, the twelve horsemen who come out every hour—even though we have not yet reached the time of the twelve peers of France. . . .[30]

Another series of actions found in the basic narrative foundation concerns theological issues. In addition to the assemblies, Charles also convokes ecclesiastical councils. Here, again, the object is often to assert himself in the face of an enemy. He calls for the condemnation of the Felician heresy, according to which Christ was only God's adopted son. For his purpose Charlemagne employs a new weapon, the same one used in the *Annals*, that is, writing: ". . . and a book to refute [the heresy] was written following the unanimous order of the bishops and signed by all" (794). But the following sentence perhaps truly reveals what was at issue: "As to the synod called up a few years previously in Constantinople by Constantine and his mother, Irene, and named by them not only the seventh council but also a universal council, it was declared [by the council of Frankfurt] to be neither the seventh nor universal and was decreed entirely invalid by all."

Frequent exchanges of ambassadors and gifts between the empire of the Orient and that of the West could not hide a tension that occasionally led to combat. But the fight was in part waged in writing—indeed by the *Annals*, themselves. The entry for the year 812 notes that Charles received the ambassadors sent from Constantinople, who addressed him as *basileus* and emperor, something that the Byzantines always refused to do.

Rome, Constantinople, Jerusalem, Aix-la-Chapelle (Aachen): these places appear often, laden with meaning. And the *Annals* as a whole form a series of meditations on the central figure of Charlemagne, a series structured by time. Yet it remains fragmented as if it were made up of the beads of a rosary running down the course of the years, with each bead taking up and repeating certain key elements. It is worth emphasizing this resemblance between prayer and the *Annals*. Although we don't perceive a unified portrait in them, there is nonetheless a coherence that is forged through the repetitions and the variations of basic narrative elements that keep time, as it were, to the rhythm of life.

Wisdom Incarnate: Einhard's *Life of Charlemagne*

No text on Charlemagne is better known or had greater influence on later interpretations than that of his famous biographer, Einhard. Most likely, Einhard did not give the *Frankish Royal Annals* their "definitive" form, but he certainly made use of them while writing his *Life of Charlemagne*. Einhard came to Charlemagne's court in 791 or 792. He knew Charlemagne at the height of the emperor's glory and ultimately became a member of the group of scholars Charlemagne gathered around him, some of whom came from distant lands. This group was known as the Palace School. Younger than the emperor, Einhard was closer in age to Charles's son Louis. Following Charles's death, Einhard experienced his greatest success at court, which he left, moreover, around 828 when relations between Louis and his sons began to deteriorate. It was probably at that time, in the tranquility of his monastic retreat—although he continued to be perfectly aware of the developing political crisis—that Einhard began to write his life of Charlemagne, whose reign was already beginning to appear as that of a golden age. Einhard's text, more than any other, served to establish a certain image of Charlemagne that was to survive for centuries. Its influence was enormous, and, in this sense, the famous clerk indeed fulfilled his self-appointed mission, that is, "to perpetuate the memory of the famous great man" by describing "his life, his customs, and his principal deeds [*res gestae*]."[31]

Einhard obtained much of his information, particularly that concerning the great emperor's conquests and external policies, from the *Annals*.[32] But he was careful to categorize his biography as a living account; his authority as narrator derived from his status as an eyewitness: ". . . aware that I was in a position to bring more truth than anyone else, since I participated in the events I am telling, that I was, as they say, an eyewitness" (p. 2). In contrast to the *Annals*, there is a first person here who makes himself known and places himself in relation to his subject, his lord who *nourished him* (domini et nutritoris mei Karoli). This expression was common usage referring to upbringing, but in Einhard's text it takes an added force in that this gift of "nourishment," of life, but also of an entire culture, of an up-bringing, establishes an obligation that the author is doing his best to honor. "The debt I have incurred toward him and toward his memory is such that I would rightfully be taken for an ingrate if I kept silent about the glorious and illustrious deeds of the one to whom I owe so much."

Einhard repays the gift of life with that of remembrance: he provides a representation of Charlemagne for future generations. As in the logic of the potlatch, the exchange of gifts proves to be a means to affirm one's power and greatness: Charlemagne, by welcoming scholars from near and far—thereby laying the foundations for cultural renewal; Einhard by using this culture to expand the influence of his benefactor through time if not over space. The sword conquers space, the pen conquers time: an old idea that is reborn in Charlemagne's own policies and practices. In addition to the *City of God*, "histories and deeds of the ancients were read to him" [lege-bantur ei historiae et antiquorum res gestae].[33] These works might have in-cluded Suetonius's *Lives of the Twelve Caesars*, by which Einhard—as has been shown—was greatly inspired while writing his life of Charlemagne.[34] Charlemagne, concerned with reestablishing ties, with giving new life to the Roman Empire, took inspiration from the ancient *gesta*.

To the circle of reciprocity between the sovereign and his subject and its replication as a dynamic of author and literary object, we must also add the hermeneutic circle of ancient literary models for conduct, which Ein-hard described via textual borrowings from ancient sources and representa-tions. We can understand better the importance Einhard attributes to language and writing at court, as well as the strange reference to Charle-magne's fruitless attempts to learn to write.[35] Writing, transferring, trans-lating: these are three means of preserving, renewing, and fashioning the image of sovereignty and legitimacy.

The reciprocal relationship between power and knowledge are laid out as a fundamental theme in representations of Charlemagne. Some ten centuries later, the great author of popular fiction, Eugène Sue, indeed captures this very conscious connection to writing at the service of royal power. In his novel *Mystères du peuple*, Sue slightly distorts facts by placing the biographer alongside Charlemagne and by having him write by order of the emperor, practically copying down what Charlemagne dictates to him. Two Gauls, claiming to be victims of repression, are complaining to Charlemagne. "Karl turns toward Einhard and says: 'You who are writing the facts and deeds of Karl, August Emperor of the Gauls, Caesar of Ger-many, Patriarch of the Romans, Protector of the Sueves, Bulgars, and Hungarians, you shall write this: that an old man spoke to Karl with unbe-lievable audacity and that Karl could not but respect the candor and the courage of the man who was speaking to him thus.'"[36] Here, Charlemagne himself is seen as constructing the image of his own greatness to be handed down to future generations.

The representation of Charlemagne that emerges from Einhard's writing uses the data from the *Annals*, but reorganizes and amplifies them according to the logic of biography. Biographical narrative, more than any other genre of writing, aims to capture the identity of an individual. In this case, the shape of the narrative and to a certain extent the image of the personage are fixed in advance: Charles will be, so to speak, the "thirteenth Caesar."[37] We are not concerned here with knowing which features are faithfully revealed through the Suetonian veil; the "distortions" introduced by such a foreign image have been often criticized. What must be emphasized is that this first "complete" representation of Charlemagne already implies a process of mythifying appropriation and projection. Although the form transmitting this image is not that of the epic, it is clear that Charlemagne's identity is molded along heroic and conquering lines. Thus, we would be justified in seeing so early on the introduction of an *epic distancing* in a portrayal "of the best and greatest king of his time and of his exploits, which are *almost unmatchable today*."[38] Here we already see Charlemagne set in a time that is "other," that of the "in-between." He is both the prolonger and the renovator of ancient traditions (that of the Franks, of the *imperium romanorum*, the *imperium christianorum*) and the creator and innovator of a new era from which we derive without being able to equal it.

Einhard thus sets out to tell the story of the life of this unique man. In principle, biography is subjected to time; the beginning and the end are determined in advance. The narrative is born and dies with the man. Unlike annals, there are definite points of departure and of arrival. Louis Halphen has shown well the extent to which Einhard conforms to the Suetonian model: a few pages on family, childhood, and adolescence; a study of the official life—military campaigns, foreign policy, public works; then family life—marriage, children, friendships; a physical description, style of clothing, the use of time, and even a description of sleeping habits, intellectual pursuits, religious beliefs, and, finally, pages devoted to omens announcing death, the emperor's death itself, and the funeral.[39] Thus, except for the beginning and the end, the basic organization of this biography is thematic rather than strictly chronological. We go from the public to the private, thus progressing toward an increasingly intimate acquaintance with the man.

A thematic organization enables a greater coherence in the description of intentions and causes, notably in the account of war exploits. After a few pages in which he discusses the heroism and legitimacy of Charlemagne's ancestors, Einhard says he knows nothing of his hero's childhood, and thus turns directly to his military life. Here Charlemagne's image is defined first and foremost *against* his enemies and through conquest and victory. But instead of describing a Charlemagne running constantly from one end of his empire to the other to deal with endlessly erupting crises in every direction, Einhard describes military actions along geographical lines rather than by the years in which they occurred. It is space that organizes war narratives, each war having its own logic and leading to a victorious end.[40] In conclusion, Einhard lists the successes of the war policy of the *rex potentissimus:* he doubled the territory of the kingdom he had inherited. Even though the emperor's biographer attributes some of the conquests already achieved by Pepin the Short to him, and somewhat inflates the list of conquered lands,[41] what is important is that the conquests defined both a hero and a geographical entity.

Far from confining himself to a simple listing of victories, Einhard portrays Charlemagne building a coherent policy of successive wars that led to the acquisition and definition of a new space, as well as to the resolute reduction of his enemies. The battles against the Saxons, for example, are grouped into a single narrative section. Einhard points out that this war was waged for thirty-three consecutive years and that "none was longer, more horrible, harder for the Frankish people."[42] However, because it is described in a single narrative section, the war no longer appears as a series of annual battles, but acquires the unity and coherence that narrative can give to an event. The story of this war is constructed as a function of its ending: "And we know that the war, after so many years of fighting, only ended when the Saxons accepted the conditions imposed by the king: their renouncing of the worship of demons and their national ceremonies [*patriis caerimoniis*], their adoption of the Christian faith and sacraments, and their being joined with the Franks into a single people" (chap. 7, p. 14). It was Charlemagne who had decided on this outcome and succeeded in imposing it. The religious and the "national" objectives are closely intertwined here. But most important, the quote ends with the idea of a collective entity: the Frankish people assimilate another people.

The presence of the Franks is significant. Much more than in the *Annals*, Charlemagne's deeds are undertaken as a function of a "people." At the beginning of his work, Einhard himself insists on his own status as one of Charlemagne's subjects; he is the great monarch's creature just as would be, in a way, this new collectivity issued from the fusion of two peoples. However, the role of the collectivity, of the "people," in Einhard's work increases as compared to their role in the *Annals*. For Einhard, war does not start because Charlemagne decrees it but because the *Franks*, angered (*Franci sunt inritati*) by the Saxons' looting and perfidious acts, decide (*judicarent*)—note the plural form—to wage an open battle.

Einhard points out that very often Charlemagne did not participate personally in the battles: "In the course of this war, in spite of its length,

Charles fought the enemy in person only twice." When he does fight, his success is of course dazzling, but here Charlemagne is not primarily depicted as a warrior king. What then is his function in a narrative in which war has nonetheless a "definitional" force, since it is foremost through war that Charlemagne's greatness is established? Let us take a look at the final passage describing the war in Saxony:

> It finally ended after thirty-three years during which so many great wars were fought against the Franks in various parts of the world and were conducted so ably by the king that one does not know which to admire more: his endurance or his success. . . . The king who surpassed all of the sovereigns of his time in wisdom and greatness of soul [*magnanimitas*], in order to ensure the success of an enterprise, never avoided any endeavor or any danger: having learned to adapt to circumstances, he knew how to resist adversity or, when fortune smiled upon him, how to prevent himself from being won over by its seductions. (Chap. 8, p. 15)

Here Charlemagne's greatness mainly becomes internal ("wisdom and greatness of soul"). Even more than geographical space, the expanse of his spirit in a certain sense becomes the essential yardstick. His moral values—constancy, courage, adaptability, moderation—enable him to rise above the moment, to rise above the temporal. This ethical transcendence embodied in the new Caesar turns out to be extremely important. Whereas a policy of conquest defined geographical space, it is moral qualities—*auctoritas*, the essential trait of the Roman Emperor—that render possible the good management of that space.[43]

We have noted the significance the *Annals* attribute to promises and oaths. In a society where the solemn word constitutes an essential mode of social functioning, the legitimacy of that word, its effectiveness, is developed here in relation to a certain interiority. Charlemagne is the pole around which promises and oaths gravitate; he is their ultimate guarantor. Thus he must embody the values that enable the gift of the word, and, in doing so, also embody the temporal existence of the community. This moral existence corresponds to the progression of the *Vita*: from external to internal geography, from public life to the great emperor's private life.

This explains Einhard's emphasis on constancy as an essential value: "I will now speak of his moral qualities, of his extraordinary constancy in all happy or unhappy circumstances, and generally of all that bears on his private and family life [*interiorem atque domesticam vitam*]" (chap. 18, p. 31]. Constancy in all its forms—patience, perseverance, loyalty—dominates Charlemagne's internal landscape just as it dominates his external policy;

the same man is found again at every level. It is constancy that ultimately ensures that the word given will be the word kept, and it is constancy that allows us to go beyond the moment and guarantees duration. But it is important that the figure of Charlemagne not be reduced to an abstraction. Einhard also describes the monarch in concrete terms: his ways of eating, of dressing (in the Frankish style), of sleeping. Nothing highlights the emperor's humanity better than the description of his sensitivity, when he is moved to tears at the loss of a child or a friend.

Yet, the picture of Charlemagne's private life includes many public activities. His piety inspires him to have the Aachen basilica built, to reform the clergy, and to provide financial support to Christians overseas (in Syria, in Egypt and in Africa, in Jerusalem, and in Alexandria). The section on his private life also includes the account of his coronation by Pope Leo III. The surprise and discomfort shown by Charlemagne during this event serve to emphasize a certain modesty as well as the moral qualities that characterize this figure: "He nonetheless withstood *with great patience* the jealousy of the Roman emperors who were indignant at the title he had taken."[44] And it took him a long time to overcome the hostility of the emperors of the Orient.

Einhard's placement of these observations shows how indistinct the boundaries between the private and the public man truly were; this is all the more understandable in that the economy of oaths and given words is based on a lack of distinction between the two levels or, at least, on the absence of boundaries separating private and public domains. Charlemagne exhibits all the attributes that make up the portrait of an ideal monarch: magnanimity, clemency, a sense of justice. Added to these qualities that were handed down through the legacy of the classical age is his exemplary piety, more proof of his concern with that which transcends the temporary and the immediate: in the realm of Charlemagne, king of the Franks, the *imperium christianorum* is fused with the *imperium romanorum*. His qualities make him a magnet for the friendship of other peoples and monarchs such as the one Einhard calls "King of the Irish [*Scottorum*]" (chap. 16, p. 26) who at times go so far as to bow down to him and recognize him as their sovereign.

Remaining within the context of the theme of constancy, Charles's main moral quality, and that of duration, it is important to reiterate the emphasis we placed on Charlemagne's preoccupation with writing. Writing is, so to speak, the best way to "keep" one's word, to ensure its longevity. It began to appear necessary to put down a tradition in writing. To this end, the emperor ordered that the laws which had up to then been handed down by the spoken word be collected and written down. So as to preserve the memory of them, he also ordered that the age-old barbarian poems that recounted the history and wars of the ancient kings be put down in writing (chap. 29, p. 48).

Thus, Charlemagne figures at the origin of the very complex interdependent relationship between writing and the spoken word. In a society that favored the oral—promises, oaths, all that was spoken—the great king could make use of writing to secure tradition, to stabilize it, and to reinforce it, thereby ensuring control over it. Einhard does precisely the same thing when he puts his representation of the sovereign, the source of political authority and legitimacy, into written form. The private man's moral values as they are described and preserved in Einhard's account ensure the political morality which must rule across the realm; and it is on this morality that the good functioning of society depends. Thus the biographer's act of writing down his account of the emperor's life, based on the model from Roman times, mirrors Charlemagne's act of ordering the writing down of the history and wars of the old Frankish kings: here again we see the fusion of two cultures.

Charlemagne's concern with mastering time is seen in his naming the twelve months of the year "in his maternal tongue," just as his naming the winds shows a desire to use language to "frame" space. Even the supernatural events that appear in the text of the *Annals* are given a place that reinforces the message of transcendent permanency. Einhard groups them at the end of the biography as so many omens of Charlemagne's death. They suggest, albeit without any explicit claim, the idea of a divine consciousness concerned with this hero's destiny. The end of the narrative describes the end of Charlemagne, and on the occasion of this double death the text mimics, on a reduced scale, the end of the world.

It is no coincidence that Einhard, at that moment, becomes silent and allows a text from beyond the grave to speak: in conclusion, he adds Charlemagne's testament, which enables the emperor to outlast death. The will is a model of generosity and wisdom; it is Charlemagne's last gift. But this last act also evokes, as it were, the biographer's own work of representation in that his work also aims to transmit to posterity the monarch's true legacy, his real value: the immortal image of the sovereign who ensures the definition, the preservation, and the duration of the entire collectivity.

NOTKER: THE POWER AND THE GLORY

Einhard's representation of Charlemagne endows a monumental identity upon the great emperor. Its influence during the Middle Ages was enormous. But there is another "source" text that completes some of the aspects of what might be called the narrative identity of the heroic king, although in a more intimate, less structured way. This text was little known at the time it was written; it was rediscovered during the twelfth century, and provides us with the best known anecdotes about Charlemagne. Guizot, in his 1824 translation, chose to see it as a "naive painting," as "what was said and told about [Charlemagne] seventy years after his death."[45] Chateaubriand readily compared this narrative to stories later told by some of Napoleon's grenadiers. Indeed, the text in question has long been situated at the heart of what had been labeled popular discourse, the "it is said" of the people. Its authenticity was linked to its oral connection, to its lack of structure, its spontaneity. However, it appears, rather, that we are dealing with a work produced on a specific occasion and addressed to none other than a Carolingian emperor who, too, was searching for remembrances of things past.

Notker, nicknamed Balbulus (the Stammerer), a monk from the monastery of Saint Gall, wrote the work known as the *Gesta Karoli Magni* for the emperor Charles the Fat, who ruled the whole of western Christendom—as Charlemagne had done—for the first time since Louis the Pious and for the last time ever. Charles the Fat had spent three days at Saint Gall in December 883, and it is probable that Notker, to entertain the emperor, told him some of the stories he would later incorporate into his *Gesta*. Crowned in 881, Charles the Fat was deposed in 887, and the work of the monk from Saint Gall never reached him, which explains why this text remained unknown for so long.

Notker himself was supposed to have heard these stories from Adalbert, a veteran of the Carolingian wars, who participated in the victory over the Avars, and from his son, who became a monk at Saint Gall monastery. But it is certain that Notker also used sources that included the *Annals* and above all Einhard's *Life of Charlemagne*. There are extant manuscripts going back to the twelfth century that combine Notker's work, Einhard's *Vita*, and the *Royal Frankish Annals*, and form a kind of anthology or compendium on Charlemagne. These three texts complement each other—in the case of the compendium following the logic of accumulation—thereby constructing more fully the great monarch's identity. Einhard's biography places Charlemagne in the tradition of Suetonius's great Caesars, whereas Notker's *Gesta* paints his portrait in a less haughty, less "statuesque" light. The narrator willingly places himself among the common people, the little people who look to the emperor with wonderment. This does not, however, keep him from peppering his text with citations from the Bible, Virgil's *Aeneid* and the *Eclogues* as well as from hagiographical literature (Paulinus of Milan's *Life of Saint Ambrose*, Sulpicius Severus's *Life of Saint Martin*). The references to religious and epic heroes add a sort of grandiose counterpoint to a story that is constantly noting its modesty and simplicity. Notker stresses the role played by eyewitnesses, claiming he is dealing with *real* history. He did not actually witness the events himself: his gaze is an indirect one, since the facts about the hero have been transmitted by word of mouth before being set down in writing.

At first glance, Notker's work appears to be a collection of anecdotes structured only by its division into two parts, the first pertaining to the emperor's piety, particularly to his ecclesiastical policy, and the second focusing on Charlemagne's war exploits. Notker refers to a third part dealing with Charlemagne's private life, but he either never completed it or it has been lost. However, it is significant that in Notker's work facts relating to religion achieve independent status and are differentiated from those pertaining to the emperor's private life.

In Notker's text the narrator favors digressions and insists on the spontaneous and nonstructured aspects of his stories, which appear at times to be linked only through an association of ideas or even a simple admission of neglect: "I forgot to say . . . I will repair this omission with a few words" (book 1, chap. 7, p. 181). Following this logic, narrative pieces could accumulate as long as the narrator could draw on collective "memories." Here, the narrative "I" frequently intervenes, ostensibly in the guise of a man remembering a sovereign's deeds; thus the text assumes the form of a series of meditations whose order is governed not by impersonal chronology but by the movement of subjective narration. Notker's representation is rendered more intimate in that the image does not appear to be imposed by a preestablished form but through a moving spirit borrowing form and tone—sometimes epic, sometimes biblical, sometimes hagiographical, sometimes anecdotal—suitable to a given moment or action. We might speak of a personalized identity in the sense that the vision of the sovereign appears to have been interiorized rather than monumentalized.

When we look closer, though, we notice that two of the elements we have already seen in Einhard, that is, space and morality, play a fundamental structural role. Notker tells us next to nothing regarding time; we don't know when the events he recounts occur. Time is simply the time of Charlemagne. In contrast, at the start of each story, the Monk of Saint Gall is careful to specify the places where the events occurred. The first sentence of the *Gesta* establishes a north-south axis by evoking the fall of the Roman Empire and the rise of the Frankish one. The second sentence defines an east-west axis by limiting the empire to the west and stating that knowledge traveled from west to east: "At the time when this monarch began to reign alone over the western regions of the world, the study of letters had everywhere fallen into almost complete oblivion: chance brought from Ireland to the coasts of Gaul. . . ."[46] Charlemagne ceaselessly travels along these two axes.

In the entire first part of Notker's work those travels are not aimed at war, as they are in Einhard, but have an ethical and cultural objective. The intent is foremost to teach, and the first anecdote Notker recounts tells of the arrival of two scholars from Ireland (Clement and Dungal) accompanied by some "Breton" merchants. They immediately begin to imitate the merchants by announcing that they have knowledge for sale. Charles, "ever filled with an insatiable love for knowledge," quickly "buys" their product and keeps them close at hand by "nourishing" or sustaining them at his court. The great monarch attracts scholars and places value on acquiring knowledge. He takes knowledge out of the free market and transforms it into a privileged instrument of unity (book 1, chap. 1, pp. 173–74). This policy succeeds so well that "the Gauls, or today's Franks, have become the equal of the Romans and Athenians of olden times" (book 1, chap. 2).[47]

Here we see the beginnings of the theme of *translatio studii*, which was to become increasingly important in France beginning in the twelfth century. Notker affirms the cultural unity of the Franks and the Gauls, that is, those "moderns" who, due to Charlemagne's policies and Alcuin's knowledge, rose to the stature of the ancients, that is, the Greeks and the Romans.

We may thank Notker for the story of the monarch seen questioning students himself, praising the hard-working schoolboys from "the middle and lower classes" (*mediocres igitur et infimi*) and scolding the rich pupils:

> Then turning an annoyed face toward the students remaining on his left, bringing terror to their conscience with his angry look, haranguing more than speaking, he threw at them words filled with the bitterest irony: "As for you, nobles, sons of the Notables of the nation, delicate and soft children, resting on your birth and fortune, you have neglected my orders and the care of your own glory in your studies and preferred to give yourselves over to softness, to games, to laziness and to futile occupations. . . ."[48] Though the king of heaven has allowed others to admire you, I give you no credit for your birth and beauty. Know and remember that if you fail to hasten, through constant efforts, to make up for your past negligence, you will never get anything from Charles." (Book 1, chap. 3, p. 176)

Thus the great king separates knowledge from the economy of the market as well as from considerations of class and birth.

A concern with preventing abuse of privileges is noted again in the second part of the text when the notables go hunting, dressed in elegant clothes that are ruined in the course of the day's activities. Charles forces them to wear the same damaged clothes again the next day, and this provides him the opportunity to lecture the notables on the uselessness of inappropriate elegance and luxury (book 2, chap. 17, pp. 260–61). These parables show the monarch *personally* praising members of the lower classes and punishing the abuses of the notables. It is true that many of the stories deal with abuses by bishops and that the Monk of Saint Gall is no doubt aiming to support the cause of the monasteries, particularly his own. There is thus a context and a specific ideology for Notker's work. In order to have his political message accepted, Notker links the bishops to the notables and the monks to the common folks. The narrator's gaze on the monarch is a vertical one, originating from below. As regards his immediate concerns, Notker seeks royal protection. As for what he wishes to pass on to future generations, Notker presents Charlemagne as a protector of the common folk and the poor against the abuses of the powerful.

Through his many travels, the emperor ensures the uniform dissemination and assimilation of a certain Christian culture. While in Trier or in Metz to celebrate Christmas, he listens to the singing of the monks sent by the pope to teach Frankish clerks to sing as they do in Rome. The following year finds him in Paris or in Tours during the same season; while listening to the monks' chanting, he notices the chants are different from those he heard sung in Trier. He thus uncovers the Roman monks' plot to corrupt the way the monks of the *regnum Francorum* sang in order to prevent them from acquiring the Roman monks' knowledge. The king then enters into an agreement with the pope to send two Frankish monks to Rome (we see that Charlemagne also encourages others to travel) to learn the Roman art of singing. Upon their return, they teach their art to their fellow monks. Charlemagne causes harmony to reign in singing just as he does among men. In fact, such harmony is established and maintained only through his travels. And this is Charlemagne's primary role in Notker's series of tales, stories, and parables: Charlemagne is the man whose existence creates the conditions for the possibility of community, the man whose presence guarantees order, harmony, and well-being in a geographical space whose cohesion he ensures.[49]

As in Einhard, Notker's narrative setting suggests strategies for power. Most of the time, the opposition to Charlemagne's authority is not associated with political issues or metaphysical differences but with a psychological and moral attitude. The emperor's enemies are driven by *invidia*.[50] Envy proves to be the driving force behind the disorder against which Charlemagne tirelessly struggles, a force that is at the origin of all divisiveness, including that which is tearing the Church apart.

The collective identity Charlemagne has forged incorporates and assimilates a great deal of diversity and many different peoples. It is Christian and its heart is *Francia*. But it extends well beyond that land, and Notker sometimes calls the Empire Europe—a term that was later to be replaced by that of Christendom.[51] And yet, while Charlemagne's *regnum* has been established and justified through faith and for the Faith—*imperium chris-tianum*—the emperor's sovereignty is also asserted in opposition to the Church. The Monk of Saint Gall describes how, during a gathering of rep-resentatives from throughout Europe, Charlemagne puts a stop to the pre-tensions of a bishop who is envious of the emperor's power. While Charles was away waging war against the Huns, this bishop had dared to ask of Queen Hildegard if he could substitute his own episcopal cross with the golden rod that "the incomparable emperor had turned into the symbol of his authority" (book 1, chap. 17, p. 193). Upon the emperor's return, Hil-degard tells him of the bishop's request.

> The whole of Europe had, so to speak, gathered [*cum autem cuncta pene Europa*] to celebrate the emperor's triumph over the redoubtable nation of the Huns. The prince then said in the presence of the magnates and the men of lower ranks [*maiorum et minorum*]: "Bishops should despise things of this world and, through their own example, lead other men to desire only celestial goods. But now they have let them-selves be so corrupted by ambition that one of them, not satisfied with the most important episcopal see of Germany, has wanted, in place of the bishop's staff, to appropriate without our knowledge the golden scepter we carry as mark of our authority [*rigiminis nostri*]." (Book 1, chap. 17, p. 193)

Notker's careful depiction of the scene draws our attention to the sym-bols of royal and ecclesiastical power. To the horizontal axis (the whole of Europe) is added a vertical axis (different social ranks). Thus the notion of identity and coherence can be realized in the celebration of Charlemagne's power. Clearly, Notker adheres to Benedictine monastic politics in setting the bishops against the emperor, but it is also true that he is promoting a community coherence that is being threatened by an essentially moral cor-ruption.[52]

While the festive gathering around Charlemagne can be interpreted as a condensed image of unity, the establishment of a vast network to facili-tate travel and communication between the different parts of the empire can be seen as the expanded image of this unity. Notker writes of the con-struction of bridges, ships, passages, and paths; the bridge over the Rhine in Mainz uniting two separated lands best illustrates the idea of a union in the process of being established.

This bridge, which burned in 813, sparked the imaginations of its con-temporaries. It is mentioned in the *Annals* as well as in Einhard's *Life*. In Notker, the bridge acquires the symbolic value of the double union, hori-zontal and vertical, that I mentioned earlier. Construction works of rela-tively limited scope were entrusted to the people of lesser rank but when it came to larger works, particularly new constructions, dukes, counts, and bishops were always expected to participate. This can be seen in the arches of the bridge at Mainz, which were built with the orderly cooperation of all of Europe (quem tota Europa communi quidem sed ordinatissime participationis opere perfecit) (book 1, chap. 30, p. 213). The schema is similar to the one at work in the celebration mentioned above: all social strata are mobilized in the construction of a bridge that unites them together. Notker transfers the order of the architectural project onto the overall activity itself: it is not just the bridge's arches that are regularly ordered but also the activities of men.[53] Whether he is teaching or building, Charlemagne is the creator of orderly community harmony. This oneness presupposes more than the simple circulation of the given word, it implies an ontology of presence, that of individuals present to each other so as to constitute a community.

The collective entity is thus defined through scenes emblematic of union and unity, of constructive order and coherence. Charlemagne creates this geographical-cultural ensemble and he also embodies it. His sovereignty is established not only in relation to different internal forces: it must also strive to conquer externally in order to be established and recognized by peoples outside its realm.

And that sovereignty must also exist in time. In the second part of Notker's work, which the monk claims to be devoted to war exploits, only one third of the episodes deals with the wars waged by Charlemagne, another third includes the exchanges of ambassadors, and a third deals with Charlemagne's lineage. In the exchanges with other kingdoms, we again find the logic of the potlatch. In contrast to the *Annals*, Notker places less emphasis on Charlemagne as the recipient of gifts than on the emperor as a great giver. But in Notker's text, the most important function of foreign ambassadors to Aachen consists in being eyewitnesses to the sovereign's glory. This is because Charlemagne, through the very act of making an appearance, creates the existence of that which he represents. To external viewers, there can be no distinction between Charles and the Church; there can only be one greatness, that of the Christian emperor. Thus Notker chooses the celebration of Easter to illustrate the identity radiating from Charlemagne, an identity in the process of establishing itself through him before the world.

Persian ambassadors arrive in Aachen during the last week of Lent and Charlemagne receives them on the eve of the great Easter celebration. "The very great Charles *appeared* to them so much more imposing than any other mortal that they thought they had previously *not seen* any king or emperor." Charlemagne granted them the favor of circulating freely and allowed them to "*see all things*, ask questions, and collect information" on every subject. But these ambassadors, "carried away and ecstatic . . . preferred over all the riches of the Orient the happiness of not leaving the emperor, of ceaselessly *contemplating and admiring* him. They climbed into the gallery that went round the basilica and looked down upon the clergy and the troops, and time and again returned to the emperor"; they displayed a sort of joyous astonishment. The next day, they were invited "on this very holy day, to the opulent Charles's sumptuous dinner with the magnates of France and Europe, but [the ambassadors], seized with astonishment at all that they were *seeing*, left the table almost without having eaten a thing" (book 2, chap. 8, pp. 233–34). The performative role of appearing could not be emphasized more. Charles is what there is to see. Everything else fades; clergy, troops, "all things" are only extensions of he who gives them reason for being. Here again, a confirmation of the collective being occurs during a celebration, which brings together society's constitutive elements (warriors and priests), and again we find a geographical reference to the space of the community (*Francia*, Europe).

Rather than an autonomous collective self-awareness, we should speak of that self-awareness occurring through the great monarch—the community's awareness of itself necessarily passes through the figure of Charlemagne. Charlemagne's constitutive function in relation to the social body affects a whole set of different entities—from the "nation" in the limited sense (*Francia*) to the empire, and from Europe to the West. Even more than with words (Einhard and Notker mention the weakness of Charlemagne's voice), this presence asserts itself through its gaze. In the poems on Charles and Leo III, Charlemagne is portrayed as the beacon of Europe, he who enables people to see by spreading his light, and who, through his stature and radiance, attracts our own gaze.

The act of appearing is Charlemagne's primary way of asserting his sovereignty. Although there is no war between the empires of the East and the West, the two emperors nonetheless engage in a symbolic struggle. The ambassador Charles sends to Constantinople is received coolly but ultimately proves his superiority through his intelligence. When the Greek emperor's ambassadors arrive in Aachen, they are required to pass through three rooms in each of which they encounter a Frankish notable surrounded by courtiers. In each room the Greeks mistake the notable for the emperor and prostrate themselves before him. On each occasion their naïveté is emphasized when they are told that the emperor is much greater than those whom they have seen up to then. Finally, after their ordeal, they are introduced to the emperor of the West. The presentation is most impressive:

> Charles, the most illustrious of kings, radiant as the rising sun and all resplendent with gold and jewels, was sitting next to a window which

let in much daylight . . . ; around the emperor, standing in a circle like celestial troops of angels, were his three sons, joined in his rule, his daughters, and their mother, no less resplendent in her wisdom and beauty than in her clothing; prelates of unequaled appearance and virtue; priests as distinguished by their nobility as by their saintliness; dukes even more impressive than Joshua when he made his appearance in Gilgal's camp. This assembly, like the one that repelled Cyrus and his Assyrians from the walls of Samaria, just as if David were present in its midst, could have rightfully sung: "All you kings and peoples of the world, all you that are princes and judges on earth, young men and maids, old men and boys together; let them all give praise to the Lord's name." (Ps. 148:11–12;[54] book 2, chap. 6, pp. 230–31)

Confronted with a rival power, Charlemagne transforms himself into a monument to be beheld: the sun king, the king in glowing majesty, immobile, framed by the window, the solar radiance complemented by that of his gold and jewels. Richness, splendor, family, church, nobility—all is arranged in a harmonious circle reflecting celestial harmony. As seen in the biblical reference, the relationship between King Charlemagne and the celestial king could not be any more explicit. We might also note in this description elements of the *aura* that surrounded Germanic kings before Christianization.[55] Such an amalgam turns Charlemagne's subjects into God's chosen people: the new Israel. It does not matter that this scene probably occurred in 812 and that Charlemagne had lost his wife in 800 and only one of his sons was still alive in 812. What is important is not chronology but a mythifying vision. Charlemagne prevails here through the simple act of allowing himself to be seen. His power lies in the act of presenting itself, whether it be in a biblical representation or an epic and conquering one. In Notker's work, Charlemagne fights against the Huns, the Saxons, the Normans, and the Lombards. In describing the conquest of Pavia, the Monk of Saint Gall uses the same schema he used to describe the three stages preceding the emperor's appearance before the Greek ambassadors. Desiderius, king of the Lombards, rises up against Charlemagne when the emperor rejects his wife, a Lombard princess, the daughter of Desiderius, as she is "always ill and unable to give him children" (book 2, chap. 17, p. 255). At Desiderius's side is a magnate from Charlemagne's kingdom, a certain Ogier (Ogger), who is on very bad terms with the emperor.[56] The two are waiting together, watching for the arrival of the king of the Franks. Three times Desiderius, seeing the impressive waves of approaching troops, asks Ogier if it is Charlemagne who is coming. Three times Ogier answers in the negative and explains that Charlemagne will arrive when the rivers Po and Tessin inundate the city with waves blackened by iron.

He had barely finished saying these words when one could begin to see in the direction of the west something like a dark cloud similar to the one raised by the northwest wind or *borea*, which can transform the clearest of days into terrifying shadows. But as the emperor approached ever closer, the brilliance of the weapons illuminated for the people barricaded in the town a day that was darker than any night. Then Charles himself appeared, this man of iron, his head covered with an iron helmet, his hands covered with iron gloves, his chest of iron and his shoulders of marble protected by iron armor, his left hand gripped an iron lance raised high in the air and his right hand held his invincible sword. The outside of his thighs . . . was covered by plates of iron. What might I say about his boots? His entire army always wore boots of iron. . . . On his shield one could only see iron. His horse was of the color and strength of iron. . . . Iron covered fields and roads. The iron blades reflected the rays of the sun. This iron that was so hard was worn by a people whose heart was even harder. The gleam of iron spread terror into the streets of the city.[57] (Book 2, chap. 17, pp. 257–58)

Confronted with this vision, Ogier faints, and Charlemagne is able to take the town the next day without any bloodshed. The hammering of the rhetorical figure of the polyptoton (*ferreus, ferrea, ferreis*, etc.) translates well the force of the vision. In war, the sun king radiating with gold becomes the iron conqueror spreading a dark light, and it takes only one glance at him for him to be able to win the battle. The great monarch's presence guarantees the extension of the community, just as it ensures its internal cohesion. Here we are close to the epic vision of Charlemagne as found in the *chansons de geste*, and it is noteworthy that Notker already presents a prince's revolt against the great monarch, a revolt that threatens the unity of the Empire.

Up to now, the emperor has appeared only as the object of another's gaze. But there is also the gaze that emanates from the great prince. In Notker's account this look is sometimes filled with anger; it can cause terror like God's gaze in the Old Testament. It is primarily a gaze from which nothing escapes. To be within Charlemagne's space is to be constantly under his gaze. He becomes a sort of living eye that unites and controls everything within its field of vision. The construction of Aachen is significant here because Notker describes the architecture of the capital as a *panoptikon* organized around the great chief's gaze:

For the dwellings of all the persons of dignity [were] built around the palace according to the plans of the shrewd Charlemagne in such a way that the emperor could, from the windows of his quarters, *see what everyone coming or going was doing, even the most hidden things.* The dwellings of the Notables were moreover suspended, so to speak, above ground. Under these houses, not only officers and their servants but all sorts of people could find shelter against the ravages of wind, snow, rain, heat or cold, albeit *without being able to escape Charles's vigilant gaze.* (Book 1, chap. 30, p. 214)

The structure of this city, the symbol of Charlemagne's glory, helps us understand how the collectivity's self-awareness is conceived primarily in relation to Charlemagne. The social order is mirrored in the different heights of the buildings, the tallest towering above the others as if detached from them. Charlemagne himself defines the layout of this space, establishing analogous relationships between the city he has built and the society over which he reigns. The city is a hierarchical, but also, for the emperor, a transparent place, because Charlemagne's gaze sees everything, encompasses everything, and in so doing ensures order, coherence, and conformity. This gaze is often extended by that of his faithful subjects, who tirelessly watch for him.

The power of Charlemagne's gaze is transmitted from father to son. Although the Monk of Saint Gall makes scant mention of time, he does devote one third of the second part of his work to Charlemagne's lineage. It is in this section, moreover, that the parallel between Charlemagne's gaze and that of the God of the Old Testament is made most explicit. As Notker notes in regard to Charlemagne's grandson Louis the German, "the anger of his gaze alone was punishing, like what is written about the eternal judge who sees within us [*quod de eterno internoque iudice scriptum est*]: A king, sitting on the throne of his dominion [*in solio regni sui*] dissipates all evil by his mere gaze or scrutiny [*intuitu vultus sui*]" (book 2, chap. 11, pp. 243–44; Prv. 20:8). Like Charlemagne, his descendants do not simply see men's actions, they penetrate into their consciences to shape and control their intentions.

Notker likens the accession of Louis the Pious to Charlemagne's throne to that of "peaceful Solomon" to the throne of the "bellicose David" (book 2, chap. 19, p. 263). But in the text of the Monk of Saint Gall the Norman menace makes its presence felt as the always clairvoyant Charlemagne foresees the danger of external threat, the end of the union of which he is himself the linchpin. Seeing the ships of Norman pirates in the distance, the emperor stands up and goes to the window facing east, "and stayed there for a very long time, his face bathed in tears. I am deeply sorrowful, he explains, that in my lifetime they came so close to landing on this shore, and I am troubled by violent pain when I foresee the evils they will inflict on my nephews and their peoples" (book 2, chap. 14, pp. 251–52). Charlemagne's tears begin to flow very early on—well before the *chansons de geste.* Einhard had located this proof of human sensitivity within the context of Charlemagne's private life (the loss of a friend); Notker extends it, one might say, to the public person.

The King and the Magnates: Hincmar

The establishment of an identificatory figure, a source of legitimacy, of harmony, of well-being, and of glory occurred in a world torn by centrifugal forces. References to the great king resonated in the rituals and ceremonies of the Church and the monarchy, the only two institutions that not only possessed structures that could preserve and promote the memory of this ideal monarch, but that also had similar needs for legitimacy in order to protect themselves against the splintering and disintegrating forces threatening them both.

King Charles III (the Fat) was succeeded by Odo (Eudes) (888–898), the first non-Carolingian king of western *Francia*, that part of Charlemagne's empire which resulted from the Treaty of Verdun in 843 and which would later become France. The first king of western *Francia* was Charles the Bald (840–877), a son of Louis the Pious. Events led this grandson of Charlemagne, filled with dreams of his great ancestor, eventually to be crowned emperor on Christmas Day 875, the anniversary of the coronation of the first Carolingian. Charles the Bald was crowned by Pope John VIII in the Basilica of Saint Peter in Rome, only to die less than two years later at Avrieux in Savoie, broken by illness from his pursuit of the dream of a reconstituted "universal" empire.

In 882 Hincmar, the archbishop of Reims, wrote a description of Charlemagne's reign. It provides the best illustration of the stresses and needs of that period of constant uprisings. It was Hincmar who persuaded the episcopate to support Charles the Bald against the treason of the archbishop of Sens, Wenilo, the Ganelon of epic, the very man who personifies treachery in the *Chanson de Roland* and for a long time afterward. After the death of Louis III, son of Louis II (the Stammerer) who had directly succeeded Charles the Bald in 877, Archbishop Hincmar wrote a "letter" to the bishops, to the powerful of the kingdom, and to King Carloman in order to instruct the young ruler. Hincmar had helped negotiate the agreement putting an end to a rebellion of the magnates against Louis the Stammerer (877–879). It was he who had crowned Louis in 877 at Compiègne, a city that even a hundred years later was still called Carlopolis, and that Charles the Bald had wanted to make the seat of his power, just as Charlemagne had done at Aachen.[58] Making a virtue of necessity, Hincmar depicts the functioning of the Carolingian monarchy as one in which the powerful of the kingdom play a primary role and in which consultation with them comprises a fundamental part of royal policy.

Up to now we have looked at representations portraying Charlemagne as a great hero in many domains: war, religion, letters, justice, morality. But we have not seen him act as a political man. Embodying that which he was creating, he had no need to consider wills other than his own. Willing and acting, conceiving and executing, appearing and being—everything formed a whole. The mention made of the general assemblies in the *Royal Frankish Annals* included neither procedure nor content. There were no obstacles to the transparency and immediacy of Charlemagne's reign. But, in Hincmar, these assemblies are endowed with a real meaning and function, and suddenly a radically different image of the emperor comes into view.

Hincmar's new mirror of the prince does not define the king in relation to external forces, nor in terms of a policy of expansion and conquest, nor even of defense against an outside aggressor, but rather in terms of a concern with internal functioning and stability. I have chosen to examine Hincmar's text here for three reasons. The first involves a teleological concern: Hincmar's text was to play a primary role in representations of the figure of the emperor Charlemagne during the Ancien Régime. The second involves the novelty of the representation in relation to the preceding texts. The third concerns a strategy of narrative analyses, because, with Hincmar, we close a cycle of narrative developments with an anti-narrative text. It is anti-narrative insofar as it aims to attain an equilibrium consisting of repetitions without reference to temporality: a state of stasis. And yet, Hincmar's work still includes an epic presence. At the beginning of his letter, Hincmar evokes Leonidas, Alexander's mediocre tutor, who had taught some bad habits to his illustrious student.[59] Later on Alexander was able to conquer many kingdoms, but "he could not conquer himself." Hincmar thus wants to prevent the irreparable, that is, the relaxed morals and the disorderly conduct Alexander had never been able to overcome. Hincmar wishes to speak of that which, once it is set up the way it should, must never be changed.

One might expect a moral pedagogy with the idea of it being instilled over time, but, in fact, the archbishop immediately launches into a description of a political structure. We go from a moral viewpoint to a constitutional one. In doing this, Hincmar bases his ideas on information he has obtained directly from Louis the Pious's advisers, as well as from the *De Ordine Palatii*, a text by Adalhard, once abbot of the monastery of Corbie and "kin to My Lord Charles the Great" (chap. 12, p. 33). The primary aim of the "historian" Hincmar is, in a sense, to stop history, to halt its movement at the point where things were done the way they should be, that is, in a reconstructed time of Charlemagne.

According to Hincmar, there are two powers participating in the government of the world: "the sacred authority of the popes and the royal power" [*auctoritas sacra pontificum et regalis potestas*] (chap. 5, p. 15). Hincmar begins by attributing a primary role to the Church, mostly to the bishops. It is the Church that confers legitimacy on the king through sacred anointing. Bishops have the function of moral trustees and, above all, in Hincmar they assume the function of the scrutinizing gaze, "since the Greek word *episcopus* [*episkopos*, "bishop"] means overseer" (chap. 5, p. 17). Their function is to watch over the lives and morals of their flock. As for the king, he must in all respects follow ecclesiastical rules (chap. 9, p. 25). Hincmar then describes each of the monarchy's functions, and he presents *The Organization of the Palace* by Adalhard as the source for his prescriptive vision. He describes a timeless system whose authority is based on that of the government that functioned under Charlemagne. The king was constantly surrounded by a great number of nobles, always "in sufficient number to manage affairs as expected by reason and dignity, and there was never a dearth of competent advisers" (chap. 25, p. 65).

The key to this government lies in the debates that were held within the assemblies, for it is there that the affairs of the kingdom were determined. The assemblies were held twice a year: one included all the notables, whether they were clerics or laymen, and the other was a gathering of the "greatest among the great" (*cum senioribus tantum et praecipuis consiliariis*) (chap. 30, p. 77). The larger assembly was divided into two groups, one made up of the clergy, the other of laymen. "No event could alter" the decisions made by the larger assembly (chap. 19, p. 73). As to the smaller assembly, its members decided what issues were to be discussed by the larger one. The king submitted propositions in the form of protocols, later issued as capitularies. Discussions, which could take several days, "occurred without the king's presence; the latter remained with the crowd, received gifts, greeted notables, talked with those he rarely saw, commiserated with the aches and pain of the elderly, rejoiced with the young men, and dealt with similar things in both the spiritual and secular realms" (chap. 25, p. 91).

In this system, which Hincmar presents as an originary constitution or form of government, the king proposes, learns, and carries out the decisions taken. Much more than the embodiment of the collectivity, Hincmar's Charlemagne is the arbiter, the mediator, and the executor of the decision makers' will. As in the other texts I have analyzed, we find a social harmony here, a sense of collectivity, though now the collectivity is defined through the consensus of the notables, which the king must facilitate and to which he submits. Rather than a great warrior, Hincmar's king is ultimately an able statesman adept at maintaining equilibrium and the status quo. His principal function is to ensure and guide debate, deliberation, and discussion.

This document is important because it reflects what might be described as a primitive stage in the development of a "national" consciousness (*Nationalbewußtsein*) in France. For Hincmar does not situate his work in relation to an external world, but seeks to identify a mode of political functioning that is aimed at maintaining internal peace and justice—one specific to the empire of the Franks in the West. In fact, rather than calling it a national feeling, one might speak of a consciousness of the particularity (*Eigenbewußtsein*) of a group of people enjoying a certain geographical coherence, albeit an unstable one, and defining itself in terms of a set of political practices (and not only in terms of a dynasty). In this context, Charlemagne's capitularies appear less the result of the king's will than of a collective consensus in which the monarch participates.[60] This Carolingian tradition of a shared rule (*Mitregierung*), in which a smaller or greater part of the collectivity collaborates, was later to play an important role in the development of republican thought in France.

The construction of an identity for this figure who in some ways created the community he embodied took place on several levels. This process drew more from the idea of regeneration than from that of ex nihilo creation. Yet, at the same time, it located the genesis of the collective entity in the fusion produced by conquest. We have gone from the fragmented vision of the *Annals*, which derives its coherence from repetition, to the narrative coherence of biography, ranging from a monumental representation to a subjective evocation, from a vision of total power to one of an essentially mediating function. We have thus seen some of the main features of the construct that has endowed the figure of Charlemagne with the prestige of a historical moment that was both originary and exemplary.

Warrior, protector of Christendom, guarantor of justice, defender of the poor, legislator, able and adept statesman, renovator of the arts and letters: Charlemagne not only fulfilled all these functions, but he also embodied them with magnificence and radiance, and represented them on very different levels. He was king and emperor; he ruled over *Francia* and the empire of the West; he was all powerful and respectful of other peoples' rights; he was an active, formidable force unto himself, *and* a mediator. More than anyone at that time, he linked the local and the particular to the universal; that is, he linked the Frankish entity, whose legacy was to become that of France, to eternal and transcendental values. The symbolic potential of the figure of Charlemagne stems from its simultaneous presence on all fronts, from the whole spectrum of values it reflects and transmits. The great emperor is made to embody a mission that transcends immediacy and will justify conquest. In short, the figure of Charlemagne crystallizes a collective identity by the values it represents.

But already the golden age that Charlemagne was to have achieved has assumed very diverse forms in the collective imagination. These different, often competing visions nevertheless maintain the emperor as a common reference point. And so this rallying figure, this figure of legitimacy and unity also became the focal point of polemics, and even of contention. In the texts we have just seen, Charlemagne is invoked to affirm the way things ought to be—they project a desire for a collective ideal and a sense of loss upon the veil that was already beginning to cover his features.

T W O

Poetic Space,
Political Reflection

POETRY AND HISTORY

Through the decline of the Carolingians and the establishment of the
Capetian monarchy the transformation envisaged by Hincmar in an idealized fashion continued at the expense of royal power. During Louis VI the
Fat's (r. 1108–1137) coronation at Orléans, not only the duke of Normandy,
King Henry I of England, but also the dukes of Aquitaine and Burgundy
refused to swear allegiance to the young king. The magnates, the "barons,"
intended to do as they pleased. With its loss of prestige, the royal house,
having become only one among others, turned in on itself. As was the case
with other princes, the king's power now rested on that which he held pri-
vately: his domain, his lands, his *hommes de corps*. And yet, the system of obligations in the Carolingian tradition, a system based on notions of loyalty
and service, still survived to some extent. Starting with Louis VI, heading a
royal house freed from the influence of the powerful, there began a renewal of the monarchy that accelerated through the reigns of Louis VII
(1137–1180) and Philip Augustus (1180–1223). From the viewpoint I have
adopted here, this rise was based on two key elements: on the one hand, the
close-knit solidarity between monarchical and ecclesiastical institutions
and, on the other, the development and establishment of a more strictly defined feudal-vassalic law. Louis VI called upon the bishops to return peace

to his kingdom. Louis VII was the first to participate in the Crusades. The aristocracy also rushed in only to be massacred while the royal house consolidated and aggrandized itself by pursuing an advantageous matrimonial policy. As its power grew, the monarchy took advantage of the establishment of knightly morality. This morality, grounded in a notion of loyalty, became the cornerstone in a process of bolstering the king in his role of suzerain or feudal overlord. He was suzerain not only of the powerful but, beginning in 1202, of their own vassals—or *arrière vassals*—as well. In short, the monarchy used feudality and vassalage itself in order to assert itself over the great lords.

Throughout this evolution, there were increasing appeals to the figures of Charlemagne. The primary role played by Abbot Suger of Saint-Denis, that high place of Carolingian symbolism, accentuates a tradition that went back to the great conqueror. Charlemagne's reign came to represent a reference point that could not be bypassed. From the greatest to the lowest, kings and nobles as well as bishops, priests, and monks called upon him to justify their status, to legitimize their privileges, to support their demands. The *chansons de geste*, which developed and spread beginning in the twelfth century, provide the best evidence of Charlemagne's symbolic power. But we have seen that the figure of Charlemagne encompasses a very broad range of values and is able to serve very different ideals. Thus, far from being either simple celebrations of a heroic figure or condemnations without possibility of appeal (as we will see in the songs of the "revolted" barons), the *chansons de geste* form a locus of debate on the nature and limits of political power and legitimacy. Machiavelli later had to invent his prince in order to reflect on the monarch's role. In the Middle Ages, in this period when the very nature of the monarchy was changing, the figure of Charlemagne became established as a privileged mirror of the prince, as a locus of reflection on the nature of the monarchy. "[Q]uoniam et mendacia poetarum serviunt veritati [since even the poets' lies serve the truth]," writes John of Salisbury.[1]

The mythified history told in the *chansons de geste* proved to be a means for medieval poets—and for those who listened to them and who commissioned their work—to think about power by examining its contours and to look critically at how key elements of a social order functioned in the midst of transformation. Out of the dynamics of the narrative there emerges a description of putting the feudal-vassalic system in its entirety to the test, including its relation to a theocentric vision. The narrative form enables an acting out of the play of social mechanisms; it enables one to depict responses to challenges coming from the outside as well as from the inside, and, within the movement of the narrative, to examine the consequences of these responses.

E. R. Curtius has already pointed out the distinctive trait of the French epic, its close ties to history. Others have spoken of an epic distance in relation to contemporary history.[2] Since the publication of *Histoire poétique de Charlemagne* by Gaston Paris (1865), no one has doubted the predominance of the figure of Charlemagne in medieval French—or even European—epic poetry. And yet the great philologist purposely excludes from his poetic history any work not having roots in popular oral tradition. Because of this, he rejects all texts composed in Latin—the language of clerks and of official culture. Thus, he excludes the *Royal Frankish Annals*, along with Einhard's and Notker's narratives, Hincmar's letter, and the Latin epic "Karolus Magnus et Leo papa." Paris also disregards certain texts in the vernacular that had too much of a "priestly feel" for his taste, including the famous chronicle of Pseudo-Turpin and the *Journey to Jerusalem*. Works by chroniclers whose main subjects did not derive from a poetic vision met the same fate. For Paris, the role of the French people in the national epic was of primary importance. According to him, the *chanson de geste* was a collective creation. Without going into too much detail now, since I will come back to this point later, it should simply be noted here that the issue of the origins of these *chansons* dominated critical debate at the end of the nineteenth century and for a good part of the twentieth.[3]

The methodology I am adopting here enables us to bypass the possibly unsolvable issue of the genesis and first composition of the *chansons* and to avoid the constraints imposed by separating poetic tradition from all others. By proceeding with a study of some important representations in order better to understand their later uses, we can avoid the constraints of the distinction between the poetic tradition and other types of representation that, in a general manner, continues to rule the study of medieval literature on Charlemagne. Such differentiations are today linked less to political stances than to disciplinary divisions: history, literature, philology. Nonetheless, it is also true that Charlemagne's historical persona has in some ways been left to the Germans while France continues to claim its literary legacy, that is, Charlemagne's poetic history, one more reason to maintain a separation of traditions. I would thus like to put these distinctions aside and approach the body of epic poetry by incorporating it into a more general category that would, at least in principle, include everything that has been written on Charlemagne. In this chapter, I will examine the *chansons de geste*, composed of course in the vernacular as well as the famous Latin pseudodesignation of "Turpin" which also circulated in Old French and was one of the most important vehicles of the great emperor's mythified history.

THE *CHANSON DE ROLAND*: A FRAGILE EQUILIBRIUM

At a crucial moment in the *Chanson de Roland*, at the start of the traitor Ganelon's trial, the *chanson* sends us back to the *geste*:

Il est escrit en l'anciene geste
Que Carles mandet humes de plusurs teres.
Asemblez sunt ad Ais, a la capele.

———

[It is written in the old geste
That Charles summons vassals from many lands.
They have assembled at Aix, in the chapel.][4]

The term "*geste*" recurs several times in the *chanson* to designate the "official" writing on which the epic narrative is based in its attempt to spread its "history."[5] In a sense, the circulatory model which the *chanson* utilizes parallels the social structure it describes: the authority of the written word legitimizes the poetic narrative just as the sovereign legitimizes feudal society. Behind this reference to the written word the image of Charlemagne as depicted in the *Annals* and in Einhard appears, as does the emperor of the Franks' own concern with fixing in writing the ancient barbarian poems telling of the exploits of the old kings.

The *Chanson de Roland* suggests better than any other text the extent to which Hincmar foreshadowed the feudal reality that was to blossom fully in the course of the eleventh century. In both works the aim is to depict a happy, but fragile, equilibrium. However, the differences between these two texts are evident. Hincmar describes a *state* of stability. The narrative dynamics of the *Chanson de Roland*, developed around the First Crusade during a time of monarchical weakening, depicts the dangers encountered by a monarchy that must find its place between God and the kingdom, between its own will and that of its barons, between the external enemy and internal treason.

Hincmar's text focuses exclusively on an internal situation, whereas the *chanson* unfolds during a war of conquest, but it also evokes the behavior of the powerful toward each other and toward the king. Charlemagne's primary identity here echoes that found in Einhard: the victorious king/ emperor. But what in Einhard was only a small reversal in a glorious campaign, a trap laid by a band of perfidious, cowardly Basques,[6] in the *Chanson de Roland* becomes a way of exploring the strengths and weaknesses of Charlemagne's power confronted with the Other—the infidel—and with the feudal society of which he is the leader. The question can be summed up as follows: what threats and challenges can royal sovereignty as embodied by Charlemagne, here shown essentially as having no defects, bear and overcome? In short, what are the limits of the social order?

In this *chanson*, which Pierre Larousse called the "Marseillaise" of Old France, binary oppositions structure a view of the conflicts (Christians/ Saracens, vassal/king, Roland/Olivier, Roland/Ganelon, Charlemagne/

Baligant) while the narrative unfolds displaying triadic dynamics that lead the sovereign, a conqueror in the first moment, into a second moment in which he is confronted by two dangers: the internal one of Ganelon's treason and the external one of the defeat at Roncevaux. This threatens his sovereignty's very existence, but then the narrative, in a third moment, reestablishes Charlemagne's authority in the face of the enemy (his victory over Baligant) and over internal challenges (treason).

The clarity of the oppositions is somewhat diminished by the confusion resulting from links of kinship among the characters. Roland is not just a vassal; he is also the emperor's nephew; he is from the same family. Not only does the private keep arising in the midst of what we would designate as the public, the very fate of the kingdom itself ultimately depends on a fortunate confusion between those two aspects of a man's life. What is essential is to avoid *excess* in all things and thus not to go beyond the limits that the *chanson* itself defines while testing them along the way.

Charlemagne's strength stems, on the one hand, from his privileged relationship with God and, on the other, from his vassals, who support and advise him. As a figure incorporating two profoundly different ideologies, one feudal-vassalic and the other theocentric,[7] Charlemagne is the sovereign and suzerain synthesis of those ideologies without which the social being would cease to exist in relation to both internal forces and external hostilities. Only he is vassal to no one; through his very existence, Charlemagne creates the ethical and juridical space necessary to the oath and to the circulation of speech.

But Charlemagne's weakness also stems from this function: he is the one who must listen and believe in the sworn word because he depends upon it, just as all of the feudal-vassalic society depends upon it. Here, the great king's constancy becomes a tragic element: his permanence in itself makes him old (two hundred years) and vulnerable ("Charlemagne is old and decrepit," says one of the Saracens; v. 905). His duty to listen and to believe in the given word, a duty inscribed in his very function, inexorably leads to his betrayal ("He cannot prevent misfortune from befalling him there"; v. 9). It is by listening to the advice of his own barons that he lets himself be fooled by Marsile. The Saracens' false gifts and lies, which Charles accepts at face value on the recommendation of those who are sworn to support him, illustrate a systematic flaw such that only resorting to force will make it possible to reestablish justice. Charlemagne's plight is defined by "perfidy," a word used repeatedly in the *Annals*.

The perfidy is Ganelon's betrayal: he gave his word, but to the Saracens, and he thereby stepped out of the realm of legitimacy. The components of the symbolic exchange between Ganelon and the Saracens are the same as those of legitimate exchanges: oaths and gifts. But Ganelon's are outside the framework of the moral space created by Charlemagne. The traitor's motives remain fairly obscure: greed, personal vengeance against Roland, weariness with the battling constantly demanded by the emperor. In any case, during the *plaid* or trial, he denies all accusations of treason:

> . . . Fel sei se jol ceil!
> Rollant me forfist en or e en aveir,
> Pur que jo quis sa mort e sun destreit;
> Mais traïsun nule n'en i otrei.

> ----

> [Ganelon said: "I'll be damned if I hide it!
> Roland wronged me in a matter concerning gold and wealth,
> Which is why I sought his death and suffering;
> But I submit no treason was committed here."][8]

The common elements in the proposed explanations—greed, fatigue, personal revenge—all belong to the private sphere. Ganelon, as he, himself, says, has fought loyally on Charlemagne's side, and he has a perfect right to take revenge for Roland's perfidy toward him. As in Hincmar, Charlemagne listens to his barons, who, instead of supporting him, take Ganelon's side and advise the king to acquit him. In the face of this challenge to his will, Charlemagne's sole response is to lower his head sadly and to lament. Even though he should avenge the death of his nephew and could use the same sort of justification Ganelon used, Charlemagne doesn't intervene. Within the boundaries separating the public from the private, the sovereign's will yields before the collective will, that of his barons. Charlemagne defers to the magnates to the point of not imposing his own will, even in the face of a council he considers "felonious." His own judgment however is enough to convince Thierry, the "short dark one," to fight in the name of the king. In doing this, the emperor's defender clearly articulates the lines between loyalty and treason, between public duty and private vengeance, when he says to Charlemagne:

> Bels sire reis, ne vos dementez si!
> Ja savez vos que mult vos ai servit.
> Par anceisurs dei jo tel plait tenir:
> Que que Rollant a Guenelun forsfesist,
> Vostre servise l'en doüst bien guarir.
> Guenes est fels d'iço qu'il le traït;
>   Vers vos s'en est parjurez e malmis.

> ----

[Dear lord king, do not show such signs of distress!
You know very well that I have served you long.
Out of loyalty to my ancestors I must pass this judgment:
Even if Roland had wronged Ganelon,
The fact that he was serving you was sufficient to safeguard him!
Ganelon committed a felony because he betrayed him,
    He perjured himself and broke his oath of fealty to you.][9]

Royal dignity is saved in the nick of time, and the guidelines marking personal rights and duties toward the sovereign are more precisely defined. An extreme case has been explored, a point of stress resolved. We see to what extent the equilibrium is fragile and to what extent Charlemagne finds himself forced to compromise with those whom he has nonetheless been chosen by God to lead. The ramifications of Charlemagne's actions are heavy with consequences because they involve Charlemagne's ability to face an external enemy as well as society's ability to function as a community and to avoid individual and familial atomization.

It is only with the arrival of Thierry that we know that Charlemagne will survive; the emperor gives free rein to his anger only after the judicial duel when he finds himself free to punish in the name of justice and of God's will. It is only then that we understand Charlemagne's anguished cry at the sight of Roland's body: "How my strength and ardor will fail! I shall have no one to fight for my honor" [Cum decarrat ma force e ma baldur! / N'en avrai ja ki sustienget m'onur] (vv. 2903–2904).[10] In fact, Charlemagne overcomes the loss of his right-hand man and in Thierry, described as the physical antithesis of the Frankish hero—small, dark, almost scrawny—he finds a support that transcends the narrow circle of the emperor's lineage and of his private affairs to accede to a new register of generalized community.

The internal judicial duel finds its counterpart in the externally waged war.[11] God's judgment intervenes in both cases. But in the realm of war, the duties of the community must be established, and here Charlemagne's role is primordial. It is he who calls up, commands, and rewards with his largesse. And it is in times of war that Charlemagne gives the clearest statement revealing the imperial nature of his character ("Carles li reis, nostre empere magnes") as well as his privileged relationship with God. Already in the time of his reign, Charles was treated as *rex christianissimus*; in the *Chanson de Roland*, God intervenes directly to stop the course of events, or he sends the angel Gabriel to protect the leader of the Christian forces.[12]

The close link established here between the emperor of the Franks and the emperor of France has been noted many times. Léon Gautier has culled 170 passages where France is identified with the empire.[13] Although France (*Francia*) is located in the geographical and ideological heart of the poem, the Empire is defined and delimited in great part in a negative manner, in relation to that which it opposes, to that which it is not. The inventory of enemy forces, a mixture of real and fictitious peoples, vaguely outlines a large geographical expanse dominated by Arabs and including Persians, Turks, and others, but also including Eastern European peoples (Sorbs [*Wends*], Slavs, Huns, Hungarians, etc.).

In fact, as has often been noted, the Saracens constitute a reverse image of Charlemagne's forces. They are all that Charlemagne's people are—they have the same qualities, and the same defects—except that they are pagans and thus, by definition, evil. Nothing reveals this reflective aspect more clearly than the description of the Emir Baligant:

> Li amiralz ben resemblet barun.
> Blanche ad la barbe ensement cume flur
> E de sa lei mult par est saives hom
> Et en bataille est fiers e orgoillus.

> ———

> [The Emir looks a good deal like a true knight.
> He has a beard that is white as a flower.
> He is very knowledgeable about his religion;
> In battle he is fierce and bold.][14]

Thus there are two leaders with white beards, and they take care to spread them out over their broignes (coats with metal rings) during the great battle! A representation of the Christian West is conveyed through the symbol of a great man, Charlemagne, struggling, as it were, against a negative image of himself. But behind this play of mirrors the fact remains that the Other comes from elsewhere. Out of that reality comes the need to define spatial boundaries.

Charlemagne embodies and illustrates the three types of relationships that make up the very essence of the monarchical institution: the sacred relationship with God; the juridical/political relationship with his Own—his subjects; and the relationship with the Other—the stranger, the heathen. Priest, politician, judge, conqueror, the king/emperor maintains a delicate equilibrium that is always threatened, always fragile; thus we have the image of Charlemagne in tears. "'God,' said the king, 'my life is so full of suffering!' / His eyes are brimming with tears, he tugs at his white beard" (vv. 4000–4001). Thus ends the *Chanson de Roland*. In the end, the moral value that ensures legitimacy comes from a privileged relationship with God, a relationship ensured through a coronation, an event occurring outside of "literature" and the written word. The angel Gabriel announces to Charles that he will have to defend the Christians against other pagans from other lands. As it closes, the song points to Charlemagne's universal mission, a mission defined more by defense than straightforward conquest.

THE *PSEUDO-TURPIN CHRONICLE:* FRANCE AND SAINT-DENIS

Charlemagne's relationship with God is at the center of the most famous medieval forgery. It was written around the same time as the *Chanson de Roland*; some believe it was written earlier, and others, later, in any event, toward the end of the eleventh century or the beginning of the twelfth. Its author was probably a monk with close ties to Saint-Denis who lived in the southwest. The *Historia Karoli Magni et Rotholandi*, or *Pseudo-Turpin Chronicle*, passed for authentic history for three centuries.[15] It relates Charlemagne's conquest of Spain; Charlemagne was believed to have undertaken this war in order to free Saint James's tomb from the Saracens. This account aims to increase the prestige and authority of the Church in general and, more specifically, of Saint James of Compostela and particularly of Saint-Denis. As J. Horrent has noted, the *Chronicle* moves, as if pulled by a magnet, along on the path of Saint James's pilgrimage.[16] A. de Mandach, following other critics, points out the parallel between the primary events narrated in the *Historia* and certain facts in the life of Alfonso VI (including a "stellar vision of the Milky Way"). This king, in 1086, controlled a large part of Spain, but not Saragossa.[17]

The Pseudo-Turpin's text endows a whole range of institutions with the prestige of their founder—Charlemagne. But this work goes even further: it provides a portrait of the king/emperor as being above all else the defender of the Church. Here, the *regnum* is subservient to the *sacerdotium*. Written in Latin prose in order to appear more credible, this chronicle was incorporated into the book of Saint James (*Liber Sancti Jacobi*),[18] and it circulated from the end of the twelfth century throughout the thirteenth in various Latin and French versions. Reprinted in various major compilations, we find it, for instance, in the *Speculum historiale* of Vincent de Beauvais (d. 1264); in Primat's *Grandes Chroniques de France* (second half of the twelfth century), in the *Chronique rimée* of Mousket (d. 1243); and in the visual compilation of the window devoted to Charlemagne in Chartres cathedral.[19] The *Pseudo-Turpin Chronicle* and the *Chanson de Roland* served as the matrix for *chansons de gestes*.[20]

It has often been pointed out that the *Historia Karoli Magni* is a work of propaganda. And because it represents a conscious manipulation of the legend of Charlemagne, Gaston Paris excludes it from the poetic history of the king. However, this is the account that represents Charlemagne as the model of the Crusading King, an image that was later adapted for expeditions to the Holy Land. The author assumes the name of the prestigious bishop who is narrating the events which he, himself, was supposed to have witnessed. In some manuscripts he introduces his text with a letter. It is of course fictitious, addressed to someone called Leonprand, docent of the cathedral of Aachen. The aim of this ruse is to make the text appear greater, more authentic, as well as to situate it alongside the official word of the *Annals*. Turpin thus writes from Vienne, where he is recovering from his injuries:

> *Quoniam nuper mandastis mihi*—Since you have asked me recently . . . to tell you in detail how Charlemagne freed from Saracen power the land of Spain and Galicia, I hasten to write and to communicate the most important of his prodigious feats and the story of his great victories over the Saracens. In my travels with him and his armies in Spain and Galicia for fourteen years, I have seen these events with my own eyes [*propriis oculis intuitus sum*]. But you wrote me that you do not find in the royal chronicles of Saint-Denis the complete account of these great and famous feats and deeds the king accomplished in Spain. You should understand that the chronicler, either because these high exploits would have taken too much space or because, since he has never been in Spain, he did not know about them, did not record them in their entirety. There is however no contradiction between his account and this new volume [which fills in the gaps . . .].[21]

Turpin preaches, he fights, he writes. The letter, added at a later date but corresponding perfectly to the spirit of the narrative, is meant to give an appearance of authenticity to this reworking of the figure of Charlemagne, to introduce a form of writing which supplements—and to some extent competes with—the official annals.[22] In these circumstances the most efficient tactic is that of direct testimony. The *Pseudo-Turpin Chronicle* is not, as is Notker's text, comprised of a series of anecdotes that clearly occupy a marginal position, that seduce with their humility and follow the twists and turns of the author's narrative. Nor is it akin to the works of the *jongleurs* composed in the vulgate, the language of everyday life, of games, of lies. It is not surprising then that the *ego Turpin* comes up so often in the narrative. Indeed, Turpin can write not only because he was an eyewitness but mostly because he had a close relationship with Charlemagne.

It is that relationship that grants the Pseudo-Turpin the necessary authority to write. Since official power was defined in relation to the founding figure of Charlemagne, and the "official" annals emanated from that power, it was as if any other voice speaking about the one who "authorized" writing had to invent a special connection to that figure in order to claim the right to speak. The conditions for this type of writing—that which seeks to redefine official power through a representation of its origins—depends on its relationship with that power. The Pseudo-Turpin thus attempts to present a view of the epic Charlemagne different from that of the *Chanson de Roland*, a view in which a theocentric system predominates.

As we know, the impostor succeeded and created a truth that was uncontested for several centuries. Translated into the vulgate, the Pseudo-Turpin's account maintained the prestige of its original Latin even as it enjoyed extraordinary diffusion. More than a century later, Mousket put the vulgate translation into verse and, driven by the logic of accumulation, incorporated it almost in its entirety into his *Chronique rimée*. From now on, I will cite from this rhymed chronicle since it is this form that brings us closest to an idea of the *doxa*, of that which "was said" about Charlemagne that endured for centuries.

We are dealing with the same story that is found in the *Chanson de Roland*, but here the perspective is larger and the battle of Roncevaux constitutes only the second part of the work. Although the *Chronique* portrays Charlemagne as the elect of God and in the service of the Church, it does nonetheless explore the limits of his power. It does this first in terms of geography. The narrative begins with a list of the places Charlemagne has conquered: "France, England, Germany, Bavaria, Lotharingia, Brittany, Lombardy, Burgundy, and all the lands of the sea of Brindisi [Apulia] all the way to the Atlantic."[23] At the beginning of the work, Charlemagne seems only to be thinking of resting and living in peace. Then, while he is sleeping, he has a dream that inspires him to conquer Spain: Saint James appears to him and asks him to take his tomb back from the Saracens. In exchange, the saint promises Charlemagne the crown of heaven and glory on earth till the end of the world. The first element of this dream is a path made up of stars, the Milky Way, "that begins from the sea of Frisia [the North Sea] and passes through France, Germany, and Lombardy, and then between France and Aquitaine, through Gascony, the land of the Basques, and Navarre, and goes to Spain all the way to Galicia where the body of Saint James, our lord, is buried unbeknownst."[24] Thus, in the space of one paragraph, the components of an entity are listed, as if to define and fix that entity, one which the emperor of the West is attempting to weld together, an entity that roughly corresponds to Europe.

Charles appears in the narrative as a conqueror who has a favored relationship with God (through the intermediary of Saint James). Although the text celebrates the theocentric aspect of Charlemagne's power, it is also careful to establish the limits of his power as it relates to God. Analogies between Charlemagne and the triumphant Christ are plentiful. "Because just as Jesus Christ our Lord along with his twelve apostles subdued the world, so Charles, emperor of Rome and king of France, along with his twelve peers conquered Spain in honor of God."[25]

Two miracles serve to illustrate this liminal function of the narrative. Before a battle against the forces of the pagan Agoulant, the lances of the Christian soldiers who were to die that day took root and grew branches. On the eve of a second battle, Charles prayed to God to point out those who were destined to die by marking them with a cross on the right shoulder. Charles decided to protect them by putting them in a chapel away from the battle. But when he returned to the chapel once the battle was won, he found them all dead. The emperor's relationship with God gave him foreknowledge, but not the power to change the course of events.

The Pseudo-Turpin's Charlemagne is not only a conqueror, he is also a liberator within his own kingdom. He follows an Augustinian politics aimed at reinforcing internal unity when confronted with a common enemy. In order to face Agoulant's army, the great king calls up his people from near and far and orders that all serfs who had been mistreated and ruled by cruel lords be freed (*franc*), along with all their descendants. Those who went to battle would be given their freedom. "He freed all prisoners and paid the poor and clothed the naked. He reconciled those who hated each other, he restored the disinherited within their families and returned them their honor. . . . And those who through some fault were estranged from him, he drew them back with his love."[26] No more discord, no more hatred, the Christian emperor's rule became the rule of harmony and love. Here the moving force of union derives from the enemy's existence; it is by defining oneself *against* the other that Charlemagne's reign is realized. And here the ideal state rests on an alliance between the monarch and the common people of the kingdom.

In the Christian society established by Charlemagne, a concern for the poor proves to be a crucial element since it is a reflection of that society's moral exemplarity. The Pseudo-Turpin insists on this obligation when he tells of Agoulant's arrival in the middle of a royal dinner in order to be baptized, as had been agreed. Seeing the magnificence of the meal, he asks who the guests are. The guests belong to the first two estates, the clergy and the nobility, and they occupy the places of honor. There are also twelve poor guests seated on the ground without a table who have been offered only a bit of meat and drink. When Agoulant asks Charlemagne who these people are, Charles answers that they are there in memory of God and his twelve apostles. Outraged by such treatment of the poor, Agoulant refuses to be baptized. Charles then realizes how unjust he has been. "And all the poor that he then found in his army he had clothed and had them eat and drink well for Agoulant, who then accepted baptism."[27] The Other's gaze thus leads to a betterment of one's self; standing before the infidel, any lack of moral exemplarity comes to the fore. Here the shortcoming is all the more serious in that it undermines a fundamental quality expected of the king: largesse.

This anecdote, which is also found in Germany concerning Widukind,[28] deals with and reinforces the ties between Charlemagne and the poor on the one hand and, on the other, highlights a hagiographical element of the emperor's portrayal: his fallible humanness and his ability to better himself. Like any human being, Charlemagne can be wrong and can repent, even in his public role in the *Pseudo-Turpin Chronicle*. This is true as well in his private life, as in the legend of Saint Gilles, where God forgives Charlemagne his "unspeakable" sin (that of having had incestuous relations with his sister Gille who, as a result, became pregnant with the future Roland) by sending an angel to put a charter on the altar where Saint Gilles is celebrating mass.[29] Neither of these events leads to a challenge to his right to rule. On the contrary, the Pseudo-Turpin appears to enjoy drawing parallels between the tests endured by Charlemagne and the tribulations ordinary people encounter in life. The emperor's weaknesses are part of the attraction (and thus the force) of the image of the official power that is based on him. The struggle against the Saracens becomes analogous to the struggle each individual must lead against sin.

> Because, just as Charles's knights put on their arms for the battle, we too must put on goodness and virtue and take off bad vices so as to wage battle against the devil. Because one who has good faith against wrong belief, charity against hatred, generosity against avarice, humility against pride, chastity against lust, prayers against the devil's temptations, poverty for God's sake against riches, perseverance against fickleness, silence against quarrel, obedience against false courage, that one shall have his lance green and leafy on Judgment Day. Ah! God! The victor's soul, the one who has loyally fought against all his bad vices, shall be beautiful, green, and flowering.[30]

Charlemagne represents the legitimacy of power, but he also represents each of us in our daily struggles and weaknesses. He is the very principle of the collectivity; thus the collectivity assumes the characteristics of a person, and is equipped with a psychology similar to that of an individual. Charlemagne's story, the story of his kingdom, is also the story of each one of us. The technique of analogy carries a moral lesson, but it is one that, at the same time, enables a greater internalization of the foundations and representation of political power.

The victory over the Saracens is a victory over Evil. For an individual, the prize for one's victory over sin is Paradise. But what is the equivalent prize for the collectivity? The transcendent value of a victory as the judgment of God is obvious. But what is to be made of defeat? The Pseudo-Turpin's chronicle gives clear answers to the ambiguities we uncovered in the *Chanson de Roland*. Ganelon betrays for personal gain, like Judas did before him. The French lose at Roncevaux because they gave in to the sins of drunkenness and lust, and they have to buy back their souls through martyrdom. But this does not explain the fates of Roland and those close to him, since they had neither drunk nor fornicated. And this is even more troubling since in principle the Christian victory rests on the heroic acts of knights such as Roland. In this case, too, the answer makes it possible to establish the boundaries between collective duty and individual interest. God caused Roland and his companions to die, explains the archbishop of Reims, so as to prevent them from sinning after they returned home; it is thus a sort of preventive death.

The tension between individual salvation and the salvation of the chosen people becomes clearer in texts with a more "national" orientation. The contradiction remained unspoken in the *Chanson de Roland*, or rather it was masked by Roland's pride. But it is dealt with clearly in the *Pseudo-Turpin Chronicle*, even if only to point out God's wisdom and Roland's ultimate happiness. In fact, this conclusion contributes to the further glorification of Charlemagne who, by bringing the martyrs' remains back to his kingdom where he buries them (Roland in Blaye, Oliver in Belin, others in Bordeaux), turns those places and his kingdom into a land made holy by the presence of new martyrs.

In the very center of this land, no longer in Aachen but in Paris and Saint-Denis, the Pseudo-Turpin reveals the boldest facet of his representation of the king, one that shows Charlemagne as being unique in having the prestige and fundamental authority to offer Saint-Denis the gift of his kingdom: "Omnem Franciam in praedio eius ecclesiae dedit" [he gave ownership of the whole of France to Saint-Denis].[31] Moreover, Charlemagne orders all the kings of France (*omnes Franciae reges*) and all the bishops to obey God and Saint-Denis and stipulates that henceforth no king is to be crowned nor any bishops received or condemned in Rome without Saint-Denis's approval. With this declaration the kingdom is given as a fief to Saint-Denis and its rights are simultaneously asserted in relationship to those of Rome. Playing on a constellation of words rooted in the Latin word "*francus*" meaning "free" and found in old and modern French ("frans," "affranchir," etc.), the author shows how through this submission to Saint-Denis, along with an annual tribute of four deniers, the kingdom achieves freedom and Gaul becomes France. "And it came to pass that those who gave the IV deniers good-heartedly and willingly were called 'the free of Saint-Denis' [*frans Saint Denise*] because they were freed from any other services by order of King Charles, and they were all called

'François,' while the land that had been called Gaul before this came to be called France [*Franche*]."[32]

We will later see that Philip Augustus and Saint Louis gave four gold *besants* to fulfill the duty stipulated by Saint James, a duty performed for the first time by Charlemagne in the *Pseudo-Turpin Chronicle*.[33] In this text, the emperor is present when France is first named, when a "Gaulish" church enjoying a degree of independence from Rome is established, and when a monarchy henceforth at the service of that church is founded. After these events the Pseudo-Turpin has Charlemagne continue on the road to Aachen, where his narrative rejoins Einhard's with the building of the basilica and with Charlemagne's efforts to restore learning by disseminating the teaching of the trivium and the quadrivium—occupations dear to the monks of Saint-Denis.

In the *Pseudo-Turpin Chronicle*, which was received as truth for hundreds of years, Charlemagne establishes his kingdom in France. In this same text, he also claims the universality of his mission. "Because, says Charles, Jesus Christ, maker of heaven and earth, elected our Christian people to be lord over all others and over all things, I have as much as I could converted pagan people to our law."[34] The Latin text, preserved in the Cathedral of Saint James at Compostela, uses the age-old logic of the dictu, *nomen est omen* to describe even more explicitly the scene in which the emperor's deeds turn Gaul into France: "Quapropter Francus liber dicitur, quia super omnes alias gentes et decus et dominatio illi debetur."[35]

EMPEROR OF THE WORLD

The vision of universal sovereignty that France acquired through Charlemagne is also expressed in the more secular contexts of the *chansons de geste*. As we will see, it is in the *chanson* that looks the closest at the temporal duration of the monarchy that the range of Charlemagne's sovereignty, whose kingdom is explicitly identified here with France, becomes limitless:

> Quant Deus eslut nonante et neuf reiames,
> Tot le meillor torna en dolce France.
> Li mieldre reis ot a nom Charlemaine;
> Cil aleva volentiers dolce France;
> Deus ne fist terre qui envers lui n'apende;
> Il i apent Baiviere et Alemaigne
> Et Normandie et Anjou et Bretaigne
> Et Lombardie et Navarre et Toscane.[36]

[When God elected ninety-nine kingdoms,
He put the best of all in sweet France.
The best king was called Charlemagne;
With all his heart he aggrandized sweet France.
God made no land that didn't depend on him,
Neither Bavaria nor Germany,
Nor Normandy nor Anjou nor Brittany,
Nor Lombardy nor Navarre nor Tuscany.]

There is a claim to unlimited sovereignty in the *Couronnement de Louis*, but the list of countries and the description of the area of activities emphasizes "European" Christendom. Possibly lurking behind these claims is a reaction to German activity, since the emperor Henry V had attempted to take Reims in 1124 in order to punish the king of France, Louis VI, for supporting the pope. Feeding on the interacting circumstances that it transcends, the notion of "France," as it develops through the representation of Charlemagne, comprises the founding element of the notion of a universal mission.

And yet, Charlemagne's image is haunted by the image of a possible Christian rival, by another emperor who is just as legitimate: the emperor of Constantinople, this selfsame Other. The most widespread translation into French of the *Pseudo-Turpin Chronicle* is that by Johannes (thirty-two manuscripts preserved), which, in an abridged version, tells another story of a crusading Charlemagne, a story that appears to parallel the narrative of his journey to Spain.

Johannes's narrative, the *Descriptio qualiter Karolus Magnus clavum et coronam Domini a Constantinopoli Aquisgrani detulerit qualiterque Karolus Calvus hec ad sanctum Dionysium retulerit* [How Charlemagne Brought the Lord's Nail and Crown to Aachen and How Charles the Bold Gave Them to Saint-Denis] dates from the end of the eleventh century and aims to explain the presence of relics from the Holy Land in Saint-Denis.[37] In this text, upon the request of the emperor of Constantinople, who was himself in a situation that made it impossible to help the patriarch of Jerusalem, Charlemagne goes to free the Holy City from the Saracens. The *Annals* had already placed the keys to Jerusalem in Charlemagne's possession, but here he takes the city back from the Saracens by force of arms. The effective completion of his mission to the Holy Land enables Charlemagne to bring back relics to the West, in this case to Aachen, relics that would endow his city with the spiritual capital that had up until then always been the patrimony of the East. After this, explains the writer of the *Descriptio*, Charles the Bald, heir to Charlemagne, gave these relics to Saint-Denis.

War certainly constitutes the most common means used to illustrate the spread of Charlemagne's power, but it is not the only one. We have seen the importance of gifts and of appearance. Confronted with another Christian civilization, recourse to war would lack legitimacy and seems thus to have been rejected. However, when he was confronted with a culture that was considered to be richer in material possessions and knowledge, Charlemagne could not claim his superiority either through gifts or through the magnificence of his court. Thus the issue of Charlemagne's relationship with Constantinople is a touchy one. In the *Descriptio*, Charlemagne intervenes in Jerusalem only upon Constantine's request. There is no shortage of accounts or evidence of the rivalry and tensions that existed between the two empires throughout the course of history. A Christian emperor, the rightful Defender of Rome, the *basileus* is a particularly apt figure for our examination of the question of limits, because in Western ideology he was neither completely "one of us" nor "one of them." There is no text that better reveals this peculiar reality than the *Pèlerinage de Charlemagne à Constantinople et à Jérusalem* or *Charlemagne's Journey to Constantinople and Jerusalem* which, according to Gaston Paris, dates from the last quarter of the twelfth century[38] and explains in its own way the transfer of the relics and the construction of the West as a new Holy Land.

We know that royal appearance is a fundamental element of royal efficacy. As we have seen, appearing is an action that is important in and of itself because it enables Charlemagne to impose himself without recourse to violence and thus becomes one of the foundations of the social order. The *Pèlerinage* develops this theme in a comic mode, a mode that in itself tends to sublimate violence. At the beginning of the *Pèlerinage*, Charlemagne is holding court in Saint-Denis and asks his wife if she has ever seen a king wear the sword and the crown, the two objects that symbolize his power and legitimacy, as well as he does. The queen answers that he overestimates himself and that she has heard of an emperor who wears the crown better, Hugh the Strong, the emperor of Greece and Constantinople. Furious, Charlemagne replies that he wants to see this for himself and that if she is wrong she will have to pay for her comment with her head. Such royal anger might appear to be exaggerated here, but in spite of the humor of the scene, the queen's quip is in fact inopportune because it questions the king's appearance, that is, royal dignity itself, before the entire court.[39] And what might be a joke in private becomes a crime of lèse-majesté in the public arena of the court.

It is precisely such limits, among others, that the text seeks to test: what then is the place of laughter in the evocation of the monarch? Although the narrative never ridicules Charlemagne to the point of making him an object of our laughter and although the emperor always triumphs in the end, the text offers us many occasions to smile at his expense. Here we again find a familiar structure: Charlemagne's power/a challenge to his power/the reestablishment of his authority. Royal power can tolerate a certain amount of humor and emerge stronger, for there is no doubt that Charlemagne's image will be aggrandized in the end. We are left with a fundamental question: the queen mentions another emperor who might be better than Charlemagne at mastering the symbolic aspect of power. The queen's remark challenges an essential element of Charles's sovereignty as well as his claim to universality. The locus and the nature of speech, and the symbols of power: these are the two axes that orient the narrative.

When Charles assembles his knights to announce their departure, he speaks mainly of a pilgrimage to Jerusalem to worship the cross and the Holy Sepulchre. He equips his forces following the logic of the gift ("He gave them much fine gold and silver"),[40] but the journey is not one of conquest by arms. Rather than swords, Charles gives his men pilgrim staffs and travel sacks, thereby resorting to the symbolism of spiritual pilgrimage. Upon arriving in Jerusalem, Charles enters a church, accompanied by his twelve peers. Seeing twelve seats laid out and a thirteenth in the middle, Charles and the twelve peers sit down to rest and are convinced that it is here that Christ himself and his apostles celebrated mass. By chance, a Jew passes by, and "when he saw Charlemagne he began to tremble / so proud was the emperor's face, he didn't dare look upon him." In this scene, reminiscent of one described by Notker, the king's appearance so greatly impresses the Jew that he believes him to be God himself and runs to the patriarch to convert. The patriarch goes to the church to inquire about the strangers, because usually no one enters it without his permission. "Sire, my name is Charles, in France I was born / twelve kingdoms I conquered by force and prowess [barnage] / I am seeking a thirteenth of which I have heard."[41] Charlemagne then explains that he has come to Jerusalem to worship the cross and the Holy Sepulchre.

In this scene the impact of the king of France's appearance, even without his sword, is confirmed, as are his close ties to God. "Sire, you are very brave [ber]," exclaims the patriarch. "You are sitting on the very throne where God sat! You will be called Charles the Great over all crowned kings."[42] All of the elements of the Frankish king's power are gathered here: his power as conqueror, his ties to God, the effect of his appearance, the universality of his sovereignty, and his greatness (the attribute "magne" joined to his name). Charlemagne, as warrior king and as priest king, continues his journey toward Constantinople, after the patriarch presents him with gifts of numerous relics, including the shroud of Christ, a nail that was used in the Crucifixion, and the crown of thorns.[43]

Less than one third of the poem is devoted to the pilgrimage to Jerusalem; the largest portion consists of the confrontation with Charlemagne's other self: the emperor of Constantinople. The Byzantine capital proves to be an Eldorado: abundance, riches, arts, peace, lack of crime, and the technological know-how that can master the elements and turn storms into harmony: the wind sets the palace spinning while horns, drums, and bells fill the air with exquisite music. The French are so in awe that they fall to the ground, and the author takes pleasure in pointing out how small Charles the "Great" feels in the face of all this splendor: "Charles saw the great palace and riches; / His own possessions seemed worthless to him."[44]

While Charles combines the functions of warrior king and priest king, in Hugh, as Griswald has shown, he encounters a king who carries out the third function of the tripartite scheme elaborated by Dumézil, that of abundance and fertility. Charles finds the emperor Hugh seated on a golden chariot plowing a field; his hospitality is perfect, the meals are exquisite, and the wine excellent.

Indeed this wine ultimately gets the French into trouble. Once led back to their lodgings, they relax by engaging in one of their native customs and boast in an exaggerated manner at the expense of their host. Charlemagne himself initiates this sort of game known as "gab." He claims to have such prowess that he could make mincemeat out of any of Hugh's knights. Roland claims to have such powerful lungs that he could destroy Constantinople simply by blowing on it. Oliver could make love to the king's daughter one hundred times in one night. Another could pick up a steel ball so big that thirty men couldn't lift it, and he would throw it so that it would destroy the palace walls. The rules of this boasting game are obvious, except to the spy that King Hugh has hidden in the chamber of his French guests. He listens to everything they say with growing indignation and reports it to Hugh. We can sense the confusion of the situation: the French are overwhelmed by the marvels they have seen, and the Greeks do not recognize a custom that is only a word game. They share enough similarities to welcome each other in a friendly manner, yet they are different enough not to understand each other and to see each other as strangers. The author uses this moment of confusion to look at Charlemagne and his men in a new way.

The king of Constantinople, outraged by this lack of respect toward himself and the rules of hospitality, decides to punish the French by having their heads cut off unless they can successfully accomplish all the exploits they bragged about the night before. This is the same punishment with which Charlemagne threatened his wife at the beginning of the story. The circle is complete; Charlemagne's crime is not very different from that of his wife: like her, he has spoken lightly and disrespectfully of the established authorities. But there is a fundamental difference: Charlemagne and the twelve peers' bad jokes were exchanged in a private context, far from the court. The exaggeration of the drunken talk is, in a way, overshadowed by the indiscretion of Hugh's indirect gaze.

God intervenes to help the contrite Charlemagne and his men accomplish the impossible, including the boast of sexual prowess by Oliver (though not one hundred times), and all this to the dismay of the emperor of Constantinople, who ultimately submits to Charlemagne. The unity of Christendom is confirmed to the benefit of the emperor of the Franks, the priest and warrior king: in a final procession celebrating mutual friendship and alliance that takes place before the French depart from Constantinople, "Charlemagne wore the great golden crown, King Hugh his own but not so well."[45] Charlemagne, after having fallen and repented, emerges even greater and returns to France, where he distributes the relics and forgives his wife.

The author uses a representation of Charlemagne to affirm the universality of the mission of France's great king, but at the same time he explores the function of ludic speech in the margins of power. One case, that of the queen, is unacceptable because it challenges the very function of the monarch. The other case involves Charlemagne as Hugh's guest and is more discreet, more removed from the ceremonial and public sphere and thus does not pose a threat to established authority, even though the latter is caught up in the humorous gameplay. But is that not part of the ludic intention of the text? For it seems to be exploring the limits of humor and seriousness in the context of political authority even as it displays profound respect for that authority, a respect that ultimately serves to reinforce the authority by associating it with joyful laughter.

GALIEN: FROM RONCEVAUX TO CONSTANTINOPLE

The story of the *Pèlerinage* was adopted and developed in a very popular *chanson de geste: Galien li Restoré*. There is a specific type of narrative logic that uses an unexplained or poorly explained element of a *geste* as the basis for a new story. This logic was no doubt at the origin of a *chanson* that brings together and seeks to harmonize the different themes we have already seen at work. Very little is known about *Galien*. Only reworked versions have survived; the oldest one, in verse, dates from the fifteenth century and is perhaps the result of a work in prose that was put into verse, the prose work itself possibly having been produced from a work in verse![46] This sort of transformation helps to illustrate the fluidity of the discourse on Charlemagne, which flows back and forth between Latin and vulgate languages, between poetry and prose. It is thus difficult to speculate on the exact conditions of the genesis of *Galien*, which is believed, albeit without certainty, to date from around 1200.[47] I am examining it here because, on the one hand, it combines the material of the *Chanson de Roland* and the *Pèlerinage* and, on the other, due to the immense success it enjoyed throughout the centuries, it was, along with the *Pseudo-Turpin Chronicle*, the main vehicle for transmitting the story of the *Chanson de Roland*, the manuscript of which was lost until its rediscovery in 1835 by Francisque Michel.[48] Thus, from the perspective of my teleological approach, *Galien*, which became part of the "Bibliothèque bleue" (to be discussed later), turns out to be extremely important in the conveyance of an epic image of Charlemagne.

In a way, *Galien* asks the same question as does the *Chanson de Roland*: can Charlemagne survive a defeat such as the one at Roncevaux? But here the answers lead to a broader synthesis, one more comprehensive than that in the *Chanson de Roland*. Who is Galien? He is Oliver's illegitimate son, the fruit of the night Oliver spent with Jacqueline, the daughter of Hugh, emperor of Constantinople. The child was named after the fairy Galienne, who assisted at his birth, and he is called *li restoré* "because he was to restore Charles and his barons, / people will call him Galien Restoré."[49] One of the essential components of *Galien* is its detailed retelling of the *Chanson de Roland*. I cannot recount *Galien* in its entirety here. In short, the narrative centers around young Galien's quest for his father and thus for legitimacy. Galien is to be both *restored* in his own right and the *restorer* of Charlemagne in the sense that he will help him overcome the defeat at Roncevaux.[50] Events lead him from Constantinople to France and from there to Spain, where Charlemagne is leading the crusade against the Saracens. It is there that the young knight rejoins his father in the midst of the battle of Roncevaux, just in time to be recognized by him and to watch him die. Here, as in the *Pseudo-Turpin Chronicle*, the reason for the betrayal is clearly stated, but in *Galien* the main motivation is an attempt to seize power rather than money: "You will see me soon crowned in France / Because my lineage has great authority, / And Charles has not sired any man from his wife. / Noble royalty will go to his sister, / And she has married me. / Thus I will rule as king of France."[51] In spite of appearances, this passage does not lead into the issue of succession, a subject dealt with in the *Couronnement de Louis*. Instead, it points out that the threat posed by the traitor is all the more grievous as he is linked to Charlemagne through ties of marriage.

The *Chanson de Roland* tended to separate the realms of the public and the private in regard to Charlemagne. The same issue is at work in *Galien* in that Charlemagne is able to move beyond the death of his nephew and right-hand man and to overcome the danger posed by Ganelon. But *Galien* puts more emphasis on Ganelon's ties of kinship with the king. During the trial, Charlemagne causes right and justice to prevail. The only people to defend Ganelon are members of his family (*li parens de Ganelon*). In *Galien*, Gondebeuf le Frison is entrusted with the judicial duel, whereas Thierry intervenes only to catch Ganelon when the latter tries to flee. However, if we look closely, we notice that rather than asserting the distinction between the public and the private, *Galien* makes it an object of reflection. Although Charlemagne is positioned above private concerns, there appears to be no attempt to set any limit between the two domains. On the contrary, their inextricable mingling seems to have been recognized and accepted as legitimate in the king's political functioning and power, a mingling of which he makes full use.

Galien can be understood as an inquiry into the role of the personal and the familial in the realm of politics. This explains the importance of Galien's quest and possibly also the idea of attributing Galien's origins to the private discourse uttered before Charlemagne, that is, the "gab" during which Oliver brags about his sexual prowess which he then, so to speak, puts at Charles's service. This also explains why love replaces the *geste* as the reason for fighting: "And think of the love that you desired so much; / Jacqueline the beautiful with looks so fair," says Roland to incite Ganelon to be brave in battle; "For the love of her, show the pagans how proud you are, / And I will show as much for your sister, / Because no man is brave unless he has a lover's heart."[52] They are fighting less for their reputation than for their love, a notion that incorporates at once courtly values and familial politics. Galien's quest for his father is a personal quest that turns, almost "naturally," into a defense of the king and the kingdom.

Charles adds the prestige of the sacred to that of the warrior. He has gone to Jerusalem (where he sat in God's chair, surrounded by his twelve men). Upon his return, he defeats a Saracen army with a single prayer. He brings the relics back to France. His status as "national" hero is confirmed when he fights in person against Baligant.

> Moy ou le Turc sera du tout deshonnourés;
> Ou je le conquerray, sachés par verités,
> Ou en champ m'occira, car n'en seray sevrés.
> Priés trestoulx a Dieu qui est mon advoués,
> Que l'honneur de France y soit trestout guardés.[53]

> ———

> [Either I or the Turk will be completely dishonored;
> Either I will conquer him, know in truth,
> Or in the field of battle he'll kill me, for I shall not abandon it.
> Pray all to God who is my protector
> That the honor of France will be maintained.]

Charles dubs Galien, who then becomes his direct vassal. Thus Galien replaces Roland as Charlemagne's right-hand man when Charles is directly threatened by the Saracen forces: "And the French are very happy and strengthened / When they see Galien Restoré / Coming to battle; they are all reassured."[54]

Galien's ties of kinship lead to a consolidation and a genuine union within Charlemagne's empire. This occurs primarily through marriage. The king's forces lay siege to the castle of Monfusain where Guimarde, Baligant's niece, resides. Galien asks the emperor for her hand in marriage: "Noble [*franc*] king, [says Oliver's son to Charlemagne] listen to me! / I beg you for God's sake to give me the Beauty / And also Monfusain, if this be your will."[55] Confronted with the French attack, Guimarde "came to an agreement with Charles / And put herself in his hands, and Charles gave her / To his vassal Galien, who married her."[56] She converts, and, thanks to Charlemagne's gift, Galien becomes Guimarde's husband and lord of Monfusain. Thus the battle is indeed a means of conquest, but the marriage arranged and approved by the king enables Galien to claim and practice his sovereignty in order to secure both conversion and peace: Galien "kept the land in peace and protected it."[57]

There are other benefits of this marriage. Galien is also Emperor Hugh's grandson. Because his mother, Jacqueline, is being mistreated by Hugh's sons, Galien returns to Constantinople, where he restores order (another restoration!) and ends up being crowned emperor of Constantinople. Thus, due to ties of kinship and vassalage, the much dreamed-of unification of the two empires is achieved under Charlemagne's suzerainty. Although he himself is above familial and personal dependency, functioning almost as a principle rather than a person, the great king takes ample advantage of the feudal-vassalic system, of ties of kinship between his vassals, and of his clever marriage policies.

The *chansons* I have discussed up to now all show Charlemagne in a favorable light, overcoming challenges to his power through various means. The mythified history of the great emperor strengthens his image as a source of legitimacy and royal authority. Nothing illustrates this positive image better than *Le Couronnement de Louis*, written during Louis VII's reign. This poem deals with the issue of the hereditary succession of the crown and looks at an extreme case when the crown is passed on to an unworthy king.

Charlemagne wants his crown to be handed down to his son Louis, who proves to be a coward. The hero of the poem, William, protects Louis against traitors who want to depose him and against the external enemy that is attacking Rome. Even though the last verse of the poem tells us that Louis never showed any gratitude to William for all that the loyal baron had done for him, the hereditary principle is never questioned. There is nothing more frightening than a *mutatio regni*. Those in power must defend the monarchy even when the king's lack of virtue does not reflect the image of the monarchy as established by Charlemagne.

Although it criticizes the unfit king as an individual, the poem fundamentally supports royal ideology. The paradox of having Charlemagne be the source of legitimate Capetian heredity does not appear problematic, and thus highlights both the force of the great emperor's image and the power of the Capetians. The memory of the *mutatio regni* that brought the Capetian monarchy into power gradually faded in the course of their long reign: Louis VII was already the sixth Capetian king. As to the external threat, it does not come from very far: a certain Guy of Germany tries to take Rome. Is this an echo of Emperor Henry V's attempt in 1124 to take Reims in order to punish Louis VI for supporting the pope? Perhaps. What is clear is that the figure of Charlemagne truly begins to dominate *chansons de geste* beginning around 1170.

CHARLEMAGNE BETWEEN FRANCE AND THE EMPIRE

Several elements combine to make this latter part of the twelfth century a fundamental time for representations of Charlemagne. We are now in the "second feudal age," a time when the hierarchical feudal institution was being perfected. It was a hierarchy based on oaths spoken between two men, on a certain courtliness, and, at the top of the hierarchy, on the figure of the king. Royal power was increasingly consolidated under Louis VII and particularly under Philip Augustus. The highest-ranking nobility lost many of its members during the Crusades, and thus gave Philip the ever-greater opportunity to draw his advisers from the lower nobility and to surround himself with people who owed him their wealth and social ascent.[58] We are in the midst of a period of exaltation of the Empire, when Frederick I (Barbarossa) dramatically claimed a connection between his empire and the first Germanic emperor: on December 29, 1165, Charlemagne was canonized by the antipope Pascal III. Charlemagne's grave was once again opened and his body was transferred—"translated"—to another location: an excuse to seize the great emperor's remains and solemnly to show the relationship between God and the emperor Frederick.

According to the imperial charter, Frederick, wanting to display his visionary powers, learned through "divine revelation" the location of the tomb that had been lost or perhaps "forgotten" since the time of Otto III. Robert Folz has shown well the dual implications of this action.[59] In the context of the schism, the first German emperor's canonization was a way of reinforcing, in the face of internal and external opposition, the ties between Germany and the antipope, of consolidating Frederick's moral authority by emphasizing the right and power that had devolved to him from Charlemagne in matters concerning the election of the pope. But this gesture was also aimed particularly at the Capetian monarchy, which continued to claim a connection to Charlemagne and its universality as the kings of God's chosen people and as the privileged defenders of the Church, although these claims had yet to be accompanied by the power to back them up. Not only does the *Chanson de Roland* come to mind here but also the more official *Gesta Dei per Francos* [God's Deeds Accomplished by the Franks] and the entire tradition surrounding Saint-Denis.[60]

The background of the diffusion of the *chanson de geste* might be explained as a triptych. One panel would be the rivalry between the kingdom of France and the Holy Roman Empire, accompanied by the development of a more clearly territorial conception of the states (although Philip Augustus continued to call himself *rex Francorum*, and not *rex Franciae*). A second panel would be made up of the affirmation and consolidation of royal power inside the kingdom, and the third would be the continuation of the Crusades.

The richest period for the epic genre corresponds approximately to Philip Augustus's reign (1179–1223), but the *chansons de geste* remained popular throughout the thirteenth century, declining in popularity only after 1300. During the final years of the reign of Louis VII and particularly under Philip Augustus a less glorious image of Charlemagne began to appear, a Charlemagne in conflict with barons whose demands sometimes appear to be justified. Critics have long seen in these *chansons* the products of aristocratic ideology glorifying the nobility at the expense of the king.[61] But, as Dominique Boutet points out in his admirable study on epic and romance literatures of this period, "deidealization" (*Entidealisierung*) does not mean demythification.[62] In this period of major transformations and the restructuring of political power, the topos of Charlemagne became a privileged locus for questioning the nature and the limits of power, including cases in which the king is in the wrong, in which the person who embodies sovereignty abuses it. Whereas in a document such as Hincmar's treatise the opinion of the nobles is expressed in the course of debates during assemblies, in the *chanson de geste* it assumed a form appropriate to the norms of the heroic genre: the focus is continually on the conflictual aspect of relationships.

However, it should be noted at the outset that in none of these stories is Charlemagne's monarchy overthrown. Regardless of the importance and the intensity of the confrontation, the old king retains legitimate power and continues to embody sovereignty. The epic makes it possible to open a debate on power even as it affirms a collective identity in the face of external enemies. It is no accident that this kind of epic began to be produced at a spectacular rate in the years following Charlemagne's canonization and that the struggle for Christendom is the context in which they were written. The dialectic of the Same and the Other is again at work here for, although it is not always possible to know what we are, it is easier to agree on what we are not.

As has already been noted, it is not possible to examine the whole spectrum of medieval epic production. And yet it is important to define the parameters of the questioning of political power found in this genre, a genre that provides both enjoyment and an interpretation of the history of the time. In many respects, the epic genre ensures Charlemagne's survival on very different levels: the discourse on origins is always coupled with an agreeable narrative, and a desire to learn more is spurred by an enjoyment of the tale, even though, as we will see, the Renaissance was soon to denounce this troubling mixture. I will limit myself to three *chansons* in which we can see conflictual relationships develop between Charlemagne and his vassals: *Fierabras*, *La Chanson d'Aspremont*, and *Renaut de Montauban*. The selection criteria are basically the same. In the light of the teleological approach I am taking, *Fierabras* and *Renaut de Montauban* (this latter was known for a long time under the title *Quatre Fils Aymon*) played an important role in the transmission of the figure of Charlemagne. As for *La Chanson d'Aspremont*, it is distinguished both by the bitterness of the revolt against Charlemagne and by the concept of territory that it explores.

FIERABRAS AND LA CHANSON D'ASPREMONT

Fierabras, which dates from around 1170, is the first *chanson* that somewhat darkens Charlemagne's image. It is a legend presented in the form of a prose romance that was extremely popular throughout the years and especially during the fourteenth and fifteenth centuries. The poem adopts the theme of Charlemagne as protector of the Church. The Saracens have attacked Rome and seized the relics: the holy crown, the nails from the cross, and the lance that pierced Christ's side. The events described in the poem thus occur prior to those described in the *Chanson de Roland*.

Fierabras once again explores the issues of loyalty and treason through the characters of Oliver, Roland, and Ganelon. Oliver is the perfect knight: though wounded, he agrees to fight the giant Fierabras. Throughout the confrontation, the two warriors show exemplary respect for each other, perfect courtliness, and complete compliance with the rules of combat. In fact, Oliver has to fight because Roland has refused to take up the challenge delivered by the great Saracen. Roland's refusal leads to an angry scene between the emperor and his nephew during which Charlemagne strikes him on the nose with such force that he draws blood. Roland reacts by exclaiming that he would just as soon tear the emperor to pieces as fight Fierabras, and he starts to draw his sword against Charlemagne. Naime and Ogier must intervene in order to prevent the situation from taking a very bad turn. Roland's resistance is the result of something Charles had said the day before: in a moment of drunkenness, Charles praised older warriors at the expense of the younger ones. It was probably a "gab," and Roland's reaction is very similar to that of Hughes in *Le Pèlerinage à Jérusalem et à Constantinople:* since you say that old knights are better, prove it by accepting Fierabras's challenge and fighting with the old knights.

> Puis te vantas le soir, quant to fus enivrés,
> Que li viel chevalier c'avoies amené
> L'avoient moult miex fait que li joule [les jeunes] d'assés;
> . . . .
> Or i parra com vous esploiterés.[63]

> ----

> [Then you bragged in the evening when you were drunk
> That the old knights you had brought with you
> Fought many times better than the young ones.
> . . . .
> So let's see what you can do.]

Charlemagne's excessive anger, which leads him to strike one of his barons, is caused not only by Roland's refusal but also by the fact that Roland is his nephew and thus should have been the first to support him. In both cases we find an element that is the result of an inappropriate mixture of the public and the private. Charlemagne should not have made such statements at court. His excessive anger arises from his status as uncle while he is carrying out his imperial functions. This private aspect (including getting drunk) is one of the most frequent causes of Charles's abuses of power: the individual person encroaches upon the function.

The same theme arises again after Oliver and five of the peers are captured by Saracen troops and brought back to Aigremore, the citadel belonging to Balan, Fierabras's father. Charlemagne assigns Roland to go there as ambassador. Roland unsuccessfully tries to avoid the assignment and then breaks down in tears at the danger of such a mission. The five remaining peers intercede with the emperor on Roland's behalf by arguing that the loss of Roland would cause the weakening of Christendom. Again the emperor explodes in anger, and he orders all five peers to accompany Roland. The narrative emphasizes the arbitrariness of the orders given in royal anger: the king is close to resembling a tyrant. The rest of the peers are also captured by Balan. Charlemagne is now deprived of all his twelve peers, in great part through his own fault. He is thus forced to take matters into his own hands and recover not only the relics but the most important men in his kingdom, as well. Can Charlemagne rule and wage war without his twelve peers? He asks this question during an assembly of barons and offers to abdicate.

> Baron, dist l'emperere, quel conseil me donnés?
> Perdu ai mes barons, moult en sui abosmés,
> Moult en sui afoiblis et mes pris avillés;
> Je vous rent la couronne dont je sui couronnés:
> Jamais jour de ma vie n'en tenrai l'ireté.[64]

> ————

> [Baron, said the emperor, what advice can you give me?
> I have lost my barons; much I feel this loss,
> Much I am weakened and dishonored.
> I give you back the crown that I wear;
> Never again will I have the right to hold it.]

The barons are all aghast; and yet it is Charlemagne who has put himself in such a vulnerable position. The storytelling *jongleur* depicts Charlemagne in a situation where he must give up his crown so that the narrative can explore not only the boundaries of proper royal behavior and the king's power, but also the boundaries of the loyalty and service owed him.

In the category of individuals linked to treasonous activities we again find the familiar pair Roland/Ganelon, but, in this work, the ethical contrast between the two characters is less clear. Appearing in turn arrogant and cowardly, in these scenes Roland behaves as the opposite of a good knight, looking out first for himself. As for Ganelon, his case is more complex. He will do all he can to weaken his companions: he supports the decision to send Oliver to fight Fierabras because Oliver is wounded and thus risks losing his life. He advises Charlemagne to renounce his efforts to liberate the relics and the twelve peers. According to Oliver—and he is not the only one to hold this opinion—the emperor asks his men to go to war far too often. As in the *Chanson de Roland*, Ganelon is the advocate of a peace that would mostly serve his personal interests. However, when in the heat of battle Alori suggests that he betray the emperor, Ganelon refuses outright and fights with valor:

> Ne plaice Dieu, dist Guenes, le pere onipotent,
> Que ja vers mon seigneur faice traïtrement [fasse trahison];

Trop serai recréans [lâche] se je sa mort consent.
De lui [tenons] nos teres et nos grans casement,
Si [Ainsi] li devons aidier et bien et loiaument;
N'i a celui ne soit à lui par serment.[65]

———

[May it not please God, our almighty Father,
That I were to betray my lord.
Too much a coward would I be if I consented to his death.
From him we hold our lands and titles;
Thus we owe him good and loyal aid,
We all who are all bound by oath to him.]

The distinction between treason and loyalty, perfidy and keeping one's word is not any clearer than that between excessive personal rage and rightful royal anger, between tyranny and strict integrity. But in spite of these ambiguities and the tension between a certain nascent individualism and a vision of collective unity, Charlemagne asserts his role as guarantor of the social order. When an argument erupts between supporters of Ganelon who are in favor of abandoning the war and Regnier's followers who support the emperor's will to pursue it, Charlemagne fills his role as mediator and impartial judge well by intervening between the opposite sides in the name of peace and in the interest of restoring order. Moreover, in spite of his failings and the obstacles to his policy, Charlemagne is victorious: he returns the relics to Saint-Denis and saves his barons' lives. Thus, God does not abandon him in his trials. Further, even if his victory is due in part to Balan's daughter Floripes's love for Guy of Burgundy, Charlemagne takes advantage of the influence of this love interest on the collective destiny. Similarly, he benefits from a softening of mores and the development of a certain courtliness, the one portrayed in the way Oliver and Fierabras treat each other.

We get a better idea of how the private and the intimate can contribute to collective goals when we look at an epic poem in which the most glorious image of a crusading Charlemagne fighting for the defense of Christendom coexists with the tale of a relentless revolt carried out against the emperor. In *La Chanson d'Aspremont*, Girard of Vienna recognizes neither Charlemagne's sovereignty nor his suzerainty. His first reaction in learning that the emperor is setting out to wage war is to declare that he, Girard, will seize the lands of his archenemy, the emperor himself. The motive for this stubborn revolt lies in his notion of the dignity of his lineage.

The *jongleur* storyteller is careful to emphasize how imposing Charlemagne's appearance is to those who see him, and his descriptions are reminiscent of Notker:

Balans esgarde enbrons, le cief enclin:
Voit par la sale tant riche palazin,
Vestus de vair et de gris et d'ermin,
Blïaus de soie, de palie, d'osterin,
Tels siet cens coupes que d'argent que d'or fin
Qui furent feites del tresor de Constentin.
. . . .
Voit par ces tables tant baron de bon lin,
Tant grant mantiel, tant coltiel acerin,
Come cascuns parole a son voisin;
Balans en jure Mahon et Apollin
Que tolt rois sont assés povre et frarin;
. . . .
Balans manjuë et regarde sovent
Con Carlemainnes ets fiers sor tolte gent.[66]

———

[Balan looks with lowered head
And sees in the room so many rich nobles
Dressed in miniver and ermine
And wearing robes of silk and other precious cloths.
[There were] seven hundred goblets of gold and silver
Which came from Constantine's treasure.
. . . .
He sees around the tables so many highborn barons,
So many great coats, and so many steel blades.
He sees how each speaks to his neighbor.
Balan swears by Mahomet and Apollo
That all the other kings are very poor and miserable.
. . . .
He eats and keeps seeing
How Charles is excellent above all the rest.]

The importance of the gaze and the impact of appearance cannot be stressed too strongly: just seeing the emperor in his court makes Balan renounce his pagan gods and adopt the Christian religion.

Girard, however, has an entirely different attitude: when he looks at Charlemagne, he sees only a dwarf's son. "Say, sir priest," Girard responds to Turpin, who has come to beg him to help Charlemagne, "you should be ashamed before God. You are kin to me, you should love me instead of coming back with such a message asking me to pay homage to a dwarf's son! His father, Pepin, just look at him! He was so small one could have rolled him and played a game of *bocci*[67] with him!"[68] He is so angry that he throws a knife at Turpin and almost kills him. His reaction is strangely reminiscent of Charlemagne's reaction to Roland's refusal in *Fierabras*. We are dealing with family politics oblivious to the community. Thus it is not an external reason that leads Girard to change his mind, but his wife's words. To convince him to act on behalf of others, she invites him to look deeper into himself:

> Sire Gerars, que est cho tu dis?
> Li rois de France est sor tols poëstis:
> Dex le commande en lois et en escris.
> . . . .
> Ja as tu fait tans peciés maleïs [mauvais]
> Églises arses, homes mors et honis,
> Tans grans peciés, dont tu iés si garnis.[69]

> ———

> [Sire Girard, what are you saying?
> The king of France rules over all;
> God orders it in laws and in writings.
> . . . .
> You have sinned so badly,
> Burned churches, killed and dishonored men;
> So many great sins you are bearing.]

Then Girard begins to reflect on his sins and worries about the fate of his soul. Thus, it is not the priest but his spouse who helps bring this entirely individual concern to the fore, a concern that leads him back to the general interest, the one Charlemagne so brilliantly represents throughout the romance.

The nobles' practice of retiring to monasteries away from the world might have tempered the threat to their souls, but in this story the compromise lies in reconciling family politics, personal salvation, and the needs of the state. The solution it proposes is the result of both human will and a structural effect: the action is, so to speak, overdetermined. The concept of the social as expressed in this *chanson* includes a movement toward equilibrium, a movement that reaches out to embrace the most recalcitrant elements. God's order is imposed in the most hidden of ways. It is through Girard's wife that the message embodied by Charlemagne reaches him.

And so what does the emperor represent in this *chanson* composed shortly before 1190, the year marking the beginning of the Third Crusade, a *chanson* that was even sung before the army of crusaders in the streets of

Messina?[70] He is the syncretic figure of union in the face of external threat. He is the "king of France," the "king of Saint-Denis," even though his capital is located in Aachen, the seat of the Holy Roman Empire.[71] His generosity provides for the poorest knights, raising them to the level of those in power by enabling them to fulfill their functions with honor and dignity. But at the same time he does not hesitate to encourage the rise of other persons from lower ranks and thus to mix commoners (*villeins*) with the nobility, including those wielders of words, the *jongleurs*.

> Vignent avant li bacelier legier,
> Keu de cuisine [cuisiniers], senscal, botellier,
> *Et demoiseax, jogleor et harpier,*
> Et tos iceux qui se poront aidier,
> L'auberc vestu et le hialme d'archier,
> L'espee çaindre et monter en destrier:
> En cest besoing seront tuit chevalier.
> S'en dolce France poïons repairier,
> Je lor ferai les fiés [fiefs] d'alberc baillier;
> *Tos lor lignages i avra recovrier.*
> . . . .
> *Chevalier fist le jor de maint lignage.*[72]

> ─────

> [Come forward, carefree young men,
> Cooks, servers, cup bearers,
> *And young men, jongleurs and harp players,*
> And all those who could help him,
> Be outfitted with chainmail [*auberc*] and the archer's helmet,
> A sword to carry and a horse to mount:
> In this struggle they will all become knights
> When they come back to sweet France,
> I'll give them fiefs,
> *To them and to all their lineages.*
> . . . .
> *On that day, he made many lineages noble.*]

Charlemagne's thoughts and actions transcend class and family interests in the name of a union that overrides all other concerns. He clearly explains what is at stake to the men he has assembled. "You need to understand our situation well," he tells them, "This is a war like no other. If I got into a fight with my neighbor, he might take one of my castles, I might put him in prison, or he might do likewise."

S'il me caçoit a coite d'esperon,
Jo revenoie la nuit a ma maizon;
Mais cist paien, ou nos nos conbaton,
Se il nos cacent, dites ou nos fuïron.
Nos somes pris, quel part que nos tornon.[73]

———

[If he chased me on horseback,
I would come back that night to my house;
But these pagans we are fighting,
If they chase us away, tell me where could we go?
If we are captured, who would help us?
We are caught whichever way we turn.]

They are fighting for their collective existence, and the outcome of the war will manifest God's will. But although the Other's difference is defined in terms of religion, in the *Chanson d'Aspremont* it also involves a geographical element that the poet continuously brings up. In describing Charlemagne's forces, the poet goes through the usual litany of the kingdoms of Christendom: Germany, Apulia, Lombardy, France, Brittany, Aquitaine, England, Hungary. The description of the enemy is more interesting. At the very beginning of the *chanson*, Balan, dispatched as ambassador by his father Agolant, arrives at Charlemagne's court. To explain his mission he begins with a course in geography, in which he draws the map of the world:

Sire emperere, faites moi escolter.
Il sont trois tieres [terres] que jo sai bien nomer:
Aise [Asie] a non [nom] l'une et Europe sa per [son égale]
La tierce Alfrique, l'on n'en puet puis [plus] trover,
Icés trois tieres departent [sont séparées] par la mer
Ki fait les tieres des illes desevrer
La mellor a mes sires a garder
L'autran [Naguére] i fisent paien un sort jeter.
Les dos [deux] devoient a la tierce acliner.[74]

———

[Sire, emperor, let me tell you,
There are three lands that I can name:
Asia is the name of one, and Europe is its equal.
The third one is Africa;
Here the three parts are separated by the sea,
Which turns the lands into islands.
The best one is for my lord to keep,

As it was given to the pagans in the past.
The two others must bow down to the third.]

Thus the world is divided into three continents. Agolant is the leader of Africa, and he promises his son Heumont sovereignty over Europe. Saracens are often called Africans, "the people of Africa," and their war cry has a geographical connotation: "Aufrikque" (v. 5389). As for Charlemagne, he is the leader of Europe: he represents a religious union, that of the Christian faith, but also a geographical unit, the one called Europe here. In this *chanson*, claims to universality come up against the reality of regional differences, differences that are beginning to be localized in terms of territorial boundaries.[75] The unity embodied by Charlemagne who has been given a sacred mission is manifest primarily vis-à-vis the enemy. Standing before Girard, the emperor can only be considered an equal among his peers. After the war is over, the duke of Vienna refuses any gifts from the emperor because he prefers to keep his independence and does not want to be beholden to him in any way. *La Chanson d'Aspremont* succeeds in reconciling the most positive image of Charlemagne and his power with the most radical refusal to recognize him as sovereign. This is possible only because dreams of identity feed on an obsessive fear of the Other.

SONGS OF REVOLT

What happens when, in spite of his legitimacy, a monarch stops behaving according to the values he should embody, when he is no longer acting for the common good, when his gaze turns away from the collectivity? This relates to another extreme case, one Dominique Boutet has aptly called "royal blindness."[76] This blindness can come from drunkenness, from greed (the inverted image of the gift), from sensuality, or simply from weakness—all such examples can be found in *chansons* that have been collectively labeled "songs of the revolted" such as *Chevalerie Ogier, Doon de Mayence,* and *Renaut de Montauban.* It should be emphasized that the exploration of these different forms of moral weakness corresponds to a reflection on the structural weakness of a political system in which royal power continues to grow. Given Charlemagne's founding image and legitimizing function, choosing him as a model is a radical means of depicting and pondering such failings. But it must be remembered on the one hand that in a feudal-vassalic context war is a juridical process, whereas on the other that in the epic genre war fulfills an aesthetic need. Thus depicting a war waged against the great emperor expresses less a refusal of the system he embodies than an expression of the conflictual relationships existing within this system. And indeed none of these *chansons* end with the overthrow of Charlemagne.

Composed around 1200, *Renaut de Montauban* illustrates well the tension between loyalty and protest.[77] Charlemagne threatens Beuves of Aigremont with harsh punishment for not having participated in the campaigns against the Saxons. He orders his son Lohier to demand that Beuves carry out his responsibility toward the king. Beuves kills Lohier. Charlemagne is threatened here not only in his attempts to wage war, but also as regards his lineage because, in this case, his succession becomes problematic. However, he is wrong when he disregards judicial procedure and has Beuves killed in an ambush. Blinded by the advice of traitors as well as by his desire for personal revenge, Charlemagne, the guarantor of the given word, nonetheless does not respect it. Disorder ensues, albeit quickly overcome through reconciliation and a new peace. A variation on the same theme appears shortly afterward in the famous scene in which Renaut, Beuves's nephew, kills Bertholai, himself Charlemagne's nephew, by splitting his skull with a chessboard. In fact, Bertholai had slapped Renaut, who had begged Charlemagne for permission to punish the insult. Renaut goes much further in his request: he asks justice for Beuves's murder, which means resuming a conflict that was thought to be settled and to expose the king on another level. This request triggers a long war during which Charlemagne proves to be so pitiless that he loses sight of the common good as well as the law. These are the circumstances in which we see him affected by Maugis's magic: his crown, his weapon, and finally he himself are seized in various episodes of the plot. However, his person is never threatened. And Aymon, the wronged man's father, remains faithful to Charlemagne even when, torn between his role as father and his function as vassal, he happens to give a modicum of help to his children. Charlemagne's inflexibility drives his barons to abandon him, particularly when his royal anger overrides the given word, that is, when he tries to force his men to break their oaths. On these occasions, Charlemagne is forced to compromise. But when he tries to give back the crown, the reaction is unanimous: his frightened barons beg him to remain king. The final peace is the result both of Renaut's submission and of the barons' threat to abandon the king if he persists in his decision to have Renaut hanged.

In the end, what emerges is a conflictual system, but one that is also in its own way efficient, in other words, a system that functions according to epic norms and enables the resolution of disagreements that at first appear unsolvable. In spite of being rigorously put to the test, the principle of sovereignty is maintained in the person of Charlemagne, and although the protagonists must sometimes define themselves in opposition to the great monarch, that definition is still developed *in relation* to him.

It has often been pointed out that these *chansons* contain parallels between Charlemagne's behavior and the policies of Philip Augustus, notably his policies toward the nobility. In *La Chanson d'Aspremont*, for instance,

Charlemagne relies less and less on those in power and increasingly more on members of the lower nobility. In *Renaut de Montauban* he wages punitive wars aimed at confiscating the lands of the highest lords who have not fulfilled their vassalic obligations. Likewise, in 1202 Philip Augustus ordered John, king of England, duke of Normandy and Aquitaine, to appear in judgment before him as his vassal on the basis of the king of France's suzerainty over Aquitaine. The spectacular victories of 1204, when Philip took the duchy of Normandy and the fiefs to the north of the Loire River from John, reflected the execution of a similar sentence.

Louis VI had already claimed the right to order nobles to appear in judgment before him in 1126. Philip Augustus's reign is marked, on the one hand, by the will and the power to have these orders executed and, on the other, by his determination to define homages and vassalic oaths more specifically by setting them down in writing. These feudal ties often went back to the Carolingian period. But under Philip Augustus, the given word turned increasingly into the written word.[78] Already in 1194 he created the royal archives. His efforts to turn writing into another weapon of royal authority are impressive. He understood what the Church had known for a long time and what had also been inscribed in Charlemagne's *geste*: writing is a means of mastering speech and of ensuring one's authority. This is perhaps one of the reasons why Philip Augustus hated *jongleurs* and *chansoniers* so much, because, in a way, they represented speech that was not controlled, that went in other directions, but which still dealt with the relationship between the king and his vassals. Yet, the later *chansons de geste* should not be seen as reflecting an antiroyalist ideology, although they did raise questions about the relationships of power within a society that defined itself in terms of two ideologies that were sometimes mutually reinforced, and sometimes in opposition: one theocentric and the other feudal-vassalic.

KAROLINUS: RETURN TO CAROLINGIAN STOCK

We have seen that the figure of Charlemagne was quite prevalent during the late twelfth century, both as regarded relations between the kingdom of France and the Empire, and the waging of the Crusades. It is therefore not surprising that during two crucial moments of his reign Philip Augustus carried the banner of the Abbey of Saint-Denis, which was equated with the *oriflamme* traditionally associated with Charlemagne. Philip Augustus carried it against the infidels during the Crusade of 1190 and, in 1214, against the emperor of Germany at the battle of Bouvines.

Charlemagne's presence was also manifest in dynastic ideology, not so much to legitimize the Capetian dynasty itself—its legitimacy had not been questioned for a long time—but to support the kingdom of France in its efforts to increase and consolidate its territory and its power.[79] We are familiar with the story of the *reditus regni ad stirpem Karoli*; following Vincent de Beauvais's *Speculum Historiale* (1244), the *Grandes Chroniques de France* expounded at length on the return to the Carolingian race that was believed to be realized through Louis VIII, Philip Augustus's son. The *Grandes Chroniques* tells of Saint Valery's apparition to Hughes Capet to tell him that the Capetians were to rule over the kingdom of France for seven generations. Philip Augustus, the seventh Capetian king, could claim Carolingian descent through his mother. He married Isabel of Hainaut, whose father, Baldwin V, count of Flanders, himself claimed to descend from Carolingian blood. Baldwin collected manuscripts of the *Historia Karoli Magni* by the Pseudo-Turpin (who, according to Baldwin, was not "pseudo"), and his sister Yolande commissioned the first translation of the Pseudo-Turpin's *Chronicle*.[80] More translations soon followed. Thus under Philip Augustus this famous work began to circulate in the vulgate. Isabel of Hainaut, raised in that family's culture, gave birth to Louis in 1187. This child, destined to become Louis VIII, thus descended from the Carolingians on both sides of his family and represented a return to the Carolingian dynasty. It is probably this ancestry that inspired Gilles de Paris in 1195 to compose a long poem entitled *Karolinus*, which he intended to present to the young Louis on the occasion of his thirteenth birthday in 1200.

Gilles's epico-moral poem can be placed, on the one hand, in the context of the *reditus* and of a certain identification of Philip Augustus's monarchy with that of Charlemagne, and, on the other, in the context of a discourse, both aesthetic and critical, in which the figure of the great emperor enables an examination of the nature and limits of the monarchy. In the *chansons de geste* we have seen that a critique of the prince often takes the form of a criticism of his morality, and the systematic weakness of the monarchy is assimilated to the king's moral shortcomings (even if this only involves his listening to wrong advice, i.e., that of traitors). Gilles takes care to differentiate his writing from the *jongleurs'* lying tales. But although he openly sets himself apart from the *mithmi*, he does borrow their aesthetic methods so that the pleasure of the poetry can facilitate the learning of the moral truths he wishes to impart to the young prince.[81] However, this author does not go so far as to accept the *jongleur's* language; he retains his Latin, the language of the Church's truth.

He is primarily concerned with recentering the figure of Charlemagne. Rather than examine the limits of the monarchy, he strives to anchor it in ethics. The poet relegates the story of Charlemagne's life and deeds to the abstract category of morality; thus the great king's life journey is a lengthy illustration of the four cardinal virtues. Gilles divides his poem into five books, the first four of which deal with the classical virtues: *prudentia, justitia, fortitudo,* and *temperantia,* while the fifth focuses on the *utilitas* and the ways to attain virtue. However, although the four virtues provide the rationale for the main divisions of the poem, the poem itself unfolds following the rules of biographical narrative, and the virtues are illustrated through deeds of war. The moral monarch appears through the conquering monarch. Further, the fact that these wars were waged in distant lands is interpreted as reflecting additional valor, because this was how Charlemagne doubled the territory of his kingdom.

> O magnum meritis o propter facta perenni
> Dignum laude uirum cuius preconia numquam
> Enarranda satis, qui non in proxima martem
> Sustinuit girare suum sed in extera regna;
> Longanimes longe distantibus intulit iras.[82]

> ----

> [O man great through your merits, and worthy by your deeds of perennial praise, and about whom one could never say enough, and who waged war not against nearby kingdoms but against far-flung ones: he has carried his anger to distant [enemies].]

Under his light, France is powerful, good, sweet, and free; beloved of God, she causes a kind of *pax franca* to reign on earth.[83] Yet the unity and peace the emperor creates through so many wars are essentially European: he triumphs over the Italians, the Saxons, the Frisians, the Slavs (those from the West), the Bavarians, the Russians, the Norwegians, the Avars, the Huns, and of course the people of Spain. In Gilles's text Roncevaux does indeed occur, Roland does sound the horn and break his sword, but, as in Einhard, it is Basques, and not Saracens, who are attacking. Charlemagne renders Rome its ancient glory. And Gilles describes how the "great Gaul" (*Gallicus Magnus*), whose ancestry went back to the people of Troy, conquers England, which elevates him above Rome and Caesar.[84] As for war, Gilles's concerns should be classified as territorial rather than universal: at the center of this territorial unity, France/Gaul. Of course, the Orient also makes its presence known but only through gifts, signs of respect; here again, we find the famous clock sent by the king of Egypt.

Although force is necessary and Charlemagne proves to be all-powerful, the very essence of monarchical authority must rest upon an ethical foundation. From this perspective, Charlemagne represents the *panarethos*, the moral entity (chap. 4, v. 63), all of whose actions and laws, in short, its whole being exists and acts for the common good and happiness ("Ut princeps per cuncta bonus, per cuncta beate / Conditionis homo meritique per omnia magni") (chap. 4, vv. 114–15). While extolling Charlemagne's fault-less virtue, Gilles expresses a number of criticisms against Philip Augustus's reign, particularly concerning his policies toward marriage, which resulted in a break with the Church, as well as his refusal to listen to others, to ask for advice, to be approachable.[85] But to whom should he listen and how should the chosen advisers serve the king in their function as *consilium*? By being virtuous themselves, of course.

In Gilles the issue of public opinion (*communis opinio*) is raised explic-itly for the first time, I believe, and this in a text whose main purpose is to provide a description of Charlemagne. In one passage, Gilles addresses a colleague, William the Breton, who composed the famous *Philippide*, an epic poem in which in his dedication to Louis he refers to Philip Augustus by the name of "Karolide." In the *Karolinus*, Gilles criticizes William for traveling to Rome to have Philip's divorce accepted. All of William's knowledge is worthless if it cannot recognize what is useful. To obtain the support of public opinion it must be put ahead of one's own pleasure: "Et pro te uigeat communis opinio, quam tu / Dilectis prepone tuis."[86] William takes pleasure in being in Rome, which, in this context, separates him from virtue. However, William seeks only to fulfill the king's will. It is for this reason—the king's moral failing—that the *panarethòs* must be sung by Gilles himself. Thus there is an implied justification of his own work. Gilles the good adviser is contrasted with William the bad guide.

In this early depiction of public opinion, the author appears for a moment to attribute a positive role to it. Logically, if the good adviser pays attention to public opinion, then the behavior of the king, who listens to him, should also be guided by it. But this does not, in fact, occur, because for the king to submit to public opinion would also be for him to submit to error: the uncontrolled speech of the *mithmi* from which Gilles seeks to distance himself is an example of this. Ultimately, what is at issue is know-ing who has the right to speak and, in this case, who has the right to repre-sent Charlemagne, the ideal representation of the monarchy. And here Gilles associates the work of the *jongleurs* with that of public opinion, which he sees as the opposite of a transmission of history.

> . . . ego quomodo, quero,
> Id facturus eram? nec enim que mithmica pangunt
> Commenta aut meminit communis opinio uulgi,
> Historie tradit brevior per singula textus.[87]

> ———

> [How should I proceed? The less prolix text of history does not trans-mit what the fictions of the *jongleurs* tell, nor what is remembered by the common opinion of the public at large.]

The only valid "public" opinion is extremely limited; speech deserving to be heard is the one Charlemagne listened to. The illustrious predecessor took care to exclude buffoons and *jongleurs* (*scurrae et mithmi*) because he refused "to be praised by shameful people just as he did not want to be praised for shameful things."[88] Instead, he demanded that serious things be read to him: the deeds of the ancestors (*gesta patrum*), the chronicle of the kings (*cronica regnum*), and of course *The City of God*. Gilles believes that this is the kind of text he is writing: serious, true, the very opposite of *communis opinio vulgi* and the lies of the *chansons de geste*; just what is needed to convey a new Charlemagne at the moment young Louis holds the promise of a *reditus regni ad stirpem Karoli*.

Gilles's poem is an attempt to reclaim the history of the great emperor from the "free" domain of the *chansons de geste*. Therefore, he must turn away from the issue of limitations and focus the discourse once again on the true strength of the monarchy: the king's moral righteousness. Following his own logic, Gilles stipulates at the end of his *Captatio* that his poem could never be published without the king's authorization. It is up to the king, that is, the young Louis, to determine which account has the right to circulate, which image of Charlemagne may see the light of day.[89] It is also up to him to set the limits of a discourse on origins.

But there appears to be one final contradiction resulting from the criteria upon which Gilles so strongly insists. He has to be truthful, to give the correct representation of the emperor based upon very sparse documentation. Gilles thus complains of the terseness of eyewitnesses who left so many of the things they had seen in obscurity.[90] But they did worse: Gilles reproaches the ancients for having written only what they pleased ("Hec uero minus attendens tantum illa uetustas / Quod uoluit scripsit").[91] Yet, this is exactly what he himself proposes when he gives the king the power to choose the words that may survive. Gilles wanted to operate in all these fields at once: to write an epic and history, to reject the *mithmi* and use their aesthetics, and to produce a truthful account and subject it to royal censorship. But he was also the first to begin a criticism of the sources in which the figure of Charlemagne is represented. Of course, at that time, one had no choice but to submit to royal authority, but such criticism later reemerged in very different circumstances during the Renaissance.

Gilles's work is significant because it highlights the "struggle for authority" concerning representations of Charlemagne, and it does so on several levels.[92] Within the kingdom, at the time of the "return" of the monarchy to the Caroligian race or "stock," the issue was not only how to represent Charlemagne, but who should do so. For us, it is most important to examine the many efforts at representation which, as has just been noted, are sometimes in contrast, and at other times complement each other. Court *jongleurs*, chroniclers, and poets revived and reinvented Charlemagne's history according to their needs, as even William the Breton does in referring to Philip as "Karolide" in the dedication accompanying his great poem, the *Philippide*.

At the time of Louis VII's reign, apocalyptic literature again became concerned with the Sibylline prophecies that had originally turned toward Byzantium in the hope that a new Constantine would emerge to redress all the Germanic emperors' wrongs and to bring about unity and peace before the end of the world. Adapted to thirteenth-century realities, this anticipated emperor became French, and his actions were directly inspired by Charlemagne.[93] In the cathedral of Chartres, the famous window devoted to Charlemagne's exploits was completed around 1225. These examples, chosen from among the clearest, suffice to illustrate how diverse were the efforts to represent the great emperor.

Beyond the kingdom, the Empire and the papacy also attempted to appropriate the figure of Charlemagne. Pope Innocent III (1198–1216), taking advantage of conflicts surrounding the succession to the Empire, emphasizes the importance of Leo III's act when he crowned Charlemagne, thereby ensuring the transfer of the Empire. Such an interpretation emphasizes the pope's role at the expense of that of the emperor, who became a servant of the pontiff with the principal mission of defending the Church. In 1215, during celebrations on the occasion of his second coronation, the emperor Frederick II chose the date of July 27, thus one year after the victory of Bouvines (in which he was allied with Philip Augustus against John Lackland and Otto IV), solemnly to place Charlemagne's bones in a magnificent reliquary decorated with small statues and bas-reliefs illustrating the legend of Charlemagne. The emperor took the city of Aachen under his protection and confirmed and broadened the privileges granted by his predecessors. As in the case of Barbarossa, these acts were directed in part at the subjects of the Empire, but, at the same time, it is clear that Frederick II was reacting against the impressive proportions that Charlemagne's image had assumed in France. At any rate, for centuries to come, each one of the elements in the France-Empire-papacy triangle would, depending on circumstances, draw on the myths of the great emperor to assert its authority over the others.

It is important to note, however, that in France, at a time when what might be called a certain "national consciousness" was awakening—even if territorial borders were ill-defined—the multifaceted and complex figure of Charlemagne continued to be a key point of reference. This complex mixture of history and legend proved to be a genuine "motivating myth" for the French identity that was then being formed, deriving its power from its multidimensional representations.[94] As a politico-ideological affirmation, a locus of debate and even of laughter, and an aesthetic construct, Charlemagne's influence spread from the courts of the powerful to churches and public squares. We should not underestimate the element of pleasure that governs Charlemagne's aura, a pleasure that lies in talking about oneself, in inventing oneself, in repeating one's history as members of a collectivity.

THREE

Rewriting History

The creative energy of the *chanson de geste* gradually waned in the course of the thirteenth century. The prestige of poetry became eclipsed by the rise of prose, which, beginning in 1250, increasingly became the sole vehicle of truth. This was also the period of the great historical compilations. Vincent de Beauvais and Primat undertook their works within a few years of each other. The tradition of accumulation put itself at the service of governmental power. What was Charlemagne's role within this cultural and political evolution?

In a way, his role at the end of the Middle Ages is less obvious than it was in preceding periods because there were fewer bodies of work devoted exclusively to him as were the *chansons de geste*. Furthermore, in this phase of the transmission of the story of Charlemagne's life we see fewer variations in how the story is told, and instead find a great stability through the retelling and the repetition of events. These documents are nonetheless very interesting in that they enable us to see what was received and transmitted and what aspects of Charlemagne's representation were used as a foundation for the establishment of a national identity. The "efficacy" of this personage endures through stained glass windows, paintings, and the "translation" of the *chansons de geste* into prose. It traveled through the slow deterioration of the feudal-vassalic system, the transformation of the alodia estates into fiefs and of fiefs into property. It nourished the image of the kingdom held by the monarchy as well as the fourteenth century's nostalgia for chivalry; it survived the devastation of the Hundred Years' War and returned in force at the dawn of the Renaissance.

In this chapter I will look at texts and images that provide testimony to the stability and the power of the figure of Charlemagne, but I will also examine the role that figure played in the eschatological anguish that characterized the close of the Middle Ages. In these works Charlemagne is represented as the promise of a new stability and as the inspiration and justification for a European policy that was to mark the beginning of the Renaissance in France. The story of Charles VIII, a pivotal figure between the late Middle Ages and the nascent Renaissance, offers us a striking example of the impact Charlemagne's heroic representation had on the experiences of those who held political power.

ACCUMULATING GLORY: PHILIPPE MOUSKET'S CHRONICLE

Let us begin by looking at how the representation of Charlemagne gained strength and was transmitted through the amalgams created by these compilations. The desire to "make history" again, to "re-do" it, arises from the "re-telling," the repeating of sources and the concomitant transformation of them. The creation of the great compilations soon became an "official" task encouraged and supported by the monarchy. The Abbey of Saint-Denis was the privileged repository of such documents.[1] These works include the famous chronicles that are often invoked in the *chansons de geste* to bolster their claims to truth, chronicles that constitute the main source of a cumulative truth. These great prose works drew from the authority and legitimacy of the monarchy and, reciprocally, lent support to that authority and legitimacy; thus they played an important role in the definition and consolidation of an "official" identity.

The taste for accumulation was not limited to prose, and it extended beyond the circles of the court and the monasteries. I thus plan to begin my examination of these chronicles with a discussion of a transitional work, a massive compilation in verse, the *Chronique rimée* by Philippe Mousket. For a long time there was some confusion as to the identity of the author; he was at one time believed to have been the bishop of Tournai in the 1280s. In fact, Philippe Mousket was only a rich burgher from that town, and he probably died in the year 1243, the year when his *Chronique* comes to a sudden stop.[2] In the prologue to his poem, he explains why he has undertaken to put into verse the entire history of France that he found in the Latin texts stored at Saint-Denis, and he notes that no one requested that he undertake this work, meaning that he did not have a patron and that "neither praise nor criticism" will cause him to stop before its completion.

Mousket's project of composing a rhymed history went against the trend of his time, but he was doing it mainly for his own pleasure, which consisted of telling his history and amusing himself by rhyming it. And this pleasure goes on for more than thirty-one thousand verses! We know little about the success this work might have had, although the fact that it survived in a beautiful manuscript leads us to assume that it must have had some impact. Rather than speculating on who its readers might have been let us focus on discovering how this bourgeois from Hainaut who was absolutely loyal to the French monarchy understood history. His work gives us an excellent idea of what constituted the stock of common knowledge (the "on-dit") about history, insofar as it translates what a lay amateur of the past had to say about it. It is quite clearly not the work of a "professional": in spite of his claims, Mousket does not draw directly from the Latin sources but gets his information from chronicles written in French. Mousket's narrative begins with the Trojans and ends with his own time. Out of the thirty-one thousand octosyllabic verses that tirelessly follow each other, almost ten thousand are devoted to Charlemagne, whereas Philip Augustus, the other important personage of the account, whose life and deeds we would have expected to take up more room, is granted only about half the space of his famous ancestor. Thus the true hero of Mousket's chronicle is Charlemagne.[3]

How does Mousket depict the figure of the great emperor? Throughout Mousket's history we again find many of the sources we have already discussed, although they are used here in their secondary, translated versions: Einhard, the Pseudo-Turpin—which had been translated into French many times since the beginning of the century[4]—the *Descriptio*, the *chansons de geste*, and elements from *Fierabras*, *Aspremont*, and *Renaut de Montauban*. He used other *chansons*, as well, as seen in the important place he gives to the wars against the Saxons, the "Saisnes." Mousket surpasses the work of the "official" chroniclers in his attempts to incorporate the entire range of texts written on Charlemagne into his history of France. The author strives to impose a certain order on this mass of information, but his primary concern is clearly to accumulate as many sources, as many other histories as possible.

The logic of accumulation does not preclude contradiction. Thus we get two versions of the battle of Roncevaux: that of Einhard, in which the "Gascons," i.e., the Basques, are attacking the French, and that of the Pseudo-Turpin, in which the Saracens attack following Ganelon's treasonous activities. We also find familiar details: the gift of the clock, Charlemagne in his bath, at court. Mousket takes pains to list all of the conquered countries, from the Holy Land to England, but he is more concerned with European Christendom: Saxons are often treated as Saracens, an indication that the opponents of the hero of unity can only come from "elsewhere."

From the amalgam of such a great number of narratives there emerges an image of the emperor that corresponds to Mousket's historical sensibility. In many respects, our author was no different from the great compilers who sought examples of conduct in history. The chronicles are, in Beauvais's and Primat's words, "mirrors of life," where each person can find "good and evil, the beautiful and the ugly, sense and folly, and profit from all the examples of history."[5] And yet, although Mousket exalts the exploits of the barons and the peers of France, he constantly returns to Charlemagne's relationship with the common people, the untitled of his kingdom. In Mousket, Charlemagne becomes the image of power, of power on *every* level it can be found:

Pour çou, vous roi, vous haut princier,	v. 3528
Ki devés tières justicier,	
Devés prendre garde à Karlon	
. . . .	
Et là devroient garde prendre	v. 3546
Roi, conte et duc et prince entendre,	
et li pape et li kardenal,	
Pour tout le peule oster de mal,	
Li prélat, et li arcevesque	v. 3550
Arcediakène, doiien, vesque,	
Abé, primat, et tous clergiés	
Et tous li peules baptisiés,	
Ki sor autre gent a pooir.	
Cascuns devroit, pour Dieu le voir,	v. 3555
Docement maintenir sa gent,	
Et repartir or et argent	
As povres, en lor sostenance,	
Et castoier, *pour ramenbrance*	
De Dam-el-dieu et de Karlon,	v. 3560
Ki par sa boine entension	
Maintint sa gent et son païs	
Si qu'il ne fu onqes haïs	
. . . .	
Ainc commanda que cascuns om	v. 3580
Ewist son droit jusques à som.	

[Because of this, kings, high princes, who must judge the kingdoms, *you must keep in mind Charles* . . . and there should kings, counts, dukes and princes, popes, and bishops remember to protect the people from harm;

and prelates, archbishops, archdeacons, doyens, bishops, abbots . . . and all the clerks, and *all baptized persons having power over others. Everyone should* in the name of the true God support his people with gentleness and give gold and silver to the poor for their sustenance and administer justice *in memory of God and of Karlon,* who, through his goodwill maintained his people and his country; thus he was never hated . . . but ordered that every man receive his due.] (my emphasis)

One must study and understand Charlemagne in order to incorporate the meaning and the psychology of responsibility, since responsibility alone can shed light on the art and the manner of wielding power *on all levels of society.* The complete fusion of the triumphant hero and the morally exemplary sovereign is achieved through the multiple accounts of Charlemagne's story. Mousket constantly compares Charlemagne to Greek and biblical heroes. Among the French combatants are new Hectors and Maccabees; never, even for the sake of the beautiful Helen, had the Greeks or Trojans raised such armies nor accomplished such feats of arms as did the French for their lord and their honor (vv. 7225–7234). It is true that Mousket does mention revolts by the barons and other internal strife, but such occurrences are in general less significant than they appeared in the original *chansons:* the affirmation of a collective identity is clearly more important than the exploration of the limits of monarchical power. And this identity is definitely an epic one: the French are a great people, as were their genealogical ancestors, the Trojans, and their spiritual ancestors, the Jewish people. Such is the basic content of the ten thousand verses devoted to Charlemagne.

Although Mousket minimizes the importance of internal discord, he nonetheless clearly describes the dangers that threatened the Christian sovereign. Charlemagne is different from his epic predecessors precisely because of his Christianity. His intimate and private life holds an important place in Mousket's work, and even though Charlemagne proves to be an exemplary man in terms of the Roman model adopted by Einhard, he is nonetheless prey to human weakness. Thus tempted by the flesh, he tries to take a young woman by force, and only a miracle prevents him from committing a sin: God intervenes and causes him to break an arm while he is trying to overcome the woman's resistance! In another scene an "unspeakable" sin Charlemagne has committed is forgiven by God through an encounter with Saint Gilles. Likewise, his generosity is marred by temporary lapses: the Pseudo-Turpin's Agolant denounces Charlemagne's stinginess toward the poor, and the king makes amends. The inclusion of these episodes serves to point out that King Charles is also a man. Be it by miracle or personal effort, the king of the French manages either to change or be forgiven. Like any other man, Charlemagne has the right to sin, to make mistakes, to err; he nonetheless remains a perfect Christian and sovereign over "all other earthly kings" (v. 4014).

In addition to projecting an image of Charlemagne as "everyman,"[6] Mousket develops an image of Charlemagne as Christ. Faithful to the Pseudo-Turpin's narrative, Mousket shows us the emperor as a victim of Ganelon's treason, just as Christ suffered from that of Judas. But in Mousket, the tragedy befalling the Christian king appears in some ways to be worse. Charlemagne's mourning after the defeat at Roncevaux is the subject of about five hundred verses (vv. 8385–8913). Roland, the barons, and many other French soldiers perished at Roncevaux because that was God's will, and God acted for the salvation of their souls and their eternal happiness. God's will brought happiness to the dead, but unhappiness to Charlemagne and his kingdom, for the great king depended on the great and the valorous. "It seems that God hates me / and that he has toward me anger and hatred / and resentment and great hatred / that he has taken from me my power, my virtue and my support" (vv. 9376–9381).[7] Mousket's rhymes play upon the verb "to hate" to emphasize the blows that fate dealt the emperor. How is he to rule, to defend Christendom if the best in his kingdom now belong to the kingdom of God?

In the twelfth century, as Augustianism was slowly waning, Mousket's *Chronique* brought to light the contradictions that weighed upon the destiny of this new chosen people of God: human happiness was not realized in this world but in the next. In his lamentations Charlemagne finds his fate much worse than that reserved for the great heroes. Even Priam, who saw the destruction of his wife, his children, his city, and his people, was consoled by dying with them (vv. 8878–8884). Charlemagne's particular unhappiness comes from not dying; his sacrifice thus consists in continuing to live. Individual happiness is refused him or, we might say, constantly postponed—since it is upon him that the survival of the collectivity in the face of the pagan enemy depends, it is he who must defend the path to heaven.

CHARLEMAGNE ACCORDING TO PRIMAT: THE *GRANDES CHRONIQUES DE FRANCE*

Although Mousket gives us an interpretation of this amalgam of historical hearsay, that is, the stock of common knowledge (the "on-dit") about history, the more "official" works in fact fix the image of Charlemagne in the period leading up to the Renaissance. They also proceed through accumulation. The great stained-glass window devoted to Charlemagne in the cathedral of Chartres is a good example of the "translation into glass" of several accounts of the great emperor's life (fig. 5). The possible meaning of the scenes depicted has been debated for a long time. Today there is general agreement that they represent three great episodes: the trip to Jerusalem (the *Descriptio*), the expeditions to Spain (the *Historia* of the Pseudo-Turpin), and the legend of Saint Gilles and Charlemagne's sin. This last subject is placed at the very top of the window: Charlemagne is a sinner, but he is forgiven by God due to a saint's mediation. This scene dominates the whole, while the emperor as crusader and defender of the Church is the subject of the other scenes.[8]

Indeed, the epic vision plays a crucial role in the great works of compilation that were undertaken under the auspices of the court and the Church. Such compilations were to be alternatively discredited and revalorized until the Renaissance when they were rejected and looked upon as mere collections of tales. In contrast, La Curne de Sainte-Palaye, the leader of a group of eighteenth-century medievalists exploring and re-evaluating the Middle Ages, expresses an opinion closer to that which we hold today:

> In order to assess [the works] we have to consider the authors' intention in writing them, and to transport ourselves to the centuries when they were composed. The aim was to assemble into a single book all that was spread out in several volumes and to omit none of the main facts regardless of their nature. . . . To carry out this project, what better way to proceed than to choose the oldest, the most accredited, and the most thorough historians and draw from other historical pieces all that could serve as supplements? This is what was done.[9]

The most accredited medieval historians were chronicler clerks such as Aimoin de Fleury (*Historia Francorum*) and Sigebert de Gembloux. They drew from some of the sources we have already discussed as well as from others that had often been inspired by earlier ones.[10] In his *Miroir historial*, Vincent de Beauvais emphasizes the fusion embodied by Charlemagne, a fusion that brought together the Greek, Roman, and German ancestry.[11] Charlemagne accomplishes this fusion on the cultural plane, as well, by ensuring, thanks to the learned Alcuin, the transfer of the *translatio studii* from Rome to Paris, thus complementing an earlier movement that had brought literature from Athens to Rome.[12]

France's claim to the glory of learning, study, and culture became increasingly stronger from the twelfth century on. Although France could not lay claim to the *translatio imperii*, the University of Paris was enjoying uncontested prominence and authority throughout Europe. Around 1288, Alexander de Roes, a canon of the Church of Saint Mary at Cologne, adopted the idea of the *translatio studii*, but this time using it to the benefit of Germany. In his view, Charlemagne had bequeathed the hereditary monarchy to France and "the great schools of philosophy and liberal arts that he transferred from Rome to Paris," but the Empire, with its elective royalty, is reserved for Germany.[13] In this schema Charlemagne would have granted a distinct function to each member of the France-Empire-papacy triad: to Germany the Empire, to France the *Studium*, and to the Romans the sacerdocy, that is, the papacy.

It is likely due to this rivalry between the three powers that Vincent is eager to differentiate Charlemagne the king from Charlemagne the emperor. The story of the royal personage occurs at the end of book 24; that of the imperial figure opens book 25. It is as if this arrangement were meant to reflect a significant change in register. Sigebert serves as the primary source for the description of royal life, whereas the *Descriptio* and the Pseudo-Turpin are the sources for imperial events.[14]

When he attained the title of Emperor, Charlemagne truly became an epic personage, but he was first an incomparable king. This distinction makes it possible to differentiate clearly between the prerogatives of the king and those of the emperor. Thus simply arranging certain elements in one part rather than in another suffices to show, for instance, that Charlemagne had acquired his true power over the Church as king of France and not as emperor. Charlemagne had to ratify the nomination of the bishops and even the election of the pope for their posts to be considered effective; Charlemagne's role was also a way to ensure the independence of the French monarchy in regard to the Church and the Empire. In this sort of symbolic struggle, true power was sometimes less important than the "ideological" value of the entities concerned: the Empire may have been in decline, but it retained its prestige. In other cases, the assumption of these positions had important ramifications and served to justify a right or a privilege.

Vincent de Beauvais's *Speculum historiale* was often recopied; it became available throughout Europe and was translated into French at the end of the sixteenth century: thus the image of Charlemagne it projected was seen far and wide. Yet it is Primat's *Roman aux rois*, later renamed *Grandes Chroniques de France*, that ensures the transition from the historical culture written in Latin to that written in French. More than any other, this monastic, royal, and nationalist history, compiled at the request of Louis IX (Saint Louis), translates and transmits an "official" vision of the history of France. It enjoyed a wide audience that included some elements of the bourgeoisie, and its influence lasted beyond the fifteenth century.[15] In Primat, the symbolic continuity of the monarchy is established around the figure of Charlemagne. Though the history of the French goes back to the Trojans, in a monarchy in which sovereignty is based increasingly on ties of blood, on heredity rather than on the coronation ceremony, the *reditus regni ad stirpem Karoli* acquires a symbolic importance. This is evidenced in the *Grandes Chroniques* in a passage that Bernard Guenée holds to be the "key to the work":[16]

> Here ends the lineage of the great Charlemagne and the kingdom passed into the hands of the heirs of Hugh the Great, named Capet, who was a duke of France at the time. But it [the Carolingian lineage] was restored, at the time of the good king Philip Augustus when he married, with the express intent of restoring the line of the great Charlemagne, Queen Isabel, who was the daughter of Count Baldwin of Hainaut. . . . One could certainly say that the valorous king Louis [VIII], son of Philip, . . . was of Charlemagne's lineage and in him the line was restored. (GCF, V, 1–2)

During the marriage ceremony, Count Baldwin "carried before the king Joyeuse,[17] the sword of the great king Charlemagne" (VI, 103). Thus, in the *Grandes Chroniques*, it is no longer the lineage of Clovis that must be recovered, but that of Charlemagne. Primat insists on this fact when he writes of the beginning of the reign of Louis VIII and tells his readers about Saint Valery's prophecy according to which the Capetians were to rule for seven generations. This prophecy is realized with the advent of Philip Augustus's son, who then brings the return of the monarchy to the Carolingian line. Indeed, while Charlemagne is the "key to the history," it is not because he begins the monarchy but rather because he represents the irruption of an ideal into the course of history and crystallizes the values of the collectivity whose evolution Primat traces.

We know which primary sources the Benedictine monk used to write about the reign of the great emperor: the *Royal Frankish Annals*, Einhard, Notker, the Pseudo-Turpin, and the *Descriptio*. As we have already seen in other works, the Charlemagne of the *Grandes Chroniques* inherits the main traits attributed to him by previous documents. Primat, a conscientious compiler, strives to remain invisible behind the witnesses he chooses. He first has Einhard speak to us to tell the accomplishments and deeds "of the glorious Charlemagne the great" [du glorieus prince Kallemanne le grant] (III, 3). Just as in the original text, the biographer tells us that little is known about the childhood of the great king. But Primat's Einhard adds that the child lived in Spain with King Galafre, a reference to the *chansons de geste* that filled the void left by the emperor's biographer.[18] The Charlemagne presented by Einhard in the *Grandes Chroniques* speaks French; he dresses "in the French style" (*à la manière de France*), he rides horseback and hunts "in the manner of the French custom" (*selonc la costume françoise*). He "knows and writes down himself the chansons that are sung about the deeds and the battles of the ancient kings" [sot et escrist, il meesmes, les chanz de diverses chançons que l'on chante des faiz et des batailles des anciens rois] (III, 151–54).

Under Einhard's authority, some anecdotes from Notker—who was probably considered less reliable—concerning culture and education are incorporated into the *Grandes Chroniques*. We are shown Charlemagne welcoming monks who have come from Scotland to "sell" their knowledge; we see him founding schools and having children from all social classes attend them ("whether they were sons of noblemen or lesser ones"), protecting and encouraging Alcuin thanks to whom "the fountain of doctrine and wisdom is in Paris just as it was in the past in Athens and in Rome" (III, 156–58). The theme of the *translatio studii* completes the comparison between Paris and Athens that had previously appeared in the prologue, "because the city of Athens was in the past the wellspring of philosophy and in Greece the flower of chivalry."

The great king represents much more than a simple knot binding dynasties together; he becomes the point of intersection of an entire civilization. Precisely through this work of fusion and transfer (*translatio*) Charlemagne is at the origin of French culture and accedes to the status of founder. It is not surprising, then, that the man who continued the chronicles, William of Nangis, at the end of the thirteenth century points out that Joyeuse, Charlemagne's sword, was brought to Philip III (Philip the Brave), the son of Saint Louis, during his coronation. This weapon, which had up to then been the sword of justice, thus becomes the sword of Charlemagne.[19]

We are familiar with the role played by the barons, those "flowers of chivalry," throughout the *Grandes Chroniques de France*, and the section devoted to Charlemagne is no exception to this rule. Nevertheless, we should not underestimate the role of the people in the chapters on Charlemagne. As we have seen, the king is not only the founder of schools, thus giving even the sons of "lesser ones" access to knowledge, he is also the legislator king who regularly assembles the people and the barons in the "general parlement." The presence of the "people" in Primat's work comes from the word *populus* in the *Annals*, though the intention of the great chronicler was rather to enhance the barons' role, since most of the time he translates expressions such as *generalem populi sui conventum* or *generalem conventum* with a sentence such as: "the king assembled the general parlement of the barons and the people."[20] In the *Annals* the word *populus* designated the military men participating in the "general *plaids*." In the *Grandes Chroniques*, the *populus* splits in two: "people" and "barons" thus reflecting the social reality of the two estates. The addition of the term "barons" probably stems from an attitude favorable to the nobility, but it is nonetheless true that in the *Grandes Chroniques* the "general parlement" called up by Charlemagne brought two groups together: the people and the nobility.

I am not attempting to prove here that Primat had a precocious consciousness of the role the "people" were to play in the construction of France; rather, I wish to show that, even in the *Grandes Chroniques*, the role of the people remained one of the possible elements that could be infused into a portrait of Charlemagne—on the condition, as would later happen, that the sources be interpreted, or rather misinterpreted, in such a manner. The same can be said regarding Charlemagne the crusader, the warrior protector of the Church. Although the famous episode of the freeing of the serfs to go fight against the pagans is not in the Pseudo-Turpin manuscript that Primat used for his translation, that manuscript does include the episode in which Agolant refuses to convert because of the mistreatment of the poor. Primat faithfully translates the emperor's realization that he has committed a wrong, and of the ethical obligation to the poor held by every man.[21] It is easy to see how much this image of the crusading king learning to become a perfect Christian corresponds to Saint Louis's deepest aspirations. Socially, politically, culturally, and genealogically, Charlemagne appears in the *Grandes Chroniques de France* as a founding figure accomplishing fusion and coherence: this is the image that was to dominate French historiography until the Renaissance.

CHARLEMAGNE AND SAINT LOUIS

This synthetic figure, who came to include many different Charleses (Charles Martel, Charles the Bald), continued to be used, both explicitly or implicitly, in the service of ideological and political aims throughout the fourteenth and fifteenth centuries, and well beyond. Internally, the aim was to legitimize, to support, and to glorify the king. In terms of external politics, it was a way for the monarchy to assert itself in relation to the emperor and the pope. Charlemagne, the illustrious emperor, would help crystallize and justify the claims of the French kings to the imperial crown, just as he would serve as a pretext for the monarchy's intervention in Italy. During the reign of Philip the Fair and his conflict with the pope, who was forcefully promoting a "Caesarist" vision of the papacy, jurists sought to ensure the autonomy of the French monarchy with the famous phrase *rex imperator in suo regno*. After his victory over Boniface VIII, Philip proposed that his brother Charles Valois wear the imperial crown. Charles Valois, having married the granddaughter of Baldwin II, the last Latin emperor of Constantinople, already harbored aspirations to the Greek empire. If Charles had been elected emperor, the old dream of the reunification of the two empires could have finally been realized. At the same time, Pierre Dubois, in his *De Recuperatione Terre Sancte* (*circa* 1306), proposes a project for a universal monarchy with the king of France at its head. Charlemagne, whose reign is believed to have lasted 125 years, provides him with the model of the wise king, but also of the warrior king who is said to have found the best route of attack during his conquest of the Holy Land.[22] This pamphlet writer, advocating a strong monarchy, claims that Charlemagne, in the fourteen years he was emperor, accomplished more than he did during his entire reign as mere king.[23]

In fact, all of these "candidates" for the imperial crown are thwarted by the same obstacle: no one wants to see French power attain the rights and prestige of an empire. In contrast, as Gaston Zeller has shown, the kings of France, from Philip the Brave to Louis XIV, all coveted the Empire, and, it should be noted, they all claimed to be heirs to Charlemagne.[24] This aspiration is found in Charles V's request on the occasion of his coronation in 1364 for a scepter topped with a small statue of Charlemagne, a gesture that Napoleon was to repeat more than five hundred years later.[25] Christine de Pisan, in her description of Charles V, shows well how important the figure of Charlemagne was to this king, as it unavoidably imposed itself as a point of reference:

Just as the Romans acquired seigniories and lands through their intelligence rather than through force, our king did likewise, he who conquered more, made more alliances, had the greatest armies, paid his men better, had more buildings built, gave great gifts, held court magnificently, spent more, did less harm to the people, and governed most wisely in all areas and paid more greatly for all expenses than had any king of France according to the texts, I dare say, since the time of Charlemagne, who for the greatness of his prowess was called Charles the Great. Thus on account of his virtue and wisdom he must forever be known as Charles the Wise.[26]

In addition to greatness, Christine de Pisan suggests another similarity between the two kings: their knowledge and culture. Charles V practiced the seven liberal arts and encouraged writing just as Charlemagne had done. Knowledge and policies that encouraged the acquisition of knowledge became increasingly important attributes in the definition of a good monarch, and they occupy an important place in this portrait. Christine de Pisan adopts Notker's anecdote on the origins of scholarship and schools in France and links them to Charles V's supportive policy toward the University of Paris, "his beloved daughter" (2:47). This monarch's fond memories of his illustrious predecessor also have a religious impact: in imitation of Aachen the royal chapel begins to celebrate the feast of Saint Charlemagne on January 28 and the anniversary of the emperor's canonization at the end of July.[27]

From Charles V's rather personal devotion, there was only one step toward an official cult. That step was taken by Louis XI in 1475: "At that time," writes Jean de Roye in his *Chronique scandaleuse*, "the king, having a great affection for the saintly deeds and the great virtue of Saint Charlemagne, willed and ordered that on the twenty-eighth day of January the feast of Saint Charlemagne should be celebrated."[28] From that year on, January 28 became a holiday at the Chatelet and the Parlement and it continued to be celebrated until the Revolution. In 1478, the members of the faculty of arts organized a confraternity in the honor of the Virgin and Saint Charlemagne. In their written request to do this they evoked the "transfer" (*translatio studii*) of the University of Athens to Rome and then, thanks to Charlemagne, from Rome to Paris. In contrast, the religious cult of Saint Charlemagne failed to take root in France: the cult was of Germanic origins, the sainthood of the emperor having been proclaimed by the antipope at Aachen on the initiative of Emperor Frederick I (Barbarossa). The French clergy never recognized a canonization that the Vatican itself did not accept.[29]

But Charlemagne's ties to the university on the one hand and to the Parlement of Paris on the other, were to remain very important in the centuries to come. In 1477, the same Louis XI had the statues of Saint Louis and Charlemagne removed from their locations among the immense statues of the kings in the Great Hall of the royal palace (today the Palais de Justice), and had them installed in a prominent position on either side and above the Parlement's chapel, which he had had remodeled.[30] With this act, Louis XI was simply continuing the iconographic policy established during the reign of his predecessor, Charles VII.

Indeed, around 1454, a painting of the Crucifixion was created that included the figures of Saint Louis and Charlemagne. This painting was destined for the Great Hall where the Parlement of Paris held its sessions (fig. 6). The tradition of placing a picture of Calvary in courtrooms went back to the fourteenth century, and its purpose was to remind people of the superiority of divine judgment over that of human beings.

With the end of the Hundred Years' War, Paris regained its place as capital of the kingdom and Charles VII decided to merge the parlements of Poitiers and Paris into one. The Parlement of Paris had already become more important under Charles V and was regaining its place in the life of the kingdom. It is likely that Charles VII wanted to place his mark—royal, national, and personal—on the institution. But this triptych, known by the title *Retable du Parlement*, found a permanent place only after the remodeling of the Great Hall during the reign of Louis XII. This "political" work is particularly important for us because, on the one hand, it forcefully brings together a certain number of themes that are at the heart of our subject matter and, on the other, the members of Parlement saw it on the wall of their main meeting hall until the end of the Ancien Régime (figs. 9, 10, and 11).

The drawings and engravings representing the *lits de justice* of 1715 and 1723—the term *lit de justice* referring to extraordinary sessions of Parlement presided over by the king himself—give us a very precise idea of what the triptych looked like.[31] It was crowned by three small statues that have since been lost; on each side of the great gable were two figures, each holding an escutcheon bearing the arms of France. In the engraving Poilly made from the drawing by Delamonce, this work was placed above the heads of the members of Parlement and at the side of the throne where the king was seated. The subject as well as the positioning of the painting associating divine power with earthly power had been chosen to reinforce the image of authority when the king was present and, one might add, also perhaps to *represent him* in the Parlement in the king's absence. Above the painting, painted directly on the wall and forming a sort of predella, we can make out three panels. The one in the center, placed directly under the crucified Christ, shows a king, probably Louis XII, on his throne, holding his scepter in his hand. On either side two injunctions from the Bible are inscribed telling the members of Parlement to "practice judgment and justice" so as to avoid divine punishment (Jeremiah 12:3, 5) and to be careful with their actions because they are handing down justice in the name of God (2 Chronicles 19:6).

The Crucifixion takes up the central panel. Above the cross there is the dove of the Holy Ghost and the image of God the Father; together they form the Trinity. At the foot of the cross the Virgin is lamenting, surrounded by a holy woman and Mary Magdalene; at the right is Saint John. Behind the cross are some buildings of Jerusalem. On the left panel we see John the Baptist next to the Virgin. The prophet is turned toward Louis IX as if to reveal some holy news; his right hand points toward the *Agnus Dei*.[32] On the far left is Saint Louis, wearing a royal mantle decorated with fleurs-de-lis; he holds a cross in his right hand. This is perhaps Saint Eloi's cross that King Dagobert gave to the Saint-Denis Abbey. Saint Louis, to whom Charles VII lent his facial features, is standing partly sideways so as to hear John the Baptist's prophecies. The crusading king's gaze is directed toward Jerusalem. Behind these two figures we can see the Seine river and the Louvre.

But the panel on the right is of greatest interest here (fig. 7). Next to Saint John, Saint Denis, with his executioners behind him, holds his severed head in his hands as blood is streaming down his neck. At the far right of the panel is the figure of Charlemagne whose strangeness draws our attention.

The great king appears to occupy a separate space. He is, in fact, the sole figure to face the viewers frontally. His gaze, which seems to reflect the biblical commandment "*videte quid faciatis*," is aimed straight at the spectators as if his extremely wide-open eyes had to watch over the people practicing law in the Great Hall. In his right hand, he holds the sword of justice, in his left the globe. Like Saint Louis, he is dressed in a sumptuous mantle decorated with fleurs-de-lis, but the neck opening shows a suit of armor beneath it. Thus Charlemagne simultaneously represents unity (the globe), justice, and strength. His stern gaze, which is not turned toward Jerusalem, is aimed, above all, at those he is observing.

These various elements, in addition to the painting's dominant position in the hall, offer us a vision of Charlemagne akin to that in Notker: Aachen's *panoptikon* finds its reflection in the gathering place of the Parlement of Paris. Directly behind Charlemagne the painter chose to put a condensed image of the palace, including the part of the building with the Great Hall where the painting was displayed and justice was rendered.[33] He thus reinforced the inconographic links between the judge-king Charlemagne and the Parlement. The scenes of Paris that appear on either side of views of Jerusalem also aim to establish visually a parallel between the holy city and the capital of the kingdom of France. Seated in front of the emperor-king of France is a small dog, perhaps the symbol of loyalty and vigilance, who, like his master, stares at us fixedly. In fact, the figure of the great emperor is differentiated from the others by its "oriental" appearance.[34] This might be an allusion to his synthetic qualities: he embodies the dream of a universal monarchy uniting the empires of Europe and of Constantinople. Thus, up until the French Revolution, sessions of Parlement were held in this hall on the most solemn of occasions under Charlemagne's gaze, a gaze endowed with a complex range of meaning. As we will see, the figure of Charlemagne became increasingly important to the French Parlement as that institution attempted to enlarge its functions and power within the monarchy.

KNIGHT: THE PROTECTOR OF CHRISTENDOM

There was an undeniable fascination with Charlemagne during the second half of the fifteenth century and the beginning of the sixteenth. One example of this intense interest can be found in the elliptical and insistent evocation of Charlemagne by the poet François Villon in his "Ballad of the Lords of Olden Times." The theme of *vanitas mundi* is combined with a yearning for the great heroes (the topos of *ubi sunt*), with the rhythmic refrain : "But where is the brave Charlemagne?" [Mais où est les preux Charlemagne?].

This infatuation with the past can also be seen in the *Croniques et conquestes de Charlemagne*, a large compilation originating at the brilliant court of Philip the Good, duke of Burgundy, whose author is believed to be David Aubert. Since the *Grandes Chroniques de France*, which were still being copied and read at the time, had omitted many sources and did not devote as much space to the great king's exploits as it was felt they deserved, Aubert was intent on making up for this lack by using the *chansons de geste*. The result is a vision that blends myth and history in which the "epic" element comes through with greater force than it does in the *Grandes Chroniques de France*. Aubert's approach in his *Croniques* is fairly close to that of Mousket in his work, although Aubert appears more concerned with reconciling the process of accumulation with a certain narrative coherence. Thus Aubert's work once again confirms the stability of historical hearsay as regards Charlemagne. Aubert's work, completed in 1458, aims to provide examples and models of chivalry and, at the same time, to offer the pleasure of an "enjoyable reading" (*lecture heureuse*). In this project, where ethics and aesthetics come together, we can see another manifestation of a yearning for glorious times that were located both in history and beyond it. The *Croniques et conquestes de Charlemagne* was part of a more general trend attempting to bring back the glorious days of chivalry.

Whereas Aubert's work did not reach a very wide audience (only one copy has survived), this was not the case with the *chansons de geste*, which continued to be translated into prose throughout the fifteenth century, a process that intensified beginning in 1450.[35] The fate of *Fierabras* is a wonderful example of the success that these "derhymed" *chansons de geste* could have. Put into prose at the end of the fourteenth century and incorporated into Aubert's *Croniques*, *Fierabras* was reworked again by Jean Bagnyon upon the request of Henri Bolomier, canon of the cathedral of Lausanne. The result was an extraordinary publishing success. Between 1478, the date of its first publication, and 1588 there were twenty-six editions of this book.[36] Once again, we see the strength and longevity of historical hearsay—the "on-dit"—about Charlemagne.

Bagnyon belongs to the tradition of literary compilation. In addition to the material from *Fierabras*, he incorporates in his work elements from Vincent de Beauvais's *Miroir historial*, from Einhard's *Vita Karoli*, from the Pseudo-Turpin, and from the *Descriptio* of the journey to Constantinople and Jerusalem. I will come back to these prose narratives in the context of the "Bibliothèque bleue," but for now it is important to note the enormous popularity of these works in which the line separating legend and history is barely discernable. These hybrids of royal *gesta* were conduits for transmitting a vision of a heroic Charlemagne, a figure embodying the values of power and social cohesion, ruling over an epic France and fighting for Christendom.

As the fifteenth century was coming to a close, the power of the epic vision acquired its full political dimension. Since, on the whole, in France "making history" meant accomplishing "epic" deeds, the same could be said of certain kings, among whom perhaps the most striking example is Charles VIII. As we have seen, Charlemagne was often used for internal political aims. And yet, for Charles VIII's immediate predecessors, grandiose ambitions could be only a dream, since they already had enough to do in just maintaining the unity and integrity of the kingdom. For that purpose Charlemagne was invoked mostly with regard to Salic law, either as its originator or as the one who definitively confirmed it.[37] However, once the French kings had emerged victorious from this period of conflict and instability, they could again put things in a larger perspective. The taking of Constantinople by the Turks in 1453 made the emperor "with the flowing white beard" relevant once again because the successful defense and the consolidation of the kingdom had awakened a new sense of power in the monarchy. Before looking to more distant horizons, the royal gaze came to rest upon Italy, for the preservation of Christendom was always considered in relation to Italy. It goes without saying that the arrival of the Ottomans in Italy in 1480, even though they were driven out in 1482, was cause for great concern.

Louis XI had been content with his role as mediator with regard to trans-Alpine affairs. In contrast, Charles VIII wanted to "make history." His external politics were constrained neither by immediate interests nor by the pressure of real danger coming from outside the kingdom. Whereas the Holy Roman Empire of Germany was directly threatened in Hungary by the Osmanlis, the same was not true for France. In fact, the deeds accomplished in Italy by Louis XI's successor must be seen as emanating from an epic vision dominated by the figure of Charlemagne.[38] Charles VIII's aim was not only to have the rights of the House of Anjou recognized but also to act as the protector of Christendom by fighting the infidels and reconquering the Holy Land. In short, his aim was to fulfill a symbolic role in the West and in Christendom.

The term "symbolic role" does not imply that it was "imaginary" or "unreal." Quite to the contrary, it was perceived as true and was at the core of the very real motivation that structured Charles VIII's policies. To wear the crown of Constantinople was a way of getting around the "symbolic" difficulty raised by the existence of a Germanic emperor whose real power continued to diminish even as it became increasingly identified with a territorial kingdom. In a way, it was as if Charles VIII were appealing to Constantine and attempting to turn the clock back to the time before the *translatio imperii* in order to accomplish in another way the past exploits of the greatest king of France, Charlemagne, and, in doing so, to renew the symbolic capital of the French monarchy.

We have seen how the epic vision was maintained throughout history, and we have looked at some texts and images that played an essential role in the transmission of that vision. I would like now to devote a few pages to a "case" in which the re-presentation of the great king assumes particularly strong significance. This is the case of Charles VIII, whose life and politics were indeed influenced by those of Charlemagne. Charles VIII was strongly attracted to the great emperor as a source of inspiration, motivation, and justification. This can be observed in very different arenas. During this period of conflicts and transformation, French power was consolidated and France affirmed itself in the political life of Europe. But the endemic instability and insecurity were the cause of a general eschatological anguish that often sought answers in prophecies and predictions in which the figure of Charlemagne occupied an important place. Charles VIII grew up in just such an atmosphere. Thus the king's personal affinities were confirmed and strengthened by the constant repetition of tales of Charlemagne that permeated his environment.

At a very young age, Charles's father gave him the *Grandes Chroniques de France* to read or to have read to him. His patron saint was in fact Charlemagne, and while he was passing through Chartres in 1484 the young king probably had the opportunity to become even further immersed in the lessons of the *Chroniques* by looking at the stained-glass window depicting the journey of the great emperor to Jerusalem.[39]

Charles VIII's first task was to deal with the revolts of the magnates. One of the fruits of his victories over the nobles was his marriage to Anne of Brittany, a bride he essentially stole from the future emperor Maximilian.[40] As she entered Paris on February 9, 1492, the new queen was welcomed on the road by a man representing Charlemagne who preceded her on horseback as far as Notre Dame. Among this figure's entourage were an elephant and a camel—or animals disguised as such—reminders of the gifts from the king of Persia, but which also served as signs of a certain interest in oriental themes.[41]

In fact, Charles already had projects in mind that were to lead him far from France. Very early on, ten years before he carried out his plans, he had begun the process by ordering a study of the documents that established his rights over the kingdom of Naples. Since 1277, the king of Naples held the title of king of Jerusalem. Thus, for Charles to claim his rights to the crown of Naples was an essential step toward his reconquest of the Holy Land.[42] Furthermore, the kingdom of Naples had for a long time been associated with holy war. It was there, in Calabria, that Charlemagne and Roland fought against Agolant's forces in the *Chanson d'Aspremont*. In fact, people confused the Saracens with the Turks: thus for André de La Vigne, a poet of the court, a historiographer to the king and eyewitness to the events of the campaign of Italy, Charlemagne did fight against the Turks.[43]

The young king's leanings toward epic feats were certainly fanned by the Calabrian hermit Francis of Paola, whom Louis XI had brought from Italy and whom Charles then kept on in Blois. The saintly man had a great influence over the young king, describing Aragonese oppression in Naples, and his influence can also be seen in the name that was chosen for the son of Charles and Anne of Brittany: Charles-Orland. Thus baptized, the dauphin (who, had he not died prematurely in 1495, would have worn the French crown) symbolically joined in himself the double tradition of the knighthood of Roland and the power of Charlemagne. The very Italian form of his name suggested a privileged relationship with France's Transalpine neighbor, and one of his pages was named Aspremont.[44]

The transmission of a myth and its impact on political reality could not be more strikingly evident. Like the Charlemagne of the legends, Charles VIII took the oriflamme and went to the kingdom of Naples, the first stage of the journey he hoped would lead him to Constantinople and Jerusalem. And he also wanted to be like the Roland of the *chansons de geste*, for this young king wished to "go to Naples to do like Roland," as André de La Vigne puts it.[45] It is significant that during these early beginnings of royal absolutism, the king seemed to want to play both roles at the same time: that of the king and that of his best vassal.

Charles VIII's fascination with Charlemagne found considerable support in Italy. We are well aware of the French tradition in which the monarchy claimed to be the protector of the Church and sought to reconquer the Holy Land. The "universal mission" was a part of the monarchy's historical identity, and it was largely through that history that the monarchy defined itself. We also know that Charlemagne's role in this "mythistory" was fundamental,[46] for the continuous appeals for help and protection the popes made to the French kings were seen as originating above all during his reign.

But we also find him at the center of other early writings that added their voices to this polyphonic ensemble drawing France beyond the Alps, or which at least served to legitimize such a course of action. In Florence, Charlemagne was depicted as the restorer of the city's freedoms: he was supposed to have freed the Florentines from the yoke of the Germanic barbarians and to have granted them privileges ensuring their independence. The Florentines and the figure of Charlemagne came to be inextricably linked in the minds of the Italians during the rise of the House of Anjou in Italy.

Prophecies turned the German emperor into the Antichrist and predicted the advent of one last emperor who would be named Charles and who was to come from the Carolingian line and the House of France; he was to become "the prince and monarch of the whole of Europe."[47] Prophecies of a new Charlemagne returning like the Messiah are linked to the conflicts that existed between the Guelfs, supporters of the pope, and the Ghibellines, supporters of the emperor. During the fourteenth century, such prophecies developed in the name of a Guelfism that defined itself as the party of liberty, of Latinness, and of true piety against imperial power and Germanic barbarism. After 1375 and the war between Florence and Pope Gregory XI, prophecies predicted a king of France who was to be elected emperor of the Romans and monarch of the whole world.[48] Thus this Charlemagne, who was fundamentally anti-German and the true heir of the Roman tradition, became the embodiment of freedom and empowerment,[49] the holder of the power and legitimacy necessary to give others mastery over their own fates.

Italian historians also see the French emperor as the liberator and restorer of Florence, something Giovanni Villani had already done in the fourteenth century in his *Istorie Fiorentine*.[50] The topos of Charlemagne then emerges in diplomatic language. Threatened by Alfonso of Aragon in 1451, the city of Florence sends Agnolo Acciaiuoli to Charles VII with the hope of obtaining his support. The envoy's mission is to acknowledge the debt the Florentines owe to France: "The very glorious kings of this very Christian House were the founders of our city. No one can ignore that our country, ravaged by Totila and the Huns and reduced to a desertlike state, was reestablished and restored by the very glorious Charlemagne. It is he who freed our city, the Roman Church, and the whole of Italy from these barbarian nations."[51]

Similar speeches were given in Tours on December 30, 1461, by an Italian delegation sent to congratulate Louis XI on the occasion of his coronation: Charlemagne, Louis's illustrious predecessor, had freed the Italians from "the harsh yoke of Germanic servitude." They mentioned his victory over Didier, king of the Lombards, in Pavia, his virtues and his piety that earned him the name "Great One," and the continuity of his very "Christian race" that is perpetuated to the present time. During this same reception, Donato Acciaiuoli presented Louis XI with the *Vita Caroli Magni* he had written for the occasion.[52] "We are living in our own fatherland, we have magistrats, laws, a state [*civitas*]: we can see that all these things we received go back to Charlemagne and we must continually celebrate his very pleasurable memory."[53] The great sovereign was "not only the glory of France: he was the honor and the light of the whole world."[54] He should serve as an example to all heads of state in both their private and public lives.

Around this same period (1461) Luigi Pulci began his great epic poem *Morgante Maggiore*, the first part of which he published in 1478 and the entire work in 1483. This new version of the Carolingian epic was highly successful and began a trend that led to the *Orlando innamorato* (1494) by Matteo Boiardo and to *Orlando furioso* (1516, 1521, 1532) by Ariosto. These works, particularly Ariosto's, had a great impact in seventeenth-century France. The fusion of epic material with that from knightly romances, which had already been accomplished in *Galien*, enabled a new exploration of the relationship between the private and the public, between the power of the state and the power of the heart, in the light of a still very present medieval tradition and a humanism that was endowing new status upon the individual. We will return to Pulci's work but, for the time being, let us note the emphasis he places on the exemplarity of Charlemagne's court, a model of civilization that Florence should imitate:

> But, blind and ignorant, the world does not
> esteem his virtues as I'd like to see.
> And yet some of his greatness you still own,
> O Florence, and can yours forever be:
> every good custom, all the courtesy
> a man on earth could ever gain and keep
> through wisdom or through treasure or through lance
> has come out of the noble blood of France.
> (Canto I, octave 7, p. 4)[55]

Pulci proposes an ideal system of moral and cultural values that is specifically French and goes back to Charlemagne, although Pulci ultimately poses serious questions, albeit with much humor, concerning the modes and the limits of that ideal. During these same years, probably around 1468, Ugolino Verino began his *Caroliade*, an epic poem in fifteen volumes and very much a political panegyric. It was dedicated to Charles VIII in 1494, the year of Charles's first expedition to Italy.[56]

ITALIAN ADVENTURES

The Italian "crusade" Charles VIII undertook in 1494 gave rise to a number of prophecies, such as the one Guillaume Guillauche included in his poem predicting that Charles would wear the "double crown," meaning that he would be named king of the Romans, "Regardless of Germans' will, / . . . And then later, through his own means / All men and Christian kings / will submit to him forever." Then he would conquer Greece and the crown of Constantinople. After becoming "king of France, . . . of the Romans / And the Greeks," he would go to Jerusalem where we see him pray on the

Mount of Olives.[57] In short, Charles is described as a kind of new Galien. But did he truly harbor the ambition to wear the imperial crown as has so often been claimed?

The answer would seem to be yes, if we were to judge by Charles's solemn entry into Naples on May 12, 1495, while holding the globe in his right hand and the scepter in his left. However, as Labande-Mailfert has shown, these insignia were those of the kingdom of Naples—the globe symbolized the "land" of the kingdom. The fact that Charles was carrying them does not mean that he wanted to compete against Emperor Maximilian. Despite the fairly widespread interpretation of the time, no doubt shared by Maximilian, Charles VIII never aspired to any empire, whether Germanic or Byzantine. The latest research makes this clear.[58] And yet, André de La Vigne set the tone in describing the king on that day "in imperial clothes, named and called Augustus."[59] A few years later Pierre Desrey, the translator and follower of Gaguin, went even further and explained that the pope "had elected Charles, king of France, emperor of Constantinople."[60] This interpretation of the facts and of Charles's intentions survived until the twentieth century.

Although it is true that the mistaken beliefs of Charles VIII's contemporaries reveal a certain "horizon of expectations" that were grounded in historical hearsay about Charlemagne, the reality was no less revealing. The reality indicates that Charles's will to imitate Charlemagne in no way involved his being a candidate for emperor. Like Charlemagne, the king of France had a universal mission; he was heir to the notion of *Gesta Dei per Francos*. But the imperial dignity as such in some ways became detached from the figure of Charlemagne. It became incidental to Charlemagne's trajectory, to the outcome of his exploits as king of France. Thus Charles VIII pursued aims that might be described as "universalist" or "imperialist" without, however, aspiring to become emperor. Moreover, these same years witness the appearance of the imperial crown (with closed sides) in representations of the kings. As king of France and a most Christian king (*roi très chrétien*), Charles did intend to lead a crusade against the infidels, but he only wanted to be emperor over his own kingdoms: France, Naples, and Jerusalem.

The Italian undertaking demonstrates the power of the epic vision that focused on the figure of Charlemagne—a vision that was political, ethical, and aesthetic. This is the vision that gave a meaning to Symphorien Champier's narrative in which Bayard dubs François I a knight. Bayard himself, the "fearless and irreproachable knight" had distinguished himself in 1495 in the famous battle of Fornova during which Charles VIII, retreating to France, succeeded in forcing his way through the advance guard of the enemy coalition made up of Venice, Milan, Austria, and Aragon.

Thus the king left Italy, a king who, much like Pulci's Charlemagne, had not listened to what the powerful of that country had to say concerning the proper way to govern. . . . Before interrupting his *Orlando innamorato*, Boiardo exclaims:

> But while I sing, redeemer God,
> I see all Italy on fire,
> Because these French—so valiant!—
> Come to lay waste who knows what land,
> So I will leave this hopeless love
> Of simmering Fiordespina.
> Some other time, if God permits,
> I'll tell you all there is to tell.[61]

———

> [Mentre che io canto, o Iddio redentore,
> Vedo la Italia tutta a fiama e a foco
> Per questi Galli, che con gran valore
> Vengon per disertar non so che loco;
> Però vi lascio in questo vano amore
> De Fiordespina ardente a poco a poco;
> Un'altra fiata, se mi fia concesso,
> Racontarovi il tutto per espresso.]
>
> (III, IX, 26)

Boiardo ends his poem abruptly with these verses. It is a poem in which the force of love makes light of existing political authorities, in which the courtly romance invades the epic, and Turpin's authority—that "eyewitness" account on which countless narratives had relied since the twelfth century—is exploded. Nonetheless, in Boiardo's poem too, Charlemagne continues to rule and to fight. The poem's conclusion is a desperate cry triggered by a French king trying to imitate the same hero who was used by the Italian poet to ponder the relationships between political power and individuals. It is one of the ironies of history that this playful epic centered on Charlemagne's life should be interrupted by a king who had taken too seriously the stories about the heroic emperor with the flowing white beard.

In a sense then we can say that the great Italian wars were started under the sign of Charlemagne. The figure of the great king was strongly present at the dawn of a new *translatio* or rather at the time of an initiation to Renaissance culture which the French discovered in Italy and brought back home to France. When, some years later, Ariosto adopted the same theme in his *Orlando furioso*, he restored complete dignity to the figure of the emperor, a dignity that, moreover, Ariosto also attributed to a "new Charlemagne," Charles V, the very king who put an end to François I's hopes of wearing the imperial crown himself.

FRANÇOIS I AND THE DREAM OF A EUROPEAN UNION

While its significance should not be overstated, François I's claim to the imperial crown should be understood within the context of the conflicts with the House of Hapsburg and of the continuing influence of the images we have discussed so far. We are now at a time when imposing visual representations of Charlemagne were being created. The famous painting of Nuremberg that Dürer did between 1512 and 1513 focuses on the emperor's saintliness, but the Charlemagne the artist shows us is young and virile (fig. 14).[62] The rejuvenation of Charlemagne corresponds to a transformation in the way power was portrayed, a transformation that can also be seen in the Vatican fresco titled *The Coronation of Charlemagne* done in 1516 and 1517 by members of Raphael's workshop upon the request of the Medici pope, Leo X (fig. 12).

However, the political intent is obvious here. Following the concordat of Bologna, which put an end to the "Gallican schism," the pope gave striking proof of his support for François I's imperial project by having Charlemagne represented with François's features while lending his own face to Pope Leo III.[63] There was a genuine fear of the Turks, and Leo X was hoping to unite the princes of Christendom around François I and undertake a crusade against the new "Saracens."

The "journey of Charlemagne to Jerusalem" (the *Descriptio*) was once again invoked: old prophecies concerning the new emperor from the House of France were unearthed and applied to the new monarch. François, being the first of his name to be king of the French as well as the link between *François* and *français* ("French"; spelled "*françois*" at the time), was believed to be the harbinger of a new era. Thus we find the same motifs we saw with regard to Charles VIII in a letter François I's illustrious predecessors sent to him from beyond the grave titled "Letter sent from Paradise to the very Christian king of France, François, the first of his name, by the emperors Pepin and Charlemagne, his magnificent predecessors, and presented to him by the transfigured knight who carried it"(1515):[64]

> . . . you and we are one and the same,
> Your glory rests in ours,
> Through our glory, yours will come forth,
> And through yours, ours will grow.

But when honor shall be given you,
When you will be crowned emperor,
And you will have by your mind and goodness
Put order in Christendom,
Then for the faith you shall go fight
And Mahomet and his law destroy,
And take back the worthy Holy Land,
What God did by his benign grace,
And you will make all peoples believe in him
In order to achieve immortal glory.
. . . .

For it has been prophesized a long time ago
That a French king valued over all others
Will subjugate, according to the prophecy,
All the peoples of Africa and Asia.
Indeed, among our French kings,
there was never one called François.[65]

In this prophetic poem, the "transfigured knight" draws the king's attention to his servant's "poverty" and reminds him of the duty to be generous to "men of arms," that is, the nobility, who, like the valiant men of old, "would give their bodies, possessions, and arms to serve you."

Jean Thenaud began the *Triomphe de Justice* in 1518 and completed it in 1519, the year the new emperor was to be elected. Just like the fresco *The Coronation of Charlemagne* in Rome, it focused on the parallel, on the one hand, between Charlemagne and François I—who, it was thought, was soon to be elected emperor by the German electors—and, on the other, between Leo III and Leo X, who believed he would be crowning the French king.[66] But all the efforts made by Louise of Savoy to ensure a majority of the electoral college votes led nowhere; even the pope failed to support her, and the French king had to withdraw from the race.[67]

Nonetheless, during the sixteenth century royal propagandists continued to turn the king of France into a new Charlemagne,[68] although it should be stated that this identification was not central to representations of the kings of that period. In fact, the genealogical argument of having descended from the great emperor was also just as easily used as a weapon against the reigning king, as the dukes of Burgundy had already shown in claiming their own links to Charlemagne. As we will later see, it became very risky to play the genealogical card: on the one hand, there was the ascension of Charles V, who was thought to be a new Charlemagne and, on the other, there was the duke of Guise who, in the course of the wars of religion in which he was at the head of the Holy League, claimed to be a descendant of Charlemagne so as to legitimize his own pretensions to the crown of France.

And yet, although an identification with Charlemagne was no longer of primary importance it still existed in the background and constituted an important element in the sense of a "national" identity. The dream of a universal monarchy maintained Charlemagne as its centerpiece. In his *Illustrations de Gaule et singularitez de Troye*, Jean Lemaire de Belges sees in Charlemagne the very image of the union between Germans and French, between "these two houses and nations of eastern and western France that would today be called Hungarians, Germans, Burgundians on the one hand and French and Bretons on the other."[69] Lemaire's mythistory is embedded within the context of the Crusades, with the effort to save "our Europe" from Turkish hands. In Lemaire, Charlemagne is the father of Europe, the original proof of its political and genealogical unity, and the condition and possibility of its future unity. The Germans, the Gauls, and the Burgundians are one and the same people. The Trojans represent a fixed, distant starting point, but Charlemagne is the one who was able to overcome the fragmentation imposed by circumstances and realize the destiny of Europe for the first time. "The sole intention of this third treatise is to show how the illustrious blood of all the named noble lineages, that of the western and eastern French, the Burgundians, and the Austrasians, all together partake of the genealogy of the Most Christian Emperor Caesar Augustus Charles, the great monarch, king of France, of Austria, of Burgundy, the one from whom has descended the nobility as a great source and fountain of his posterity."[70]

The Capetians, descendants of Widukind, usurped the crown of France but, as was predicted by the Valerian prophecy, there was a return to Carolingian stock, thus realizing the fusion of the Houses of Saxony and France. All the differences within Christendom are resolved and disappear, and at the head of this new union, there is the king of France: "And the two nations begin to love each other, to blend in . . . as they used to do in the time of the emperor Charles the Great. . . . King Louis XII is in many ways comparable to the emperor [Charlemagne]," explains Lemaire in his conclusion.[71] The European epic thus returns to its point of departure: Louis XII rejoins Charlemagne, a union that was the result both of a sense of history, and of a certain aesthetics.

No one pushed the idea of universal monarchy further than Guillaume Postel did around the middle of the century, that is, at the moment when Henry II resumed the wars in Italy against the pope and the emperor. In his *Raisons de la monarchie. Et quels moyens sont necessaires pour y parvenir . . .*, the famous Orientalist goes well beyond the European framework to claim that "the Gallic people," by their rights and the ancient law, "should lay claim to the universe."[72] In the name of universal harmony and peace, Postel be-seeches the king to have his rights recognized "so that in consequence as well as by desire there would be but one world under one God and under one king and sovereign pontiff, one faith and one law and one common consent."[73] This great monarchy originated with Caesar; it was reformed by Constantine and found "its true confirmation under Charlemagne."[74]

It is difficult to differentiate between the dream of union and grandiose delusions in this work, and it is not likely that these sorts of arguments were taken seriously. And yet, despite their exaggerations, they do nonethe-less highlight the universal mission that was believed to belong to France, and of which the figure of Charlemagne was a key element. The exaggera-tions and hyperbole are never ending in the representations of this figure of power, legitimacy, and unity. They form a fulcrum between the grandiose and the comical, between loyalty to the state and patriotic delirium. And, as we shall see, it was precisely against the scandal of lies and exaggeration that historians rebelled during the Renaissance.

The symbolic power of the great conqueror was largely affirmed during this period of consolidation and unification of the kingdom, a period that marks the end of the Middle Ages. The great compilations as well as the transposi-tion of the *chansons de geste* into prose brought about a new fusion of history and legend. This mythical-historical discourse stimulated a brilliant literary production in Italy and erupted into political "reality" under Charles VIII. Even in sixteenth-century France Charlemagne remained at the center of dreams of a transcending unity, of a universal monarchy that would ensure harmony in Europe and beyond. But, as we will see, these dreams were shat-tered as they encountered the many stumbling blocks of a new European reality. Charles V came to embody these aspirations better than did the French king. New historical and philological methodologies, as well as the pull of religious differences were exploding the age-old mythistorical fusion. In a France torn apart by wars of religion, the figure of Charlemagne became increasingly transformed into a site of contention where different groups in search of historical legitimacy confronted each other.

FOUR

A Call for Reality,
a Need for Myth

It is a commonplace to say that the French brought the Renaissance back from their wars in Italy. Drawn and redrawn throughout the Middle Ages, the image of the great conquering king at the head of a universal monarchy was ever-present during these Transalpine adventures. The sixteenth century, however, marks a time when representations of Charlemagne began to be radically reconfigured.

Two fundamentally opposite trends were at play in this evolution. On the one hand, the rediscovery of Antiquity and the idealization of its forms led to a historiographical style modeled on that of the ancients. This was the beginning of a vision of history and of the historian's work that persisted throughout the French classical age, an oratorical history that attributed to historical personages forms of public speaking—"harangues"—that demonstrated the best of the classical rhetorical style: a knowledge of how to speak and to act, a proper style of language, and good moral tenor. Thus, like so many others, Charlemagne began to speak like the heroes of Antiquity. National history was asserted and acquired its dignity by way of a metaphorical identification with the qualities of the ancients: in short, people saw themselves as being like those ancients. In this desire for resemblance, the past lost its specificity and acceded to an atemporal state where "eternal" values of good speech and good conduct ruled over human behavior.

On the other hand, the methodology of humanistic philology uncovered the otherness of Antiquity: in short, the ancients were quite different from us. Guillaume Budé's attack on scholastic jurisprudence caused the Justinian code to lose its status as referent in the rendering of justice. Thus devalued, the code ceased to be the expression of right reason and was seen rather as a text that had been inherited from the ancient world, a foreign document that had to be interpreted in the light of humanist philology and hermeneutics. Thus it came to be seen as a collection of heteroclite laws that had been enacted within a specific historical context bearing no relation to current European political and legal conditions. The development of humanist methodology and the critique of scholastic jurisprudence led to a new interest in customary laws and practices. A *mos docendi Gallicus* developed in Bourges; it was the French way of teaching law, in which the authority of custom and tradition assumed increasing importance. What began as an inquiry into the principles of the law opened up a debate on historical precedents. The hearsay, lies, and fables of the Middle Ages were denounced, whereas the old capitularies regained popularity. Although during the sixteenth century a direct identification with Charlemagne was generally relegated to the margins of royal propaganda, Charlemagne was often at the center of debates that sought an understanding of the past as a specifically "national" past.

And yet, this period of "national definition" also became a time during which the fabric of the kingdom came unraveled as debates on historical precedents turned into polemics on the ancient constitution. The complex interactions between the Renaissance and the Reformation and the violence of the wars of religion led to the emergence of a different image of the great king. Instead of supporting and legitimizing a monarchy that was attempting to assert itself and to increase its hold over the kingdom on all levels, the "new" Charlemagne joined the camp of his adversaries, that is, those who for various reasons and at various times wished to limit the power of the monarchy, sometimes quite radically. For the first time there was a Charlemagne embodying a different type of sovereignty, ruling according to practices inherited not from Rome, but from the German forests.

In representations of the great monarch showing the intersection of German and Roman influences, we can detect the beginnings of a polemic on "ethnic" origins that grew in importance within the nobiliary movements at the end of the seventeenth century and even more so during the eighteenth. Two central themes in constant interaction emerge from these debates and conflicts: that of national identity in relation to other European countries and that related to the form and nature of government.

At the turn of the fifteenth century the fury of the wars of religion was well in the past. Although, as we have seen, the optimism that characterized military operations in Italy fed off a "fabulous" history of the great emperor, a new historiography sought to distance itself from legends and popular rumors. Already under Charles VIII, a period when myth was an integral part of political reality, we can see the first elements of this reorientation: the beginnings of a fundamental change in the way Charlemagne was perceived. Although he did remain a great warrior—his function in the external policies of Charles VIII bears witness to this—the emphasis shifted increasingly toward Charlemagne's role as founder of a culture: cultural development began to be valued more highly than military conquests.

Robert Gaguin's work is telling evidence of this process. Like many others, Gaguin, a leader of the French humanists, presented Charles VIII with a biography of Charlemagne.[1] This work has been lost, but the content of it is probably included in his *Compendium de Francorum origine et gestis*. Published for the first time in 1495, the book met with an immediate and enduring success. There were five editions during the author's lifetime and fourteen more by 1586. Gaguin has often been criticized for not going further in his attempt to renew historiography. Indeed, the very title as well as the organization of his history places him closer to the medieval taste for accumulation and its vision of the king as the true mover of history and the nation.

In Gaguin's work kings embody national glory, and the history of France unfolds in the succession of its monarchs. Following this logic Gaguin aims to give France heroes comparable to those of Antiquity. In this sense, the portrait of Charlemagne Gaguin paints is inspired by humanist currents. The emperor is the antibarbarian liberator who triumphs over the Saxons from the north and who, in the south, chases the Germans (the Lombards) out of Italy. He restores Florence, takes Genoa under his protection, allows Venetians to live "*according to their own laws*," and is no less a benefactor to all other towns in Italy.[2] Although when it comes to the consolidation of the "national" territory, Charlemagne fights and wins (in Aquitaine, Gascony, Brittany), his role in Italy is described as that of an anti-Germanic hero involved in reclaiming the great Italian cities for their inhabitants rather than conquering them. Without him, Italy would have remained the victim of the corruption to which it had fallen prey.

However, at the time Gaguin was writing, Charlemagne's French identity was no longer taken for granted. In the context of developing national sentiment in Europe, Charlemagne's identity as both French and universal began increasingly to be questioned outside of France. Already during the twelfth century, Godefroi de Viterbe had claimed that Charlemagne was born in Ingelheim and that he was essentially German.[3] With the rise of a more territorial concept of the "nation," place of birth became a crucial point. From the Italian side, Petrarch had been only too happy in 1333 to include among the Germanic barbarians: "King Charles, whom they dare equate to Pompey and Alexander by giving him the surname 'the Great.'"[4] Petrarch was notably the one who spread the famous anecdote about Charlemagne having fallen prey to a morbid love for the dead body of his mistress at the expense of affairs of state.[5] According to the story a voice from heaven informs the bishop of Cologne that a magical ring is hidden under the tongue of the dead woman. The bishop removes the talisman, but then Charlemagne falls in love with him. In order to get rid of the ring and to prevent it from falling into the wrong hands, the bishop throws it into a bog near the site of the future Aachen, where the emperor was with his court. This episode was believed to mark the moment when Charlemagne fell in love with the place where he had the "new Rome" built. Quite unlike the sublime devotion that Petrarch held for Laura after her death, the depraved love the poet attributes to Charlemagne depreciates the origins of Aachen. Moreover, this narrative, which Petrarch claims to have heard at Aachen itself, shows Charlemagne's private life to be unhealthy, to say the least. More than a century later, Gaguin remained resentful of the Italian poet who from his stay at Aachen "learned only a shameful fable about Charlemagne."[6]

Gaguin reacted most adamantly against accusations of barbarism. For him the greatest deeds accomplished by the true Charlemagne were in the field of letters and culture. Exemplary in his private life, the king was educated, had a true thirst for knowledge, wrote his thoughts down on wax tablets, and, even more important, founded the universities of Paris and Pavia. The historian places much emphasis on Charlemagne's creation of the institutional framework that enabled France to assert its national culture and knowledge not only in comparison to those of Italy, but also to those of England. It was indeed at the University of Paris that Ebritus "learned from the French the science of governing" before he became king of England.[7] But Gaguin scarcely mentions the university again in the rest of the *Compendium*. What really matters to Gaguin is the originary moment. In those early times, the creation of the university was one of the exploits of the founding monarch. Cultural heroism was seen as a way of exercising sovereignty, a genuine way to ensure the survival of a society whose king remained the source and the center of that society.

A central function of the university was to preserve and to transmit knowledge that specifically included a remembrance of the sovereign. In a letter to the bishop of Marseille, Gaguin explains that the great emperor "felt that *everything great he had done would remain in obscurity* if he did not establish this famous university in Paris, this home of wisdom, this academy of letters, believing that he would thus leave with posterity *a memory more splendid and more glorious through what he did for letters than by his fame as a warrior.*"[8] Of course Gaguin's position served the interests of the institution to which he himself belonged. In fact, an institutional policy merges with a national policy here because for Gaguin a university serving the king was a university serving the nation; ensuring an acquisition of knowledge proved to be a way of ensuring royal and national glory.

Although this Parisian academician turned Charlemagne into a source of glory for France, Gaguin nevertheless participated in the movement that began to question aspects of the great emperor's identity. True, Gaguin had no doubts regarding the nationality or the private life of this founding figure who, in his eyes, remained a model for all sovereigns. However, as a French historian, influenced by the sort of critical analysis inherited from the Italian humanists, he subjected the most fantastic epic elements of Charlemagne's history as it was told in the great compilations to close critical scrutiny.

Gaguin begins with the elements that had motivated Charles VIII's interventions in Italy. These interventions proved to be harmful to France since "no part of Italy has kept with constancy its faith toward the Gallic name [*nulla italie pars fidem gallico nomini constanter servet*]."[9] It is better not to get involved with this people whose habitual way of functioning is treason. As for the tendency among certain "nationalist" circles in Italy to classify the French among the barbarians, Gaguin counters with the French accusation of corruption and moral decay rampant in Italy. This sort of critique, formulated here within the framework of a national ideology, was to reappear later in Reformation circles.

Gaguin first directs his critical gaze at Charlemagne's journey to Constantinople and Jerusalem. He finds Charlemagne's entire oriental trip incredible. When could it have happened? Is it possible that a great conqueror would wander around all night with his army only to be saved by a bird speaking the language of human beings? Likewise, he rejects Turpin's narrative. Is it conceivable that the walls of Pamplona would have fallen at the sound of the trumpets? Was Charlemagne really so strong that he could split a man in two from head to toe with a single blow of his sword? Did he really fight against a giant called Ferragus? Gaguin raises doubts about the credibility of the "chronicler of Saint-Denis" by claiming not to believe in these blatantly exaggerated exploits.

And yet, although Gaguin excludes these stories from the realm of history, he seems to want to save a place for them in the realm of culture. Even though these "poetic fictions" should not be believed, their characters are giants similar to those in the fables of the ancient poets. Our fantastic stories about Charlemagne are like those invented in Antiquity about Jupiter or Anteus. Thus Gaguin opens the door, albeit cautiously, to the "myths" about Charlemagne to which he accords a certain dignity and greatness by comparing them to the myths of the ancients. This was the beginning of a vision of Charlemagne that explicitly made him both a founder and a collective dream.

Against Fantastic History

Although the time was not ripe for exploring Charlemagne's poetic dimension, it definitely was the moment to begin tracing the boundaries of history. In this process of definition, myth becomes the Other of History. This is why the great emperor played such an important role in the affirmation of the identity of a discipline that took on the task of understanding, revealing, and preserving the truth of a national identity.

Because the figure of Charlemagne was so steeped in myth, he himself in a way became a target of History. One of the most consistent characteristics of sixteenth-century histories of France is their denunciation of scandals concerning lies about Charlemagne. The *chansons de geste* and the Pseudo-Turpin narrative came to be seen as so many inventions that served only to mask the truth, to confuse people, to misinform them about their own origins. Hyperbole was definitely to be banned from descriptions of ruling figures. The truth of the nation, its identity, was affirmed through its history. National memory had to be purged of fables and exaggerations. From Paul-Émile to Étienne Pasquier to Bernard Du Haillan, the most prestigious historians of all schools of thought made it a rule and a pleasure to denounce Charlemagne's fantastic history. The stakes were all the more important in that he essentially remained the model king, the monarch who deserved to be revered and imitated above all others. Thus, the real historical personage should not be sullied by fiction, his memory should not be distorted by the imaginary. Du Haillan's assessment at the end of the century summarizes well the dominant feeling toward the great king:

> Charles had in him all the qualities that make a prince laudable, so that he must be proposed to all princes as a patron, a mirror, and an example of the virtues worthy of them, as having the faith, the valor, the happiness, the justice, the knowledge, the eloquence, the promptness, the clemency, the wisdom, and the liberality that are precious pearls with which princes must adorn themselves and make everything shine. Beautiful, great, and admirable was in his time the state of the affairs of France, which was rich and opulent, honored with countless victories,

decorated and supported by justice, ornamented with religion, praised for all virtues, and aggrandized and augmented by arms.[10]

At that time there was another general strategic trend with regard to Charlemagne: this involved attempts to gradually detach him from the Empire and from the power of the pope. The Vatican fresco depicting the crowning of Charlemagne did endow the first emperor with the face of a ruling king of France, but that king is shown kneeling in front of the pope who crowns him. The painting, which was commissioned by Leo X, represents royal grandeur, but also its submission to the papacy. French historians of all schools were conscious of this "danger" and represented Charlemagne first and foremost as the king of France. In the sixteenth century, the *Rex Francorum* became the king of the Gauls, a king who brought back the Empire to the West and who served the Church well, although without ever subjecting himself to it. At a time when historians were aiming to "embellish" and "aggrandize" a "Gallic" nation that was increasingly defined in relation to a culture and a territory, their depiction of Charlemagne enabled them to assert their independence from the myth, that is, to claim a status as bearers of truth, while their approach in turn reinforced the "truth" of the independence of France.

As noted, this new "critical" and national history developed on two fronts, thus making Charlemagne a locus for the meeting of different traditions. On the one side, "oratorical" history painted a picture based on the "classical" past of the great Roman and Greek heroes. On the other, there was a "Gallic" history that was more institutional and even "ethnological," that tended to bring out a non-Roman specificity to French culture. The first tendency included historians such as Paul-Émile, François de Belleforest, and Bernard Du Haillan; the second, men such as Claude de Seyssel, François Hotman, Charles Du Moulin, and Étienne Pasquier.[11] And yet, the dividing line between the two tendencies was not firmly fixed, as can be seen in the works of Du Haillan, who drew largely from both.

CHARLEMAGNE THE CIVILIZER

"Oratorical" or "rhetorical" history remained fairly constant in its representation of Charlemagne. In its efforts to embellish history and provide moral teaching through beautiful examples drawn from the national past, this form of history consciously aimed to seduce the reader: "The pleasure accumulated and received from the narration of beautiful things . . . is so great that the one who has once been attracted by the sweetness of histories . . . can never leave them and is nailed and attached by the ear to them."[12] And one was to be seduced by truth and not by imaginary fables. Yet, although this type of history rejected hyperbole, the mechanisms of metaphor and comparison were essential to it. The truth of French history would become apparent to the extent that it rose to the level of that of the ancients. Heroes, great men, were the driving force of the history of France, just as they were of the history of the ancients. In Belleforest's *Histoire des Neuf Roys Charles de France*, which he presented to Charles IX, Belleforest expresses well this vision that viewed Antiquity as the yardstick of French facts and deeds:

> You can bring up the Macedonian phalanx or the Roman legions; you can compare the feats of Alexander and of the consuls of the city founded by Romulus with the deeds of this bellicose prince; you can compare periods, the force of men, the happenstance of things: I am certain that the fortune, the time, and the virtue of Charlemagne will have the advantage over the former, no less than the religion in which he believed, which was above that held by these first monarchs, who were more scourges of the world than true ministers of justice and preservers of the peace of their people.[13]

A distancing from medieval "fables" corresponds to a rapprochement with the histories and legends of the ancients. While there is a demythification of Charlemagne on one level, there is a remythification of him on another (fig. 15). He is in turn the "Roman Fabius," a "Mark Antony," the "Gallic Caesar," the "Gallic Mars"; he is "as eloquent as Ulysses in Homer," "like the idea and the figure of the reign of Augustus when the whole living world lived in peace and the Sun of Justice, our Savior Jesus Christ was born."[14] The use of metaphor and comparison could not be more evident. Charlemagne is identified with the greatness of all these heroes; he becomes a metaphor himself, a "figure" for all the values they embody, and he is a reflection of the image of Christ through the proximity of the savior and through the metaphor of the "sun of justice" so often used as a royal epithet. But there is distancing as well as a rapprochement, since Charlemagne is seen at the same time as being different from his illustrious predecessors; he is even above them, not only because he is Christian but also because he benefits from the popular support the others lacked:

> Alexander, Caesar, and Augustus: they achieved their glory through tyranny, whereas this Gallic Caesar, king of countless provinces, did well by his people, was gentle to the vanquished and the weak, was religious and devoted to sacred things, achieving his honor through the common voice of the people and the voluntary election of princes and the legitimate approval of the Roman pontiff.[15]

The emperor Charlemagne had every level of society on his side: the pope, the nobles, and the people. His crusades to the Holy Land having been rejected as fables and the war against the Saracens having been reduced in importance (for instance, there is no mention of Roncevaux), the "epic of the north," the war against the Saxons—the other holy war—assumes a much more important place in these "oratorical" histories. Triumph over his German enemies is total, and, like the image of the avenging God of the Old Testament, the fury of Charlemagne's army is merciless.

Paul-Émile is Belleforest's and Du Haillan's source for Charlemagne's harangue to his troops after the Saxons surprised them in their camp and massacred a great number of French soldiers. Charlemagne's speech incites his army to seek vengeance that would spare neither woman nor child. "The eyes big, green, and shining like jewels, terrible and furious to all he looked at when he was angry. . . ."[16]

Whereas Charlemagne acts as God's avenging conqueror when he confronts pagans, whether they be Saracens or Saxons, when it comes to Italy, Charlemagne arrives as a liberator: "Here it was necessary that Rome see the flamboyant arms of the Gauls, coming for the freedom of Italy" and for that of the Church.[17] But the enemy in Italy is also German, and Charlemagne's triumph is that of civilization over barbarism. The new Caesar restores the laws and returns Italy to its "ancient authority, strength, beauty, and magnificence."[18]

The hero's connection to the Roman ideal that nourishes him is evident in all of his words and deeds. This is the true meaning of *translatio imperii;* he brings back to the West a set of moral and cultural values. In this sense, he is the one who makes "oratorical" history possible, because he is the one who was able both to renew and to preserve. He is the fulcrum between prehistory and history. His work as the creator of schools and of the university, as the builder of architectural monuments, and his practice of the seven liberal arts are cast in that light. His relation to history, his consciousness of its importance, are leitmotifs in the works of these historians.

Belleforest goes even further in this direction by depicting Charlemagne himself as being emblematic of the historian concerned with good style. In Belleforest, the great king becomes a poet who rewrites "in nice phrasing and sweet style certain ancient verses that were rude and barbarian" about the facts and deeds of the kings and governors of Gaul. This poet-king wants everyone to learn these verses by heart so as to render the memory of great men immortal. In this, too, he is better than his successors, who emphasized action over words, actions over language and history. This concern with language and culture is, of course, characteristic of the Renaissance in France, but it is interesting to note the extent to which rhetorical history considered itself the prose poetry of the nation and looked upon ancient poetry as a primitive form of history.

Did those historians, who saw kings as the true driving forces of history and of nations, set limits on Charlemagne's power? What was Charlemagne's policy toward the "people" of the kingdom? Three features emerge from these texts. The first is a constant reference to the general assemblies (*plaids*) held before each military campaign and referred to either as "parlements," or as "Estates-General." Wars of conquest had a transcendent justification in that they were waged in the name of a mission that was both religious and civilizing, but they were also linked to internal political necessities, as they proved to be the best means of maintaining virtue and peace within the kingdom:

> . . . knowing that the French become impatient with a long rest in which they might either end up indulging in voluptuousness or fighting among themselves when they cannot fight against foreigners, [Charlemagne] knew it was necessary to use them somewhere. He thus offered them a good occasion for a cause that came up to wage war in Spain.[19]

Thus we begin to see certain psychological characteristics of the French people emerge; they were warriors by nature but also irreducibly attached to their freedom. Indeed, it was that attachment that restricted Charlemagne's power. In a speech addressed to the emperor by a native of Gascony, we again find traces of the barons' uprising. In oratorical histories as in the *chansons de geste*, revolt, or the threat of revolt, was the vehicle for reflections on liberty. We see the same situation in Paul-Émile, Belleforest, and Du Haillan; the same speech, with slight variations, in all three texts: Charlemagne attempts to impose imperial laws throughout the Empire, including France. Du Haillan emphasizes that the restorer of the Empire of the West undertakes this reform because he hopes to achieve the "glory of the ancients," in other words, he wishes to be like them.[20] The emperor believes that, in order to govern the entire world it is necessary to have a center from which all laws originate: this is the old dream of universal unity.

The French react negatively to this project in a scene that brings into play their status with regard to the Empire, as well as the limits of imperial *and* royal power. It is here, at this originary moment, that oratorical history chooses to restrict the scope of the metaphor ruling its narrative. While Charles seeks to emphasize his resemblance to the Romans as strongly as possible, the French adamantly proclaim their difference, a difference defined in terms of their right to freedom.

But they have very little room to maneuver, as their position lies between the necessity of maintaining an adherence to the universal mission while refusing to accept the consequences of it for themselves. Of course, the right to conquer is accompanied by a transcendent justification. "You began in Rome," says the Gascon to Charlemagne, "to be the emperor of other nations: but you were born prince and king of the French, whose valor, though I know not by which fate, all foreigners envy and consider that our freedom is the cause of their servitude, in spite of the fact that before your reign only a small part of the earth could call itself free."[21] Other lands must submit in order to be free. The French are liberators through the very act of subjugating them.

When Charlemagne plans to impose the laws of the Empire on the French, those with power object and are prepared to take up arms should Charlemagne refuse to alter his plans. "We are complaining about one point only, O most illustrious and victorious Augustus. It is that you wish to turn into serfs the ones you had found free."[22] In other words, that which frees others would turn the French into slaves. This is because even if, thanks to Charlemagne, the Empire is now in the hands of the French, it is not certain that it will stay that way. The idea of the *translatio* itself implied that the same thing could happen again and that the Empire could be controlled by others. Thus the Empire is placed under the banner of mobility and the temporary, whereas the monarchy is established as permanent. The French refuse to obey an order given by Charlemagne the emperor and thereby clearly state that there are things that even the king cannot order. Charlemagne's greatness consists of his ability to listen to those words, to recognize the wisdom of the complaints, and to accede to them.

The speech is repeated from one history to the next and also reveals a deep distrust of the office of emperor since it might lead the French king to pursue a policy that did not take into account specific national differences. The emperor might forget his own people for the sake of a universal vision. Although this prose poetry of history sings of conquest and victory as being essential traits of a nation, it does not integrate the ideal of empire, an ideal with which the French identity could never be confused. In a manner of speaking, Charlemagne is made to remember himself by his own nobles. Indeed, although aspiring to control an empire was part of the foreign policy of French kings, it did not generate much enthusiasm in their own country. In spite of the aspirations of Henry II, Charles IX, and Henry IV, who drew inspiration from Charlemagne's legacy,[23] the general trend in the histories we have been examining, which reflect a strong royalist stance, is to express mistrust toward Charlemagne in his role as emperor even as they affirm claims to the great man as king of the French.

A New Model of the King: Claude de Seyssel

There is an alternative school of historiography in contrast to these "Romanizing" tendencies that proclaim the greatness of France and even its superiority over Italy while turning Charlemagne into a hero modeled on those of Antiquity. This alternative, "Gallican" current brings together and gives coherence to a fairly broad set of conceptions about the history of France. The historians of this school undertook in-depth studies of French traditions and institutions. They favored straight talk over metaphors and tended to move the dynamics of national evolution to the north. As Jean Du Tillet writes in his *Recueil des Roys de France*:

> Those who wrote that the French were of German origin honored them more than those who thought they had come from Troy since honor is only due to virtue. Because there has been no nation that has less suffered corruption in its morals and that has so strongly and for a long time maintained its liberty than the German nation.[24]

Here, too, the figure of Charlemagne is a point of reference, even if it is used only to highlight differences in relation to him. In general, this school fed off the works of jurists, such as Du Tillet, Du Moulin, Pasquier, and Hotman, all of whom were trained in the philological methods of the *mos Gallicus* school and all of whom were influenced by Protestantism. The historians in this group sought to free France from the influence and corruption of the Church. They no longer sought to prove French superiority by turning Charlemagne into a hero who was supposed to have been even more Roman than the Romans but rather by making him the fulcrum between Germanic traditions and the kingdom of France in all its greatness. In this context we might rightfully speak of a sixteenth-century rehabilitation of the barbarians.[25]

By raising doubts about a set of "fables" concerning the emperor, philological criticism to a certain extent helped to sever the ties that closely linked the conqueror to Rome and to the Church. By focusing on the capitularies and the work of the councils that Charlemagne convoked, this criticism shows him as a legislator concerned with establishing institutions as well as with reforming religion, the true leader of the Church in his kingdom. Indeed, at the heart of a Gallican tendency we find great value placed on institutions, traditions, and customs at the expense of the facts and deeds surrounding the hero-king. For some time already, the functioning of institutions and cultural components had been increasingly important in representations of Charlemagne; in the sixteenth century it became primordial.

This change in emphasis had important consequences in how the great king was represented. For the first time in the history of the kingdom, a major part of sociocultural dynamism and creativity was attributed to the community, a community that was understood as a whole, as an ensemble of traditions, customs, and institutions. The story of its origins and the narrative of its history were no longer necessarily reduced to the story of the lives and reigns of its successive kings. Charlemagne's place in this history was thus seriously threatened. The greatness of the hero could compete with that of the collectivity: the dazzle of his deeds threatened to overshadow the force and constancy of customs and traditions. Hence the growing emphasis on the limitations of the man and on circumscribing his place in history in order not only to give more weight to institutions and traditions but also to bring the community to life.

In fact, the first expression of such a vision of France goes back to the time of the wars in Italy. In many respects, Claude de Seyssel, a jurist and adviser to Louis XII, remained unaffected by humanist currents. His attachment to Roman traditions and to the Justinian code did not prevent him from granting an important place to specifically French institutions.

In his *Grand'Monarchie de France*, addressed to François I, he devotes several chapters to the "three constraints" (*trois freins*) to the authority and power of the king: religion, justice, and the police. Ordinances and laws that comprise the "police" emanate from the king himself who submits voluntarily to their authority; "this moderation and restraint of the absolute power of kings is to their great honor and benefit."[26] Seyssel strives to understand this monarchy as an institution "better organized than any other." Already in his *Histoire singulière du roy Loys XII*, a work written immediately following the session of the Estates-General of 1506, respecting those laws and ordinances was, in the eyes of Seyssel, an important policy of the king.

In addition to his "institutional" perspective, Seyssel introduces in this book (which was very popular in the sixteenth century) an image that was to endure for a long time and that reveals the birth of a new way of conceiving the entity France. Seyssel borrowed the image from Florus's *Epitome*; it is a metaphor that portrays the history of the kingdom as though it were an individual's biography.[27] France is supposed to have passed through four ages: childhood, adolescence, maturity, and old age. The development of France is thus akin to that of an individual. There appears to be no doubt in Seyssel's mind that the king remains the sine qua non condition for the collectivity, but this theoretician of the monarchy nevertheless conceives of this community as having lived *as a collectivity* the adventures of a human individual. This concept projects a new organic unity onto the nation, a unity whose dynamism spreads out over time. The kingdom/nation becomes the true hero of history. In Seyssel's work, the age of Charlemagne corresponds to the period of maturity when the man/kingdom could draw on fully developed physical strength and on a certain restraint that it ignored during its adolescence. The old age of the kingdom, marked by greater weakness of the body but also by greater wisdom ("virtue" and "experience"), begins with the advent of the Capetians.[28]

Seyssel assesses Louis XII's reign by comparing the king to some of his predecessors; the comparison of Charles VIII's successor with Charlemagne is the most developed. This is a daring comparison but it allows Seyssel to contrast the hero-king, a notion that many continued to find appealing, and another type of king who was less concerned with glory and more respectful of laws and regulations tempering his power. Louis XII's biographer is forced to concede Charlemagne's superiority in a number of categories, albeit while making excuses for it. If Charlemagne was more learned and eloquent than Louis, this was due to "the ignorance of the present time" affecting not only the king but the whole of the nobility as well.

> When it comes to Charles the Great, I cannot deny that the strength and valor of his person, [his knowledge] of science and doctrine, his strength and agility, his heart and greatness, his lordship and high and victorious deeds are to be preferred over the modern king, but I have to say that the modern king can be reasonably preferred over Charles the Great on account of his charity toward his predecessors, his goodness and love toward his family, his desire to treat his subjects well and to maintain them in peace and quiet, his good administration of justice, his constancy and sobriety, and the happiness of his reign.[29]

Louis XII represents progress for the kingdom. It is true that Charlemagne was a great conqueror, but he spent his whole reign waging war. "Though this is something that is much respected in the acquisition of human glory, a wise prince tries not to spend his whole life that way." A prince should fight neither for glory nor to enlarge his kingdom. Only defensive war can be justified. This is why Charles was wrong in wanting to accede to the Empire, a source of troubles and instability, while Louis, to whom Maximilian had offered the Empire, had the wisdom to refuse it.

Rejecting the idea of a universal monarch, of a transcendent unity, Seyssel chooses to emphasize the intermediary powers and institutions that were unique to the French monarchy. Louis XII himself created parlements in Normandy and in Provence. The historian points out that Charles did not have "sovereign courts," that is, parlements, without which it is impossible, for instance, to prevent the strong from oppressing the weak. Seyssel collects a set of emblematic symbols of the great epic hero in order to bring his abuses of power to light: "And thus we still find to this day privileges and lands given by him [Charlemagne] in the presence of Roland and Oliver and sealed with the handle of his sword along with his promise to protect them with its blade." Here Charlemagne is showing largesse, backed by his most faithful vassals as well as his own warrior strength: a strong image mixing myth and history that sums up obsolete values in order to help us understand "that, at that time, they made more use of force and absolute power than of reason and justice."[30]

Charles's abuses even include the murder of a religious. And Seyssel deploys historical hearsay against the great emperor: "And it is even said that he killed with his own hands an abbot of Lagrasse, in Languedoc country, as he was standing before the altar, because the abbot had refused to welcome and feed an old soldier in his abbey."[31] If Seyssel seems unconcerned with ascertaining what might and might not be true in Charlemagne's story, in spite of his advocating a policy of respect for the letter of the law, it is because fables illustrate abuses even better than reality can, and it was, to a great extent, the fables that supported the idea people had of this great man who embodied a certain conception of the monarchy.

According to Seyssel, it was in order to expiate the great wrong he had committed that Charlemagne built a large number of churches and given them substantial lands and income. However, this attempt at reparation was also only an arbitrary act; it was an abuse of power that Louis could not have committed *even if he had wanted to*, as the laws of the kingdom forbade him from giving away any of his domain or from rendering justice on a whim. Charlemagne was not able to separate the private from the public. He took his own glory to be the happiness of his people, and his largesse was out of place because he was using it to expiate a wrong that was in any case unacceptable for a king. Louis's greatness lay in his knowing how to defer to the law and to the authority of the courts, in wanting to administer rather than to conquer, to use reason and kindness rather than force and violence.

Throughout this long comparison, Seyssel goes to great lengths to present his readers with a new model of the king, a model that would keep its distance from epic values and would recognize the limits of its power and the importance and value of submitting to laws and institutions. The seductive qualities of the conquering all-powerful figure had to be rejected. Charlemagne belonged to another age. In the meanwhile another entity had come of age, that of the collectivity understood metaphorically as a person; the drama of this comparison lay in the struggle between the grandeur of tempered monarchy, as an institution, and that of the greatest of kings. The distance between the present and the past was growing. The biographical metaphor underscores the impossibility of going back, as well as the idea of progress. It was no longer desirable to return to outdated values.

CHARLEMAGNE'S ABUSES AND SINS: ÉTIENNE PASQUIER

Among the "radical" critiques of Charlemagne, the most rigorous is that found in Étienne Pasquier's *Recherches de la France*.[32] Whereas Seyssel wrote during an age of optimism, when royal policy favored a certain "decentralization" with the setting up of new provincial parlements,[33] Pasquier lived in a kingdom that had fallen prey to financial and religious crises. The end of the Italian wars had left the warrior class idle and with their coffers empty, and the monarchy had little means to compensate those who had fought for the services they had rendered. Bestowing honors and selling offices became the preferred means to ensure the loyalty of subordinates and to fill the royal coffers. In this atmosphere of crisis, the intermediary powers and institutions gained in importance. The sale of offices swelled the ranks of the members of the parlements that were, at the same time, acquiring more definition and coherence. In particular, the Parlement of Paris proclaimed its role as defender of the Gallican church and began to express itself forcefully on affairs of state. As for the monarchy, driven by a need for money and a crippling debt, it resorted on a number of occasions either to the Estates-General or to assemblies of Notables.

Within the context of an increasingly contested and vulnerable monarchy, Pasquier shows a certain optimism in his examination of a France whose identity and power went beyond the figure of the monarch and were rooted in traditions and institutions in a national culture that went back to the time of the Gauls. As institutions take center stage and constitute the governing principle of the *Recherches*, the figure of Charlemagne is diminished due to its fragmentation among the different books and chapters devoted to the multiple aspects of French institutions and laws. In a sense, there is no longer a history of Charlemagne; with the loss of the coherence of a continuous narrative he seems to have lost his power. He has his place among the institutions, to be sure, and Pasquier does recognize a certain genius in him. Thus early treatments of him are stronger, more positive. In Pasquier, Charlemagne maintains a certain defining value for France above all when it is a question of other European peoples.

For Pasquier, there are only three great peoples in the history of the world: the Gauls, the Germans, and the Saracens. He doesn't include the Romans on his list, for "since Charlemagne and a long time before [the Italians] have never stood up to us, but plotted according to the times and occasions, at times submitted to our devotion, at times dispensing with it, without dismissing thoughts of returning to it."[34] When dealing with France's identity in relation to Italy, or even to the Germans in the guise of the Lombards, Pasquier freely calls on "our valorous Charlemagne."[35] The great hero serves as a support in forging an identity against neighboring nations. The French are heirs to the Gauls, themselves strengthened by the arrival of the Franks, who freed them from Roman tyranny.[36] Thus France originated in a time that long preceded the arrival of the Franks, well before writing as well, in an era of oral culture. The "invention of the Gauls" enables Pasquier to anchor national identity in a time that predates the monarchy.[37] In this context, the discourse on origins centered around

Charlemagne becomes problematic in relation to the one that focuses on the Gauls.

It quickly becomes apparent to the reader that when it comes to the essence of the country, that is, its institutions and culture, Pasquier goes to great lengths to deny the conquering king any originary function. Ironically, the result is that Charlemagne is ever-present in the *Recherches,* since the author keeps repeating that the great king was not the founder of any of the great institutions: not the Parlement, "the principal support of our monarchy" and the real hero of the history of France, nor the university. It is as if Pasquier has taken on the task of freeing these institutions from the hold of the great king. The implications are important because, in Pasquier's concept of France, the institutions and the civilization of that nation obey a logic and dynamics that go beyond any individual's impact, no matter how great he might be. Thus Pasquier systematically refuses to attribute any of the great institutions of the monarchy to the impact of a single individual.[38] From this perspective, the fact that Charlemagne is mentioned so many times in the *Recherches* allows us to appreciate the importance of the tradition that made him a founding father.

However, Pasquier mentions another reason to deny Charlemagne his function as originator: the absolute power of the figure. This reasoning in some ways parallels that of the priority Pasquier accords to institutions over any single individual. Far from seeing Charlemagne as a monarch who submitted to the laws and the advice of the nobles, Pasquier likes to point out that it was, in fact, Charlemagne who held all the power. Pasquier expresses himself very clearly in this regard when he deals with the institution of the peers as a possible mediating force:

> Most people take for very true history that the emperor Charlemagne, to ensure his state and win over the hearts of his people, gave almost the same authority as his own to twelve of his magnates, though on the condition that he would retain the main voice in discussions. . . . However, it seems to me that those who were of this opinion did not really understand Charlemagne's power, nor how the affairs of France were decided in his time; as for me, I would never agree with them. It must be said that this belief stemmed more from the fabulous ignorance of our Romans than from any authentic history. It is certain that Charlemagne ruled his country by his sole authority and not by that of the dukes and counts, who then were only simple governors that he could dismiss at will.[39]

There are two points to be noted in this passage. First historical hearsay is caught in the act of inventing and distorting. Pasquier, with the help of good historical and philological arguments, shows that what "the greatest part" of people believe could not have been true in Charlemagne's time. Here again, the romances spread falsities, and Pasquier acts as a redresser of wrongs. Charlemagne's absolute power, on which the author dwells, foreshadows Pasquier's exposé of the all too often hidden abuses of the great monarch.

Pasquier is completely uninterested in the hero's glory. He very rarely uses adjectives such as "valorous" and "great," and he does not compare Charlemagne to a "Gallic Mars" or a new "Augustus." He discredits the honor of Charlemagne being a patrician of Rome and an emperor by denigrating the pope's and Charlemagne's motives and lowering the level of language he uses to describe the relationship between them: "Thus they split the cake between the two of them"; "in this way the pope and the king, passing the ball to and fro, enriched themselves from the spoils of the Empire."[40] Charlemagne is often referred to simply as "Pepin's son," as if his readers were unaware of his prestige and were to define him mainly in relation to his father. Thus the relationships between the lesser known and the less famous, on the one hand, and the best known and the most praised on the other, are inverted.

In the fifth book, Pasquier begins the chapter entitled "Chute de la seconde famille de nos Roys" [The Fall of the Second Family of Our Kings] by explaining: "I leave to other historians the conquests, the glorious victories and superb exploits of this second family: as for me, I now take its ruins as my share."[41] Here we learn that even the beginning of Charlemagne's true reign—that is, when the two parts of the kingdom were united after the death of his brother Carloman—came about through underhanded means, because that union was achieved at the expense of his brother's legitimate heirs. Pasquier wonders why this first act of cruelty is never mentioned. "This history is in no way touched upon by our annalists and is put in the category of forgotten sins as if it were a peccadillo to have deprived his nephews of their father's inheritance."[42] Pasquier puts the fate of the second race under the sign of this wrong; the sin might be forgotten, but "nonetheless it was strongly avenged *on his family by a just judgment of God*."[43] This reference to God's vengeance is surprising in a historian putting so much emphasis on entirely secular causality.

God, Fate, and Fortune: these subjects are frequently mentioned in the *Recherches* and blend together in the rhetoric of an author eager not to offend the exacerbated religious sensibilities of his contemporaries.[44] These transcendent forces play a crucial role in Pasquier's portrayal of the development of France. Indeed, they give a tragic structure to the discussion of the Carolingian reign. Pasquier again insists on the role of these concepts, a mixture of religion and humanism, in the chapter on "la fatalité qu'il y eut en la lignée de Hugues Capet au préjudice de celle de Charlemagne" [the fatality that was in Hughes Capet's line to the detriment of that of Charlemagne].[45] It should be noted that when it comes to the decline of the second royal line, Charlemagne is immediately promoted to uncontested leader of the dynasty and, above all, to the status of the one who sowed the seed of his own family's decline. Though Charlemagne's wrong against his nephews was a grievous one, the "sins" upon which Pasquier dwells pertain to the emperor's sexual inconstancy. His repudiation of Didier's daughter, his many wives, but mostly his mistresses and concubines are all dealt with in turn. Pasquier chooses to attack the great king in the realm of his private life, specifically in his sexual behavior.

Charlemagne, overwhelmed by his good fortune and holding absolute power, was in a way his own worst enemy, the only one he could not defeat. It was not only he but his own daughters as well who indulged themselves shamelessly "so that this great emperor's court was nothing but a bank of shame." To back his argument, this ardent apologist of France brings up the anecdote told by the very anti-French Petrarch about the emperor's morbid love for the dead mistress with the magical ring hidden under her tongue. Pasquier emphasizes that already when she was still in good health, Charles fell so madly in love with her that "he forgot not only the affairs of the Empire but also the care of his own person."[46] Pasquier exhibits an obvious satisfaction in discussing this episode at length; he shows us Charlemagne adoring the cadaver, "kissing it and holding it the same way as he did before her death," in spite of the growing decay. Then comes the scene of his attraction to Bishop Turpin after the bishop discovers the ring and removes it; this is followed with Charlemagne's love for the site of Aachen after the ring was thrown into the bog.[47] At the end of the tale, just before he draws his conclusions about Charlemagne's immorality, Pasquier reveals in passing that he cannot say whether this story is true any more than Petrarch could, and that he is just reporting "what it is: a *common rumor*."[48] Not satisfied with telling the anecdote a single time, Pasquier comes back to it in the sixth book and devotes an entire chapter to it entitled "D'un amour prodigieux de Charlemagne envers une femme" [Of Charlemagne's Incredible Love for a Woman] (book 6, chap. 32).

Using any means possible in his fight against the hero-king, the scholar Pasquier, though experienced in the methods of philology, obviously has no qualms about drawing on historical hearsay, especially since he repeats himself by telling this secondhand story twice. It is clear that Pasquier, who had previously denounced the scandal of forgetting and hiding, knows full well the impact and the seduction of such an anecdote on the reader. Regardless of its veracity, the author achieves his goal simply by telling the tale and using it directly in his argument. He then goes straight to his conclusion:

No matter how great the sovereignty of a king, since he is a man he fails at times. All of his thoughts should be turned to God, and he must believe that He is the true judge of our actions, that He sometimes punishes us in our lifetime, or our children after our death. This you will find true in what I am about to describe. Thus you can expect from me in the story of our present subject only injustices, partiality, and divisions between fathers and sons, civil wars between brothers, uncles who mistreat their nephews, treachery mixed with cruelty, all of it punished by the just judgment of God.[49]

Pasquier ends the fifth book in this biblical tone. God punished Charlemagne's children, and the story of his family became a long "tragic history." Thus the author of the book clothes himself in the authority of the author of the world so as to make us see Charlemagne not as a founding father but rather as the one "who laid down the first foundation of ruination."[50] He who ruled alone, who held all the power, was above all the originary figure in the decline of his own dynasty.

But the ruin of the reigning family in no way involved that of the kingdom. Pasquier is certainly aware of the irony of depicting this champion of the Church and of religion as the object of divine vengeance. This irony also resonates in the fulfillment of the family's destiny. Even the "epic" of the north, the great victory over the Saxons and their leader Widukind turns out to be an illusion. Pasquier is obviously pleased with the Capetians' claims of descent from the old Saxon leader, the one who breathed "nothing else in his soul than the ancient liberty of this land."[51] Far from constituting a liberation, the victory over the Germanics was only an act of tyranny, the fate of which was retribution in making the crown of France pass from the Carolingians to the Capetians.

Pasquier constantly belittles Charlemagne and assumes the task of demythifying the figure of the hero-king and the epic vision of the monarch. And yet Pasquier is not against the monarchy. He is fighting against a history of the origins of France that sees one man as the driving force of that history. Although Pasquier constantly searches for the foundations of the monarchy, he rejects any idea of a founding father. This is why Charlemagne occupies such an important place in the *Recherches:* he embodies a vision of history and of the nation that Pasquier rejects, and he embodies it best, most powerfully, and thus most dangerously. From this perspective, Pasquier's attack, focusing on the private life of the great king, proves to be a particularly effective way to reveal the limitations of the all too human king. Such an approach reveals the failings of the king as a man, but it also makes it possible to separate morality from politics.

Charlemagne's tragic flaws resulted in other abuses and in the suffering and the fall of his own family, but France emerged triumphant from all these trials. Just as a powerful figure cannot build a kingdom alone, a powerful wrongdoer cannot lead to its downfall. In the long run, he or his heirs will suffer the consequences of his actions. The constellation God-Fate-Fortune is bound up with a civilization, a culture, a set of institutions, a people: this transcendent triptych, like the author himself, stands solidly on the side of France. "Strange mysteries of God!" writes Pasquier in another passage, "that a greatness built on so much wrongdoing . . . would have such a happy ending."[52]

And yet Pasquier does not entirely reject the heroic vision, and he does not deny Charlemagne's role in establishing certain institutions. The historian grants the founding prestige of the great king a certain functionality. The example of the Parlement is perhaps the most significant one in this regard. Far from being the fruit of honest and wise reflection on the best form of government, the Parlement originated out of a royal ruse. The mayors of the palace created assemblies with the aim of masking their usurpation of all the power of the Merovingian kings and to avoid an uprising: "The mayors of the palace [*maiores domo*], so as to fool the people, had introduced their use." And Pepin and Charlemagne were the first to call upon them "without ruse" for the most important affairs.[53] This scheme is typical of Pasquier's work: an obscure origin accompanied by a dubious intent, then the gradual transformation and improvement of an institution.

Charlemagne does have a place in this process, but it is a limited one. As to his relations with the Church, he is depicted as the precursor of the Gallican church. Even if Charlemagne's intentions pertained mostly to his desire for riches and power ("in this way, the pope and the king, passing the ball to and fro, enriched themselves from the spoils of the Empire"), the result of his maneuvers and manipulations was to obtain for him and his successors the right to confirm the pope and the agreement that no archbishop or bishop could be anointed in any part of his kingdom without having first been invested by the king—all privileges that were to be lost under Louis the Pious.[54] Even while he attacks Charlemagne's role as a founder, Pasquier uses it indirectly: according to Pasquier, this exceptional reign constituted a first draft of a France that had a parlement and practiced a Gallican religion.

THE GOLDEN AGE AND THE POWER OF THE PEOPLE: HOTMAN

The ideological importance of national origins continued to grow within the context of religious conflicts. "This kingdom of France has been and is above all others like the kingdom of Israel, instituted by God in the person of David," exclaims the famous jurist and theologian of feudalism, Charles Du Moulin.[55] Like the people of Israel, those of France were facing the temptation of idolatry and corruption. And this was not the first time. France had already experienced a similar crisis in the earliest days of its existence. And here Charlemagne, having become in this context a sort of proto-Protestant, in councils and through his capitularies, was able to bring the nation back to the truth of the primitive church. Because "this very wise and heroic prince knew well that the true religion . . . depends totally on the word and law of God, and not on any secondary cause, and that it is not possible for man, nor angel, nor any other second cause or any creature to add or subtract anything from it."[56]

Pasquier belonged to the moderate pro-monarchy "party," which rejected both Catholic and Huguenot extremism and advocated instead a primary role for the Parlement of Paris in the government of France. In contrast, more extreme individuals preferred to set their sights on the Estates-General. The monarchy had attempted to use this assembly to have new taxes approved, but it reflected too many of the divisions of the kingdom to be effective. Among the second estate, religious oppositions were tied to tensions between the old nobility and the new, that is, between the sword and the robe. From the time of Henry II's death in 1559, there were a number of factors that seemed to contribute to the breakdown of order in the kingdom; these included the monarchy's growing inability to control a gradually intensifying, explosive political situation, and to cope with an increasingly ruinous economic and financial situation, with the violence that was erupting almost everywhere as a means to settle conflicts, and with the increasingly open revolt of those in power who had split into clans under different religious banners. The onset of war led to the neglect of the common good and to behavior driven purely by personal interest. One of the most blatant examples of this can be found in combatants who changed their religious adherence depending upon the needs of the moment.[57] But such cynical actions were only one side of the coin. For there also existed a deep eschatological anguish that manifested itself in the irruption of prophetic and iconoclastic violence, in the need to rediscover the purity of origins. Huguenots and members of the Catholic League sought to purge the country from the evil that was destroying it.

This was a period when the legitimacy of both the Church and the monarchy was being questioned. It is not surprising, therefore, that those who were most blatantly living an ideology of *reformation*, of a return to the source, and of a more direct relationship with God, albeit a God who was not manifesting himself very much in human affairs at that time, were the first and the most vocal in propounding the notion of popular sovereignty representing the origins of France.

The search for a primitive constitution corresponded to a search for the purity of the primitive church. In both cases there was an impulse to return to the past, the dream of rediscovering that originary time "ruled by the Law, and thus by atemporality."[58] The historical optimism of a politically aware moderate like Pasquier, who saw history as a process of becoming in which France never ceased to assert itself, was no longer maintainable. The present seemed only decadence, corruption, and the loss of essential values. Thus Seyssel's biographical metaphor becomes inverted in François Hotman: just like men, "republics" also die of sickness, of external blows, or of old age.[59] Without pushing the image to an extreme, the logical outcome of which could only leave France without hope, Hotman, who had already written a treatise on the status of the primitive church, proposes a return to the primitive constitution, to the purity of origins, as the only sure political remedy for current ills.[60] Published shortly after the massacre of Saint Bartholomew's Day, his treatise fits into the context of the Huguenots' demands that the Estates-General be convened.

According to the Protestant historian, a look back in time would reveal among the Gauls prior to the Roman conquest and among the Franks a government in which the general assembly—the *Champs de Mai* (Fields of May)—played a primordial role in the guidance of the kingdom. Basing his argument on passages from Tacitus and Caesar, Hotman depicts a free people who elected their kings. The Gauls themselves had called on the Franks to free them from the tyranny and the corruption of the Romans, the only true invaders.[61] Thus in Hotman's view, the Franks acquire the status of "the authors of liberty." The word "Frank," he argues, is Germanic and has nothing to do with Turpin's fables about the relationship between Charlemagne and the church of Saint-Denis.[62] The idyllic system where the assembly of the people is primary in the government of the country was preserved during the reign of the first two dynasties. The advent of the Capetians ruined the system.[63]

And yet, in spite of Hotman's attempts to diminish Charlemagne's role as originator, he nonetheless allows the great monarch to keep a privileged place in his scenario. This is because Charlemagne helps to maintain the strength of the immemorial tradition of freedom. In fact, Hotman uses Charlemagne's greatness to emphasize the greatness of the Franco-Gallic people. Citing as evidence the *Royal Frankish Annals* conveyed by Aimoin and Sigebert, the advocate of the Estates-General explains:

Aimon speaks constantly of King Charles, who, having acquired almost the whole of Europe for his kingdom with his great exploits [*magnis suis rebus gestis*], was consequently called "the Great" by the consent of all. *Nonetheless, Charlemagne was not able to take away from the Franks their primitive rights and freedom, nor did he undertake anything of import without soliciting the opinion* [iudicium] *of the people and the authority of the magnates* [optimatrum auctoritas].[64]

At the height of its power and with its most powerful king, France-Gaul kept its primitive laws and freedom as defined by tradition. Thus Charlemagne's age is conceived as an ideal moment when a strong king and an assembly that had preserved all of its rights were able to function harmoniously together. It is not only the power of this king that led the devoted Protestant author, experienced in the methods of philology, to endow him with such an important place; it is also because Charlemagne left more evidence, more documents, more writing than any king before him. His will, his capitularies, and his biography reinforce and augment what we learn from the chronicles. This enables Hotman to draw on the deeds of Charlemagne in his discussion of the most essential elements of his ideal government: laws and legislation, the succession of the crown, and justice.

In the making of laws, the power of the people (*potestas populi*) under Charlemagne was such that laws could not be amended without first consulting the people (*populus interrogetur*) and securing their consent before adding new clauses. Thus Charlemagne's capitularies prove that even under his reign the people of France (*populus Franciae*) were only required to obey laws they had already approved in the assemblies (*quas in comitiis suffragiis suis sanxerant*).[65] Regarding the succession to the throne, Charlemagne's testament provides the first example of the role the assembled people played in the choice of the sovereign. The will specifies that since his successor would not be chosen on the basis of heredity, the decision must come from the assembly.[66] Thus Charlemagne's testament is a key element in Hotman's argument because it clearly shows that the great king respected the ancient constitution and preserved "the right of the Frankish people to constitute its kings."[67] Louis the Pious's sovereignty was not established on the fact that he was Charlemagne's heir but on his election by the general assembly. Just as he did in the legislative realm, Charlemagne maintained the tradition of exercising direct justice in the judicial domain. Hotman, resolutely hostile to the parlements, argues that, far from having created a court from which modern parlements might claim to originate, Charlemagne was the model of the judge-king. He had the opposing parties come before him and judged their conflicts himself.[68]

Thus an essential element in Hotman's representation of Charlemagne is this tension between the greatness of the king and the preservation of a tradition. Hotman puts scholarship in the service of Huguenot propaganda demanding the convening of the Estates-General. The figure of the great king made it possible to rival the ancients on the level of glory while affirming the power of specifically Germanic customs. Hotman develops a passionate and forceful representation of a "republican" vision of the primitive constitution, one that functions as a kind of political parallel to that of the republic of letters. On the one hand, Hotman's representation betrays a classicism influenced by the literature of Antiquity; on the other, there is a German influence that harks back to an older spoken tradition.

In this second tradition, Charlemagne becomes the fulcrum between the spoken word and writing. Detached from his role as protector of the Church, he provides written traces of the existence and transmission of practices found in the ancient republic of the north (the one described by Tacitus) and proof that this republic could not only survive Roman imperialism but could also become more glorious than Rome.[69] In this sense, Charlemagne's reign functions as a golden age still close enough in time to enable dreams of a possible return to the glory of it. Hotman assigns a concrete function to sessions of the assemblies: they produced the capitularies. These documents were repeatedly published during the sixteenth century (in 1545 by Vitus Amerpachius, in 1545 by Jean Du Tillet, and in 1588 by Pierre Pithou),[70] and they became crucial for illustrating the "people's" actions, rights, and power.

CHARLEMAGNE VERSUS SAINT LOUIS: THE LEAGUE

The new myth of a golden age when the "people" played a crucial role in choosing the king and in leading the country influenced all opponents of royal policy during this period of troubles and wars.[71] The "zealots" of the Catholic League denounced the abuses of Henry III's court, his moral failings, his corruption, and his weakness in the face of the spread of heresy. For these League zealots the country needed to be cleansed, to be returned to its original purity: purity in law and in faith. To the chagrin of the Huguenots, the Catholics in their turn adopted the notion that the Estates-General should pick Henry III's successor because he did not have a direct heir, and the closest one, Henry of Navarre, was Protestant. As the religious struggle was compounded by the uprising of the nobility, the figure of Charlemagne was invoked as an example of genealogical legitimacy. The League was led by the Guise family of the House of Lorraine, who claimed to have descended from Charlemagne, and thus to represent the survival of the Carolingian line. According to this logic, the Capetians were nothing but usurpers. The remedy would be found in a return to origins:

> But it seems that God has prepared and disposed . . . the parties, the judges, and the occasion to reintegrate the Crown to the true successors of Charlemagne . . . robbed of their temporal inheritance by force and violence. . . .

It is evident that the race of the Capets has abandoned itself in the forbidden way: some of them suffered from a weak mind; they were stupid and inconsequential people. Others were damned by God and men for their heresy and condemned and forbidden from the Holy Ecclesiastical Communion.

On the contrary, Charlemagne's descendants are blossoming, loving virtue, filled with strength in spirit and body, ready to accomplish high and virtuous deeds.

Wars served to raise them in honor and prominence: but peace will return to them their ancient legacy of the kingdom, with the consent and the election of the whole people.[72]

Henry III's degeneracy, like Henry of Navarre's heresy, were so many signs of the curse afflicting the Capetians. The return to the dynasty of Charlemagne would occur through the participation of all the people in an election, just as in the old *Champs de Mai* (Fields of May). This was the plan outlined in the summary of a secret meeting held in Rome in 1576 and discovered in the luggage of David Jean, a League envoy sent to the Holy See.[73] The document fell into Huguenot hands, and they quickly published it so as to denounce the Guisard plot. In 1580, François de Rosière, the archdeacon of Toul, published his *Stemmatum Lotharingiae*, in which he demonstrates the existence of the Carolingian ascendants of the House of Lorraine. Pamphlets and arguments from both sides referred to the Guises as the descendants of Charlemagne. As late as 1597, Philippe Emmanuel, duke of Lorraine, the most committed member of the League, had a long epic poem, *L'Espagne conquise, par Charles le Grand, Roy de France* dedicated to himself.[74]

With the Guises claiming the great king as one of their own, the Valois monarchy risked losing a pillar of Capetian legitimacy. In other words, Charlemagne threatened to cross over to the House of Lorraine. And this was occurring at a moment when the figure of the great king appears to have been regaining importance in the cultural arena. We should remember that in 1582 Robert Garnier, inspired by Ariosto, produced a representation of the emperor in his *Bradamante*. In this tragicomedy, which was reprinted a number of times, Charlemagne, reigning "in this court where all things prosper,"[75] succeeds in reconciling the stringency of the given word, the interests of his kingdom, and the union of a divided Christendom.

The play ends with two weddings: that of Roger and Bradamante, Aymon's daughter and Renaud's sister, and that of Leon, the son of Constantine, "emperor of Greece," and Leonor, Charlemagne's daughter. These marriages achieve the "private" happiness of love as well as the public happiness of the union of two empires. In a France that was being tragically torn apart by the wars of religion, Garnier uses the idea of the universal monarchy to create a Charlemagne who is able to pursue a policy that unites western and eastern Europe in the bosom of Christendom. Garnier's message is clear, and his use of the old king could only add to Charlemagne's symbolic worth at the very moment when the members of the League were attempting to use him to question Henry III's legitimacy.

Confronted with these dangers, the Capetian heirs invoked Saint Louis. The two sovereigns, who were so often shown together to represent the foundations of the monarchy, as was seen in the *Retable du Parlement*, were now pitted against each other. The Catholics also set out in search of origins and of a fundamental law. As they conceived it, that law required the king of France to be Catholic and, like Charlemagne, to be the protector of the Church. Therefore Henry of Navarre had to be excluded from the succession, and the stage was set for a new *reditus regni ad stirpem Karoli*, this time by way of the Estates-General. The growing power of the Guises worried Henry III as much as it did the Huguenots.

> O God, through what good path
> This good League is leading us!
> These offsprings of Charlemagne,
> Good Zealots, are ruining everything:

> ———

> Let us find out what we can,
> And then we will strike.[76]

Henry III himself decided to strike, and he aimed at the heads of the opposition: those who embodied that other legitimacy, the Carolingian line. The assassination of the duke of Guise and his brother, the cardinal, followed by the imprisonment of Charles, the cardinal of Bourbon, in public opinion eliminated the concessions made to the members of the League during the meeting of the Estates-General in Blois in December 1588. What remained was a striking affirmation of royal absolutism in matters of politics and justice. The League was far from disarmed, as the events that followed show, but the king did inflict a harsh blow by removing its head. When it was Henry IV's turn to rule, he found it prudent not to release the cardinal of Bourbon, who ultimately died in captivity.

Henry IV: Exiting from History, Marginalizing Charlemagne

The monarchy proclaimed its power, so to speak, in opposition to the figure of Charlemagne. Afterward, Henry IV showed little interest in establishing any substantial identification with the great king.[77] In fact, in the course of this eventful century, the image of the emperor with the flowing white beard suffered greatly in its relationship with the French monarchy. He had now become the hero of another vision of France, one involving a greater role for intermediary governing institutions and thus one that did not invest the person of the king with all national sovereignty.

Huguenots and Catholics in turn conceived of the power of the monarchy as being broader, less absolutist than that which the monarchy itself advocated. Charlemagne became the one who, "without ruse," could govern with assemblies that were the prototypes of the Parlement or the Estates-General. At the time of the *chansons de geste*, the great king became a vehicle for exploring the limits of royal power. In the sixteenth century, Charlemagne was squarely at the center of a debate on the nature and limits of the monarchy, but he had somehow crossed over to the side of those "in revolt." At least in the realm of domestic policy, Charlemagne was the one who knew how to share, or who was forced to agree to share his sovereignty to a certain extent. But the devaluation of the figure of the great emperor in relation to the monarchy is in some ways overdetermined since it was carried out within several domains in the course of the century.

Looking first at foreign policies, after the failure of François I's quest for the imperial crown in the first half of the century, Charles V put life back into the ideal of a universal monarchy. The people who placed their hopes in him saw this new emperor as Charlemagne's true heir. Boiardo ends his poem with a complaint against the king of France, Charles VIII; in the fifteenth song of his *Roland furieux*, it is the emperor from the house of Hapsburg that Ariosto glorifies:

> Of Arragon and Austria's blood I see
> On the left bank of Rhine a monarch bred;
> No sovereign is so famed in history,
> Of all whose goodly deeds are heard or read.
> Astraea reinthroned by him will be,—
> Rather restored to life, long seeming dead;
> And *Virtues* with her into exile sent,
> By him shall be recalled from banishment.

> ----

> For such desert, Heaven's bounty not alone
> Designs he should the imperial garland bear,—
> Augustus', Trajan's, Mark's, Severus', crown;
> But that of every farthest land should wear,
> Which here and there extends, as yet unknown,
> Yielding no passage to the sun and year;

And wills that in his time Christ's scattered sheep
Should be one flock, beneath one Shepherd's keep.[78]

Thus the House of Austria, the main enemy of the French monarchy, succeeded in capturing and exploiting Charlemagne's prestige. And although the Hapsburgs were unable to maintain their universal claims for long, the kings of France, increasingly mired in internal troubles, were in no position to take the initiative with regard to visions of imperial glory.

Moreover, as we have seen, as the century unfolded the imaginary realm occupied by the great emperor fell under the combined attacks of philologists and historiographers and continued to diminish. Charlemagne, having once occupied a prominent place in mythistory, became a prime target in attempts to separate the myth from history, falsehood from truth. This new history conveyed a different representation of Charlemagne, one that was closer to Hincmar's than Turpin's. The great king's connections to Germany were indeed a way of affirming French identity in the face of Rome. But although valuing institutions and a culture that issued from tradition and customs was certainly not *unavoidably* anti-monarchical, it did provide religious polemics with a resonance and an effectiveness that benefited both Huguenots and Catholics. Instead of being an affirmation of a collective identity, the discourse on origins had itself become a source of division, an object of debate: what had once been a given had in some ways become a battle zone. At the dawn of modernity, the Guises' Carolingian claims and the League's rebellion, itself partially shaped by Huguenot ideology, brought about Charlemagne's inclusion in a camp that was basically hostile to that of rising absolutism.

Given the uncertainties of the times and the multifaceted nature of representations of Charlemagne, it is not surprising that Henry IV essentially turned away from history and from any identification with Charlemagne. Far from serving to strengthen the monarchy, history seemed to take it to task; rather than focusing national unity on the figure of the king, history seemed mainly to emphasize divisions and legitimize very diverse visions of the monarchy. Were the countless victims of the civil wars not proof enough of its destructive impact? It was better to ignore history and to depict the king's authority using references sheltered from inopportune legitimizing returns to the past. Thus Henry IV was more of a new Hercules than a new Charlemagne. The difficulties and ambiguities of a personage partaking of both the myth and the history of the kings of France could thus be avoided. Hercules belonged to the absolute atemporality of myth, a territory that had no relation to the horrors of contemporary history. Like Charlemagne, Hercules was a two-sided hero: he was both a warrior and a cultural figure, for he represented not only physical force and the art of combat, but also the art of language and of rhetoric. Like that the old emperor, the myth of the Gallic Hercules made the history of ancient Gaul and that of ancient Rome resonate in unison.[79] However, the link between Henry IV and Hercules was primarily metaphorical. Bringing them together glorified the king who was likened to a demigod of Antiquity, without raising the issue of genealogical legitimacy or the issue of his relationship with the Church. In freeing the image of the monarch from those ties, the Herculean identification gave a new purity to the image of the monarch leading his country out of the trap of history.

Henry IV's royal appearances visually emphasized his identification with Hercules. But there is also a text that is a particularly strong example of how the representation of the king was transposed and retranscribed.[80] This work illustrates the passage from the history of the kingdom to the classic myth of Hercules. In *Les Trois Visions de Childeric, quatriesme roy de France, pronostics des guerres civiles de ce Royaume* [The Three Visions of Childeric, Fourth King of France, Foreseeing Civil Wars in the Kingdom], Pierre Boton narrates the prophecies on the future of France that were supposedly made by Childeric's wife, Basine. Thus from the start the poem is solidly rooted in the history of the kingdom.

The queen, in a visionary trance, sees the parade of the successive reigns of Clovis, Charles Martel, Charlemagne, Saint Louis, Philipe the Brave, and Henry IV pass before her eyes. The place of honor is given to Charlemagne, who was to unite the Roman Empire to France, hold the earthly globe in his hand, and acquire the greatness of the "universal world." "During his reign were to triumph the brave Olivers, / Rolands, Renauds, all immortal warriors."[81] The great emperor was to cross the Pyrenees and chase the Saracens out of Spain. When the author comes to Henry IV, he shows him lifting up the scepter again, righting the kingdom, and bringing it out of chaos. Henry IV's resemblance to Charlemagne is evident, though implicit, in this striving for a new order. In the passage on Henry IV Charlemagne's name is not mentioned; and yet, like Charles, Henry de Bourbon "was to be nicknamed 'the Great'," and like Charles he "was to go and conquer Pamplona and [assert] his rights," this time not against the Saracens but against the usurping "tyrant." In contrast, the identification with Hercules is explicit and Biron becomes a new Achilles. Thus Henry IV *implicitly* participates in Charlemagne's greatness, but this greatness was to be recontextualized in relation to classical myths. In this sense, Henry IV represents the end of history, the introduction of an atemporal stability.[82]

In spite of some meager attempts to integrate the national past into the realm of literature, Greco-Roman culture already largely prevailed over the medieval legacy. The *chansons de geste* were looked upon as primitive forms of history (thus prey to the scandal of lies and errors) and were denied the dignity of great epic poetry. Moreover, the Renaissance objected to the "imperfections" and the "crudeness" of the language of earlier periods. The "myth" that remained alive in the realm of literary production was the one that dealt with Trojan origins, as seen in Ronsard's *La Franciade*. The legend of Francus was aimed primarily at linking France to the epic greatness of Antiquity. Thus Charlemagne appears to have been erased from the realm of literature as well as from that of a certain political culture. At the dawn of the great classical century and the establishment of absolute monarchy, Charlemagne was no longer a major pillar of legitimacy in royal discourse, largely because he was used heavily in explorations and discussions on the nature and the limits of royal power. We will see that this rejection was not universal and that Charlemagne remained a presence in the margins of culture and politics before coming back in full force at the end of the seventeenth century.

PART TWO

FROM UBIQUITY
TO
OBLIVION

FIVE

The National Past in
the Classical Age

KING OF FRANCE: HERCULES, ALEXANDER, AUGUSTUS

The establishment of absolutism continued throughout the seventeenth century, and had all the ingredients of a long epic: revolts of the powerful, plots and betrayals, wars of religion, foreign wars. It took time for the monarchy to triumph over a nobility clinging to its legacy, its prestige, its privileges. It was not until 1659 that the duke of Condé fully rallied behind the king. The aftermath of the wars of religion continued to tear the country apart. Campaigns against the Huguenots were sometimes waged in locations that were permeated with memories of the old *chansons de geste*: in 1621, there was the temporary defeat of the royal armies during the siege of Montauban. The threat of a return to the chaos of the preceding century was ever present. Facing frequent challenges, the monarchy went to great lengths to reflect an image that was apparently impervious to the passing of time, as well as to the ambiguities of identifying with aspects of history. Rather than return to its origins, the monarchy was represented as a form related to an Antiquity freed from the weight of history. Associating itself increasingly with Greco-Roman mythology and with the heroes of ancient Greece and Rome, the monarchy avoided the minefield of national history in order to accede to an atemporal and universal ideal. In a movement begun by Henry IV, the kings of France increasingly had themselves depicted with the traits of Hercules, Alexander, or Augustus.[1] The success of this effort to escape history, to transcend it, to settle down into a timeless, ideal present can be measured by the constancy of later generations in seeing the seventeenth century as a period of classical stability, hence the term by which this period has come to be known: the "classical age."

In many respects, the monarchy drew on the discoveries of humanism to develop a new manner of representing itself. Even as it adapted and became secularized, this new image preserved many of the universalist elements contained in the ideology that had previously made France the eldest daughter of the Church and its king the main defender of the true faith. The monarchy was thus claiming for itself a more neutral ground. Freed from the constraints imposed by the truth of the faith, it was able to assume the guise of the gods and demigods of classical mythology as well as that of the deified Roman emperors. A number of images come to mind. There is the one found on Saint Martin's gate representing Louis XIV–Hercules dressed as *imperator*. There is also Le Brun's painting, which shows the king wearing the *imperator* robes in the Hall of Mirrors at Versailles. Elsewhere we see the king as Jupiter and, of course, as Apollo.[2]

In its own manner, identification with these deities emphasized the sacred nature of the monarchy. It also made it possible to avoid the thorny question of the morality of the king's private life. By gathering all power and all symbols of that power into himself, the monarch reduced the gap between his symbolic and his "private" selves.[3] In this type of context, the laxity of royal morals presented a thorny problem. It was always felt that the moral lapses of Charlemagne or Henry IV needed to be excused or explained. In contrast, the pagan gods could behave in the most scandalous manner, without their immorality sullying the monarch for whom they served as models. Such recourse to Antiquity also had other benefits, notably in relation to the finality of actions. At a time when the notion of "reason of state"[4] was in the process of developing as an end in itself, a reference to Antiquity diminished the problems raised by Christian teleology. From the absolutist perspective, Augustus acted for the greatness of Rome and for his own glory, and these two aims were actually one and the same thing. The images of Antiquity put in the service of the monarchy reinforced the autonomy of politics relative to religion.

As the monarch was increasingly projected as the unique center, the sole wellspring of the kingdom, he also transcended the history of France to assume the prestige and the grandeur of Antiquity. The kings of France embodied the timeless virtues of the ancient gods and heroes, and these universal values were accepted well beyond France's boundaries. Descartes's beliefs contributed philosophical support to this ideological drive to banish history: the Cartesian *ego* was in no way defined in relation to history. For the philosopher, history was an impossible science, a practice devoid of truth or usefulness.

> And even the most accurate of histories, if they do not change or exaggerate the importance of things in order to render them more worthy of being read, almost always at least omit the more base and less notable circumstances thereof: hence the rest does not appear such as it is, and those who regulate their mores by the examples that they draw therefrom are liable to fall into the extravagances of the paladins of our romances and to conceive of plans that exceed their powers.[5]

Descartes's reduction of the best of history to fables about knights is a rejection of national history and its myths. Such a claim was quite logical in a system of thought that postulated an isolated individual as the point of departure for all philosophical reasoning, a system that, consequently, did not account for society as a collective subject.[6] This contrasts with the monarchy's efforts to define itself as the embodiment of the will of this collective subject. Thus, even though an isolated Cartesian self might disregard history, history constituted an essential element of the monarchy.

And yet, the desire to transcend history became an established component of absolutism throughout the seventeenth and eighteenth centuries. Whether the monarchy was modeled on Antiquity or was conceived as an absolute and unprecedented paradigm, as was the reign of Louis XIV at the apex of his glory, or was presented as an interpreter, indeed as the very incarnation of reason, as Voltaire and the physiocrats wished, the absolutist monarchy constantly strove to position itself on a terrain other than that of history. But its own past could never be fully abandoned. This conflict pitted a necessary and radical dependency on history against a need for freedom from it, a freedom that would enable the king to settle into a discursive place from where he could dominate absolutely the various contrasting elements of society.

This new and fundamental conflict concerning its nature and raison d'être would sap the coherence of royal ideology in the seventeenth and eighteenth centuries. In fact, the monarchy seemed to tack with the winds, changing direction depending on the imperatives and the opportunities of any given moment. It attempted to make use of history without ever truly making an effort to occupy the historical terrain in a consistent manner. Relying perhaps too much on a tradition it believed to have been established once and for all, the monarchy failed to renew history to serve new needs, that is, to develop a coherent interpretation of the national past that could be adapted to modern circumstances. Others were to do this in its stead.

Later, on the eve of the Revolution, knowing it had become vulnerable for its lack of interpretation of history, and recognizing that without historical legitimacy it was losing its raison d'être, the monarchy assigned J. N. Moreau the task of writing a royal history that could refute both republican and aristocratic arguments. Moreau did as he was asked, but, as we will see, with a startling frankness he exposed the fragility of an institution that was unable to adapt its vision of history in order to confront the diverging interpretations of the kingdom's ancient constitution. Thus, as to the way the monarchy conceived and represented itself, the very same discursive displacement that had helped the monarchy overcome the troubles of civil war, religious protests, and the plotting of the powerful, was to contribute to its downfall almost two centuries later.

The marginalization of history associated with the establishment of absolutism has direct consequences for the organization of the present study. In order better to understand the place held by the national past, we must look at where it was at issue. Instead of following the neatly drawn line of a strong and clearly defined thematic, we must assemble different fragments and examine them as so many pieces of a jigsaw puzzle, whose meaning can only emerge when all the pieces are put in place. Taken individually, their importance is not evident because the "sites" where the national history is mentioned are scattered. But when examined as a whole, we can better grasp the weight of the national past in the classical age. Focusing on the figure of Charlemagne assures us of a certain coherence. By the very range of significant issues connected to it—France vis-à-vis Germany, France vis-à-vis Rome, the nature of the monarchy, the role of culture, the epic deeds and accomplishments of the great king—Charlemagne's presence resonates like a basso continuo not only at key moments but throughout the century.

We will see that references to the great king multiplied throughout the seventeenth century, reaching a crescendo in the 1660s. At that time the monarchy, feeling more secure, cautiously began to turn toward history again, a history in which Charlemagne played a crucial role. As we will see, there was a myriad of factors, of motives, and of manifestations that ranged from foreign policy to institutional claims, from politics of language to reflections on religion and the human condition. Alongside reassuring images of Louis the Great's illustrious ancestor, other portraits began to be drawn, portraits that raised essential questions about the fundamental assumptions of absolutism. These early attempts at developing an alternative image of the monarchy foreshadowed the great constitutional debates of the eighteenth century in which Charlemagne recovered his central position to such an extent that, as the nation took the path toward Revolution, the old emperor again became one of the strongest images of national consciousness. In the present chapter, we will examine the beginnings of this evolution.

In fact, the monarchy never really attempted to deny the historical nature of its legitimacy. Charlemagne, often accompanied by the Capetian Saint Louis, continued to play a central role in all ceremonial activities. A sword and a crown said to have belonged to Charlemagne were presented during the coronations of Louis XIII, Louis XIV, and during all subsequent coronations up to the Revolution. The 1610 *lit de justice*,[7] whose function was to inaugurate young Louis XIII's reign and, at the same time, to confirm Marie de Medici's regency, was held at the convent of the Grands-Augustins where the Parlement of Paris was meeting due to the preparations taking place in the royal palace (today the Palais de Justice) for the crowned queen's entry into the city. In an anonymous drawing depicting the scene, next to the *lit* (the royal seat) the artist adds a little imaginary detail to give the ceremony a more authentic look: it is a depiction of the famous retable representing Saint Louis and Charlemagne, which was in fact located in the palace (fig. 9).[8] This royal pair, depicting the monarchy's lasting durability, can be found in numerous locations. The *lits de justice* celebrating the coming of age of Louis XIII (in 1614), of Louis XIV (in 1651), and of Louis XV (in 1723) were all held under the gaze of the two ancestors (fig. 10). In 1641, Richelieu held the first mass in Saint-Louis-des-Jésuites[9] on an altar framed by the statues of Charlemagne and Saint Louis. In short the enormous weight and inertia of tradition enabled the monarchy to benefit almost effortlessly from the symbolic capital accumulated over the centuries even as it was busy forging links with Antiquity.

Although the king was increasingly represented as *imperator*, he also maintained his image as Great Monarch.[10] From this perspective, Charlemagne often appears in the histories of the kingdom as the connecting or intermediary figure between the Roman Empire and the French monarchy, between the history of the kingdom and atemporal myth.[11] "Here is a reign of greatness, saintliness, and justice under a great, saintly, and just king," writes Scipion Du Pleix at the start of his narrative on the life and reign of the emperor in his *Histoire générale de France* (1621). "Here is a century of martial arms under the government of a hero. Here is the honor of the Muses under an Apollo. Here is the advancement of French conquests under a conquering prince. Here is the glory of the French empire under a very August emperor."[12] "In sum, the one who wants to draw a good portrait of the prince," writes Mézeray in his *Histoire de France depuis Faramond jusqu'à maintenant* (1643), "should take that of Charlemagne as model . . . because he demonstrated far more piety than all those who wore the crown, and, in my opinion, he matched the beautiful exploits of Caesar and Alexander."[13]

In these works, critical scholarship gives way to rhetorical and moral concerns. The technique of likening Charlemagne to ancient gods and heroes takes the great king out of the historical time frame while creating a link between mythical time and the history of France. In fact, the triumph of humanistic style and oratory was perfectly suited to the needs of a monarchy seeking to make use of its history without having to reinvent it. The French empire partook of the glory of the great empires of the past while surpassing them on the plane of religious truth. The Great Monarch differentiated himself from the *imperator* through his religion.

But religion, of course, raises the issue of morals. This explains the virulence with which Du Pleix attacks Pasquier for turning the emperor "into a goat in his old age, his court into a brothel, his palace into a seraglio of concubines, and his daughters into prostituting wenches."[14] In Du Pleix's opinion Pasquier was a bad Frenchman as well as a bad Catholic when he retold Petrarch's "imposture" about Charlemagne's insane love. Louis XIII's historian was well aware of what was at stake. If one held, as he does, that "the will of the sovereign is an independent law that is absolute and not subject to any control,"[15] any wayward turn of the mind or the senses was akin to a political wrong turn.

During the seventeenth century, royal sexuality, that is, the "private" body of the king, became the dominant metaphor that translated an obsessive concern that the royal will might be only the will of a man. There was no place for "reasons of the heart" in the kingdom of the "reason of state." Thus, under no circumstances should one admit that this great and saintly ancestor, in order to satisfy personal desires, might forget the good of his people and the salvation of his conscience. At times, historians chose to recognize the august emperor's weaknesses while pointing out that he made up for them with his piety and penance. Thus religion appears to have been the only constraint against abuse of power. Sometimes, references that turned Charlemagne into an ancient-style hero seem to excuse and even justify his sexual appetite.

Du Pleix appears to waver between the two interpretations. Having strongly insisted on Charlemagne's piety and on the mortifications he put himself through, he explains that inconstancy is "a vice fairly common in martial temperaments: because . . . natural heat predominates in them, they are of a hot temperament and consequently of an amorous one."[16]

The process of distancing oneself from the critical practice of history that began in the sixteenth century continued to grow, and the legends about Charlemagne became more important in the histories compiled during the seventeenth century. Du Pleix gives a detailed account of the Pseudo-Turpin's narrative on the conquest of Spain even as he points out its fabulous nature. Mézeray goes further. The famous historian completely ignores the separation between history and myth when, having told of the battle between Roland and the giant Ferragus and having discussed Charlemagne's fights against Marsile and Baligant, he suggests that the whole of the story up to Ganelon's treason could be true.[17] In fact, since the "truth of history" had become less important for the monarchy, the distinction between myth and history also lost some of its significance. Thus in the histories of France written throughout the seventeenth century, there is a recurring narrative that in its own way continued to promote and cultivate the glorious image of the conquering emperor.

The writing of absolutist history reached its highest point with Father Daniel. In the preface to his *Histoire de France*, he outlines a restrictive formula that summarizes the way he conceives of his work: "The history of a kingdom or a nation has as object the prince and the state; there is the center to which everything must be directed and referred; and individuals should have a part in it [i.e., history] only in so far as they have relations with one or the other."[18] This representation of national history, developed during the establishment of absolutism, was retained by the eighteenth-century monarchy. Father Daniel's work was published for the first time in 1696 and was reprinted many times in the first half of the following century.[19] Distancing himself from many of Mézeray's excesses, the Jesuit historian discards Turpin's fables and draws mostly from Einhard. However, even though he criticizes the errors and the abuses of his "humanist" predecessors, he still adds an element of marvel to his description of the era of the great ancestor. At this moment when the criterion of verisimilitude ruled not only history but fiction and theater, Father Daniel uses a comparison that allows him to function in two registers at once. In other words, he succeeds in maintaining the image of a certain methodological rigor even as he suggests a divine intervention with regard to Charlemagne: "Even though this sudden birth of a torrent is not unprecedented, . . . it was looked upon as *miraculous*"; "the next day, the French, seeing the path open *as if by a sort of miracle*, entered the plain"; "a panicky terror *that was attributed to the Saint's protection* . . ." (my emphasis).[20]

When it came to morals, the logic of absolutism refused to admit any contradiction between public demeanor and the private behavior of the one embodying the reason of state and the will of the nation. Being the center toward which "everything must be directed," the king could not escape from his subjects' constant gaze. Le Moyne expressed this well in 1665, in his *De l'art de régner*: "The virtue of princes is not constrained and narrow like that of private individuals, who only get to show it in their own homes. The prince has the whole of the kingdom as his theater, and all of his subjects are its spectators."[21] Instead of having to excuse Charlemagne's possible carnal failings, Father Daniel simply turns him into a "model for all of his subjects," filled with respect, tenderness, and solicitude for the queen and concerned with his children's education.[22] Charlemagne, a model for all his subjects, is also a model for all times, since he and Louis XIV occupy the place of "the two greatest princes that ever sat on the throne of France."[23] One might add that this was a model among many potential others. In a regime that emphasized its relationship with Antiquity and that claimed to be an absolute model, the importance of the figure of Charlemagne becomes entirely relative. Moreover, in terms of national history, other examples might seem more appropriate: Saint Louis, who did not generate any dynastic conflicts, or Henry IV who reunited a divided nation and had, in addition, the advantage of existing in very recent history.

In the Service of French Expansionism

There was, however, a domain in which Charlemagne surpassed all other kings, a domain that rendered him a precious and necessary reference for the monarchy: the realm of conquest. Daniel is well aware of this, and he begins his presentation of Charlemagne on that point:

> The kingdom of the French reached the highest level of power it had ever had: a great part of Spain and almost the whole of Italy were conquered; the Saracens were tamed; the boundaries of French domination and that of Christianity had been pushed well beyond the Danube and the Theisse; Dacia, Dalmatia, and Istria had been brought into subjection; barbarian nations as far as the Vistula had been made to pay tribute; the empire of the West with all its prerogatives had been transferred to the House of France; a state of such breadth was governed with conscientiousness and authority and policed by the most beautiful civil and ecclesiastical laws; finally, there had been a continual series of victories and conquests in the space of forty-six years: that is the portrait of the glorious reign of Charlemagne.[24]

There is no reference here to the heroes of Antiquity. A long list of the conquered countries follows with the claim that the rights and prerogatives of the Empire had been transferred (*translatio*)—within a time frame that Father Daniel leaves vague—to the kings of France. With the brief mention of the quality of the reign and the laws, this is how Father Daniel begins his history of the great ancestor. Thus the historian situates Charlemagne's exploits primarily in relation to the Other: the countries of Europe and the Saracens. When the author discusses these vast territories, it is to emphasize their place under French domination. At this point Daniel's use of a collective noun hides the dynastic issue and unavoidably causes him, as if it were an afterthought, to mention Christianity, whose interests he saw as identical to those of France. In fact, Father Daniel's introductory paragraph summarizes a whole current of monarchical reflection and propaganda that was first developed in the second third of the century, shortly after the "Day of Dupes" (November 10, 1630) and the consolidation of power in Richelieu's hands.

The "Dupes" were the queen-mother, Marie de Medici, and the king's brother, Gaston of Orleans, who were forced to flee and to seek refuge with the Hapsburgs in the Netherlands. Richelieu then mobilized his propagandists to help in his aim of strengthening royal policies. These propagandists were writers who elaborated a political and juridical justification for the internal and external policies carried out by the prime minister. As long as war was being waged against the Huguenots, Richelieu was able more or less to maintain the support of the party of the *Devots*. But after La Rochelle was taken and Richelieu adopted a resolutely anti-Hapsburg policy, he faced opposition from the queen mother and from Gaston of Orleans, who tried to reverse that policy. Emerging victorious from this crisis, which ultimately led to the Day of Dupes, Richelieu worked to have the defeat of Marie de Medici and the duke of Orleans pass as a triumph over the Spanish party. Surrounded by the Hapsburgs, France was in a very delicate diplomatic situation. Within the Empire, Ferdinand II had been gradually strengthening his power during the Thirty Years' War at the expense of the Protestants.

Richelieu was constantly attempting to improve France's position within Europe, and, to do this, he often called upon history. Unless he were simply to accept the ideology of "might makes right," he had to find a justification for his very broad view of French interests. At a time when the idea of international laws that might rule the affairs between different countries had scarcely been born, only historical and genealogical justification could be called upon to establish claims and rights. And military might would still be needed to have those rights prevail. In the meanwhile, Richelieu prepared the ground by assigning writers and jurists the task of defining the rights of France in relation to her neighbors.[25] And here the figure of Charlemagne as conqueror proved to be ideal.

The strategy essentially consisted of using early conquests as legal justification and then of developing a fundamental distinction between those early conquests and later "usurpations." In 1624, Richelieu appointed a commission that included Pierre Dupuy and was headed by Cardin Le Bret to investigate usurpations of lands in the bishoprics of Metz, Toul, and Verdun. In 1627, the king ordered Jacques de Cassan, the head lawyer of the presidial court of Beziers, to research the king's rights to "several estates, duchies, counties, towns, and rural areas" that had been taken from the sovereignty of the king of France.[26] In his *Mémoire sur l'origine des maisons et duchés de Lorraine et de Boulle-le-Duc* [Report on the Origins of Houses and Duchies of Lorraine and Boulle-le-Duc], Louis Chantereau-Lefevre strives to prove that the House of Lorraine did not descend from Charlemagne. Putting the science of diplomatics in the service of the king, the jurists Dupuy and Théodore Godefroy searched the archives in order to turn Richelieu's territorial claims into rights.[27] Although other kings are mentioned, Charlemagne's name appears most often for the good reason that he had conquered the largest territories and because, as we have seen, many charters and documents cite him as the source of rights and privileges.

Such treatises touted the principle of inalienability of the royal domain. Kings held the crown in trust, and under no circumstances could they grant anyone else rights over any of the territories of the kingdom. The fact that those rights originated in such a distant time did not weaken them, "on the contrary, this deep antiquity adds to their strength," states Jacques de Cassan in the most famous of the treatises, *La Recherche des droicts du Roy, et de la Couronne de France sur les royaumes, duchez, comtez, villes et pays occupez par les Princes estrangers: Appartenans aux Roys Très-Chrestiens, par Conquestes, Successions, Achasts, Donations, et autres Tiltres legitimes. Ensemble de leurs droicts sur l'Empire, et des devoirs et hommages deus à leur Couronne, par divers Princes Estrangers* [Research on the Rights of the King and the Crown of France over the Kingdoms, Duchies, Counties, Towns, and Rural Areas Occupied by Foreign Princes and Belonging to the Most Christian Kings through Conquests, Successions, Purchases, Donations, and Other Legitimate Titles. This along with Their Rights over the Empire and the Duties and Homages Owed to Their Crown by Various Foreign Princes]. Thus, "in spite of their ancientness, Charlemagne's rights have been transmitted to His Majesty." Any treaty or pact proposing a renunciation of these rights would be invalid, because the crown could not be subject to the twists and turns of fortune. Although Cassan does not hesitate to cite Clovis, Charles Martel, and even Brennus, the first emperor of the West is the one who held the key to a good portion of national rights. In the opinion of this advocate of the French monarchy, Spain, Portugal, and Italy belonged to France. Going from south to north, he shows that Lorraine, of course, was French, but also all of Germany was an "ancient member of the kingdom of France."[28] The litany goes on without end, and at times it almost sounds like a *chanson de geste:*

> During Charlemagne's reign, the Saxons, a people impatient with rest and peace, in order to gain back their freedom, decided to emancipate themselves from the duty of obedience in the year 768. The war was

long and bloody, but in the end Charlemagne with the help of a lord of the area called Widukind, won a victory over them. . . . The Huns and the Avars, who were also Hungarians and had waged war on France for eight years, were subjugated and vanquished and their country united with the kingdom of France. In addition, the Sunois, the Sorabes, Abrodites, and Westphalians, who had made an alliance in this war with the Hungarians, were powerfully tamed by Charlemagne, who by his glorious and illustrious victories enlarged the limits of his kingdom to the farthest countries of the North: because Hungary, Austria, Valachia, Bohemia, Transylvania, and Poland, conquered by his valor, enriched his treasures, which were more beautiful and larger than those of the great Alexander. Denmark was also a part of the state of Charlemagne.[29]

There was still the problem of the imperial crown, and here Charlemagne's case raises more questions than did Clovis's or Philip Augustus's. The jurist, "adviser to the king," responds in several ways. He claims that all of these territories belonged to Charlemagne as king of France and not as emperor. Reducing the great conqueror's accession to the imperial crown to an epiphenomenon, Cassan alternates between denigrating the imperial function, whose seat was not even established, and denouncing German usurpation: "The imperial crown belongs legitimately to the Most Christian kings, exclusive of all other princes, in view of the fact that it was given to Charlemagne's successors by the pope."[30] Of course, Cassan emphasizes the continuity and the permanency of the French monarchy and, like the *Grandes Chroniques*, he claims Philip Augustus belonged to Charlemagne's line.[31] The usurpation of the Empire only occurred at the cost of its transformation into an elective crown, which made it "an aristocratic state rather than a monarchical one" and which led to its decline.[32] In sum, according to these arguments, the logic of the principle of non-alienability of royal possessions combined with the rights gained through early conquests gave France sufficient justification to intervene almost anywhere it wanted! It was up to Richelieu to choose the place and the time in relation to the balance of power at any given moment.

Richelieu's opponents decried these justifications of his aggressive policy, which was leading to so much public misery. *La Voix gémissante du peuple chrétien* [The Wailing Voice of the Christian People] criticizes the prime minister: "It is in vain that you strain your mind to recover the loss of the first successors of Charlemagne and unearth these old quarrels of which history has barely been able to preserve any intact vestige or any untroubled light."[33]

But while the regime's detractors pointed out the arrogance of the undertaking, the frequency with which Cassan's treatise was brought up shows it must nevertheless have had a certain effectiveness. Published for the first time in 1632, it was reprinted on numerous occasions during the 1630s and 1640s. The needs of the state brought the mythistory of Charlemagne's empire back to life by investing it with a certain juridical value. Cassan himself pushes his argument to logical limits when, in the dedication of his work, he suggests that the cardinal should "bring back to the royal power all of these states that were usurped" and even "extend the limits of France to the ends of the earth."[34] However, the acquisition of the imperial crown was not foremost among Richelieu's and Louis XIII's concerns. Their goal was rather to clear a safe path through the quicksand of European politics in this first half of the seventeenth century. For Richelieu, that path was to lead the kingdom of France to a dominant position relative to its neighbors without resorting to the title of emperor.[35]

Louis XIV's intentions were much more concrete. An entire cultural war machine backed a diplomatic and military policy aimed at ensuring French domination over all of Europe. But France was not the only nation dreaming of hegemony. The House of Austria still threatened to unite the imperial crown to the Spanish throne. Under the Sun King, France's foreign policy could be looked upon either as essentially defensive or as fundamentally aggressive and warlike. Regardless of how we might view this issue, Louis XIV's claims to the empire and the maneuvering in that direction by Mazarin and the king were motivated more by an anti-Hapsburg policy than by a real desire to wear the imperial crown.[36]

Louis glorified the French monarchy while depreciating the imperial crown. In his *Mémoires pour l'année 1661*, Louis XIV raises the issue of the Empire and notes that he found it of little interest. Instead of seeing Charlemagne as a link between the Roman Empire and the French monarchy, Louis XIV states that the great French king founded a new empire. "He rose to that high point of glory not by being elected by a few princes but by his courage and the victories that are the election and the votes of Heaven itself when he resolved to submit the other powers to a single one."[37] Thus Charlemagne's greatness, which he forged as king of France, founded the title of emperor. And yet, while the French monarchy endured and maintained its prestige, the Empire did not. In fact, Charlemagne's empire ceased to exist shortly after the great warrior's death. Though the Germans appropriated the title, their empire had nothing to do either with the Roman Empire or with that of the great king. "Because in truth they should be looked upon only as chiefs and captains of a Republic of Germany."

This effort to inflate his own glory and to increase his prerogatives at the expense of the imperial image inspired a genuine ideological campaign that Louis undertook in the 1660s. Just as Richelieu did before him, the king's aim was to justify the broadest possible range of expansion. Tactics involving language differed little from those used by Cassan, but the tone of the message grew bolder and bolder as the years went by. Charles Sorel, who was also the author of the *Histoire comique de Francion*, having succeeded his uncle in the office of royal historiographer, states in his *Traités sur les droits et prérogatives des rois de France* that the "king of France is the first king of the universe and that he has the immemorial right to take precedence over all others."[38] Like Cassan, he walks us through Europe to assert the rights of the French kings to reclaim the territories France had conquered in the past. And, of course, Charlemagne becomes the cornerstone of his argument. The great king vanquished the Spaniards, conquered Italy, overcame Germany. He did not dominate the Saxons as much as he freed them. Charlemagne created the empire, and France has maintained its right to the imperial crown. In fact, the seat of the empire of the West should be in France, not in Germany. But regardless of where it is located, according to Sorel, the preeminence of the French monarchy has never been in doubt. Its absolute nature is proof of its superiority, because the French monarch is chosen by God and not elected by men. As for England, not only were its kings Charlemagne's vassals but if one goes back far enough in history one discovers that "to it [England] are attributed quite ancient kings, but their names and deeds seem to be works of the imagination and are more beholden to fable than to history."[39] As for Charlemagne, the fact that he belonged to history seems to justify having recourse to legend.

The most famous work devoted to the preeminence of the French monarchy was that of Antoine Aubery, *Des justes prétentions du Roy sur l'Empire* [The Legitimate Claims of the King to the Empire]. This treatise was published during the first months of 1667 during preparations for the War of Devolution, and it provoked an angry reaction from the German side.[40] It is of interest not only because of its imperialistic aims but also because of its conscious attempt to associate Antiquity with the history of France, while aiming to establish the juridical legitimacy of France's expansionist policy. In his dedicatory epistle to the king, Aubery points out:

> In all times Kings were looked upon as Heroes and Demigods, and it was always thought that their appearance exuded a radiance that imprinted in the heart of their subjects respect and religion. And what should be noted, Sire, is that these positive feelings and expressions were not only part of the style of paganism but also of the language of councils and the Holy Fathers, who did not hesitate to treat Sovereigns as Sacred Majesties and to name their gaze celestial splendor, in a word, to prostrate themselves at their feet or, to use their own words, to worship the footsteps of their Saintliness.[41]

The author develops the metaphor of the Sun King in his epistle and this leads him, at the beginning of the first chapter, to praise Paris, "rightfully the rival of the old and new Rome, whose glory it has not only equaled but surpassed."[42] Having already outlived the combined duration of the Roman Republic and Empire, the French monarchy, the first and most ancient of all, has in some ways surpassed time itself and has reached a stage where "it does not grow old, and whose age, always young and flourishing, promises it an eternity equal to that of the stars."[43] In this argument, longevity is used as a springboard to leap out of time, while the mixture of Greco-Roman antiquity and Christian modernity supports the arguments of "juridical" right and eternal glory. Even though the France of Louis XIV is unique in the history of the world, it has nonetheless inherited all the prestige and all the prerogatives accumulated by its ancestors since Clovis.

Aubery proves to be resolutely modern: nothing has ever surpassed the immediate present. Even the great emperor with the flowing white beard, to whom Aubery frequently turns in matters of right, "is too weak a model compared to *our own* [king], whose heroic actions will make posterity recognize that he has successfully erased Charlemagne's glory and surpassed by far all the kings, his predecessors, in valor and wisdom."[44] Only precedents remain of this history that is abolished in the present. However, without the detour through history, it would be impossible to distinguish between the two kinds of possession—"one *de facto* and the other *de jure*"—between usurpation and legitimacy.[45]

There is little difference between most of Aubery's arguments and those of Cassan. The first part of his treatise deals with the ancientness of the French monarchy. Institutionally, the monarchy is the same under Louis XIV as it was under Clovis. The only limit imposed on the power of the king is the prohibition to alienate his realm. In the second part of his treatise, the apologist for the prerogatives of the king of France states that Germany "is the patrimony and the ancient legacy of the French princes."[46] But he goes further than other propagandists when, drawing from Einhard, he claims that the French and the Germans, just like the French and the Saxons, are "one and the same people."[47] In the third and final part, Aubery shows the inferiority of the imperial dignity in relation to the title of king. The French monarchy is that which succeeded the Roman crown. Although Charlemagne acceded to the Empire, his elevation was due to his conquering virtue more than to his coronation by the pope.

History, rights, dignity: in all areas France is triumphant. It comes as no surprise then that the Germans reacted strongly against such an argument. In his *Bouclier d'Estat et de Justice, contre le dessein manifestement découvert de la Monarchie Universelle, sous le vain pretexte des pretensions de la Reyne de France* [Shield of the State and of Justice against the Designs for Universal Monarchy under the Vain Pretext of the Pretensions of the Queen of France], the baron de Lisola denounces these justifications of aggression and conquest and calls upon Europe to be vigilant.[48] Rather than surpassing history, he warns, the French will repeat it: this is proven by the insistence with which they connect themselves to Charlemagne.

IN THE SERVICE OF SCHOLARSHIP AND LETTERS

Paralleling this expansionist policy and rhetoric, there was a substantial amount of literature supporting and justifying the internal policies of absolutism. In this domain, arguments relied only to a small extent on historical precedents. Thus Charlemagne's name remained marginal though he was not totally absent. Under Richelieu, the policy of confrontation with regard to the Hapsburgs was a necessary complement to the prime minister's attempt to consolidate and strengthen the monarchy within the kingdom. The threat posed by the enemy was used to legitimize the state's increasing power, that is, the power of the king and his agents. Action was necessary to prevent harm: "On the basis of a simple suspicion," writes Guez de Balzac in *Le Prince* (1632), "on the basis of a slight doubt, on the basis of a dream of the prince, why should he not be permitted to deal with his factious subjects and ease his mind by meting out their own rest [death] as punishment?"[49] Government must thus have pure intentions, and the prince owes that purity to "the force of his reason, assisted by the grace of God."[50] In this kingdom, where the sovereign "sees in a mode different from our own" and where "he is guided by a purer light than that of ordinary reason,"[51] prudence wins out over justice so that evil can be uncovered and prevented from causing harm. "Justice only pertains to the actions of men, but prudence has a right over their thoughts and their secrets. It looks far into the future, it looks to the general interest."[52] In the name of the general interest, there must be complete transparency. In other words, the prince has a right to an absolute gaze, as elsewhere he has the right to hide and disguise the truth, because the end justifies the means.

Controlling thoughts required institutional support. Three years before the creation of the French Academy, Cardin Le Bret, another theoretician of absolutism, claimed that no "company," no corporate body could be constituted without the authority of the sovereign. According to Cardin Le Bret, the good prince filters all forms of knowledge which circulated around him. For this, he had to establish proper institutions himself, and he had to deal particularly with the education of the youth to "prevent them from being taught maxims contrary to Religion and to the fundamental laws of the state."[53] And yet, such a notion already implied a history of privileges and benefits. Hadn't the various institutions been in existence forever in France? Le Bret demonstrates that the main body for teaching, the university, was created by Charlemagne. The great monarch, "appearing as a new sun in the world, dissipated the clouds of ignorance and reignited in the heart of the French the desire to study, through the great honors he bestowed on men of letters and the establishment of this famous University of Paris he organized with so much good sense and prudence that, since then, it has served as model for all the great princes and republics of Europe."[54] The great French emperor marked the end of barbarism and the beginning of a new era throughout Europe, and his sovereignty over the university enabled the proper diffusion of knowledge. One cannot find a better example of the extent to which the creation of institutions served both a policy of glory and of control.

In this corporatist society reclaiming one's past had not lost its legitimizing value. Whereas the monarchy could accept exiting from history, this was not the case for corporate bodies and the other institutions under its authority. Inside the kingdom, institutions behaved toward each other a bit like sovereign countries on an international scale. In an absolute monarchy the relative distinction of institutional bodies depended on their ancientness and their proximity to the monarchy. As the king founded new institutions, older ones attempted to show that they had existed since time immemorial and that they too had been created by the king. A striking example of these discursive strategies is seen in the institutions responsible for defining and diffusing knowledge.

At the end of the sixteenth century, the University of Paris had lost much of its power and lustre. Already under Charles VII the ordinance of 1445 put it under the jurisdiction of the Parlement, in spite of its claim to be directly under royal authority. There were other universities in Orleans, Angers, Poitiers, Bourges, Bordeau, and Reims that were competing more and more with the University of Paris, which was also unhappy with the privileges granted to the Royal College. In addition, the Jesuits, the Oratorians, and the Benedictines continued their attempts to have their teaching functions increased. Since 1635, the star of the French Academy had continued to rise. Confronted with these very diverse rivals and in order to regain its preeminence, the university resorted to its claims of ancientness, as well as its proximity to the king. In 1661, the rector, Du Boulay, tried to reestablish the feast of Saint Charlemagne. In a meeting held on December 16, 1661, the faculty of arts ordered all the directors (*principaux*) of the collèges to celebrate the *Carlomagnalia* on January 28. The faculty then gave an institutional twist to that day by ordering the rector to publish written instructions on the solemn celebration every year. From that time on, as a school holiday instead of a religious one, the feast of Saint Charlemagne turned into a custom that survived the Ancien Régime as well as several restorations and republics, and fell into oblivion only at the end of the first half of the twentieth century.[55]

In his *Histoire de l'Université de Paris* (1665), Du Boulay retraces the glorious past of this institution. In his dedicatory epistle, the rector-historian claims that the university's origin went back to "the one who submitted Italy, the Saxons, Germany" and who attracted people from as far as Greece and England as well as from Spain and Italy to France. The author points out the parallel between the *Rex Augustissimus* and his illustrious predecessor.[56] In spite of Pasquier and the "demythifications" of the sixteenth century, the *translatio studii* is reborn under the pen of the defender of the university.[57] Paris had taken Rome's place, just as Rome had surpassed Athens. Charlemagne was the "parent, the teacher, the founder" of this "first Academy"; he was the one who knew how to draw knowledge out of obscurity and put it in the light, who drew it out of private cells to put it into the public arena (*è* [sic] *privatis cellusis in publicum forum*).[58]

Du Boulay tries hard to emphasize the relationship between the university and the state, between the institution, bearer of true culture, and the monarch. Because of this relationship Charlemagne turned Paris into a cultural seat, attracting scholars from all over the world to the city. Thus Du Boulay attempts to reinforce the image of the university relative to a whole gamut of institutions, including other centers of knowledge and erudition such as monasteries. The dark "cells" of the monasteries had hidden knowledge, whereas the "eminent Academy" brought it back to the secular public place and put it within everyone's reach.

One cannot help thinking that Mabillon had these sorts of passages in mind when he evokes the figure of Charlemagne in his *Traité des études monastiques* (1691). This Benedictine scholar devotes a great deal of space to the emperor for Charlemagne's reestablishment of the study of letters and for his having restored discipline in the monasteries and abbeys. In his treatise, Mabillon develops an apologia for a conception of monastic life that placed scholarship at the center of monastic activities. He argues that engaging in scholarship is not an end in itself, since monastic communities were set up to be "academies" of virtue. But scholarly discipline is a necessary component of religious perfection, to such an extent that, without it, monasteries would sink into dissipation and commerce with the world, in short, would follow a path leading to "the total ruin of the monastic spirit."[59]

The scholarly mission goes back to Charlemagne. Mabillon cites a circular letter the emperor had addressed to the abbot of Fulda, calling for the restoration of letters. Mabillon believed that Charlemagne had sought to impose a "life that would be regular and that conformed to the rules of good morals prescribed by religion" as well as to ensure a proper understanding of the Holy Scriptures, without which one falls "into errors of sentiments." Thus the erudite monk returns to an originary moment, in this case the reestablishment of learning that put an end to barbarism, in order to legitimize the scholarly activities of Benedictine monks. But given the widespread view that knowledge belonged in the public domain and was in the service of the state (Le Bret and Du Boulay come to mind here), Mabillon faced the objection that scholarship was not an appropriate activity for monks and clergy in general. Mabillon's assertion that the recommendation to study applied not only to monks but also to the clerics and canons of the cathedrals was not sufficient to refute the argument. This great scholar foresaw an objection that threatened to pervert the very origin of scholarship, that is, Charlemagne's intention: "Some might say that these sentiments were fine coming from the mouth of an emperor because his primary consideration was *political* and that, not knowing the purity of monastic life, he wanted to establish schools in the monasteries *less for the particular benefit of these institutions than for public usefulness.*"[60] Without denying that the great prince did have some political motivations, the Benedictine monk insists on the fact that "the main motive pertained to the *particular usefulness* for the monasteries and the monks" (my emphasis).[61] Thus Mabillon carefully blends a corporatist element with his historical justification in an attempt to refute criticism from within the Church itself. In this context, an argument based solely on the general interest would have weakened his position. It was necessary for him to show that concern for the monks' specific welfare lay at the heart of Charlemagne's intentions.[62]

The Survival of Roland

The texts we have just examined enable us to understand better in what way and to what extent history counted in seventeenth-century society. Whenever the collectivity was discussed, and particularly when one was attempting to determine one's respective place in it (or to mask it in order to occupy a different one), the need arose to look to the past. Thus, although classical culture triumphed in that century, the national past was never discarded.[63] Although individuals could well have themselves represented as heroes or gods of Antiquity, when it was a matter of showing one's credentials, Romans and Greeks could not compete with French ancestors.

The survival of the French hero was not limited to legal or propaganda documents. In French, the word for romance is the same as the word for novel, both being designated by the word *roman*. During this period, as the modern novel begins to come into its own, the *chansons de geste* were considered as old *romans* (*vieux romans*) and were often associated without much distinction with the Italian works translated into French. In his novel (*roman*), *Histoire comique de Francion*, Charles Sorel writes at length about his hero's passion for such readings when he was a young man. When Francion tells of his life at college in Paris, he describes how he spent his money:

> I bought those books called *romans* that told of the prowess of certain knights. Sometime previously one of my companions had talked me into reading one about Morgant the Giant that completely enchanted me, because I had never read anything besides Cicero's letters and Terence's comedies. I was told of a bookstore of the Palace that sold several fabulous stories of the same kind, and it was there that I brought my money; but I assure you that I was a good customer, because I was so afraid of never getting my hands on what I was burning to buy, I gave all that the merchant asked. . . . In short, I had nothing anymore in my mind but encounters, tournaments, castles, orchards, spells, deliciousness, love affairs, and when I told myself that all that was only fiction, I said that it was nonetheless wrong to censure the reading of them and that henceforth we should follow the lifestyle described in my books; and then I often started to blame the vile occupations of the men of this century, [occupations] by which I am completely horrified today.[64]

In this novel, then, the hero's taste for *vieux romans* or what we would call romances is born, so to speak, under the sign of the legend of Charlemagne. Pulci's work had been translated as early as the sixteenth century, but it was reprinted in Troyes in 1618 and in 1625, just before Sorel inserted the reference to *Morgant* in a new edition of his novel published in 1626.[65] Sorel himself claimed ties to old nobility; he boasted of a genealogy going back to the old kings of England.[66] In fact, he came from a bourgeois family of lawyers, and his father had fought on the side of the League during the wars of religion. It is not surprising that he bought a position as royal historiographer and even claimed to be "first historiographer to the king." In order to show off his function, Sorel, in his *Traité de la charge d'historiographe de France* [Treatise on the Office of Historiographer of France], begins the presentation of his predecessors by mentioning Einhard.[67]

The *Histoire comique de Francion* belongs to the genre of tales of initiation: its hero is a young noble of old stock who despises the newer nobility of the "robe." But Sorel's novel also reveals traces of the legacy of the *Fronde*. For Morgant describes an uprising of nobles led by Renaud de Montauban. Charlemagne falls under the influence of flatterers headed by Ganelon. Here the traitor is the very embodiment of hypocritical flattery in his mastery of language and his sacrifice of the good of the kingdom for his own gain. This work almost seems to describe the *Fronde* before its time when we see Charlemagne forced to flee his palace and go into hiding to avoid being overthrown, perhaps even murdered, by the insurgent nobles. Roland comes to the rescue, but not before admonishing him:

> Sire and Uncle, says Roland, you well know that you are to blame for the ills that have befallen you because everyone knows that my cousin Renault along with Astolfo, the lord of England, and those of their lineage have served you loyally and in many places and have put their bodies on the line and their lives in danger against the Saracens and others many times so as to defend your rights and support your kingdom and keep you in peace, and, as sole reward, upon the request of some flatterers and traitors who never did anything for you but harm, you banish them from your court, and, worse, you want to have them killed at the gibbet as if they were petty crooks: this is why I am not surprised that Renault and his kin want to seek vengeance, since they are strong and powerful, and I do not know of anyone, no matter how small they might be, who would not call for revenge on those who repaid the good they themselves have done with harm.[68]

Throughout the seventeenth century, prose translations of the *chansons de geste* continued to be published, often in Troyes. *Les Quatre fils Aymon* [The Four Aymon Sons], a romance dealing with Renaud de Montauban's revolt, was published in 1613, 1625, and 1708; *Fierabras* in 1640, 1664, and 1705; *Galien* in 1606, 1622, 1640, 1679, and 1709.[69] As the references to them in Sorel's novel demonstrates, the "Bibliothèque bleue," a series of "popular books" reached a fairly large and relatively educated audience.[70] (Let us not forget that Francion was the son of a country nobleman whose origins were "among the noblest and most ancient.")[71] During a period marked both by uprisings and by a heightening of national sentiment, the sword and the robe could both find something to their advantage in these romances.

But the works were also able to please the royalists, or at any rate their content did not inspire the monarchy to pursue a policy of censorship, for in the end Charlemagne is always triumphant in these tales. Even before coming to the subject of the emperor with the flowing white beard, *Fierabras* tells the whole "mythical" history of France from the time of Francus and the ancient origins of the kingdom through Clovis's conversion and the story of the holy Ampulla, that is, through the sacred origins of the monarchy. Furthermore, the *chanson de geste* gets to its subject matter only after presenting a description of the life of Charlemagne as that of a model king.[72] Incorporating elements from various sources such as Einhard, Pseudo-Turpin, Vincent de Beauvais, and the *Descriptio* of the journey to

Constantinople, the tale retraces the path of the great emperor who through his power doubled the territory of the kingdom of France, defended the faith, sent his advisers everywhere in the country to render justice to all and to protect everyone's rights, and made people respect the law.

The popularity of the old romances was rooted in the interstices of the culturally hegemonic place occupied by Antiquity. There were two currents that led the people of the seventeenth century toward the old national literature: a yearning for a grander, more elevated ethos than that of the present and the quest for an epic poetry worthy of the glory of France. Thus two very different and in some sense almost contradictory feelings converged in a gaze that was directed at a specifically French past: a rejection of the mores of the century and an affirmation of national values.

Sorel laments the vile behavior of his century and suggests that the world should be changed so as to make it similar to the one found in the romances. In his *De la lecture des vieux romans* (1647), Jean Chapelain states that upon reading the old romances filled with chivalrous defenders of women and orphans we can see "how the centuries closest to our own, as they have progressed toward enlightenment [*lumière*], have gotten farther away from virtue and into what disorders of life and corruption souls have fallen."[73] This awareness of an ethical legacy reconciling reasons of the heart with reasons of state drew much more on courtly romances than on the epic matter of the *chansons de geste*. Chapelain, the famous academician, appears as a character in a dialogue composed by Jean-François Sarasin that constituted a sequel to *De la lecture des vieux romans*. In *S'il faut qu'un jeune homme soit amoureux* [If a Young Man Must Be in Love] (1649), the character Ménage sees in Roland's story an example of the nefarious effects of love. If we go back to those people from "the good old days," those "brave ones elevated above all others through their great deeds," to the century "when nothing in the world was as great as our court, where Charlemagne ruled the empire of the West and could almost count the days of his reign by the number of his victories, where paladins preserved justice, protected widows, and, finally, did more good for men with their swords than the combined pens of Plato and Aristotle," we discover a Roland crazed with love, abandoning his uncle to the mercy of the infidels, a knight who, for personal reasons, wanders around in the East at the moment when Paris is threatened.[74] Later, the character of Chapelain argues that his friend is not speaking of the old French romances but of a deformation foreign to the French tradition. Ariosto is no more deserving of trust than are the Spanish novelists and "our worst romances," including that of Archbishop Turpin, who claimed that Roland ruptured "the main vein of his heart by blowing too hard on his horn."[75]

In his own treatise, Chapelain turns away from the Carolingian epic in favor of the courtly romance. He discovers France's own Hercules in

Lancelot, and its own Homer in the author of *Perceforêt*.[76] In these French romances, love makes knights brave, and the more they love, the greater their valor. These works provide us with "perfect images" of French ancestors' morals and customs and constitute a "supplement to the annals."[77] By showing us what lies at the "bottom of their souls," they allow us to go beyond appearances and simple events. In *Le Vray Théâtre d'honneur et de chevalerie ou le miroir héroique de la noblesse*, Vulson de la Colombière focuses primarily on the Arthurian cycle and on the tradition of the Round Table. The courtly tradition is seductive precisely because it teaches proper morality, it is an education that can reconcile the needs of the individual with those of the city. The key is that these romances tell not only about feats of arms but also explore the inner feelings of individuals.

Nevertheless, Charlemagne's nephew does survive and even triumphs in the seventeenth century. If there is an element of the Middle Ages that succeeds in holding its own against the heroes, gods, and demigods of Antiquity, it is the adventures of the valiant Roland and Renaud as told by Ariosto and Tasso.[78] While Tasso's *Jerusalem Delivered*, an epic poem about the First Crusade, takes place after the time of Charlemagne, the adventures of Ariosto's, Pulci's, and Boiardo's Rolands occur during the great emperor's reign. In fact, Charlemagne's history survives in "worldly" culture to the extent that it blends epic material with that of courtly romances.

Ariosto was the main inspiration for plays centered on Charlemagne. In general, they raise the issue, unavoidable in the seventeenth century, of the relationship between love and politics, between individual happiness and collective salvation, but also that of the relationship between the nobility and the king.[79] During Louis XIV's reign, Calprenède borrows the story of Bradamante from Garnier in a tale in which Bradamante refuses a marriage that her father wants to impose on her. Her father, Aymon, turns to Charlemagne and laments his lack of power:

> I will not complain that I have one hundred times
> For the good of the State sweated under the harness,
> . . . .
> If you let blood and reason act,
> If I were absolute master in my own house,
> . . . .
> I intercede in vain with an ingrate daughter,
> Instead of being absolute master over my whole family.[80]

There is tension here between the king and the nobleman as well as between the father's vision of familial duty and the daughter's desire for happiness. The king mediates all relationships, even those within the family. Leon clearly expresses the king's relationship with the "great knights" when he addresses Charlemagne: they "do well add to the shine of your crown, / But it is above all from you that it receives its luster."[81] The monarchical reading of Ariosto also resonates in Jean de Mairet's *Roland furieux*. This play depicts a Roland who claims he is to be pitied more than Charlemagne. For although the great king and his court are threatened by the Saracens, the enemy is outside the walls whereas he himself "has love in his stomach" eating at him night and day. At the end of the play, Astolphe strongly scolds the emperor's nephew (Roland) who, because of his preference for "the love of a Pagan / over the salvation of France and the Christian faith," has come to neglect his duty and lose his senses.[82]

CHARLEMAGNE AT THE COURT OF THE SUN KING

Representations of Charlemagne were scarce in the courtly milieu prior to the time Louis began to rule personally. However, the defeat of the *Fronde* and the strengthening of the monarchy appeared to have reduced the risks posed by historical references. Thus in the 1660s there was a renewal of interest in the great emperor.[83] The development of a "historical" justification of Louis XIV's foreign policy corresponded to the beginning of a return to national history domestically as well.

In 1661, the court was eagerly awaiting the completion of *Hercule amoureux*. This opera was to celebrate both the wedding of Louis XIV with Maria Theresa of Austria and the Treaty of the Pyrenees. To help distract the court during the long wait, the *Ballet de l'impatience*, dealing precisely with the theme of the frustration of waiting, was created. Benserade wrote the story and the verses introducing each character. The plot featured Charlemagne, who was filling in for a tardy Hercules: perhaps a mere coincidence, but also a sign foreshadowing the future. Condé was among the nobles who were dancing in this ballet, and Benserade took advantage of his presence to slip in an allusion to the defection and recent submission of this prince of the royal blood. In the third part of the ballet, the king plays the role of a "knight of the old chivalry" (*Chevalier de l'ancienne chevalerie*). When the poet is ready to designate the new queen by name, he points out that her "lover" is descended from Charlemagne.

> Here is the fine flower of chivalry
> Who surpasses by far our fabulous heroes
>   In brave deeds as well as in gallantry;
> Indeed, this marvelous Prince
> Whom love follows everywhere, whom glory accompanies
>   Is of the pure blood of Charlemagne.

———

Whether he is dancing or fighting, as soon as he appears
We can see his heroic greatness above all others;
He is the honor and support of the order to which he belongs.
   Knighthood is ancient,
Dating, I believe, from the time of my first ancestors;
   But the Knight is not old.

———

War and discord he has stifled in our time;
Without his head and his hands they would still be on the rise.
He turned their fall into his trophy,
   In short, he pacified everything:
By giving us peace and giving himself *Theresa,*
   He made us all feel at ease.[84]

The queen surely noticed the allusion. Confronting the Hapsburgs, to whom he would henceforth be united by marriage, Louis XIV reclaimed his relationship with his ancestor Charlemagne. In 1664, a play by Gabriel Gilbert, drawing very freely from Ariosto, was performed at the Hôtel de Bourgogne. Although Charlemagne does not appear in it, the play's characters mention him often. At the end of the play all the players turn toward this prince, who is to "turn the whole world into a single province":

But let us honor the hero of the French,
The wisest of mortals and the greatest of kings,
Who is renowned in peace as well as in war,
Who has just shared the empire of the world,
Whose rare virtue shines everywhere,
Whose standard shows lilies intertwined with eagles.[85]

This play was dedicated to Louis XIV and, in its own way, upheld the king's claims to the Empire. In his dedicatory epistle, Gilbert praises Louis XIV by stating that his reign was to be no less great than that of his illustrious ancestor, who was able to make flourish both letters and arms. Now all that was needed was a man to write down his valorous exploits, as had been done for the Greeks and the Romans. Then, "antiquity would have nothing to reproach us, and our age would be comparable to the heroic times."[86] In May of this same year, during the knightly carousel enacted for the famous performance of the *Plaisirs de l'Ile enchantée,* the king and a group of nobles played Ariosto's characters, who themselves were competing in the Pythian games played to entertain the queens. Singing of the greatness of the kingdom of Louis XIV, Apollo compares it to that of Greece in valor, merit, and skills. But the sun god also points out that the time of Antiquity is past and that now he shuns it in favor of France, whose destiny, thanks to the queen, is universal monarchy.

A thousand different climates are seen under the power
Of all the demigods who gave it birth,
Yielding as much to its [France's] merit as to the demands of duty,
They will find themselves one day united under its power.
The greatness that France and Spain had,
The rights of Charles V, the rights of Charlemagne,
With their blood happily transmitted,
Will give back the whole submitted universe to its throne.[87]

These verses foreshadow the waging of the War of Devolution that broke out in 1667. There could be no clearer connection between the idea of the greatness of modernity and the plan for European domination.

The whole spectacle was clearly meant to impress all those who had gathered at Versailles, as well as to those influenced by the various accounts of it. But it was also a play in which the nobility performed. The king himself played the role of Roger, the duke of Noailles played Oger the Dane, and the duke of Guise played Aquilant the Black. The role of the emperor's nephew was reserved for the duke of Enghien, the Great Condé's son:

Roland's name will be heard far and wide;
Glory will become his faithful companion.
He comes from a blood burning to spill out
When the plan is to wage a campaign;
And to tell the truth,
It is the pure blood of Charlemagne.[88]

A performance inspired by the story of Roland, the king himself playing the role of a noble, and the duke of Enghien embodying the "pure blood of Charlemagne": all this would certainly have appealed to the nobility. After all, the play situated the nobility at the center of the great royal entertainment and of its glorious "past." However, viewed from another angle, it was also a means of showing the nobility's ineptness when it came to governing. Roland is the one who turns away from the state to seek personal happiness. Nobility lets itself be distracted from its essential task, and this distraction could only be pleasing to the monarchy. Later, in 1685 when Quinault adopted the story of the mad Roland it is indeed that aspect of Roland's character that he emphasizes. As the lover himself states at the conclusion of the play:

Heaven! how could I without shame think
Of the disorder to which love had reduced my soul?
Wandering, crazed, enraged,
I made of my weakness an odious spectacle.[89]

In the great festival of *l'Île enchantée*, the multifaceted nature of the figure of Charlemagne is illustrated in a particularly striking manner: foreign policies; nobility that is both exalted and demeaned—and this occurs within a framework that satisfied the prevailing taste for Antiquity (as evidenced by the presence of Apollo, a figure placing the Sun King beyond time) while at the same time reviving national history.

There is no doubt that during the 1660s there was a "rebirth" of Charlemagne's mythistory and that it was encouraged by the monarchy. It was during this same period that Sorel and Aubery published their treatises and Du Boulay wrote the history of the University of Paris. The emperor did not disappear in the following years, either. In 1681, Father Alexandre published a dissertation on Charlemagne's coronation in which he shows that the great conqueror did not receive any power from the pope other than that which he already possessed.[90] The Jesuits had the play *Carolus Magnus* performed for Louis XIV in 1684 and again in 1698; it was a tragedy in Latin, dealing with the conquest of Saxony.[91] Shortly after being named tutor to the young duke of Burgundy (who became heir to the throne for a brief period before succumbing to illness himself), Fénelon, who at the time was still Bossuet's brilliant protégé, wrote a history of Charlemagne that has since been lost. But he wrote about it in a letter to his friend, the duke of Beauvillier: "Charlemagne had the advantage of being Christian, which put him above pagan heroes, and that of having always been successful in his plans, which makes him a better model than Saint Louis. I do not even think that one could find a king more worthy of being studied in all his aspects, nor a greater authority to use to teach those who must rule."[92]

As we have seen, the great emperor was useful to the kingdom both externally and internally, and there are good reasons to believe that Fénelon's history of Charlemagne was commissioned within the context of conflicts with the pope.[93] The French monarchy's relationship with the Vatican was often tense, and it worsened in 1682 with the *Declaratio Cleri Gallicani*.[94] In 1687, Innocent XI excommunicated the marquis de Lavardin, the French ambassador to Rome; and the following year the pope secretly informed Louis XIV that he and his ministers had also been excommunicated. The Sun King decided simply to ignore the sanction, although the enmity lasted well beyond Innocent XI's death. Fénelon was called upon to help justify the king's policy. In his *Mémoire sur la cour de Rome*, completed before the fall of 1688, the young cleric summarizes some of the points in his essay by noting that the pope played only a formal role in Charlemagne's coronation and had no real power in the temporal sphere of sovereigns or in their election.[95] The conflict between the papacy and Paris no doubt also explains a proposal by La Teulière, the director of the Academy of France in Rome, made to Edouard Colbert, the superintendent of buildings. In 1691, La Teulière submitted a proposal to Colbert, marquis de Villacerf, to have copies made of two paintings representing respectively Charlemagne's coronation and Leo III's oath. These paintings were located in the Vatican in a hall that had been cluttered with scaffoldings for at least twenty-five years. La Teulière suspected that the Vatican wanted to "hide the most well established truths." According to him, the Romans were calling Charlemagne's coronation *The coronation of François I by Leo X*, and they were hiding the subject matter of the painting representing Leo III's oath. La Teulière thus suggested using copies of these works to commission two tapestries from the Gobelin works to be made.[96] The superintendent liked the idea very much and noted "it is important for the king to remember [it] so as to evidence the good things his predecessors did for the Church and the power that the kings of France had in Rome in the past."[97]

AN EPIC HERO

Whether dealing with Rome or the Empire or Europe, France continued to use the emperor with the flowing white beard to define itself vis-à-vis the Other. Since international legitimacy was measured by the yardstick of tradition, precedent, and historical justification, the great conqueror provided a broad foundation for a range of geopolitical claims. He inspired memories, albeit increasingly vague ones, of a past unity. Dissociated from the Empire, his image conveyed the idea of a French Europe. There was thus a uniformity in the interpretations of Charlemagne's reign when it came to France's foreign relations, but when domestic matters were concerned, his reign gave rise to the most varied of interpretations.

The figure of Charlemagne comes to function as a springboard as much for debate on the nature of the ancient constitution as for an affirmation of common identity. We will see that these divergent interpretations continued to increase. But already during the period of unrest and of open or latent uprisings that followed the wars of religion, the monarchy discovered it could not call upon the hero without the risk of finding itself confronted with a very different, oppositional image of the figure. History had become a trap, and then, of course, so had the figure of Charlemagne. The situation was different in the 1660s. By then the monarchy was sufficiently imposing and powerful to be able, without running too great a risk, to initiate a return to national history. Moreover, the king who embodied that history was aiming to reign as a hero. If the "domestic" image could be made to harmonize with "foreign" propaganda, it would mean one more step toward the dream of unity had been taken. This did not mean that the king had to renounce the advantages offered by a connection to Antiquity. The monarchy could indeed encourage the opening of a "modern" path even as it maintained classical associations; the king could be Apollo and still call upon Charlemagne.[98]

For King Louis XIV, a champion of letters and the arts, who saw scholarship and artistic creation as an extension of his own glory, this two-sided identification did not pose any problems. In a painting by Henri Testelin (1666–1668) depicting Louis XIV as the protector of the Academy of Painting and Sculpture, we see him seated on his throne, surrounded by objects of modern science. On his right are a globe and a sculpture of Minerva's head, and there is a building of ancient-style architecture behind him. In his right hand, highlighted so as to attract the viewer's gaze, is Charles V's scepter topped with a figurine of Charlemagne, which, in turn, is holding a scepter in his right hand and a globe in his left.[99] This mixture of Antiquity and the national past is also found in the *Plaisirs de l'Ile enchantée*, where, as we have seen, the king could act on many different levels in evoking the history of his illustrious ancestor. Most enlightening in this regard are the attempts that were made during this same period to construct a theory and practice of the epic. Between 1664 and 1687 Charlemagne was the subject of three epic poems. These are not of interest so much for their poetic quality but on the one hand for what they say about how national culture was conceived and, on the other, for how they depict royal power in its most triumphant of forms.

The two authors had connections to the aristocracy, and their poems are not dedicated to the king but to their protectors. Louis Le Laboureur puts his Charlemagne under the patronage of the prince of Condé (known as the Great Condé). Le Laboureur had already supported Condé in his writings during the *Fronde*, and an impassioned pamphlet attacking the prime minister Mazarin has been attributed to him. The pamphlet accuses the prime minister of dark perfidy, of unprecedented injustice for having the prince imprisoned.[100]

Le Laboureur's epic poem was published the same year the king was attempting to flatter the Condés by emphasizing the kinship between them and the great conqueror during the celebration of *Ile enchantée*. The epic poem, in which Le Laboureur in his own way celebrates the return to favor of the repentant Great Condé, also glorifies the greatest of the king's ancestors. From the beginning of the poem, the tension between the affirmation of the great nobleman's glory and the necessity of subordinating it to that of the king must be resolved. In the old *chansons de geste* this tension was so central that it became the very subject matter of the poems. In somewhat abstract terms, the *chansons de geste* developed around the dual problematic of the relationship with the Other and of the identity of the Same. The victory over the Other was doubtful only to the extent that the identity of the Same lacked strength. This identity was, so to speak, constructed through the dynamics of the poems themselves. Under an absolute monarchy, identity was a given: it was unitary, it was developed around the king alone.

Epic poems of that time reached the somewhat paradoxical point where the best way to sing the glory of one's aristocratic patron was to show him submitting to the king or to describe him celebrating royal glory. Le Laboureur had scarcely completed a few lines of praise for the Great Condé, describing him as "overshadowing the names of the greatest heroes," had scarcely begged this "Mars, lover of scholarship" to deign to accept the fruits of his latest efforts, when he comes to what was, in fact, the greatest deed his glorious benefactor ever accomplished: bowing down before the monarch. This self-effacement is manifest even in the size of the printed letters in the poem:

> Now, the Great CONDÉ shows me the KING.
> . . . .
>
> On his knees, I see him, greeting his person,
> Let us no longer fear so many precipices.
> For us this demigod declares himself today,
> He is the support of the saintly poets.
> We see him now, this supreme potentate,
> Relax with them from the care of the crown
> And taking pleasure in their learned discussions
> Open up to them his palace and even his treasures.
> . . . .
> Of the French Apollo, whom I beg
> To light me with the divine flame.
> O CONDÉ, you are the one who showed me this beacon!
> Under him I have no fear of losing my muse. . . .[101]

Obviously, the writer seeks royal benevolence in its most concrete form. The raising of Louis XIV to the status of a demigod shows the true orientation of the poem. In Nicolas Courtin's poem, published two years later, the king is the model for the subject of the poem itself. Courtin addresses the king directly:

> But I believe that in this Hero whose image I trace
> It is you that I contemplate and you that I see.
> . . . .

And while Charlemagne is the object of my late-night work,
While I raise my voice to sing his marvels,
It is in you I contemplate in noble excess
The same virtues and the same successes.
Are you not what he was? . . .[102]

Both authors point out that their works should remind the pope of all that he owes to the French monarchy. In his *Charlemagne, ou le Rétablissement de l'Empire romain*, Courtin goes even further and claims that, as heir to the great conqueror, Louis has the right to the Empire that one day he will win "along with the entire world."[103] These sorts of statements might lead us to see the poems as mere propaganda devoid of any real significance beyond showing the strong return of Charlemagne's figure on the political scene during the 1660s as well as Louis XIV's encouragement of comparisons between himself and Charlemagne.

And yet, before sending them back to the oblivion to which history has sentenced them, we should look at these epics in the light of what they reveal about the changing national times. Louis Le Laboureur produced one of the most radical formulations of the nascent cultural nationalism, whereas, in contrast, Nicolas Courtin returned to the emperor in a later work, *Charlemagne pénitent*, to depict him as a mere man. There he presents him as an individual subject to the human condition, and thus his description shortens the distance separating the monarch from others.

In between these two works that, on the one hand, exalt conquest and cultural triumph and, on the other, describe the passing of glory as the ultimate trial and inexorable fate, we find a series of attempts at constructing a French epic focusing on a Charlemagne who has been revised and corrected to suit the tastes of the time and to reflect the image of Louis XIV. Of course, the great emperor was not the only hero to be dealt with in this way: there was *Saint Louis ou la sainte couronne reconquise* [Saint Louis, or the Reconquest of the Holy Crown] by Le Moyne (1658),[104] *Clovis ou la France chrétienne* [Clovis, or Christian France] by Desmarets de Saint Sorlin (1656),[105] and Chapelain's famous failure, *La Pucelle* [The Maiden] of 1656.[106]

All these attempts stemmed from a "modernist" conception of culture. In this view, French Christian civilization would establish its superiority over Antiquity only after proving itself through the most prestigious genre: the epic. The legitimacy of the nation, of its identity, was in some way tied to the existence of an epic. The sixteenth century had already raised the issue and sought a response in the extension of the myth of Trojan origins. But here we see the first moments of a quest that was to be completed only with the rediscovery of the Oxford manuscript of the *Chanson de Roland* in the nineteenth century.

The seventeenth-century approach consisted of turning the Middle Ages into "our modern antiquity," as Chapelain calls it in his treatise *De la lecture des vieux romans*.[107] This approach sometimes involved reworking medieval literature, or it sometimes aimed to create new works that drew their subject matter from the national past. Each of these approaches had their disadvantages. In order to defend old French literature, it was necessary to deal with the poor, even "barbarian," nature of Old French. In order to reinvent the epic, one had to confront the anachronism of the "marvelous" (*le merveilleux*) and the issue of its appropriateness for Christian readers.[108] The classicism of the seventeenth and eighteenth centuries favored the second approach. Le Laboureur's *Charlemagne* indeed reflects the consequences of this choice. It contains, existing side by side, angels, fairies, allegoric characters, Germanic gods, and gods of Antiquity. Magical tricks and spells abound. Dream leads to delirium which in turn becomes a revelatory vision during which Charlemagne is witness to the creation of the world, flies over it in the present, and foresees its future. All of this constitutes the action that leads to the triumph over Widukind, his subsequent conversion, and the incorporation of Saxony into the French empire.

CHARLEMAGNE AND LOUIS THE GREAT

Thus that heroic poem depicts a conquering Charlemagne endowed with all the qualities that create the greatness of France: strength, daring, justice, prudence, knowledge, and reason, but also clemency, sensitivity, kindness, and love. The poem seems to collapse under the weight of all these different elements. We can obtain a better understanding of the logic of such accumulation when we look at it in terms of how language was viewed. The modern epic hero could not be conceived without a language that was itself epic and conquering. A few years later, in 1667, Le Laboureur returned to his *Charlemagne* within the context of a debate on the education of the crown prince. Should the young prince be fed on "Latin muses," as Du Périer argued, or on "French muses," as the author of *Charlemagne* argued? In his treatise, *Les Avantages de la langue françoise sur la langue latine*, Le Laboureur drew on his heroic poem to illustrate his defense of the French language:[109] the king should be brought up with modern French and in the image of a hero of modern antiquity.

Thus at the heart of Le Laboureur's argument there is an opposition between Latin, a dead language, and French, a living one. The organic metaphor that Le Laboureur uses to turn language into a living thing then takes on decidedly virile and triumphant overtones. The French language was supposed to have gained in strength by drawing from other languages such as Latin, Spanish, German, Italian, and even "by extending its conquests to the Greeks."[110] It traveled through the ages to finally reach "the force of virility [*la force de d'âge viril*]".[111] In Le Laboureur, the politics of language and the language of politics were linked because French already reigned in the courts of the north and, he states, "I promise you that the way our King is extending the boundaries of his empire he will bring the French language farther than the Latin language ever went."[112] While the conquering king was able to impose the French language, that language in turn was proving to be robust enough to sing of the wars of conquest even in their most horrific moments, as seen in his own *Charlemagne*: "I found that our French muses neither trembled nor grew pale in the midst of blood and carnage. . . . The Huns came at night to attack Charlemagne's camp in his absence; they planned the deed with all its accompanying horror and made of it a picture with the most vivid colors they could possibly use."[113] The power of the hero king was matched by the triumphant power of language, and both affirmed, over and against the culture of the Ancients, the value of a modernity and a specifically French identity.

But Charlemagne was also a hero of knowledge, "a prince intelligent and studious, to whom we are beholden for the establishment of letters in France."[114] This leads Le Laboureur to include a "course of natural philosophy" in his epic and to use his defense of French as an opportunity to insert scientific details in his *Charlemagne* that prove that French is strong enough to be the language of the conquest of knowledge. The following quote reveals the kind of shoals on which Le Laboureur's modern epic foundered:

> You might have heard of the Poem of Charlemagne; I will quote you only sixteen verses at most, verses describing the state of enthrallment of this hero; where, so as to let you know what was this spell that had put him in a terrifying sleep, I discuss the circulation of blood; where I explain the course of the spirits rising from the heart to the brain; and where I show how awakening and sleep occur; and how the pores being closed and not transpiring anymore, this prince did not need food anymore and could stay a long time in this state without dying. This is how I satisfactorily deal with so many difficult things.[115]

To a language capable of expressing everything there corresponded the epic poem whose mission was to summarize an entire modern civilization destined to conquer the universe. Both Le Laboureur's epic and his defense were based on a rejection of "foreign merchandise,"[116] and yet the king and the language, both conquerors, were able to take from other cultures, that is, from Antiquity, Italy, and Germany, what they needed to gain in strength and to create a synthesis that enabled them to prevail over the entire world.

The power and greatness of the epic language, the power and greatness of the hero king: this was a system uniting power and its expression. We can indeed understand the role the monarchy assigned to the figure of Charlemagne and why it allowed its medieval roots to grow again. In 1675, Cordemoy brought many of these themes together before the *Académie Française* while noting the resemblance between the ancient conquering king and Louis XIV. According to him, Charlemagne's "academy" was a first draft of the French Academy. Knowing that it is through language that the memory of a nation is preserved, the founding king carried out a vigorous linguistic policy while waging three wars. The absence of a language capable of promoting his glory and that of the kingdom was a major concern for him:

> Charlemagne, who was uncontestably the greatest captain, the wisest of princes, and one of the most learned men of his time, had so well recognized this lack that after he had collected everything written up to then about the French people he himself began a grammar of their language, and it was apparently one of the subjects of learning that led him to establish in his palace this beautiful Academy that all the persons of his court in which he had noticed good manners and the love of letters were called to.[117]

Thus, as with Louis XIV, concern with language had led to an institutional policy. Perhaps only Charlemagne could be compared to the Sun King, but it was nevertheless always a way to show how basically Louis XIV was beyond comparison. "What was attempted in vain under the reign of Charlemagne was gloriously completed under the reign of Louis XIV."[118]

Bossuet appointed the learned academician to the post of "lector" for the crown prince, and Montausier, the prince's governor, asked him to write a history of Charlemagne for the young prince's instruction. This project broadened into a history of the first two dynasties. Cordemoy turned the great king primarily into a model of piety. But it must be noted that this "Cartesian" historian, committed to ridding history of fables, wrote a long laudatory description of Charlemagne's palace inspired mainly by Notker's "fabulous" history. Cordemoy surprisingly ends up describing a palace resembling Versailles, and the all-inclusiveness of the place emerges under his pen as an emblem of absolutism.

> This palace was magnificent; an author who wanted to show its greatness and comforts wrote that there were porticoes under vaulted galleries

under which all the soldiers and other persons used to being at court could take cover; that the lords had apartments above these galleries and that everything was laid out so that Charles could see from his own apartment all who entered or exited from the other apartments.[119]

Charlemagne as Jansenist

Almost all the themes relating to Louis XIV's monarchy could reflect the image of the great monarch from the distant past. As long as this image emanated from the court or was directed toward it in order to assert close ties, the general way the numerous elements comprising it were utilized remained relatively stable. However, the multifaceted nature of the personage soon allowed him to escape the constraints of royal ideology. Very soon he was seen as a counterexample and became the inspiration for critical reflection on the nature of the monarchy. Even the quest for the epic, adorned with all of its "national" significance, led to an image that was, in a sense, the opposite of that of unbounded greatness. This contrasting image was that of a humbled monarch, the victim of his position in which his dual status as man and king was the origin of a tragic dissociation.

We know almost nothing about Nicolas Courtin, the author of two long poems on Charlemagne. He was, apparently, a professor at the Sorbonne, where he dedicated his first poem, *Charlemagne, ou le Rétablissement de l'Empire romain*, to Pierre du Cambout de Coislin, bishop of Orleans and chief almoner to the king and, later, great almoner of France and cardinal. It is possible that, perhaps for religious reasons, Courtin had to distance himself from the court at a later date.[120] At any rate, he set out to use the hero's life to create "Christian poetry." He shows his disinterest in church benefices and in the protection of the powerful by dedicating his poem to a repentant David instead of a living being. In 1687, the same year Perrault read his famous *Siècle de Louis le Grand* to the Academy, a work in which he argues that the century of the Sun King can be compared to that of Augustus, Courtin published his *Charlemagne pénitent*, in which he depicts the greatest of the royal ancestors prey to his own human misery.

In this poem, whose beauty has been largely overlooked, psychomachy replaces the warrior's exploits. Like Louis XIV after his recent "conversion," Courtin's Charlemagne adopts an extremely pious stance. This poem resonates with Jansenist influences as Courtin reflects on the pitfalls of pride and reminds his readers that even the masters of the world cannot rise above the human condition. In a Christian universe, there can be no demigods, and, from the point of view of salvation, there is no middle ground between the Supreme Being and common mortals. Jansenism widens this divide. And yet, by putting God at a greater distance from human beings, by emphasizing their fundamental powerlessness, by reducing the importance of their actions through the doctrine of predestination, Jansenism opens a new door to freedom. As the hidden God is not manifest in the field of politics, politics then becomes a human responsibility. In contrast to the hostility of Cartesianism toward history, Jansenism perceives the past differently through its insistence on God's radical transcendence, a view that in some ways heightens God's otherness. The issues of humankind's past and of the origin of society acquire an entirely different meaning through this loosening of ties of dependency on God. This view proved to have a powerful appeal that continued to grow during the eighteenth century.[121] Although Courtin's work does not deal with all the consequences of this argument, it does already reveal certain fundamental themes that are implied by the existential repositioning of human beings.

The Charlemagne to whom we are introduced at the beginning of the poem is already nearing the end of his reign, and he has already performed acts of penitence: shameless behavior and the pleasures of the flesh have been banished from the court. But penitence and even charity appear as ruses in which each act of renunciation, each act of generosity, becomes in its turn a source of pride. "The infinite distance between bodies and minds symbolizes the infinitely more infinite distance between minds and charity, for charity is supernatural," writes Pascal.[122] This view is echoed in the verses Courtin devotes to the dangers of pride:

> If he has a temple or a monastery built,
> With his name on the façade in brilliant letters,
> Engraved by a clever sculptor,
> It shows that Charlemagne is the founder.
> If he feeds the poor, if he takes care of the sick,
> These humble exploits this prince displays;
> If he wants to reform the abuses of his time,
> There is pride mixed with these excellent concerns.[123]

The author heightens the tension between both the different forms assumed by the ideal of royal glory and yearnings born of Christian practice. Driven by his religious fervor, Charlemagne renounces his scepter; he accepts with a resignation matching that of Job the loss of his sons and the premonition of the fall of his line. And yet, renouncing the throne is in itself a visible act, a source of prideful satisfaction. For the true penitent:

> The more his merit is rare and his virtues shine,
> The more his actions make his name famous,
> The more he must hide its value and luster.[124]

In the quicksand of lust and pride, the sole source of legitimacy comes from divine grace; the only possible action is to accept human pain, a pain that turns the crown into true asceticism. "Thus sovereigns on high thrones / Can do less for themselves than private men."[125] Living in a continuous state of penance, Charles prepares for his death; the only trace left of his pride, his only sin, one serious enough to cause his damnation, is his failure to have his engraved name taken off the wall of one of the temples he had founded. Only divine intervention saves him: thunderstorms, described since Einhard's life of Charlemagne as the precursory sign of the emperor's impending death, destroy the facade of the temple, thus reducing "Charlemagne's name and title to dust."[126] Charlemagne will not be remembered; he has not founded nor left anything with his name on it. It is only at this cost that he avoids falling into the trap of his pride. The individual must be completely effaced; yet this effacement can never be entirely achieved and must be constantly repeated; in a way, it is by annihilating his own heroic figure that Charles accedes to immortal glory.

Thus we should not take at face value the obligatory praise included in Courtin's *Charlemagne pénitent* in which the author claims that during Louis XIV's reign there is a rebirth of the happiness and glory initiated by the hero of ancient France. Indeed, the marked reduction of the distance separating the king from his subjects is much more important. Like Christ, who had to become a man, the king must also endure the fate of common mortals, and even worse. Thus the "existential" critique of the king's status also leads to a political vision:

> The one whose destiny was to rule
> Is more slave than master of his scepter.
> He doesn't belong to himself, he belongs to his vassals;
> He owes them his advice, his care, and his labor.[127]

The phrasing is significant: the king belongs to his vassals and not to all of his subjects as one might have expected, particularly given the author's Christian viewpoint. Courtin still maintains a pro-noble perspective, even though he is somewhat distant from high society. His penitent Charlemagne helps us understand how a Jansenist type of reflection could nonetheless create a history that reflected aristocratic concerns with limiting royal power.

In the eighteenth century, as Jansenism became increasingly politicized, the image of Charlemagne became increasingly marked by the notion of a transcendence beyond any particular individual, beyond all concerns for personal benefit. Paradoxically, as we already see in Courtin's emphasis on the humanity of his protagonist, the more the great monarch is like other men, the higher he rises above them and, consequently, the freer he is to give himself entirely to them. To retire from the world in order to devote oneself to one's individual salvation, is to be overly concerned with one's own interests. It also implies an attempt to exercise one's will in a realm that ultimately lies beyond the realm of human endeavors: let us not forget that, in the end, Charlemagne is saved only due to God's intervention. The margin for actions open to human beings is narrow because an excessive concern with glory, even if it is manifest through acts of generosity, reveals too great a concern with one's self and one's personal interests. A righteous attitude implies relinquishment: "He no longer belongs to himself," but to the collectivity.

This is the vision of Charlemagne that was to become popular during the Age of Enlightenment. In Courtin's time, though, when this view was still developing, the community in question was defined in a very restricted manner. In the eighteenth century, however, the circle of this society continued to widen. But we are jumping ahead, so let us for now note the alliance of Jansenist thought with an aristocratic viewpoint. In the most glorious manifestation of this alliance, that is, in Courtin's vision of Charlemagne, to whom in his earlier epic, *Rétablissement de l'Empire romain*, he attributes the creation of the institution of dukes and peers,[128] the monarchy does have obligations toward the nobility.

In fact, already in Le Laboureur's work, in spite of the praise he lavishes on the Sun King, *Charlemagne* did offer the opportunity to meditate on the limits of royal power, but without leaning on Jansenist ideas. As we have seen, the supporters of the most radical absolutism gave the king the right to an unrestricted gaze, a gaze that, as Guez de Balzac believed, should penetrate the most secret thoughts of men. Like Guez de Balzac, Le Laboureur thought that the king "does not see the same way as we do." But the Great Condé's protégé nonetheless does attribute limits to the royal gaze. At the close of a long scene in which, during the emperor's trance, an angel shows him the secrets of creation and of the universe, Charlemagne remarks that there is only one thing left for him to learn about the world, and it is a crucial one:

> But to us kings this point is important:
> It is to know man and to see what he is thinking;
> Make me able to penetrate his heart
> And add to all your gifts this supreme happiness.[129]

This wish to know the hearts of others, to make their hearts transparent to the king's gaze, is met with the angel's refusal. The inwardness of human beings cannot be ruled. The heart is a privileged locus that individuals open only to whom they please and give only when they themselves will it.

But before trusting it [the heart], you must see clearly
Whether it is giving itself or only pretending to do so,
As it often misleads, and thinks it may do so
When it doesn't like its burden and it is not carrying it willingly:
It then thinks it is not breaching the laws
But merely is gaining back its rights.[130]

The transparency of men's hearts is linked to rights and freedom. It is not within the power of angels to give this gift to the king; this power belongs to human beings, and when they feel wronged they can resort to putting on masks and lying. This involuntary burden that led to rebellion had weighed heavily on Le Laboureur's protector. Should one thus reign according to the will of men—be it only the nobility—and to their interpretation of their rights? Le Laboureur stops short of carrying his argument to that point in this poem in praise of Louis XIV and celebrating the reconciliation of the king and the *Fronde* leader. But he uses these reflections to point out kings' dependency on God, because "with God you shall win over men, demons, and spells."[131] Nothing could be truer in the logic of conquest and of the divine right of kings, a logic that implies an intersubjective limit to absolutism: human beings are not immediately intelligible. But the monarch does not really require hearts to be transparent, because the only true legitimacy comes from God. Ultimately, absolutism is different from tyranny through its recognition of this fundamental impregnability and of the need to have recourse to God. But a question arises: what is to be done when God abandons the monarch and other human beings, when he no longer intervenes as a mediating force between the king and his people? As we will see later, in that case the transparency of hearts would become an ideal that continued to grow in importance throughout the eighteenth century.

CHARLEMAGNE, THE DUKES, AND THE PEERS

The attempts made in the second half of the seventeenth century to see in Charlemagne the image of a different kind of monarchy, one less absolute, less distant with regard to the "nation," were not limited to a few epic poems that navigated between gratitude toward an aristocratic patron and praise for an all-powerful king. In the 1660s a debate began that was the seed of a pro-aristocratic movement the scope of which continued to grow during the eighteenth century. In the beginning this movement did not voice any opposition to the king; rather it took the form of a struggle for preeminence within the nobility. The rivalry was similar to the type of conflict we have seen at play between the various rival educational institutions that expressed their demands exclusively in function of their proximity to the king rather than in terms of a critique of the monarchy. This was, after all, the time of the triumph of absolutism. But the conflict that opposed dukes and peers to the presidents of the Parlement was significant because the logic deployed was to become that of a radical critique of absolute monarchy. It had already led the dukes and peers to commission Jean Le Laboureur, Louis Le Laboureur's brother, to research the ancient nobility, and the report resulting from Le Laboureur's research circulated for a long time in manuscript form before it was finally published in 1740. The study aimed to rehabilitate the feudal system, and, in the eighteenth century, it contributed indirectly to the development of a certain aristocratic republicanism. But such an idea was still quite remote in 1662 when, during the *lit de justice* assembled by Louis XIV to register a treaty by which Lorraine came under the control of the crown, the dukes and peers abstained from giving their opinion because they had not been requested to do so ahead of the Parlement's presidents *à mortier*, that is, those of its members entitled to wear crown-shaped hats and who were assigned the task of leading discussions and setting agendas.[132]

On that occasion, the highest-ranking members of the noble estate wanted to assert and exercise their preeminence in circumstances when the presence of the king, in the dukes' and peers' opinion, elevated the Parlement to its highest function, that of a court of peers. In ordinary meetings, the position of the Parlement presidents entitled them to speak before anyone else, including princes of the royal family and even the crown prince. However, the king's presence changed everything, and the elite of the nobility claimed that, for the *lits de justice*, the titles of "those whom birth, merit, and great deeds have elevated above other men" should have preeminence over rank within the Parlement itself.[133]

The presidents *à mortier*, another elite that claimed a rank superior to that of other royal officers, claimed that the Parlement was not a court of peers but the court of the king, and thus the king's officers should be the first to voice their opinions. In response to this argument, the peers claimed to be the king's advisers by birth, and only they were equal to each other in rank, authority, and power. Inseparable from the king, they were *pars corporis principis*.[134] This controversy unfolded following an agenda that we have already seen at work: to be nearer to the king, to situate oneself as close to him as possible. The peers sought to show their preeminence through this strategy and thus differentiate themselves not only from the king's officers but also from the rest of the nobility of the sword. The conflict lasted two years and ended with a decision by the king's council to maintain the peers' right to give their opinion before the presidents *à mortier* during the *lits de justice*. It is thus the king who made the decision, possibly as a delayed punishment for the Parlementarians' role in the *Fronde*.

The peers supported their view of their status with a range of royal acknowledgments of their privileges, of genealogical status, and of immemorial traditions. Among these traditions, of course, there was the legend of Charlemagne and his twelve peers. Although historians were absolutely denying the connection between the great emperor and the institution of peerage, the myth still resonated for the nobility. This is seen in Courtin's praise for the Coislin family, when, while addressing Pierre du Cambout de Coislin in the dedication of his *Charlemagne, ou le Rétablissement de l'Empire romain*, he mentions the emperor's brother: "If it is true that Charlemagne instituted dukes and peers, would he not see with joy that the greatest of his successors recompensed with such an important title the services of my lord your brother?"[135] Indeed, Armand de Coislin was named peer of France in 1663.[136] The hypothetical "if" says a lot about the way a certain "genealogical consciousness," in this case Charlemagne's legend, supplemented true genealogical research.[137]

In their conflict with the presidents *à mortier*, the dukes and peers needed more than a vague legendary justification for the peerage. They turned to historical documents to back their claims. Jean Le Laboureur probably helped them by preparing the reports that supported their rights.[138] In March 1664, they formally asked him to conduct research on their history and, if the opportunity arose, to use his pen to defend their interests. Thus, having been made secretary of the syndicate of peers, Jean Le Laboureur ultimately wrote a history of the peerage and the Parlement, *Histoire de la Pairie de France et du Parlement de Paris*, a study that circulated in manuscript form until its publication in 1740.

However, regardless of the approach the peers took, there was no way to claim that the establishment of their institution as such went back to the time before the fall of the Carolingians and the creation of hereditary fiefs. The true beginning of their history thus corresponded to the seizing of power by the Capetians with the support of the highest-ranking members of the nobility. Such an origin had the disadvantage of situating the founding of peerage during a period of usurpation of royal power by the great feudal lords, and, at any rate, that time frame appears to preclude Charlemagne's role as founder. However, Le Laboureur's study is nonetheless of interest for that very reason, since the peers' advocate places the great emperor in a prehistory ruled by a protofeudal logic. Jean Le Laboureur thus managed to diminish the impact of the idea of aristocratic usurpation that was so negatively affecting feudalism in a regime that was increasingly absolutist. But he did even more, since he began to sketch a political idyll set in a time when constitutional practices corresponded to the natural order of things.

Of course, he was not the first, nor the only, person in the seventeenth century to see something in the distant past that was not an absolute monarchy. Mézeray, for instance, turned the first two dynasties into elective monarchies. In order to clear Charlemagne of the accusation that he usurped the rights of his brother Carloman, Mézeray even argues that "there is no Empire more legitimate than that given with the universal consent of the people."[139] As a consequence of having voiced his overly noble bias, Mézeray lost his position as historiographer to the king.

Le Laboureur shied away from such claims. However, in order to bolster the status of the peerage, he had no choice but to rehabilitate the feudal past. To do this, he attempted to show that the roots of that past, just as the roots of the peerage, went back to a time well before the Capetians. In order to prove the ancientness of the peerage, he brings up the outcome of the Frankish conquest and turns the idea of the peers of France into "a right naturally acquired by the French nation for each one to be judged by a peer, that is, his equal."[140] At that time, he argues, there were only two orders: the clergy and the nobles. The nobles were those who, on account of their birth, had to respond to the king's orders and take up arms to defend the fatherland.[141] In addition to these free men, there were serfs. Thus the ancient parlements were only assemblies of peers, in the broad sense of the term, who appeared in their function as judges. Therefore the origin of the peerage goes very far back in the past. But having established the basis for an argument that could be used to place all nobles on an equal footing, Le Laboureur takes care to introduce the first element of a hierarchy. The change occurs very soon:

> The peerage thus created, one could not claim that the name of peer is new: if all the nobles of a state were peers, if all the members of the clergy were peers and equal to each other, and if they were each other's judges . . . , then we need not question the antiquity of the name of peer: we see it used in the seventy-first of Charlemagne's capitularies, "quicumque ex his, qui beneficium principis habent, Parem suum contra hostes communes in exercitu pergentem dimiserit, et cum ire, vel stare noluerit, honorem suum et beneficium perdat." Whichever way one interprets the word peer in this passage, it does pertain to the peerage in which parity existed between the nobles on the basis of their status, and we can well see that in all this there was the subordination of a peer who followed another peer [all the way] to the one who led, this either out of personal merit or of dignity [status].[142]

For Le Laboureur, Charlemagne's capitularies were privileged documents that make it possible to establish the ancientness of the peerage in the judiciary sense of the term. But he quickly adds that a hierarchy headed by the most powerful had already been put in place at the time of the great emperor. With the change in dynasty, the institutionalization of a state of affairs that had already existed during prehistory was a natural consequence of the more ancient practices. After a long decline of the monarchy, those in power had to intervene directly to ensure the survival of that monarchy: "It was up to them to support the monarchy upon the end of the race of Charlemagne, which had declined so much in power and merit that it had not only lost the respect it had enjoyed but forgot its own greatness."[143] Indeed, Hughes Capet became king by being elected by the peers. This proximity to power was reaffirmed during the coronation, since the monarchy had been in a state of "personal vacancy" and was believed to exist only in the persons of the peers. Their participation in the monarchy "ended with Hughes Capet's election as first peer of France"; thus "the figure of the same monarchy that they represent in this ceremony expires again in the person of the peers of France immediately after the coronation of our kings."[144]

Le Laboureur's history made the preeminence of the peers an originary given that became institutionalized at the beginning of the third dynasty. Judges, advisers to the king, and warriors very early on, the peers participated in the greatness of the monarchy by carrying out its most essential tasks: justice, sovereignty, and the defense of the kingdom. The laws they uncovered and exercised alongside the prince went back to the laws and customs they had previously observed in Germany. Made up of high-ranking barons, the "court of the king," in the image of the ancient Fields of Mars (*Champs de Mars*), still survived as the Parlement, "representing the French nation in its ancient state."[145] But Le Laboureur speaks of a parlement that would be made up essentially of the king and the peers of France. In fact, this convenient continuity between prehistory and history was not maintained. The enemy came from without, not from the battlefields but from the field of culture. The ancient institution was gradually transformed by the addition of clerks to the ranks of parlementarians, "all of them persons of letters and leisure," stubbornly propounding the use of Latin and marked by "the affectation of appearing knowledgeable of foreign laws." In addition, military duty forced the nobles to be absent for long periods of time. When they returned to the Parlement, "the same language was no longer spoken there."[146] Since common sense and natural equality were no longer enough, the nobility "lost its customs and its rank in the Parlement and became enslaved to the laws of the foreigners they had chased out of Gaul."[147]

Le Laboureur laments a lost Germanic culture in the face of a classicist monarchy and a new, Latinizing body. A new body and a foreign language had taken over one of the principal arenas of the greatness of the nobility. Henceforth, the nobility was no longer at home in the Parlement. In this context, the old national culture acquired a strategic value. The basis of the nobility's legitimacy, the Middle Ages, that antiquity of modernity, emerged as a cultural source from which, due to a host of reasons, it became necessary to draw nourishment. It is therefore not surprising that Jean's brother used the history of Charlemagne to extract the necessary ingredients in order to depict, in the language of unpretentious people of common sense, the true glory of the French monarchy. The great emperor's reign was in the process of becoming the golden age of the French monarchy. It was sufficiently detached from contemporary history to acquire a certain autonomy in relation to immediate issues, yet it was nonetheless sufficiently linked to that history to become the illustration of what "ought to be." More and more often Charlemagne's story was sung to the tune of an idyll.

SIX

Saving the Monarchy,
Establishing the Republic

THE ENLIGHTENMENT AND HISTORY

In 1677, Baluze published the first laws of the kingdom, the capitularies, in his monumental *Capitularia Regum Francorum*. His readers probably took little notice of the frontispiece of the first volume that shows two women seated on a pedestal with the title of the book engraved on it. Behind them, there are pillars between which a large piece of cloth covered with fleurs-de-lis is waving. One woman is holding a sword, and the other a cross. With their other hands, they are holding onto a large medallion that bears the inscription "Karolus Magnus Imperator." In the eighteenth century, with the publication of this type of scholarly work, the conquering king came to be transformed into a law-making king. Baluze dedicated his book of ancient laws to Colbert, who was not only a great architect of the absolute monarchy and a fierce enemy of the parlements but was also one of the supporters of historical research, which he believed would benefit the monarchy. But this is one of the ironies of history: these capitularies were to feed a lengthy debate on the ancient constitution of the kingdom, a debate that continued to sap the historical foundations of absolutism and ultimately turned Charlemagne into a model anti-absolutist king.

The polemics, the conflicts between the different governing bodies, and a return to history that the monarchy initiated during the seventeenth century all foreshadowed the language and the arguments of the great constitutional debates of the eighteenth century. The Sun King's decline and death contributed to the process of viewing the national past in a new way. With the death of the great king, the nature and the intensity of historical arguments underwent a fundamental change; visions of the past assumed different significance. Resorting to a regent had always raised constitutional issues that had bearing on the very nature of the monarchy. But these issues, arising at a time when absolutism, while increasing the power of the monarchy, had also isolated it, were so wide-ranging and were expressed with such vigor that they fed various currents of protest up to the time of the Revolution.

Until recently, these "retrograde" protests were accorded only minimal importance in the way in which the eighteenth century was viewed by later generations. After all, the eighteenth century was the Age of Enlightenment, the era of philosophers and their faith in the future and progress. But the philosophers showed little concern with history. They preferred to focus on universal laws, on "Man" in general, and on knowledge and understanding of human society. Or else they were concerned about the problem of the alienation, the humbling dependency, the isolation and powerlessness of the individual in the midst of the great social "pantomime." Looking from a distance, we are puzzled by the two apparently contradictory elements in their thinking, divided as it was between an exploration of the infinite spaces of universality and a definition of solitude. Rameau's nephew (*Le Neveu de Rameau*) thumbs his nose at the *Encyclopédie; Les Rêveries du promeneur solitaire* leads us far away from the *Social Contract*. These opposing eighteenth-century tendencies, as well as a progressive vision of the world, encompassed the two poles of the bourgeois experience as it emerged later on. In that eighteenth century, there was no longer any room for a Charlemagne. And we can search in vain for an entry about him in the *Encyclopédie*. The policies of the editors, at least at the beginning of the project, were to refuse the "great men" of the past an entry in the *Encyclopédie*.

Recent historiography has shown that, between the two extremes of the individual and the universal, a school of thought developed concerning collectivities and their historical becoming. This thinking was developed primarily within entities that disappeared with the Revolution, and it has remained so long in the shadows because it was deeply anchored in particularisms, which later fell into disgrace. And yet it is here that we find the first signs of a language of the "nation" and the first interpretations of a national history that were coherent enough to rival the vision propagated by absolutist monarchy. We also discover here that, although the value of modernity and the idea of a certain human autonomy in the world were evident in the eighteenth century, the medieval past was increasingly defined as the antiquity of modernity. Of course, the classical world of the Greeks and Romans provided moral, aesthetic, and political models that were all the more tempting in that they seemed outside of, or above, history. And yet, the Middle Ages emerged as a direct source of the nation, its vital origins. Antiquity was still a privileged locus for the perspective it offered on a universal human being, but the Middle Ages provided what was required to understand the national entity and its institutions. Therein lies the significance of the rekindling of the quarrel between the Ancients and the Moderns at the beginning of the century. But the rigid distinctions defining the two camps ultimately lost their edge and the arguments tended to move from the field of aesthetics to that of politics. This pattern is best illustrated by the evolution of Father Du Bos, who went from writing a critical work on poetry and painting, *Réflexions critiques sur la poésie et sur la peinture* (1719), to writing a critical history of the rise of the French monarchy, *Histoire critique de l'établissement de la Monarchie française* (1734). The eighteenth century was ultimately, after all is said and done, a time of triumph for history.

One can therefore see the emergence of two different eighteenth centuries. One espoused modernity, was open to the future, and rejected the past in which it saw only a long series of abuses and errors: Voltaire was its most militant representative. The other was turned toward the past where it sought the foundations for the existence and the legitimacy of the present as well as a possibility of reform: Boulainvilliers and the parlementarians are examples of this perspective. One of these eighteenth centuries was generally believed to have lost the contest and was largely forgotten, whereas the winner was thought to have opened the doors to the Revolution. But if we look closer, we are struck by two facts that alter the apparent simplicity of this analysis. First, there were many attempts to combine the "retrograde" and the "progressive" positions. Such attempts assumed various forms: the retrojection of certain moral or political ideals into history— the application of the language and the doctrine of natural rights to the origins of the nation, for example; the simultaneous evocation of the right of conquest and of natural rights; attempts at combining largely incompatible analytical approaches, for example, a development of universal laws with a historical analysis of political and institutional contingencies, an approach brilliantly pursued by Montesquieu. Second, the "future oriented"/"past oriented" distinction disappears in the light of the momentum historical discourse acquired. Therefore those who sought to avoid turning history into a principal battleground—such as the monarch or the physiocrats, among others—felt forced to return to it in order to be heard by a public whose support they increasingly considered to be necessary. We too often forget that, although the Revolution was seen as the advent of enlightenment and the universal rights of man, it was initially experienced as a reform of the constitution of the nation as a historical entity. Regenerated humankind had had to fall before it could rise again; this movement of decline was located within the specific context of the immemorial collectivity that was France.[1]

Toward the middle of the century, at a time that was in many ways a turning point, the marquis de Mirabeau summed up well the type of amalgam we have been discussing. He wrote a famous work that was one of the first to pull the word "regeneration" out of its religious context and place it in the realm of politics:

> *The laws of creation, preservation, and regeneration are always the same:* they are a great model for us. Sovereigns, the images on earth of the divinity, could never imitate this respectable uniformity enough. But just as according to the laws of nature itself the physical mass diminishes within certain parts while it gains strength in others, the political body experiences similar variations, and the general steward must be concerned with following these changes in detail so as to remedy unavoidable harm and bring back the possible good. (my emphasis)[2]

In this quote the language of the Enlightenment is intertwined with that of an aristocratic reaction suggesting a return to the purity of origins. The religious metaphor leads to a comparison drawn from contemporary science. Change becomes deterioration here only when it creates disequilibrium, that is, when it benefits only certain parts of society and harms society as a whole. It is this type of change that requires an intervention "to bring back the possible good." Thus regeneration is basically only a form of conservation. Humankind has acquired autonomy and the power to repair evil and reconstitute good. However, if left to itself, the historical process would be one of degeneration, of a movement of fragmentation resulting from a set of forces with the power of destiny. This is a puzzling mixture of faith in humankind and its powers and pessimism about the movement and forces of history. The things that can be changed are located at the level of society as a whole, and it is at this level that things must be made right again. Who is the man who rises above the fray to save the situation? He is the king, the general steward, the disinterested redemptor, the only one, in the end, who is fully concerned with the general good and who is able to avoid the traps set by the "unavoidable harm" engendered by the movement of history.

We are familiar with the optimistic elements of this passage, since they are linked, of course, to the movement of the Enlightenment in the eighteenth century. As for the historical pessimism, we can perceive a religious resonance in it along with elements of a monarchical language concerning the king's function. But the *perception* of history as a *process* of degeneration and decline seems somewhat foreign in the context of the eighteenth century. In fact, the roots of this idea are found in the period spanning the end of the seventeenth century and the beginning of the eighteenth. It developed within the context of an aristocratic consciousness that was beginning to take form, for instance, in the writings of Jean Le Laboureur, a consciousness that assumed its most radical form around 1716 in the works of Henri de Boulainvilliers.

We have seen that in the quarrel between the Ancients and the Moderns, the Moderns were celebrating the triumph of absolute monarchy and that the monarchy itself was cautiously turning again to national history, that is, to its own history, which had been contested so heatedly during the wars of religion. The monarchy had encouraged historical research and sustained the hope for an epic worthy of the nation. In reaction to these activities, a pessimistic aristocratic vision gradually emerged that decried the subversion of fundamental principles and the perversion of the original constitution of the monarchy. This vision was backed by a theory concerning the conquest of Gaul by the Franks, and it conceptualized the nation as a victim of the movement of history. It drew abundantly from the documentation provided by the historical research of Duchesne, Baluze, Du Cange, and other members of the Académie des Inscriptions et Belles Lettres with the support of the monarchy. The crucial documents used as evidence in the various revisionist theories include the works of Tacitus on the Germans, the collections of the old laws of the kingdom, particularly Baluze's *Capitularia Regum Francorum* (1677) and Hincmar's *De ordine palatii*, a work of the greatest significance in the eighteenth century, as it provides long descriptions of general *plaids* and of the intense participation of the nobility in the government.[3] Already in the seventeenth century, Jean Le Laboureur wrote of the "naturally acquired right of the French nation."[4] And yet, it was Boulainvilliers who had a decisive impact on the way in which national history would be conceived in the eighteenth century.

Idyll of the King of a Nation of Nobles: Boulainvilliers

Henri de Boulainvilliers rejected the monarchical historiography that viewed the kingdom's past as a long unbroken chain transmitting legitimacy through the ages. Instead, he propounded the notion of a nation of conquerors, victims of the forces of history.[5] Through an unrelenting process in which the nation itself participated, the nation witnessed the gradual usurpation of its primitive rights by a monarchy greedy for power.

In the beginning, goes the story as told by Boulainvilliers, there was a French republic, a nation of equals who gathered on the Champs de Mars in the General Assemblies of the Nation to elect its chiefs, "to whom they gave the name of kings, so as to execute the laws they themselves had made."[6] Legislative authority was in the hands of the nation, that is, the Franks. In contrast, the Gauls, a conquered and submitted people, were not included in these assemblies. In the beginning, the king, in this nation of equal citizens, was only the foremost among his peers. But, under the second dynasty, the kings turned away from the general interest to advance their own particular interests by increasing the power of the monarchy at the expense of the rights of the nation. This conflict was inscribed in the very heart of society: the kings, in seeking to mislead French citizens either through force or lies, became despots, usurpers. Thus things turned bad very quickly, and the natural tendency of history, which led each individual to exploit every situation to his own advantage, led to the fall of the French republic. Already under Pepin, we witness a degraded nation:

> *They are no longer the French, born free and independent,* attached to their ancient laws more than to their own lives, *who elected their kings and their generals in perfect freedom* and who enjoyed with glory and tranquility a conquest they owed solely to their valor and perseverance in a most difficult project; *they in their turn became the conquest, not of a foreign nation but of a particular family. A family that shared the same origins but was more ambitious and more active and knew how to pursue its own advantage in all the events and circumstances that occurred during a century.* (my emphasis)[7]

In Boulainvilliers, there is a paradox in that his ideal society already contained forces that were to lead to its own destruction.[8] The threat does not come from the outside; it is inherent in the social organization itself. In this regard, the kings' main flaw was to be too much like everyone else, except that the kings were the only ones to have at their disposal disproportionate means to achieve their aims. The sole source of power and legitimacy lay in the French nation itself. In this sense, kings were public persons. But these kings were, by definition, men like any others, hence they shared the same needs and motivations. For monarchs, their public side was entrusted with the task of controlling and constraining the private side, the one Boulainvilliers identifies with passions. An oppressor is a "prince who has abused his power, who, *giving in to his passions and doing good only for himself, separated himself from the body of society so as to enjoy alone advantages* that should remain common lest their removal lead to the political destruction of this same society" (my emphasis).[9] As soon as the king committed such abuses, all of society followed him on the path of corruption. In fact, any noble, that is, any Frankish citizen, naturally sought to aggrandize himself; it was precisely in behaving like the greatest of the lords, instead of remaining above the fray, that the king became a despot.

We can clearly see that this was the very struggle described in the old *chansons de geste*, except that the genre had changed: epic was replaced by tragedy. For Boulainvilliers, history was but one long and painful process of degeneration. It was the tragedy of duplicitous kings, who abandoned the public good by giving in to the passions of their private interests, and that of the misled French people, who allowed themselves to be corrupted and denatured and ended up forgetting their rights, their dignity, and even their own identity. This vision of the history of France shares many aspects with the one Rousseau was creating for all humankind. It is clear, moreover, that this conception of national origins owed much to classical republicanism.

Boulainvilliers's work was a crucial step toward a conception of the Middle Ages as the antiquity of modernity. The work offered a passionate projection of certain values associated with the Greco-Roman world onto the national past as well as the identification of numerous documents that helped to justify his vision. The resulting representation of history offered both the possibility of laying claim to the originality and the specifically European origins of monarchical government, and of viewing that original monarchy as an ideal against which one might judge the failings and abuses of the present state of affairs. And yet, in contrast to Rousseau, Boulainvilliers did not offer a "philosophical" analysis of the tragedy of history. He was an activist writing a practical document: he wanted to persuade his readers and Philip of Orleans himself that the Estates-General should be called so as to bolster the legitimacy of the Regency. To this end, he compiled a genealogy establishing the link between the Champs de Mars, viewed as the general assemblies of the nation, and the Estates-General.

And yet this description of relentless decline risked conveying a paralyzing pessimism rather than a call to action. It is at that point that the figure of Charlemagne emerges, a figure capable of bringing the text and the nation out of a historical impasse. "I thus say again that we should go back to this century of Charlemagne, to find this happy time. It is there that we see a close union of the members with their chief, a perfect unanimity of feelings and a mutual accord for the common good. The prince was thus as attentive to preserving the rights of his subjects as the subjects were eager to advance the glory and power of the prince."[10] Boulainvilliers turns this reign into a political idyll, the reign of this "hero of the first order and without doubt the greatest king . . . to ever rule in France," "the only one of all our kings to merit the beautiful surname of Great."[11]

Charlemagne is important because he came after an earlier decadence to restore the ancient rights and freedoms and to reestablish in "the French

1. Alfred Rethel, *Otto III Visits the Tomb of Charlemagne*. Used by permission of the Staatliche Kunstsammlungen, Dresden (see pp. 5–6).

2. Alfred Rethel, *Otto III Visits the Tomb of Charlemagne*, detail of the veiled head. Used by permission of the Staatliche Kunstsammlungen, Dresden (see p. 6).

3. *Otto III as Christomimetes*, from the
dedicatory page of the Aachen Gospel
Book (*Ottonisches Evangeliar*),
Reichenau or the School of Otto III.
Photograph by Ann Münchow.
© Domkapital Aachen
(see p. 6).

4. The elephant from Charlemagne's
chess set. Used by permission of the
Bibliothèque nationale de France, Paris
(see pp. 306–7 n. 29).

5. The Charlemagne window
in Chartres cathedral,
late twelfth to early
thirteenth century.
Used by permission of
Edouard Fievet,
Chartres
(see pp. 90–91).

6. *Le Retable du Parlement de Paris*, fifteenth-century Tournai, Musée du Louvre, Paris. © Réunion des Musées Nationaux/Art Resource, New York (see pp. 97–98).

7. *Le Retable du Parlement de Paris,* detail of the panel with the image of Charlemagne, Musée du Louvre, Paris. © Réunion des Musées Nationaux/Art Resource, New York (see pp. 98-99).

8. Charlemagne, "patron" of Louis XII, before 1498. Photographic reproduction by the Photographic Laboratory of the Biblioteca Nacional, Madrid. Used by permission of the Biblioteca Nacional, Madrid (see p. 322 n. 39).

9. *Lit de justice* of 1610 (visible on the wall is *Le Retable du Parlement de Paris*), anonymous. Used by permission of the Bibliothèque nationale de France, Paris (see p. 98).

10. *Lit de justice* of 1614 (visible on the wall is *Le Retable du Parlement de Paris*), anonymous. Used by permission of the Bibliothèque nationale de France, Paris (see p. 98).

HERAVS DARMES. L'ARRIVEE. DV ROY AV PALAIS. MONSIEVR FRERE DV RO

11. *Lit de justice* held by Louis XV in the Great Hall of the Parlement on September 12, 1715, engraving by Poilly after the design by Delamonce. Used by permission of the Bibliothèque nationale de France, Paris (see p. 98).

12. *The Coronation of Charlemagne in Rome*, school of Raphael, the Vatican. Used by permission of Scala/Art Resource, New York (see pp. 108–9).

13. Jacob Jordaens (1593–1678), *Charlemagne Receiving the Ambassador of Hārūn ar-Rashīd at Aachen*. Used by permission of the Musée des Beaux-Arts, Arras (see p. 341 n. 83).

14. Albrecht Dürer
(1471–1528),
*Charlemagne,
Charles the Great
(747–814), King
of the Franks,
Emperor of the
West, in His
Coronation Robes*,
oil on canvas,
ca. 1512. Used by
permission of the
Germanisches
Nationalmuseum,
Nuremberg,
Germany/
Bridgeman Art
Library
(see p. 108).

15. H. Müller (1540–1617), *Charlemagne, Conqueror of the Saxons in 782*. Used by permission of the Bibliothèque nationale de France, Paris (see p. 119).

(see p. 119)

16. Roman image. Used by permission of the Bibliothèque nationale de France, Paris.

17. Franco-Gallic image. Used by permission of the Bibliothèque nationale de France, Paris.

EMPIRE DE CHARLEMAGNE.
Année 814.

A la mort de Charlemagne, l'Empire français comprenoit, outre l'ancienne Gaule, environ le tiers de l'Espagne, c'est-à-dire, cette vaste étendue de terre, qui a formé depuis les royaumes de Navarre et d'Arragon avec le comté de Catalogne. Dans la Méditerranée les Isles de Majorque, de Minorque, de Corse et de Sardaigne; au-delà des Alpes l'Italie entière, à la réserve d'une partie du royaume de Naples, qui étoit restée aux Grecs. A l'Orient tout ce qui forme aujourd'hui l'empire d'Allemagne en y comprenant la Hongrie, la Bohême, et une partie de la Pologne, jusqu'à l'embouchure de l'Oder, le peu de Souverains indépendans, qui restoient encore en Europe, étoient plutôt ses protégés que ses alliés. Cependant à peine ce Colosse de puissance étoit-il élevé qu'il commença à crouler de toutes parts. La discorde qui s'établit dans la famille impériale entre le père et les enfans, entre les frères, entre les Oncles et les neveux, rompit tous les liens de la subordination. Des Vassaux indociles et avides se partagèrent les dépouilles de leurs maîtres; et les arrières petits fils de Charlemagne, étrangers ou méconnus dans presque toutes les parties de la monarchie, conservèrent à peine la propriété de deux ou trois villes du second ordre, qui ne suffisoient plus pour entretenir leur Maison.

18. *The Empire of Charlemagne in 814*, engraving by Julien and J.-P. Lebas after Moreau le Jeune. © Roger-Voillet Collection (see p. 353 n. 88).

(*Left*)
The two "medals" in figures 16 and 17 show radically different images of Charlemagne: the consecrated emperor and the great conqueror. They appear in François Eudes de Mézeray, *Histoire de France* (Paris: M. Guillemot, 1643), 162–5 (see p. 334 n. 11).

19. Jacques-Louis David (1748–1825), *Bonaparte Crossing the Alps at the Grand Saint Bernard Pass* (Year IX, 1800–1801), Musée national de Malmaison. © Réunion des Musées Nationaux/Art Resource, New York (see p. 254).

(top right)
20. Ary Scheffer (1795–1858), *Charlemagne Receives the Submission of Widukind at Paderborn*, 1827, Musée de Versailles. © Réunion des Musées Nationaux/Art Resource, New York (see p. 272).

(bottom right)
21. Ary Scheffer, *Charlemagne Presents His First Capitularies to the Assembly of the Franks in 779*, 1827, Musée de Versailles. © Réunion des Musées Nationaux/Art Resource, New York (see p. 272).

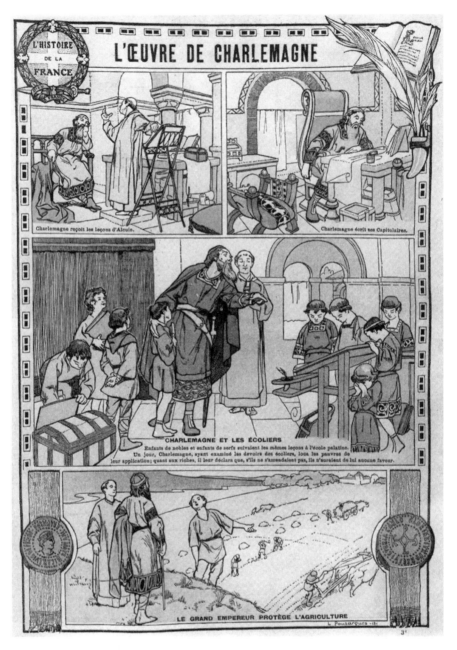

22. *The Works of Charlemagne*, engraving by L. Pouzargues from G. Gautherot, *Histoire de France*. Used by permission of the Archives Charmet/Bridgeman Art Library (see p. 299).

23. *Saint Charlemagne, the Patron of Scholars*, 1892. Engraving appeared in the *Petit Journal illustré*. Used by permission of Archives Charmet/Bridgeman Art Library (see p. 299).

24. Louis Rochet (1867–1875), equestrian statue of Charlemagne outside the
Cathedral of Notre Dame, Paris. Photograph by Raymond Depardon. Used by
permission of Magnum Photos (see pp. 294–95).

nation its true, primary, and legitimate rights."[12] Thus Charlemagne does more than provide an originary ideal: he opens the way to a return to this ideal. His existence is the condition of possibility for a true reconstitution of the French nation. Other models of government, such as for instance Lycurgus's Sparta or England, are less powerful because temporal and spatial "elsewheres" are not suitable for any direct association with French identity. The great king's government existed at home in France; it possesses the reality of a historical fact.

Thanks to scholarly works of the seventeenth century, a scholarship that continued throughout the eighteenth century, a corpus of documents covering the reign of Charlemagne—something that was impossible to achieve for kings of the first dynasty—became available. These documents enabled scholars to describe in detail, using precise references (even if the interpretation of them in fact distorted the letter and the spirit of the cited documents!), that idyllic, completely exceptional moment in French history.[13] Suddenly then, the ideal moved from the "weak" space of utopia and into the "strong" space of a true past that had "really happened."

What did Charlemagne do? He essentially restituted that which Boulainvilliers constantly refers to as "a natural right." Charlemagne recognized that the entire dignity of the nation was rooted in the parlements, that is, in the general assemblies that came to be known by another name. He agreed to share his power, to take no action until those assemblies had deliberated and given their consent. In fact, he made the assemblies more prestigious than ever before by transforming them into superb spectacles that drew the attention of the entire world. Boulainvilliers describes the reactions of the ambassadors of the caliph of Babylon who attended "one of the general assemblies of the nation." When they returned home they said that

> they had seen in Europe a people of kings to which a great number of nations were submitted; that this people had at its disposal numerous armies covered with gold and steel; that these kings had nonetheless a leader who was the king of kings, and yet he and they always wanted the same thing; they obeyed this chief even though in a sense they were free and kings like him.[14]

There could be no stronger image to express the sovereignty of the people than that of a people of kings. But in this context, how else could Boulainvilliers describe Charlemagne's position and role among his people than by borrowing biblical language and making him a king of kings? The functioning of this entity resembles a divine mystery, and the author describes it with a series of conjunctions and adverbs (*nonetheless, yet, even though*) which enables him to express the otherwise inconceivable joining of opposites. It was this republic, this nation of equals, that dominated Europe and lands beyond.

But Boulainvilliers sees Charlemagne as another Julius Caesar and does not miss a single opportunity to emphasize his greatness. Charlemagne's conquests, "in inspiring respect for his person, had made people more apt to obey him."[15] "Rome, even in its splendor, never shone brighter and had more greatness than that which the wisdom of this monarch gave his nation assembled in the Parlement."[16] Boulainvilliers then borrows from biblical language and from the stock of metaphors comparing Rome to France that Louis XIV had used for so long. This is done to explain that the act of restitution was in no way an act of weakness or a compromise imposed by circumstances. On the contrary, Charlemagne rose above the immediate situation; he, so to speak, inverted the movement of history and restored to the nation its rights and freedoms.

Boulainvilliers's image of this prince, the greatest of them all, is that of a leader whose legitimacy came from the people and whose attributes brought him closer to the divine. The "miracle" of Charlemagne is to have put the nation back into contact with itself, to have helped it overcome a state of national amnesia to which it had been reduced. Before the advent of Charlemagne, France no longer recognized itself. The great leader again made France conscious of its own transcendence as a nation in relation to its king. Thus, rather than presenting Charlemagne as a king mediating between God and men, Boulainvilliers presents him as a mediating figure between the nation as sovereign and the nation as a collectivity subjected to the laws it itself has made. This image resembles the one Rousseau presents of the legislator in his *Social Contract*, but Boulainvilliers's argument, instead of being located in the realm of the universal, is rooted in the history of France. And it is precisely this rootedness that explains both the astonishing success of this text in the eighteenth century and its subsequent fall into oblivion.

Boulainvilliers's description does, however, raise a problem: why did Charlemagne act in the way he did? After all, he was an ambitious man, as proven by his conquests. Like Christ, Charlemagne came to save men, not all men, to be sure, but all the "French." To do this he had to sacrifice absolute power, the illicit fruit of the usurpation perpetrated by his ancestors, but a power that had nonetheless been handed down to him. The aristocratic historian is at pains to emphasize that it was a *return* to legitimacy, a *restitution*. The key factor is Charlemagne's character, his *disinterestedness*. In evoking the great prince, Boulainvilliers often discusses Charlemagne's inner thoughts, his intimate motivations: "a sincere intention to do good and look after the public interest and to find glory only in the common good of all the men living in his empire."[17]

Charlemagne, a sincere and truthful prince in his intentions as well as his conduct, incapable of separating his interests from that of the state or of thinking it possible for the sovereign to earn solid glory independent of his internal administration, decided that artifice was as unworthy of him as it was inappropriate toward a nation as generous, as affectionate, and as loyal toward its king as were the French.[18]

It was his character, his moral strength, that enabled the great providential man to go beyond history in the name of justice and of right, to reestablish the legitimate order where before there had been only despotism and tyranny. The prince's authority was thus a moral one, and the great mediator drew his identity from the community itself. But the nation, too, had an inner self. It was generous, affectionate, loyal, it recognized the motivations of its leader and, thanks to him, rediscovered its true self-awareness, that is, the very meaning of the nation, of its identity and its collective being. Charlemagne was able to see through the deformation of the moment and bring out "the character and significance of his nation."[19] Thus was born the reign of reciprocity of hearts, of transparency, and of "unanimity of sentiments."[20] Even the magnates, those who, being the most powerful, benefited from the fragmentation of interests, rediscovered the well-being of the nation. "The genius of the sovereign" spilled over on his subjects, imbuing them with the morality that was the very foundation of his politics: honor, generosity, and above all this

> personal disinterestedness that in a way made up the specific nature of the century of Charlemagne; this prince did not want anything for himself that was not also for the benefit of the whole nation, and the magnates of the state, filled with trust in the wisdom of this great prince and convinced that their individual good could be found in the general good, did not desire anything for their benefit that wasn't common to the whole of the kingdom.

This reciprocal love, "this union of sentiments and will" constituted the very foundation of this ideal monarchy.[21] In returning to their original republic the French reawakened and reacquainted themselves with freedom. The great prince insisted that in the assemblies every person be free to express his opinion without constraint and that he himself should not be present during the deliberations. This was because "these parlements would not disregard justice and truth if they had the freedom to deliberate according to their conscience."[22]

Boulainvilliers borrows an image from Hincmar that endured throughout the century: that of Charlemagne receiving his subjects, speaking and listening to them with affability, kindness, and compassion while the general assemblies are deliberating. At times, when the "Parlement" met with obstacles or was divided on an issue, it called upon Charlemagne "so that his light would meld the diversity of sentiments into a single unanimity."[23] The idea of a perfect harmony, of a *complete national unanimity* underlies this vision of the Carolingian period when time seemed to stand still, when, "under the leadership of an incomparable leader, law and order burst forth everywhere and each glorious year was followed by another that was even more so."[24] If the movement of history was seen to be one of degeneration, then the reconstitution achieved by Charlemagne can in contrast be described as a sort of stasis, an idyllic state in which a feeling of well-being sprang from the love the nation had for itself through its leader.

After the great prince's reign, the nation reverted to a state of self-forgetting and moral degradation. Since Charlemagne had done all he could to reestablish political mores, his successors should have pursued the same objective to ensure the stability of the constitution. The weakness and mediocrity of subsequent kings was thus the primary cause of decline. Weighing their individual interests against those of the state, they listened to their own passions, which were "always more chaotic than those of other men because they were born into power and grew stronger in the rank and the sublime authority linked to their birth." Such a notion explains why the amorous passions of the kings acquired such great importance in the eighteenth century. They became the principal metaphor for describing the hold individual interests had over the kings at the expense of the public interest. As for the parlements, they, too, succumbed to corruption because "it is morally impossible to resist the example of kings."[25]

The nation never recovered from this fall. It remained consumed by an uncontrollable pursuit of private interests, growing fragmentation, and moral decline. In a passage expressing the pathos of this return to a downward course of history, Boulainvilliers emphasizes the rapid pace of the change and his nostalgia for the happy union of the nation. As usual, he is careful to substantiate his argument with a "document"; this time he cites one from the ninth century which gives an account of the discord between Louis the Pious's sons and of the internal wars that were tearing the Empire apart.

> Nitard . . . expressly notes that in Charlemagne's time the French people marched along a single and unique path that was that of the public interest, of peace, and of concord within the nation; but, only thirty years after his death, everyone thought solely of his individual interest and of satisfying his private passions. There resulted universal divisions that could not fail soon to cause the general ruin of the French monarchy.[26]

The glorious unity of the French people, the public interest, the concord of the nation: concepts that would mark the period of constitutional debates beginning with the Regency. These strong notions passed through all the crises of the eighteenth century to become the rallying cries of the Revolution and beyond. In fact, the utopian lyricism used to describe the Carolingian period, a lyricism tied to a pessimistic view of history, was transmitted as it was renewed throughout the century. Histories of France consistently paused to admire this utopic moment when everything seemed to stop and sociopolitical happiness became a reality. Boulainvilliers provided a coherent interpretation of the national past that rivaled the monarchical conception, and he invented a French hero who was able to draw the victim-nation out of its historical impasse. By insisting on the fundamental contrast between public and private interests, Boulainvilliers defined the axis along which a crucial element of political thought developed in France in the eighteenth century.

Most important, Boulainvilliers constructed a lasting association between the republic, the nation, and the great providential man. Although we have always been aware of the link between absolutism and Napoleon's empire, an examination of Charlemagne's role in eighteenth-century thought enables us to trace a direct line from the origins of republican thought in France to the establishment of Napoleon's empire. In doing so, we can discover other sources of that empire, including a certain overdetermination. For in order to destroy the inexorable constraints of the historical process and break free from the grip of the dominant absolutism, Boulainvilliers, and many after him, needed nothing less than the moral force and the conquering strength of the great man. Moreover, just as the earliest expressions of republican thought in France needed a Charlemagne with whom Napoleon would not fail to associate himself, so, too, did the lyricism and the primordial role that republican thought devoted to feeling and sentiment in some ways foreshadow a romanticism that would extol the union of poetry and politics and would replace "reason" of state with national sentiment. Scholars have for too long separated the reflections of the eighteenth-century nobility and its preoccupation with the Middle Ages from the medieval affinities of romanticism.[27] In fact, there is a connection here whose importance will become increasingly clear as we pursue the avatars of the figure of Charlemagne and of its relationship with the nation.

VERTOT AND THE GERMANIST THESIS

The Académie des Inscriptions also participated in the reinvention of the great king in the first half of the eighteenth century. The renowned scholar

Mabillon was appointed to the Academy in 1701 and died in 1707. His eulogy appeared in the first published volume of the *Mémoires* of the Academy, and the second volume included his paper on the ancient tombs of "our kings."[28] Mabillon's description of the tomb of the "first of our kings to love letters" presents one after another all the elements of the legend, showing the great king seated on a golden throne, the Gospels in his hands, and his face covered with a shroud.[29] This description of Charlemagne's tomb, which was erected as a monument to the glory of the first restorer of literacy, includes an explicit parallel to Louis XIV, who devoted so much attention to the institutions that promoted the arts and letters. The eighteenth century maintained the image of a restorer and broadened it to cover the field of politics. Moreover, the tales of the great monarch's efforts to create schools and academies placed him in a position to be used by those who insisted on the importance that should be accorded to public opinion in governing the realm.

In this period of serious (and less serious) scholarship, the "Germanist thesis" found constant support in the stern Abbé de Vertot. A few pages before Mabillon's essay, Vertot evokes the collections of *chansons de geste* celebrating the virtues of Germanic heroes in his "Dissertation in which an attempt is made to uncover the true origin of the French through the parallel of their mores with that of the Germans."[30] Obviously he uncovers a close kinship between the two peoples. In 1735 the Academy established a literary prize, and in the first year, the theme announced focused on "the state of knowledge [sciences] in the French kingdom during the time of Charlemagne's empire."[31] In his presentation of April 15, 1736, La Curne de Sainte-Palaye mentions Charlemagne's great love of the history of his predecessors and notes that the restorer of letters "himself had written crude poems in which the combats of the kings and the ancient peoples were celebrated; he had them read during his meals, he learned them by heart."[32] We will return to Sainte-Palaye later.

In the meantime, the essay Vertot read to the Academy on May 3, 1720, which was published in the *Mémoires* in 1729, is of interest for two reasons: on the one hand, it indicates the level of interest in the Germanist theses at the beginning of the century, and, on the other, it enables us to observe the way in which the figure of Charlemagne acquired a consistency, taking on, so to speak, the flesh-and-blood density of an attractive personage capable of rivaling Greek and Latin heroes. Since the fifteenth, and particularly the sixteenth centuries, historians had been primarily concerned with criticizing the "fables" and the mythification of the emperor of the West. In contrast, in the eighteenth century there was a certain remythification of the great king, a process that went hand in hand with the general movement of a reinvestment in national history.

Vertot was a tireless apologist of austere morals. He describes the great king as an extremely simple man whose dress during the great ceremonies of state "differed little from that of the people."[33] Here the "ethnic" definition ("the Frankish people") takes on a socioeconomic dimension that aimed to idealize the reign of the great prince to whom the first sumptuary laws of the kingdom were owed. The implicit association with Lycurgus is obvious. Clearly there was a strong need to find examples in the national past that were as edifying as those of Greco-Roman antiquity. In order to complete his portrait, Vertot draws on Notker who, translated and brought up to date, could pass for a kind of French Plutarch. We have seen how, in the *Gesta Karoli Magni,* the Monk of Saint Gall takes the side of the poor and turns Charlemagne into their protector against the nobles.[34]

Notker's parables were perfectly suited to Vertot's argument. Charlemagne becomes a moral philosopher who taught by his own example. Thus he was troubled by the luxury in which the nobles were indulging. One day, they went hunting wearing elegant clothes that became damaged. Charlemagne forced them to wear the ragged clothes again the next day. Vertot puts these anecdotes in the service of an anticapitalist bias that was typical of a certain strain of the aristocratic ideology—the clothes had been bought from "Venetian merchants." The great prince acted "to preserve among the French the ancient clothing and simplicity of the nation."[35] Charlemagne is imparting a "national"—not a Christian—morality here.

We can see the extent to which Vertot's ideas reflect the two levels of the notion of a French nation: like Boulainvilliers, he keeps both the general meaning of the term, i.e., the kingdom of France, and its "socioethnic" dimension, that is, the aristocracy, or the Frankish conquerors. In fact, during the eighteenth century the "ethnic" element, which was based on an ambiguity of translation—*Francs* (Franks) being translated *François* (French or Frenchmen)—used to designate the nobility, i.e., the descendents of the original Frankish conquerors, would be eliminated and replaced by a more general inclusive meaning comprising all classes of French. But in spite of the change in content, the basic structure of the discourse on the "French nation," however defined at a given moment, remained stable and the image of Charlemagne providing morality to the nobility easily found its place in a broadened conception of the nation that includes the lower "Gallic" ranks of society, victims of aristocratic abuse.

And yet, in spite of Vertot's telling example, the aristocratic point of view was certainly not the only one that was held within the Académie des Inscriptions. In fact, the spirit of the institution, as well as its strict dependency on the monarchy, tended toward prudence. Most of its work shied away from major political issues. However, in debates on the old constitution, Foncemagne, one of the great promoters of medieval research within the Academy, perhaps concerned with the threat Vertot's position posed for the institution, wrote a heated response. Shortly afterward, the great success of Boulainvilliers's work led Foncemagne to write a "critical examination" in which he explicitly links the theses of the aristocratic ideologue to Hotman's views.[36] The wars of religion still haunted the eighteenth century, as can be seen in Voltaire's *Henriade*. By establishing a link between Boulainvilliers and the Protestant propagandist of the wars of religion, Foncemagne aimed to show the real threat that these ideas presented for the monarchy.

Du Bos and the Roman Legacy

Confronted with the formidable challenge presented by the supporters of the Germanist thesis, the defense of absolutism developed along two drastically different axes. One of these two currents attempted to attack the nobiliary discourse on its own ground by simply denying the Frankish conquest. The other, more radical, rejected history as a source of legitimacy by reducing it to a long series of crimes, blunders, and biases. This ideological bifurcation shows well the difficulties faced by a monarchy torn between its dependence on history and the temptation to free itself from history and position itself on a more universal ground, such as reason and enlightenment. The monarchy, thus torn between the past and the future, improvised according to the needs of the moment, drawing at times from one side of the ideological divide, at times from the other, in order to cope with an increasingly stormy present. And yet, it lacked neither arms nor soldiers to conduct this ideological fight. The Abbé Du Bos provided a powerful interpretation of absolutism in history, whereas Voltaire drew up a crushing indictment of the past even as he supported the practice of enlightened absolutism. In both these cases, Charlemagne lost his position as ideal monarch.

Du Bos probably comes closest to formulating a great monarchical synthesis encompassing history and aesthetics. In a way, this theoretician of the monarchy represents the end point of a long ideological effort to liken France to ancient Rome. But his particular strength comes from the fact that he takes the "classicist" model of the monarchy that had been developed in the seventeenth century and turns it into history by claiming a relationship of uninterrupted continuity between imperial Rome and the French monarchy. Previously, the ties between these two entities tended to be located in the realm of metaphor. But gradually such a tendency invited comparison of the respective greatness of each entity and forced a choice that led straight to the tangled polemics between the Ancients and the

Moderns. For Du Bos the relationship between the two was established over a long continuum. The monarchy directly inherited the authority of the Roman emperors. There was never a conquest that caused the Gauls to submit to the Franks. Du Bos situates the foundations and the legitimacy of the monarchy in imperial Rome rather than in the forests of Germany.[37] Therefore the significance and even the reasons for all the research on the laws of the first two dynasties disappear. And what is more, the nobility's claims to some sort of original right prove to be fantasies.

In the realm of aesthetics, the famous abbé uses the notion of "taste" to show the relativity of aesthetic criteria by freeing them from their ties to reason. Henceforth, the greatness of the authors of Antiquity could be enjoyed in spite of the "backwardness" of their mores, philosophy, and knowledge. But, he adds, we can also fully enjoy modern opera and even hope for an epic worthy of the French monarchy. The subject of this epic poem would be a national event drawn from recent history; at any rate, it should not go back further than Charles VII, whose reign constituted the true beginning of national history.[38] For Du Bos, who already knew that Voltaire was working on an epic poem, the ideal figure was that of Henry IV. In this renewal of the concept of the *translatio imperii*, Antiquity and Modernity become the two poles of interest and legitimacy. Thus in Du Bos, whether in the realm of history or aesthetics, the Middle Ages—and the figure of Charlemagne—seem to disappear.

Charlemagne as Usurper and Barbarian: Voltaire

Du Bos and Voltaire chose the same hero for the national epic. Rather than choosing a conqueror who was supposed to have enlarged the national territory, they picked Henry IV, who reunited a nation that had been divided by civil war and reestablished the authority of the monarchy. For both men the king embodied national sovereignty, but for Voltaire he also embodied reason, or at least had it close at hand in the person of a philosopher advisor. For Voltaire as for Boulainvilliers, the prince as a public figure had to be above all disinterested and do his best to overcome his private passions, a theme on which Voltaire focuses in his "national epic" about Henry IV, *La Henriade*.[39] Voltaire's epicurean leanings were in contrast to Boulainvilliers's austere stoicism, so in his view it was enough that "libertine" failings of private life did not impinge on the king's public function. In fact, far from disappearing, the prince's true passions only projected themselves onto public matters: the raison d'être of the king was the happiness of his subjects, and it was his responsibility to ensure that they could peacefully enjoy cultural and material well-being in their private lives. But whereas the king could master his passions, the people were incapable of doing so, and, at least in France, there was no intermediary body to assume public responsibility.

The parlementarians never did forgive Voltaire for the description he gave in his book on Louis XIV's century, *Le Siècle de Louis XIV*, of their inability to act for the collective good. "One could not expect otherwise from a company of magistrates who, thrown out of its sphere of competence and knowing neither its rights nor its real power, nor public politics, nor war, made decisions in the midst of tumult on matters it had not thought about for even one day, decisions that would surprise it later on."[40]

Regarding the issue of origins, Voltaire seems to sweep it aside by claiming that "it is imagination alone that wrote the first histories. Not only did each people invent its origins but they each also invented the origins of the whole world."[41] At any rate, according to him, we can learn very little from history because generally, and more specifically for Europe, it is nothing but "a vast scene of weaknesses, faults, crimes, misfortunes."[42] There was never another man who labored as hard as Voltaire to cast doubt about the writing of history while devoting so much time and effort to it.

Indeed, throughout his long career, Voltaire never ceased to be a historian, constantly preoccupied with the "great men" of history: Charles XII, Peter the Great, Louis XIV. One might expect that, for Voltaire, Charlemagne would have been a precursor of the modern "great man." On the contrary, in the philosopher's writings Charlemagne becomes an "anti-model," a king of darkness: usurper and conqueror, both a despot and a fanatic. "Charlemagne's reputation is one of the greatest proofs that success justifies injustice and assures glory."[43] Voltaire's view of Charlemagne is of a piece with his belief that, before the Enlightenment, whose first light began to shine only with the Renaissance, there was nothing in Europe but barbarism. It was from this perspective that he was inspired to write that "the horrors of past centuries are the glories of the present."[44]

However, following in the footsteps of Bossuet, this apostle of the Enlightenment recognized Charlemagne's reign as an important historical moment, as can be seen in his work on universal history since the time of Charlemagne, *Essai sur l'histoire universelle depuis Charlemagne*.[45] Although he concedes to the great monarch some primitive successes in the realms of culture, trade, the arts, and sciences, Voltaire views Charlemagne's time primarily as the founding moment of ecclesiastical temporal power. It is Charlemagne's close complicity with the Church that Voltaire criticizes most vehemently. And it is precisely the opposition between ecclesiastical power and lay power that structures Voltaire's entire interpretation of the Middle Ages. Voltaire perceives a motive lurking behind Charlemagne's association with the Church: unbounded individual ambition that is severed from concern for the well-being of those he is governing. Thus, regarding the conquest of Saxony, the philosopher points out the arbitrary nature of the undertaking. There "were no accumulated riches . . . , no towns worthy of the ambition of an usurper. The aim was only to gain millions of men as slaves, men who cultivated their land in a poor climate, who fed their flocks, and who did not want any masters."[46] The great conqueror was acting as a brigand and "made laws that stemmed from the inhumanity of his conquests," instituting "a jurisdiction that was more abominable than the Inquisition has ever been since."[47] In Scandinavia, in Poland, in Moscow, pagan peoples lived "in peace in their ignorance, happy to be unknown to Charlemagne, who sold the knowledge of Christianity so dearly."[48] His actions in the name of the faith did not prevent him from forming an alliance with the Moslems of Spain: "other interests, other means."[49] Nothing renders the eloquence of Voltaire's attacks against Charlemagne better than this little-known passage from the *Annales de l'Empire*:

> This monarch, like all other conquerors, was basically an usurper: his father had been nothing but a rebel, but all historians call rebels those who refuse to bend under a new yoke. He usurped half of France from his brother Carloman, who died suddenly enough to warrant suspicions of a violent death; he usurped his nephews' inheritance and their mother's subsistence; he usurped the kingdom of Lombardy from his brother-in-law. We know of his bastards, his bigamy, his divorces, his concubines; we know he had thousands of Saxons murdered; and we made a saint out of him.[50]

As for the Germanist theory, Voltaire claims that the Gauls were "happy to be vanquished by the Romans," bearers of civilization and prosperity. In contrast, the arrival of the Burgundians, the Goths, and the Franks signaled the return to barbarism, the beginning of ruin. "What kept these newcomers from building regular structures on the Roman model? They had stone, marble, and better wood than we do. . . . If they were ignorant of all the commodities able to sweeten the bitterness of life, was it not because the savages who crossed the Rhine turned the other peoples into savages too?"[51] Voltaire does not argue against the scholars who claimed that Germanic peoples had elective monarchies because, according to him, democracy naturally leads to despotism. Thus popular participation does not lend legitimacy and dignity to a social contract among thieving barbarians:

> These immigrant chiefs were elected by a majority of votes, and it could not have been otherwise: by what right could a thief command

his comrades? A clever and bold brigand, very successful, could over time acquire a lot of influence over subordinate brigands who were less clever, less bold, and less lucky than he. They all had a right to equal parts of the loot; and this is the most unbreachable law of all the early conquering peoples.[52]

A mixture of force and of common interest imposes a form of democracy. But as the leaders' power increases, they gradually turn into despots and end up establishing hereditary succession. This is the case with Clovis, as with Charlemagne, who was himself the son of an usurper.

His only ancestors were his father, who had invaded the kingdom: he himself had usurped his brother's share and had robbed his nephews. He flattered the nobles in the parlement, but when the parlement was not in session, woe to the person who dared defy his will![53]

Du Bos attempted to establish a direct line of descent between the Roman emperors and the kings of France, whereas Voltaire saw a break of continuity between the two entities. But both authors viewed the Middle Ages and feudalism in the same way as absolute monarchy viewed it: a period of anarchy, violence, and usurpation. Though the two versions of history differ profoundly, in both there emerge two poles of transition through which legitimate authority, good taste, and "civilization" pass: ancient Rome and modern France.[54]

CHARLEMAGNE AND THE INTERMEDIARY BODIES:
MONTESQUIEU

And yet, regardless of the power of these absolutist syntheses, the monarchy was unable to stem the constitutional questions that continued to arise against a background of crises that were forcing the rethinking of the relationship between the king and his subjects. The monarchy itself sought to impose through administrative measures changes such as the reduction of fiscal privileges, the broadening of the tax base, the merger of tribunals, and the elimination of a number of offices. But it sought to do this without modifying the symbolic relationship between the different entities that comprised the kingdom. The fiscal and administrative changes envisaged had strong implications for the way in which the monarchy was conceptualized. Indeed, they led it into contradiction with itself. Although the changes still defined the king as the unique representative of the kingdom which was divided into orders, corporate bodies, and estates, the reforms tended to level the orders and to homogenize society.[55] Again, we see the monarchy torn between reason and history. The reforms were justified by the public interest; the relationships between the bodies were defined in relation to the past. The monarchy was never able to reconcile the two.

Several trends had weakened the monarchy's ability to construct a solid ideological defense. These currents can all be summed up by a single word: isolation. The symbolic gap between the monarchy and the society over which it ruled was the result of a long process, the most striking manifestation of which was the moving of the court to Versailles. But certain elements of this trend are of particular interest to us. First, it must be noted that the ties between God and king had weakened considerably. Bossuet's enormous effort at the end of the seventeenth century may be seen as representing the ultimate attempt to reclaim the power of theology over profane history. It is significant that in his *Histoire universelle*, in which Providence has a subtle and constant influence over the flow of history that brings about the establishment of absolute monarchy, Bossuet, the famous bishop of Meaux, does not go beyond Charlemagne, who, according to him, began the last, modern epoch, which continued uninterrupted until Louis XIV. Henceforth, theological historiography became increasingly interested in religious history.[56] God's withdrawal is also confirmed on the level of those symbolic acts that were used to affirm the divine nature of the monarchy. One of these had been a ceremony in which the king laid hands on the sick and thus cured them (*le toucher des écrouelles*). It is telling that Louis XV ceased to perform this ceremony after 1738.[57]

This transformation of Jansenism into a political movement represents in a sense the logical outcome of a belief that, in its insistence on the radical transcendence of God, deepened the divide separating the human from the divine. The resulting withdrawal of God had the effect of expanding the realm of the human. For in the absence of divine manifestation, it was more and more left up to human beings to run their world and to make their history. It is not surprising then to see the nobles' passion for history, revived in the seventeenth century, now find its counterpart in the growing interest of the heavily Jansenist magistracy in national history. This renewed interest in history accompanied the reinvention—what we have called the "remythification"—of origins of the figure of Charlemagne, a process that contributed to the isolation of the monarchy. From its first formulations we have seen that monarchical absolutism had a tendency to conceive of the present as the apogee of the movement of history. The metaphorical impasse of the monarchy regarding its own identity in the seventeenth century is a visible sign of this: in becoming the peerless, incomparable king, Louis XIV froze the ideal of the monarchy into that which he embodied in the present. While the monarchy could use history to show its own continuity and the greatness of the kingdom, it could not uphold the national past as an ideal against which it should be measured. By definition, the monarchy in its actual form represented the best and fullest realization of the institution. In sum, it was now the way it should be and everything it should be. The process whereby the monarchy fenced itself up in the present was fraught with consequences. It could not relate its reforms to a return to origins; the technique consisting of using past models to justify and legitimate change and reform was to a large extent unavailable to it. This was not the case for the different orders and corporate bodies. Their open access to the past helped them project onto national history the changes they were demanding and thus to legitimize their resistance to royal policy. We have seen the extent to which the nobiliary point of view drew part of its strength and its energy from the very affirmation of the nobility's decline. This affirmation was liberating in that it helped to locate a historical moment to emulate. What it lacked was the mechanism to attain it. Charlemagne's reign provided the model both for an era of well-being and legitimacy and for the providential man able to lead the subjects to it. For the great king had already demonstrated that the return so desired and so necessary to the happiness of the nation was indeed possible.

The impact of Boulainvilliers's thinking is seen in the explicit references to his work as well as in the many times his portrait of Charlemagne was borrowed throughout the century. These renderings of Charlemagne do however vary, mainly in the way they view the composition of the nation as well as the governing bodies with which the general assemblies or *plaids* were identified. The trend led to a broadening of the group of people who were considered "citizens" to include those who, in Boulainvilliers's thought, had no right to it.[58] As it became more inclusive, Boulainvilliers's thesis only gained in power.

Charlemagne's position within this movement of reinvesting in national history was singularly strengthened by the status Montesquieu gives him in *The Spirit of the Laws*. In his celebrated work, Montesquieu combines Enlightenment principles with a historical perspective in an analysis that creates a place and a function for the aristocracy within the modern monarchy. He also does away with the distinction—so fundamental in Boulainvilliers—between the aristocracy of the sword and that of the robe, and considers them as a single corporate body capable of living in harmony. In this way, Montesquieu recreates the nobiliary thesis in a form that could satisfy a much broader public than the limited caste identifying itself with the ancient Frankish "race." Placing himself at the outset between Boulainvilliers and Du Bos, Montesquieu constructs a theory of the monarchy tempered by intermediary bodies and flourishing in a complex state of interdependency which he describes with the famous maxim: *Point de monarque, point de noblesse; point de noblesse, point de monarque* [No monarch, no nobility; no nobility, no monarch]. In addition to "restoring" the corporate bodies within a modern context, he reestablishes them in history. This philosopher of the nobility extricates the Middle Ages from the black hole to which Du Bos and Voltaire had consigned it and grants it an equal or greater dignity than Greek and Roman antiquity. In his *The Spirit of the Laws*, his introduction to the book deals with "the theory of the feudal laws of the Franks in relation to the establishment of the monarchy":

> I would think my work wanting if I kept silent over an event that occurred only once in the world and that perhaps will never occur again, if I did not speak about those laws that appeared suddenly all over Europe, laws not derived from those known previously. . . . Feudal laws are a beautiful sight. An old oak tree towers; the eye sees the leaves from afar; as they come closer, it sees the stem, but it does not perceive the roots: one must dig up the ground in order to find them.[59]

The author who wrote so extensively about the Greeks and the Romans here emphasizes the truly original nature of the feudal system which acquires the solidity and greatness of an old oak tree. Montesquieu not only rehabilitates the Middle Ages but does so in a style that fits in perfectly with the norm and practices of the eighteenth-century sociability. Much has been made of the "indirection" of Montesquieu's prose in a work that begins by announcing a series of "laws" and then goes through a loosely connected succession of chapters, an approach that in its own way reproduces salon conversations and reflects a certain rococo sensitivity. The chapter on Charlemagne confirms these observations. Located in the middle of the last book, Charlemagne's portrait is striking due to the artful mixture of passionate argument and formal conciseness that distinguishes it from the rest of the text. To his discussion of the Middle Ages Montesquieu adds a sort of medallion portrait of the perfect monarch: "Charlemagne thought to keep the power of the nobility within limits, and to prevent the oppression of the clergy and free men. He *tempered so well the orders* [estates] *of the state that they counterbalanced each other and he remained the master*" (my emphasis).[60] This is the very image of Montesquieu's ideal: intermediary bodies that counterbalance each other, a moderate monarch who nonetheless remains the master. This peerless monarch created "admirable rules" and, moreover, "had them executed." Under his leadership "pretexts for shirking duties were eliminated; mistakes were corrected and abuses reformed or prevented."[61]

What is surprising in this portrait is the way the man is characterized. Montesquieu's entire work focuses on the importance of structures and forms, on the preponderant role played by forces transcending the individual. But here, on the contrary, it is the great man who dominates the whole:

> All were united by his genius. . . . His genius spread to all parts of the empire. We see in the laws of this prince a mind that foresees and understands everything and a force that carries everything along. . . . He knew how to punish; he knew even better how to forgive. His aims were large, his execution simple; there has been no one who possessed to such high degree the art of accomplishing the greatest things with ease and the most difficult ones promptly. He ceaselessly traveled throughout his vast empire, intervening wherever it was necessary. . . . There has never been a prince who was better able to face dangers, never one who was so good at preventing them.[62]

The words expressing Charlemagne's greatness and superiority unfold in a binary rhythm that expresses the power of a leader who at all times controls both sides of every issue, who can see the beginning and the end of every problem. His constant personal involvement in some ways lifts him up above the structures and the forces at work. But the lyricism singing the greatness of the man that marked the first part of the portrait is balanced by praise for the moderation of this marvelous king whose character was so gentle. This "prince who always governed by himself" is admirable even when it comes to details. "A father could learn how to rule his household from his laws." This perfect prince succeeds in reconciling two apparently incompatible ideas and institutions that kept confronting each other in the eighteenth century: absolutism and feudalism, monarchy and nobility. But Montesquieu arrives at this idyllic reconciliation only by glorifying the great man to such an extent that the beauty of the system is effaced by the exceptional individual.

Savior, Legislator, Conqueror, and Bourgeois: Le Paige and Mably

After 1750, the figure of Charlemagne often appeared in the debates on the ancient constitution. The great monarch's reign became the historical justification evoked by the detractors of absolutism, who were advocating increasingly radical "rectifications." Within this movement, two works had quite a remarkable impact: Louis Adrien Le Paige's text on the history of the Parlement, *Lettres historiques sur les fonctions essentielles du Parlement*

(1753) and Gabriel Bonnot de Mably's book on the history of France, *Observations sur l'histoire de France* (1765). Both works appeared during the growing conflict between the parlements and the monarchy. They both directly descend from Boulainvilliers's line of thought. But they are both examples of the tendency to broaden his very limited concept of the "French nation" to include a wider range of people than just the descendants of the old "Frankish" nobility, and by so doing to expand the ranks of those capable of participating in the governing of the realm.

Boulainvilliers argued for a direct descendancy between the Champs de Mars, the "parlements" under Charlemagne, and the Estates-General. Le Paige in turn attempted to make the parlements the legitimate heirs to the legislative assemblies of the first two dynasties. As he tells it, the several parlements together constituted a single body (the *union des classes*) and had acquired the right not only to represent the king before the nation but to represent the nation before the king.[63] The successor of the old "general parlements" is the "depositor and the conservator of the laws and maxims of the state; it examines and it promulgates legitimately and freely all new laws; it gives the monarch important advice for the good of his reign and that of the fatherland (*Patrie*); it even resists him, if necessary, rather than betray these dear interests: in a word, *it curbs*, as Seyssel said to François I, *the absolute power that all kings would like to use*" (Le Paige's emphasis).[64]

Thus the pamphleteer-historian of the parlements uses the historian of the monarchy to back his own argument. But he does so by affirming what Seyssel had explicitly denied in his history of Louis XII: the existence of the old parlements under Charlemagne's reign. For Seyssel, the creation of the parlements was a proof of the superiority of modern monarchy over the ancient one. In contrast, Le Paige sees the reign of Charlemagne as a period of ideal harmony between a strong monarchy and a parlement enjoying its full rights. The ease with which the militant parlementarian takes over Boulainvilliers's description of the great monarch is telling evidence as to the rapprochement of the high aristocracy with the magistracy. It needed only a bit of touching up for it to be adapted to the "parlementary" vision of the national past.

The parlementarian's Charlemagne is described as the most powerful of all kings and the most secure on his throne, but "because he was the most concerned with preserving the rights of his peoples, he was also the best loved."[65] Comparing him with Louis XV, who had recently been proclaimed "Louis the Well-Beloved" (*Louis le Bien-Aimé*), an epithet that soon doubled as an ironic reference to the proclivities of his intimate life, Le Paige presents Charlemagne as the "best loved" because of his respect for the rights of his subjects. The parlementary theoretician and polemicist, who was also a good Jansenist, draws on Hincmar to claim that under

Charlemagne the "senators of the Parlement" could "put their conscience above the king" and that "after their conscience" there was "nothing more dear to them than the real interest of the monarch and the fatherland." And while the monarchy had abandoned the greatness, righteousness, and love of public interest that had characterized Charlemagne's reign, the Parlement did not do so. "Are you not admiring, Monsieur, that for so many centuries, there still survives in the Parlement this same spirit that Charlemagne saw in it?"[66] And then Le Paige describes once again the scene in which Charlemagne circulates among the masses while the Parlement is deliberating. In fact, "the reign of this great king was really that of the opinions and directives that were always received with gratitude and that contributed significantly to the glory of his reign as well as to the happy success of his undertakings."[67] The description of Charlemagne's reign ends with words of praise that were supposed to inspire Louis XV to follow his example: "Happy are the princes who, like this great king, feel the need to be instructed in all things by the magistrates, or even by the people [*les Peuples*]! It is impossible that their states not be always flourishing and their throne not be always splendid."[68]

We can see how thin is the line between the king who feels the need to be instructed by the magistrates and the one who lets himself be instructed "even by the people," in other words, between the corporatist strategy adopted by Le Paige and a democratic logic. This was a line that the abbé Mably did not hesitate to cross in a work that had an enormous impact in the prerevolutionary period and well beyond. Indeed, his *Observations sur l'histoire de France* (1765) represents the decisive fusion of ancient republicanism with a meditation on the French past, of a philosophical tendency à la Rousseau, and a historical tendency adopted by nobiliary thinkers and parlementarians.

Mably greatly modifies the terms of the historical debate. He rejects the notion of a historical continuity and sees the national past as a long series of revolutions. Out of this idea of discontinuity and rupture in the evolution of the nation there emerges a radical critique of the concept of ancient fundamental laws toward which one could or should turn. "The fundamental law of a state is not a heap of rejected, forgotten, and neglected laws but rather it is the law that regulates, prescribes, and constitutes the form of the government."[69] Thus Mably attempts to separate the idea of fundamental law from any necessary link with origins. He also takes pain to point out that an error in the way government has been conceived had already infiltrated the monarchy in the time of Clovis. From the first coronation, there was "confusion of all ideas because of the application of the principles of divine government, which operated through miracles, to the government of the French that *God had abandoned to natural right that is common to all men*."[70]

It would be difficult to find a clearer expression of the fundamental misconception that, in this view, characterized the doctrine of the divine right of kings. Whereas the true fundamental law is universal and applies in principle to all men at all times, this error occurred in history.

Mably borrows his pessimistic vision of the national past from Boulainvilliers, a past he sees as being mired in the sacrifice of the public good for private interests.[71] Likewise, he keeps the language of the nation which in his opinion represents the true transcendent entity. He also retains the Germanist theory derived from Tacitus and setting forth an originary democracy "tempered by the power of the prince and the magnates."[72] The invasion of Gaul was more than a conquest; it was the liberation of a people subjected to Roman rule. Soon, however, the love of freedom gave way to greed. The Franks turned themselves into an aristocracy, and the country fell into chaos and anarchy. Thus history took off on a downward slope leading all the way to the present, with absolute monarchy representing only the victory of the strongest among the magnates. But, like Boulainvilliers, Mably sees Charlemagne as interrupting, even reversing, this movement of history. When the great monarch acceded to the throne he found "only citizens filled with hatred and scorn for one another and looking only after their own private interests." His greatness was to lead the French back "to the ancient principles of government their fathers had brought from Germany."[73]

Mably attempts to accomplish several things at once. Having attempted to deny any link between origins and fundamental law, he now claims that Charlemagne's achievement lay precisely in his having orchestrated a return to "the ancient principles of the government." A happy coincidence indeed between an originary moment and natural right! But what is more, after pointing out that the mistake in Clovis's time was to have confused divine government "that works through miracles" with the worldly government of the French, Mably's choice of words turns Charlemagne himself into a veritable miracle that no one could have foreseen. The historian rhapsodizes at length over the unexpected nature of Charlemagne's arrival on the scene. "From the midst of the barbary in which the kingdom of the French had plunged, there emerged a prince at once philosopher, legislator, patriot, and conqueror." The neglect of the public good had put the kingdom in the sort of deplorable condition that usually would lead a prince to believe that "the highest form of happiness consists in enjoying unbounded power."[74] The parallel with eighteenth-century France is obvious: everything was in place for the establishment of despotic absolutism. The prince needed only to let himself be carried by the current. "The French would have been lost if Charles, whom I will thenceforth call Charlemagne, had had less virtue than genius."[75]

The providential great man, whom nothing could have predicted, miraculously appears on the scene. "It would have been child's play for such a great and resourceful genius to turn to his profit the divisions between his subjects, to humiliate the different orders of the state by pitting one against the other, and to elevate royal prerogative on the ruins of their privileges."[76] In this momentous hero, the nation had found its Savior. Instead of personally benefiting from his immense power that his genius was only strengthening, Charlemagne identifies completely with the nation. He renounces the royal rights established through the tyranny of his predecessors and keeps only "those that immemorial usage had legitimized."[77] The great prince establishes himself as supreme mediator of the divided nation by convincing the three orders ravaged by hatred to "consent to have only the same interests" and to "form one single body [*former un seul corps*]."[78]

Mably emphasizes how deeply pathetic is a nation torn by its own heated passions and wracked by the division opposing private interests to the public good. Mably solicits our compassion for the fate of the principle victim, the "people," that, having been "treated with so much inhumanity since the establishment of feudal dominions [*seigneuries*] and the ruin of the ancient government and having lost all concept of its dignity and its rights, . . . was ready to accept any relief from all the ills being done to it as if it were a favor."[79] Charlemagne had for the people a deep sense of sympathy, and Mably seeks to impart to his readers "this compassion mixed with respect which ordinary men feel upon seeing a fugitive prince deprived of his power."[80] Suddenly, then, the people are transformed into a disinherited prince and the political gift Charlemagne gives to them is nothing less than the reestablishment of their "inalienable rights," that is, participation in the Champs de Mars, "which thus becomes truly the assembly of the nation."[81] This moving sight transforms the tragedy of the national history into a kind of melodrama in which, at the last minute, the hero appears, a *deus ex machina*, to free the victim from the hands of the villain.

For Mably Charlemagne's vision embraced both the past and the future and he stimulated a moral regeneration among the citizens. "It is not enough to order a people to be free for it to be so, it is not enough to bring them laws; rather, the way citizens see, feel, and think must be changed." Eighteenth-century thinkers often evoke the figure of the "Legislator" of the type Rousseau described in abstract form in his *Social Contract*. Mably found him first, as so many others did, in Antiquity in the personage of Lycurgus, then in French history itself.[82] This "legislator of the French" who was able to read the human heart, fostered a vision that transcended his time; yet he also knew that it is necessary to adapt to the mores of his time in order to make the best possible use of them. Mably also depicts a Charlemagne who, after having returned legislative power to the assembly, did not actively participate in the debates of which he was nonetheless the "soul," and only intervened "to serve as mediator."[83] The nation had been returned to itself, and the monarch only executed its will: "Charlemagne willed, ordered, commanded because the nation had willed, ordered, and commanded and charged him with proclaiming its laws, with observing them, and with being their protector and avenger."[84] In order to ensure the diffusion of the laws and the unity of the nation, the great restorer king sent his *missi dominici* to help the local assemblies that were held in the provinces. Thus was bridged the pernicious gap separating subject from citizen, the orders and corporate bodies from the nation, and private interest from the general good. "The astonished French understood from their own experience that one class of citizens could be happy without oppressing the others."[85] Thus the rule of transparency was established, and the nation, now acting as a single, unitary subject, could observe, oversee, and control its own workings and governance.

> The entire nation continually kept its eyes on each public figure. The magistrates were observed, and they learned to respect themselves: morals, without which freedom always degenerates into dangerous license, righted themselves, and the love of the public good joined to freedom made every day more productive and healthy.[86]

Thanks to Charlemagne's mediation, hatred abated and an era of unity began. For the first time love of fatherland and glory surfaced as dominant values for the French and made them into "a completely new nation." "In dividing all, says a tyrant, I will become all-powerful. Be united, said Charlemagne to his people, and we will be happy." In Mably, this quest for unity leads directly to conquest. "Acting finally with this zeal that freedom gives and with this unity that gives greater strength, the French found that nothing could resist them. They conquered [*soumirent*] part of Spain, Italy, all of these vast lands all the way to the Vistula and the Baltic sea; and the glory of the French name, like that of the ancient Romans, spread all the way to Africa and Asia."[87] A passion for freedom and unity were at the heart of the conquering force of the nation. A return to democracy led naturally to conquest and empire, and through conquest the French ended up equal in greatness and glory to the ancient Romans.[88]

This history of a Charlemagne who pulls the nation out of chaos, gives it back to itself, and leads it to the conquest of the world represents "the most intriguing, interesting, and instructive part of our modern history."[89] Charlemagne's remythification reaches its apex in this amalgam of "national" discourse, religious language, and ancient republicanism. The "Gallic" third estate has a place here in the bosom of the nation as it accedes to legislative power. Not only does Mably give us a Charlemagne savior of the nation, legislator of the French, and great conqueror, he also turns the emperor's private life into an example of the perfect bourgeois household. "Even though his wife was empress and queen of almost all of Europe, she looked after the furniture of the palace and her husband's clothes like any simple housewife would." Charlemagne administered his domains with prudence and thrift "and ordered the vegetables he could not consume to be sold."[90] The reign of harmony, happiness, and transparency was established thanks to a new vision, a new way of seeing things; political transformation depended on a moral one. We can now understand why Charlemagne's domestic life was so important. Habits, ways of seeing are formed in private life, within the family: morality and politics are made up of one and the same thing.

After Charlemagne's death, history resumed its course; the people "fell back into nothingness: new habits had not been sufficiently instilled for the people to understand its own power." The message transmitted by this passage is crystal clear: even though freedom is an inalienable right at once universal and immemorial, the French had fallen so low that they could only conceive of it as the gift of a great man.

FOLLOWING CHARLEMAGNE'S EXAMPLE: MALESHERBES

One might assume that the philosophes expressed little interest in the ongoing reinvestment in history. However, Mably's brother, the famous Sensualist philosopher Condillac, borrows his brother's statements almost word for word in his *Cours d'études.* He wrote this study manual during his stay in Parma where Louis XV's eldest daughter, having become duchess of Parma and of Plaisance, had entrusted him with the education of her son. The Germanist thesis, all of the depiction of the restitution and of the welcoming of the third estate into the assembly remains pretty much as it is in Mably, including the vision of the *ex nihilo* appearance of the providential man rising all by himself above the world that surrounds him to become its master. "It is a great wonder that there was a genius such as Charlemagne in the eighth century. He is the proof that great men rise on their own."[91] Condillac, however, does focus on one specific aspect, namely, the work Charlemagne did to promote literacy and the schools. According to Condillac, the task of the enlightened and all-powerful king is akin to that of the teacher. "But you will easily understand," he writes to his student, "that knowledge is born and develops in a whole people the same way that it is born and develops in each individual man. The history of your mind is thus a summary of the history of the human mind."[92] The great king's work with his people is like that of a teacher because great collectivities are like individuals: the more they follow opinions in harmony with reason, the happier they are.

Gradually the notion of Charlemagne as master of public opinion began to emerge.[93] The love people felt for him became a reasoned love feeding proper patriotic passions. The transparency of his reign provided the best example of proper public relations for royal administration and policy. This transparency was in sharp contrast to the veil covering the workings of a monarchy that was increasingly led by ministers or, worse, by agents and emissaries who managed to hide their many abuses. The 1771 "coup d'état" of Maupeou led to a growing awareness of both the vulnerability of the parlements and of the potential uses of the unlimited power of the absolute monarchy. Henceforth, the debate increasingly focused on the Estates-General at the national level or, that failing, on the provincial estates at the local level. The nation had to be consulted. Louis XV's death and the advent of Louis XVI gave new hope and a good opportunity to reflect on the nature of the monarchy. The figure of Charlemagne, as it was reinvented in the circles of "historians" opposed to absolutism, was redeployed in this context. Here, he became the leader who was not only able to give the nation the means to listen to itself but who himself listened to what the nation had to say.

In an atmosphere of growing crisis, the magistrates of the *cour des aides*, that is, the court of final appeal for all matters relating to taxation, who claim to be the "defenders of the people," denounced the secrecy of administrative despotism, which they claimed to be as tyrannical as oriental despotism. In their view, this government's failing lay both in its constitution and its morals. The only remedy was to lift the veil, to allow the nation itself to speak. This is what is recommended in the famous *Remonstrances* written by Malesherbes that the *cour des aides* addressed to the king in 1775. Malesherbes, the president of the court, who had frequented philosophes and used his position as director of the library between 1750 and 1763 to protect them, draws a parallel between the circulation of free speech in the assemblies of the old monarchy and the popularity printing granted to writing. "The entire nation had to acquire the taste and the habit of instructing itself by reading, so that there would be enough persons skilled in the art of writing to lend their ability to the general public, just as those who, gifted with a natural eloquence, had spoken to our fathers on the Champs de Mars or in public plaids."[94] The nation had acquired enough enlightenment to express itself intelligently on affairs of state, but it also needed to find the best way to communicate with the monarch:

> The truth should be told, Sire, that the simplest, most natural way, the one that most conforms to the constitution of this monarchy, would be

to hear the assembled nation itself; . . . no one should let you be unaware that the unanimous wish of the nation is to obtain the convening
of the Estates-General or at least the provincial estates.[95]

Malesherbes then invites the king to return to his illustrious ancestor's
practice in a passage in which the president of the *cour des aides* argues that
such an act would be an affirmation of royal power. "It is up to you to
judge, Sire, if your power would be weakened if you imitated Charlemagne, this proud monarch who so furthered the prerogatives of his
crown. Should you follow his example, you would reign over a nation the
whole of which would be your council."[96] The need is for a strong king
who is able to take in hand a government that has already exceeded the
limits of its established authority and of which the monarch is as much a
victim as the nation.

Making a Whole Nation Move: Le Trosne

In the second half of the century, the calls for a return to the golden age of
Charlemagne multiplied. Their importance can be measured first by the
fact that they were henceforth integrated into discourses that previously
had had little room for history or questions pertaining to fundamental and
originary law; and, second, by the monarchy's attempts to reappropriate a
figure it could no longer ignore. We know the extent to which eighteenth-
century rationalism could and did serve as justification for absolutism.
From Voltaire to Turgot and Condorcet we see the repetition and multipli-
cation of the ideal image of a monarchy embodying right reason and,
therefore, enjoying absolute legitimacy and power. In this view, the king
was in his kingdom as God was in the universe, enforcing an order dictated
by universal principles. Theoretically, such a point of view needs no historical justification precisely because of the ahistoricism of the legitimizing
principles found in eternal nature. Even Voltaire's obsession with the past
involves a fundamental rejection of it and all its abuses. Condorcet sums up
well the basic incompatibility between rationalist arguments and justifications drawn from history. He points out the absurdity of these historical
idealizations of the national past in his discussion of Montesquieu: "Can
the *great mind* [*grand esprit*] of Charlemagne still be referred to in the eighteenth century in philosophical discussions? Surely this must be a joke."[97]
True political philosophy had to be developed independent of history. But,
as the century progressed, having recourse to history was increasingly
common as the means to formulate fundamental reforms and above all to
conceive of their being implemented in the context of France. Thus for Le

Trosne, an ardent physiocrat, Charlemagne's epoch was the proof that fundamental reforms could be accomplished in France.

In his treatise on tax reform, *De L'Administration provinciale et de la réforme de l'impôt* in the years following the firing of Turgot, Guillaume-François Le Trosne attempts to resolve the problem of the apparently unbridgeable gap between ideal theories and political realities. Timid minds, he claims, might agree that absolute principles such as the laws of natural and social order might be true in theory and might even be applicable in a new nation, "but they would argue that there are great risks inherent in leading a nation back to them after it obeyed opposite ones for so many centuries; they would argue that such a major undertaking is dangerous" and without hope of succeeding.[98] Le Trosne's arguments are directed against this vision.

Published in 1779 and again in 1787, the work develops the main arguments of proposed physiocratic reforms: provincial assemblies and national assemblies made up of propertied citizens; free trade; unitary land tax. According to Le Trosne, respect for absolute principles of political economy has the advantage of establishing the universal good through the happiness of individuals. In this happy kingdom, sovereign authority resembles "the authority of the Supreme Master, always beloved, because his immutable will is order itself." Le Trosne conceives of this sovereign authority "as an emanation of the authority of God, as it is His most perfect image on earth."[99] In fact, the physiocrat attempts to obscure as much as possible the definition or, rather, the exact identity of the sovereign. Because principles are fixed and universal, the state becomes, in its very essence, an administrative entity: its task is to execute the laws dictated by reason, to apply the absolute rules of political economy. The assemblies made up of representatives chosen by the nation participate in this administration, and, once the nature of these laws is well understood, there could be no difference between the will of the assemblies and that of the king: there would only be a single national will.

This way of viewing things helps us understand the power public opinion could have, and why it is so necessary to inform it. Once it is enlightened on the "principles discussed and recognized to be true . . . , public opinion . . . would no doubt penetrate the sovereign bodies that are the sole channel through which the nation can express its needs today; public opinion would enlighten their proceedings, it would dictate their presentations."[100] Thus property owners must learn to recognize their true interests. But how was this to be done? All the ambiguity of the physiocrat's thought surfaces when he affirms that "it is public opinion that governs; it is thus important to become its master."[101] Le Trosne does not underestimate the magnitude of his task: "In some way everything must be destroyed so as to recreate everything, the absolute reign of liberty and property by the destruction of everything contrary to it. . . . The revolution unavoidably must hurt what in France is referred to as the *constitution* or, rather, what passes for it."[102]

To achieve this tabula rasa the nation must be enlightened and convinced; there must be formulated a plan for regenerating the nation (*plan régénérateur*) and it must be announced in its entirety from the very beginning of its implementation.[103] We must, explains Le Trosne, act with courage, speed, and determination while maintaining a broad vision of things. It is necessary to unite "all the hearts and all the wishes . . . , in a word, to turn the nation that is nothing at present into *a true living and organized body politic*."[104] Thanks to public education, public opinion, which is at present lost and fragmented by the esprit de corps of the different corporatist bodies, will change into an "*esprit national*" or a kind of "national mind."[105] Thus the nation is constituted into a living being with a body and a mind animated with a will akin to that of an individual willing to put his passions in the service of transcendent and absolute reason. In fact, the nation itself becomes the embodiment of this reason.

But who is going to act and how can the weight of habits and of the esprit de corps that are dividing the nation be overcome? "There is to be in the state only one will that orders, acts, and executes, and it must be common to the leader and to the members." How are we, asks Le Trosne, to attain this objective in the present context? Since the 1660s, notes the physiocrat, the country has been in a political impasse, the nation seems to be moribund, "deprived of life and action."[106] Le Trosne emphasizes how disastrous the present situation is. It is the constitution, that is, the present form of government itself, that induces the greatest opposition to reforms. However, he readily recognizes the paradox at the very heart of the undertaking he is proposing: "If absolute authority is necessary to overcome resistance and to bring about a great revolution through a general reform, this authority can only inspire confidence and make the plan it has executed endure if it enchains its own self and gives up the harmful power it has of destroying its own work by strengthening all the institutions apt to maintain this plan."[107]

How then can an absolute power striving to put itself in chains be conceived in such a context? Experience seems to prove the impossibility of such an exercise. Thus the physiocrat's propositions run the risk of being reduced to a theoretical daydream detached from reality. This is why Le Trosne turns to Charlemagne's remythified history: the past is the only way to plan a future revolution. In a way, the aim is to fuse the fundamental law evoked by historians and the fundamental law of universal reason. The Carolingian myth becomes not only the measure of the present, but its status as real history makes it the guarantor that reform can be achieved. Mably appears again through Condillac in the many citations Le Trosne draws from the *Cours d'étude*. In Malesherbes's *Remonstrances* of 1775, the physiocrat sees nothing less than a "monument of the patriotic spirit."[108]

Le Trosne's portrait of the great king includes many of the elements we have already seen but, because he incorporates them into an administrative vision of the government, his is the most radical representation. His Charlemagne established a provincial administrative system through the local assemblies. He took a barbarian people, civilized them, elevated them to his own level by enabling them to participate in government, and he succeeded in turning them into a national body. Charlemagne's gift becomes a gift of life. The creation of a reasoning national spirit is tied to that of a national body. In Le Trosne's eyes, Charlemagne acquires an authority that is bounded only by the absolute principle of reason, and, in a manner of speaking, he even accomplishes the work of God: Charlemagne creates the nation in man's image:

> Indeed, no single man had ever obtained authority broader than that of making a whole nation move, of uniting millions of individuals to turn them into a single body, to lead it as if it were a single man and to govern its own will by making it conform to his own.[109]

Here, unity is total: one body, one mind, one doctrine, one practice. The concept of the nation as a single man is the faithful reflection of the image of the heroic man elevated to a quasi-divine status. We should not underestimate the contribution of Sensualist philosophy to this political vision. Here, the people taken as a whole becomes a sort of wild child, and the hero-king, imbued with the right principles of political economy, has the mission of educating them. Thus Le Trosne reformulates the triple identity of the monarch, of sovereignty, and of the nation, but this time from the perspective of the Enlightenment.

Against the negativity of history, against the destructive flow of time, the providential figure intervenes and makes it possible to go back to a lost perfection, to restore the golden age. This age is no longer located outside of national history but within the very current of that history, even though it represents only an exceptional moment. The action of pulling the collectivity off its tragic and alienating course in order to return it to itself is no longer seen as occurring through a king mediating between men and God, but through a king mediating between, on the one hand, men who are lost, divided, and in a state of subjection and, on the other, these same men who have become conscious of their collective being. All these depictions show a Charlemagne who, through a disinterested act of renunciation, made it possible for the nation to go back in time. Through his association with the assemblies, regardless of their role in the various systems proposed, the most powerful king in French history also becomes increasingly anti-absolutist. Even Le Trosne's position propounding administrative absolutism is surreptitiously contrary to absolute monarchy. However, in spite of this hostility to the doctrine and practice of absolutism, there emerged, in the midst of the images of a king receptive to the nation, the idea of a power even stronger than absolute power. This power transcended any other existing powers and interests and, through the force of Charlemagne's genius, succeeded in imposing itself upon everything. This image, drawn and redrawn throughout the century, played an important role in the construction of the ideological bases upon which Napoleon would build his empire.

Charlemagne to the Rescue of the Monarchy: Moreau

The ideological onslaught that was coming by way of history, along with a seemingly never-ending series of crises, intensified the risks of a possible delegitimization of the absolute monarchy. The figure of Charlemagne confronted the eighteenth-century Bourbon kings both as a contradictory model and as the historical proof that modern monarchy had lost its way. The remythified Charlemagne became a means to imagine a radically different mode of interaction between king and subjects. He became a figure that could not be ignored in debates on fundamental law, and in discussions on the "constitution." This figure appeared in the arguments of the supporters of the nobiliary thesis, of protesting supporters of parlement, of "democrats," and even of physiocrats.

But what about the monarchy itself in the second half of the century? What was its response to the challenge posed by the golden Carolingian age? As mentioned earlier, the monarchy proceeded more in response to contingent circumstances than by following an explicit, coherent policy. It found itself trapped by its own efforts to see the present as the apex of a historical process and to conceptualize collective evolution as progress leading to the greatness of the present. The monarchy's rear guard became singularly exposed in moments of crisis when it was obvious that everything was not for the best or when it had to face harsh criticism. Given the way it conceived of itself, absolute monarchy was by definition unable to evoke a past golden age. It increasingly expressed and defended the reforms it attempted to implement in terms of present necessity and public utility, although its legitimacy, that is, the ideological foundations that authorized it to act, came from the past. This contradiction opened up a breach into which the ablest critics of absolutism eagerly jumped.

The monarchy lost the "battle for history."[110] This was not because it had failed to recognize the threats it faced. On the contrary, it made explicit the consequences of historical arguments that were used to back the claims and demands of the various governing bodies. Paradoxically, the very clarity of the monarchy's rebuttals often worked to strengthen its opponents' arguments, as seen, for instance, in the consequences of the monarchy's response to the parlements. In 1766 the king harangued the magistrates in a famous session that came to be called the Flagellation session. In his speech he explicitly brought together and articulated with surprising force and coherence the parlementarians' previously fragmented claims.

Regarding Charlemagne, the monarchy well understood the strategic importance of the great king and of his association with both fundamental law and the assemblies. The monarchy understood that it could no longer avoid the issue the way Du Bos had done, nor, like Voltaire, condemn a monarch who was so universally celebrated. The problem was all the more complex in that works of praise written with the explicit or tacit support of the monarchy only served to add to the aura surrounding the great king. Thus the Benedictine monks of Saint-Maur were composing a multifaceted image of Charlemagne in the literary history of France they were writing, *Histoire littéraire de la France,* that was looked upon favorably by the monarchy in spite of the monks' Jansenist leanings. The image of Charlemagne they created was aimed at satisfying the demands of Gallic Jansenism as much as those of monarchist absolutism.[111] In fact, certain aspects of the figure of Charlemagne had a marked "national" character that pleased adherents on all sides. But even these kinds of works that the monarchy could not avoid approving did not help it confront the "constitutional" problem posed by the great "restorer." On the contrary, these affirmations of the great king's prestige had unwanted side effects in that, in some way, they served to strengthen the position of the monarchy's critics.

The pro-parlement opposition was winning this battle thanks to its ability to fuse history with public law. The monarchy was aware of this fact as well as the possible impact these interpretations of the past might have on public opinion. In addition, the feeling of its own inadequacy in that domain led the monarchy to favor the creation of a public repository of charters. This project was proposed in 1762 by Jacob-Nicolas Moreau, a well-known antiphilosophe. The repository was to contain vast juridical and historical documentation to be used to help ministers conceive and write laws. The aim was to provide them with weapons to fight against the parlements and to provide the monarchy the possibility of developing a coherent interpretation of the past. "In this century, when the people judge everything and abuse so much of the half knowledge they have acquired, we must oppose false opinions with useful and proven truths. It seems to

me that the art of dispensing these truths as needed and the manner of ac-
crediting them deserve some of the concerns of government."[112] In this enterprise, Moreau obtains the help of the Benedictine monks, but he also
collaborates with medievalists from the Academy of Inscriptions such as
Sainte-Palaye and Bréquigny.

Moreau also attempts to write a pro-monarchist interpretation of the
national past in his *Principes de morale, de politique et de droit public, puisés dans
l'histoire de notre Monarchie ou discours sur l'histoire de France, dédiés au Roi*
[Principles of Morality, Politics, and Public Law Drawn from the History
of Our Monarchy or Treatise on the History of France, dedicated to the
King]. This enormous work is of particular interest in that it makes it possible to measure the importance Charlemagne had assumed as a figure of
opposition in monarchic consciousness. Moreau's approach consists of adopting and renewing Du Bos's Romanist thesis. In this view, the true basis of
the French monarchy lies in the ruins of the Roman empire. The fundamental principles of the Roman government ensured essential rights to all
subjects: freedom, property, and the peaceful enjoyment of possessions.
From this perspective, Charlemagne's accession to the empire becomes "the
work of a farsighted and profound policy" that reconstructs the links to the
true foundations of the monarchy. Thus, in the passage from Antiquity to
modernity, Charlemagne's reign for Moreau represents a crucial moment of
return to the source. "He was no longer king of the Franks . . . he was the
heir to this Roman power destined to give laws to the entire world; he was
successor to the Caesars, and, already in possession of their ancient legacy,
he regained all their rights."[113]

> He was not, however, the founder of the French government; but he
> was its restorer. In the principles of his administration, *we find again all
> the laws of our primitive constitution;* but after having noted the base on
> which he built his authority and after getting a deeper grasp of his
> views and having meditated on his plan, *we can forget the ferocity and the
> despotism of our first race. With him begins the reign of laws* under a
> regime in which the power of our kings and the freedom of their peo-
> ples are still in step. (my emphasis)[114]

Charlemagne made it possible to forget the kings of the first race. His
reign constituted a new point of departure, one showing that French kings
were the true heirs of the Roman emperors. Moreau argues that we need to
go back to Charlemagne to find the fundamental laws of the monarchy.
Thus he agrees to see in Charlemagne's reign what so many critics of the
government claim to uncover in him. This explains why the historian, defender of the monarchy, is not satisfied with giving only a positive vision of

the great king. He feels compelled to refute views of Charlemagne as anything other than one of the most illustrious kings to have ruled in the world, a monarch governing with the most absolute and least arbitrary power, a direct heir to the Caesars. Thus Moreau becomes a kind of Don Quixote of historiography and tilts at the greatest representatives of the various currents of eighteenth-century thought. Philosophers, aristocrats, republicans: he fights them all on behalf of the monarchy for the ideological site occupied by the figure of Charlemagne. In doing so, he inadvertently makes the power of these other interpretations more explicit and brings to light the extent to which they are threatening the legitimacy of the monarchy.

In order for Charlemagne to bear the ideological weight the monarchy's apologist was putting on him, the emperor first had to be cleared of the accusations of fanaticism and inhumanity that had been leveled against him: thus Voltaire had to be confronted. Moreau attacks the philosophe, who had seen only a man driven by ambition, having invaded Saxony "for the sole pleasure to be its master."[115] Although he acknowledges that Charles fell prey to the barbarism of his century, Moreau emphasizes how great an obstacle the Saxons were to the establishment of a wise and peaceful government and how much the great king's subjects were victims of the Saxons' repeated incursions.

And yet, though he is concerned with denouncing Voltaire's errors, his greatest efforts are aimed at responding to the arguments of Montesquieu and Mably. He discusses the urgency of his task with surprising frankness. He agrees with Mably that Charlemagne returned its originary freedom to the nation and himself set limits to his own authority. Yet Moreau also argues that if we go along with Mably and the notion that the king obeyed the assembly of the nation and only executed the laws it passed, we should then also have to assume that this assembly had the right to ask him to account for his own actions. Moreau insists on making explicit all the consequences of Mably's claims:

> Here the chain of consequences frightens me; it is terrible, it extends all the way to us: how could the successors of Hughes Capet have been able to seize little by little an authority that Charlemagne did not have? Our kings, in gathering under their crown the title to all public power, have they despoiled the nation from which they held the scepter or, on the contrary, have they only recovered the rights taken away from their predecessors, rights that are indefeasible because the indefeasible freedom of peoples required in itself that the sovereign be put back into the possession of the right to protect it? This problem was imprudently submitted to the perusal of the masses. Its solution is thus of import to our kings if they want to know the nature of their power.[116]

But, even though Moreau denounces Mably's theories, which he summarizes so concisely, and in spite of his affirmations that Charlemagne enjoyed absolute power, his rhetoric is clearly part of a defensive strategy.

Moreau well understands the implications of comparing the government of England of his time with that of France under Charlemagne, a parallel Moreau (erroneously) attributes originally to Montesquieu. Moreau takes pains to identify all of the elements used in the attempt to establish secret links between the two governments. "And we are told that this is what Charlemagne did, this is what Charlemagne was. We are asked whether, when we study the political constitution he established, we do not see it as entirely similar to the constitution of the government of Great Britain today? We are told that legislative authority was vested in one house for the clergy, in one for the nobility, and in one for the commoners. And then it is claimed that this happened under one of our greatest kings and at a period that cannot be studied enough if we care to know the true principles of the French government."[117] Moreau concludes that the argument relying on the English form of government to prove "that France, under Charlemagne, was a republic, thus cannot prove anything. Charlemagne was the master of his kingdom, and that is what a King must be."[118]

Moreau, the historian of the monarchy, cites at length from Montesquieu's ideal portrait of the great king and then uses it to attack the theory of the intermediary bodies. In his view, during the time of Charlemagne the clergy and the nobility were in conflict while the people were in danger of being crushed by the magistracy (in Moreau's imagination, already constituted at the time). Towns looked to the prince as the protector of a popular freedom that clearly did not imply the right to participate in the government. Charlemagne's masterpiece was to give back a just freedom to all the orders. By restricting the power of the magistrates he asserted his right to exercise the three functions of his authority: legislative, judiciary, and administrative. In order to weaken the magistrates he multiplied the *conventus*, or assemblies, that were held in his palace as well as in provincial capitals and elsewhere. These assemblies did not have any legislative power; they had been created to enable the king to listen directly to the people without needing the magistrates as intermediaries. They were, in short, "so many organs he lent to the public consciousness so that it could constantly inform his own." A careful examination of the laws passed at that time shows that "they all presuppose the freedom of all and the power of a single one."[119]

We can indeed understand why the monarchy ultimately gave only a lukewarm reception to a work that inadvertently proved the constitutional fragility of the monarchy. Moreau had planned an enormous project of forty volumes, but only twenty of them were published before the Revolution interrupted his work. In its unfinished state this *Discours sur l'histoire de France* appears as a testimony to the monarchy's inability to articulate its own history in the face of competing interpretations. The author nonetheless became a sort of minister of history under Louis XVI. The place he gives Charlemagne, one that is quantitatively greater than that of any other king, shows well the strategic importance that the emperor's reign had acquired in the debates on the constitution of the monarchy.

Constitution and Revolution: The Estates-General

In his discussion of the assemblies held by Charlemagne, Moreau was voicing one of the monarchy's strongest inclinations in the second half of the eighteenth century. Indeed, one of the constants of monarchic policy until the convening of the Estates-General in 1789 was the attempt to bypass the magistracy by the creation of other assemblies. It is not by chance that the quasi-official preamble to the Assembly of Notables, *Préambule sur l'Assemblée des Notables*, attempted to situate Louis XVI in direct line of descent from the great king:

> The assemblies of Notables or of citizens of all orders, called Champs de Mars or Champs de Mai because they were held in the open in the months indicated, produced, in Charlemagne's time, the fundamental laws of the kingdom: they were followed in later times by assemblies of the Estates-General, which then replaced them. . . . It was the love of the public good along with Louis XVI's permission, seconded by a minister whose prudence and righteousness are character-forming models, that revived these assemblies so apt to arouse the zeal of the nation and cement its loyalty.[120]

The attempts by the king and his ministers to recover the figure of Charlemagne failed. In the monarchy's last offensive against the parlements, the minister of justice, Lamoignon, attempted to create a "plenary court" that was to replace the parlements in registering laws and taxes. Lamoignon put forth this new project under the guise of a return to origins by claiming that this new court was a restoration of an ancient institution. Antoine Barnave, a young lawyer at the parlement of Grenoble, who was destined to have a brilliant future, denounced the ploy: 'With the reading of the edict, the first remark that comes to mind is about the miserable ruse perpetrated by using the word '*Rétablissement*' [restoration]. How could they have assumed the ignorance of a whole people?" He evokes the "primitive constitution that flourished under Charles the Great" and declares that insurrection, though it is a resource held in common by oppressed peoples, should be used only as "the last and worst resort." He ends up with a passionate request to the king, asking him to act like Charlemagne, a request that I cite at length because it sums up well both the themes woven around the great monarch and the art and manner of deploying them to mobilize public opinion.[121]

> Open your eyes, sensitive and good king; see the deep abyss in which your unworthy servants have thrown your empire, see the harmful effects of the blind and illegitimate authority they have appropriated for themselves in your name. . . .
>
> Call, call, it is time, call your loyal people to deliberate with you, only they can offer you enough light . . . they alone will offer you the proofs of this love that will bring tears to your eyes and that will fill your fatherly heart with happiness; you will see joy and acclamations take the place, in a single day, of so much pain; you will be called father of the people and restorer of the monarchy.
>
> Those who told you that this happy institution would weaken your power are cowards. Charlemagne gave its long forgotten constitution back to the nation. As the leader of an even larger empire, surrounded by untamed tributaries, gathering in his hands the threads of an immense administration, he reigned for forty years in the midst of the acclamations of a legislating people, and he died leaving behind the name of the most powerful of monarchs and the greatest of mortals.[122]

The light of reason, the warmth of sentiments, the denunciation of treason, the praise of a power so great it did not need to assert itself to the nation in any other way than by the restoration of the ancient constitution, these are so many motifs that developed throughout the century and that were resonating forcefully in the prerevolutionary period.

Charlemagne's reign is often described as the moment of true and pure constitutionality in the numerous pamphlets that were published dealing with the form the Estates-General should have.[123] The descriptions of Boulainvilliers, Montesquieu, Mably, and Le Trosne picked up, reworked, and often, despite their deep incompatibilities, merged to suit a given pamphleteer's political perspective. The power of the image of the great king stems from his ability to rediscover the ancient government and *restore* to the nation its rights. "Charlemagne, the only legislator of whom France can be proud, also conceived the project of regenerating the nation."[124] He is depicted as the king of the third estate, the one who opened the Champs de Mars to the people. We see him scolding the clergy with harangues echoing Gallican Jansenism.[125] After Charlemagne, "the greatest man since the Romans," the only real victories the kings were able to achieve were at the expense of their people. Charlemagne came before the abuses of the feudal system and is outside the space contaminated by absolute kings. Even better, he freed the monarchy from the grip of despotic ministers often identified with the mayors of the palace at the end of the first race but who reappear in the Third Dynasty as Mazarin, Richelieu, and their successors.

> Let those perverted ministers who try to distance the kings from the memory of the national assemblies by exaggerating dangers, let them read the life of this great man! Let them learn from it that no single year passed without him assembling the nation, and let them know that this nation was not limited to the boundaries of France but that he ruled over Germany and Italy! Let them learn that this hero won more battles than they [the ministers] have committed crimes and have plotted infamous and odious intrigues and that the hand that gave the law to the people and that submitted itself to its voice belonged to the same man whom his enemies could not look upon without terror and who seemed to have victory at his service![126]

These repeated references to the great king indicate that across the political spectrum, from the monarchy to the republicans, those who sought to use history to legitimize the different forms of the assemblies of the nation, resorted to the figure of Charlemagne at one time or another. The plasticity of the image of the great man is best illustrated by the debate on the secular constitution of the clergy of 1790. On May 29, in a speech to the assembly, the archbishop of Aix, Monsignor de Boisgelin, evokes Charlemagne to back his argument against the civil constitution. The next day, M. Treilhard speaks in favor of this measure in a speech blending reflections on theology and history. We can hear echoes of Jansenist Augustianism in his argument that the Church "can only be judge of that which is supernatural and divine, and . . . everything else must be submitted to temporal authority." He seeks confirmation of this claim in the politics of Charlemagne, the king who "regulated in the national assemblies all matters of ecclesiastical policy and discipline. He also pronounced on how bishops should be named and where they should serve."[127] In the prerevolutionary period, and even during the early years of the Revolution, among individuals who were otherwise adamantly opposed to each other, all seemed nevertheless to agree that under Charlemagne things were the way they should be.

In fact, as long as the monarchy was still in power, Charlemagne remained the model of a king able to practice royal power properly and the only one to restore the ancient constitution. Although he possessed a power that transcended everything around him, he was able to reign while closely collaborating with the national assemblies, whose laws he faithfully executed. After the disappearance of the monarchy with the Revolution, Charlemagne of course soon became a sort of nostalgic memory. Yet he was also seen as a means to end the growing disorder, as the model for the providential man able to put an end to the Revolution.

However, from that time on, the idea of restoration was to take on another meaning. Already in 1795, Stéphanie de Genlis, the former tutor to the children of the duke of Orleans and future inspector of elementary schools under Napoleon, chose Charlemagne's era to represent the possibility that the nation could be regenerated once again in a very different manner from the absolutely new beginning sought by the Revolution. We will return to this novelist who took advantage of a cultural and literary revalorization of the Middle Ages that was taking place at the same time, but on a different plane, so to speak, the debates on the ancient constitution. But it should be pointed out that she was also inspired by those very debates to draw a parallel between two founding moments. Her book is titled *Chevaliers du Cygne ou la cour de Charlemagne* [Knights of the Order of the Swan or the Court of Charlemagne] and its subtitle informs us that this work constitutes "a historical and moral tale . . . in which every trait that might seem to be alluding to the French Revolution is, in fact, drawn from History"—a clever way of indicating what the book is about, while disavowing it.[128] Her ploy, then, is transparent. And though her disclaimer might exonerate the letter of the text, it also draws attention to its spirit because it calls for an allegorical reading that brings together not only reality and fiction, but past and present, as well. In order to bring the country out of its present chaos, one must look to the man who had already succeeded in doing this in the past. From Boulainvilliers and Le Paige to Mably and Condillac, all looked upon Charlemagne as he who had been able to pull the country out of chaos and engineer a national reconciliation.

Stéphanie de Genlis labels her novel a "moral tale," since she sees herself as living in a time of unleashed passions, violence, and immorality, in other words, a time when the need to rekindle morality had become the overriding issue. "But if I want to depict constant and passionate love, sublime and loyal friendship, enthusiasm for glory and virtue, where can I find such perfect models? Alas! We have to look for them in history since the century in which I was born cannot offer them to me."[129] Thus she turns to the past, but she looks for her models in the national past and not in Greek or Roman antiquity. She explicitly rejects the century of the Enlightenment and goes back to the French Middle Ages, projecting the entire feudal civilization onto Charlemagne. The moral regeneration to which she wishes to contribute cannot be found through the pathways of reason nor draw its model from the wisdom of the ancient Romans and Greeks. And so her sentimental education takes Charlemagne as a model, a Charlemagne who has been reinvented and remythified over the course of the century. But in addition to these historical and political reflections that contributed to turning the Middle Ages into the antiquity of modernity, there were also efforts to explore and to revalorize medieval literature, where the emperor with the flowing white beard also played a primary role. We will now explore this second tendency in order to grasp more fully the power the figure of Charlemagne acquired in the eighteenth century.

The Old Knighthood and the Old Romances: Sainte-Palaye and the Count de Caylus

As we have seen, the slow movement toward a rehabilitation of medieval literature began in the seventeenth century. As early as 1670, the learned abbé Huet, in his treatise on the origins of romances, claims that the old romances of the lands of northern Europe were created locally rather than imported from elsewhere. He rejoices because "our nation, having ceded to others the prize for epic poetry and history, beat them so well in this genre that their best romances barely equaled the worst of ours."[130] Like the political form of the mixed monarchy studied by Montesquieu, these old romances were marked by a European, and a particularly French, originality that was different from the works of Antiquity. Thus, it is not surprising that nobiliary theoreticians were among the first to encourage the reading of medieval romances. In his history of the peerage, *Histoire de la Pairie*, Jean Le Laboureur praises these works and sees in them portraits of the olden days.[131]

A theory of feudalism was developed from examination of ancient laws and other "monuments" of the Middle Ages. A reconstruction of the "laws" of chivalry was pieced together from the chronicles and romances, which were primarily viewed as useful documents. Thus, after the long period of criticism and demythification that marked the Renaissance, a movement of recovery had begun. This recovery was not aimed at rescuing works from the aesthetic oblivion to which they had been relegated. Even in the eighteenth century no one tried to defend their formal aspects. The aim rather was to place them within the field of history. Seen as faithful accounts of the period in which they were written, they became the mirrors not of a simple political and juridical constitution but of a whole ancient French civilization with its mores, customs, and traditions.

The monarchy raised no objection to the study of old customs. After all, they related not only to the national past but they could very well be interpreted as remnants of the Roman military organization, and thus could be used to support the Romanist thesis.[132] We have already seen some examples of the way the monarchy attempted to use such customs under Louis XIV's reign. But in the eighteenth century, with the studies undertaken by La Curne de Sainte-Palaye in the Academy of Inscriptions and Letters, chivalry acquired the status and prestige of a coherent system of practices and customs, of a culture with its own modalities and goals.

Sainte-Palaye believed that the oldest "heroic or historical *chansons*" went back a very long time and that none had survived. Charlemagne himself was supposed to have written "barbarian poems," in which he celebrated the combats of the ancient peoples and kings. But in order to read the chronicles and the romances that did survive, the medievalist points out in his writings that a certain relativism is needed to help understand these works, which do not deserve the scorn in which they were held. "To judge them properly, it is necessary to think about the intention with which they were written and to transport oneself to the centuries in which they were written."[133] In the case of the chronicles of Saint-Denis, for instance, it was necessary to gather into a single book material "scattered across several volumes" without omitting any important fact, regardless of its nature. To this end, the compilers chose the most ancient historians, those best known with the best credentials. Sainte-Palaye claims that even the romances most filled with fables contain facts belonging to history. The historians of these times, on the other hand, were only interested in the narratives of major events and had no concern for common customs. Romances, then, prove to be a precious source to "unravel the origin of our practices and customs and to follow their evolution."[134] This is because the writers represented things as they existed around them. In response to the objection that one should not construct an understanding of the Middle Ages on the writings of the romancers, Sainte-Palaye points to our knowledge of the Greek and Roman world: "There are many practices of Antiquity we think sufficiently proven by the sole testimony of poets! Why should our romancers not have the same privilege?"[135] Thus, on the level of historical knowledge, the ancient romancers were worth as much as the Greek and Roman poets, an important claim in the construction of an antiquity of modernity.

These methods led Sainte-Palaye to develop a renewed vision of the Middle Ages. Although his famous essay on the old chivalry, *Mémoires sur l'ancienne chevalerie considérée comme un établissement politique et militaire* [Memoirs on the Old Chivalry as a Political and Military Institution], presented to the Academy between 1746 and 1750 and published at a later date, deals with a period later than that of Charlemagne, it is of interest for several reasons. First, Sainte-Palaye, following in the footsteps of authors such as Vulson de la Colombière,[136] albeit with a more vigorous approach, saw chivalry as a system capable of inculcating the best moral values; the practice of courtesy; the spirit of civility, valor, and other required military qualities. In this ideal world, tournaments taught the art of war; castles became schools of virtue and politeness; and narratives, *chansons de geste*, and romances were the means used to reinforce these qualities and transmit them from one generation to the next.

Implicit and explicit comparisons with Antiquity abound in descriptions of this happy world. The laws of chivalry "could have been adopted by the wisest legislators and the most virtuous philosophers of all nations and all times."[137] The tournaments equaled the games of Greece and the triumphs of ancient Rome. Regarding the credibility of the accounts of historians and romancers who told of battles being halted to accommodate individual combats between knights seeking to immortalize the beauty of their ladies, Sainte-Palaye responds with another question: "Were the Greek heroes any wiser in Homer when in the midst of the melee they suddenly stop to tell each other their genealogies or that of their horses?"[138] The military distinctions of chivalry resembled those invented by the war tactics of the Romans.

Although knightly values contrasted sharply with the "pure reason" propounded by the Enlightenment, chivalry nonetheless managed to put an end to the barbarism and anarchy that were rampant at the end of the second dynasty and to establish a civilization in which there was a harmonious balance between war and gallantry, between desire for glory and service to the state. It was, in short, an ideological economy that regulated all aspects of life:

> While politics cleverly knew how to bring to bear love for glory and love for the ladies in order to maintain sentiments of honor and bravery in the knightly order, it also knew that the tie of friendship, so useful to all men, was required to unite so many heroes among whom a double rivalry could become the source of divisions harmful to the common interest. This flaw, so often fatal to states, had been prevented by the creation of societies or fraternities of arms entered into by knighthood's children.[139]

Thus chivalry worked "usefully for the public good and for individuals."[140] Boulainvilliers had written the first version of the political idyll of ancient France; Sainte-Palaye gives us a cultural version. Having depicted an aristocratic civilization and implied that, far from being limited to a single class or order, it had universal implications, Sainte-Palaye emphasizes, as Montesquieu had done before him, its compatibility with the monarchy. "Knighthood alone—always protected by our kings, who always were its guides and models—put this kingdom in the flourishing state that we see it in."[141]

And yet, there is probably no more telling example of the deep ambivalence of the Ancien Régime toward the national past than Sainte-Palaye's essay on old chivalry. This is because once he had constructed this ideal system, depicting it in all its balance and harmony, the author finishes by harshly criticizing it in his fifth and final book, in which he describes all its defects and ultimately destroys it. Suddenly, the medieval world loses all resemblance with Greek and Roman antiquity. Knighthood produced an impetuous militia that confused ostentation with glory, foolhardiness with valor, and "which in the grip of its false prejudices would never believe that there had been wise peoples, such as the Lacedaemonians and the Romans, who punished excesses of courage the same way they did cowardice, a militia almost incapable of uniting, consequently of recouping its mistakes and its losses." Only "the absolute power," the unity of command makes it possible to keep discipline strong.[142]

These knights, who were prey to superstition, did not serve the Church any better than they did the state. "Never did one see morals more corrupted than in the time of our knights, and never was the reign of debauchery more universal."[143] Sometimes these knights competed with the sovereign or even sold themselves to the enemy. But for the most part they neglected study and letters. Finally, it was their ignorance that was their downfall; they did not take the time to "draw from the pure sources of antiquity the reasoned principles of good taste and morality."[144] Sainte-Palaye then reconnects with the language of the Enlightenment to praise literature, which gives us "the usage of right reason" and good taste.

One might think that such a dismal view would have invalidated everything that preceded and transformed it into a sort of fairy tale. But this blatant contradiction, this spectacular manifestation of the gap between the theory of chivalry and its practice, made it possible to respond more or less adequately to three very different needs. The first four memoirs give a new "cultural" dimension to the vision of the antiquity of modernity that was in the process of being constructed. They were pleasing to the aristocracy, whose legacy they were exalting. At the same time they effortlessly became part of the concept of the greatness of the national past that the monarchy wanted to promote. The final memoir made it possible to uphold royalist notions of feudalism as a period of usurpation and anarchy. But it also made it possible to conceive a modern, literate, and thinking nobility, an aristocracy that incorporated both the sword and the robe and had its place in the monarchy of Sainte-Palaye's time.

In this work, Sainte-Palaye draws from documentation dating from the thirteenth and fourteenth centuries which itself looked even farther back in time for the idealized image it gave of society.[145] But he does not place knighthood prior to the eleventh century. Stéphanie-Félicité de Genlis in turn adopted the vision of knighthood portrayed by Sainte-Palaye and projected it all the way back onto Charlemagne's time. In doing this, she made good use of works that followed in the footsteps of Sainte-Palaye and that tended to valorize the great king's reign. For example, the count de Caylus presented to the Academy of Inscriptions, probably in 1750 or 1751, a memoir on the connections between old chivalry and old romances. His aim was to "prove that Charlemagne's brilliant reign is the basis and the source of all the romances on chivalry that flooded Europe in the following centuries."[146] Sainte-Palaye had already claimed that a sort of knighthood had existed during Charlemagne's time and even earlier, albeit only in the very limited sense of the existence of a solemn ceremony during which youths destined for a military profession received their first arms.[147]

The count de Caylus saw something else in Charlemagne's reign: a model that determined the principal forms of chivalry as described in the romances and as it was practiced. "Charlemagne's valor, his great deeds, similar to those of the most renowned knights, and the strength and daring of his nephew Roland are well represented in the way of thinking of the chivalry introduced after his reign."[148] The image of Durandal, the sword with which Roland accomplishes more outstanding exploits than even those described in Homer, remains on the minds of all subsequent romancers. Neither before nor during Charlemagne's reign were knights known "by name or exploits."

Thus Charlemagne's legend rather than his history, Caylus believed, was at the origin of chivalrous civilization. But Caylus only suggests the relationship between myth and society, a relationship that, moreover, reinforces the parallel between Greek and Roman antiquity and the distant past of modernity. He believed Turpin's narrative to have been the father of all the chivalric romances and that the text of the Monk of Saint Gall also played an important role. According to Caylus, the establishment of the "laws" of chivalry was a gradual process; they were a series of reactive regulations aimed at correcting abuses and served as "restraints on men who had none."[149] He believed that the kings authorized and encouraged the rise of chivalry because it helped make nobles who were besotted with their own valor and who had become tyrants to their vassals submit to the laws of the kingdom. As with Sainte-Palaye's writings, this vision of chivalry included elements apt to please both the aristocracy and the monarchy, but it also took a more explicit "nationalist" stance in the sense that, in a period when relations with England were very strained, Caylus claims that the English, "jealous of not having produced a prince as great," wanted to give themselves a comparable king and thus invented King Arthur. Charlemagne's superiority stems from his dual status as genuine historical personage and as mythified figure.

The image of the emperor depicted in the *chansons de geste* gradually returned, and the romances were again valued as historical documents. And yet there remained an insurmountable obstacle to complete acceptance; the barbarian crudeness of the language of these works. There was no way around it: eighteenth-century good taste simply could not digest such fare. Sainte-Palaye claimed in vain that the moral of these works "is no less sensitive, no less important than the most praiseworthy, most beautiful poems of Antiquity."[150] He proposed "a general and complete series of publications of all our ancient *romans* (that is, both *chansons de geste* and chivalric romances)" and hoped that "some persons of letters would share among themselves the hard work of reading these works." The aim of this encyclopedic project would lie not so much in transmitting the plots themselves (which would be given only brief summaries) as in capturing "everything that would appear to be of some use for history, for genealogies, and for French antiquities," in short, everything that might help to gain knowledge of the national past.

The wish Sainte-Palaye expressed in 1743 was realized some thirty years later, but with a fundamental difference: medieval works were to be published in a form that would be pleasing as well as instructive. The first publication of the series *Bibliothèque universelle des romans* appeared in July 1775 with the king's patent. The series enjoyed immediate and lasting success until it ended in 1789. The flyer for the first volume announced the encyclopedic project of publishing *romans,* which in the French of the time included *chansons de geste,* romances, and novels and noted that, particularly in France, *romans* made up "the most interesting, broadest, and richest part of our literature." Their value stemmed from the pleasure of reading them, but,

> led by philosophy and embracing the general meaning of their fictional parts, [this reading] becomes the study of the most reliable and consistent means of faithfully apprehending secret history. . . . The *roman* has this advantage over history in that it depicts mores while describing actions; it gives nuances to the characters; and it represents the whole of a nation through the story of the adventures of a few citizens. All the individual elements in the *romans* form the true body of history.[151]

One can recognize here ideas that had already been formulated by Sainte-Palaye who collaborated in the project by providing various texts. The books published in the first years of the *Bibliothèque* reflected in particular the mindset of the Academy of Inscriptions. The marquis de Paulmy, who belonged to the powerful family of Argenson and who was an avid bibliophile, was the soul of the series and the main provider of texts until his abrupt departure in December 1778 following a conflict with the count of Tressan. During this initial period, the focus was primarily on the *romans* of the Middle Ages. Aimed both at scholars and the general public, the *Bibliothèque*'s primary concern was with the national patrimony.

Thus a strange hybrid of erudition and literary *re*-creation of the *chansons de geste* and romances of the past was born. This amalgam lasted well beyond the Revolution and was at the heart of "troubadour" literature, the first elements of which were already beginning to appear.[152] In the end, the problem of the perceived crudeness of the old works was overcome by adapting them to the tastes of the time. They were translated into modern French and, in the best of rococo tradition, the editors made liberal use of the art of "miniatures," that is, of excerpts and summaries.[153] Henceforth, readers could find entertainment by enjoying "good ideas and touching and agreeable situations"[154] as well as the naïveté and even the superstitions and ridiculous practices of their ancestors. The romances were useful not only for an understanding of the long chain of history, but also in order to see the superiority of the present civilization. The series offered a smoothed-over path to a Middle Ages dotted with miniatures while satisfying the public's taste for entertaining novelties and its growing passion for history.

Indeed, the *roman*,[155] the genre par excellence of modernity, became the favored conduit of knowledge of cultural history because it was uniquely able to depict daily practices, mores, and the mind-set of the people of a given period in time. It alone enabled an intimate contact with the past and helped readers narrow the gap between themselves and their ancestors while they were appreciating the differences and enjoying an exotic experience: "The tale [*fable*] will become the best commentary on history."[156] We can now see how attitudes had completely reversed: the "fable" that had been denounced as a lie and a mythification at the beginning of the century had gradually come to be viewed as the key to an essential truth, one that was deeper than the knowledge of purely factual history.

In their introduction, the editors of the *Bibliothèque* propose to classify the works into eight categories. The first category includes works translated from Greek and Latin. The second is made up of chivalric romances (*romans de chevalerie*), and the third of historical romances, "*romans historiques*" containing everything from biographies to novels. Neither of these last two genres "has a model in antiquity."[157] Taken together, they reflect French genius at the time of their writing. In the second half of the year 1777 and in 1778, the figure of Charlemagne clearly dominates the two genres. Texts include Einhard, Pseudo-Turpin, the *Pilgrimage to Jerusalem*, numerous *chansons de geste* (among others, *La Chanson des Saisnes*, *Fierabras*, *Les Quatres Fils Aymon*, *Ogier le Danois*, *Galien restauré*), more recent works (such as that of Louis Le Laboureur and a romance on Charlemagne written in the eighteenth century), a biography of Roland based on French, Spanish, and Italian romancers, books written specially for the *Bibliothèque* (the story of the love between Einhard and Imma, as well as a *Chanson de Roland*), tales such as the one of the magic ring that made Charlemagne fall madly in love with his mistress's corpse, and, of course, Italian epics (Pulci's *Morgante Maggiore*, Boiardo's *Orlando innamorato*, Ariosto's *Orlando furioso*).[158]

This historical and mythical series on Charlemagne was published in a period when the great king was being constantly evoked in political debates. Malesherbes's *Remonstrance* dates from 1775, the year when Condillac's *Etude d'histoire* was published. Le Trosne's and Moreau's works appear at the same time as the volumes of the *Bibliothèque*, in which the emperor plays an important role. Thus the name of Charlemagne was circulating among a different and broader audience than that of Le Trosne's readers, for instance. It resonated in the world of fashionable literary leisure as well as in political demands and grievances.

And yet, the overall depiction contained in the *Bibliothèque* shies away from these debates. It seems that the editors were seeking a balance aimed at pleasing different groups of readers. We must remember that every one of the sixteen volumes published yearly had to be read and approved by a royal censor. The *chansons de geste* feature a nobility in revolt against a Charlemagne indulging in gross abuses of power. Thus the publication of the *chansons de geste* threatened to reproduce in fictional form the entire debate on the monarchy and the ancient constitution.

The publication plan presented in the July 1777 edition follows the decision announced in January of the same year to focus the category of historical *romans* on the lives of the great princes of France from the nation's founding to the present. The editors also note that they will first include, as they have done with Pepin, the genuine history of Charlemagne because they are publishing the works in the chronological order of their writing.[159] The editors present a life of Charlemagne drawn mainly from Einhard and also publish a fairly detailed summary of the Pseudo-Turpin chronicle.[160] They then begin with the *romans*, in this case *chansons de gestes*, in the planned order.

In the first few pages, we see Charlemagne demanding money to finance the war against the Saxons and mobilizing his forces for the war. He encounters the "most lively" resistance of the princes and the peoples of "Hurepie." The editors of the *Bibliothèque* were careful to link this fiction to reality by pointing out that there still existed in France, near Paris, "an area called Hurepoix." When Charles sends ambassadors to resolve the problem, "[they] threatened very violent actions against Charles and his ambassadors; they wanted to declare war against the first and have the second flayed. *According to this romance, the kings of France had that little authority over their vassals at the time*" (my emphasis).[161] The princes end up agreeing to send troops but not money, and they declare that, if the king keeps on demanding it, they will wage war on him. "The wise and prudent monarch renounced his demands."[162] Kings lacking in authority, a monarch who tries to collect taxes, nobles who refuse to pay them and threaten an uprising—such a description could not fail to bring to mind the current crisis within the monarchy. The wisdom shown by Charlemagne was not attractive to a modern monarchy on a desperate quest for revenues. This text basically includes all the elements required to comfort the militant parlementary magistrates, who were increasingly supported by the old nobility in their resistance to royal policies.

We might assume that this was after all only a tale and had no impact. But in the following publication, the editors suddenly deviate from their plan. They abandon a chronological order with the excuse that they need more time to decipher the other manuscripts in their possession. As a replacement, they offer their readers more recent works in which Charlemagne is the hero. There then follow summaries and extracts from Louis Le Laboureur's *Charlemagne* and from a novel (*roman*) by Joseph Dufresne de Francheville published in 1741 and dedicated to the king of Prussia. It was certainly no coincidence that the editors chose this moment to present Charlemagne in conformity with the most absolutist ideas. We are familiar with Le Laboureur's poem. The editors criticize its prosaic nature and ridicule its style even as they claim that "the poet describes exploits and has his warriors deliver speeches worthy of Homer's heroes."[163]

Dufresne's novel on Charlemagne's first expeditions, *Histoire des premières expéditions de Charlemagne*, is of interest because it rekindles the entire debate on the nature of the constitution of the monarchy, although it locates it in Sweden. Inspired by *Telemachus*, Dufresne assumes the task of writing a work aimed at educating Frederick of Prussia, who acceded to the throne in 1740. This work includes some passages that could apply directly to the political situation in France, but it reached a broad audience only through its reprinting in the *Bibliothèque*, where it was cited at length.

The editors inform us that Dufresne's depiction of the court of a northern king named Sigefroy is in fact "that of the court of Louis XIV at its most brilliant moment. We have even added a few positive nuances to make it into the portrait of a perfect court worthy of serving as a model to all the courts in the world."[164] The summary explains that "in a well-governed kingdom, the king and the fatherland are indistinguishable; anyone who attacks one also attacks the other."[165] But the most striking passages deal with England and a constitutional debate that was supposed to have occurred in Sweden. During a stay in London, the young Charlemagne meets the learned Alcuin, who instructs him in the manner in which France should be governed: "It is a light and thoughtless nation, though basically good and sweet, toward which you should act as a wise mentor, or as a good governess does toward a child that has a good nature but is often carried away by his impulsiveness and, it has to be said, by a bit of thoughtlessness." This nation must be handled with kindness, it must be shown with few words ("because it is easily bored") that you are acting for its own good. If you have to punish it, you should embrace it immediately afterward. Above all else, the French seek entertainment; they have to be amused, distracted. Alcuin reveals to young Charles that the same could be said of the French as what used to be said of the Romans: "They need only bread and spectacles," and the latter should include the reading of "light literature in which the French engage with so much success and pleasure."[166]

The phrasing hints at the *Bibliothèque* editors' own plans and goals. Are they not, after all, undertaking precisely the task of providing the French with "light literature" to take their minds off their troubles and particularly off politics? Alcuin's lesson ends on a final word of advice on the way to govern the French: "Prevent them from indulging in this somber philosophy that is peculiar to us English; it is a product of our climate that should be consumed locally; the use that they might make of it in your country would change the admirable gaiety of the French character."[167] It reads as if the editors wanted to emphasize their remoteness from any agitation, be it political or "philosophical," and to describe themselves as the providers of entertainment able to serve as a protective barrier for the lightheartedness of the French, to keep them away from the temptation of being directly involved in the political questions concerning the public good.

In short, the French should be wary of having any political will of their own, except perhaps that of affirming the wisdom of absolutism. Called to Sweden to oust the usurper Mordac, who has seized the throne, Charles is welcomed by the Swedes as the liberator of their fatherland. But he soon discovers that there are many internal divisions. The government needs to be founded anew, and there are strident debates on the form it should take:

> Eloquent orators who seemed animated by patriotic zeal dared in Charlemagne's very presence to give a positive description of the aristocracy and an odious one of the monarchic government, which they accused of despotism. The young Charles, showing neither anger nor moodiness on a question of so much interest to him, spoke in his turn to the assembled estates and convinced them that the republican system had more drawbacks than the monarchical one. As for the people, he told them, it is better for them that they find authority gathered into a

single point and in a single man than have to depend on so many masters, whose individual interests usually predominate over the general interest.[168]

Charles intervenes in the debates to persuade the Swedes to choose a king. It is in this manner that the educational travels of the young king end; he returns to France, where he becomes "one of the greatest and wisest monarchs of the world."[169] The summary of Dufresne's novel ends on this sort of fairy tale of absolutism.

Given the nature and the political weight of the figure of Charlemagne, the debate on the ancient constitution erupts in the midst of a literary undertaking that, in principle, had no interest in broaching that subject. The editors probably felt the need to show the monarchy (and of course the royal censor, who had to approve each volume) where they stood before continuing with the publication of a body of works that often portrayed the monarchy, in the person of Charlemagne, in a negative light. As if to illustrate their desire to avoid controversy, they end this volume with an "original" composition, a short story drawn from the legend of the love between Einhard and Imma. This story tells how Einhard and Imma loved each other without being aware of it, how passion took hold of them, how, when Charlemagne confronted them, Imma fainted, how the great king forgave them and allowed them to marry, and how they lived happily ever after.

This saccharine tale already contains many of the elements of the "troubadour" spirit. It foreshadowed the method that was used by Marchangy, the future high priest of a new historical and national literature, whose *Gaule poétique* enjoyed great success when it was published in 1813. Of course, this love story provided yet another opportunity to paint a flattering portrait of Charlemagne, of his kindness, fairness, and clemency, and to plead the cause of literature by asserting that "he felt early on that the cultivation of the mind could sweeten the mores of his subjects."[170]

And yet, although the *Bibliothèque universelle* strove to curry the favor of absolutist sensibilities, it also pleased the adversaries of absolutism. The attempt to write a life of Charlemagne's heroic nephew by using French, Spanish, and Italian poets and romancers is an example of this. "The whole story of Roland has yet to be told; it will thus be a new work written from old materials."[171] Just like the figure of Charlemagne, that of Roland was to be dusted off and polished, brought up to date, and generally rendered suitable for circulation in the best salons of this second half of the eighteenth century. The nobility of the time had no difficulty recognizing itself in the impetuous and faithful servant whose cries of distress were not heard in time by Charlemagne and whose horn was to sound so powerfully after the Revolution in Vigny's poetry. The *Chanson de Roland* written by Paulmy himself was published, stripped of all its tragic elements, at the end of the second volume devoted to Roncevaux's victim. It is salon poetry serving up a moral portrait of the perfect knight as he was imagined in 1777, a model that was supposed to be followed by the nobility of the time. Roland is of course a formidable and brave warrior, "a good comrade, a loyal friend":

> When he was asked why
> The French were campaigning,
> He answered, in good faith,
> It is by order of Charlemagne:
> His ministers, his favorites
> Have discussed this matter;
> As for us, let us beat his enemies,
> This is what we have to do.
> . . . .
> With the peasant and the bourgeois
> Let us never be violent,
> Let us use the rights of war
> With kindness and propriety.[172]

He readily drinks good wine, but in moderation; he is, in short, a "good gentleman." His only flaw is to love women a bit too much. The fearless warrior is perfectly loyal to his sovereign. But Paulmy introduces in this *chanson* a barb aimed primarily at the monarchy, which some people must have relished in the political context in which there was still a desire for a new Charlemagne. He mentions the anecdote of the French soldiers who sang the *Chanson de Roland* on the day of the battle of Poitiers. King Jean the Good hears them and exclaims to an old officer of his army: "Alas, there are no longer any Rolands in France!" The officer, taking the comment as a reproach, replies: "If there were still a Charlemagne, we would still have Rolands."[173] This anecdote is emblematic of the impasse in which the nobility and the monarchy found themselves during the eighteenth century.

The figure of Charlemagne held a certain attraction for young authors seeking success. In 1789, for instance, on the eve of the first session of the Estates-General, a young, ambitious author published a long satirical epic. The future revolutionary Saint-Just had not yet found his true vocation, but in the meanwhile he was inspired by Italian works as well as by Voltaire's *Pucelle* to narrate the adventures of a bastard son of Bishop Turpin in his book *Organt*. Saint-Just uses the personage of the emperor with the flowing white beard to depict a corrupt and decadent monarchy. This king, who had at one time been so good, so loyal,

Became brutal and crazed because of his overindulged senses;
He lost his ancient prudence:
"I only want to drink and sing."
. . . .
He thirsted for gold;
To get some, he fleeced the people.
He got gold, but in exchange he lost
Glory and rest: heaven thus avenges us.[174]

Charlemagne's queen is none other than a certain Madame Cunégonde who "destroyed everything in her wanton rage." Saint-Just published his poem again upon his election to the Convention, but it never achieved any success. However, it enables us to measure the "strategic" value of the figure of Charlemagne: precisely because it was at the center of debates on the nature of government, it enticed a young author yearning for success to prepare a dish with ingredients mixing literature and history, the whole generously seasoned with coarse salt.

A RATIONAL AND SENTIMENTAL CHARLEMAGNE: GAILLARD AND STÉPHANIE-FÉLICITÉ DE GENLIS

If literary discourse incorporated the arguments of political discourse in its portrayal of the great king, the reverse was equally true. The influence of the various images of Charlemagne can be clearly seen in the enlightened synthesis that Gabriel Henri de Gaillard attempted to write in 1782 in his *Histoire de Charlemagne*. This work met with some success and became one of the main sources of documentation for Stéphanie-Félicité de Genlis. Like that of the novelist, Gaillard's career spanned the Revolution. He became a member of the Academy of Inscriptions in 1760, and was elected to the *Académie Française* in 1771. In his inaugural speech, he spoke at length of Charlemagne as the restorer of letters and founder of an academy foreshadowing the one founded by Richelieu. In year IV of the Revolutionary calendar, this prolific writer was named associate member of the *Institut de France*.

Gaillard was a close friend of Malesherbes. The figure of Charlemagne he presented in 1782 was cast to fit the Enlightenment mold. To do this, the historian split the great man in two. As a conqueror, he was a genius, who fit well into the barbarian mind-set of his time. The unchecked expansion of his empire led only to an ephemeral entity and soon sowed discord that erupted shortly after his death. Gaillard dreamt of a Europe united by the principles of reason rather than by the will of a conqueror. In contrast, according to Gaillard, Charlemagne as a legislator and restorer of the arts was a visionary, who was far ahead of his time. Gaillard deals in detail with Mably's descriptions depicting Charlemagne as the great mediator of the nation, who, instead of giving orders, proposed, advised, and suggested. It was through him that the unity of the nation was fashioned. "Charlemagne knew, judged and himself formed public opinion."[175] His "great talent . . . was to be capable of handling everything, from work to study, to pleasure."[176]

But the historian also devotes a sizable portion of his work to the study of the fictional histories of Charlemagne. "The tale [*fable*] is an essential part of the history of this monarch, and we can say that it belongs to truth by depicting the superiority of the prince over all others, the effect that his glory had on the imagination, the enthusiasm he inspired in romancers and in poets as much as in warriors."[177] Gaillard endorses the count de Caylus's conclusion, in which he sees Charlemagne's reign as the source not only of all the chivalric romances but of chivalry itself. He chooses to retrace the history of tales written about Charlemagne without taking the chronology of the works into account. Thus he creates a parallel life of Charlemagne from his birth to his death, and constructs a mirror of the great emperor's existence, this time in the realm of fable.

According to Gaillard, the negative portraits of the great monarch are often of foreign origin—Italian or Spanish—but generally, he specifies, the spirit of the chivalric romances tends to put knighthood above all else, even above Charlemagne. Thus, even though Charlemagne's many victories are recognized, he is "still more often put down, overthrown, rejected but also always freed, avenged, reestablished through the valor of his paladins, particularly that of Roland."[178] For Gaillard, however, Charlemagne always emerges victorious from these trials and denigrations because he remains at all times the most formidable prince, the "king of kings." The whole of Europe is defined in relation to him. "It is always his court, it is under him that the heroes and the paladins go seeking glory. . . . All these heroes and heroines always act for or against Charlemagne; it is he, it is his exploits, it is the great role he played in Europe, it is the institution of chivalry of which he is the author that led to this."[179] The myth outstrips the historical greatness of the man to the point of constituting the foundation of a government, a way of life, a society, and even a European identity. Paradoxically, Gaillard in the guise of a historian of events disparages the great conqueror, but exalts him through the tone he adopts in his role as historian of the legend.

Given the way in which events were unfolding at the end of the eighteenth century, Charlemagne was in fact seen to have delivered the nation from chaos in two respects: first, in his capacity as a historical figure with whom were associated—in different ways, according to the historian—conquests, the establishment of laws, the creation of schools and academies, and the reform of the Church; second, in his capacity as mythical figure, for his legend subsequently served as a model for those who sought to correct abuses, to rein in uncontrolled passions, to subject men who had become tyrants to the institutions and the laws of the land. Thus chivalry became the antidote to tyrannical feudalism, an antidote originating in Charlemagne's myth and drawing its effectiveness from it.

The trend toward more gentleness in customs played a great part in the rise of what is called "troubadour" literature toward the end of the century. The refinement of chivalry in this genre becomes an additional quality when linked to the great monarch. The historical figure acted as legislator to correct political customs. But the reign of transparency he was thought to have initiated left little room for private space. The legendary personage, stimulating the imaginations of the generations that followed him, provided inspiration to a system concerned with reconciling private interests and passions with the public good. Friendship, love, and the quest for individual glory were mobilized in the service of society. Acting on two different levels, the great king became the common locus linking politics and morality.

Stéphanie-Félicité de Genlis borrowed this vision of Charlemagne to use in her novel. Her aim was to write a work that would combine scholarship and literary creation and would have both the power of myth and the authority of history. The importance that the historical novel was to have in the nineteenth century was already apparent in this "troubadouresque" attempt. In *Les Chevaliers du cygne*, a political program accompanies the description of knightly "civilized" mores. This novel, perhaps less subtly but with more clarity than a "higher quality" piece of writing might have done, articulates the relationships between myth, history, scholarship, and literary creation that characterized one of the trends of romanticism and sustained Charlemagne's astonishing nineteenth-century success.

National history did not emerge from the Enlightenment suffering from an excess of identification with dry reason, as Greek and Roman antiquity did. Rather, by this time fully established as the antiquity of modernity it was becoming both an escape from the harsh reality of the Revolution and the realm of authentic values. It was there that warrior violence was tempered by the ideal of love; it was there that morality and politics were reconciled. De Genlis's novel is filled with tournaments, jousts, damsels in distress, tender loves, and sweet male friendships between knights, and Charlemagne plays the role that was gradually being defined throughout the century, that of the founding father par excellence: "He wanted to reign only by laws; they had to be created, because they did not exist. Only he was able to put together this great work in these vast states . . . and [he] wanted to give all the glory to the nation."[180] It was he who "realized" the nation by unifying it and giving it a juridical form. In contrast, enemy kingdoms that Charlemagne conquered and ultimately incorporated into "the nation" were governed by unjust "sovereigns" and were prey to the misfortunes of revolutions and "revolutionary" tyrants. In de Genlis, the great king is conqueror, legislator, pious Christian, and again we see him establish his famous Academy of Letters. A lover of justice and a devoted father, Charlemagne works tirelessly for the happiness of his family and his people. He is a democrat, who gathers his people in general assemblies where laws are voted on by the will of the majority.

And yet his status as archtypical founder did not stem from his being the first king, which he was not, but from his fundamental difference from all other kings.[181] Charlemagne *was* thus radically other, and so was his time. He was, so to speak, both in History and the creator of a *new* history, he was the founder of a constitutive mutation. In this sense we can speak of a mythified history; for, in a sense, this new history was part of the continuous chain of History, one that was still ongoing in modern France. In Genlis's view, this history was doubly tied to the present: by a direct chronological line that could be traced from the founding era of Charlemagne to 1795 and, as has been noted previously, by the parallels that could be drawn between the revolutionary period and Charlemagne's reign. But, in a more fundamental sense, this history was lost to modern time: there was no longer any real connection to those originary times. There were no longer heroes like those found *in illo tempore*. Genlis develops the double framework of her *Chevaliers du cygne* by playing simultaneously on these two notions of proximity and distance. On the one hand, we are linked to these men who constitute our national past. But, on the other, she explains, those men were very different from us, infinitely more courageous, more valiant, more generous, in short, infinitely greater. As a result, the distance becomes, above all, moral. We are separated from them by an ethical chasm. In this perspective, proximity makes the text credible as it links the fictional narrative to history, to the probable and the true:

> One of the great advantages of historical romances . . . is to give to morality the powerful authority of experience and example. It is not possible for an imaginary personage to have as great an impact as a [real] hero whose name has been consecrated by glory. . . . In depicting all that is noble and touching that heroism has to offer, I did not invent anything, as I was only the historian of virtue.[182]

Thus, de Genlis derives her moral authority from the accuracy of her work as historian. And this explains the surprising paratextual apparatus of her text. In the abundant notes she parades a series of references to the historians and the political theorists on which the story of the *Chevaliers du cygne* is based. There are numerous citations from Gaillard, Mably, Montesquieu, and—for everything pertaining to chivalry—to La Curne de Sainte-Palaye. The narrative authority is buttressed by historical writing; historiography provides a representation of the past, anchoring fictional discourse and enabling it to avoid the superficiality of a fable devoid of any connection to reality:

> I had the idea . . . of putting at the bottom of the page, for every accurate detail, a historical note (which does not interrupt reading) and, finally, to relegate to the end of each volume informative notes that would not have been dramatic enough to place in the body of the work. . . . This helpful innovation was used for the first time in the *Chevaliers du cygne*, and it has been generally adopted since.[183]

But using historiography as a foundation does not prevent a rewriting of history; the second function of the notes is precisely one of explaining and, in so doing, justifying the novel's distortions of history. Although tournaments did not yet exist in Charlemagne's time, de Genlis feels they are indispensable to a novel on chivalry. By protecting herself in this way against possible accusations of ignorance, by showing that she is fully conscious of the changes she has brought to historical discourse, de Genlis lays claim to the right to rewrite that history. In addition to their defensive, proleptic function, the notes also play a positive role in that they serve to clarify the parallel between history and current events. It is in the notes, for instance, that the author explains that Iliska's tyranny is as atrocious as that of Robespierre, that the Revolution, in short, is nothing but the resurgence of barbarism. De Genlis succeeds in making use both of the authority of history and the freedom of fiction to reinvent the history of Charlemagne's court. While basing her tale on historical writings, she revives that history and affirms the right—indeed, the usefulness—of participating in a conscious mythification of history, of going back to its origins and grounding moral values in what she establishes as the originary moment, a founding moment in French history.[184]

Les Chevaliers du cygne is not a counterrevolutionary work. And yet, although its author is not seeking to abolish the Revolution, she does want to set boundaries for it. According to her the Revolution should not have been pursued beyond 1789. Unfortunately, the revolutionary engine went off track and, in an attempt to stop it, de Genlis turns toward the providential man evoked in the course of the debates on the fundamental law of the monarchy, but who has been refined, or rather tamed, by "recreational" literature such as we saw in the *Bibliothèque universelle des romans.*

Many people were beginning to wish for the second coming of this man who had a power transcending all others, and, in a way, this had been a long-standing wish. The history of the figure of Charlemagne in the eighteenth century shows the extent to which throughout the century the existence of a providential man in French history was affirmed and reaffirmed. He was imagined as being stronger, more generous than others; he loved the nation, was imbued with its spirit, and was profoundly disinterested. He was able to pull the nation away from its immediate history in order to regenerate it, to restore it to itself, and in so doing to create the golden age of the French nation. The figure of Charlemagne, first invoked in contrast to the sort of absolutist rule embodied by Louis XIV, assumed an ideological importance that continued to grow until it became the object of a very large consensus. Even though on the eve of the Revolution there were great divergences of opinion regarding the constitutional changes that should or should not be made, there was, however, agreement that everything should be as it had been in Charlemagne's time.

This view of the great Carolingian also enables us to understand better an aspect of the *Fête de la Fédération* held one year after the taking of the Bastille. This celebration was held on the Champs de Mars, a place that recalled the practices of both the Romans and French ancestors.[185] The emperor of the West was himself a figure who, as we have seen, incorporated both traditions. But it was of the ancient "French" that a member of the club Société de 1789 was thinking during the weeks preceding the *Fête de la Fédération*. This club enjoyed great prestige at the time and its members included particularly influential political figures such as La Fayette, Mirabeau, Dupont de Nemours, and the abbé Sieyès. During a meeting of the club it was proposed that, on July 14, Louis XVI should not be greeted with the usual acclaims of "Long live the king!" but instead he should be given the title of emperor. The motion was made by Charles-Michel de Villette, who had been Voltaire's protégé and who welcomed the old philosopher into his home when Voltaire returned to Paris in 1778. Villette's motion shows that already in 1789 it was possible and indeed, justifiable to conceive of the nation as being led by an emperor:

> [He proposes] that on the solemn day of July 14, when the representatives of the troops and of the national guards from all the regions of France come to swear allegiance to the Federation before the representatives of the nation and the eyes of the monarch, instead of the cries of "Long live the king!" that have for so long tired our ears without ever penetrating our hearts, we should all yell together in a single voice: "Louis, emperor!" This new title would conform perfectly well to the new order of things. Spoken by the president of the National As-

sembly, it would be sanctioned by five hundred thousand souls who would repeat it together. . . . Charlemagne was proclaimed *emperor of the French* and convoked the nation in the Champ de Mars. After one thousand years the nation reclaimed its glory and its rights. . . . Let us erase the words *king, kingdom,* and *subjects* that are incompatible with the word *freedom.* The French people, in whom sovereignty is now vested and who now exercise it, are ruled by laws and are no one's subjects. The prince is their leader, not their master; *imperat, non regit.* Thus, let him come back to the Champs de Mars, the imperial crown on his head.[186]

Napoleon would not miss the opportunity to stand on the shoulders of a figure who was imbued with the glory of conquests and national reconciliation, of an emperor who had pulled France out of chaos and restored both order and the ancient democracy and had achieved the impossible synthesis of absolutism and republican ideals.

SEVEN

To Conquer and to Sing Praises

THE REGENERATION OF CHARLEMAGNE'S THRONE: NAPOLEON

"Sire, you have regenerated [*régénéré*] the Empire of the Franks and the throne of Charlemagne buried beneath the ruins of ten centuries," states a letter written to Napoleon and published in the newspaper *Moniteur* in May 1805.[1] After so many years of revolutionary fervor, a "regenerated man" found himself the subject of a new emperor, one who sought to derive his legitimacy from the reign of Charlemagne. At the end of the century, writing about Charlemagne in 1884, Léon Gautier exclaimed: "We needed a man of that stature so that the French epic would not die. Without him, we would have deserved the stupid reproach so often directed at us: 'France has no epic poem.' With him, we had a future of two hundred epics and five hundred years of epic poetry."[2] The nation that had suffered for so long from a lack of epics had at last discovered one worthy of Antiquity. The role of the great man, the bigger-than-life individual, and a quest for the national epic were two important preoccupations throughout the nineteenth century. And both cases were seen as expressions of the nation or to borrow Victor Cousin's phrase, as a manifestation of the "spirit of a people."[3] Bolstered by these two themes, Charlemagne became one of the most important images with which the emerging French nation identified in the course of the nineteenth century. "His figure," writes Gaston Paris in a work published in 1865, to which I will return at length, "as depicted in our national poetry, becomes forever the most complete symbol of the genius of a people, the epitome [*résumé*] of its aspirations, the embodiment of its ideal."[4] Here Charlemagne has become a kind of figure of the nation, a metaphor for national identity.

And yet the revolutionary "spirit" might appear to be the opposite of the image of Charlemagne. Indeed, as we have seen, although his name was often mentioned in the decades leading up to the assembly of the Estates-General, evocations of Charlemagne by members of the various republican currents in the Constituent Assembly gradually became more rare. This was only a logical reaction by a revolution that took sovereignty away from the monarch and gave it to the people, a people that thus no longer needed a hero to restore their usurped rights. For the people themselves had taken back their rights and, in one stroke, had become sovereign and heroic.

The Revolution saw itself as an originary moment, a new beginning freed from the weight of the past and oriented toward a glorious future. The old origins had been left behind and transcended by the flowering of freedom and the establishment of a renewed nation. And yet, the triumph of liberation was soon followed by the anguished fear of disorder and of the disintegration of society. In the opinion of many, the new "hero" had abused his power and transformed it into tyranny, and the Revolution remained unfinished. Thus the French continued to replay and reinterpret the Revolution throughout the nineteenth century, a period that was for France one of profound national redefinition and self-questioning. What relationship should the nation have with its history? What place should be given to its former origins in relation to the "new" revolutionary origins? In this work of reconceptualization, the figure of Charlemagne, forever located at the juncture of history, myth, and poetry, soon reappeared.

Chateaubriand raises a most penetrating issue in the passage from his *Mémoires d'outre-tombe* that I cited at the beginning of this study.[5] Charlemagne's resplendent ghost turns into dust as soon as it is touched:

> Let us respect the majesty of time; let us contemplate past centuries with reverence, centuries that memory and the vestiges of our fathers made sacred; and yet we should not try to go back to them. They no longer hold any part of our true nature, and if we tried to grasp them, they would disappear.

The lesson is clear: we should keep our distance from the past. But this lesson had been learned only in the light of the epic experiences of the beginning of the century; it seemed much less evident to the people suffering the repeated upheavals of the revolutionary years.

Although there was little room for the great emperor in republican discourse before Robespierre's downfall, he remained an ideal for those who, like Stéphanie-Félicité de Genlis, wished for a form of constitutional monarchy.[6] For the republicans, it was war that brought Charlemagne back on the scene, albeit indirectly, as he arrived, carried on the shoulders of his nephew Roland, himself recently celebrated in the *Biblothèque universelle des romans*. On April 20, 1792, the legislative assembly voted in favor of declaring war against the "king of Bohemia and Hungary," who was also the emperor of Austria. Shortly afterwards, Rouget de Lisle wrote the *Marseillaise*; as soon as he was done, he composed *Roland à Roncevaux*. Here, however, Charlemagne remains in the shadow and it is Roland who fights for the country:

> Où courent ces peuples épars?
> Quel bruit a fait trembler la terre
> Et retentit de toutes parts?
> Amis, c'est le cri du dieu Mars,
> Le cri précurseur de la guerre,
> De la gloire, de ses hasards.

> ———

> Mourons pour la patrie,
> Mourons pour la patrie!
> Mourons pour la patrie!
> Mourons pour la patrie!
> . . . .
> Je suis vainqueur, je suis vainqueur!
> En voyant ma large blessure,
> Amis, pourquoi cette douleur?
> Le sang qui coule au champ d'honneur
> Du vrai guerrier c'est la parure,
> C'est le garant de sa valeur.

> ———

> Mourons pour la patrie . . . ![7]

> ———

> [Where are these scattered peoples running?
> What is that noise that makes the earth tremble
> And echoes from everywhere?
> Friends, it is the cry of the god Mars,
> The cry announcing war,
> Its glory and its dangers.

> ———

Let us die for our country,
Let us die for our country!
Let us die for our country!
Let us die for our country!
. . . .
I am victorious, I am victorious!
When seeing my large wound,
Friends, why are you sad?
The blood that flows on the field of honor
Is the adornment of the true warrior,
It is the proof of his valor.

———

Let us die for our country!]

This same year, in the operetta *Guillaume Tell*, Michel Sedaine and André Grétry had the Swiss patriots sing a "Chanson de Roland" while they were rebelling against their Austrian oppressors. And in the play *Guillaume le Conquérant*, performed at the *Comédie-Française* in the first years of the nineteenth century, André Duval has a Guillaume de Poitiers sing a "Chanson de Roland" directly inspired by the *Biblothèque universelle des romans:*

Soldats français, chantons Roland,
L'honneur de la chevalerie,
Et répétons en combattant
Ces mots sacrés, Gloire et Patrie![8]

———

[French soldiers, let us sing Roland,
The honor of the chivalry,
And let us repeat as we are fighting
These sacred words: Glory and country!]

Duval's hymn was set to music by two different composers, Étienne Méhul and Alexander Choron, and it was hugely successful. Napoleon's soldiers sang Méhul's version, and it was included in the collection *Chants et chansons populaires de la France*, published in 1840.

Roland had something to offer to every political orientation: from a republican and imperial perspective, he was the loyal soldier who died for his country; from the aristocratic point of view, he expressed the tragic fate of the nobility. He was a romantic figure par excellence, the victim embodying the immemorial wound of the suffering nation. His unheard cries for help became the symbol of poetry itself, a swan song carrying all the pathos of war, of treason, and of abandonment in a nineteenth century in which all sides felt betrayed and abandoned. No one captured these traits better than Vigny, whose poem "Le cor" resonates as one of the highlights of nineteenth-century poetry:

> Et l'Empereur poursuit; mais son front soucieux
> Est plus sombre et plus noir que l'orage des cieux.
> Il craint la trahison, et, tandis qu'il y songe,
> Le Cor éclate et meurt, renaît et se prolonge.
>
> ———
>
> "Malheur! c'est mon neveu! malheur! car si Roland
> Appelle à son secours, ce doit être en mourant."
> . . . .
> Dieu! que le son du Cor est triste au fond des bois![9]

> [The Emperor is in pursuit, but his worried brow
> Is darker and blacker than the storms of the heavens.
> He fears treason, and as he is thinking
> The sound of the horn is born and dies, is reborn and
>   keeps on sounding.
>
> ———
>
> "Oh misfortune! It's my nephew! Oh misfortune!
> If Roland is calling for help, it must be that he is dying."
> . . . .
> Oh God, how sadly sings the horn deep in the woods!]

In 1777, as we have seen, the *Biblothèque universelle des romans* noted ironically that for there to be more Rolands in France there needed to be another Charlemagne.[10] More than twenty years later, during the Italian campaign, Napoleon Bonaparte rose to the level of his destiny and linked his military glory to that of the old emperor of the West. In 1801, David exhibited side by side two different versions of his famous painting of Napoleon crossing the Alps *Bonaparte Crossing the Alps at the Grand Saint Bernard Pass.* The painter depicts a calm Napoleon astride a spirited rearing horse on a rock on the side of a mountain (fig. 19). Through a sort of luminous fog, we see in the background only a few soldiers marching with their weapons and the French flag. Dominating his horse's fear and braving the unleashed winds, the hero points his right hand toward some distant summit to which he is leading his army, perhaps even the whole of France.

On the jutting rock beneath the horse's feet, three names are engraved in the stone: Bonaparte, Hannibal, and Karolus Magnus.

Napoleon's proclaimed link to Charlemagne is well known. Two explanations for this are commonly given. First, there was the resemblance between the two great conquerors, and, second, there was the Revolutionary hero's need to seek historical legitimacy elsewhere than among the Capetians. Napoleon could not link himself to a monarchy the Revolution had just overthrown: Louis XVI had all too often been referred to as the last king of France. And yet the ideological foundation of the filiation between Charlemagne and Napoleon drew on the legacy of the Ancien Régime as it was established by the Capetians. In many respects, the new administration represented the outcome of absolutist ideals. But the figure of Charlemagne was also heir to the republican discourse. His figure played such an important role precisely because it enabled the melding of revolutionary and absolutist elements.

Essential to this amalgam was the idea that Charlemagne had reestablished order after a period of chaos, barbarism, and moral degradation. In the wake of the atrocities of the Terror, Napoleon presented himself as the one who was able to lead the country out of anarchy and stop the disintegration of society. But the order he established was supposed to integrate and stabilize the essential achievements of the Revolution. Charlemagne had already been largely incorporated into republicanism in the eighteenth century. As we have seen, Mably and Condillac made him the restorer of the ancient originary republic, a leader capable of recognizing the rights of the third estate, of unifying Gauls and Franks, and of going back to the ancient constitution. Le Trosne saw him as the embodiment of the nation because he so perfectly represented and expressed public opinion. Indeed, popular sovereignty was conceived essentially in terms of public opinion, and Napoleon became a master in the art of exploiting this conception of the foundations of government for his own benefit. He managed to present himself as the living expression of public opinion by organizing plebiscites and manipulating the press. One citizen wrote in a letter to the citizen first consul which was published in the *Moniteur*: "What better proof of the nation's happiness than its love for its government, than its putting all its faith and hope in you, than the touching concord of all hearts and voices, than this simultaneous cry of admiration, of devotion and gratitude!"[11] Another letter exclaims: "There is only one voice and one opinion, it is that you are necessary to the state."[12] The nation saw itself represented in the person of Napoleon.

In addition to its being rooted in republican discourse as it developed in the historical arguments of the eighteenth century, the figure of Charlemagne had the advantage of being situated in a time prior to the feudal era, in a period of military, cultural, and political greatness. The august emperor emerged as the ideal ancestor not only because he made it possible to avoid referring to the Capetians, who had just been overthrown, but also because he was not "contaminated" by feudalism and the abuses linked to aristocratic privileges. According to one of the prerevolutionary pamphlets I mentioned earlier, the great emperor conceived "the project of regenerating the nation."[13] Like so many other works, this small pamphlet owes much to Mably and to Le Trosne. It sees in Charlemagne the man who has been able to return to the originary practices of the Champs de Mai and restore their birthright to the people. The foundations of this ideal regime were, in the eyes of the pamphleteer, liberty and property.

Liberty, property: these two key words summed up the contribution of the Revolution that Napoleon claimed to preserve. In fact, in the years preceding the Revolution, representations of Charlemagne made him an exemplary leader, who had undertaken a project very similar to the one proposed by Napoleon, the last guarantor and ultimate protector of the Revolution. "There is only one thing, so far as I can see, that we have really defined during the last fifty years, and that is the sovereignty of the people," Napoleon wrote from Italy in 1797. "We have been no more successful in defining what is constitutional, than in allocating the different powers in the state. The organization of the French people is only barely begun."[14] Charlemagne was not simply a conqueror, but was also the individual who was able to "organize" the French people, and this "domestic" justification constituted a crucial element in the establishment of imperial ideology.

In a speech given to the corps législatif in January 1804 after having been elected its president, Fontanes takes the first steps in a campaign aimed at establishing Napoleon as Charlemagne's heir. He is careful to refer to republican values by evoking the theme of the Champs de Mars as he draws a parallel between the first consul and "the greatest man of our history, a conqueror and founder." After "many storms" that led to social upheaval, "a firm and wise hand" eliminated "the power of all the different factions so as to add to that of the nation." Thanks to this strong hand pulling the country out of chaos, "freedom returns in the national assembly under the auspices of reason and experience."

Fontanes announced that the first consul planned to come to the legislative body himself in order to impart an air of solemnity to the opening of the sessions. In doing this, the protector of the Revolution again mirrored the policies of Charlemagne, who, "like the man who governs us, wrote amidst the tumult of the [military] camps the laws that were to maintain peace for families and planned new victories while opening the peaceful assemblies of the Champs de Mars."[15] The great difference between Napoleon and his illustrious predecessor lay in the progress of humanity since the time of the second dynasty. It was this enlightened advancement that would endow Napoleon's undertakings with a permanency that could not be achieved in the barbarian times of Charlemagne's reign. As the author of one of the countless letters—cast in the *Moniteur* as the direct expression of public opinion—wrote in praise: Napoleon was going beyond his model; "To mark this period of glory and of power, of wisdom and of happiness when, governed by a man superior to all others, the French nation rose above itself, history will not have to refer to the distant century of Charlemagne, to a century that our own resembles in so many respects just as it overshadows it in so many others. History compares: it judges, and already we can foresee from our own experience the testimony it will transmit to posterity."[16]

The first consul resisted comparisons to Cromwell and, at this point, even to Caesar. In contrast, he liked to be portrayed in the *Moniteur* as a new Charlemagne. In fact, Napoleon pursued a trajectory similar to that of Louis XIV: he, too, became the "incomparable one" par excellence. At the end of April 1803, Napoleon conceived the idea of having a statue of Charlemagne erected in the Place de la Concorde or in the Place Vendôme. His edict of October 1 specifies that a column was to be erected on the place Vendôme "like the one erected in Rome in honor of Trajan." This column would be topped by a statue of Charlemagne. The fact that this statue ended up being that of Napoleon only confirms the idea that Bonaparte had of himself in relation to this "ancestor" whose legacy he had claimed. "It is in vain," states Senator Chaptal after the victory of Austerlitz, ". . . that we seek in Antiquity names that could compare with our emperor: I see in the past neither a model he might have closely followed, nor anything resembling his glory."[17] In an "ode on the victories of Napoleon the Great," also published in the *Moniteur* in 1806, a Frenchman awakens Homer to ask him to come back to sing the glory of the hero who, through the greatness of his deeds, had effaced the great names of Antiquity and even that of Charlemagne:

> Il n'est plus pour nous de prodiges;
> J'ai vu des antiques prestiges
> S'évanouir le merveilleux;
> La fable a cessé d'être fable;
> Il n'est plus rien d'invraisemblable,
> Que les faits passés sous nos yeux.[18]

————

[There are no more prodigies for us;
I have seen the marvelous

Fade away from antique prestige;
The fable has ceased to be fable;
There is no longer anything unbelievable
Besides the facts that occurred under our own eyes.]

And yet, before becoming the "incomparable one," before discarding history and situating himself in an absolute present, Napoleon felt the need to seek legitimacy by calling upon the national past. In 1803, shortly after proposing the statue of the great emperor, Napoleon created four secondary schools in Paris, the *lycées* Imperial, Napoleon, Bonaparte, and Charlemagne. Of these four schools only the Lycée Charlemagne managed to retain its name throughout the nineteenth century without change, and it still exists as such today.[19] Before his coronation ceremony, Napoleon went to Aachen, where he stayed from September 2 to September 11, 1804. Talleyrand, his minister of foreign affairs at the time, understood well the symbolic implications of this trip. He wrote to Napoleon:

> It will appear great and just that the city that was the first imperial city for so long, that always bore the special name of the seat and throne of the emperors, and that was Charlemagne's habitual residence, experience its own magnificence through the presence of Your Majesty and bring out the resemblance in destinies that Europe has already grasped between the restorer of the Roman Empire and the founder of the French Empire.[20]

The new emperor visited Charlemagne's tomb; he contemplated the relics, the throne, the sarcophagus of the emperor of the Franks; he had a Te Deum mass sung in the cathedral. While his journey along the Rhine asserted his authority as conqueror—among other things he visited fortifications—at Aachen he performed acts that were aimed at giving his power a symbolic extension and legitimacy.

It was likely in order to demonstrate that he was as much a civilizer as Charlemagne that the new emperor issued an edict enacting a cultural policy that brings together, in a gesture directly inherited from the Ancien Régime, a "national" consciousness and the "universal" values of the Enlightenment. Dated 24 Fructidor of the year XII (September 11, 1804), the edict declares that Napoleon, "Emperor of the French . . . , with the intention of encouraging the sciences, letters, and arts," which contribute to "the glory of nations," and desiring not only that "France maintain the superiority it has attained" in these domains but also that "the century that is beginning be better than all those preceding it," orders the creation of prizes for the sciences, history, fine arts, and the best poems "having as subject matter the memorable events of our history or the deeds bringing honor to the French character."[21] In this time leading up to the creation of the empire, the national past was put in the spotlight. Already a few months earlier, the poet Parny had given a speech at the Institute (printed of course in the *Moniteur*) in which he deployed a mixture of the logic of the *translatio studii* and of conquest to support his thesis on the literary superiority of France. According to him, only literary institutions could counter the decadence that threatened from all sides: "The schools of Athens created and preserved eloquence and philosophy. After Greece's defeat, these schools became those of the victors, and Rome drew learning and taste from them that softened the rudeness of customs." After a period of barbarism, "Charlemagne attracted grammarians and poets and opened his palace to literary assemblies over which he himself presided."[22] But the enlightenment that Charlemagne, who was all too superior to his time, fostered could not dissipate for long the darkness that surrounded him. Obviously Napoleon, benefiting from all the progress since that time, was ensured of success.

The synthetic strength of the figure of Charlemagne was all the more powerful in that as emperor of the Romans, he could be used as an example and a justification for a policy of rapprochement with the pope. France's interventions in Italy had always occurred in the shadow of the emperor with the flowing white beard, protector of the Church, indeed, liberator of Italy. Bonaparte traveled those beaten paths again in order to bring the light of the republic to the peoples beyond the Alps. He quickly came to the conclusion that since the influence of Rome was "immeasurable, breaking with this power had been a serious mistake."[23] Napoleon's insistence on his kinship with Charlemagne at the moment when ties with the Church were being renewed was a way of asserting that the pope had to be under the guardianship of France and its emperor.

But it was also a way of strengthening his symbolic power over Europe. The first sense of unity in Europe took root in the idea of Christendom and the empire of the West. In 1804, in his speech to the Corps législatif on the organization of metropolitan seminaries, Portalis insisted at length on the ties between European identity and Christendom. "The long childhood of humanity lasted until Charlemagne's reign. This prince founded a vast empire with his conquests and his laws, but religion was the material with which he built Europe."[24] He was able to forge a well-balanced "sacred alliance of religion and learning." Out of this happy union of knowledge and revelation there developed a new unity within which "the various peoples ceased being strangers to each other . . . , and imperceptibly Europe, as it became enlightened, turned into one great family made up of diverse nations that . . . were united by religion, knowledge, and mores." The

Napoleonic empire would complete the historical movement initiated by Charlemagne.

All this explains why Napoleon insisted so adamantly on being crowned by the pope. This ceremony was to bear Charlemagne's imprint and thus seal the young conqueror's identification with the ancient emperor whose legacy he claimed. We know Napoleon was concerned with incorporating the "honors of Charlemagne" in the coronation, "honors" constituted by the regalia that had survived the Revolution, including the spurs, Charlemagne's sword and its sheath, and Charles V's scepter topped with a statuette of Charlemagne, along with a replica of his crown made specifically for the occasion.[25] This same scepter, slightly modified, as well as the crown were later used in Charles X's coronation. Effigies of Charlemagne and Clovis were set on top of the pillars of the gothic portico erected in front of Notre Dame for the ceremony held on the 11 Frimaire of the year XIII (December 2, 1804). The Carolingian motif was repeated in the decorations inside the cathedral in the form of tapestries representing the scepter topped with Charlemagne's statuette and the hand of justice crosswise under the imperial crown.

Two weeks later, the *Moniteur*, which had already devoted a large amount of space to the coronation ceremony, published a long report on a history of Charlemagne, *Histoire de l'Empereur Charlemagne*, conveniently translated from the German. The paper used this opportunity to remind the public of Charlemagne's deeds and, in particular, to explain why the great man decided to have himself crowned emperor: "The momentum was started, France marched towards expansion, and Charlemagne saw that unless he united on his head and in his person all the means of power and respect, he would never be able to control events and ensure the glory of his reign."[26] Beyond the kingdom, war-mongering peoples threatened the borders; inside, there was "a political system lacking harmony with rights that were in turn ignored and then recognized only to be ignored again; this system effectively barred any reform that could have contributed to the growth of wealth and internal strength."[27]

The great prince aspired to the glory of conquests only in order to improve the internal administration of the Empire. But he understood only too well the power the Empire and the Church exercised over people's minds. He thus drew support from them and accepted the imperial crown from the hands of the pontiff, a crown "that he could have also obtained from the vote of the people and the authority he already wielded."[28] At the same time, he was aware that he was inheriting the place and the rights of the ancient emperors and his empire was inspired by the history and the monuments of the ancient Romans. Charlemagne's life became an allegory for that of Napoleon. The old emperor lacked only a plebiscite, which he would have won anyway and which would have enabled him to garner the benefits of both absolutism and the republic.

Thus Napoleon's eagerness to cultivate his resemblance to Charlemagne stemmed from a whole set of motivations and provided him with symbolic capital that he could exploit in his attempt to reconcile the irreconcilable and legitimate his ascension to the imperial throne. This approach adopted an entire current of thought in which the great prince was viewed as having given back liberty and rights to the people by pulling them out of barbarism and by civilizing them. It also made it possible to avoid the Capetians and, at the same time, to establish a link with ancient Rome, of which the emperor of the West was the direct heir. Finally, it used history to foreshadow and justify not only a reconciliation with the Church but also a policy of dominating it, which was of course quite pleasing to the partisans of the old Gallican tradition. Napoleon pushed this identification to the extreme. In his instructions to his ambassador in Rome, Cardinal Fesh, on the sort of relations he expected to have with the Vatican, he states: "I am Charlemagne. Because like Charlemagne, I join the crown of France with the crown of the Lombards. . . . I therefore expect [people] to behave toward me accordingly."[29] And in 1809, he becomes angry at one point and criticizes the members of the clergy who were entrusted with settling issues with the pope for acting too independently. He finally explodes: "Messieurs, . . . you wish to treat me as if I were Louis le Débonnaire: Do not confuse the son with the father. . . . You see in me Charlemagne . . . I am Charlemagne, I, . . . yes, I am Charlemagne!"[30]

It was very tempting to complete the Carolingian symbolism by also appropriating the crown of the Holy Empire. Napoleon's making Bavaria into a kingdom (through the Treaty of Brünn, December 10, 1805), his having Eugène de Beauharnais marry the daughter of Maximilian Joseph I (January 14, 1806), his distributing duchies and principalities to his relations and kingdoms to his brothers: all this seemed to announce the reconstruction of the Carolingian empire. In the course of an hour-long meeting on January 17, 1806, Dalberg, the archchancellor of the German empire, told Napoleon of his plans to "regenerate the German constitution." After this conversation, he wrote a note in which he advocates, in order to bring the "nation" out of the anarchy into which it has fallen, the concentration of power into the hands of a great leader: "His Majesty the Emperor of Austria, François II, is worthy of respect as an individual because of his personal qualities, but in fact the scepter of Germany is escaping him. . . . He should be emperor of the East to resist the Russians and the empire of the West should be reborn in the emperor Napoleon, just as it was under Charlemagne, and should be made up of Italy, France, and Germany!"[31] François II gave up the imperial crown on August 6, 1806, but Napoleon knew better than to take it. He concentrated instead on reassuring Europe and pointed out that he was not planning to crush his allies but to protect their independence.

Though Napoleon never disowned his infatuation with Charlemagne, it did eventually lose its intensity. During the Prussian and Polish campaigns, the "barbarians of the north" were denounced while the benefits of a new Caesar were vaunted. Claims of kinship with ancient Rome replaced the notion of kinship with Germany. This turnaround is best illustrated by the lukewarm reception of the famous painting *Napoleon on the Imperial Throne* painted by Ingres for the Salon of 1806. The painter was aiming to please the new regime. To this end, he wanted to create a representation of Napoleon that would connect him to the national past without evoking the portraits of the kings of the Ancien Régime. Thus Ingres had to go very far back in history in order to avoid any bad association. Champigny, an "inspector" sent by the minister of the interior to examine the painting two weeks before the opening, noted that the "author, in adapting the images of Charlemagne, has tried to imitate the very style of that period in art."[32] The painter had emphasized the connection to the ancient emperor by centering the composition on the scepter topped with Charlemagne's statuette showing him seated on his throne. A pale and statuesque Napoleon holds this scepter in his right hand exactly the same way the small figure of Charlemagne does. Indeed, the whole attitude of Napoleon on his throne imitates that of his illustrious predecessor.[33]

We might have expected that the royalist critics who thought ill of attempts to legitimize the empire by a return to the ancient monarchy would denounce Ingres's "gothic" style.[34] But the critics who supported Napoleon attacked the painting as strongly as others did, accusing the painter of being inspired by gothic medallions. In their view, this hieratic manner of representing the new emperor diminished his status as a hero.[35] It would have been better to capture the power of epic genius than the historical legitimacy of the sovereign. Napoleon in the present or else dressed in the Roman style and thus rejoining the atemporal eternal: this was how the creator of a new Europe should henceforth be represented.

As the trend toward identification with ancient Rome advanced, references to Charlemagne in the *Moniteur* became more rare. And yet, the parallel with the old Carolingian empire, which was so strongly emphasized during the establishment of the new empire, the legitimizing recourse to the Middle Ages as the antiquity of modernity inspired an interest, even a passion, in national history that continued throughout the century and generated a great number of works in the realm of historiography as well as in the fine arts. The durability of an identification with Charlemagne was such that the change of direction that followed it did not prevent an increasing number of explicit and implicit comparisons with Charlemagne.

In the same year that Ingres was criticized for his medieval orientation, Louis Dubroca published *Les Quatre Fondateurs des Dynasties françaises ou Histoire de l'établissement de la Monarchie française*.[36] The author explicitly intended to bolster the legitimacy of Napoleon's empire by making it the extension of the immemorial French monarchy. Thus Dubroca announced that he would deal with Clovis, Pepin, Hughes Capet, and Napoleon the Great. In principle, then, there was no place for Charlemagne in such a work. And yet, immediately following his discussion of Pepin, the author goes into a long digression on the first emperor of the West. Although Charlemagne did not found a dynasty, explains Dubroca, his prestige prevents him from being ignored. It was he who gave France a greatness that made its kings into the "followers of Augustus, Trajan, Anthony."[37] But in addition to its function as the connecting point between Antiquity and modernity, Charlemagne's era comes to mind because of its affinities to the present:

> If ever the history of this great monarch was worthy of a keen interest on the part of the French, it is mostly at this present moment when everything Charlemagne gave of power and greatness to France is restored to it by a prince worthy of his glory. There have never been so many striking similarities between two centuries and two sovereigns at so great a distance from each other; never did two epochs resemble each other so much in terms of equally memorable events and glorious circumstances. The creation and now the rebirth of the French empire will constitute for history two remarkable periods to which the centuries separating them will pale in comparison.[38]

Past centuries between the two summits of the French monarchy seem to disappear before the power of the resemblance between the two reigns with the surplus of glory that characterizes them. Not only were there no breaks between the present and the national past, but that past itself paralleled the present moment, which had taken on the status of originary moment even as it remained in the continuation of a tradition fundamental to French identity.

It is the legislating prince rather than the warrior whom Dubroca sees as Napoleon the Great's illustrious predecessor. Like Napoleon, Charlemagne appears at a moment when "the troubles of the state has all the symptoms of general anarchy," when "all the mechanisms [*ressorts*] of government are broken," and when laws are shunned by the weak and violated by the strong; a time when "any attempt at reform seems impossible."[39] All the signs announcing the arrival of the providential man are clearly present: the collectivity was at a historical impasse requiring the intervention of a great man. Drawing on Mably, Dubroca proceeds with ease to attribute the republican spirit and values to Charlemagne. The sole ambition of the great prince was to "bring back the French to the ancient principles of the government that their fathers had brought from Germany"; his first concern was to establish the rule of law. Knowing the rights of the people to be inalienable, he "had for [the people] this compassion mixed with respect with which ordinary men see a fugitive prince robbed of his estates."[40] Dubroca repeats Mably's text word for word. His entire vision is the direct legacy of eighteenth-century reflection on the ancient constitution. Napoleon became the second restorer of the originary republic, the man who rose above all factions and who transcended all individual interests in order to bring France back to the truth of her distant origins.

The inspiration to compose works on "Carolingian" themes was not limited to historiography. Several epics and plays drawing parallels between the two emperors were produced during this period, including an epic in verse by Napoleon's brother Lucien. Another such epic was written by Viscount Charles Victor Prévôt d'Arlincourt, whose project Napoleon had personally encouraged. "The orders of heroes are heavenly orders," wrote d'Arlincourt.[41] He began his poem in 1806 but only published the first passages, titled "Une Matinée de Charlemagne," in 1810. The entire epic, *Charlemagne ou la Caroléïde*, was published in 1818, well after Napoleon's downfall. In the poem, the right of conquest resides in the very status of the hero. Indeed, the author's justification boils down to the circular argument that the "great man" is great because he is a "great man" and the proof of this lies in his success. Two "transcendent" values are defined in the course of the epic. The notion of glory, lifting up both the hero *and* the nation, and that of unity: Charlemagne forged a united Europe under France's tutelage.

D'Arlincourt was one of Napoleon's favorites. The emperor named him squire to his mother (*écuyer de Madame Mère*), then auditor to the Council of State, and then intendant in Spain. But later on he received an equally warm welcome at Charles X's court because his father and grandfather had been guillotined during the Revolution. D'Arlincourt enjoyed some literary success thanks mostly to his novel *Le Solitaire*. In the preface to his *Charlemagne* he adapts to the change of regime by turning his poem into a paean for the fatherland and its heroes. His text sought to remind France of its past glory, a France that, at the time, had been beaten down by defeats and "the unbearable yoke of foreign troops."[42] "And why should France not have a Homer, a Virgil, a Tasso, a Milton, since it did possess its own Sophocles, Euripides, Menander, Horace."[43] A pamphlet published by "a friend of Monsieur d'Arlincourt," included a piece in praise of Charlemagne, *Eloge de Charlemagne*, and d'Arlincourt's inaugural speech to the French Academy. The author boldly proclaims that "France finally possesses a national epic! It is the monument Voltaire could only dream of."[44]

The reason France did not have an epic prior to the publication of his *Charlemagne*, explains d'Arlincourt, is because the country was in a state of self-forgetting, of self-estrangement, caused by classicism, the unhealthy fascination with ancient Greece and Rome. "Because of a truly inexplicable, bizarre turn, French authors, instead of celebrating their nation as the Greeks and Romans did, seemed to have stubbornly taken only foreign warriors as subject of their songs."[45] The author of the epic cites Madame de Staël abundantly in his notes, particularly the passages in which she claims that the literature of the ancient Greeks and Romans is for the French a "transplanted literature," whereas chivalric literature is indigenous.[46] Thus the works in praise of Napoleon depicting him as the providential man destined to save France from chaos were able to survive his downfall because they were part of a broad movement of return to national history and of the sentiment that France lacked its own specific literature. D'Arlincourt decided to publish his epic in 1818 because he intended to take advantage of the growing trend to remythify history.

MARCHANGY AND *LA GAULE POÉTIQUE*

Developed during the postrevolutionary period, the literature of the troubadour genre was one of the first literary attempts to renew ties with the past. Based on a medievalism that had roots in the eighteenth century, this literature reveled in the evocation of a past inhabited by noble figures who combined courage and chivalry with sensitivity and poetry. We have seen an early sample in de Genlis's *Les Chevaliers du cygne*. The troubadour movement and its glorification of national history gave rise to theoretical reflection advocating the mythification of history for the sake of fostering a national historical literature. Perhaps the best-known theorist of mythified history was Louis Antoine François de Marchangy, a devoted Bonapartist or an ardent royalist, depending on the political winds of the moment. His *La Gaule poétique*, first published in 1813, enjoyed considerable success and was reprinted five times by 1834. *La Gaule poétique ou l'Histoire de France considérée dans ses rapports avec la poésie, l'éloquence et les beaux-arts* is a curious hybrid work midway between historiography and literature, taking on the self-appointed mission of mediating between national history and the literary and artistic production of the time.[47] Marchangy did not intend to produce a literary work but instead to create conditions favorable to the production of a national historical literature by providing the community of potential poets and artists with a work that evoked the national past and explained why and how these historical events should be viewed as matters worthy of literary endeavors.

In retracing the history of France from the earliest times of Gaul to the seventeenth century, Marchangy does not limit himself to historical facts, although he notes that he does not wish to invent history either. What really matters is that legends and fables, as well as facts, were given form and expression by others before him. They are now part of a tradition. Collective memory is transmitted through documents, that is, through written texts, and it is on this writing and not on individual subjectivity that the new national literature should be based. For instance, in his discussion of the origins of coats of arms, Marchangy notes that the institution is often thought to have originated in Charlemagne's time: "This view is mistaken, but it need only have been expressed by several writers for poets to [legitimately] adopt it in their poetry."[48]

Marchangy devotes the entire third volume of his work to Charlemagne, and it is here that he chooses to explore more explicitly the relationships between history and myth, between fact and fiction. He is led to do this largely because of the role he attributes to Charlemagne in the history of France. For Marchangy, the emperor is a figure symbolizing a break with the past, one marking the beginning of a new era, the passage from the ancient to the modern. With Charlemagne, through the greatness and difference of his time, the French began to develop a sense of national identity, a "national sentiment," as Marchangy puts it, that is, the consciousness of their difference from others.

But Charlemagne was not only a great historical figure, he was also a mythical one, and for Marchangy the mythical aspect of the discourse on Charlemagne deserves as much attention as the historical discourse. Whereas the heroes of Antiquity have lost their place in history, Charlemagne still leads a double existence: he is at once *in* history and *beyond* history. He has been preserved and reinvented more than any other hero of any other people. Thus the myth has penetrated his time, that is, it has penetrated French national history itself, and this blend of a collective, national past and the alterity of myth imparts to this history the prestige and power of being both the Self and the Other.

Having told Charlemagne's *history*, Marchangy then deals with myth or with what he calls "the fabulous part of his reign" as it appears through "the magical prism" of the old romances. Like the authors of the *Bibliothèque universelle des romans*, Marchangy employs the French word *roman* that is used to designate both the medieval genre of *romance* and its modern-day descendant, the novel. He relies on this ambiguity to insist on the continuity linking the two—along with the *chanson de geste* which he does not distinguish from the romance genre—in opposition to the writings of historians and chroniclers. Adapting the theses that La Curne de Sainte-Palaye and the *Bibliothèque universelle des romans* had previously propounded in the eighteenth century, he states that "historians regrettably almost always forget to describe in their works the customs and practices of the time of which they write."[49] They lose sight of the fact that the difference between periods of history is relative. Moreover, the absence of any attempt to anchor their discourse in the present—to discern a relationship between past and present—constitutes *le non-dit* (the unspoken, the unexpressed aspects) of history. The essential value of the *romanciers*—that is, the authors of medieval romances, but also, we must believe, their latter-day incarnations writing the kind of national historical literature Marchangy is advocating—is to bring this relationship to life. Seen from this perspective, incorporating history into the present is a way of establishing a connection with that history, of inserting it into a overall vision:

> *Romanciers* necessarily link the facts they are narrating to the details of public and private life: society is the backdrop on which they draw and embroider their conceptions. They draw their opinions and language from the dominant ideas, biases, habits, and ways of seeing of their contemporaries.[50]

Through their mythical reinvention of Charlemagne's history, the old epic romances become important "supplements to history" in that these works represent "the sole resources of annalists, archaeologists, and even poets and painters concerned with giving their subjects an air of truth."[51] Thus the errors in this mythical or fabulous history become the truths of the French national tradition and, as a result, they can be incorporated into the nation's new historical literature while at the same time supplying criteria by which that literature's plausibility would be judged.

But Marchangy also sees these fables as having had an ideological function that could be recovered for French literature. For him, there is a "striking similarity" between our ancestors' taste for romances and their principles of "civility."[52] This parallel is significant because, in Marchangy's view, the rules of civility blended ethics with aesthetics and politics to make everyday practices into a harmonious whole. Thus Charlemagne's mythified history acquires a unifying function: it links that originary moment to the multiple "present" moments that followed it and, in the process, it condenses and unifies the national past by integrating its different moments into Charlemagne's myth. At the same time it brings together values that would otherwise appear irreconcilable in the postrevolutionary context; politics, ethics, and aesthetics come together not as an intellectual abstraction but as a manner of being subsumed under the concept of civility. These epic tales conveyed the moral and ethical values of their civilization, a civilization that began with Charlemagne and which still constituted the foundation of France in Marchangy's time. In this sense these works could be seen as a modern creation.[53] Because French society developed and crystallized its identity in these epic romances, they represent the triumph of modernity over Antiquity: "The epic romance is a modern invention, it is almost the sole poetic genre to which Antiquity can lay no claim."[54]

For Marchangy, this triumph of modernity was above all a victory for France. The roots of epic romance lay in the mythical history of Charlemagne. Marchangy goes to great lengths to prove that the epic romance was a distinctively French invention; it was French in its form and content, in the values it expressed, and in the heroes it depicted. "These epic romances were, for five centuries, read and internalized by all the members of society from all classes, not only in France but in the whole of Europe."[55] According to Marchangy, romances conveyed a "code of public and private virtues" with a dual function that proved to be both conservative and imperialistic. Within France, this code served to crystallize the nation's identity in the ethical and political spheres: the code of chivalry described in these epic romances conveyed to the French "the kind of patriotism that supports the throne, as well as virtuous enthusiasm, which all too often has been replaced by an attitude of complacency and conceit or by the turbulent anguish of revolutions."[56] Outside France, this code transmitted French civility to other nations.

In Marchangy's view, the "exquisite civility" formulated and transmitted by chivalric romances depicted the French as a courteous, urbane people in which politeness and politics came together to constitute a highly civilized nation. Drawing on the ethical and political rules of conduct conveyed by the mythified history of Charlemagne was a way of recovering a moral legitimacy lost during the Revolution. As for his literary program, Marchangy hoped to encourage creative work that would lead to the revival of a France at home with its past as well as to political practices tempered by a long tradition of civility.

And yet, Marchangy is propounding a national ideology that is still defined in terms of absolutism, which turns one individual, Charlemagne, into the embodiment of national values and national sovereignty. Although others had created the institution of the monarchy, it was Charlemagne who forged a true collective identity and created what could be described as a *feeling* of nationhood. This explains the importance accorded to the "true" Charlemagne, the historical figure that enabled the French to think of themselves as a people and to become conscious of their identity and of their difference in relation to others. Indeed, the nation became present to itself through the figure of Charlemagne. In Marchangy's description of this immense figure through which France discovered itself, we can make out the triple identity dear to absolutism: that of sovereignty, nation, and monarch. But Charlemagne's creative act was echoed and amplified in the cycle of epic poems composed long after his reign. Indeed, the triple identity of absolutism, sovereignty, and monarch (or, more generally, of political power) was in turn bolstered by the mythifying work of social imagination as it expressed itself in popular narratives. According to Marchangy, "these popular interpretations" and "exaggerated opinions" were first transmitted by word of mouth, from father to son, but they soon enjoyed an "extensive circulation among all classes of society."[57] These oral tales were like an echo, that is, a confirmation by the voice of the people, of the great emperor's fame. Moreover, it was through these narratives that public opinion was expressed. Seen from this perspective, the transition to writing assumes a crucial importance, for it assured the transmission of a legitimacy that found its most complete expression in the global vision of the *romans courtois*, the written courtly romances of knighthood and chivalry, whose origins can be traced to oral folktales.

THE FOUNDING HERO AND THE SOVEREIGN PEOPLE

Claims of popular sovereignty and the role played by the "people"— essentially that part of the nation formerly referred to as the third estate— in French history, were refined and reinforced over the course of the nineteenth century. This trend among militant liberal historians of the 1820s has been recently described in a study by Marcel Gauchet.[58] The quest for historical legitimacy, which had long been the favorite pastime of the Right, was taken up by historians on the Left. The Right had viewed history as a continuous, dynastic sequence; the Left replaced this vision with that of a collective evolution advancing in stages. It was no longer the great actor who made history but history that made the great actor.[59] Instead of seeking to depict the great man, the historian should strive to present a total history, to *bring the past back to life*, as Michelet was to put it. Instead of seeking a determining causality in the great man's actions, the "new" historians focused on tracing the advent of the people to its new role as sovereign. In the *Social Contract* Rousseau explains that the "*public* person . . . formed by the union of all other persons was once called the *city* [city state] and is now known as the *republic*."[60] In a sense, then, Rousseau's vision was realized: sovereignty had passed from the king to the people. The sovereign people constituted a collective ego. After the Revolution, this public "person" was referred to as the nation. The personification of the nation, its identification as an individual, became one of the dominant ways of imagining and describing it, as in this remark by Michelet: "I was the first to see the nation as a soul and a person."[61] Viewed as a person, France had all the advantages of a unity of intention, of vision, and of effective action enjoyed by the great hero, the larger-than-life figure so admired during the romantic era. What, then, was the destiny of the great historical hero and founding figure, that is, of the *individual* hero, in this period in which the true hero became a collective figure, in which individuality was projected onto the nation?

Napoleon's use of the figure of Charlemagne was the all too logical result of a whole set of eighteenth-century representations of the great conqueror. And it is not surprising that the exploitation of the old emperor to legitimize the new absolutism was ill received in some republican circles whose members wished nothing more than to oust Charlemagne from his strategic position in the history of France. Indeed, Augustin Thierry, in his famous *Lettres sur l'histoire de France*, attempts to diminish the place held by the old emperor.[62] He affirms that it is only now, in the afterlight of the Napoleonic empire, that we can perceive Charlemagne's true nature.

> Perhaps, before the great and sad experience we went through thirteen years ago and with the only help of ideas prevalent under the Ancien Régime, it was then impossible to make out the true reason for the political movements into which Charlemagne's family was drawn. Maintaining the Frankish empire did not depend, as so many historians following Montesquieu have claimed, on the *wise tempering of the orders of the state, on the task given to the nobility to keep it from plotting troubles, and on the filial submission of the children of the prince.* The issue was neither the orders of the state, nor the nobility, nor the other social classifications of modern monarchy. The aim was to maintain the forced subjection of several nations foreign to each other, many of which were more civilized . . . than the conquering people.[63]

The fall of the French empire was a revelation; it made it possible to look at the Frankish empire in a new light, to see that it was about the military domination "of one race of men over other races."[64] In fact, Thierry's arguments bear an uncanny resemblance to those of Voltaire. But the philosopher had wanted to maintain sovereignty in the hands of an absolute king, albeit an enlightened one, in contrast to Charlemagne, whereas Thierry aims to show that the people took its destiny into its own hands. Thierry contrasts the French party and "the party of the *Carolingians*" supported by Germanic interventions.[65] The existence of the French nation dates from the splitting up of the empire of the Franks, an event that occurred with the advent of a "national monarchy," that of the Capetians.[66] This is the event that marks the beginning of the long evolution that would lead from the revolt of the communes to the French Revolution. In this scenario, Charlemagne is not in the least French and is relegated to the negative prehistory of France.

As Thierry pushes Charlemagne out of French history, Michelet carries out a draconian demythification of the emperor of the Franks. In the first volume of his *Histoire de France* (1833), Michelet mounts a two-pronged attack against the ancestral conqueror. First, he strips him of genius, of true greatness, and above all of his role as a founding father, and second, he differentiates and separates the empire of the Franks from the French nation. Invoking his status as head of the historical section of the National Archives, Michelet often emphasizes the importance of access to the sources he had at his disposal. Yet, however much he invokes the authority conferred by his access to "authentic" documents, his portrait of Charlemagne is drawn above all in relation to the discourse of mythified history. In fact, Michelet's project here was much more the killing of a myth inherited from the eighteenth century than the bringing of history back to life. To this end, he examines and inverts the main components of the Charlemagne topos. In his view, even the testimonies to the greatness of the emperor that are found in ancient documents were based on an error in perception; Charlemagne's long life had caused people simply to forget what had gone on before. "With Charlemagne as with Louis XIV, people spoke only of the *great reign*, which became the point of reference for institutions, the glory of the nation, and everything else."[67] Napoleon was able to work around the Capetians by using the great emperor; as we can see, Michelet aimed to link him to the most absolutist of them all.

Far from being a great innovator, Charlemagne was, in Michelet's view, little more than a cruel and vile imitator, one who was more like a priest than a king, more German than French, and a leader presiding over a period of decline and decadence rather than the birth of a nation. Seen from this perspective, any hints of a sense of unity or feeling of nationhood resulted only from a false consciousness: "We often speak of the army of the Franks," remarks Michelet. "However, the Frankish people were much like Theseus's ship: replaced bit by bit, they had little in common with what they were at the start."[68] Even images of renewal are associated with a kind of alienation rather than with the notion of fresh beginnings. The French people's inconsistency paralleled "that weak and pale representation of the Empire" that was ruled by a Charlemagne stripped of his mythified history.[69] By denying Charlemagne's status as a founding father and his role as a heroic innovator, Michelet suspends him in a kind of historical limbo, in an anti-history peopled by impalpable phantoms. By killing the myth of Charlemagne, Michelet denies him his place in history. It is thus hardly surprising, in his view, that one of the most enduring memories left by Charlemagne is that of the defeat at Roncevaux. Michelet further widens the gap between France and Germany by turning Ganelon, for instance, the traitor who betrayed Roland, into a German.

Louis-Philippe's reign did allow for the development of a liberal historiography, one that revisited French history in quest of the distant roots of the Revolution and the republic. These events had to be anchored in the national past so that they would no longer be seen as the result of a sudden rupture and instead become the product of a long historical evolution. Far from being the fruit of a rampant, unregulated, out-of-control rationalism, they could be seen as rooted in timeless traditions and customs. But the reign of the bourgeois king also encouraged a practice of history that favored national reconciliation. Thus the figure of Charlemagne was accorded an important place in historical paintings. The submission of Widukind, a moment of peace, union, and triumph, became a favorite subject entirely compatible with the infatuation for all things medieval.[70] Scheffer's painting of this subject, for example, reaffirms pictorially the predominant role of France in Europe (figs. 20, 21).

It is also from this perspective that we should understand Guizot's long reflection on Charlemagne. In contrast to Michelet, Guizot attempts to take a more European approach. In his *Cours d'histoire moderne* (1843), he states that "it is clear that a European civilization does exist."[71] However, this statement is followed very quickly with the assertion that "without flattering ourselves, we can say that France has been the center, the hearth of European civilization." Thus, he focuses primarily on a France defined as a model for the rest of Europe. Guizot, who had published a new edition of Mably's *Observations sur l'histoire de France* in 1823, explicitly raises the question of the "great man," with much of his discussion centering on Charlemagne. In his view, the figure of Charlemagne is inextricably linked to that of Napoleon: "We ourselves have seen a similar empire, one that took pleasure in comparing itself to that of Charlemagne, *and rightly so.* The fate of that empire too was linked to that of a single man, and we saw it fall with him" (my emphasis).[72] Thus, Guizot presents us again with the familiar picture of a Europe led by France, with a "great man" at the helm. What role in history did Guizot assign to the great man, and how are we to interpret that role?

Guizot notes that he avoided presenting an event-based history for all the periods prior to Charlemagne's reign. Before Charlemagne, "general developments alone" had been important in the history of civilization. Under the great monarch, however, the situation was quite different: "General developments were far less prominent than the extraordinary events dominating the scene."[73] Guizot feels compelled to change the way he presents history, that is, to speak more of events so as to capture the phenomenon of the great man. However, he does not wish to be limited to a simple narrative of great deeds, as this would mean falling back into the old technique of monarchical historiography or into that of romanesque fiction, with all the dangers of the loss of objectivity (and hence of mythification) these entailed. To emphasize his analytical distance as he presents the important events of Charlemagne's reign, Guizot has recourse to statistical tables. He acknowledges that this approach does not present a "living, animated view of society as a narrative would, but instead clearly outlines its structure and organization, thereby avoiding the problem of vague and random generalizations."[74] His goal is to avoid arbitrariness, as well as the nonanalytical subjectivity that narratives inevitably involve. After presenting a "table listing Charlemagne's principal expeditions," Guizot intersperses in the body of his text a series of tables devoted to the general assemblies held during his reign, to his capitularies, to "key documents, diplomas, letters, and acts," to "famous men who were born or who died during that period," and to Alcuin's letters to Charlemagne.[75] These tables, which merely list the items in each category or the places and dates where the events in question took place, interrupt the text to give the reader time for reflection.

This contemplative distance serves to guarantee the "scientific objectivity" of his project and to shelter it from any charge of mythification. Thus protected, Guizot launches into a description of Charlemagne that places the king at the origins of European civilization and is intended to refute "a host of moralistic commonplaces concerning the lack of power of great men, their uselessness, the vanity of their projects, and their lack of any real impact on the world."[76]

> Until the eighth century, nothing that had gone on before could continue to exist; nothing that showed promise of developing actually succeeded in materializing.
>
> Beginning with Charlemagne, the face of things changed: the process of decline ended and progress resumed. . . . Charlemagne's reign was the point at which the dissolution of the old world was finally complete. It was during his reign and under his direct leadership that European society turned itself around and, leaving behind the paths of destruction, followed instead paths of creation and renewal.[77]

Guizot emphasizes the importance of Charlemagne's personal involvement: "It was during his reign and under his direct leadership." There were no true political rights, nor was there any participation in the government on the part of the governed. The assemblies were mainly a means for the emperor to stay informed of what was happening in the different regions of the kingdom, a kingdom of which Charlemagne was "the center and soul."[78]

According to Guizot, the logic underlying the phenomenon of the great man is closely linked to the public and private aspects of the leader's character. At first, his greatness assured his success, because he understood better than anyone the needs of the society in which he lived and knew best how to gauge social forces, to take control of them, and to shape them. This is because he is at that point closer to reason, that is, to the true site of sovereignty.[79] What he undertakes during this first phase constitutes his true contribution to society. But the great man is also endowed with a strong inner vision and strength that push him to go beyond his contemporaries' needs and abilities. This aspect of the great man stems from his own egotism, dreams, and imagination, and it is precisely in this respect that his greatness works against him. For, as Guizot explains, he tries "to use public power [*la force public*] to serve his own aims and desires."[80] His inner dreams, his personal vision cause him to lose contact with his people; he becomes isolated and eventually falls. His failure occurs in the second phase because his inner dreams prevail over his understanding of reality—of his subjects' abilities and needs.

Charlemagne's egotism and dreams become apparent in his desire to force a Germanic people to conform to the Roman model of civilization, a goal that "did not at all reflect the needs or the will of the people."[81] As for Napoleon, he had "a true gift for organization and was endowed with an ardent imagination; he was an egotist and a dreamer, a schemer and a poet. He poured his energy into gigantic projects that were often arbitrarily chosen, the offsprings of his mind alone."[82] This exteriorization of an inner vision characterized the great man's arbitrary absolutism, so that in a strange way he came to resemble the poet and the dreamer. His greatness enabled him to efface momentarily the difference between private, inner space and public space, turning the world into a plaything of his imagination, an extension of his self. However, Guizot warns, identifying one's self with the nation should not stem from the projection of self onto society; rather, it must emanate from society, that is, from a true understanding of its needs and capabilities.

HUGO/SHAKESPEARE = NAPOLEON/CHARLEMAGNE

Situated at the juncture of myth, history, and poetry, the figure of Charlemagne is used to reflect on the relationships between the individual, politics, and history and also as a way of situating that reflection within a conception of Europe. No one illustrates the nature and the evolution of this notion better than Victor Hugo. His evocations of the old emperor reveal both the seductive pull of the great man and the problems raised by the figure of Charlemagne. The great writer identifies with the great conqueror, and, throughout his slow and complex journey from royalism to republicanism, Hugo returns often to this figure that had dominated his century just as Hugo hoped to dominate his own. Napoleon was the modern Charlemagne; Hugo yearned to be the new Shakespeare, for the time of weapons had been replaced by the power of the pen. Literature and culture should henceforth fulfill the civilizing mission that had, in the past, been entrusted to military action. "Why should there not now emerge a poet who would be to Shakespeare what Napoleon was to Charlemagne?"[83] The year 1830 is marked by the rekindling of the republican demands that were to endure till the advent of the Third Republic. But while riots were flaring up in the streets, the battle of *Hernani* was raging at the Théâtre-Français. In this play, in the famous meditation of Don Carlos before Charlemagne's tomb, Hugo develops his thoughts on the relationship between the present and the past, on the role of the private individual versus that of the statesman, and on the nature of power. This scene constitutes the cornerstone of the play, because it is here, while looking at history face to face, that Don Carlos achieves his greatness. It is here, in a quasi-mystical communion with his illustrious predecessor, that the king rises to the level of leader of the Empire. And, for Hugo, Charlemagne's empire represents the beginning of a united Europe that was itself only the first realization of universal thought:

> Es-tu bien là, géant d'un monde créateur,
> Et t'y peux-tu coucher de toute ta hauteur?
> Ah! c'est un beau spectacle à ravir la pensée
> Que l'Europe ainsi faite et comme il l'a laissée!
> . . . .
> Qu'une idée, au besoin des temps, un jour éclose,
> Elle grandit, va, court, se mêle à toute chose,
> Se fait homme, saisit les coeurs; creuse un sillon.[84]

———

> [Are you truly here, giant creator of a world,
> And can you lie down in it with all your height?
> Oh, the Europe you have thus made and left us
> Is a spectacle beautiful enough to stir our thoughts.
> . . . .
> An idea, needed by the times, one day flowers,
> It grows, it moves, it blends with everything,
> Turns into a man, wins over hearts, plows a row.]

Having come to this tomb to thwart a plot against him, Don Carlos, the future Charles V, sinks into a long daydream that detaches him from his immediate concerns and his manly passions and makes him see the possibility of "melding peoples and kingdoms into one to make a new Europe." But the height of his aspirations brings out the dangers of the abyss, this "ocean" of people where thrones are tossed about, these "dark waters" with their countless wrecks of great ships. Doubt and anguish seize Don Carlos, and it is then that he turns to history. Falling on his knees in front of the tomb, he exclaims:

> Charlemagne! c'est toi!
> Oh! puisque Dieu, pour qui tout obstacle s'efface,
> Prend nos deux majestés et les met face à face,
> Verse-moi dans le coeur, du fond de ce tombeau,
> Quelque chose de grande, de sublime et de beau!
> Oh! par tous ses côtés fais-moi voir toute chose,
> Montre-moi que le monde est petit, car je n'ose
> Y toucher . . .
> Apprends-moi tes secrets de vaincre et de régner,
> Et dis-moi qu'il vaut mieux punir que pardonner!
> N'est-ce pas? . . .
> Oh! dis-moi ce qu'on peut faire après Charlemagne![85]

> ——

> [Charlemagne! It's you!
> Oh, since God, for whom all obstacles vanish,
> Has brought our two majesties face to face,
> Pour into my heart, from the depth of this tomb,
> Something great, sublime, and beautiful!
> Oh, let me see everything from all sides,
> Show me that the world is small, for I don't dare
> Touch it . . .
> Teach me your secrets for winning and ruling,
> And tell me that it is better to punish than to forgive!
> Is this not so? . . .
> Oh, tell me, can anything still be accomplished after Charlemagne!]

At this point in his contemplations, Don Carlos looks to Charlemagne to justify the policy of vengeance he wants to pursue. It is then that Hugo, poetically enacting the fusion of man and history, has Don Carlos enter *into* the tomb of the great emperor. The arrival of the conspirators, that is, the direct threat to his authority, forces the king to take refuge in the vault. But when he comes out, he is no longer the same man. As we hear the cannon shots signaling his election to the Empire in the distance, the Don

Carlos who emerges from the tomb is the product of his remembrance of Charlemagne. The intimate, physical contact with his illustrious predecessor has produced a double transformation in Don Carlos. On the one hand, he goes from vengeance to clemency; the conspirators are forgiven. Thus, political unity will not be achieved through violence but through reconciliation. On the other hand, he renounces his personal desire:

Éteins-toi, cœur jeune et plein de flamme!
. . . .
L'empereur est pareil à l'aigle, sa compagne;
À la place du cœur, il n'a qu'un écusson.[86]

———

[Young heart, you must smother your flames!
. . . .
The emperor is like the eagle, his companion:
Instead of a heart, he has only a coat of arms.]

This double transcendence opens the way to the personal happiness of others. While he was submerged in the past, Don Carlos came to understand the essential nature of legitimate power and the conditions for its practice. The transformation that occurred in Charlemagne's tomb led to the sublimation of the private self, the precondition for replacing personal love with the first step toward universal love, that is, clemency. "Are you pleased with me?" asks Don Carlos as he bows in front of the monument at the end of the scene. "Have I thoroughly understood the misery of being king? / Charlemagne! Am I as emperor truly another man? . . . / Have I understood the voice speaking in your tomb?"[87] The new sovereign is to be the new embodiment of an idea that was first personified in Europe by the figure of Charlemagne.

In many respects, it is only by embracing history that Don Carlos can find in himself the power to renounce his personal passion and transcend his individual self. The goal is indeed to bring history into the present, to reappropriate it, to touch once again the purity and the greatness of origins.

In the nineteenth century, many were those who tried to understand the voice speaking from the tomb in Aachen. Of all the places that foster reflection on the memory of Charlemagne, his tomb in Aachen is mentioned most often in nineteenth-century French literature. Because of the polyvalence of that memory, which resonates with elements that are both religious and heroic, royal and imperial—and because of the concrete reality of the monument itself, Chateaubriand chose Charlemagne's tomb to illustrate the powerful fascination that the past can hold for a present in search of its origins. We have seen that Napoleon also spent moments of silence at Charlemagne's graveside, no doubt to immerse himself in the spirit of the former master of Europe while profiting from his glory. Nor did Victor Hugo fail to make his pilgrimage to the tomb. In *Le Rhin*, he recounts his trip, during which he also did what he had the hero of *Hernani* do: he entered the tomb of the great emperor, and this leads him to reflect on the role of the figure of the great man in shaping the minds and hearts of citizens.

Hugo wrote this work in the context of the crisis of 1840, when he hoped to be named a peer of France.[88] The Rhineland had again become a burning issue. In the face of an Anglo-Prussian rapprochement, Hugo proposes an alternative to a war of reconquest of the left bank of the Rhine. This alternative would be "the union of Germany and France, a union that would "dampen the friendship between England and Russia, thereby ensuring the salvation of Europe and world peace."[89] And yet, it is above all through history that Hugo reflects on the future of Europe. He sees the Carolingian empire as the first draft "of the great southern Rhenish state" that, in his opinion, is the necessary end toward which history is moving.[90] For Hugo as for Guizot, Charlemagne was the founding hero par excellence. Before him, the world had been primitive and amorphous. In a draft of a monograph on the Rhineland dating from the same period, Hugo writes: "At the climax of this transitional period, at a decisive moment in the midst of all that conflict and chaos, civilization suddenly became flesh and blood as Charlemagne appeared."[91] This founding moment had all the magic of a chemical reaction: rather than a slow evolution, the passage from chaos to civilization happened in a flash of creation. Moreover the end of history, the union of France and Germany, was already inscribed in that first moment. In this way the return to origins becomes the means of knowing and understanding the future.

And yet, as Hugo notes, to achieve such a union would require overcoming the hatred dividing the two countries. Presented this way, the political issue turns into one of emotions. Thus it is not surprising that Victor Hugo bases his authority on sincerity and good faith. "The *self* is an affirmation," he writes. Hugo establishes the authenticity of his self through intimate letters rather than through political rhetoric. *Lettres à un ami* consists of a daydreamer's reflections jotted down from day to day as he travels along the Rhine. The friendly reader, the supposed spontaneity of the style, all work together to establish the good faith of the writer, of the book, and consequently, of the political arguments. Hugo explains that "though these letters appear separate from the conclusion, they become . . . supporting documents."[92] It is by putting his inner self on display that the author gains the right to express his political views. Anticipating the question of whether the discourse of the dreamer and political discourse were really compatible, if the unconstrained expressions of the dreamer would not violate the constraints of political thought, Hugo raises the possibility of contradiction but only in order to dismiss it. "In a certain way, the dreamer's journey guided by whimsy . . . might possibly diminish the authority of the thinker." But since we are dealing with a matter of sentiments, that is, "the friendly resolution of an issue of animosity," it is of utmost importance for the writer to express his thoughts faithfully, "even the most personal and hidden ones."[93]

By identifying himself as a dreamer, Hugo frees himself from the constraints of rigorous argumentation and lays claim to a freedom of thought enabling him to link seemingly unconnected matters and to reveal unusual but profound parallels—in short, to establish symbolic analogies. When this solitary walker arrives at Aachen, he finds a church whose appearance is "hybrid and discordant," an "indecent" rococo-style chapel, and a tomb whose sanctity had been violated and that has been "given over to shameless commercialization."[94] But, before long, Hugo transforms this discord into symbolic harmony and finds in the church a parallel to Charlemagne's work:

> After a moment of contemplation, a singular majesty emanates from this extraordinary building, a monument that, like Charlemagne's work, has remained unfinished and is made up of architectural elements speaking in all styles, just as his empire was made up of nations speaking in all languages.[95]

Hugo focuses on the degraded reality before him only to transform it through the movement of dreaming thought. As he meditates in front of Charlemagne's throne, he imagines how, in the future, the holy emperor might once again be seated there just as he was before the plundering of his tomb. Restored to all his iconographic splendor, the seated Charlemagne, along with his diadem, his globe, and his mantle of fine gold cloth, would become an object of contemplation and reverie. In this way, Charlemagne's tomb would serve to remythify history. The visitor's closeness to the hero's remains would cause the discourse of mythified history to rise again and be assimilated into his or her deepest consciousness:

> It would be an awesome sight to behold and a great source of inspiration for anyone who dared venture into this tomb. People would travel there from the ends of the earth, and all sorts of philosophers would come. Charles, son of Pepin, is indeed one of those complex beings who can be looked at from several different angles. From a historical perspective, he is a great man like Augustus, Caesar, and Sesostris.

From the perspective of fiction, he is a holy crusader like Roland, a magician like Merlin. From the perspective of the Church, he is a saint like Jerome and Peter. Finally, from a philosophical perspective, Charlemagne embodies civilization itself, which is transformed into a giant every thousand years in order to cross some deep abyss—civil war, barbarism, revolution—and whose name is at one moment Caesar; at another, Charlemagne; and at another, Napoleon.[96]

Charlemagne's multifaceted exemplarity enhances his greatness to the point that, for Hugo, he comes to personify civilization as a whole. However, the intimacy of the contact imagined in this passage is crucial: through personal contact with the remains of the past, the self internalizes the discourse of mythified history to such an extent that it is able to draw from it powerful inspiration for personal action. Hugo concludes the letter about his pilgrimage to Aachen with the description of a hallucinatory reverie he had in the evening while seated on a grassy slope overlooking the town from which two distinct masses stood out: the town hall and the chapel:

> The town itself, this illustrious and symbolic city, seemed to become transformed in my mind and beneath my gaze. The first of the two black masses that I could still see, the only ones I could see, was no longer anything for me but a child's cradle, the second, merely a dead man's shroud; and at times, in the depths of the contemplation in which I was buried, I thought I saw the shadow of this giant whom we call Charlemagne slowly rise from this pale night horizon in between this great cradle and this great tomb.[97]

However, imagining or dreaming history in this way and psychologizing the process of mythification are not without risks. The collective function of the myth of origins may easily be overshadowed by the psychological processes depicted. Such proximity favors the relationship between the self and the internalized hero. Charlemagne ultimately becomes less a collective representation than a creation of the poet's ego. It is telling that, in the passage just quoted, the town disappears as a place inhabited by men and women and as a locus of civilization. It is entirely obscured by the giant shadow of the hero who is supposed to embody the community. The problem Guizot raised concerning the role of the great man in history again crops up regarding the person wishing to draw inspiration from this great man: the internalization of the great man causes the collectivity to be forgotten. Of what use then is such a vision of Charlemagne so rooted in personal writing, to the "rigorous" thinking of political writing, which attempts to examine the nation's collective destiny? The logic of politics requires a different perspective. The hero, exalted in the poet's intimate reverie, reappears in the "conclusion," but his greatness becomes so over-whelming that it ends up blocking the historical process. The hero's grandeur becomes a problem precisely at the moment when Hugo proposes the union of Germany and France and tries to demonstrate the need for this "reunification" by invoking the precedents of Charlemagne and Napoleon, that is, at the very moment he proposes a collective future for the two na-tions. Suddenly, Hugo is led to wish for a history devoid of great men:

> Perhaps the work of Charlemagne and Napoleon needs to be redone without Napoleon and without Charlemagne. These great men have the disadvantage of personifying the French nation more than the German one and, hence, of stirring up nationalistic animosities. Misunder-standings might result; people might come to think that they serve a man rather than a cause, that they serve the ambition of a single person rather than the collective good.[98]

The problem therefore is twofold. The mythification that takes place through personal writing describing intimate reveries does not pose any problem as long as it is a question of a single individual; however, as soon as it is a question of the collectivity, the type of representation that is appro-priate takes on very different dimensions, ones that relate it to society as a whole, to the nation. This point then raises the very difficulty that Hugo hoped to transcend: that of nationalities. The second part of the problem lies in the way the hero is imagined: he is a too-powerful personification of the ideal he purports to represent or, more precisely, the ideal, the true motive for action, tends to be overshadowed by his larger-than-life person-ality. Hugo attempts to establish his relationship with history not through reasoned reflection but through direct contemplation of the tomb, and he psychologizes the work of mythification as it is experienced by the writer of the "supporting documents" (i.e., the letters to a friend). As a result, he is no longer able to integrate the figure of Charlemagne into the vision he presents in his political treatise on the collective future of the two nations. When mythified history is generated through the poet's inner voice and reveries, the great hero loses his place in collective history.

In the intimacy of reverie, Hugo is tempted by hero worship. However, when he shifts to public discourse in his conclusion, he suggests that great men prevent nations from understanding the true meaning of history because the force of their personalities obscures the very ideals underlying collective identity, its true raison d'être. In the end, the poet's dream proves to be at odds with the authority of the political thinker, just as the inner self that im-poses itself on the world is at odds with a collective identity. Rather than a collective symbol, Charlemagne's figure becomes an individual's obsession.

Indeed, in the new conception of the world that was emerging during the nineteenth century, what place could there be for the great man and founding father, especially when the very idea of any one individual embodying sovereignty implied that he had somehow usurped the people's own inalienable right to sovereignty? At a time when everything was working to foster the personification of the nation, the individual personifying power could only be seen as preventing the nation from obtaining it. Be it Caesar, Charlemagne, or Napoleon, everything seemed to lead to a necessary demythification of the great men who dominated nations and eras. However, Charlemagne's case appears more complex precisely because of the myths and legends associated with him, since it was through them that the figure of Charlemagne would be resuscitated and reworked.

One of the main paths leading to a "reappropriation" of Charlemagne can be found in the affective realm, because, in spite of Charlemagne embodying a potentially overwhelming power, he can also be seen as a tragic hero. In a century when people often thought of the Terror as the result of radical rationalism and blamed the abuses of the Revolution on its refusal to acknowledge basic feelings of love and pity, the role of emotion as a source of legitimacy became primordial. In the course of the nineteenth century, the aesthetics of strong emotions took a variety of forms—from lyricism to melodrama. Again and again, authors proved their own humanity and brought out the humanity of others by giving over to emotion and being deeply moved or by deeply moving others. This aesthetics of emotion had political consequences: rather than thinking the nation, one should feel it and make others feel it too. Again, Victor Hugo helps us understand such a vision.

In *La Légende des siècles*, Hugo narrates a new version of the story of Charlemagne's conquest of Narbonne, a story in which he makes the emperor the victim of the narrow-mindedness of the nobles, who think only of their personal welfare. The tale is particularly meaningful to Hugo because it takes place after the great defeat at Roncevaux. There is an obvious parallel between the tragedy of this defeat stripping France of its bravest warriors, thus figuratively beheading it, and the upheavals of the Revolution. The taking of Narbonne becomes a way of illustrating how France's strength rebounded after such trying times.

But in Hugo's tale the emperor cannot act alone; he needs the help of the barons who survived the Roncevaux disaster. However, one after another, all of the nobles refuse him. The wise Naymes advises him to buy the town rather than conquer it. They all voice their fatigue, their yearning to return home, their desire to enjoy a bit of private happiness. "I want a nightcap. I am fed up with my helmet!" exclaims Eustache de Nancy. "I have glory to spare, O king. I am yearning for some straw."⁹⁹ Thus the greatness of the nation dissipates in the fragmentation of individual and bourgeois pleasures. There are no more conquests, only purchases.

The author leads us to support the great emperor's point of view by turning him into a victim of his own barons. Instead of depicting him with all the strength of the conqueror, Hugo chooses to emphasize the humiliation the emperor endures at the hands of his own men. Conquest is reduced to an abstraction that can be used to measure the internal unity and strength of the nation. Charlemagne gives unreservedly of himself, he exists only to embody the collective principle and its continuity.

> Allez-vous-en d'ici, car je vous chasse tous!
> Je ne veux plus de vous! retournez chez vos femmes!
> Allez vivre cachés, prudents, contents, infâmes!
> C'est ainsi qu'on arrive à l'âge d'un aïeul.
> Pour moi, j'assiégerai Narbonne à moi tout seul.
> Je reste ici, rempli de joie et d'espérance.¹⁰⁰

> ———

> [Go away, get out of here!
> I don't want you anymore! Go back to your wives!
> Go and live hidden, prudent, content, infamous!
> That's the way to reach old age.
> As for me, I'll lay siege to Narbonne on my own.
> I am staying here, filled with joy and hope.]

Then, out of the crowd, a young stranger appears whose sole qualifications are literary ("I can read Latin and I have completed my studies"). This young man naturally embodies the future of the nation, which the powerful — and very bourgeois—magnates had so shamefully abandoned. And Charlemagne is the one who knows how to inspire him to act in the service of the country. As for the conquest, Hugo recounts it in a single line, the closing line of the poem: "The following day, Aymery took the town."

Viewed solely from the perspective of his greatness, Charlemagne is overwhelming. By making him a victim suffering persecution that he overcomes through words of hope and unity rather than by force of arms, Hugo finds his way out of the impasse with which he was faced in the *Rhin*. The humiliated great man wins over the reader by calling upon his or her compassion; it is by drawing on the new strength of youth that he renews the country.

In composing this poem, Hugo draws on a body of philological research which was increasingly being popularized.¹⁰¹ By recasting one of those old romances now generally recognized as belonging to a folk tradition, Hugo reconciled the great man and the people. In so doing Hugo was participating in a larger trend that was depicting Charlemagne in a new light. His true greatness was now thought to derive from the people, because it was the people who, in singing his praises, had enabled the great man to survive.

Charlemagne: A Creation of the Nation

The evolution of Victor Hugo yet again shows the extraordinary plasticity of the figure of Charlemagne. Indeed, in the nineteenth century there was a Charlemagne for every taste. Monarchical and Bonapartist depictions of the emperor could be found in historical works, in textbooks, and even in novels.[102] And yet, it was in republican thought that the great hero's fate met with the most unexpected and significant reversal of fortune. The theory of the "great man" always ran into obstacles when confronted with the abuses of Napoleon, with the chasm separating him from the sovereign people, and with the failure and ephemerality of the great man's reign. Thus, it was through another channel, that of poetry, that is, through the national epic, that the republicans were able to recover Charlemagne. The various political idylls of the eighteenth century had been inspired by the philological studies of the seventeenth. Similarly, the republican renewal of the nineteenth century was first given form in philologists' circles. This current of thought illustrates the complex interactions at play between erudition, aesthetics, and politics. It drew its inspiration from the ideas of German thinkers such as Herder, Wolf, the Grimm and Schlegel brothers concerning the nature, role, and function of folk culture in the development and representation of national identity. A new vision of Charlemagne was to garner a force transcending the boundaries of various political beliefs and was to turn Charlemagne into the ideal figure of the nation in all its glory and unity, a figure that could be shared by all, a meeting point for all of France. This could occur because, to a certain extent, the notion of a universalist nation inherited from the Revolution could, without contradiction, join that of a nation as an organic unit enduring through time. The figure of Charlemagne derived its power and strategic position from the coexistence of these two views of the nation.

While the quest for a national epic was one of the constants in French culture from the sixteenth century on, the concept of *Volkskultur* as a folk and national voice spread in France beginning with the works of Claude-Charles Fauriel in the nineteenth century. Fauriel bridged the gaps between various trends; he knew the works of the ideologues and was the companion of Madame de Condorcet until her death in 1822. The Sensualist philosophical legacy was no doubt of help to him in the development of his ideas on the organic nature of the collective entity. He was a friend of Madame de Staël and Benjamin Constant, who put him in contact with Friedrich von Schlegel, who introduced him to German philology and its view of folk culture. Fauriel was a staunch republican, a close friend of Thierry, Manzoni, and Guizot, and he held the chair of literature that Guizot created for him at the faculty of letters in Paris. This blend of influences led Fauriel, on the one hand, to develop a theory of folk poetry as "the direct and true expression of the national character and mind,"[103] and, on the other, to create a republican reformulation of the "Romanist" thesis on the historical and cultural foundations of national identity.

In 1824, Fauriel published his *Chants populaires de la Grèce moderne* in the context of the Greek uprising. In this work, he describes a genre of poetry that seldom exists in the "often artificial life of books," but is alive "in the people itself."[104] This poetry, in which "popular imagination manifests itself with the greatest variety, freedom and effect," consists of war songs that are sometimes put into a narrative form and sometimes into lyrical form.[105] Sung by wandering blind rhapsodists, these poems, whose authors remain anonymous, emanate from the "spontaneous flow of folk genius."[106] They represent the continuation of the ancient folk poetry of Greece. This folk poetry had thus always existed; it conveyed an ancient tradition, constantly keeping it alive and renewing it. Fauriel then depicts the idyll of a Greece crisscrossed by Homer-like minstrels singing and thereby giving voice to what was in effect the expression of the national character. "Those songs were heard and learned in the midst of a crowd, in the open, in the gaiety of a feast in which they [the rhapsodists] were taking part, in one of those moments when the exaltation of life brings out the charm of its most humble impressions. We think they must have been enriched by all those reminiscences with which they were associated."[107] There are deep Rousseauean resonances here: the author's aim is in some way to form, consolidate, and maintain a general will that is nourished by memories and is reexpressed constantly through the harmony of these songs.

In the eighteenth century, Du Bos had forcefully argued the Romanist thesis, which held that the Gallo-Roman civilization was the continuation of Roman civilization. His apologia of absolutism turned the king of France into the direct heir of the Roman emperor. Fauriel also looks to Roman civilization, though he emphasizes culture over politics. He locates the cradle of French civilization in southern Gaul. It is there that Roman civilization survived the longest, that it was transmitted even as it was renewed, that a new language was built from Latin—"ancient Provençal . . . , the first language in the great Romance family, polished, civilized, and able to express the subtlest feelings" and to have its own poetry.[108] This Gallo-Roman culture had the power to assimilate the Visigoths and the Burgundians. But the Midi was conquered by Germanic barbarians, led mostly by the Franks. Fauriel invites his readers to empathize with this Midi, this great victim, which never ceased to rebel nor to be conscious of its identity. The Frankish people had crude customs; they were a people "still completely barbarian," which sought only to satisfy or to exalt "the natural passions of the barbarian, that is, greed, cruelty, the unbridled need for material pleasures."[109] Thus, in a vein similar to Thierry's support for the vanquished Anglo-Saxons, Fauriel gives his support to the beaten Midi, which carried the legacy of Roman civilization even as it gave it new form.[110]

According to Fauriel, the true folk poetry of the nation developed there, in southern Gaul. In a series of articles published in 1832 in *La Revue des Deux Mondes*, he attempts to show that "Carolingian romances" as well as those of the Round Table are only degraded forms of the original Provençal poetry; that is, they are less "popular" and more artificial. Discussing at length the case of *Renaut de Montauban*, Fauriel argues that the romancer mostly sought to show the insubordination, the lack of solidarity, the out-of-control individualism of a hero acting only for his own benefit and "having no other goal than his own glory."

Fauriel contrasts this "barbarian heroism" to the "civilized heroism powered by disinterested concerns for the common good."[111] In his view, the Charlemagne who is depicted in these *chansons* proves to be so unworthy of admiration that one has trouble understanding his influence and authority. The origin of these romances should be sought elsewhere; we should go back to the ninth century and look to "the Provençal-speaking peoples." There one finds folk romances involving the Arabs of Spain, that is, the Saracens of the *chansons de geste*. Thus the Carolingian epic, "a spontaneous development from old historical *chansons* on the wars of the country against the Moors,"[112] experienced its greatest development and its greatest complexity in Provençal poetry. It is there that it took on a truly popular and national character; it is there that it sang of civilized heroic deeds performed solely for the collective good. The Franks took their epic from the Provençals and deformed it to sing of barbarian individualistic values. And yet, the fact that the Franks borrowed this Provençal lyrical and epic poetry is in itself a testimonial to the triumph of Latin culture:

> Of all the countries that welcomed Provençal poetry, France was without a doubt the one where this poetry had the greatest chance of complete success. Spatial proximity, political relations, linguistic affinities, the memories and the persistent effects of the old Gaulish entity, all that facilitated the adoption in France of the poetic system of the South, *an adoption that was as complete as possible.*[113]

Fauriel's theories had a great impact. There was, however, a major flaw in his system. There was no proof, because no surviving piece of this great epic edifice in Provençal had been found. Could the Carolingian epic flourish among the Provençal people and then disappear without a trace? The search and the need for these missing pieces explains the success of Eugène Garay's literary forgery. Like Macpherson, who, a century earlier, had produced a fake "translation" of a nonexistent Gaelic poem, Garay took the pen name Garay de Montglave and published a "folk song" in the Basque language, along with its translation into French. Garay was supposed to have seen a transcription brought back originally from the Pyrenees by La Tour D'Auvergne, a transcription that had since conveniently disappeared. This short song describes a scene from the battle of Roncevaux: the Franks, led by Charlemagne, were invading, pushing back the natives, who were simple and brave mountain dwellers who later put their adventures to song. "Run away, King Carloman, with your black feathers and your red cape. Your nephew, your bravest, your darling, is lying there, dead."[114]

The influence of theories of the folk origins of epic continued to grow. At times, there were attempts to combine that subject with reflections on the "great man" who was supposed to have left his mark on his century. For instance, in a passage from Chateaubriand's *Études Historiques* cited by Achille Jubinal in his article "Some Romances among Our Forefathers," published in the *Journal du Dimanche*, Chateaubriand speculates that Notker's narratives might be akin to "stories told by one of Napoleon's simple grenadiers about the Egyptian campaign."[115]

In his *Histoire littéraire de la France avant le douzième siècle*,[116] J.-J. Ampère, a professor at the Collège de France, who was also well informed of the recent ideas on folk culture being developed in Germany, describes the role of the historical figure of Charlemagne. He attributes to Charlemagne all the positive traits of a founding hero and the feats of an individual who transformed the world: "Yet, this tremendous change was accomplished by a single man, and no other example could better demonstrate the powerful influence of great men on the masses."[117] In his view, only the four great figures of Alexander, Caesar, Charlemagne, and Napoleon have surpassed all others in history and attained mythical stature. Alexander and Charlemagne were the greatest of these four in that they were able to follow the "flow of civilization" and understand the movement of history.[118] Whereas nothing remains of the traditions of imperial government established by Napoleon, the light that Charlemagne rekindled "never went out and will only be extinguished with the sun."[119] Why? Because, Ampère argues, what distinguishes great men and true heroes from others is the fact that they are celebrated in popular poems and songs: "Humanity has not been ungrateful toward its benefactors, and these two names, more than any others, have been enshrined in legends and popular songs [*chants popu-laires*]."[120] Ampère maintains that poetry and legends can vouch for true heroes and help distinguish them from false ones. The true hero is elected and recognized in the harmony of the folk song, in the poetic expression of the collective will. Thus, the true hero's legitimacy became increasingly rooted in public opinion that was spontaneously manifested in medieval folk songs.

This mind-set helps us to understand the extraordinary importance of the publication in 1837 of the *Chanson de Roland* based upon the manuscript discovered in England by Francisco Michel. In the long article Pierre Larousse devoted to it in his *Grand Dictionnaire universel*, he heralded this epic as "the first national monument erected by the French muse."[121] Unlike other Carolingian poems that often stage rivalries or tensions between historical figures, the *Chanson de Roland* is distinguished by its expression of "love of country" centered around the figure of Charlemagne. Indeed, the power of this epic poem is derived from Charlemagne's character, which dominates the poem and constitutes its central core and unifying thread:

> The author of the *Chanson de Roland* invests the figure of Charlemagne with authority, grandeur, and majesty. The poet glorifies this imposing figure in order to glorify the fatherland [*patrie*]. He portrays him as beloved and obeyed by all, supremely just and all-powerful. . . . We should therefore not be surprised to learn that the *Chanson de Roland* was for several centuries the *Marseillaise* of old France.[122]

But it is nevertheless a long way from a poet celebrating his homeland in a national epic to the nation using that epic to express its own identity: the first instance represents an individual creation, whereas the second forms part of the collective realm of public opinion. Research into medieval philology helped republican thought reclaim the figure of Charlemagne in two different ways. First, Fauriel's argument on the origins of the *chanson de geste* led to the inversion of Charlemagne from *creator* of the nation to Charlemagne as *creation* of the nation. Second, the Romanist thesis propounded by Fauriel disappeared in favor of an entirely republican fusion of Romanist and Germanist theses. In both cases the key author was Gaston Paris, who emphasized the distinction on which Gaillard had insisted at the end of the eighteenth century in his history of Charlemagne.[123] Paris synthesized the arguments of folk and national poetry, republican ideology, and Romanist and Germanist theses of French culture and identity.

In his *Histoire poétique de Charlemagne* (1865), Gaston Paris, well versed in the ideas and methods of German philology, resolves to distinguish history from legend: "The mythical history of a great man has its own place alongside true history."[124] For him, the point of departure is without question a Germanic one:

> The Austrasian Franks had become for ninth-century Europe what the Romans had been at the time of their power, a superior race destined for supremacy over all others. . . . The Franks were the ones who sang of their heroes after the victory; they also preserved for centuries the old popular epics that Charlemagne had ordered to be collected.[125]

However, Paris nonetheless insists on the fact that "Charlemagne must have been celebrated while he was alive and immediately after his death *in Germanic- and Romance-language songs*" (my emphasis).[126] In any case, France's poetry derives from the north; it is the work of the peoples who lived there and was in no way imported or inherited from southern populations. Finally, whereas true history sees in Charlemagne a personage who was as much German as he was French,[127] poetic history uncovers a primarily French mythical figure. The best proof of this is the fact that it was the Romance-language version—not a Germanic or Provençal version—that became the most important.[128] In contrast to the theories of a Roman or Germanic legacy, Paris fashions a specifically French solution: he argues that Romance-language culture derives from both Germanic and Provençal cultures but rises above them and contains the seed of a French identity.[129]

In Paris's view, the poetic history of the great man is a creation of the "popular imagination"; it is a collective representation.[130] This poetic creativity derives from the popular imagination and is given expression in the originary moment of a national poetry that is the first expression of "national sentiment" and thus plays a constituent, legitimizing role. "It is through this national poetry that a people becomes conscious of itself. It alone, in these distant times of political reflection, can give to the members of the nation the strong and constant idea of their brotherhood and their originality."[131] This sense of national identity does not stem from individuals but instead from the collectivity itself through the creation of poetry. Usually, this process is triggered by contact with another nation; one's own identity is forged only *in relation* to another. The epic then arises in the course of a second phase; it is a genre that consolidates and refines the materials of national poetry. Paris adds that this transformative work occurs only among Aryan peoples and is not achieved "with premeditation, but spontaneously."[132]

> In order to develop, the epic requires a people to possess a remarkable poetic ability and a vivid sense of the concrete, which gives it the power

to personify its aspirations and passions by idealizing them. The epic needs to draw from a strongly rooted national identity.[133]

The role of the individual in the creation of the epic is therefore reduced to being almost nothing. Paris ascribes the poetic faculty leading to the production of the epic directly to the people, perceived as a collectivity. In Paris's view, it is precisely when "personal fantasy" starts to dominate the epic that it loses its authenticity.[134] In turn, the collectivity functions as an individual, in this case a poet, and it does so precisely in order to depict itself as a heroic individual. This self-portrait as a heroic individual enables the collectivity to express its fundamental unity and the immanence of its spirit. This leads to a healthy identification of the unified will of the collective self—its "general will" (to adopt Rousseau's expression)—with the heroic prince, who serves to personify this spontaneous creation of the collective imagination. It is as if Paris wished to attribute the function of the first social contract to this spontaneous creation of the collective imagination. In his view, the harmony of the epic form expresses a harmony of feeling. Moreover, because an epic narrative, like a song, implies a connection that escapes the laws of logical debate and of conflictual oppositions, the epic organizes and structures the founding, constitutive event in its own way. The epic thus takes on a "constitutional" role.

It was within this theoretical framework that Gaston Paris undertook his work on the poetic history of Charlemagne, which he viewed as the "organic center" of the French epic. Seen in this light, the importance he attached to the notion of authenticity becomes understandable, as do the issues that were raised by the arbitrary distortions and deformations that were introduced into the nation's epic poetry over time and in no way represented the expression of that originary, constitutive general will. According to Paris, spontaneity is the fundamental criterion for establishing a document's authenticity and for determining whether it constituted a canonical element of that poetic history:

> Spontaneity is the main quality that poetic history requires of its monuments. It attaches only minor importance to the artificial productions of refined poetry. As soon as a work is willed into existence and arbitrarily composed, it loses all value as a document in poetic history.[135]

In Paris's view, the purest form of the epic is the *chanson de geste*. Intended to be sung, this type of poem was fundamentally linked to oral tradition. Paris contrasts spontaneous productions with deliberate productions, "popular poetry" with "artistic poetry," national collectivity with the individual, and, implicitly, the general will with the private will. He excludes historical writing (including chronicles) from the category of poetic history, because it derives from the domain of the real. He dismisses "literary" writing from the category of poetic history as well. Since the era of oral literature was long gone, Paris's exclusion of literary writing from the canon of poetic history had the effect of delegitimizing any attempt to rewrite or alter the mythified history of Charlemagne. For, as Marchangy pointed out, after a certain period of "crystallization,"[136] rewriting Charlemagne's poetic history could no longer be spontaneous but only a deliberate act producing an artificial, "artistic" composition—the expression of a private self devoid of any collective value. According to Paris, Charlemagne's poetic history is henceforth closed and set off limits *in illo tempore*—in a time that is other, sacred, the moment of the nation's origins.

But it is this unbridgeable distance itself that ensures the value of Charlemagne's poetic history: the expression of nascent national identity is specific to the founding moment. Due to the plenitude that Paris attributes to the oral tradition, the texts that express that originary collective identity take on a sacred, hieratic aura; they resume, so to speak, their true "constitutional" function. These texts are spontaneous creations, "crystallizations" arising from the people's will to constitute itself as one people. However, Charlemagne's poetic history can be seen as the expression of public opinion only if a unique value is attributed to this moment of consensus—to a unity of opinion that can no longer be personified in the individuality of the epic hero. Later creations drawn from historical hearsay—the *on dit*—can no longer be the expression of national identity, for it is always the voice of someone, and not that of everyone.

Henceforth we can only try to understand this collective voice that has fallen silent. When I spoke earlier of the "sacred aura" of these epic texts, I was referring to a sense of the sacred that arose within the context of a belief in science. Removing poetic history from the realm of literature was a way of defining it better and, in the process, of setting it apart as a focus of study. "My work was far more scientific than literary," states Paris.[137] Integrated into the discourse on science, poetic history thus became an object of scientific study, which served to define its limits and resolve the issues of authenticity that it raised. It was thus science, with all its authority, that was fostering a new process of mythification, but with the crucial difference that the originary national collectivity, of which Charlemagne's poetic history was a spontaneous production, acquired "mythic" status as a creative force. And, as a result, the voice of science became the only legitimate vehicle for properly understanding and interpreting the meaning of this founding period of French history.

This conclusion has weighty implications not only for any attempt to create a national historical literature with a collective value, but also for any historical writing undertaken before the emergence of a critical science of history. Before the impersonal voice of science was discovered, a voice that could express the truth of originary moments in the national collectivity, no attempt to express that truth could escape the traps of deformation set by individuals or special interest groups. As we can see this was a time when the various currents that dominated in the nineteenth century were converging and often seemed to be in conflict: republicanism inherited from the Revolution, romantic nationalism, the no less romantic fascination with the great hero, and scientific positivism.

Gaston Paris and the "republicans" were not the only philologists interested in Charlemagne who were imbued with the idea of positive science. The figure of Charlemagne, its long evolution in the nineteenth century and due mainly to the growth of philology, acquired a symbolic force that turned its representation into the embodiment of originary France. In the third quarter of the century, there was general agreement on the constitutive function of the Carolingian epic. The "mythification" of Charlemagne's legend made it possible to claim a primordial identity and harmony. It was through him that the collectivity found a way to create its own representation of itself. The spontaneous creation of the epic and its continuation can be understood as a process through which the nation became conscious of itself. This "crystallization" of identity elevates Charlemagne as the figure of the nation.

The movement of symbolic reinvestment in the great emperor, the end point of the slow development of the Middle Ages into the antiquity of modernity, reached its apex in the 1860s. The Catholic medievalist Léon Gautier also saw Charlemagne as the center, the hero of the national epic. Like Gaston Paris, Gautier viewed this epic, now vouchsafed by science, as ensuring that France's primitive poetry held first rank among literatures in Romance languages.[138] Gautier was also strongly imbued with the methods of German philology, and he wanted to establish an essentially Germanic origin and nature for the *chansons de geste*. In fact, "no other national element has joined the Germanic element in the composition of our poems."[139] This idealization of Germanness went hand in hand with a mythification of the historical personage of Charlemagne. Without him, France would not have a national epic: "A man of this stature was needed to keep the French epic from perishing."[140]

> Charlemagne saved our national poetry in the past as well as in the future. . . . Yes, Charlemagne saved the future French epic, he saved it voluntarily and involuntarily. Voluntarily by ordering the compilation of these ballads [*cantilènes*] from which one day our first *chansons de geste* were to arise naturally. Involuntarily through the magnificent spectacle of his grandeur, of his conquests, of his glory. He only had to show himself, and our epic came into existence.[141]

To a greater extent than Paris, Gautier undertook the mission of popularizing philologic knowledge. Aiming to create a sort of philologically sound "Bibliothèque bleue," Gautier wanted to emphasize national and religious values that he felt should be shared by all French people. In his introduction to Alphonse Vétault's *Charlemagne*, Gautier sees the advent of the great emperor as the result of God's intervention to save Christianity and to make France the beacon of Christian Europe. Gautier puts France's universal mission into a Catholic perspective, while claiming on the other hand that the French inherited their customs, bravery, and virility from the Germanic peoples.

This movement of the remythification of Charlemagne and of the idealization of the national function of the *chansons de geste* of the Carolingian cycle goes beyond any particular political stance. While there most certainly was no political consensus in France at that time, everyone seemed to agree on Charlemagne's function as the creator of national identity and on the importance of highlighting its value. However, the German invasion of 1870 interrupted this growing attachment to the figure of the great emperor, although the strength of the attachment maintained it for yet a little while. In these years of crisis, the nation turned away from Charlemagne. The ties between his poetic history and the republican and nationalist discourse began to loosen after the advent of the Third Republic. Soon, France no longer recognized itself in the figure that had for so long dominated the multiple visions France had of itself. Stuck in the crossfire of different nationalisms and penetrated by the multiple and specialized gazes of the human and social sciences, the discourse on Charlemagne lost its cohesion and its identifying power. Suddenly, Charlemagne's relationship to France began to be questioned as he began to be considered too close to the German Other, seen henceforth as a people, an ethnic unit. During this period, the belief in France's universal mission lost much ground, and there was a turning away from the figure that had for so long and in so many different ways embodied the meaning of that mission. During the Third Republic, Charlemagne was still in view, but, increasingly, it was through the gaze of specialists who shed a truer light on the different aspects of Charlemagne's life, his reign, and his legend. More knowledge had been gained, but the overall figure became fainter, hidden as it was by the multiple layers of scientific knowledge.

EIGHT

Final Comments: The Waning Power of the Figure of Charlemagne

The symbolic aura surrounding the figure of Charlemagne gradually diminished after France's 1870 defeat in the war against Prussia and the establishment of the Third Republic. Of course, the reinvestment in the figure of the emperor during the years preceding the war still motivated scholarly work on this topic during the 1870s, but the momentum was broken. There were three different sets of processes at play here. First, there was the effect of the defeat: Charlemagne's profound identification with France was increasingly challenged as he became identified more and more as being German. Second, on the conceptual plane, the legend had definitely been detached from living history and relocated to the realm of scholarly philology. Finally, the development of a specialized field of political science reduced the legitimizing role of this kind of historical justification. A new identity came to the fore in all of these cases. Germany's political nationalism posed a profound challenge to the old universalist ideal. In addition, the growth of the new scientific disciplines radically reconfigured knowledge.

There is no better illustration of Charlemagne's waning status as a national founding hero than the story of the imposing equestrian statue of the emperor located to the right of the Cathedral of Notre Dame, on the banks of the Seine (fig. 24). Although it is present every day in the shadow of the giant cathedral, this imposing twenty-five-foot-tall statue, half hidden by the trees surrounding it, often goes unnoticed. This paradox is emblematic of the "absent presence" that has become the hero's fate.

In 1852, Louis Rochet, a sculptor specializing in equestrian statues, decided to create a statue of Charlemagne. What could be more appealing, during the reign of Louis Bonaparte, who was so proud of his ties to his imperial uncle, than a statue of the figure with whom Napoleon himself had identified in order to legitimize his empire? In a move that seemed to echo that imperial history, Rochet chose to depict Charlemagne's triumphant entry into Saragossa. The sculptor died without completing his work, and in 1878 his brother Charles, who had been helping him, wrote a pamphlet on the project but, in the new political climate of the Third Republic, decided to attribute the inspiration for the statue to republican influences. According to Charles Rochet, Louis had been inspired by the works of historians such as Augustin Thierry and François Guizot.[1] The sculpture was different from the traditional equestrian genre; its originality lay in its monumental façade, with two squires standing in front of Charlemagne and holding the reins of his horse. In his 1878 essay, Charles identified the two squires as Roland and Oliver, thereby linking the statue to the *Chanson de Roland.*

The statue was first executed in plaster and exhibited at the artist's expense at the 1867 World's Fair. A bronze casting was then exhibited at the 1878 World's Fair, but the work did not attract a buyer from either the public or private sector. In was in the hope of saving the statue that Charles Rochet wrote the essay proclaiming the "truth" of his brother's work. But what, we must ask, could he write about Charlemagne so soon after France's defeat by Germany? First, Rochet insisted that the great hero was indeed born in France, contrary to German claims: "It was there, in the territory later called Ile-de-France, that Charlemagne was born, at the place the troubadours celebrated as the cradle of French civilization" (38–39). Second, he argued that the statue deserved a place of honor because it represented a founding father who had played a key role in the nation's history. Finding a suitable location for it would thus serve the nation well: "It is a work of the greatest national significance, recalling one of the least known periods of our history, that of the founding and true birth of our country, which has been called France only since then" (40). Moreover, he continued, in a France that had again become a republic, one should not forget that Charlemagne was not one of those "barbarous and cruel" Germanic Franks but a Frank integrated into "our Gaul," a "Gallicized" Frank, a "Gallic Frank." In short, "this monument, created in France, was truly a monument for France" (42). The French should therefore take care of it!

Meanwhile, in the hope of finding a buyer, the Thiébaut foundry, where the bronze statue had been cast, asked the Paris city council for permission to exhibit Rochet's Charlemagne in the square in front of Notre Dame. The commission in charge of the fine arts, which included Viollet-le-Duc, was asked to study the proposal. However, the commission's report gave only lukewarm support to the Thiébaut's request:[2] "The figure of Charlemagne is only of minor interest to the city of Paris. The great emperor of the West was neither a Parisian nor even a Gaul." The report further claimed that Charlemagne was not always treated with respect in the *chansons de geste*, which often presented him somewhat satirically, thus clearly showing "that, at that time, the Gallic spirit still reacted against the absolute domination by this master of the West." The report went so far as to state that "before undertaking such a work, the sculptor should have more carefully considered the nation's view of Charlemagne; he should have asked himself if this work really belonged in a French city." Thus the report represents Charlemagne both as an absolutist (hence an enemy of the republic) and as a foreigner (hence an outsider). Yet, although the commission voiced serious reservations on both historical and aesthetic grounds, it nevertheless considered the "aspects of the statue that might be of technological interest to Parisian industry." From this perspective, the commission noted that the statue was a "unique work, one of a kind in all of Europe," and it recommended that authorization be granted to exhibit the work for a period of three years. Technoindustrial interests appear to have carried the day.

The request to exhibit the statue led to an intense debate when it was discussed at the Paris city council meeting of January 25, 1879. A republican council member protested the fact that the city council, "after having refused to authorize the erection of a statue of Voltaire, who contributed so much to the progress and enlightenment of civilization, was now authorizing the erection of a statue of Charlemagne . . . who above all symbolized absolute power." Another council member declared that it certainly was not the council's mission to "glorify the conquerors of nations." In the end, the council dismissed the counter-arguments that Charlemagne should be regarded as the "personification of the Latin races" and that the statue should not be seen as a tribute to the monarchy but rather as "an affirmation of nationhood." The commission's recommendation was therefore denied.

The situation changed rapidly when Hérold, the new prefect of the Prefecture of the Seine, proposed the erection of two other statues. One was to be of Voltaire and would be placed in front of the town hall of the eleventh *arrondissement*, and the other would be a monument to the republic.[3] The latter was to be erected on the square then known as Place du

Château-d'Eau, which would be renamed Place de la République, and the street leading to it would be renamed Avenue de la République. In the city council meeting of February 5, 1879, the proposal to place the statue of Charlemagne on the square in front of Notre Dame was finally approved. "Since Voltaire was going to have his statue," notes an observer, "no one expressed any further opposition to the statue of Charlemagne."[4] It is ironic that it was Voltaire, who was so virulent in his denunciation of the great conqueror in the eighteenth century, who made it possible for Charlemagne to have a place in the streets of Paris at the end of the nineteenth! But contrary to what republican thinking in the Age of Enlightenment might have wished, no one considered placing Charlemagne's statue on the Place de la République itself. Thus the passionate arguments that the placement of the statue unleashed reveal the deep ambivalence that has continued to surround the figure of Charlemagne as a possible symbol of national identity.

In the realm of historiography, the process of detachment is very clear. This distancing is first manifest in the attempts to deny that there was any Germanic influence at work in the achievements of the great emperor. In 1876, Fustel de Coulanges, in an article first published in *La Revue des Deux Mondes*, attempted to show that Charlemagne's empire "was in no way Germanic" and refuted the idea that Charlemagne presided over a republican government with national assemblies.[5] The Romanist theory reappeared in Fustel de Coulange's writing: Charlemagne established a completely absolutist and centralized monarchy, and it was during the reign of the Roman emperor that the term *respublica* was used again and that "the government again took on . . . all the traits of the old empire."[6] Lucien Double best illustrates this movement of rejection in the 1881 publication of his *Empereur Charlemagne*. He points out that "legend is not always history" and that the true Charlemagne was "quite different from the character of the romances." Double expresses his surprise at the "unbelievable infatuation history has always shown for this German who did not even have the bloody merit [*mérite sanglant*] of victorious conquerors,"[7] and he denounces the use of brute force and the barbarism of a conqueror whose empire disappeared without a trace. According to Double, the emperor of the Franks had definitely lost his identificatory power for the French. He felt this role had increasingly fallen to Joan of Arc. She was the heroine of invaded France, a daughter of the native land, and a figure clearly originating from the people.

But, even though they were still of some importance, these reinterpretations of history had little impact in the face of the reconfiguration of historical knowledge. Gaston Paris's philological work occupied an important place in this movement. In 1878 and in 1882, Alfred Duméril and

Albert Sorel published studies aimed at unmasking the role played by Charlemagne's legend in the history of France. Their goal was to explore the origins of absolutist tendencies, on the one hand, and, on the other, of territorial expansionism or the spirit of conquest, which had for so long characterized France. The two historians attempt to uncover the long-term specificity and ideological function of the legend or the "popular tradition." Duméril referred openly to Gaston Paris's distinction between history and legend. But while the philologist was seeking the expression of an originary national unity in the myth formed around Charlemagne, Duméril found only abuses in it. Instead of analyzing the "spontaneous" birth of these folk narratives, Duméril focused on the uses of the great man's legend for political ends. His goal was precisely to prevent this sort of exploitation by unmasking the wrongful use of the myth and especially by insisting on the radical distinction between history and legend. He saw the ways in which Charlemagne had been used throughout history as the weaving of a veil used to hide the fundamental contradiction that has always plagued the nation, that of tyranny practiced with "a scepter of iron in the name of the French nation."[8]

Albert Sorel takes up the same idea and sees the issue as being at the origin of conflicts with Germany: "This political position was determined by geography: national instinct suggested it before reason of state advised it. It is founded on one fact: Charlemagne's empire. The point of departure of this great process occupying the whole of the history of France is the unresolvable conflict around the emperor's succession."[9] Instead of laying the groundwork for the unity of Europe, Charlemagne's legend served to encourage competition and aggression.

In this way, the myth of Charlemagne, now construed as an object of knowledge, became the objective correlative, so to speak, of absolutist and expansionist policies that had been pursued by France from the time of Philip Augustus to that of Napoleon. Duméril expressed the hope that one day there would be a true political science that would allow us to avoid such ideological deformations. But for the time being, he sought to neutralize the myth by ending his essay with a pronouncement of the death of the ideological force of the figure of Charlemagne: no doubt "his legend will be reinvented many a time. But I do believe that it will no longer be possible to use it to prepare and to end a revolution."[10]

The connection between the poetic history of Charlemagne and the republican and nationalist discourse was definitely severed with the advent of the Third Republic. However, the relationship of Charlemagne's history to public education, a main issue in republican doctrine, remained important. Textbooks continued to call upon the figure of Charlemagne to promote some of the fundamental values of the Republic. "This great reign was not useless for humankind, and under Charlemagne's leadership our ancestors were of great service to Western Europe."[11] There are two particularly striking elements in end-of-the-century interpretations: at a time when the structures of a modern republican administration were being put in place, Charlemagne was presented as a great "administrator," and at the time when free public education was being organized, he was depicted as the founder of the first free school (figs. 22, 23). But of these two legacies, it is mostly the link with schools that survives to this day. And even into the 1960s, schools celebrated the feast day of "Saint Charlemagne" by organizing a banquet for students.[12]

With the rise of the social sciences, ideological justification based on originary discourses gradually decreased in importance. The figure of Charlemagne, so long representative of French identity, was gradually expelled from national history. Moreover, the strong identification of the personage with the French nation became increasingly challenged—the defeat of 1870 having been a decisive factor in this development. But even though the French rejected Charlemagne partly because he was too German, it would be a mistake to think that the Germans adopted him as the emblem of their new power. Wilhelm II chose to be crowned emperor at Versailles rather than in Aachen. And Charlemagne, he who had massacred so many Saxons, and who had attempted to impose a Latin way of life in the midst of Germania, simply could not become an uncontested symbol of modern German identity. Widukind, who resisted Charlemagne's invading power with so much courage and tenacity, was at least as attractive, if not more so, as the emperor of the Romans. Moreover, it was the legend of the Nibelungs that occupied center stage in the German epic realm. There were of course attempts at reappropriation. But these were motivated by a will for hegemony rather than by an identificatory ideology of national solidarity. It was mainly in relation to the "Other," that is, to France, that the Germans were sometimes tempted by the figure of Charlemagne. We should therefore look upon the famous collection of studies devoted to Charlemagne and published in 1935, *Karl der Große oder Charlemagne* in that light.[13] When in 1944 the Germans decided to name after Charlemagne a division of the SS consisting of Frenchmen serving the Hitlerian cause, they were perfectly aware of the ideological resonance the name had for the French. Yet this act was more a provocative propaganda ploy than evidence of any real identification.

Rejected by the French, never adopted by the Germans, the figure of Charlemagne settled into a kind of neutral *Zwischenland*. Such "neutrality" placed Charlemagne above specific national identification and opened up the way to a "European" reappropriation of the great man. Charlemagne endures through a European awareness of its "Carolingian organizing core."[14] Charles de Gaulle, nicknamed "Le grand Charles" (great/tall Charles), never looked to the figure of the emperor to justify his domestic policies. But he did invoke him in a press conference in 1950 when he spoke of the possible construction of a unified Europe:

> I see no reason why the German and French peoples—if they overcome their reciprocal contentions and territorial intrigues—should not end up united. In short, it would amount to picking up Charlemagne's project, this time on modern economic, social, strategic, and cultural grounds.[15]

Such a conception of a Europe whose driving force would be a Franco-German alliance is not too far removed from what is actually happening today. And there are numerous signs announcing a European reappropriation of the great hero. Each year Aachen's Charlemagne Prize is awarded to a personality of outstanding merit in the cause of European integration. In 1992 the Paris mint produced a coin with the image of Charlemagne on it to celebrate the "creation of Europe." These examples indicate a redeployment of a symbol that is now relatively detached from a national framework and has been erected as "the father of Europe." Seen from a European perspective, the *chansons de geste* and the genres derived from them in which Charlemagne plays a fundamental role could now take on the appearance of a European rather than a national phenomenon.

And yet it remains true that in the past the figure of the great founder of Europe was most often invoked to justify war and conquest. Perhaps, as Hugo suggested, the work of Charlemagne and Napoleon does need to be accomplished anew but this time without Charlemagne and without Napoleon. Instead of reappropriating history, perhaps it would be better this time to keep it at a distance sufficient to ward off blind adherence. Since the eighteenth century, there have been continuous calls for a political science and endless announcements of its arrival. In principle, this science should make it possible to keep one's distance from history, to renounce the need to see the future through the past. But the dream of a purely conceptual political science has always been upset by the collectivity's need to represent power and legitimacy in flesh and blood form. The ideal of politics cleansed of the imaginary and the figurative finds its nightmarish realization in the regulatory bureaucracies of the twentieth century. Might not some of the most strident voices of present-day resistance to the creation of a unified Europe stem precisely from this lack of symbolic investment?

The best way to maintain a safe distance from history, while recognizing the need for symbolic projections that draw on the past, is to be as aware as possible of past appropriations. Examining past representations enables us to see more clearly than simply reappropriating history would do. In any case, simply expelling the figure of Charlemagne from French identity as though it had not played an important role is perhaps not the wisest course; after all, he managed to maintain his strategic position in the French sociopolitical imagination for more than ten centuries. At a time when so many nationalistic passions that were thought to be dead are once again resurfacing, what better way to avoid their dangerous effects than by studying those past projections that had placed the figure of Charlemagne at the center of a collective ideal? What better way than to listen to this discourse that has now fallen silent?

NOTES

INTRODUCTION

Unless otherwise noted, all translations from French into English are my own. Though I have not always been able to provide a poetic translation of these texts, I have at times left some archaic elements in them so as to give the reader at least an inkling of their original flavor. *Trans.*

1. J. C. L. Simonde de Sismondi, *Histoire des Français* (Paris: Treuttel and Wurtz, 1821), 2:217.

2. Charlemagne's nickname probably originally meant something like "flowing beard" in Old French. He retained his nickname as time went by, though, in modern French, its meaning changed to that of "flowery," the present-day English translation of *fleuri*. Today, most people in France assume that his nickname meant he had a bushy beard.

3. Gaston Paris, *Histoire poétique de Charlemagne* (1865), p. 8 (see below, chap. 2, n. 29).

CHAPTER ONE. THE MAGIC OF ORIGINS

1. Michel de Certeau, *L'Écriture de l'histoire* (Paris: Gallimard, 1975), 18.

2. François Auguste René de Chateaubriand, *Mémoires d'outre-tombe*, ed. Maurice Levaillant, centennial ed. (Paris: Flammarion, 1948), 1:316–17.

3. Josef Ponten, *Alfred Rethel*, "Klassiker der Kunst" (Stuttgart: Werke, 1911), 18:187; cited by Herbert von Einem in "Die Tragödie der Karlsfresken Alfred Rethels," in *Das Nachleben*, vol. 4 of *Karl der Große: Lebenswerk und Nachleben*, ed. Wolfgang Braunfels, 306–25 (Düsseldorf: L. Schwann, 1967), 320.

4. See Ernst H. Kantorowicz, *The King's Two Bodies: A Study in Medieval Political Theology* (Princeton, N.J.: Princeton University Press, 1957), 71–72.

5. *Chronicon*, book 3, chap. 32, in *Monumenta Novaliciensia Vetustiora. Raccolta degli atti e delle cronache riguardanti l'abbazia della Novalesa*, ed. Carlo Cipolla, "Fonti per la storia d'Italia" (Rome: Forzani e C. Tipografi del Senato, 1901), 2:197–98. The Latin text is as follows:

> Intravimus ergo ad Karolum, non enim iacebat, ut mos est aliorum defunctorum corpora, sed in quandam cathedram ceu vivus residebat. coronam auream erat coranatus. sceptrum cum mantonibus indutis tenens in manibus, a quibus iam ipse ungule perforando processerant. erat autem supra se tugurium ex calce et marmoribus valde compositum. quod ubi ad eum venimus, protinus in eum foramen fecimus frangendo. at ubi ad eum ingressi sumus, odorem permaximum sentivimus. adoravimus ergo eum statim poplitibus flexis ac ienua. statimque Otto imperator albis eum vestimentis induit, ungulasque incidit, et omnia deficentia circa eum reparavit. nil vero ex artibus suis putrescendo adhuc defecerat. sed de sumitate nasui sui parum minus erat. quam ex auro ilico fecit restitui. abstraensque ab ilius ore dentem unum, reaedificato tuguriolo, abiit.(Cited by Helmut W. Beumann, "Grab und Thron Karls des Großen zu Aachen," in Braunfels, *Karl der Große*, 4:10.)

There are three main sources for this anecdote: the chronicle of Thietmar von Merseburg (1012–1018), the history of the Franks by Ademars de Chabannes (around 1030), and Novalesa's chronicle (1027–1050). Scholars have for a long time now agreed that Charlemagne was not buried on his throne. According to Beumann, Thietmar's version is the closest to the truth. Otto III had decided to visit Charlemagne's tomb, not to pray but to do what he believed Caesar had done with Alexander. In the eyes of some people, Otto's action was sacrilegious, and it was for this reason that the location of the vault was not conserved. Thus Frederick Barbarossa required a vision to find it again in 1166. He took out some bones and had them put in the reliquary that is now in the choir of the Church of Saint Mary in Aachen.

6. See Benedict Anderson, *Imagined Communities: Reflections on the Origin and Spread of Nationalism* (London: Verso, 1983), particularly chapters 1 and 2.

7. For an eloquent and forceful argument concerning Louis the Pious's importance, see Karl Ferdinand Werner, "*Hludovicus, Augustus*: Gouverner l'empire chrétien—Idées et réalités," in *Charlemagne's Heir: New Perspectives on the Reign of Louis the Pious (814–840)*, ed. Peter Godman and Roger Collins (Oxford: Clarendon Press, 1990), 3–124. Here I am only restating a commonplace concerning Louis rather than making any historical claim about his true role.

8. "Karolus Magnus et Leo papa," in *Monumenta Germaniae historica: Poetae Latini aevi carolini*, ed. Ernst Dümmler (Berlin: Weidmann, 1881), 366–70. On this poem by Angilbert, see Robert Folz, *Le Souvenir et la légende de Charlemagne dans l'Empire germanique médiéval* (Paris: Les Belles Lettres, 1950), 1–3. In a recent article, Hans Hubert Anton places the composition of this poem at a later date, *after* Charlemagne's coronation; see "Beobachtungen zum Fränkisch-Byzantinischen Verhältnis in Karolingischer Zeit," in *Beiträge zur Geschichte des Regnum Francorum*, ed. Rudolf Schieffer (Sigmaringen: Thorbecke, 1990), 77–119.

9. For instance, at a much later date, Mousket in his *Chronique rimée* (1243) saw in the name the words *car de lumière*, that is, "chariot of light." See *Chronique*

rimée de Philippe Mouskès, ed. Frédéric August Ferdinand Thomas, Baron of Reiffenberg (Brussels: M. Hayez, 1845), 1:456, v. 11861. It should be noted that in Slavic languages the word for "king" is derived from "Charles" (Karl > *kral* in Czech; *król* in Polish; *korol* in Russian).

10. The numbers are impressive: 27 cathedrals, 232 monasteries, 65 palatial compounds built between 768 and 814, as noted by Stéphane Lebecq in his excellent book *Les Origines franques, Ve–IXe siècle*, vol. 1 of *Nouvelle histoire de la France médiévale* (Paris: Éditions du Seuil, 1990), 271.

11. See for example Arthur Jean Kleinclausz, *Charlemagne*, new edition, with a preface by Régine Pernoud (Paris: J. Tallandier, 1977; first edition, Paris: Hachette, 1934).

12. Colette Beaune's fine work, *Naissance de la nation France* (Paris: Gallimard, 1985) comes to mind, and it makes little mention of Charlemagne.

13. The same is not true in Germany, where an impressive number of studies on Charlemagne have been published focusing both on Germany and France. See the works of Braunfels, Schramm, and Schneidmüller cited below. It is significant that the best study done in France since World War II on representations of Charlemagne focuses on Germany. See Folz, *Souvenir et légende*.

14. Bronislaw Baczko, *Les Imaginaires sociaux: Mémoires et espoirs collectifs* (Paris: Payot, 1984).

15. For ideological uses of Charlemagne during the Middle Ages, see primarily Percy Ernst Schramm's monumental work, *Herrschaftszeichen und Staatssymbolik: Beiträge zu ihrer Geschichte vom dritten bis zum sechzehnten Jahrhundert, mit Beiträgen verschiedener Verfasser* (Stuttgart: Hiersemann, 1954–1956), and *Kaiser, Könige und Päpste: Gesammelte Aufsätze zur Geschichte des Mittelalters*, 4 vols. (Stuttgart: Hiersemann, 1968–1971). See also Stephen G. Nichols, Jr., *Romanesque Signs: Early Medieval Narrative and Iconography* (New Haven, Conn.: Yale University Press, 1983); Jacques Monfrin, "La Figure de Charlemagne dans l'historiographie du XVe siècle," in *Annuaire-Bulletin de la Société de l'histoire de France* (1964–1965): 67–78. For the ninth century, see Bernd Schneidmüller, *Karolingische Tradition und frühes französisches Königtum: Untersuchungen zur Herrschaftslegitimation der westfränkisch-französischen Monarchie im 10. Jahrhundert* (Wiesbaden: Franz Steiner, 1979); Andreas Bomba, *Chansons de Geste und französisches Nationalbewußtsein im Mittelalter: Sprachliche Analysen der Epen des Wilhelmszyklus* (Stuttgart: Franz Steiner, 1987). See also André de Mandach, *Naissance et développement de la chanson de geste en Europe*, vol. 1, *La Geste de Charlemagne et de Roland* (Geneva: E. Droz, 1961). (Book 1, "La Préhistoire de la geste de Charlemagne et de Roland," 21–73, discusses the confusion of Alphonso VI with Charlemagne.) For the German empire there is Folz's authoritative book *Souvenir et légende*.

16. Around 1250 French prose acquired the prestige of being a truth-telling medium.

17. There are two versions of the *Annals*, an early version and a reworked or "definitive" one. I am citing the revised one here. They were printed for the first time in Cologne in 1521. During the seventeenth and eighteenth centuries we find them again in André Duchesne and Dom Bouquet's series. As to the reworking, there were stylistic revisions up to 812. A useful discussion can be found in Bernhard

Walter Scholz and Barbara Rogers's translation *Carolingian Chronicles: Royal Frankish Annals and Nithard's Histories* (Ann Arbor: University of Michigan Press, 1970); see especially P. D. King, *Charlemagne: Translated Sources* (Lancaster, 1987). I am basing my discussion here on Friedrich Kurze's edition, *Annales Regni Francorum et Annales q[ui] d[incuntur] Einhardi*, "Scriptores Rerum Germanicarum in usum scholarum ex monumentis Germaniae historicis separatim editi" (Hanover: impensis bibliopolii Hahniani, 1895; 1930). Since Guizot plays an important role in making this text available in the nineteenth century and since we will discuss him again in chapter 7, I cite his translation here: François Pierre Guillaume Guizot, *Collection des mémoires relatifs à l'histoire de France, depuis la fondation de la monarchie française jusqu'au XIIIe siècle; avec une introduction, des suppléments, des notices et des notes* (Paris: Brière, 1823–1835). There is a very good introduction in *Charlemagne* by Georges Tessier (Paris: Albin Michel, 1967), 123–91.

18. See Hayden White, *The Content of the Form: Narrative Discourse and Historical Representation* (Baltimore, Md.: Johns Hopkins University Press, 1987), chap. 1, pp. 1–25 (previously published under the title "The Value of Narrativity in the Representation of Reality," *Critical Inquiry* 7, no. 1 [1980]).

19. Guizot, *Collection des mémoires*, 3:13–15.

20. Ibid., 15.

21. Regarding the fact that Charlemagne doesn't become God's elect in Latin literature, see Karl-Heinz Bender, *König und Vasall: Untersuchungen zur Chanson de Geste des XII. Jahrhunderts* (Heidelberg: Carl Winter, 1967), chap. 1, "Die Idealität des Karlskönigtums in der Chanson de Roland," 9–42.

22. Guizot, *Collection des mémoires*, 3:49.

23. On the sending out of the *missi* see, for instance, the capitularies of 789 and 802.

24. "Rex autem, *ne quasi per otium torpere ac tempus terere videretur*, per Moenum fluvium ad Saltz palatium suum in Germania iuxta Salam fluvium constructum navigavit atque inde iterum per eundem amnem secunda aqua Wormaciam reversus est" (Kurze, *Annales Regni Francorum*; my emphasis).

25. By sovereignty I mean the form of the practice of power inherited, to an extent that has remained uncertain, from Frankish royalty and the Roman *imperium*.

26. See Georges Dumézil, *L'Idéologie tripartie des Indo-Européens*, vol. 31 (Brussels: Latomus, 1958). This thesis was adopted by Joël H. Grisward in *Archéologie de l'épopée médiévale: Structures trifonctionelles et mythes indo-européens dans le cycle des Narbonnais* (Paris: Payot, 1981) and recently by Dominique Boutet in "Mythes et idéologies de la royauté dans la littérature médiévale (1100–1250): Charlemagne et Arthur" (Ph.D. diss., University of Paris III, 1991), published under the title *Charlemagne et Arthur, ou Le Roi imaginaire* (Paris: H. Champion, 1992).

27. Marcel Mauss, "Essai sur le don: Forme et raison de l'échange dans les sociétés archaïques," *Année Sociologique*, 2d ser., 1 (1923–1924); reprinted in *Sociologie et anthropologie* (Paris: Presses universitaires de France, 1950), 143–279.

28. Kurze, *Annales Regni Francorum*, and Guizot, *Collection des mémoires* (my emphasis).

29. The legend of the gift of elephants has probably been kept alive by the four elephant chess pieces that are part of the chess set said to be Charlemagne's.

The set was preserved for a long time at the Abbey of Saint-Denis, and it was believed that it had belonged to Charlemagne, who was thought to be an unbeatable chess champion. It is obvious that Charlemagne was born too early ever to have played chess. See Michel Pastoureau, *L'Echiquier de Charlemagne: Un Jeu pour ne pas jouer* (Paris: Éditions Adam Biro, 1990), 5 (see fig. 4).

30. See Carlo M. Cipolla, *Clocks and Culture, 1300–1700* (London: Collins, 1967), and Peter F. Dembowski, "*Li Orloge amoureus* de Froissart," *L'Esprit créateur* 18, no. 1 (1978): 19–31.

31. Louis Halphen, ed. and trans., prologue to *Vie de Charlemagne,* by Einhard (Paris: Champion, 1923), 2; in addition to the excellent introduction to this translation, see *Études critiques sur l'histoire de Charlemagne: Les Sources de l'histoire de Charlemagne, la conquête de la Saxe, le couronnement impérial, l'agriculture et la propriété rurale, l'industrie et le commerce* (Paris: Alcan, 1921), 60–103.

32. Other documents accessible to Einhard included Paul the Deacon's *Historia episoporum Menttensium* (ca. 784), diplomatic correspondence, and, of course, Charlemagne's will, which Einhard included at the end of his biography.

33. Halphen, *Vie de Charlemagne,* chap. 24, p. 42 (p. 29 in the Latin text). Halphen's translation: "On lui lisait l'histoire et les récits de l'antiquité."

34. Einhard has often been criticized for supposedly having distorted or neglected the truth about Charlemagne the man. See, for instance, "Einhard," in Wilhelm Wattenbach and Wilhelm Levison, *Deutschlands Geschichtsquellen im Mittelalter: Vorzeit und Karolinger,* ed. Wilhelm Levison and Heinz Löwe (Weimar: H. Böhlaus, 1953), 2:266–80; and Helmut Beumann, "Topos und Gedankengefüge bei Einhard," *Archiv für Kulturgeschichte* 33 (1951): 337–50. See also the beginning of Hans-Joachim Reischmann, *Die Trivialisierung des Karlsbildes der Einhard-Vita in Notkers "Gesta Karoli Magni": Rezeptionstheoretische Studien zum Abbau der kritischen Distanz in der spätkarolingischen Epoche* (Constance: Hartung-Gorre, 1984) for a good summary of various points of view. Among French scholars, Halphen criticizes distortions of the model: originality either falls into exaggeration or naïveté, or else a mixture of the two (Halphen, *Vie de Charlemagne,* 9–10). See also Matthew S. Kempshall, "Some Ciceronian Models for Einhard's Life of Charlemagne," *Viator* 26 (1995): 11–37.

35. He "applied himself to the study of foreign languages and learned Latin so well that he could express himself in that language as well as in his native tongue. . . . He also tried to learn to write, and he was in the habit of placing under his pillows tablets and sheets of parchment so as to take advantage of moments of leisure to practice tracing letters; but he started this too late and the result was mediocre" (Halphen, *Vie de Charlemagne,* 43–44). Recently it has been suggested that this passage refers to calligraphy—an interesting speculation but without any proof. For other references to language and writing see Einhard's chapter 29.

36. *Mystères du peuple, ou Histoire d'une famille de prolétaires à travers les âges* (Paris: Administration de librairie, n.d.), 5:237.

37. In his edition of Einhard, Halphen painstakingly examines the connections between the *Annals* and Suetonius's *Lives of the Twelve Caesars.* We must bear in mind however that, in Einhard, Charles also remains the king of the Franks, a concept deeply rooted in Frankish tradition.

38. Einhard, *Vie de Charlemagne*, ed. Halphen, 2. On the idea of epic distancing, see R. Van Waard, "*Le Couronnement de Louis* et le principe de l'hérédité de la couronne," *Neophilologus* 30 (1946): 52–58; Jean Frappier, "Réflexions sur les rapports des chansons de geste et de l'histoire," *Zeitschrift für Romanische Philologie* 73 (1957): 1–19; and K.-H. Bender, *König und Vasall*, where the concept is mentioned often.

39. Halphen, *Vie de Charlemagne*, "Introduction," x.

40. Even Roncevaux is depicted as only a temporary setback due to an ambush during a war whose conclusion was a happy one for the king of the Franks. As if to reinforce this fact, Einhard begins the passage directly following the story of Roncevaux with the sentence: "Charles *also* triumphed over the Bretons [*domuit et Brittones*]"; my emphasis (Halphen, *Vie de Charlemagne*, chap. 10, p. 17).

41. See Halphen's notes in *Vie de Charlemagne*, chap. 15, pp. 24–25. Halphen's comments are aimed primarily at identifying the distortions that Einhard constantly employs to aggrandize his hero. However, Halphen, who published his work after World War I, seems primarily concerned with diminishing Einhard's reputation by pointing out his mistakes in relation to the facts as well as his distortions—mostly due to naïveté—of the Suetonian model.

42. "Quo nullum neque prolixius neque atrocius Francorumque populo laboriosius susceptum est" (Halphen, *Vie de Charlemagne*, chap. 7, p. 12; p. 9 in Latin text).

43. Robert Folz points out the importance of the *auctoritas*, very different from the *potestas*, in the conception of the empire; see *L'Idée d'Empire en Occident du Ve au XIVe siècle* (Paris: Aubier, 1953), 13–15.

44. Halphen, *Vie de Charlemagne*, chap. 28, p. 47 (my emphasis).

45. Guizot, "Notice sur le traité des faits et gestes de Charlemagne," in *Collection des mémoires*, 169–70.

46. Notker (alias Balbulus), *Taten Kaiser Karls des Großen*, "Monumenta Germaniae Historica: Scriptores Rerum Germanicum," ed. Hans F. Haefele, new series, vol. 12, book 1, chap. 1 (Berlin: Weidmann, 1959). Regarding geography as well as "anthologies," I refer primarily to Haefele's comments in his introduction (pp. xvii–xxi). Here I am citing from Guizot's translation in *Collection des mémoires*, 3:173. In my references, the first two numbers refer to the book and the chapter of the edition of this text in the series Monumenta Germaniae Historica (MGH); the third number refers to the page in Guizot's translation.

47. This sentence is missing in the translation; see MGH, 3. On the theme of the *translatio studii*, see Étienne Gilson, who cites the sentence in *Les Idées et les lettres* (Paris: J. Vrin, 1932; 2d ed., Paris: J. Vrin, 1955), 183. A. G. Jongkees has summed up the issue very well in his study "*Translatio Studii*: Les Avatars d'un thème médiéval," in *Miscellanea Mediaevalia in memoriam Jan Frederik Niermeyer* (Groningue: J. B. Wolters, 1967), 41–51, which points out, among other things, the equivalence of the ancients and the moderns. Alcuin himself was very conscious of a renewal, a cultural rebirth that was able to occur due to Charlemagne's policies. In fact, the moderns were to surpass the ancients because they were to have a knowledge based on the true faith. "If your example, O king, were to be followed by many others," wrote Alcuin in 799 in a letter to Charlemagne, "a new Athens could spring up at Aix, in the kingdom of the Franks, an Athens that, illuminated by the

grace of our Lord Jesus Christ, will eclipse the wisdom of the Academy. The other Athens shone only through Plato's teachings and through the culture of the liberal arts. The new Athens, enriched with the gifts of the Holy Spirit, will surpass all profane knowledge" (MGH, Epp. Karol, Aev., 2:279, cited by A. G. Jongkees, "*Translatio Studii*," 46–47). See also Heinz Löwe, "Das Karlsbuch Notkers von St. Gallen und sein zeitgeschichtlicher Hintergrund," *Schweizerische Zeitschrift für Geschichte* 20 (1970): 269–302.

48. It is Guizot who inserts the reference to the "nation," "*fils des principaux de la nation*"; in Notker, Charlemagne says, "*vos primorium filii.*"

49. Marshall David Sahlins, *Islands of History* (Chicago: University of Chicago Press, 1987).

50. On the role of envy in Notker, see the excellent study by Reischmann, *Trivialisierung*, 36: "Neid ist die Kontinuität und der rote Faden, der sich als Ursache aller innerkirchlicher Parteiungen durch die historische Dimension des Papsttums zieht. Damit setzt Notker eine irrationale, psychologisierende Kategorie als Prämisse."

51. On the relationship between Christendom and Europe, see Denys Hay, *Europe: The Emergence of an Idea* (Edinburgh: Edinburgh University Press, 1957, 1968), 16–36. According to Hay (p. 29), the term *Christianitas* began to be used in the time of the popes Nicolas I (858–867) and John VIII (872–882). During the latter's term, the word was used in the context of the Saracen threat (*defensio Christianitatis*). It was only during Gregory VII's papacy (1073–1085) that the term took on a geographical meaning.

52. It should be noted that Notker generally resorts to personalization. Thus evil sometimes takes on the personalized form of the devil, just as miracles here stem from God's direct intervention.

53. In his introduction to the *Gesta*, Hans F. Haefele notes that neither the *Annals* nor Einhard see the burning of the bridge as the result of hostility toward Charlemagne. It is significant that Notker attributes it to thieves wanting to loot merchandise. Haefele notes that the *Annals of Fulda* for the year 886 mention a similar fire in Frisia. Notker might have thus confused the two events for the sake of his narrative (see MGH, xv–xvi).

54. English citation from *Holy Bible*, trans. R. Knox (New York: Sheed & Ward, 1956), Ps. 148:11–13.

55. See Marc Léopold Bloch, *La Société féodale: Les Classes et le gouvernement des hommes* (Paris: Albin Michel, 1940), 152; Bender in his *König und Vasall*, 10–12, brings out certain "Germanic" aspects of Charlemagne's figure, notably his relationship with God.

56. This person was probably Otker (Autcarius), who ran away from Carloman's court with his widow. He was at that time in Verona, and not in Pavia. See L. Duchesne, ed., *Le Liber Pontificalis: texte, introduction et commentaire* (Paris: E. Thorin, 1886), 1:488, 495.

57. This is the passage in Latin:

His necdum finitis primum ad occasum circio vel borea cepit apparere quasi nubes tenebrosa, que diem clarissimam horrentes convertit in umbras. Sed

propiante paululum imperatore ex armorum splendore dies omni nocte tene-
brosior oborta est inclusis. Tunc visus est ipse *ferreus* Karolus, *ferrea* galea
cristatus, *ferreis* manicis armillatus, *ferrea* torace *ferreum* pectus humerosque
Platonicos tutatus, hasta *ferrea* in altum subrecta sinistram impletus. Nam
dextra ad invictum calibem semper erat extenta; coxarum exteriora . . . in eo
ferreis ambiebantur bratteolis. De ocreis quid dicam? Que et cuncto exercitui
solebant *ferree* semper esse usui. In clipeo nihil apparuit nisi *ferrum*. Caballus
quoque illius animo et colore *ferrum* renitebat. . . . *Ferrum* campos et plateas
replebat. Solis radii reverberabantur acie *ferri*. Frigido *ferro* honor a frigidiori
deferebatur populo. Splendissimum *ferrum* horror expalluit cloacarum.
(Notker, MGH, book 2, chap. 17; my emphasis).

This citation comes from the critical edition by Haefele, pp. 83–84. In spite of
some differences between Guizot's translation and the Latin version, the image of
iron functions the same way.

58. On the relations between Compiègne and the Carolingian tradition, see
Schneidmüller, *Karolingische Tradition*, 101–105.

59. Hincmar, *De Ordine Palatii: Texte latin, traduit et annoté*, ed. Maurice Prou
(Paris: Vieweg, 1884), chap. 1, p. 7. See also the standard modern edition: Hinc-
marus, *De Ordine Palatii*, "Monumenta Germaniae Historica: Fontes Iuris Ger-
manici Antiqui," ed. Thomas Gross and Rudolf Schieffer, vol. 3 "Prologue," p. 34,
I. 26. Concerning Hincmar's motivations and sources see Heinz Löwe, "Hinkmar
von Reims und der Aprocrisiar; Beiträge zur Interpretation von *De ordine palatii*,"
in *Festschrift für Hermann Heimpel*, "Veröffentlichungen des Max-Planck-Instituts
für Geschichte" (Göttingen: Vanderhoeck & Ruprecht, 1972) 3, 36, 197–225.

60. See Joachim Ehlers, "Karolingische Tradition und frühes Nationalbewußtsein in Frankreich," *Francia: Forschungen zur Westeuropäischen Geschichte* 4
(1976): 213–35; his discussion of Hincmar can be found on pages 215 and 216. On
the role of Carolingian tradition in the tenth and eleventh centuries, see Schneidmüller, *Karolingische Tradition*. The kingdom of the West was called the *regnum
Karoli* in Widukind of Corvey's chronicle. This name points to a Carolingian tradition linked geographically to the west and recognized by the eastern Franks—
which remains true, as Schneidmüller points out, even if, as argues Margaret
Lugge, the reference to Charles refers rather to Charles the Bald (ibid., pp. 43–44).
On Widukind of Corvey, see Folz, *Souvenir et légende*, 54–56.

CHAPTER TWO. POETIC SPACE, POLITICAL REFLECTION

1. John of Salisbury, *Policraticus*, ed. Clement Webb (Oxford: Clarendon
Press, 1909), 1:186.

2. Ernst Robert Curtius, *Gesammelte Aufsätze zur romanischen Philologie*
(Bern: Francke, 1960), 177. On epic distance, see chap. 2, n. 19.

3. Joseph Bédier argues in his study *Les Légendes épiques: Recherches sur la formation des chansons de geste*, 3d ed. (Paris: H. Champion, 1926–1929 [1st ed., vol. 1

and 2, 1908; vol. 3 and 4, 1913]), that, on the contrary, the *chansons de geste* originated in Latin and clerical literature (and thus not in "popular" literature). The best discussion of this issue can be found in Bender in his *König und Vasall*, a work in which he points out certain "Germanic" aspects of Charlemagne's figure, notably his relationship with God. See also the excellent study by Dominique Boutet, *La Chanson de geste: Forme et signification d'une écriture épique du Moyen Âge* (Paris: Presses universitaires de France, 1993).

4. For the French, Joseph Bédier, ed., *Chanson de Roland* (Paris: H. Piazza, 1922); for the English, Gerard J. Brault, ed. and trans., *The Song of Roland: An Analytical Edition* (University Park, Penn.: Pennsylvania State University Press, 1978), vv. 3742–3744.

5. Here as elsewhere in the text the French word *histoire* raises translation problems because it can stand for either "story" or "history" or both. The translator is thus forced to make a choice that at times impoverishes the semantic benefits of the ambiguity at play in the French term. *Trans.*

6. See Einhard, *Vie de Charlemagne*, chap. 10, p. 17. Karl D. Uitti emphasizes this victorious context in "*ço dit la geste*: Reflections on the Poetic Restoration of History in *The Song of Roland*," in Rupert T. Pickens, *Studies in Honor of Hans-Erich Keller: Medieval French and Occitan Literature and Romance Linguistics* (Kalamazoo, Mich.: Medieval Institute Publications, 1993), 1–27; see also Uitti's very useful chapter "The *Song of Roland*" in his *Story, Myth, and Celebration in Old French Narrative Poetry, 1050–1200* (Princeton, N.J.: Princeton University Press, 1973), 65–127.

7. See Dominique Boutet's fundamental work *Charlemagne et Arthur*. Limiting himself to the "poetic" tradition, Boutet points out the "experimental" aspect of the *chansons de geste*, which put the monarchy to the test against various destructive forces. He elaborates several times on the relations between the two ideologies.

8. Bédier, *Chanson de Roland*; Brault, *Song of Roland*, vv. 3757–3761.

9. Ibid., vv. 3824–3830.

10. The polysemy of the word *onur* should be noted. It can mean "good" or "power" as well as "honor."

11. For the function and description of war (which is different from *werra*), see Georges Duby, *Le Dimanche de Bouvines (27 juillet 1214)* (Paris: Gallimard, 1973), 190–208 (English translation: *The Legend of Bouvines* [Berkeley: University of California Press, 1990]).

12. Folz, *Idée d'Empire*, 26.

13. Léon Gautier, "L'Idée politique dans les chansons de geste," *Revue des questions historiques* 7 (1869): 70–114; *La Chevalerie* (Paris: Victor Palmé, 1884). See Gaston Zeller's article "Les Rois de France candidats à l'Empire: Essai sur l'idéologie impériale en France," *Revue historique* 173 (1934), no. 2 (March-April): 273–311, and no. 3 (May-June), 497–534, reprinted in *Aspects de la politique française sous l'Ancien Régime* (Paris: Presses universitaires de France, 1964), 12–89; I refer here to p. 14.

14. Bédier, *Chanson de Roland*; Brault, *Song of Roland*, vv. 3172–3175.

15. On the *Chronicle*, see among others André de Mandach, *Naissance et développement de la chanson de geste en Europe*, vol. 1, *La Geste de Charlemagne et de Roland*. (Mandach retraces in detail the paths of diffusion and the different versions

of the text.) Jules Horrent, *La Chanson de Roland dans les littératures française et es-pagnole au Moyen Âge* (Paris: Les Belles Lettres, 1951). On its importance in Germany, see Folz, *Souvenir et légende*, 215–25. For the editions of the *Chronicle* I rely on Cyril Meredith Jones, ed., *Historia Karoli Magni et Rotholandi ou Chronique du Pseudo-Turpin: Textes revus et publiés d'après 40 manuscrits* (Paris: E. Droz, 1936); in translation, those of Ronald N. Walpole, *The Old French Johannes Translation of the Pseudo-Turpin Chronicle: A Critical Edition* (Berkeley: University of California Press, 1976); *An Anonymous Old French Translation of the Pseudo-Turpin Chronicle: A Critical Edition of the Text Contained in the Bibliothèque Nationale, MSS fr. 2137 and 17203, and Incorporated by Philippe Mouskés in his Chronique rimée* (Cambridge: Mediaeval Academy of America, 1979).

16. Horrent, *Chanson de Roland*, 85–87.

17. De Mandach, *Naissance et développement*, 33–35; on the vision, see p. 38.

18. The *Liber Sancti Jacobi* (also known as the *Codex Calixtinus*) preserved at the Library of Santiago de Compostela, contains the oldest known version of the *Pseudo-Turpin*; it constitutes the fourth of the five books of the *Liber.*

19. Clark Maines, "The Charlemagne Window at Chartres Cathedral: New Considerations on Text and Image," *Speculum* 52, no. 4 (October 1977): 801–23.

20. Boutet, *Charlemagne et Arthur*, 215.

21. This is the passage in Latin:

Turpinus, Domini gratia archiepiscopus Remensis, ac sedulus Karoli magni imperatoris in Yspania consocius, Leoprando decano aquisgranensi, salutem in Christo. Quoniam nuper mandastis mihi apud Viennam cicactricibus vul-nerum aliquantulum aegrotanti, ut vobis scriberem qualiter imperator noster famosissimus Karolus magnus tellurem yspanicam et gallecianam a potestate Sarracenorum liberavit, mirorum gestorum apices eiusque laudanda super ys-panicos Sarracenos trophea, quae propriis occulis intuitus sum XIIII annis perambulans Yspaniam et Galleciam una cum eo et exercitibus suis, pro certo scribere vestraeque fraternitati mittere non ambigo. Etenim magnalia divul-gata, quae rex in Yspania gessit, sancti Dionisii cronica regali, ut michi scrip-sistis, repperiri plenarie auctoritas vestra nequivit; igitur auctorem illius aut pro tantorum actuum scriptura prolixa aut quia idem absens ab Yspania ea ig-noravit, intencio vestra intelligat minime in ea ad plenum scripsisse et tamen nusquam volumen istut ab ea discordasse. Vivas et valeas et Domino placeas. Amen. (Jones, *Historia Karoli Magni*, 87)

See p. 36 for the details on the letter written by Arnauld du Mont announcing his discovery of this manuscript in 1173. I thank my colleague Michael I. Allen for this translation. On the passage, see Ronald N. Walpole, *Le Turpin français, dit le Turpin I* (Toronto: University of Toronto Press, 1985), ix. This letter is not included in any of the French translations.

22. See Jones's comment in his edition of *Historia Karoli Magni*, 258.

23. Mainly in order to facilitate my "teleological" approach, I cite from the French translation here: Walpole, *Anonymous Old French Translation*, 39–40: "France, Angleterre, Allemagne, Bavière, Lotharingie, Bretagne, Lombardie, Bourgogne et toutes les terres de la mer de Brindise [Pouilles] jusqu'à la mer d'oc-

cident." To make reading easier I have modernized the spelling at times. The Jones Latin edition differs from the Old French version. For example, England comes before France and the Brindisi Sea is not mentioned: "Angliam scilicet, Galliam, Theutonicam, Baioariam, Lothoringiam, Burgundiam, Italiam, Britanniam, ceterasque regiones *universasque* urbes a mari usque ad mare" (p. 88).

24. Ibid., 40: "qui commençait dès la mer de Frise et venait entre France, Allemagne et Lombardie, et passait entre France et Aquitaine, parmi Gascogne, la terre des Basques et Navarre, et allait parmi Espagne jusqu'en Galice ou le cors monseigneur saint Jacques gisait inconnu." The first reference to France here does not exist in the Latin text.

25. Ibid., 52. The Latin text reads: "Ut enim Dominus noster Ihesus Christus una cum duodecim apostolis et discipulis suis acquisivit mundum, sic Karolus rex Gallorum et Romanorum imperator cum his pugnatoribus Hispaniam adquisivit ad decus nominis Dei" (Jones, *Historia Karoli Magni*, 126). The transformations of *rex Gallorum* into "King of France" as well as that of *cum his pugnatoribus* into "with his twelve peers" should be noted.

26. Walpole, *Anonymous Old French Translation*, 49–50: "Touz les emprison- nez delivra et les povres enrichi et les nuz revesti. Ceuls qui s'entrhaoient accorda; les desheritez et les echis rapela et mist en leur heritages. . . . Et ceuls qui par aucun forfet estoient esloignié de lui, it les atrest a s'amour"; Jones, *Historia Karoli Magni*, 120.

27. Walpole, *Anonymous Old French Translation*, 57: "Et touz lez pauvres qui il trouva ensuite en l'ost, il fist revestir soufisamment et bien les fit manger et boire pour Agoulant qui pour telle occasion laissa de prendre baptesme"; Jones, *Historia Karoli Magni*, 136, 138.

28. See Folz, *Souvenir et légende*, 119.

29. On the legend of Saint Gilles, see Folz, *Souvenir et légende*, 167–68, and Gaston Paris, *Histoire poétique de Charlemagne: Reproduction de l'édition de 1865 aug- mentée de notes nouvelles par l'auteur et par M. Paul Meyer et d'une table alphabétique des matières* (Paris: E. Bouillon, 1905; new ed., Geneva: Slatkine Reprints, 1974), 378. The story can be found in *Karlamagnus-Saga*. As he is required to do by the char- ter, Charlemagne has his sister marry Milon d'Angers.

30. Walpole, *Anonymous Old French Translation*, 46; Jones, *Historia Karoli Magni*, 112. This is the Old French text:

> Car ausi conme li chevalier Charle s'apareilloient d'armes contre la bataille, ausi nous devons nous apareillier en bien et en vertuz et oster les mauvés vices de nous qui devons fere la bataille contre le deable. Car qui bone foi a contre mescreance, charité contre haine, largesce contre avarice, humilité contre orgueil, chastée contre luxure, oroisons contre temptacions de deable, poverté pour Dieu contre riquece, perseverance contre legerie, silence contre tençon, obedience contre mauvés corage, sachiez que cil avra sa lance vert et fueillie au jour dou juise. Ah! Dieus! Tant sera l'ame dou venkeor bele, vert et florie qui loyalement avra estrivé en terre contre ses mauvés vices.

31. Jones, *Historia Karoli Magni*, 218; Walpole, *Anonymous Old French Trans- lation*, 84: "dona a Saint-Denis toute France en alleu."

32. Walpole, *Anonymous Old French Translation*, 85: "Puis avint que qui donnoit les IIII deniers de bon cuer et de bon gré, qu'il estoit appielés 'frans Saint Denise' pource qu'il estoit frans de touz autres services par le commandement le roi Charle, et par ce si furent touz apielé 'François' et la tere 'Franche' qui devant estoit apelée 'Gaule'"; Jones, *Historia Karoli Magni*, 218, 220.

33. "Rursum post plurima dona praecepit ut eidem ecclesiae unusquisque possesor uniuscuiusque domus totius Galliae quattuor nummos annuatim ad aedificandam ecclesiam darent" (Jones, *Historia Karoli Magni*, ms. A. 6, 218).

34. Walpole, *Anonymous Old French Translation*, 54: "Pour ce, dist Charles, que Jhesu Crist, fesierres [faiseur] dou ciel et de la terre, eslut notre gent crestienne seur toute autre gent, et seur toutes choses vost qu'il eussent [veut qu'elle eût] seignorie, et ai de ta gent paienne convertie a nostre loi tant conme je puis." Here is the Latin text: "Ideo, inquit Karolus, quod Dominus noster Iesus Christus, creator celi et terrae, gentem nostram, scilicet christianam, prae omnibus gentibus elegit, et super omnes gentes to[t]ius mundi eam dominari instituit, tuam gentem sarracenicam legi nostrae in quantum potui converti" (Jones, *Historia Karoli Magni*, ms. A. 6, 130). The Latin differs somewhat from the Old French: "Wherefore the Frank is called 'free,' because over all other peoples both glory and dominion are owed to him."

35. Ibid., 220: "Wherefore 'Franc' means free, because France must rule over all other peoples."

36. Ernest Langlois, ed., *Le Couronnement de Louis: Chanson de geste du XIIe siècle* (Paris: H. Champion, 1920), vv. 12–19; a translation into modern French is by André Lanly, *Le Couronnement de Louis: Chanson de geste du XIIe siècle, Traductions des classiques français du Moyen Âge* (Paris: H. Champion, 1983), 17–18.

37. In the introduction to his edition of *The Old French Johannes Translation*, Walpole explains that an abridged translation of the *Reductio* was inserted in Johannes's translation a year or two after the latter finished his work (xvii).

38. Gaston Paris, "La Chanson du *Pèlerinage de Charlemagne*," *Romania: Recueil trimestriel consacré à l'étude des langues et des littératures romanes* 9 (1880): 1–50; for dating, see pp. 41–43.

39. On this point, see Jules Horrent, *Le Pèlerinage de Charlemagne: Essai d'explication littéraire avec des notes de critique textuelle* (Paris: Les Belles Lettres, 1961).

40. Paul Aebischer, ed., *Le Voyages de Charlemagne à Jérusalem et à Constantinople: Texte publié avec une introduction, des notes et un glossaire* (Geneva: Droz, 1965), v. 78.

41. Ibid., vv. 151–153. Here is the Old French text: "Sire, jo ai nun Karle, si sui de France nez. / Duze reis ai conquis par force e par barnez: / Li treizime vois querre, dunt ai oï parler."

42. Ibid., v. 39: "Sire, mult estes ber! / Sis as en la chaere u sist meïmes Deus: / Aies nun Charlemaine sur tuz reis curunez!"

43. Joel H. Grisward has convincingly studied the *Pèlerinage* from the viewpoint of the Indo-European trifunctionality presented by Dumézil: "Paris, Jerusalem, Constantinople in the *Pèlerinage de Charlemagne*: Three Cities, Three Functions," in Daniel Poirion, ed., *Jérusalem, Rome, Constantinople: L'Image et le mythe de la ville au Moyen Âge*, Colloque du Département d'études médiévales de l'université de Paris-Sorbonne (Paris IV) (Paris: Presses de l'Université de Paris-

Sorbonne, 1986), 75–82. Jules Horrent shows that all the relics mentioned were worshipped in the Middle Ages, and he makes a survey of the locales where they were kept; see his *Pèlerinage de Charlemagne*, 40–41.

44. Aebischer, *Voyage de Charlemagne*, vv. 362–364: "Karle vit le paleis e la richesce grant; / La sue manantise ne priset mie un guant."

45. Ibid., vv. 809–810: "Karlemaine portat la grant corone a or, Li reis Hugue la sue, plus basement un poi."

46. The verse version is contained in manuscript 26092 at Cheltenham, located between *La Geste de Monglane* and extracts from *Chronique de Saint-Denis*. I am citing here from David M. Dougherty and Eugene B. Barnes, eds., *Le Galien de Cheltenham* (Amsterdam: John Benjamins, 1981). In spite of its shortcomings, this edition is enhanced by its aim to render the manuscript faithfully without seeking to complete it. I am also referring, in addition to Dougherty and Barnes, to another, more accessible, edition, that of Edmund Stengel, *Galïens li restoré: Schlußtheil des Cheltenhamer "Guérin de Monglan"* (Marburg: Elwert'sche, 1890); the page references are to the pages of this edition. There are four older versions in prose that have been examined recently (see Dougherty and Barnes's introduction, p. xi, and Jules Horrent, *Chanson de Roland*).

47. Horrent, *Chanson de Roland*, 377–412.

48. According to Jules Horrent, the decline in popularity of the *Chanson de Roland* "is due to competition by another work that too tells the story of the battle of Roncevaux: the geste of *Galien le Restoré*." See *Chanson de Roland*, 377.

49. Dougherty and Barnes, *Le Galien de Cheltenham*, pp. 14–15, vv. 356–357.

50. On the double meaning, active and passive, of the word *restoré*, see the article by Peter F. Dembowski "Whom and What Did Galïen Restore?" *Olifant* 10, no. 3 (fall 1983–summer 1984): 83–98.

51. Dougherty and Barnes, *Le Galien de Cheltenham*, pp. 95–96, vv. 1292–1296: "Vous me verréz tantost de France couronné; / Car mon lignaige est de grant auctorité, / Et Charles n'a nul homme en sa femme engendré. / Si viendroit a sa soeur la noble royaulté, / Et celle est ma moulier, elle ma espousé. / Ainsi seray je roy de France le regné."

52. Ibid., vv. 1724–1728: "Et pensés à l'amour que vous desirés tant, / Jacqueline la belle qui a la doulz [doux] semblant" "Montrés pour son amour a paiens fier semblant, / Et j'en monstreray pour vostre seur autant, / Car ja homs n'est hardis s'il n'a vray ceur d'amant." Jules Horrent links these heroes' attitude to that of the heroes of knightly romances; see Horrent, *Chanson de Roland*, 401–402.

53. Dougherty and Barnes, *Le Galien de Cheltenham*, pp. 355–56, vv. 4403–4407.

54. Ibid., p. 347, vv. 4245–4247.

55. Ibid., p. 270, vv. 3491–3493: "Frans rois, or entendés! / Je vous prie pour Dieu, la belle me donnés / Et Monfusain aussi, ce [si] c'est vo[stre] grés."

56. Ibid., p. 271, vv. 3512–3514: "Charlon s'acorda, / Et se mit en sa main et Charles la bailla / Au vassal Gualien qui adonc l'espousa."

57. Ibid., p. 365, v. 4707: "le païs tint en paix et sa terre guarda."

58. See John W. Baldwin, *Philippe Auguste et son gouvernement: Les Fondations du pouvoir royal en France au Moyen Âge* (Paris: Fayard, 1991), 170; translated and

updated version of *The Government of Philip Augustus: Foundations of French Royal Power in the Middle Ages* (Berkeley: University of California Press, 1986). For a more general picture, see Robert Bartlett, *The Making of Europe: Conquest, Colonization, and Cultural Change, 950–1350* (Princeton, N.J.: Princeton University Press, 1993).

59. Folz, *Souvenir et légende,* 203–13.

60. See Beaune, *Naissance de la nation France,* and Bernard Guenée, "Les Grandes Chroniques de France: Le Roman aux roys (1274–1518)," in Pierre Nora, ed., *Les Lieux de mémoire,* vol. 2, book 1, *La Nation* (Paris: Gallimard, 1986), 189–214.

61. This critical tradition started with Léon Gautier, but Karl-Heinz Bender most thoroughly developed the thesis of the deidealization of Charlemagne in his *König und Vasall.*

62. Boutet, *Charlemagne et Arthur,* 567.

63. The meaning of this last verse ("Or i parra com vous esploiterés") is: "So we shall see how you [the old ones] are going to behave"; A. Kroeber and G. Servois, eds., *Fierabras, chanson de geste: Publiée pour la première fois d'après les manuscrits de Paris, de Rome et de Londres* (Paris: F. Vieweg, 1860), 6; it is Roland who addresses Charlemagne here.

64. Ibid., 133. The word "ireté" means the right, literally, the inheritance, the property.

65. Ibid., 151.

66. Louis Brandin, ed., *La Chanson d'Aspremont: Chanson de geste du XIIe siècle, texte du manuscrit de Wollaton Hall* (Paris: H. Champion, 1970), 1:14, vv. 411–428.

67. Ancient game played with metal or wooden balls thrown and rolled on the ground, still widespread in Mediterranean Europe. *Trans.*

68. Here is the Old French text from Brandin, *Chanson d'Aspremont,* vv. 1127–1133: "Dites, dans priestre, Dex vos puist vergonder. / Mes parens estes, deüssiés moi amer / Et tel message revenés aconter, / Del fil au nain homage demander! / Pepin, son pere, quil volsist esgarder, / Tant estoit grans qu'il peüst roëler: / Come pilote en peüssiés joër." See also de Mandach, *Naissance et développement,* vol. 3, *Chanson d'Aspremont: Manuscrit Venise VI et textes anglo-normands inédits, British Museum additional 35289 and Cheltenham 26119* (Paris: Droz, 1975), 103–104, vv. 1335–1353.

69. Brandin, *Chanson d'Aspremont,* 1:47, vv. 1438–1449.

70. Bender, *König und Vasall,* 133–36; he is drawing from Van Waard's work, "*Le Couronnement de Louis* et le principe de l'hérédité de la couronne"; Philip A. Becker, *Grundriß der altfranzösischen Literatur,* vol. 1, *Älteste Denkmäler: Nationale Heldendichtung* (Heidelberg: C. Winter, 1907); and Curtius, *Gesammelte Aufsätze zur romanischen Philologie.*

71. See Boutet, *Charlemagne et Arthur,* 470–71.

72. Brandin, *Chanson d'Aspremont,* 2:38, vv. 7270–7279, 7443.

73. Ibid., 1:161, vv. 5018–5022.

74. Ibid., 1:9, vv. 243–251.

75. This geographical recognition uses the voice of those who have come from elsewhere, because it is the Africans who utter the word "Europe" in the chanson.

76. Boutet, *Charlemagne et Arthur,* 92–102, 372–402.

77. I am using Jacques Thomas's edition, *Renaut de Montauban* (Geneva: Droz, 1989).

78. See Baldwin, who strongly insists on the importance of writing for Philip Augustus: *Philippe Auguste,* 333–39, 386; on the order to John Lackland to appear at Philip Augustus's court, see pp. 339–40.

79. E. R. Brown, "The Quest for Ancestry in Later Medieval Europe: Myths of Origins and Genealogies in Capetian France," in the proceedings of the conference *Legitimation by Descent,* Paris, 1982 (unpublished manuscript), and particularly Gabrielle M. Spiegel, "The Reditus Regni ad Stirpem Karoli Magni: A New Look," *French Historical Studies* 7, no. 2 (fall 1971): 145–74.

80. See Walpole's introduction to *Anonymous Old French Translation,* 28; according to Walpole, between 1195 and 1205, Yolande, countess of Saint-Pol-en-Ternois, had one of her clerks, Nicolas de Senlis, translate the *Pseudo-Turpin Chronicle.* The latter translated the chronicle from a manuscript that Baldwin had left to his sister. Johannes's translation dates from around 1205, and the one used by Mousket also dates from that period.

81. M. L. Colker, ed., *The Karolinus of Egidius Parisiensis,* in *Traditio: Studies in Ancient and Medieval History, Thought, and Religion* (New York: Fordham University Press, 1973), 29:199–325. "Hunc preter dictata stilo iam trita soluto / Affectans seruansque modum quia tradita uersu / Pro metrico dulcore sonant iocundius auri / Et leuius capiuntur et intus firmius herent" (chap. 4, vv. 390–393).

82. Ibid., 2:265, vv. 129–133.

83. "Francia, donec eras tante subiecta lucerne / Et radiis radiosa suis, tu Francia pollens, / Tu bona tu dulcis tu libera uertice recto, / Tu multum dilecta Deo feixque fuisti, / Tu propter titulum pacis, quam sola gerebas / Quamque dabas aliis per signa preambula terris, / Sensifica uoce bene nomen adepta togate" (ibid., 2:266, vv. 144–150).

84. "Nec timide ostensis uastata Britannia tergis / Insultare potest, nam pars fit et ipsa triumphi. / Gallicus hic potuit plus Roma et Cesare Magnus" (ibid., 2:276, vv. 436–438). On Trojan ancestry, see vol. 1, vv. 360–361.

85. Ibid., vol. 5, vv. 73–85.

86. Ibid., vol. 5, vv. 209–210.

87. Ibid., "Captatio Beniuolencie," pp. 322–23, vv. 133–136.

88. "Hoc quoque continuit sacro obseruamine Magnus / Ut quia palpones blando sermone resoluant / Corda auditorum cum dira pereffluit aures / Pestis adulandi, scurras icirco cauendos / Duceret, icirco nebulones quoslibet a se / Sedulus arceret, nullosque admitteret huius / Nequicie mithmos, laudari a turpibus ipse / Sic fugiens sicut laudari ob turpia nollet" (ibid., 4:290–92, vv. 21–28).

89. "Hactenus hec. tu deinde iube, sequar ipse iubentem / Facto quid sit opus, nam sunt qui muneris usum / Huius habere uolunt sed non, nisi iusseris, umquam / Diuulgandus erit, potius mittendus in ignem" (ibid., "Captatio," p. 235, vv. 220–223).

90. ". . . tunc ipso cognita uisu / Plenius et melius scripto mandanda fuerunt" (ibid., "Captatio," p. 322, vv. 120–121).

91. Ibid., "Captatio," vv. 122–123.

92. *Karolinus* is far from being alone in this regard. Among other elements, in translations from Latin into French of narratives such as that of the Pseudo-Turpin, we must see evidence of the same "struggle" as found in these lines of Nicolas de Senlis in the Pointevin translation (around 1200): "Li bons Baudoins, li cuens de Chainau, si ama molt Karlemaines. Ni ne vont onques croire chose que l'on en chantast; ainz fist chercher totes les bones abaies de France et garder par totes les aumaires por saver si l'on i troveroit la veraie estoire" ("Der sogenannte poitevinische Pseudo-Turpin," ed. Auracher, *Zeitschrift für romanische Philologie* 1 [1877]: 262).

93. See Zeller, "Rois de France" (1964), 16–17, and Folz, *Souvenir et légende*, 138–40.

94. On the idea of "motor myths" see Anthony D. Smith, *The Ethnic Origins of Nations* (Oxford: Basil Blackwell, 1986), 21–32. Smith notes that he is indebted for this concept to John Jay Armstrong, *Nations before Nationalism* (Chapel Hill: University of North Carolina Press, 1982). The term used by Armstrong originates with Ramon D'Abadal I de Vinyals; see his "A Propos du legs visigothique en Espagne," in *Caratteri del secolo VII in Occidente*, vol. 2, Settimane di Studio del Centro Italiano di Studi sull'Alto Medioevo, V (Spoleto: Presso La Sede del Centro, 1958), 541–85.

Chapter Three. Rewriting History

1. On the role of Saint-Denis, see C. Beaune, *Naissance de la nation France*, chap. 3, "Saint-Denis: Un Patronage contesté."

2. The actual bishop was named Philippe Mus or Meuse; he was born in Ghent. See Peter F. Dembowski, "Philippe Mousket and His *Chronique rimée* Seven and a Half Centuries Ago: A Chapter in the Literary History," in *Contemporary Readings of Medieval Literature*, ed. Guy Mermier, Michigan Romance Studies (Ann Arbor: University of Michigan Press, 1989), 8:93–113; Ronald N. Walpole, "Philip Mouskés and the Pseudo-Turpin Chronicle," ed. S. G. Morley, Rudolph Altrocchi, J. E. de la Harpe, and L. M. Price, *University of California Publications in Modern Philology* 26, no. 4 (1947): 327–440.

3. See Dembowski, "Philippe Mousket," 94.

4. Walpole published the translation of the Pseudo-Turpin that Mousket used and that was probably done in the 1230s. He lists no fewer than five translations of this work done between 1200 and 1230 (Walpole, *Anonymous Old French Translation*, 28).

5. Jules Viard, ed., *Les Grandes Chroniques de France* (Paris: Société de l'histoire de France, 1920), 1:3.

6. In English in original French text. *Trans.*

7. "Il me semble que [Dieu] me hait / et qu'il a envers moi colère et haine / et ressentiment [male amour] et grande haine / qu'il m'a retiré ma puissance, ma vertu et mon soutien."

8. On this stained-glass window, see Clark Maines, "The Charlemagne Window at Chartres Cathedral," as well as Isabelle Rolland, "Le Mythe carolingien

et l'art du vitrail: Sur le choix et l'ordre des épisodes dans le vitrail de Charlemagne à la cathédrale de Chartres," in *La Chanson de geste et le mythe carolingien: Mélanges René Louis* (Saint-Père-sous-Vézelay: Musée archéologique régional, 1982), 1:255–77. On the visual transcriptions of the legend of Roland, see the wonderful work of Rita Lejeune, "Une Allusion méconnue à une *Chanson de Roland,*" *Romania: Revue trimestrielle consacrée à l'étude des langues et des littératures romanes* 75 (1954): 145–64. See also Linda Seidel, *Songs of Glory: The Romanesque Façades of Acquitaine* (Chicago: University of Chicago Press, 1981).

9. "Mémoire concernant les principaux monumens de l'Histoire de France, avec la Notice et l'Histoire des Chroniques de Saint-Denys," in *Mémoires de littérature tirez des registres de l'Académie royale* . . . , Assemblée publique, 15 avril 1738 (Paris: Imprimerie royale, 1743), 611.

10. The best general work on the art of the chroniclers and historians is that of Bernard Guenée, *Histoire et culture historique dans l'Occident médiéval* (Paris: Aubier Montaigne, 1980; 2d. ed., 1991).

11. "*Ex Chronicis*. Iste Pipinus, vt dictum est, ex regalis aulae praefecto in Regem promotus, in ecclesia sancti Dionysii cum multa fuit honorificentia tumulatus, foelix victoriarum successibus Regumque Francorum eximius. Huius filius extitit Carolus ex Berta filia Heraclii Caesaris. Vnde in ipso genus Graecorum et Romanorum, ac Germanorum concurrit. Vnde merito ad ipsum postea translatum est Imperium" (Vincent de Beauvais, *Speculum historiale, dans Bibliotheca mundi. Speculum quadruplex, naturale, doctrinale, morale, historiale* . . . , 4 vols. [Duaci: Ex officina Baltazaris Beller, 1624; reprint, Graz, Austria: Akademische Druck- und Verlagsanstalt, 1964], vol. 4, book 23, chap. 161, "De quibusdam gesti Pipini Regis, et de morte eius," 956).

12. "Hoc itaque monasterium post hoc, ut dictum est, donante Carolo suscepit regendum Alcuinus, scientia vitaque praeclarus, quoia sapientae studium de Roma Parisios transtulit, quod illuc quondam a Graecia translatum fuerat a Romanis" (ibid., "De Alcuino, qui et Albinus," chap. 173, p. 960).

13. Herbert Grundmann and Hermann Heimpel, eds., *Memoriale de praerogativa Imperii romani*, in *Die Schriften des Alexander von Roes*, vol. 4, Deutsches Mittelalter des Monumenta Germaniae Historica (Weimar: Hermann Böhlaus, 1949), chaps. 14 and 15, p. 48; cited in Folz, *Souvenir et légende*, 389, whose analysis I follow.

14. See M.-C. Duchenne, "Un Historien et sa source: L'Utilisation de la Chronique de Sigebert de Gembloux par Vincent de Beauvais," in *Spicae: Cahiers de l'Atelier Vincent de Beauvais* (Paris: Éditions du Centre national de la recherche scientifique, 1986), 4:33–80.

15. Guenée, "Les *Grandes Chroniques de France*: Le *Roman aux roys* (1274–1518)," 204–208; Guenée employs the French term "le nœud de l'histoire."

16. Ibid., 192.

17. "Joyful." *Trans.*

18. The Pseudo-Turpin's chronicle twice mentions this childhood spent in Spain, which proves, as Gaston Paris notes, that the narrative already existed around the middle of the twelfth century. We find other references in *Renaut de Montauban*, and *Garin de Monglene*, as well as, of course, in the German poem, *Karl Meinet*. On this issue see Paris, *Histoire poétique de Charlemagne*, 230.

19. See Beaune, *Naissance*, 114.

20. Here are a few examples: Primat III, p. 22, which corresponds to the year 770 in the *Annals*; Primat III, p. 36 (777 in the *Annals*); Primat III, p. 45 (782 in the *Annals*).

21. J. Viard notes—contrary to the opinion of Paulin Paris, who saw this passage as an indication of Primat's position—that this passage is also missing in the manuscript that Primat used to do his translation (see Viard, *Grandes Chroniques*, 226–27).

22. Pierre Dubois, *De Recuperatione Terre Sance*, ed. Charles Victor Langlois (Paris: A. Picard, 1891), 5. Dubois mentions the length of Charlemagne's reign within the context of an argument that the old should rule since they are wiser than the young. However, he also concludes with the Thomistic idea that reason at the service of free choice is the best defense against the infidels' diabolical machinations. It must be noted that Dubois's pamphlet was not "official" propaganda. However, this text is significant, written as it was by an accomplished bourgeois jurist who had represented the third estate during the general assembly held by Philip the Fair.

It is during the same period (1301–1306) of intense propaganda that Girart d'Amiens composed his *chanson de geste* entitled *Charlemagne*. It comprises over 23,300 verses (alexandrins). See Antoinette Saly, "La Date du *Charlemagne* de Girart d'Amiens," in *Au Carrefour des routes d'Europe: La chanson de geste, Sénéfiance* no. 21 (Aix-en-Provence: Université de Provence [Centre d'Aix], 1987) II, 975–981.

23. Dubois, *Recuperatione*, 130.

24. Zeller, "Rois de France," is still the best source of information on this topic. See also Folz, *Idée d'Empire*.

25. See Danielle Gaborit-Chopin, *Regalia: Les Instruments du sacre des rois de France, les "Honneurs" de Charlemagne* (Paris: Ministère de la Culture et de la Communication, Éditions de la Réunion des musées nationaux, 1987); Blaise de Montesquiou-Fézensac and Danielle Gaborit-Chopin, *Le Trésor de Saint-Denis* (Paris: A. and J. Picard, 1973–1977). See the catalog for the exhibition *Le Trésor de Saint-Denis: Musée du Louvre, Paris, 12 mars–17 juin 1991* (Paris: Réunion des musées nationaux, 1991); and *The Coronation Book of Charles V of France (Cottonian ms. Tiberius B. VIII)*, ed. Edward Samuel Dewick, Henry Bradshaw Society Publications, vol. 16 (London: Harrison and Sons, 1899).

26. Christine de Pisan, *Le Livre et bonnes meurs du Sage roy Charles V*, ed. Suzanne Solente (Paris: H. Champion, 1936), 1:133:

> . . . si comme les Roummains plus acqueissent seigneuries et terres par leur sens que par force, semblablement le fist nostre roy, lequel plus conquesta, enrichi, fist aliences, plus grans armées, mieulx gens d'armes paiez et toute gent, plus fist bastir edifices, donna grans dons, tint plus magnificent estat, ot plus grant despense, moins fist de grief au peuple et plus sagement se gouverna en toute policie, et plus largement [fu] furnie toute despense que n'avoit fait roy de France, selon le raport des escriptures, je l'ose dire, depuis le temps Charlemaine, qui, pour haultece de sa proece, fu appellé Charles le grant. Ainsi, pour la vertu et sagece de cestui, lui doit bien perpetuelment demourer le nom de Charles le sage. . . .

27. Robert Folz, "Aspects du culte liturgique de saint Charlemagne en France," in Braunfels, *Karl der Große*, 77–99; my reference here is to p. 79.

28. Jean de Roye, *Journal de Jean de Roye, connu sous le nom de Chronique scandaleuse, 1460–1483*, ed. Bernard de Mandrot (Paris: Librairie Renouard, H. Laurens, 1894–1896), 1:323.

29. Even though the cult of Saint Charlemagne was not adopted by the French church as it had been by the Germans, we nonetheless find a certain number of references to Saint Charlemagne in the texts of that period; see, for instance, Juvénal des Ursins, *Audite Celi*, in *Écrits politiques de Jean Juvénal des Ursins*, ed. P. S. Lewis and Anne-Marie Hayez (Paris: Klincksieck, 1978), 156; Jean de Roye, *Chronique scandaleuse*, 2:134; Madeleine Jeay, ed., *Les Évangiles des quenouilles: Édition critique, introduction et notes* (Paris: A. J. Vrin, 1985), 100; Philippe de Commynes in his *Mémoires*, ed. Joseph Calmette and G. Durville (Paris: H. Champion, 1924), 1:145.

30. Jean de Roye, *Chronique scandaleuse*, 2:62. I thank my colleague Katherine Taylor for giving me this information.

31. I would like to thank Sarah Hanley for her help in locating these images.

32. This work, painted in the Flemish style and showing the influence of Roger van der Weyden, has been the subject of numerous commentaries. Among the most interesting I note Emile Clairin, "Le Calvaire de la Grand'Chambre du Parlement," *La Nouvelle Revue* 56 (November–December 1921): 3–17; Albert Châtelet, "Le Retable du Parlement de Paris," in *Art de France: Études et chroniques sur l'art ancien et moderne*, ed. Pierre Berès and André Chastel (Paris: Hermann, 1964), 4:60–69; and Charles Sterling, *La Peinture médiévale à Paris: 1300–1500* (Paris: Bibliothèque des arts, 1990), 2:37–49. Albert Châtelet (p. 62) provides the two Latin inscriptions: "Facite judicium et justitiam. Quod si non audieritis verba haec, in memet ipso juravi, dicit Dominus, quia in solitudinem erit domus haec" (Jeremiah 12:3, 5) and "Videte, ait, quid faciatis. Non enim hominis exercetis judicium, sed Dei: et quodcumque judicaveritis in vos redundabit" (2 Chronicles 19:6). Scholars question the painter's identity; Charles Sterling believes he is from Tournai, possibly Louis Le Duc, who worked in Paris around 1454. It is relevant to our study to note that another *Crucifixion* existed in which Saint Louis and Charlemagne were added on either side, but their positions were inverted. This painting, done at a later date than the *Retable du Parlement de Paris*, was displayed in the main office of the treasury and was of clearly inferior quality; it was destroyed by fire in 1737.

33. See Châtelet, "Le Retable," 67.

34. I believe Sterling was the first to note this "oriental" aspect (see *La Peinture médiévale à Paris: 1300–1500*, 38).

35. Georges Doutrepont, *Les Mises en prose des Épopées et des Romans chevaleresques du XIVe au XVIe siècle*, Mémoires de l'Académie royale de Belgique (Brussels: Palais des Académies, 1939), 40:355.

36. Monfrin, "Figure de Charlemagne," 68; see also the introduction to the work of J. Bagnyon, *L'Histoire de Charlemagne*, ed. Hans-Erich Keller (Geneva: Droz, 1992), v–xxxi.

37. See, for instance, Juvénal des Ursins, *Audite celi*, in Lewis and Hayez, *Écrits politiques*, 156.

38. Yvonne Labande-Mailfert describes very well this "epic atmosphere" in her *Charles VIII et son milieu (1470–1498): La Jeunesse au pouvoir* (Paris: Klincksieck, 1975), 185–92, 224. See also Anne Denis, *Charles VIII et les Italiens: Histoire et mythe* (Geneva: Droz, 1979); and Henri François Délaborde, *L'Expédition de Charles VIII en Italie: Histoire diplomatique et militaire* (Paris: Firmin-Didot, 1888).

39. See fig. 8. This miniature painting was done for Charles VIII, but the face is that of Louis XII. Robert Scheller believes that the face was repainted after Charles VIII's death. See his excellent article "Imperial Themes in Art and Literature of the Early French Renaissance: The Period of Charles VIII," *Simiolus: Netherlands Quarterly for the History of the Arts* 12, no. 1 (1981–1982): 5–69, particularly pp. 24–25.

40. In the hope of being able to fend off Charles VIII's armies, Anne of Brittany wed by proxy Maximilian, duke of Austria, on December 19, 1490. This marriage was annulled in 1493 by Pope Alexander VI after Anne of Brittany's marriage to Charles VIII in December 1491.

41. Here is a description of this scene found in Jean Nicolai:

> After these things being done in that manner, behind the said city gate [la Porte aut Paintres] next to Saint-James-the-Hospitaler, there was a personage representing Charlemagne mounted on a big horse that was about fifteen feet tall and with a girth that matched its height, covered with purple blankets, half of which were decorated with the royal arms and the other half with ermine. And the representative of the said Charlemagne was about one lance high and had the girth to match his height, holding in his right hand a naked sword, tall and wide according to the height of the said personage, and in the other hand the golden globe topped by the cross. The said personage wore a real crown, and on the crown was a golden cross meaning that in his time he submitted and exacted obedience from the greatest part of the world. This said king, mounted on a horse with a blanket decorated with fleurs-de-lis, saluted the queen and made her a beautiful speech for her happy arrival; and in this state he traveled in front of the noble lady all the way from the door of the painters to Notre Dame of Paris, having pages in front and in back of him, dressed the same, leading him and his horse. / And behind him were other people leading an elephant, and others a camel, both covered with blankets close to their skin that such beasts must wear; these beasts were led by big chains, woven and golden, whose links were round and big. / In this state the noble lady entered Paris, accompanied by lords of such greatness that it is impossible to assess them. (Text published in the *Bulletin de la Société de l'histoire de France* [1845–1846]: 111–21; this passage is on pp. 117–18)

Such a scene did not lack irony, because Charles VIII had just "taken" Anne of Brittany from her husband, the emperor Maximilian. On the queen's arrival in Paris, see Robert W. Scheller, "Imperial Themes in Art and Literature of the Early French Renaissance: The Period of Charles VIII," 18.

42. Labande-Mailfert, *Charles VIII et son milieu*, 171–75.

43. André de La Vigne, *Le Voyage de Naples: Edition critique avec introduction, notes et glossaire*, ed. Anna Slerca (Milan: Università cattolica del Sacro Cuore, 1981), p. 246, vv. 4338–4341.

44. Labande-Mailfert, *Charles VIII et son milieu*, 189–91; and, by the same author, *Charles VIII: Le Vouloir et la destinée* (Paris: Fayard, 1986), 158.

45. André de La Vigne, *Le Vergier d'honneur, nouvellement imprimé à Paris: De l'entreprise et voyage de Napples . . . Ensemble plusieurs choses faictes et composées par Révérend Père en Dieu, Monseigneur Octavien de Sainct-Gelais . . . et par maistre Andry de La Vigne* (Paris: P. Le Noir, n.d.).

46. The first instance of the use of the term "mythistory" is found in Julius Capitolinus and Flavius Vopiscus, the two presumed authors of *Historia Augusta*. In fact, these are two pseudonyms used by an unknown author who, probably toward the end of the fourth century, wanted to have his *Historia* pass as a continuation of Suetonius. This impostor cites sources and documents that never existed and also denigrates other authors by accusing them of having only written *mythistories* (see *Historia*, "Opilius Macrinus" chap. 1, and "Firmus, Saturnus, Proculus, et Bonosus," chap. 1). In the sixteenth century, François Baudouin used the term to speak about epic poetry; see Donald R. Kelly, *Foundations of Modern Historical Scholarship, Language, Law, and History in the French Renaissance* (New York: Columbia University Press, 1970), 136; more recently, Jean-Marie Apostolidès uses the term in *Le Roi-Machine: Spectacle et politique au temps de Louis XIV* (Paris: Éditions de Minuit, 1981), "La mythistoire," chap. 4, pp. 66–92.

47. "De Carolingis, id est de stirpe regis Caroli et de domo regnum Franciae imperator suscitabitur Carolus nomine qui erit princeps et monarcha totius Europae," cited in Alexander de Roes's treatise and taken up by Zeller, "Rois de France" (1964), 26. These prophecies were attributed to a priest from Calabria, Joachim of Flora. There were two versions of them: one predicted the arrival of a new Charlemagne and the other, pro-German, announced the arrival of a new Frederick. On the role of prophecies in Florence, see Donald Weinstein, "The Myth of Florence," in *Florentine Studies: Politics and Society in Renaissance Florence*, ed. Nicolai Rubinstein (Evanston, Ill.: Northwestern University Press, 1968), 15–44; on the role of prophecies, see Marjorie Reeves, *The Influence of Prophecy in the Later Middle Ages: A Study in Joachimism* (Oxford: Clarendon Press, 1969); and Franz Kampers, *Kaiserprophetieen und Kaisersagen im Mittelalter* (Munich: H. Lüneburg, 1895; reprinted in 1969 under the title *Die Deutsche Kaiseridee in Prophetie und Sage*); see particularly pp. 145–53, regarding Florence. For a good discussion of the relationship between prophecies in Germany—where Frederick II's figure replaced Charlemagne—and those in France, see Folz, *Idée d'Empire*, 178–84.

48. D. Weinstein, "Myth of Florence," 24. It should also be noted that the voice of Savonarola joined these prophecies, since he saw Charles as the instrument of divine vengeance.

49. "Empowerment" is in English in original French text. *Trans.*

50. Monfrin, "Figure de Charlemagne," 70; see also Constance Jordan, *Pulci's Morgante: Poetry and History in Fifteenth-Century Florence* (Washington, D.C.: Folger Shakespeare Library; London: Associated University Presses, 1986), "The Idea of Empire in Florentine History," in the introduction, 18–27. It goes without saying that Charlemagne's founding role pertains as well to other countries such as Spain; see, for instance, Paul Freedman, "Cowardice, Heroism, and the Legendary Origins of Catalonia," *Past and Present* 121 (November 1988): 3–28.

51. Cited by Monfrin, "Figure de Charlemagne," 71, from the draft of the speech that the ambassador was supposed to give, preserved in Italian in the records of the deliberations of the seigniory.

52. Ibid., 71–72. The delegation included Filippo dei Medici, the archbishop of Pisa; Piero dei Pazzi; and Bonnacorso Pitti.

53. Johann Burckard Mencke, ed., *Scriptores Rerum Germanicarum* (Lipsiae: Impensis Ioannis Christiani Martini, 1728–1730), 1:827: "Quod enim in solo patrio sumus, quod liberi vivimus, quod magistratus, leges, civitatem habemus, ea omnia Carolo accepta sunt referenda, ac eius memoria tam grata recordatione perpetua celebranda."

54. Acciaiuoli in Mencke, *Scriptores Rerum Germanicarum*, 813; Monfrin translation, p. 72.

55. Luigi Pulci, *Morgante: The Epic Adventures of Orlando and His Giant Friend Morgante*, trans. Joseph Tusiani, introduction and notes by Edoardo A. Lebano (Bloomington and Indianapolis: Indiana University Press, 1998). "E tu, Fiorenzia, della sua grandezza / Possiedi, e sempre potrai possedere / Ogni costume ed ogni gentilezza / Che si potessi acquistare o avere / Col senno, col tesoro o colla lancia / Dal nobil sangue è venuto di Francia" (Luigi Pulci, *Morgante*, with an introduction by Enrico Bianchi, vol. 1 [Florence: Salani, 1965], p. 15, song 1, st. 7, vv. 9–14).

56. Jordan, *Pulci's "Morgante,"* 22–23; on Verino, see Alfonso Lazzari, *Ugolino e Michele Verino: Studii biografici e critici*, Contributo alla storia dell'umanesimo in Firenze (Turin: C. Clausen, 1897), 158–85.

57. "Oultre le vouloir des Germàins, / . . . Et puis après, par son moyen, / Tout homme et Roy chrestien / A luy tousiours se soubsmectra" and "Roy de France . . . , des Rommains / Et des Grectz." Claude de Cherrier published this prophecy as an appendix to his *Histoire de Charles VIII, roi de France, d'après des documents diplomatiques inédits ou nouvellement publiés* (Paris: Didier, 1868), 1:488–89.

58. Labande-Mailfert, *Charles VIII et son milieu*, 364–66; Scheller, "Imperial Themes," 18.

59. De La Vigne, *Voyage de Naples*, p. 266, v. 183.

60. Robert Gaguin, *La Mer des croniques et miroir hystorial de france . . . editio princeps*, ed. Pierre Destrey (Paris, 1514); cited by Scheller, "Imperial Themes," 63.

61. Translation by Charles Stanley Ross (Berkeley: University of California Press, 1986), p. 849.

62. On this painting, see the article by Paul Schoenen, "Das Karlsbild der Neuzeit," in Braunfels, *Karl der Große*, 274–305 (on Dürer see pp. 274–76).

63. See ibid., 286–87, and Anne-Marie Lecoq, *François Ier imaginaire: Symbolique et politique à l'aube de la Renaissance française* (Paris: Macula, 1987), 264–68.

64. "Épistre envoiée de Paradis au très chrestien roy de France Franscoys, premier de ce nom, de par les empereurs Pepin et Charlemaigne, ses magnifiques predecesseurs, et presentée audit seigneur par le chevalier Transfiguré, porteur d'icelle."

65. . . . toy et nous n'est qu'unne mesme chose,
    Dont nostre gloire ent la tiengne repose,
    Et par la nostre la tienne aparoistra,

Et par la tienne la nostre se croistra.
  Mais, quant l'honneur te sera lors donné
Que tu seras empereur couronné,
Et qu'aras mis par tes sens et bonté
Grosse police en la crestienté,
Lors pour la foy combattre t'en iras,
Et Machommet et sa loy destruyras,
En recouvrant la saincte terre digne,
Ce que Dieu doint par sa grace benigne,
Et tous peuples en luy tu feras croyre
Pour parvenir a immortelle gloire.

. . . .
Car long temps a qu'il est prophetisé
Q'un roy françois sus tous aultres prisé
Subjuguera, selon la prophetie,
Tous les peuples et d'Africqué et d'Asie.
Or n'y eust-il, entre nous rois françois,
Jamais ung seul qui fust nommé Fransçoys.

This text has been edited by Anatole de Montaiglon, *Receuil de poésies françoises des XVe et XVIe siècles: Morales, facétieuses, historiques* (Paris: P. Jannet, 1856), 4:180–92; Lecoq analyses it in her *François Ier imaginaire*, 271–74. The emperor's election was held in 1519.

66. Lecoq, *François Ier imaginaire*, 448. She also notes that Jean Thenaud dedicates the first letter of the second volume of *Triumphes de Vertuz* to the king: "Francisco Francorum Regi Maximo et Optimo, Imperatori Proximo Imperiique Turcorum Eversori Invinctissimo" [To François, very great and very good king of France, future emperor and destroyer of the Turkish empire, invincible]; ibid., 268.

67. See Zeller, "Rois de France" (1964), 56–58.

68. See, for instance, Symphorien Champier, *De Monarchia Gallorum campi aurei ac triplici imperio videlicet romano, gallico, germanico una cum gestis heroum ac omnium imperatorum* (Lyon: Ex officina M. and G. Trechsel fratum, 1537); and Charles de Grassaile, *Regalium Franciae libri duo, jura omnia et dignitates Christianiss, Galliae regum continentes* (Lyon: Apud haeredes S. Vincentii, 1538). In the prophetic genre there appeared in 1523 *Mirabilis liber qui prophetias revelationesque necnon res mirandas praeteritas praesentes et futurus.*

69. Jean Lemaire de Belges, *Œuvres*, vol. 2, *Les Illustrations de Gaule et singularitez de Troye*, ed. J. Stecher (Geneva: Slatkine Reprints, 1969; reprint of the Louvain edition 1882–1885), 422: "deux maisons et nations de France Orientale et Occidentale, lesquelles vous nommez auiourd'huy Hongres, Allemans, Lansquenets, d'une part: François et Bretons de l'autre."

70. Ibid., 422: "Toute l'intention de ce troisieme Traicté n'est que de monstrer, comment la tresparfonde illustrité de tous les nobles lignages dessusdits, du sang des Francs Orientaux et Occidentaux, des Bourguignons et des Austrasiens, ou Austrichois, eurent tous ensemble concurrence en la genealogie du treschrestien Empereur Cesar auguste Charles, le grand monarque, Roy de France, d'Austriche

la basse et de Bourgongne, et de luy est derivee et procedee ladite noblesse, comme d'un grande source et fontaine à sa postérité."

71. Ibid., 474: "Et se commencent ces deux nations à sentreaymer, et sentre-accointer . . . comme ilz faisoient du temps de l'Empereur Charles le grande. Le . . . Roy Loys douzieme est en plusieurs choses comparables audit empereur."

72. Guillaume Postel, *Les Raisons de la monarchie. Et quelz moyens sont neces-saires pour y parvenir, la ou sont comprins en brief; Les tresadmirables et de nul iusques au iourdhuy tout ensemble considerez Privileges et Droictz, tant Divins, Celestes, comme hu-mains de la gent Gallicque, et des Princes paricelle esleuz et approuvez* (Paris: [1551]), ii. See the article by Michel François, "L'Idée d'Empire en France à l'époque de Charles Quint," in *Charles Quint et son temps* (Paris: Éditions du Centre national de la recherche scientifique, 1959), 23–35.

73. Postel, *Raisons de la monarchie*, ix–x.

74. Ibid., xii.

CHAPTER FOUR. A CALL FOR REALITY, A NEED FOR MYTH

1. Gaguin speaks of a "small book on the deeds of the glorious emperor and saintly king Charlemagne" ("Les Commentaires de Jules César"), in *Roberti Gaguini Epistole et Orationes: Texte publié sur les éditions originales de 1498, précédé d'une notice biographique et suivi de pièces diverses en partie inédites*, ed. Louis Thuasne (Paris: Émile Bouillon, 1903), 2:301; this passage has been cited by Mireille Schmidt-Chazan in her article "Histoire et sentiment national chez Robert Gaguin," in *Le Métier d'historien au Moyen Âge: Études sur l'historiographie médiévale*, ed. Bernard Guenée (Paris: Université de Paris I, Centre de recherches sur l'his-toire de l'Occident médiéval, 1977) 233–300; see p. 179. My discussion of Gaguin owes much to Schmidt-Chazan.

2. Robert Gaguin, *Compendium Roberti Gaguini super Francorum gestis* (Paris, 1511), fol. 54r; translation: *Les Grandes Croniques, excellens faitz et vertueux gestes des très illustres, très chrestiens, magnanimes et victorieux roys de France . . .* (Paris: Galliot Duprez, 1514), fol. 41r.

3. See Folz, *Souvenir et légende*, 254–58, 414–18, 554–57. In the fourteenth century, Lupold de Bebenbourg developed the thesis of Charlemagne's German origins. Moreover, according to him, "there is perfect continuity between the Frankish state and the German state: Franks and Germans are one and the same people" (ibid., 414).

4. Francesco Petrarca, "To Giovanni Colonna, Cardinal of the Roman Church, Description of a Journey," in *Rerum familiarum libri I–VIII*, translated into English by Aldo S. Bernardo (Albany: State University of New York Press, 1975), 26, letter 4. See also Frances A. Yates, "Charles Quint et l'idée d'Empire," in *Les Fêtes de la Renaissance*, vol. 2, *Fêtes et cérémonies au temps de Charles Quint* (Paris: Édi-tions du Centre national de la recherche scientifique, 1960), 57–97; see p. 71. On Petrarch, see Theodor E. Mommsen, "Petrarch's Conception of the 'Dark Ages'," *Speculum* 17, no. 2 (April 1942): 226–42.

5. Francesco Petrarca, *Rerum familiarium libri*, book 1, 26–28, letter 4. On this anecdote see Gaston Paris, "*Der Ring der Fastrada: Eine mythologische Studie, von Dr. Jur. August Pauls, Aachen*," *Journal des savants* (November–December 1896): 637–43, 718–30.

6. Cited by Schmidt-Chazan, "Histoire et sentiment national," 246.

7. Gaguin, *Compendium*, fol. 54r; translation: *Les Grandes Croniques*, fol. 41r.

8. "A dominum episcopum Massiliensem," in Thuasne, *Roberti Gaguini Epistole et Orationes*, 2:126; cited in Schmidt-Chazan, "Histoire et sentiment national," 287.

9. Gaguin, *Compendium*, fol. 54v; translation: *Les Grandes Croniques*, fol. 41v (the translator substitutes "French name" instead).

10. Bernard de Girard Du Haillan, *L'Histoire de France* (Paris: P. L'Huillier, 1576), 227: "Charles eut en luy toutes les graces qui rendent un Prince louable, de façon qu'il doit estre proposé à tous Princes, comme un patron, miroir & exemple des vertuz dignes d'eux, comme ayant la religion, la vaillance, le bonheur, la iustice, le sçavoir, l'eloquence, la promptitude, la clémence, la sagesse, & la liberalité, qui sont les perles precieuses, desquelles les Princes se doivent parer & faire par tout reluire. Beau, grand & admirable fut de son temps l'Estat des affaires de France, qui estoit riche & opulante, honoree d'infinies victoires, decoree & soustenue de la iustice, ornee de la religion, louee de toutes vertuz, & agrandie & augmentee par les armes."

11. On historiography in the sixteenth century see George Huppert, *The Idea of Perfect History: Historical Erudition and Historical Philosophy in Renaissance France* (Urbana: University of Illinois Press, 1970); for Gallican history, see Kelley, *Foundations*. I owe much to Kelley's study for my argument on the "Gallican" tendency. For a rapid overview of Charlemagne's image in European historiography, see Arno Borst, "Das Karlsbild in der Geschichtswißenschaft vom Humanismus bis heute," in Braunfels, *Karl der Große*, 364–402. For a broader study of the role of the Middle Ages in French historical thought, see Jürgen Voss, *Das Mittelalter im Historischen Denken Frankreichs: Untersuchungen zur Geschichte des Mittelalterbegriffes und der Mittelalterbewertung von der zweiten Hälfte des 16. bis zur Mitte des 19. Jahrhunderts* (München: Wilhelm Fink, 1972).

12. Du Haillan, *Histoire de France*, "Épistre."

13. François de Belleforest Comingeois, *L'Histoire des Neuf Roys Charles de France: contenant la fortune, vertu, et heur fatal des Roys, qui sous ce nom de Charles ont mis à fin des choses merveilleuses* (Paris: Olivier de P. L'Huillier, 1568), 18: "Or qu'on m'allegue icy les Phalanges Macedoniens, ou legions des Romains: qu'on mesure les faicts d'Alexandre, & des Consuls de la ville fondée par Romule, avec les gestes de ce belliqueux Prince: Qu'on face comparaison des temps, de la force des hommes, des occurrences des choses: ie m'asseure que la fortune, heur & vertu de cestuy [Charlemagne] aura l'avantage sur les precedents, non moins que la religion de laquelle il faisoit profession, tenoit les dessus sur celle de ces premiers Monarques: qui ont esté plustost les fleaux du monde que les vrais ministres de justice, ou autheurs du repos du peuple à eux commis."

14. Ibid., 8, 48, 62, 15.

15. Ibid., 50: "Alexandre, Cesar & Auguste: lesquels tyraniquement avoient attaint cest gloire: là où ce Cesar Gaulois, Roy d'infinies provinces, bien merité des

siens, doux aux vaincus & debiles, devot & religieux aux choses sacrées, parvient à cest honneur, par la voix commune du peuple & election volontaire des Princes, & l'approbation legitime du Pontife Romain."

16. Du Haillan, *Histoire de France*, 227.

17. Belleforest, *Histoire des Neuf Roys*, 11.

18. Ibid., 58.

19. Du Haillan, *Histoire de France*, 157: ". . . cognoissant les François impatiens d'un long repos, avec lequel il fault, ou qu'ils s'addonnent aux volutptez, ou qu'ils s'entrequerellent eux mesmes, quand ils ne trouvent à se battre contre les estrangers, il cogneut estre necessaire de les employer en quelques endroicts. Il s'en offrit doncq une belle occasion par une cause qui survint d'aller faire la guerre en Espaigne."

20. Ibid., 213.

21. Ibid., 214: "Tu commenças à Rome d'estre Empereur des autres nations: mais tu es né Prince & Roy des François, sur la vaillance desquelz par ie ne sçay quel destin, tous estrangers portent envie, estimans nostre liberté cause de leur servitude, combien que devant ton regne une seule partie de la terre n'eust peu se dire libre." In Belleforest: "*You took in Rome the title of emperor for the subjection of foreign nations.* But for us, you were born and nourished and crowned king and Augustus of the French. It is the fate of your nation to be envied for its valor by the cowardice and pusillanimity of others, *so much so that our liberty is the servitude of foreigners: there is no nation that could call itself free when you started to control the Empire*" (de Belleforest, *Histoire des Neuf Roys*, 76).

22. Ibid.

23. See Zeller, "Rois de France" (1964), 64–73.

24. Jean Du Tillet, *Recueil des roys de France . . . ensemble le rang des grands de France* (Paris: J. Houzé, 1602; first edition, 1580), 1: "Ceux qui ont escrit les François avoir esté d'origine vrays Germains, les ont plus honnorez, que ceux qui les ont estimez estre venus des Troyens, puisque l'honneur n'est deu qu'à la vertu. Car il n'y a eu nation qui moins ait souffert de corruption en ses bonnes mœurs, qui si fortement et longuement ait conservé sa liberté par armes que la Germanique."

25. The rehabilitation of the barbarians is a theme well developed by Kelley, *Foundations*, 203. The distinctions between Celtic, Gallic, and Germanic tendencies were important in the political context of the time. But since they have little impact on Charlemagne's representation, I chose not to develop them here.

26. Claude de Seyssel, *Grand'Monarchie de France* (Paris: Galliot Du Pré, 1557; first edition, Paris: R. Chauldière, 1519), chap. 12, fol. 13.

27. Claude de Seyssel, *Histoire singulière du roy Loys XII . . . faicte au parangon des règnes et gestes des autres roys de France ses prédécesseurs, particularisez selon leurs félicitez ou infélicitez* (Paris: G. Gorrozet, 1558), 8–9. First published in Latin in 1506, Seyssel published a French version (*Les Louenges du Roy Louis XII de ce nom . . .*) in 1508; in later editions the work was given the title *Histoire singulière*. See the preface that Jacques Poujol wrote in his edition of *La Monarchie de France* (Paris: Librairie d'Argences, 1961), 20–21; and Michael Sherman, "The Selling of Louis XII: Propaganda and Popular Culture in Renaissance France, 1498–1515" (Ph.D. diss., University of Chicago, 1974), 133–58. On the metaphor that turns the kingdom

into the body of a man, see Jean Céard, "Les Visages de la royauté en France, à la Renaissance," in *Les Monarchies*, ed. Emmanuel Le Roy Ladurie (Paris: Presses universitaires de France, 1986), 73–89.

28. Claude de Seyssel, *Histoire singulière*, 8–9. Needless to say, Seyssel does not push the metaphor to its logical consequence, death.

29. Ibid., 15: "Je ne veulx point pourtant nier qu'iceluy Charles le grand, & de force & de vaillance de sa personne, de science & doctrine, de vigueur & haltesse, de cueur & de grandeur, de seigneurie & de hault & victorieux faictz ne soit préféré au Roy Moderne, mais je veulx bien dire qu'iceluy roy Moderne en charité envers ses prédecessurs, en bienveillance & amour envers ses parens, en désir de bien traiter ses subiectz, & de les tenir en paix & en repos, en bonne administration de iustice, en continence & attemprance, & en félicité de son règne peult raisonnablement estre préféré audict Charles le grand."

30. Ibid., 25.

31. Ibid.

32. The first book was published in 1560. My references are to the Trévoux edition, *Les Œuvres d'Estienne Pasquier, contenant ses recherches de la France* (Amsterdam: Compagnie des libraires associez, 1723); reprinted in Geneva (Slatkine Reprints, 1971) and titled *Œuvres complètes*. See vol. 1 of the Slatkine edition. Among the studies on Pasquier the first that should be cited is that of Huppert, *Idée de l'histoire parfaite*, chap. 3, "Les recherches d'Estienne Pasquier," 31–76; see also the important article by Corrado Vivanti, "Les *Recherches de la France* d'Étienne Pasquier: L'Invention des Gaulois," in Nora, *Lieux de mémoire*, vol. 2, *La Nation*, part 1, 215–45.

33. See J. Russell Major, *From Renaissance Monarchy to Absolute Monarchy: French Kings, Nobles, and Estates* (Baltimore, Md.: Johns Hopkins University Press, 1994), 19–22.

34. Pasquier, *Recherches*, vol. 1, book 2, p. 12; on the three great races, see book 1, chap. 3, p. 11.

35. Ibid., book 2, chap. 1, p. 43: "And the Lombards, who under the same emperor at the instigation of Narses took over [the area of] Gaul on this side of the Alps, [an occupation that ended] only under our valorous Charlemagne, lasted only two hundred and ten years."

36. Here is the passage in which Pasquier strives to reconcile the grandeur of the Gauls and the arrival of the Franks: "The Gauls first took over a part of Germany. Then, with the coming of the Franks [*François*], the Germans then did the same to us. Since then, under Clovis and fairly long afterward under Charlemagne, Germany was reduced to complete submission [*obéissance*] to Gaul, and this situation lasted until around the time of the Ottonians. Thus kingdoms go from hand to hand, without, for all that, being lessened [*vilipendez*]" (ibid., book 1, chap. 7, p. 22).

37. Vivanti was the first to write of the "invention of the Gauls" by Pasquier in *Recherches*; on the same topic, see also Claude-Gilbert Dubois's *Celtes et Gaulois au XVIe siècle: Le Développement littéraire d'un mythe nationaliste. Avec l'édition critique d'un traité inédit de Guillaume Postel: De ce qui est premier pour réformer le monde* (Paris: J. Vrin, 1972).

38. The influence of the treatise of Étienne de la Boétie is quite clear here. In his *Discours de servitude volontaire*, tyranny is precisely the collective resignation of a people, who become dependent on the "will of a single person"; hence the second title of the treatise, *Contr'un* [Against One].

39. Pasquier, *Recherches*, book 2, chap. 9, p. 95, "De l'Ordre des douze Pairs de France et s'ils furent instituez par Charlemagne, comme la commune de nos Annalistes estime" [On the order of the twelve peers of France and whether they were instituted by Charlemagne, as our annalists generally believe]:

> La plus grande partie du peuple tient pour histoire trés-certaine, que l'Empereur Charlemagne pour asseurer son Estat, & gaigner le cœur des siens, donna presque semblable authorité qu'à soy à douze de ses principaux, à la charge toutesfois de se retenir la principale voix en chapitre. . . . Toutesfois il me semble que ceux qui ont esté de cet advis, ne digererent oncques bien la puissance de Charlemagne, ny comment les affaires de France se demenoient de son temps; car de ma part je ne presteray jamais consentement à ceux-cy. Et croy à bien dire que ce discours ait esté plustost emprunté de l'ignorance fabuleuse de nos Romans, que de quelque histoire authentique. Qu'ainsi ne soit, il est certain que Charlemagne gouvernoit ses pays de l'authorité de luy seul, & non de la necessité des Ducs & Comtes, lesquels pour lors n'estoient que simples Gouverneurs, & tels qu'il les deposoit à sa volonté . . .

See for instance book 2, chap. 2, p. 45, "Du Parlement Ambulatoire, et premiere introduction d'iceluy"; and book 3, chap. 29, p. 272, "De l'Université de Paris."

40. Ibid., book 3, chap. 6, pp. 172, 173.

41. Ibid., book 5, chap. 29, p. 507.

42. Ibid., book 5, chap. 29, p. 508.

43. Ibid.

44. This is the opinion of George Huppert, who, for instance, sees "a concession to the orthodox reader" (*Idée de l'histoire parfaite*, 46).

45. Pasquier, *Recherches*, book 6, chap. 1, p. 511.

46. Ibid., book 5, chap. 29, p. 509.

47. See above, pp. 115. It should be noted that here the bishop is Turpin instead of the bishop of Cologne as in Petrarch's story.

48. Pasquier, *Recherches*, book 5, chap. 29, pp. 510, 511.

49. Ibid., 510: "Quelque grandeur de souveraineté qui soit en un Roy, ores que comme homme, de fois à autres il s'eschape, si doit-il tousjours rapporter ses pensées à Dieu, & croire qu'il est le vray juge de nos actions, pour le punir quelquesfois en nous de nostre vivant, ou bien à nos enfans aprés nos decez. Chose que trouverez averée en ce que je discourray cy-aprés. N'attendez doncques de moy au recit de ce present suject, que des injustices, partialitez & divisions entre les peres & les enfans, guerres civiles de freres à freres, oncles qui malmenerent leurs neveus, tromperies entremeslées de cruautez, le tout basty par juste jugement de Dieu."

50. Ibid., 507.

51. Ibid., book 6, chap. 1, p. 511.

52. Ibid., book 5, chap. 25, p. 499.

53. Ibid., book 2, chap. 1, p. 46.

54. Ibid., book 3, chap. 4, p. 173.

55. Charles Du Moulin, *Traicté de l'origine progrez et excellence du royaume et monarchie des François et couronne de France*, in *Omnia quae extant opera*, vol. 2 (Paris: J.-B. Coignard, 1681), chap. 81, par. 1037.

56. Ibid., chap. 201, par. 1049. "The said Charlemagne . . . made a sacred and Catholic law, which is that only the books of the Holy Scriptures should be read in church. . . . Moreover, the said Charlemagne . . . instructed the bishops and priests . . . on the preaching of God's word, ordering these bishops not to allow the preaching to the people of any new thing they might have concluded that was not found in the Holy Scriptures [Ledit Charlemagne . . . a fait une sainte & Catholique Loy, sçavoir est, qu'en l'Église fussent leus les Livres de la Sainte Écriture seulement. . . . Davantage ledit Charlemagne . . . instruit les Évesques & Curez . . . à la predication de la parole de Dieu, enjoignant mesmes aux Évesques, qu'ils ne permissent aucuns controuver & prescher au peuple chose nouvelle de leurs sens, & non selon les Écritures Saintes]" (chap. 104, p. 1039). On Charlemagne as "Protestant prince" in Du Moulin, see Kelley, *Foundations*, 180.

57. On these combatants, see J. H. M. Salmon, *Society in Crisis: France in the Sixteenth Century* (New York: St. Martin's Press, 1975), chap. 9, "The Drift to Anarchy, 1574–1784," 198–233.

58. Denis Crouzet, *Les Guerriers de Dieu: La Violence au temps des troubles de religion, vers 1525–vers 1610* (Seyssel: Champ Vallon, 1990), 1:641. This work is essential for understanding of the wars of religion. In this passage the reference to an "impulse to return to the past [*une dynamique de retour en arrière dans le temps*]" is a citation that Crouzet took from A. Dupront, "Réformes et 'modernité,'" *Annales E. S. C.* 39, no. 4 (1984): 747–68; I am referring here to pp. 758–59.

59. François Hotman, *Francogallia*, text in Latin transcribed by Ralph E. Giesey, translated into English by J. H. M. Salmon (Cambridge: Cambridge University Press, 1972), 142; see also the translation into French, *La Gaule françoise: Nouvellement traduite de Latin en François. Édition premiere* (Cologne: Hierome Bertulphe, 1574), v; or the reprint, *Franco-gallia: Traduction de l'édition française de 1574*, ed. Antoine Leca (Aix-en-Provence: Presses universitaires d'Aix-Marseille, 1991; published without a date). Hotman first wrote this text in 1567 but did not publish it until 1573.

60. Hotman, *Francogallia*, 142: "ut mihi quidem nequaquam dubium esse videatur, quin ab illa certissimum tantorum malorum remedium petendum sit."

61. This theme is repeated often; for instance: "Nunc, ut ad institutum revertamur, incredibile dictu est, quam indigne atque acerbe Galli Romanorum latrocinia tulerint, quamque crebrae ab iis defectiones rebellionesque numerentur; quanquam cum per se satis virium ad depellendam Romanorum tyrannidem non haberent, vetus institutum tenebant, ut Germanos mercede conductos ad suum auxilium evocarent" (ibid., 178).

62. Ibid., 202, 208. Hotman borrows Tacitus's expression.

63. In his introduction to *Francogallia* Giesey points out that Hotman's attitude regarding the epoch in which the old constitution was supposed to have been lost, and particularly regarding the role of the assembly that the Estates-General was to embody later, remains somewhat inconsistent (ibid., 72, 87).

64. Ibid., 392–94.

65. Ibid., 346.

66. Ibid., 220.

67. Ibid., 242: ". . . eundem Carolum in suo testamento ius regum constituendorum populo Francico integrum illibatumque servasse." Hotman mentions the will often; see also pp. 264, 342, 390.

68. Ibid., 506. On Hotman's hostility toward parlements, see Giesey's introduction, 60, 72.

69. In fact, the only negative part of Charlemagne's reign, as Hotman describes it, lies in his imposition of a liturgy following the rites and customs of Rome.

70. On the publication of the capitularies, see Étienne Baluze, *Capitularia Regnum Francorum* (Paris: Quillau, 1780), 41–48.

71. While no one is talking about a real democracy, there are certainly sketches of an aristocratic republic not necessarily limited to the nobility in the narrow sense of the term.

72. Simon Goulart, *Mémoires de la Ligue, contenant les événemens les plus remarquables depuis 1576, jusqu'à la Paix accordée entre le Roi de France et le Roi d'Espagne, en 1598* (Amsterdam: Arkstée and Merkus, 1758), 1:3:

> Mais il semble que Dieu ait préparé & disposé . . . les Parties, les Juges, & l'occasion, pour réintegrer la Couronne aux vrais Successeurs de Charlemagne, . . . spoliés de l'héritage temporel par force & violence. . . .
>
> Il se voit à l'œil que la race des Capets est du tout abandonnée à sens réprouvé: les uns étans frappés d'un esprit d'étourdissement, gens stupides & de néant: les autres réprouvés de Dieu & des hommes, pour leur hérésie, proscrits & rejettés de la Sainte Communion Ecclésiastique.
>
> Au contraire les rejettons de Charlemagne sont verdoyans aimains la vertu, pleins de vigueur en esprit & en corps, pour exécuter choses hautes & louables.
>
> Les guerres ont servi pour accoître en dégrés, en honneur & prééminence: mais la paix les remettra dans leur ancien héritage du Royaume, avec le gré, consentement & élection de tout le peuple.

73. On this episode, see Frederic J. Baumgartner, *Radical Reactionaries: The Political Thought of the French Catholic League* (Geneva: Droz, 1975), 59. Baumgartner notes that the attribution of this document is at times controversial. But he argues that even if the Huguenots changed certain passages, the content agrees with other "Guisard" documents and thinking. The haste with which the Huguenots published this document might also point to the inefficacy of the Guises' strategy. In any case, Protestants saw in it a means of turning public opinion against the Guises.

74. Abbé Nicolas de Montreux, *L'Espagne conquise, par Charles le Grand, Roy de France: Première partie . . . par Ollenix du Mont-Sacré . . .* (Nantes: P. Doriou, 1597). Like Garnier and many others, the author was clearly inspired by Ariosto. See Alexander Cioranescu, *L'Arioste en France: Des origines à la fin du XVIIIe siècle* (Paris: Les Presses modernes, 1939; new edition, Slatkine, 1970), 199–200.

75. Robert Garnier, *Bradamante: tragi-comédie; Les Juifves: tragédie*, Classiques Garnier Series, ed. Marcel Hervier (Paris: Bordas, 1991), 108 (act V, scene

VII, v. 1878 in *Bradamante*). See Daniel Ménager, "Charlemagne dans la seconde moitié du seizième siècle: Entre l'histoire et la légende," in *La Chanson de geste et le mythe carolingien: Mélanges René Louis*, 2:1277–95.

76. This Huguenot propaganda poem is cited by Pierre de L'Estoile (December 1585) in *Mémoires-journaux*, ed. Gustave Brunet, Aimé Louis Champollion-Figeac, Eugène Halphen, et al. (Paris: Librairie des bibliophiles, 1875), 2:284.

77. However, he did not entirely reject him. In 1594 a response to the *Stemmatum* of François de Rosière was published, titled: *Extrait de la généalogie de Hugues, surnommé Capet, roy de France, et des derniers successeurs de la race de Charlemagne en France* (Paris: M. Patisson, 1594), which is attributed by Thou to Pontus de Tyard. It seeks to prove that the Capetians were Charlemagne's descendants on both sides (on the father's side, "Vidichind, the first king of the Saxons," is supposed to have married Berte, the daughter of Carloman). We should look at the book by Johann Wilhelm Stucki in the same light: *Carolus Magnus redivivus, hoc est Caroli Magni, Germanorum, Gallorum, Italorum et aliarum gentium monarchae potentissimi, cum Henrico M., Gallorum et Navarrorum rege florentissimo comparatio* . . . (Zurich: J. Wolphius, 1592). Stucki establishes a Plutarchan form of comparison between the great emperor and Henry IV, the new Charlemagne. The historian Thou criticizes the weakness of this genealogical and bookish response (see Frances A. Yates, *The French Academies of the Sixteenth Century* [London: Warburg Institute, 1947], 217).

78. Ludovico Ariosto, *Orlando Furioso*, trans. William S. Rose, ed. Stewart Baker and A. Bartlett Giamatti (Indianapolis and New York: Bobbs-Merrill, 1968), Canto XV, 25–26, p. 137.

79. See Corrado Vivanti, "Il mito dell'Ercole Gallico e gli ideali monarchici di *renovatio*," in *Lotta politica e pace religiosa in Francia fra Cinque e Seicento* (Turin: Giulio Einaudi, 1963), 74–131. In the case of Charlemagne, ancient traditions needed to be preserved; see also Philippe Desan, *Penser l'histoire à la Renaissance* (Caen: Paradigme, 1993), chap. 1, "Nationalism et histoire," 29–78.

80. See C. Vivanti, "Il mito," and D. Crouzet, *Les Guerriers de Dieu*, 2:574–84.

81. Pierre Boton, *Les Trois Visions de Childeric, quatriesme roy de France, pronostics des guerres civiles de ce Royaume* . . . (Paris: F. Morel, 1595). The poem is dedicated to Biron, marshal of France.

82. On this poem, see D. Grouzet, *Les Guerriers de Dieu*, 2:574–76.

CHAPTER FIVE. THE NATIONAL PAST IN THE CLASSICAL AGE

1. See the recent works on the classical models adapted by the monarchy: Jean-Pierre Néraudau, *L'Olympe du Roi-Soleil: Mythologie et idéologie royale au Grand Siècle* (Paris: Les Belles Lettres, 1986); Chantal Grell and Christian Michel, *L'École des princes ou Alexandre disgracié* (Paris: Les Belles Lettres, 1988).

2. See Néraudau, *Olympe du Roi-Soleil*, 63. Among the numerous depictions of Louis XIV as Apollo, the *Triomphe de Louis XIV* (1664) by Joseph Werner is a

spectacular example of this practice. As to Louis XIII, in the course of his *entrée* into Paris to celebrate the surrender of La Rochelle, we see him as Hercules on one of the triumphal arches; the frontispiece of the *Prince* by Guez de Balzac shows him dressed as *imperator*.

3. See Apostolidès, *Roi-Machine*, 8.

4. Literally, "for reasons of state." These are state policies that can be unjust or arbitrary and need not be justified to the public. *Trans.*

5. E. Gilson, ed. (Paris: Librairie philosophique J. Vring, 1947), 7, cited by Krzysztof Pomian, "Le Cartésianisme, les érudits et l'histoire," in *Archivium Historii Filozofii i Mysli Spolecznej* (1966), 12:175–204; see p. 182: "Même les histoires les plus fidèles, déclare-t-il dans son *Discours de la méthode*, si elles ne changent ni n'augmentent la valeur des choses, pour les rendre plus dignes d'être lues, au moins en omettent-elles presque toujours les plus basses et moins illustres circonstances; d'où vient que le reste ne paraît pas tel qu'il est, et que ceux qui règlent leurs mœurs par les exemples qu'ils en tirent, sont sujets à tomber dans les extravagances des Paladins de nos romans, et à concevoir des desseins qui passent leurs forces."

The English quotation used here is from René Descartes, *Discourse on the Method*, edited, translated, and introduced by George Heffernan, bilingual ed. (Notre Dame, Ind.: University of Notre Dame Press, 1994), 19–21. *Trans.*

6. Pomian, *Cartésianisme*, 184–85.

7. The *lit de justice* was a session of the parlement presided over in person by the king. *Trans.*

8. See Sarah Hanley, *The "Lit de Justice" of the Kings of France: Constitutional Ideology in Legend, Ritual, and Discourse* (Princeton, N.J.: Princeton University Press, 1983), 237–38.

9. This is the church of Saint-Paul-Saint-Louis, located in Paris on rue Saint-Antoine in the 4th *arrondissement*, next to the *Lycée* Charlemagne.

10. See Apostolidès, *Roi-Machine*, 76. On the *Retable du Parlement*, see this chapter, below.

11. The ambiguity concerning the issue of Charlemagne has never been better conveyed than by the frontispiece to Mézeray's chapter on his reign, which depicts a Roman Charlemagne face to face with a Franco-Gallic Charlemagne (figs. 16 and 17).

12. Scipion Du Pleix, *Histoire générale de France avec l'état de l'Église et de l'Empire* (Paris: C. Sonnius, 1939; first edition, 1621–1628), 297.

13. François Eudes de Mézeray, *Histoire de France depuis Faramond jusqu'à maintenant, œuvre enrichie de plusieurs belles et rares antiquitez et d'un Abrégé de la vie de chaque reyne, . . . le tout embelly d'un recueil nécessaire des médailles qui ont été fabriquées sous chaque règne et de leur explication* (Paris: M. Guillemot, 1643), 205.

14. Du Pleix, *Histoire générale*, 353.

15. Ibid., 298.

16. Ibid., 391.

17. De Mézeray, *Histoire de France*, 174.

18. Father Gabriel Daniel, preface to *Histoire de France depuis l'établissement de la monarchie française dans les Gaules*, vol. 1 (Paris: J.-B. Delespine, 1713; first edition, 1696), unnumbered page.

19. 1713 (first complete edition), 1722, 1729, 1742, 1755–1757.

20. Daniel, *Histoire de France*, 1:433, 441, 486.

21. Pierre Le Moyne, *De l'art de Régner* (Paris: Cramoisy, 1665), 42: "[L]a Vertu des Princes n'est pas contrainte & resserrée, comme celle des Particuliers, qui ne se déploye que dans leur Cabinet. Elle a tout le Royaume pour son Theatre, & tous les Sujets du Prince pour Spectateurs."

22. Daniel, *Histoire de France*, 1:555.

23. Ibid., "Épître au Roy," unnumbered page.

24. Ibid., 425:

Le Royaume des François parvenu au plus haut point de puissance où il ait jamais esté, une grande partie de l'Espagne, & presque toute l'Italie conquise; les Sarazins domptez; les bornes de la domination Françoise, & celles du Christianisme poussées bien au-delà du Danube & de la Theisse; la Dacie, la Dalmatie, l'Istrie soumises; les Nations barbares jusqu'à la Vistule, renduës tributaires; l'Empire d'Occident, avec toutes ses prérogatives, transferé dans la Maison de France; un État de cette étenduë gouverné avec application & autorité, & policé par les plus belles Loix tant Civiles qu'Ecclésiastiques; enfin une suite continuelle de victoires & de conquestes pendant l'espace de quarante-six ans, c'est là la carrière que m'ouvre le glorieux Règne de Charlemagne.

25. On these issues, see William Church, *Richelieu and Reason of State* (Princeton, N.J.: Princeton University Press, 1972); and the classic work by Étienne Thuau, *Raison d'État et pensée politique à l'époque de Richelieu* (Paris: A. Colin, 1966).

26. Letter of Louis XIII dated June 15, 1627, cited by Zeller, "Rois de France" (1624), 74.

27. See Church, *Richelieu*, 358–64. Among these jurists, Church cites Christophe Balthasar (or Balthazard), *Traité des usurpations des Roys d'Espagne sur la Couronne de France depuis Charles VIII. Ensemble un Discours sur le commencement, progrez, desclin et démembrement de la Monarchie Françoise, droits et prétentions des Roys Très-Chrestiens sur l'Empire* (Paris, 1625; enl. ed., 1626); Charles Hersent, *De la Souveraineté du Roy à Mets, pays Metsin, et autres villes et pays circonvoisins: qui estoient de l'ancien Royaume d'Austrasie ou Lorraine. Contre les prétensions de l'Empire, de l'Espagne et de la Lorraine, et contre les maximes des habitans de Mets, qui ne tiennent le Roy que pour leur Protecteur* (Paris, 1632); and, of course, Pierre Dupuy's work *Traitez touchant les droits du Roy Très Chrestien sur plusieurs estats et seigneuries possédés par divers princes voisins et pour prouver qu'il tient à juste titre plusieurs provinces contestées par les princes estrangers. Recherches, pour monstrer que plusieurs provinces et villes du royaume sont du domaine du Roy. Usurpations faites sur les trois éveschez Mets, Toul et Verdun; et quelques autres traitez concernant des matières publiques* (Paris, 1655); see also the analysis of Etienne Thuau, *Raison d'État*, 300–303.

28. Jacques De Cassan, *La Recherche des droicts du Roy, et de la Couronne de France sur les royaumes, duchez, comtez, villes et pays occupez par les Princes estrangers: Appartenans aux Roys Tres-Chrestiens, par Conquestes, Successions, Achasts, Donations, et autres Tiltres légitimes* . . . (Rouen: F. Vaultier et J. Besonge, 1643; first edition, Paris, 1632), 489.

29. Ibid., 493–94:

Sous le regne [de Charlemagne], les Saxons, peuple impatient de repos & de paix, pour se remettre en liberté, se voulurent emanciper derechef du devoir de l'obeyssance l'an 798. La guerre fut longue & sanglante: mais en fin Charlemagne avec l'assistance d'un Seigneur du pays nomme Vvidichind, remporta sur eux la victoire. . . . Les Huns & les Avares aussi qui sont les Hongres, lesquels pendant huict ans avoient fait la guerre à la France, furent subiuguez & vaincus, & leurs pays uny au Royaume de France. Les Sunois en outre, Sorabes, Abrodites, Vvesphales, qui avoient fait alliance en ceste guerre avec les Hongres, furent puissamment domptez par Charlemagne, lequel par ses glorieuses & illustres victoires, estendit les limites de son Royaume iusques aux plus reculees contrees du Nord: Car la Hongrie, l'Austriche, la Valachie, la Boëme, la Transsylvanie, la Pologne conquestees par sa valeur, enrichirent ses trophees, plus beaux & insignes que ceux du grande Alexandre. Le Danemarch aussi faisoit une partie de l'Estat de Charlemagne. . . .

30. Ibid., 497.

31. On the *reditus rex ad stirpem Karoli*, see above, pp. 79, 93.

32. De Cassan, *Recherche*, 508.

33. *La Voix gémissante du peuple chrestien et catholique accablé sous le faix des desastres et des misères des guerres de ce temps: addressée au Roy tres-chrestien par un François desinteressé* (Paris, 1640), 240; cited by Rudolf von Albertini, *Das politische Denken in Frankreich zur Zeit Richelieus* (Giessen: Simons Verlag Marburg, 1951), 154 n. 4, and reused by Thuau, *Raison d'Etat*, 303. I am following Thuau's analysis here.

34. De Cassan, *Recherche*, "Épître à Monseigneur le Cardinal de Richelieu," unnumbered page.

35. This plan of domination extended as far as the Ottoman Empire. W. Church and E. Thuau point out how the notion of France heading a new crusade against the Turks was in no way foreign to Richelieu's thought. Church, *Richelieu*, 292; Thuau, *Raison d'État*, 282–86.

36. On this issue, see Henri Vast, "Des tentatives de Louis XIV pour arriver à l'Empire," *Revue historique* 65 (September–December 1897): 1–45; and the article by Zeller, "Rois de France" (1964), 76–82.

37. *Louis XIV Mémoires, suivi de Réflexions sur le métier de Roi, Instruction au duc d'Anjou. Projet de harangue*, ed. Jean Longnon (Paris: Tallandier, 1978), 68. This is the point of view taken by Jacques Bénigne Bossuet in his *Discours sur l'histoire universelle*, written for the dauphin, as were Louis's memoirs: "I give you this establishment of a new empire under Charlemagne, as the end of ancient history, because it is here that you will see the final end of the Roman Empire" (*Discours sur l'histoire universelle* [Paris: S. Mabre-Cramoisy, 1681], 6).

38. Charles Sorel, *Divers traitez sur les droits et les prérogatives des roys de France tirez des Mémoires historiques et politiques de M.C.S.S.D.S.* (Paris: Société des marchands libraires du Palais, 1666), 2. On Sorel, see Orest Ranum, *Artisans of Glory: Writers and Historical Thought in Seventeenth-Century France* (Chapel Hill: University of North Carolina Press, 1980), 129–47.

39. Sorel, *Divers traitez*, 30, 57.

40. We know that the baron de Lisola wrote a response to Aubery, *Bouclier d'Estat et de Justice*, between May and July of 1667. See Paul von Schmidt, "Deutsche Publizistik in den Jahren 1667–1671," in *Mitteilungen des Instituts für österreichische Geschichtsforschung* (Innsbruck: Wagner'sche Universitäts-Buchhandlung, 1907), 28:577–630; on the controversy regarding the date of writing of *Bouclier*, see p. 584.

41. Antoine Aubery, *Des Justes Prétentions du Roy sur l'Empire* (Paris: A. Bertier, 1667), "Epistre au roi," unnumbered page:

> l'on a de tout temps considéré les Roys comme les Heros & des Demy-dieux, & l'on a toûjours creu que leur aspect avoit quelque chose, pour ainsi dire, de rayonnant qui imprimoit dans le coeur de leurs Sujects du respect & de la religion. Et ce qui est à remarquer, SIRE, ces sentimens & ces expressions avantageuses n'estoient pas le stile seulement du Paganisme, mais aussi le langage des Conciles & de Saints Peres; qui n'ont pas fait scrupule de traiter les Souverains de Sacrées Majestez, de nommer leurs regars splendeur celeste, en un mot de se prosterner à leurs pieds, ou pour user de leurs propres termes, d'adorer les pas de leurs Saintetez.

Already in 1649, Aubery had published a similar treatise, *De la Prééminence de nos roys, et de leur préséance sur l'empereur et le roy d'Espagne, traité historique* (Paris: M. Soly, 1649). Extracts from his *Justes Prétentions* were translated and published in German. On Aubery, see Charles Ancillon, *Mémoires concernant les vies et les ouvrages de plusieurs modernes célèbres dans la République des Lettres* (Amsterdam: Wetsteins, 1709), 357–77. Sorel's *Divers traitez* have also been translated into German. Emile Roy cites two editions, the first in 1668, the second in 1680 (*La Vie et les œuvres de Charles Sorel* [Paris: Hachette, 1891]).

42. A. Aubery, *Des Justes Prétentions*, 3.

43. Ibid., "Épistre au roi," unnumbered page.

44. Ibid., 15.

45. Ibid., 72.

46. Ibid., 43.

47. Ibid., 45, 60.

48. Baron François Paul de Lisola, *Bouclier d'Estat et de Justice, contre le dessein manifestement découvert de la Monarchie Universelle, sous le vain pretexte des pretensions de la Reyne de France*, new ed., 1667. In "Deutsche Publizistik in den Jahren 1667–1671," Paul von Schmidt cites among others Nicolaus Martini, *Libertas aquilae triumphans, sive De jure quod in imperium regi Galliarum nullum competit schediasma nuperis Auberii, Parlamenti parisiensis advocati, impugnationibus oppositum* (Frankfurt: C. Gerlachius and S. Beckenstein, 1668).

49. Jean-Louis Guez de Balzac, *Le Prince* (Paris: T. du Bray and P. Rocolet, 1632), 128–29: "Sur un simple soupçon, sur une legere deffiance, sur un songe qu'aura fait le Prince, pourquoy ne luy sera t'il pas permis de s'asseurer de ses Sujets factieux, & de se soulager l'esprit en leur donnant pour peine leur propre repos?"

50. Ibid., 80.

51. Ibid., 175.

52. Ibid., 130.

53. Cardin Le Bret, *De la Souveraineté du Roy* (Paris: J. Quesnel, 1632), 659.

54. Ibid., 658.

55. See Charles Jourdain, *Histoire de l'Université de Paris au XVIIe et au XVIIIe siècle* (Paris: Hachette, 1867), 218. Elsewhere in this work, Jourdain notes how a first attempt to make use of the Carolingian legacy occurred in the months following Louis XIII's victory at La Rochelle. In January 1629, Le Maistre, then rector, ordered the celebration of the feast of Saint Charlemagne in all of the schools of the university. His order was mostly ignored, thus proving that the time to reconnect with the great emperor had not returned (see p. 124).

56. César Egasse Du Boulay, *Historia Universitatis Parisiensis*, vol. 1 (Paris: F. Noel and P. de Bresche, 1665–1673), dedicatory epistle, unnumbered page.

57. In fact, all through the seventeenth century the university made use of any suitable occasion to mention its establishment by Charlemagne. Du Boulay seeks to provide decisive proof of these claims.

58. Du Boulay, *Historia Universitatis Parisiensis*, 1:91. "Nos igitur cum nouem prope seculorum fide indubitanter afferimus Carolum verè Magnum, omnium Regum maximum, sapientissimum, litteratissimum esse huius principis Academiae verè Parentem, Institutorem et Fundatorem. Non quod nullae fuissent omnino ante ipsum Litterae Lutetiae, fuisse enim supra demonstratum est; sed quia paucis cognitas et in Cœnobiis ac Claustris Episcopiisque latentes eduxit in lucem, seculares quodammodo reddidit et communes, easque proposuit omnibus ad amplectendum, quae solis fere viris Ecclesiasticis et Cœnobitis antea patebant." See also the dedicatory epistle: "Non enim ille Studiorum aeternitatem quam Barbarae Gentes in Galliam irrumptentes interruperant, restituendo, nominis duntaxat sui gloriam quaesivit, aut Regni Gallicani splendorem, sed id maximê, ut *apertâ publicâ litterarum Officinâ*, propositisque Privilegiis et Beneficiis ex omnibus Orbis Christiani partibus studiosos alliceret . . . ," unnumbered page; the *princeps Academia* is also the *Praecellens Academia* (1:92).

59. Jean Mabillon, *Traité des études monastiques divisé en trois parties, avec une liste des principales difficultez qui se rencontrent en chaque siècle dans la lecture de Originaux, et un Catalogue de livres choisis pour composer une Bibliotéque ecclesiastique* (Paris: Charles Robustel, 1691), 48.

60. Ibid., 52.

61. Ibid.

62. Mabillon often refers to Charlemagne in his works. In his article on Charlemagne and the University of Paris, Inge Jonsson shows that Mabillon did not reject all the ties between the Palace School founded by Alcuin and the Parisian schools. However, he did distinguish between these "academies" and the university ("Karl den store och Paris-universitetet," in *Vetenskapens träd: Idéhistoriska studier tillägnade Sten Lindroth* [Stockholm: Wahlstrom and Widstrand, 1774], 7–27); see pp. 22–23 on Mabillon.

63. Nathan Edelman describes well the extent to which the Middle Ages remained vital in the seventeenth century. His study *Attitudes of Seventeenth-Century France toward the Middle Ages* (New York: King's Crown Press, 1946) is still the best starting point for research on the medieval presence in the classical age. I owe many of the references on the following pages to him.

64. Charles Sorel, *Histoire Comique de Francion*, ed. Émile Roy (Paris: Hachette, 1924), 1:179–81:

> J'en achetois de certains livres que l'on appelle des Romants, qui contenoient des prouësses de certains Chevaliers. Il y avoit quelque temps qu'un de mes compagnons m'avoit baillé à en lire un de Morgant le Geant qui m'enchanta tout à fait: car je n'avois jamais rien leu que des Épistres familieres de Ciceron et les Comedies de Terence. L'on m'enseigna un Libraire du Palais qui vendoit plusieurs Histoires fabuleuses de la mesme sorte, et c'estoit là que je portois ma pecune: mais je vous asseure que ma chalandise estoit bonne, car j'avois si peur de ne voir jamais entre mes mains ce que je bruslois d'acheter, que j'en donnois tout ce que le marchand m'en demandoit. . . . Bref, je n'avois plus en l'esprit que rencontres, que Tournois, que Chasteaux, que Vergers, qu'enchantements, que delices, qu'amourettes: et lors que je me representois que tout cela n'estoit que fictions, je disois que l'on avoit tort neantmoins d'en censurer la lecture, et qu'il falloit faire en sorte que doresnavant l'on menast un pareil train de vie que celuy qui estoit descript dedans mes livres: là dessus je començois souvent a blasmer les viles conditions a quoy les hommes s'occupent en ce siecle, lesquelles j'ay aoujourd'huy en horreur tout a fait.

The first edition of the *Histoire comique* was published in 1632. It did not contain the reference to *Morgant le Géant*. Sorel added it to the 1626 edition, and it remained in all subsequent editions (twenty-two in all by the end of the seventeenth century) till Roy produced a critical edition based on the 1623 version. On Pulci, see above, p. 104–5.

65. *L'histoire de Morgant le geant et de plusieurs autres chevaliers et pairs de France, lequel avec ses freres persécutoient souvent les Chrestiens, et serviteurs de Dieu. Mais finalement furent ses deux freres occis par le Comte Roland, et le tiers fut chrestien, qui depuis ayda grandement à augmenter la saincte foy Catholique, comme entendrez cy après* (à Troyes, chez Nicolas Oudot, imprimeur demeurant en la rue nostre Dame, à l'Enseigne du Chappon d'Or Couronné, 1625).

66. See Roy, *La Vie et les œuvres de Charles Sorel*, 3–6.

67. This treatise was published in 1646 at the beginning of his *Histoire du roi Louis XIII* (Paris: Augustin Courbé, 1646), unnumbered page, by his uncle Charles Bernard, from whom Sorel had bought the position; see Ranum, *Artisans of Glory*, 132.

68. *Histoire de Morgant le geant*, chap. 43, "Comment Astolfo fut délivré d'estre pendu par Rolland et Regnault," unnumbered page:

> Monsieur & oncle, dit Roland, vous sçavez bien que vous estes cause des adversitez qui ores vous surviennent, car chacun sçait bien que mon cousin Regnault, & Astolfo le Seigneur d'Angleterre, & ceux de leur lignage vous ont servy loyallement, & en plusieurs lieux, & plusieurs fois vous ont exposé leurs corps, & mis leurs vies en danger contre les Sarrazins, & contre autres pour deffendre vostre droict, & pour soustenir vostre Royaume, & vous tenir en pax, & pour toute recompense à la requeste d'aucuns flatteurs & traistres, qui ne firent iamais que pourchassez vostre dommage, vous les bannissez de vostre Cour, & qui pis est les voulez faire mourir au gibet, comme si c'estoient des

larrons: parquoy ie ne suis pas esbahy, si Regnault & ses parens se veulent venger, veu qu'ils sont forts & puissans, car ie ne sçache si petit, qui n'appellast vengeance de ceux qui leur font mal pour bien.

69. We know these dates thanks to surviving copies. It is possible that other editions existed that did not survive. *Huon de Bordeaux* was also frequently published in the seventeenth century (1606, 1626, 1634, 1636, 1666, 1675, 1676, 1679, 1683, 1705). See Léon Gautier, *Les Épopées françaises: Étude sur les origines et l'histoire de la littérature nationale*, 2d ed., 5 vols. (Paris: Société générale de librairie catholique, 1878–1897). It should be noted that the 1525 edition of *Galien* had a more pessimistic ending in that Guimarde, Galien's wife, did not produce any heir. Thus the union (through ties of vassalage) of the empires of the East and the West does not last. At the death of his wife, Galien, overcome with grief, returns to Roncevaux to die. Thus Roncevaux ends up by taking away even this hope of renewal of the aristocracy (*Les Nobles prouesses et vaillances de Galien restaure filz du noble Olivier le marquis, et de la belle Jacqueline fille du roy Hugon empereur de Constantinople* [Lyon: Claude Nourry, 1525], Arsenal 4 B.L. 4265). Though works dealing with Charlemagne continued to be published, the number of different romances diminished during the seventeenth century. See Edelman, *Attitudes of Seventeenth-Century France*, 152–54; and Doutrepont, *Les Mises en prose des Épopées et des Romans chevalresques du XIVe au XVIe siècle*, chap. 1.

70. On the issue of the readers of this literature, which has at times been too easily classified as "popular," see especially Henri-Jean Martin, "Culture écrite et culture orale, culture savante et culture populaire dans la France d'Ancien Régime," *Journal des savants* (July–December 1975): 225–82; Roger Chartier, "La Culture populaire en question," *Histoire* 8 (1981): 68–90; Raymond Birn, "Deconstructing Popular Culture: The *Bibliothèque bleue* and Its Historians," *Australian Journal of French Studies* 23, no. 1 (January–April 1986): 31–47.

71. Sorel, *Histoire comique*, 1:148.

72. See above, p. 100.

73. Jean Chapelain, *De la lecture des vieux romans*, ed. Alphonse Feillet (Paris: Aubry, 1870), 27: "combien les siècles plus voisins du nôtre, à mesure qu'ils se sont approchés de la lumière, se sont reculés de la vertu, et considérer dans quels désordres de vie et de corruption les âmes y sont tombées."

74. Paul Festugière, ed., *Œuvres de J.-Fr. Sarasin* (Paris: E. Champion, 1926), 2:146–232; I am quoting here from pp. 172–73.

75. Ibid., 208–209.

76. *Perceforêt* is a vast anonymous composition in prose dating from the middle of the fourteenth century.

77. Chapelain, *De la lecture*, 12, 16.

78. I should mention the enormous popularity of *Amadis de Gaule*, which in its own way cultivated the taste for the Middle Ages.

79. On Ariosto's fate in the seventeenth century, see Cioranescu, *Arioste en France*.

80. Gautier de Coste de la Calprenède, *La Bradamante, tragi-comédie* (Paris: A. de Sommaville, 1637), 9: " Je ne me plaindrois pas d'avoir cent mille fois, / Pour

le bien de l'Estat sué sous le harnois, / . . . /Si vous laissiez agir le sang & la raison, /
Si j'estois absolu dans ma seule maison. / . . . / J'intercede sans fruit pour une ingrate fille, / Au lieu d'estre absolu sur toute ma famille."

81. Ibid., 15.

82. Jean de Mairet, *Le Roland furieux, tragi-comédie* (Paris: A. Corbé, 1640),
act 5, p. 104; the permit is dated February 1631. It is thought that the play was performed in 1638; see Cioranescu, *Arioste en France*, 1:339–40; and Henry Carrington
Lancaster, *A History of French Dramatic Literature in the Seventeenth Century*, 5 parts
in 9 volumes (Baltimore, Md.: Johns Hopkins University Press, 1929–1942), part 2,
The Period of Corneille, 1635–1651, 1:225–27.

83. In this period, when Versailles claimed to be the capital of the world, Jordaens painted his famous painting *Charlemagne Receiving the Ambassador of Hārūn
ar-Rashīd at Aachen* (fig. 13).

84. Cited by Charles I. Silin, *Benserade and His Ballets de cour*, Johns Hopkins
Studies in Romance Literature and Languages (Baltimore, Md.: Johns Hopkins
University Press, 1940), extra volume 15, 282–83:

> Voicy la fine Fleur de la Chevalerie,
> Qui passe de bien loin nos Heros fabuleux
> En belles actions comme en galanterie;
>   Enfin ce Prince merveilleux,
> Que l'Amour suit par tout, que la Gloire accompagne,
>   Est le pur sang de Charlemagne.

> ———

> Qu'il danse ou qu'il combate, aussi-tost, qu'il paroist
> L'on voit par dessus tout sa grandeur heroïque;
> C'est l'honneur & l'appui de l'Ordre dont il est,
>   La Chevalerie est antique,
> Et je la croy du temps de ses premiers Ayeux;
>   Mais le Chevalier n'est pas vieux.

> ———

> La Guerre & la Discorde en nos jours étouffées,
> Sans sa Teste & son Bras seroient encor debout,
> Il a fait de leur chûte un comble à ses Trophées:
>   Bref il a pacifié tout:
> Et nous donnant la Paix, & se donnant *Therese*,
>   A mis tout le monde à son aise.

> ———

85. Gabriel Gilbert, *Les Amours d'Angélique et de Médor, tragi-comédie* (Paris:
G. Quinet, 1664), 70–71.

86. Ibid., unnumbered page.

87. *Les Plaisirs de l'Ile enchantée, fêtes galantes et magnifiques, faites par le Roi à
Versailles, le 7e mai 1665*, in *Œuvres de Molière*, ed. Eugène Despois and Paul Mes-

nard, Les Grands Ecrivains de la France (Paris: Hachette, 1878), 4:89–128; see p. 120: "Mille climats divers qu'on vit sous la puissance / De tous les demi-dieux dont elle prit naissance, / Cédant à son mérite autant qu'à leur devoir, / Se trouveront un jour unis sous son pouvoir. / Ce qu'eurent de grandeurs et la France et l'Espagne, / Les droits de Charles-Quint, les droits de Charlemagne, / En elle avec leur sang heureusement transmis, / Rendront tout l'univers à son trône soumis."

88. Ibid., 115. See Néraudau, *Olympe du Roi-Soleil*, 52–53.

89. *Roland, tragédie-lyrique en cinq actes*, in *Œuvres choisies de Quinault*, vol. 1 (Paris: Didot, 1811), act 5, scene 3, p. 216. Étienne Gros thinks that Quinault made use of Mairet's *Roland furieux* (*Philippe Quinault: Sa vie et son œuvre* [Paris: E. Champion, 1926], 584 n. 1).

90. Father Noel Alexandre, "De Translatione Imperii à Graecis ad Carolum Magnum," in *Selecta historiae ecclesiasticae capita, et in loca ejusdem insignia dissertationes historicae, chronologicae, criticae, dogmaticae* (Paris: Antonius Dezaller, 1681), 15:1–20.

91. Joseph de Jouvancy, *Carolus Magnus* (Paris: Ex typographia Antonii Lambin, 1684), also attributed to Father Jacques de La Baune; see Edelman, *Attitudes of Seventeenth-Century France*, 197. A copy of the manuscript of this tragedy is kept in the archives of the city of Paris.

92. Letter to the Duke of Beauvillier (between 1690 and 1695), in *Correspondance de Fénelon: Lettres antérieures à l'épiscopat 1670–1695*, ed. Jean Orcibal, vol. 2, *Texte établi* (Paris: Klincksieck, 1972), 320.

93. Orcibal believes that it was Seignelay, Beauvillier's brother-in-law and state secretary for the navy and the house of the king, who asked Fénelon to write Charlemagne's history.

94. There were several reasons for this animosity: the extension of the *régale* to the whole of the kingdom, that is, the king's right to collect revenues (temporal *régale*) and to appoint benefices (spiritual *régale*) as each episcopal see became vacant, as well as tax-free status for the neighborhood around the French embassy in Rome. On the relationship between church and state during this period, see Jean Orcibal, *Louis XIV contre Innocent XI: Les Appels au futur concile de 1688 et l'opinion française* (Paris: J. Vrin, 1949).

95. Orcibal, *Correspondance de Fénelon*, vol. 3, *Commentaires*, 475–76.

96. La Teulière, letter to M. de Villacerf, Rome, August 1691, in *Correspondance des Directeurs de l'Académie de France à Rome avec les Surintendants des bâtiments*, ed. Anatole de Montaiglon (Paris: Charavay frères, 1887), 1:209–11. As we have seen above (p. 108), the Italians were not completely mistaken in thinking that François I was the subject of the painting representing the coronation. To my knowledge, the plan of having two tapestries made of the copies of the paintings was never carried out.

97. "Note de Mignard [?] pour M. de Villacerf, 27 septembre 1691. Réponse à la lettre escrite par M. de la Teulière, dattée de Rome le 28e aoust 1691," in Montaiglon, *Correspondance*, 222. This topic recurs in the correspondence all through the years 1692 and 1693.

98. On the polemic between the ancients and the moderns and "public opinion," see Marc Fumaroli, 'La République des Lettres (IV): De Descartes à Fontenelle: La Querelle des Anciens et des Modernes,' in *Annuaire du Collège de*

France, 1990–1991, résumé des cours et travaux, 91st year (Paris: Collège de France, 1991), 505–32.

99. The Academy of Painting and Sculpture had been reorganized in 1664. Already in 1660, in his painting *Allégorie de l'alliance de Louis XIV avec Philippe d'Espagne,* Van Thulden had represented Louis XIV holding "Charlemagne's scepter." On the scepter, see above, p. 96 .

100. Louis le Laboureur [?], *Response au libelle intitulé: Bons advis, sur plusieurs mauvais advis* (n.p., 1650).

101. Louis le Laboureur, *Charlemagne: Poëme heroïque* (Paris: L. Billaine, 1664), 2–3:

Voicy le Grand CONDÉ qui me montre le ROY.
. . . .
   Á genoux, je le voy, salüons ses auspices,
Et n'ayons plus de peur de tant de precipices.
Pour nous ce demy-Dieu se declare aujourd'huy,
Il est des Chantres saints le Soutien & l'Appuy.
On le void maintenant, ce Potentat supréme,
Se delasser chez eux des soins du Diadéme,
Et prenant ses plaisirs à leurs sçavans accords
Leur ouvrir so Palais, & méme se Thresors.
. . . .
De l'Apllon François que je viens d'implorer,
C'est le divin flambeau qui veut bien m'éclairer.
Qu'à propos, ô CONDÉ tu m'as montré ce Phare!
Sous luy je ne crains point que ma Muse s'égare. . . .

This edition includes a long theoretical preface on the nature of the epic and the first three *chansons.* A second edition enlarged with three *chansons* appeared in 1666. The poem would be summarized in prose, along with both harsh critiques and praise, in the *Biblothèque universelle des romans* (August 1777); see below, pp. 237–40.

102. Nicolas Courtin, *Charlemagne, ou le Rétablissement de l'Empire romain, poème héroique* (Paris: T. Jolly, 1666), 3:

Mais croy qu'en ce Heros dont je forme l'Image,
C'est toy que je contemple, & toy que j'envisage.
. . . .
Et que si Charlemagne est l'objet de mes veilles,
Si j'éleve ma voux pour chanter ses merveilles,
C'est qu'en toy je contemple avec un noble excés
Et les mémes vertus, & les mémes succés.
N'est-tu pas ce qu'il fut? . . .

Courtin dedicates his poem to Pierre du Cambout de Coislin.

103. Ibid.

104. A first draft of the poem was published in 1653 under the title *Saint Louis ou le héros chrétien*. This first version included only seven books. These were heavily edited for the 1658 edition, which included eighteen books.

105. Another version was published in 1673.

106. On seventeenth-century epic poetry, see David Maskell, *The Historical Epic in France: 1500–1700* (London: Oxford University Press, 1973).

107. Chapelain, *De la lecture*, 13.

108. On these issues, see Maskell, *Historical Epic,* and Marc Fumaroli, "Entre Athènes et Cnossos: Les Dieux païens dans Phèdre," *Revue d'histoire littéraire de la France* 93, no. 1 (January–February 1993): 30–61 (see especially pp. 30–45).

109. Louis le Laboureur, *Les Avantages de la langue françoise sur la langue latine,* 1st ed. (Paris: Florentin Lambert, 1667; 2d ed. enl., Paris: Guillaume de Luyne, 1669); I am using the 1669 edition. On this topic, see the fine article by Marc Fumaroli, "L'Apologétique de la langue française classique," *Rhetorica: A Journal of the History of Rhetoric* 2, no. 2 (summer 1984): 139–61; I am referring here to page 147; see also Fumaroli, "République des Lettres."

110. Le Laboureur, *Avantages,* 16.

111. Ibid., 19. In his study "Apologétique," Fumaroli brings out the maternal element that emerges from Le Laboureur's description of the French language. Though I am not denying the presence of the maternal aspect, I emphasize in contrast here the focus on the virile and conquering nature Le Laboureur attributes to the French language. In fact, Le Laboureur's French possesses all the advantages of androgyny.

112. Le Laboureur, *Avantages,* 25.

113. Ibid., 205–206.

114. Le Laboureur, preface to *Charlemagne,* unnumbered page.

115. Le Laboureur, *Avantages,* 40: "Vous avez pû entendre parler du Poëme de Charlemagne, je ne vous en diray que seize vers tout au plus, qui parlent de l'enchantement de ce Heros; où pour faire entendre ce que c'étoit que ce charme qui l'avoit horriblement assoupy, je touche la circulation du sang; où j'explique le cours des esprits qui montent du cœur au cerveau; & où je montre comme se fait la veille et le sommel; & comme enfin les pores étant fermez, & ne se faisant plus de transpiration, ce Prince n'avoit pas besoin de nourriture, & pouvoit demeurer, longtemps en cet état sans mourir. C'est ainsi que je satisfais à tant de choses difficiles."

116. Ibid., 12.

117. Géraud de Cordemoy, "Discours prononcé le même jour 12 Decembre 1675 par Monsieur de Cordemoy, lorsqu'il fut reçû à la place de Monsieur de Balesdens," in *Receuil des harangues prononcées par Messieurs de l'Académie Françoise dans leurs réceptions, & en d'autres occasions differentes, depuis l'establissement de l'Académie jusqu'à present* (Paris: Jean-Baptiste Coignard, 1698), 274–80; I am quoting here from p. 275: "Charlemagne qui fut sans contredit le plus gran Capitaine, le plus sage Prince, & l'un des plus sçavans hommes de son temps, avoit si bien reconnu ce défaut, qu'aprés avoir fait recuëillir tout ce que l'on avoit écrit des François, jusques alors, il commença luy même une grammaire de leur langue, & ce fut apparemment un des sujets qui l'obligerent à former dans son Palais meme cette belle Académie, où toutes les personnes de sa Cour, en qui il remarqua de la politesse & de l'amour pour les belles lettres, furent appellées."

118. Ibid., 276.

119. Géraud de Cordemoy, *Histoire de France par M. de Cordemoy, Conseiller du Roy, lecteur ordinaire de Monseigneur le Dauphin, de l'Academie Française* (Paris: Jean-Baptiste Coignard, 1685), 579: "Ce Palais étoit magnifique; & un Auteur, pour en marquer la grandeur & les commoditez, dit qu'il y avoit des portiques sous galeries voutées, sous lesquelles tous les soldats & les autres personnes qui avoient accoûtumé d'être dans la Cour, se pouvoient mettre à couvert: que les Seigneurs avoient des appartemens audessus de ces galeries; & que tout étoit disposé de sorte, que Charles pouvoit voir de son appartement, tous ceux qui entroient dans les autres appartemens, ou qui en sortoit." This description draws from Notker; see above, pp. 36–37.

120. Perhaps Courtin sought Coislin's protection because of the latter's tolerance. Issued from an old family from Brittany, Coislin distinguished himself through his great piety but also through his efforts to ward off the king's persecution of the Protestants after the Edict of Nantes.

121. On the question of the heightening of God's transcendence leading to a "loosening of the dependence toward him," see Marcel Gauchet, *Le Désenchantement du monde: Une Histoire politique de la religion* (Paris: Gallimard), chap. 3, "Dynamique de la transcendance," 47–80.

122. The English translation is from Pascal's *Pensées*, translated and with an introduction by Martin Turnell (New York: Harper and Brothers, 1962), 283. The French is from *Pensées sur la religion et sur quelques autres sujets*, ed. Louis Lafuma, 3 vol. (Paris: Éditions du Luxembourg, 1952), vol. 1, 196: "De tous les corps et esprits, on n'en saurait tirer un mouvement de vraie charité cela est impossible, et d'un autre ordre surnaturel." On the connection between Pascal's thought and the representation of the king, see Louis Marin, *Le Portrait du roi* (Paris: Éditions de Minuit, 1981), chap. 1.

123. Nicolas Courtin, *Poésies chrétiennes. Charlemagne pénitent. Les IV fins de l'homme, où il est traité de la Mort, du Jugement dernier, du Paradis, et de l'Enfer avec La chute du Premier homme* (Paris: Charles de Sercy, 1687), 9–10:

> S'il fait bâtir un Temple, ou fonde un Monastere,
> Son nom sur la Façade en brillant caractere;
> Gravé par le ciseau d'un habile Sculpteur,
> Apprend que Charlemagne en est e Fondateur.
>   S'il nourrit l'Indigent, s'il a soin du Malade;
> De ces humbles emplois ce Prince fait parade;
> Et s'il veut reformer les abus de son tems,
> Un peu d'orgueil se mêle à ces soins éclatans.

124. Ibid., 16: "Plus son merite est rare, & son prix éclatant / Et plus ses actions rendent son nom illustre, / Plus il en doit cacher la valeur et le lustre."

125. Ibid., 79.

126. Ibid., 119.

127. "Celuy que les Destins pour regner ont fait naistre, / Est du Sceptre qu'il tient plus esclave que maistre, / Il n'est plus à luy-même, il est à ses Vassaux; / Il leur doit ses conseils, ses soins, & ses travaux."

128. Courtin, *Charlemagne*, "A Monseigneur l'illustrissime et révérendissime Pierre du Cambout de Coislin . . . ," unnumbered page.

129. Le Laboureur, *Charlemagne*, 75: "Mais à nous autres Rois ce point est d'importance, / C'est de connoistre l'homme, & de voir ce qu'il pense; / Fay-moy comme par tout penetrer dans son coeur, / Et joins à tant de biens ce suprème bonheur."

130. Ibid., 76: "Mais avant qu'on s'y fie, il faut bien discerner / S'il se donne en effet, ou feint de se donner; / Car il trompe souvent, & croit le pouvoir faire / Si son joug l'incommode, & n'est pas volontaire: / Il ne croit point alors pecher contre les loix, / Mais se faire justice, & rentrer dans ses droits."

131. Ibid.

132. I owe a great deal in the following discussion to Harold A. Ellis, *Boulainvilliers and the French Monarchy: Aristocratic Politics in Early-Eighteenth-Century France* (Ithaca, N.Y.: Cornell University Press, 1988), 41–44. See also Sarah Hanley, *The "Lit de Justice" of the Kings of France*, and Roland Mousnier, *Les Institutions de la France sous la monarchie absolue: 1598–1789*, vol. 1, *Société et État* (Paris: Presses universitaires de France, 1974), 120–25.

133. This quote is taken from the letters of the peerage-duchy of Chatillon of 1648; quoted by Father Pierre de Guibours Anselme de Sainte Marie, *Histoire généalogique et chronologique de la Maison royale de France, des pairs, grands officiers de la Couronne, et de la Maison du Roi et des anciens barons du royaume*, 3d ed. (Paris: La Compagnie des libraires, 1726–1733), 5:784 (reprints: Paris: Éditions de Palais Royal; New York: Johnson Reprint Co., 1967); quoted by Jean-Pierre Labatut, *Les Ducs et pairs de France au XVIIIe siècle* (Paris: Presses universitaires de France, 1972), 33. On the conflict between the dukes and the peers with the presidents *à mortier*, see pp. 407–19.

134. "But when [the king] is present in person, then they do not represent him anymore and cease to preside; and it is [the king] who presides over the peers as well as the rest of the assembly, [the king] being accompanied by his peers, who are his first advisers and the principal members of the body politic of which the king is the chief and who can never be separated from each other" ("Second memoire des pairs de France," in *Recueil des écrits qui ont esté faits sur le differend entre Messieurs les Pairs de France et Messieurs les Présidens au Mortier du Parlement de Paris, pour la maniere d'opiner aux Lits de Justice, avec l'arrest donné par le Roy en son Conseil en faveur de Messieurs les Pairs en 1664* [Paris: n.p., 1664], 4); see also Labatut, *Les Ducs et pairs de France*, 411, and Ellis, *Boulainvilliers and the French Monarchy*, 42.

135. Courtin, *Charlemagne*, "A Monseigneur l'illustrissime et révérendissime Pierre du Cambout de Coislin," unnumbered page.

136. Séguier, the chancellor of France, instead of accepting the king's first inclination to make his domain of Villemor into a peerage-duchy, begged Louis XIV to confer instead this dignity to Armand du Cambout, "eldest son of his eldest daughter" (Labatut, *Les Ducs et pairs de France*, 97).

137. The expression "genealogical consciousness" comes from Ellis, *Boulainvilliers*.

138. André Grellet-Dumazeau thinks that Le Laboureur himself wrote the briefs of 1664 (*L'Affaire du bonnet et les Mémoires de Saint-Simon* [Paris: Plon-Nourrit, 1913], 27); see also Ellis, *Boulainvilliers*, 39–40.

139. De Mézeray, *Histoire de France*, 164; see also, for instance, the chapter devoted to Clovis, "Clovis elected with the consent of the people and the armies," 29.

140. Jean Le Laboureur, *Histoire de la pairie de France et du Parlement de Paris, où l'on traite aussi des électeurs de l'Empire et du cardinalat* (London: S. Harding, 1740), 1–2.

141. Ibid., 2.

142. Ibid., 17.

143. Ibid., 79.

144. Ibid., 81.

145. Ibid., 86.

146. Ibid., 149.

147. Ibid., 150.

CHAPTER SIX. SAVING THE MONARCHY, ESTABLISHING THE REPUBLIC

1. Mona Ozouf, "La Révolution française et la formation de l'homme nouveau," in *L'Homme régénéré: Essai sur la Révolution française* (Paris: Gallimard, 1989).

2. Victor Riqueti, marquis de Mirabeau, *L'Ami des hommes, ou Traité de la population* (Avignon: n.p., 1756, first edition 1744), part 2, chap. 3, p. 34: "*Les loix de la création, conservation et régénération sont toujours les mêmes*: c'est pour nous le grande modèle. Les souverains, images ici-bas de la divinité, ne sçauroient trop l'imiter dans cette respectable uniformité. Mais de même que selon les loix mêmes de la nature, la masse physique s'altere en certaines parties, tandis qu'elle profite dans d'autres, le corps politique éprouve de semblables variations, et l'attention du régisseur général doit être de le suivre dans ses changemens de détail pour remédier au mal inévitable, pour ramener le bien possible." On the theme of regenerated man at the time of the Revolution, see Ozouf, "Révolution française," 116–57.

3. See above, pp. 38–42. On the development of historiography during the seventeenth and eighteenth centuries, see the works of Blandine Barret-Kriegel, *Les Historiens et la monarchie*, particularly vol. 1, *Jean Mabillon*, and vol. 3, *Les Académies de l'histoire* (Paris: Presses universitaires de France, 1988); Madeleine Laurain, "Les Travaux d'érudition des mauristes: Origine et évolution," in *Mémorial du XIVe centenaire de l'abbaye de Saint-Germain-des-Prés* (Paris: J. Vrin, 1959), 231–71; Henri Duranton, "La Recherche historique à l'Académie des inscriptions: L'Exemple de l'Histoire de France," in *Historische Forschung im 18. Jahrhundert: Organisation, Zielsetzung, Ergebnisse*, ed. Karl Hammer and Jürgen Voss, Pariser Historische Studien (Bonn: Ludwig Röhrscheid, 1976), 13:207–35; and, in the same volume, Bruno Neveu, "Mabillon et l'historiographie gallicane vers 1700: Érudition ecclésiastique et recherche historique au XVIIe siècle," 27–81.

4. See above, pp. 184–87.

5. Denis Richet, "Autour des origines idéologiques lointaines de la Révolution française: Élites et despotisme," *Annales E.S.C* 24 (January–February 1969): 1–23; François Furet, "Deux légitimations historiques de la société

française au XVIIIe siècle: Mably et Boulainvilliers," in *Atelier de l'histoire* (Paris: Flammarion, 1982), 165–85; Johnson Kent Wright, "Les Sources républicaines de la Déclaration des droits de l'homme et du citoyen," in *Le Siècle de l'avènement républicain*, ed. F. Furet and M. Ozouf (Paris: Gallimard, 1993), 128–64; see particularly pp. 128–36.

6. Henri de Boulainvilliers, *Histoire de l'ancien gouvernement de France, avec XIV lettres historiques sur les parlements ou états généraux* (The Hague and Amsterdam, 1727), 210.

7. Ibid., 69: "*Ce ne sont plus les François, nez libres & indépendans*, attachez à leurs anciennes Loix plus qu'à leur propre vie, *qui élisoient leurs Rois & leurs Généraux avec une parfaite liberté*, & qui jouissaient avec gloire & tranquillité d'une conquête qu'ils ne devoient qu'à leur seule valeur & à leur perseverance dans une entreprise infiniment difficile: *ils sont à leur tour devenus la conquête, non pas d'une Nation étrangere, mais d'une famille particuliere, pareille aux leurs dans son origine, laquelle plus ambitieuse & plus active a su tirer ses avantages de tous les évenemens & de toutes les circonstances qui se sont passés durant un siecle.*"

8. See Harold A. Ellis, *Boulainvilliers and the French Monarchy*, 92–206.

9. Boulainvilliers, *Histoire*, 224.

10. Ibid., 207: "J'en reviens donc à dire qu'il faut remonter au siècle de Charlemagne, pour trouver cet heureux tems. C'est là où l'on voit une intime union de tous les Membres avec leur Chef, une parfaite unanimité de sentimens, & une correspondance mutuelle pour le bien commun: le Prince ayant été aussi attentif à conserver les Droits des Sujets, que les Sujets zélez à concourrir à la gloire & à la puissance du Prince."

11. Ibid., 72, 213–14.

12. Ibid., 217.

13. On the importance of finding the originary moment in history, see Brian C. Singer's interesting comments in *Society, Theory, and the French Revolution: Studies in the Revolutionary Imaginary* (New York: St. Martin's Press, 1986), 100–103.

14. Boulainvilliers, *Histoire*, 217: "qu'ils avaient vu en Europe un Peuple de Rois, auquel obeissoit un grand nombre de Nations; que ce Peuple avoit en sa disposition de nombreuses armées couvertes d'or & de fer; que ces Rois avoient pourtant un Chef qui étoit le Rois des Rois, & que néanmoins eux & lui ne vouloient jamais que la même chose; qu'ils obeissoient pourtant tous à ce Chef, quoiqu'en un sens ils fussent libres & Rois comme lui."

15. Ibid., 108.

16. Ibid., 109–10.

17. Ibid., 209.

18. Ibid., 219.

19. Ibid., 113.

20. Ibid., 226; see also, for instance, p. 239.

21. Ibid., 240, 245.

22. Ibid., 116.

23. Ibid., 236.

24. Ibid., 230.

25. Ibid., 116–17.

26. Ibid., 271–72.

27. Lionel Grossman, *Medievalism and the Ideologies of the Enlightenment: The World and Work of La Curne de Sainte-Palaye* (Baltimore, Md.: Johns Hopkins University Press, 1968); see, for instance, p. 279.

28. "Discours sur les anciennes sépultures de nos rois," in *Mémoires de littérature tirés des registres de l'Académie Royale des Inscriptions et Belles Lettres* (*MAI*) (Paris: Imprimerie royale, 1717), 2:684–700.

29. On this legend and its origins, see above, pp. 5–8.

30. "Dissertation dans laquelle on tâche de démêler la véritable origine des François par un parallele de leurs mœurs avec celle des Germains,"*MAI*, 2:611–50; on Charlemagne, see pp. 635–36.

31. *MAI*, 12:2.

32. "Mémoire concernant les principaux monumens de l'histoire de France, avec la Notice et l'Histoire des Chroniques de Saint-Denys," in *MAI*, 15:580–616; see p. 584.

33. "Dissertation de l'establissement des lois somptuaires parmis les français," in *MAI* (Paris: Imprimerie royale, 1729), 6:727–38. Essay read to the Academy on May 3, 1720. On Charlemagne, see pp. 729–32; here I am quoting from p. 729.

34. On Notker, see above, pp. 27–38.

35. Vertot, *MAI*, 6:730.

36. On January 25, 1726, for instance, Foncemagne read an essay that aimed to prove that the monarchy was already hereditary in the first dynasty: "Pour establir que le Royaume de France a esté succesif-héréditaire dans la Première Race" (*MAI*, 8:464), in which he responds to Vertot's claims; on April 22, 1732, he presented a critique of Boulainvilliers: "Examen critique d'une opinion de M. le Comte de Boulainvilliers sur l'ancien gouvernement de la France," in *MAI*, 10:525–41. See above, pp. 134–36.

37. Jean-Baptiste Du Bos, *Histoire critique de l'établissement de la Monarchie françoise dans les Gaules*, new ed., revised, corrected, and enlarged, 2 vols. in 4 (Paris: Didot, 1742), 2:382–90; on the alliance between the Franks and the Romans, see 1:168–73. On Du Bos and the Romanist school, see Alfred Lombard, *L'Abbé Du Bos: Un Initiateur de la pensée moderne (1670–1742)* (1913; reprint, Geneva: Slatkine Reprints, 1969), part 3, chaps. 3–5.

38. Ibid., 292.

39. Voltaire expresses his view of Louis XIV as follows: "He did not separate his own glory from the good of France, and he did not look upon his kingdom the same way as a lord looks upon his land from which he takes all he can so as to live only for pleasure. Any king who loves glory also loves the public good." Voltaire, *Le Siècle de Louis XIV*, in *Œuvres historiques*, ed. René Pomeau, Bibliothèque de la Pléiade (Paris: Gallimard, 1957), 977.

40. Ibid., 659.

41. Voltaire, *Dictionnaire philosophique*, "Histoire," sec. 2, in *Œuvres complètes*, ed. Louis Moland, 52 vols. (Paris: Garnier, 1877–1883), 19:352–56; see p. 353.

42. Voltaire, *Annales de l'Empire depuis Charlemagne*, in *Œuvres complètes*, 13:615 (first ed., 1754).

43. Voltaire, *Essai sur les mœurs et l'esprit des nations et sur les principaux faits de l'histoire depuis Charlemagne jusqu'à Louis XIII*, ed. R. Pomeau (Paris: Garnier Frères, 1963; first edition, 1756), 1:324.

44. Voltaire, "Lettre à Madame la duchesse de Saxe-Gotha," Colmar, March 8, 1754, quoted at the end of *Annales de l'Empire*, in *Œuvres complètes*, 13:618. On the oppositions light/darkness, present/past in Voltaire, see Suzanne Gearhart, *The Open Boundary of History and Fiction* (Princeton, N.J.: Princeton University Press, 1984), 32–56.

45. Bossuet's *Le Discours sur l'histoire universelle* ends with Charlemagne. The great king inaugurates the modern era that lasts up to Louis XIV's reign. It is only later that Voltaire changed the title of his work to *Essai sur les mœurs . . .*

46. Voltaire, *Essai sur les moeurs*, 1:326.

47. Ibid., 1:328.

48. Ibid., 1:363.

49. Ibid., 1:329.

50. Voltaire, *Œuvres complètes*, 13:240: "Ce monarque, au fond, était, comme tous les autres conquérants, un usurpateur: son père n'avait été qu'un rebelle, et tous les historiens appellent rebelles ceux qui ne veulent pas pliers sous le nouveau joug. Il usurpa la moitié de la France sur son frère Carolman, qui mourut trop subitement pour ne pas laisser de soupçons d'une mort violente; il usurpa l'héritage de ses neveux et la subsistance de leur mère; il usurpa le royaume de Lombardie sur son beau-père. On connaît ses bâtards, sa bigamie, ses divorces, ses concubines; on sait qu'il fit assassiner des milliers de Saxons; et on en a fait un saint."

51. Voltaire, *Essai sur les mœurs*, 1:338.

52. Ibid., 1:342.

53. Ibid., 1:343.

54. Rome is, of course, the cultural heir of Athens. No one expresses this modern version of the *translatio imperii* and of the *translatio studii* better than Voltaire in *Le Siècle de Louis XIV*.

> Louis XIV's century has been compared to that of Augustus. It is not that the government and the events are similar. Rome and Augustus were ten times more important in the world than Louis XIV and Paris. But it must be remembered that Athens had been the equal of the Roman Empire in all things that are not linked to force and power. We also should ponder that, even though there is nothing in the world like ancient Rome and Augustus, nonetheless all of Europe together is very superior to the whole of the Roman Empire. There was in Augustus's time only a single nation, and today there are several, policed, armed, enlightened, that possess arts of which the Greeks and the Romans were unaware; and among these nations there is only one that has shone more brightly in all things for about a century: the nation that was in a way formed by Louis XIV. (Voltaire, *Siècle de Louis XIV*, 982–83)

55. See Keith Michael Baker, "Representation Redefined," in *Inventing the French Revolution: Essays on French Political Culture in the Eighteenth Century* (Cambridge: Cambridge University Press, 1990), 224–51.

56. See Chantal Grell, *L'Histoire entre érudition et philosophie: Étude sur la connaissance historique à l'âge des Lumières* (Paris: Presses universitaires de France, 1993), 151.

57. On Louis XV's giving up the public use of his healing touch (originally because of his adulterous affairs), see the remarkable biography by Michel Antoine, *Louis XV* (Paris: Fayard, 1989), 485–87. This process of the desacralization of the monarchy began very early on; see Ralph E. Giesey, "The King Imagined," in *The Political Culture of the Old Regime*, ed. Keith Michael Baker (Oxford: Pergamon Press, 1987), 41–59, and Ralph E. Giesey, *The Royal Funeral Ceremony in Renaissance France* (Geneva: E. Droz, 1960). There is a good summary of the research on this issue and that of the increasing lay nature of the monarchy in Roger Chartier, "Déchristianisation et laïcisation" and "Le roi désacralisé?" in *Les Origines culturelles de la Révolution française* (Paris: Éditions du Seuil, 1990), 116–66.

58. On the process of making citizenship more inclusive, see D. Richet, "Autour des origines idéologiques lointaines de la Révolution française: Élites et despotisme," 10–11.

59. Montesquieu, *De l'esprit des lois*, "Livre trentième, Théorie des lois féodales chez les Francs dans le rapport qu'elles ont avec l'établissement de la Monarchie, chapitre premier, des lois féodales," ed. Robert Derathé (Paris: Garnier, 1973), 2:299: "Je croirais qu'il y aurait une imperfection dans mon ouvrage, si je passais sous silence un événement arrivé une fois dans le monde, et qui n'arrivera peut-être jamais; si je ne parlais de ces lois que l'on vit paraître en un moment dans toute l'Europe, sans qu'elles tinssent à celles que l'on avait jusqu'alors connues. . . . C'est un beau spectacle que celui des lois féodales. Un chêne antique s'élève; l'œil en voit de loin les feuillages; il approche, il en voit la tige; mais il n'en aperçoit point les racines; il faut percer la terre pour les trouver."

On Montesquieu's perspective, see Louis Althusser, *Montesquieu: La Politique et l'histoire* (Paris: Presses universitaires de France, 1959).

60. Montesquieu, *De l'esprit des lois*, vol. 2, book 31, chap. 18, p. 383: "Charlemagne songea à tenir le pouvoir de la noblesse dans ses limites, et à empêcher l'oppression du clergé et des hommes libres. Il mit *un tel tempérament dans les ordres de l'État, qu'ils furent contrebalancés, et qu'il resta le maître.*"

61. Ibid., 383.

62. Ibid., 382–83:

Tout fut uni par la force de son génie. . . . Son génie se répandit sur toutes les parties de l'empire. On voit, dans les lois de ce prince, un esprit de prévoyance qui comprend tout, et une certaine force qui entraîne tout. . . . Il savait punir; il savait encore mieux pardonner. Vaste dans ses desseins, simple dans l'exécution, personne n'eut à un plus haut degré l'art de faire les plus grandes choses avec facilité, et les difficiles avec promptitude. Il parcourait sans cesse son vaste empire, portant la main partout où il allait tomber. Les affaires renaissaient de toutes parts, il les finissait de toutes parts. Jamais prince ne sut mieux braver les dangers; jamais prince ne les sut mieux éviter.

63. Roger Bickart, *Les Parlements et la Notion de Souveraineté Nationale au XVIIIe siècle* (Paris: Félix Alcan, 1932); see particularly pp. 86–142; Dale Van Kley, *The Damiens Affair and the Unraveling of the Ancien Régime (1750–1770)* (Princeton, N.J.: Princeton University Press, 1984), 187–89; Dale Van Kley, "Church, State, and the Ideological Origins of the French Revolution: The Debate over the General Assembly

of the Gallican Clergy in 1765," *Journal of Modern History* 51 (December 1979): 629–66; and Baker, "Representation Redefined," 224–51; see particularly pp. 232–34.

64. Louis Adrien Le Paige, *Lettres historiques sur les fonctions essentielles du Parlement: Sur le droit des pairs, et sur les lois fondamentales du royaume*, 2 vols. (Amsterdam, 1753–1754), 1:151–52: " le dépositaire & le conservateur de Loix & des maximes de l'État; qui examine & qui promulgue légitimement & librement toutes les Loix nouvelles, qui donne au Monarque les avis importans au bien de son service, & à celui de la Patrie; qui lui résiste même, s'il le faut, plutôt que de trahir des intérêts si chers; *qui refrène* en un mot, comme le dit du Seissel [*sic*] à François Ier, *la puissance absolue dont voudroient user les Rois*."

65. Ibid., 156.

66. Ibid., 158–59.

67. Ibid., 167–68.

68. Ibid., 168.

69. Gabriel Bonnot de Mably, *Observations sur l'histoire de France*, in *Collection complète des œuvres de l'abbé de Mably* . . . (Paris: Imprimerie de Desbière, Year 3 of the Republic [1794–1795]), 1:125. On Mably see Johnson Kent Wright, *The Political Thought of Gabriel Bonnot de Mably, 1709–1785* (Ph.D. diss., University of Chicago, 1990 [Stanford University Press, forthcoming]).

70. Mably, *Observations*, 1:216.

71. Ibid., 155: ". . . after the conquest, each Frenchman thought he had done everything once he acquired a patrimony and indulged in the pleasure of showing off his new possessions or of disturbing his neighbors in theirs. The public good was sacrificed to private interest, and this change in mores announced a forthcoming revolution."

72. Ibid., 133.

73. Ibid., 249.

74. Ibid., 221.

75. Ibid., 221–22. The text is filled with expressions of this type, all of which emphasize that "Charlemagne pulled his nation out of chaos" (p. 245).

76. Ibid., 222–23.

77. Ibid., 240.

78. Ibid., 250.

79. Ibid., 240: "traité avec tant d'inhumanité depuis l'établissement des seigneuries et la ruine de l'ancien gouvernement, [et] ayant perdu toute idée de sa dignité et de ses droits, . . . étoit disposé à recevoir, comme une grâce, tout le mal qu'on voudroit ne pas lui faire."

80. Ibid., 224–25.

81. Ibid., 225.

82. On page 248 (vol. 1) Mably labels the great king "the legislator of the French." On Lycurgus's role in Mably, see Wright, *Political Thought*, 1:227–28.

83. Mably, *Observations*, 1:227–28.

84. Ibid., 228.

85. Ibid., 245.

86. Ibid., 233: "La nation entière avoit les yeux continuellement ouverts sur chaque homme public. Les magistrats, qu'on observoit, apprirent à se respecter

eux-mêmes: les mœurs, sans lesquelles la liberté dégénère toujours en une licence dangereuse, se corrigèrent, et l'amour du bien public, uni à la liberté, la rendit de jour en jour plus agissante et plus salutaire."

87. Mably, *Observations*, 1:234: "Agissant enfin avec ce zèle que donne la liberté, et avec cette union qui multiplie les forces, rien ne put résister aux Français. Ils soumirent une partie de l'Espagne, l'Italie, toutes ces vastes contrées qui s'étendent jusqu'à la Vistule et à la mer Baltique; et la gloire du nom Français, pareille à celle des anciens Romains, passa jusqu'en Afrique et en Asie."

88. A good example of this image of Charlemagne as conqueror can be found in *L'Empire de Charlemagne en 814*, the last entry in a series of fourteen aimed at "fixing in the memory of youth our laws, our mores, and our customs" (*Les Figures de l'Histoire de France*, published in 1785 under the direction of Jean-Michel Moreau, engravings by Julien and J.-P. Lebas after Moreau le Jeune; see fig. 18).

89. Ibid., 221.

90. Ibid., 247.

91. Georges Le Roy, ed., *Œuvres philosophiques de Condillac* (Paris: Presses universitaires de France, 1948), 2:134.

92. Ibid., 2:160.

93. Lucian Hölscher, "Öffentlichkeit," in *Geschichtliche Grundbegriffe: Historisches Lexikon zur politisch-sozialen Sprache in Deutschland*, ed. Otto Brunner, Werner Conze, and Reinhart Kosselleck, 7 vols. (Stuttgart: Klett-Cotte, 1972–1992), 4:413–65, and especially Jürgen Habermas, *L'Espace public: Archéologie de la publicité comme dimension constitutive de la société bourgeoise* (Paris: Payot, 1993), have explored the role of publicity and public opinion in the eighteenth century. See also the important contribution of Baker, "Public Opinion as Political Invention," in *Inventing the French Revolution*, 167–99; R. Chartier, "Espace public et opinion publique," in *Les Origines culturelles de la Révolution française*, 32–52; M. Ozouf, "Le Concept d'opinion publique au XVIIIe siècle," in *Homme régénéré*, 21–53.

94. Élisabeth Badinter, ed., *Les "Remontrances" de Malesherbes: 1771–1775* (Paris: Flammarion, 1985), 273.

95. Ibid., 265.

96. Ibid., 275: "C'est à vous à juger, Sire, si ce sera affaiblir votre puissance, que d'imiter en cela Charlemagne, ce Monarque si fier, et qui porta si loin les prérogatives de sa Couronne, C'est à son exemple que vous pouvez encore régner à la tête d'une Nation qui sera tout entière votre Conseil."

97. *Observations inédites de Condorcet sur le 29e livre du même ouvrage*, in Comte Antoine Louis Claude Destutt de Tracy, *Commentaire sur L'Esprit des Lois de Montesquieu* (Paris: T. Desoer, 1822), 379; on this issue, see Élie Carcassonne, *Montesquieu et le problème de la constitution française au XVIIIe siècle* (Paris: Presses universitaires de France, 1925), 297–350. On the authenticity of these *Observations*, see Keith Michael Baker, *Condorcet: From Natural Philosophy to Social Mathematics* (Chicago: University of Chicago Press, 1975), 221 n. 97.

98. Guillaume-François Le Trosne, *De l'Administration provinciale et de la réforme de l'impôt* (Basel: Pierre J. Duplain, 1787; 1st ed. 1779), 1:121: "mais ils soutiendront qu'on ne peut sans risque y ramener une Nation qui, depuis des siecles, en a suivi de contraires, qu'une si grande innovation est dangereuse."

99. Ibid., 136.

100. Ibid., 139.

101. Ibid., 195.

102. Ibid., 196, 210.

103. Ibid., 199–200.

104. Ibid., 205.

105. Ibid., 207.

106. Ibid., 534.

107. Ibid., 206.

108. Ibid., 541.

109. Ibid., 543–44: "En effet, quelle plus grande étendue l'autorité d'un seul homme peut-elle jamais obtenir, que de faire mouvoir toute une Nation, de réunir des millions d'individus pour n'en faire qu'un corps, de le diriger comme un seul homme par une impression directe, et de gouverner même sa volonté en la conformant à la sienne."

110. On the monarchy's failure in the "battle for history" in general and on Moreau's role in particular, see K. M. Baker, "Controlling French History: The Ideological Arsenal of Jacob-Nicolas Moreau," in *Inventing the French Revolution*, 59–85.

111. "The beginning of Charles's reign was like a rising sun, first piercing the night of ignorance, and, before [the sun] reached its apex, it had completely dissipated the darkness and given back a brilliant light to the sciences. . . . The state was flourishing. Everything contributed to its greatness. Glorious successes ensured its tranquility. Abundance was everywhere. The government was kind and friendly, joy was everywhere" (Des Religieux Bénédictins de la Congrégation de Saint-Maur, *Histoire littéraire de la France*, ed. M. Paulin Paris [Paris: Victor Palmé, 1866], 4:4–14; see pp. 6, 7). On *Histoire littéraire* see François Fossier, "*L'Histoire littéraire de la France* au dix-huitième siècle, d'après les archives des Bénédictins de Saint-Maur," *Journal des savants* (July–December 1976): 255–83; Bruno Neveu, "*L'Histoire littéraire de la France* et l'érudition bénédictine au siècle des Lumières," *Journal des savants* (April–June 1979): 73–113.

112. "Réponse de Moreau aux observations de Bertin, 14 août 1762," in Xavier Charmes, *Le Comité des travaux historiques et scientifiques (Histoire et documents)*, 3 vols. (Paris: Imprimerie nationale, 1886), vol. 1, p. 47, no. 8, cited by Dieter Gembicki, *Histoire et politique à la fin de l'Ancien Régime: Jacob-Nicolas Moreau (1717–1803)* (Paris: A.-G. Nizet, 1979), 96; B. Barret-Kriegel devotes a chapter to Moreau in *Les Historiens et la monarchie*, vol. 1, *Jean Mabillon*, 211–67.

113. J.-N. Moreau, *Principes de morale . . .* (Paris: Imprimerie royale, 1778), 6:137–38.

114. Ibid., 7:3: "Il ne fut pourtant pas le fondateur du gouvernement François; mais il en fut le restaurateur. Dans les principes de son administration, *nous retrouverons toutes les loix de notre constitution primitive*; mais après avoir bien constaté la base sur laquelle il appuya son autorité, après avoir approfondi ses vues & médité son plan, *nous pourrons oublier & la férocité et le despotisme de notre première Race. Avec lui commence le règne des loix*, sous le régime desquelles marchent toujours d'un pas égal la puissance de nos Rois & la liberté de leurs peuples."

115. Ibid., 6:277.

116. Ibid., 13–14:

Ici la chaîne des conséquences m'effraie; elle est terrible, elle s'étend jusqu'à nous: car enfin les successeurs de Hugues Capet ont-ils pu s'emparer peu à peu d'un autorité que n'eut point Charlemagne? Nos Rois, en réunissant à leur Couronne le titre de toute Puissance publique, ont-ils dépouillé la Nation, dont ils tenoient le Sceptre, ou n'ont-ils fait au contraire que recouvrer des droits enlevés à leurs Prédécesseurs, des droits imprescriptibles, parce que l'imprescriptible liberté des peuples demandoit elle-même que le Souverain se remît en possession du droit de la protéger? La solution de ce problème que l'on a trop imprudemment soumis à l'examen de la multitude, importe donc aux Rois s'ils veulent connoître la nature de leur pouvoir.

117. Ibid., 2:198.
118. Ibid., 7:211.
119. Ibid., 7:260.
120. *Préambule sur l'assemblée des Notables, du 29 janvier 1787, suivi de la liste de ceux qui doivent la composer* (n.p., n.d.), cited by Carcassonne, *Montesquieu*, 554–55: "Les Assemblées de Notables ou des Citoyens de tous les Ordres, appelées *Champs de Mars ou Champs de Mai*, parce qu'elles se tenoient en plein air et aux mois indiqués, ont produit, du tems de Charlemagne, les loix fondamentales du Royaume: elles ont été suivies dans des tems postérieurs d'Assemblées d'États Généraux, et les on ensuite remplacées. . . . Il étoit réservé à l'amour pour le bien public, et à la franchise de Louis XVI secondé par un Ministre dont la prudence et la droiture forment le caractère, de faire revivre ces Assemblées si propres à animer le zele et à cimenter la fidélité de la Nation."
121. Antoine Pierre Joseph Barnave, *Esprit des édits, enregistrés militairement au Parlement de Grenoble le 10 mai 1788* (n.p., 1788), 2, 16.
122. Ibid., 23–24:

Ouvre enfin les yeux, Roi sensible & bon; vois l'abîme profond où d'indignes Serviteurs ont précipité ton Empire, vois les funestes effets de l'autorité aveugle & illégitime qu'ils ont voulu s'attribuer sous ton nom. . . .

Appelle, appelle, il en est temps, ton peuple fidèle à délibérer avec toi, lui seul pourra t'offrir assez de lumieres . . . ; lui seul t'offrira ces preuves d'amour qui feront couler les larmes de tes yeux & qui rempliront de délices ton cœur paterne; tu verras la joie & les acclamations prendre, en un jour, la place de tant de douleurs; on te donnera les noms de pere du peuple & de restaurateur de la monarchie.

Ils sont lâches, ceux qui t'ont dit que cette heureuse institution affoibliroit ta puissance. Charlemagne rendit à la Nation sa constitution long-temps oubliée; chef d'un Empire plus vaste encore, environné de tributaires indomptés, ralliant dans ses mains les fils épars d'une immense administration, il régna pendant quarante ans au milieu des acclamations d'un peuple législateur, & mourut, laissant après lui les noms du plus puissant des monarques & du plus grand des mortels.

Barnave evokes more briefly Henry IV and Saint Louis.

123. For an excellent discussion of the role of the debates on the ancient constitution in prerevolutionary pamphlets, see Jeremy Popkin and Dale Van Kley, eds., *Le Débat prérévolutionnaire*, Les Archives de la Révolution française, ed. Colin Lucas, sec. 5 (Oxford: Pergamon Press, 1990); see also Raymond Birn, "The Pamphlet Press and the Estates-General of 1789," in *The Press in the French Revolution*, ed. Harvey Chisick, Ilana Zinguer, and Ouzi Elyada, vol. 287, Studies on Voltaire and the Eighteenth Century (Oxford: Voltaire Foundation, 1991), 59–69.

124. *À un ami, sur les craintes de la nation, sur ce que doit déterminer l'Assemblée des Notables, au sujet des États-Généraux* (Paris, 1788), 12 (the author dates this "letter to a friend" December 1).

125. *De la Forme de Délibérer: Discours célèbre de Charlemagne* (n.p., 1789), 8–11.

126. Emmanuel Henri Louis Alexandre de Launay, comte d'Antraigues, *Mémoires sur les Etats Généraux, leurs droits, et la manière de les convoquer* (n.p., 1788), 67–68:

> Que les ministres pervers qui chercherent à éloigner les rois du souvenir des assemblées nationales, en leur exagérant les dangers, lisent donc la vie de ce grand homme! qu'ils y apprennent qu'il ne se passa pas d'années qu'il n'assemblât la nation, & qu'ils sachent que cette nation n'étoit pas circonscrite dans les limites de la France, mais qu'il régnoit sur l'Allemagne & l'Italie! qu'ils y apprennent que ce héros gagna plus de batailles qu'ils n'ont commis de crimes, qu'ils n'ont ourdi d'infâmes & odieuses intrigues; & que cette même main qui présentoit la loi au peuple & se soumettoit à sa voix, étoit la même que ses ennemis ne pouvoient fixer san effroi, & qui sembloit avoir enchaîné la victoire!

127. M. J. Mavidal and M. E. Laurent, eds., *Archives parlementaires de 1787 à 1860*, May 29 and 30, 1790, vol. 15 (Paris: Paul Dupont, 1883); see especially p. 749.

128. Stéphanie-Félicité, comtesse de Genlis, *Les Chevaliers du cygne ou la Cour de Charlemagne: Conte historique et moral pour servir de suite aux "Veillées du chateau," et dont tous les traits qui peuvent faire allusion à la Révolution Françoise sont tirés de l'Histoire*, 3 vols. (Paris: Lemierre, 1795).

129. Ibid., 1:2–3.

130. Pierre-Daniel Huet, *Traité de l'origine des romans* (Paris: Jean Mariette, 1711; 1st ed. 1670), 208–210, 261.

131. See Le Laboureur, above, pp. 184–87.

132. On this point and on the whole issue of medieval studies in the eighteenth century, see the indispensable study by Lionel Gossman, *Medievalism and the Ideologies of the Enlightenment*.

133. Sainte-Palaye, "Mémoire concernant les principaux monumens de l'Histoire de France Avec la Notice et l'Histoire des Chroniques de Saint-Denis," in *MAI*, 15:611.

134. Sainte-Palaye, "Mémoire concernant la lecture des anciens romans de chevalerie," December 13, 1743, in *MAI*, 17:787–99; see p. 793.

135. Sainte-Palaye, "Mémoires sur l'ancienne chevalerie considerée comme un établissement politique et militaire," in *MAI* (1753), 20:597–697; see third *Mémoire*, p. 659.

136. See above, p. 166.

137. Sainte-Palaye, "Mémoires sur l'ancienne chevalerie," in *MAI*, 20:619; see second *Mémoire*.

138. Ibid.; see third *Mémoire*, p. 654.

139. Ibid.; see third *Mémoire*, p. 655: "Si la politique savoit habilement mettre en œuvre & l'amour de la gloire & celui des Dames pour entretenir des sentiments d'honneur & de bravoure dans l'ordre des Chevaliers, elle savoit aussi que le lien de l'amitié, si utile à tous les hommes, étoit nécessaire pour unir tant de héros entre lesquels une double rivalité pouvoit devenir une source de divisions préjudiciables à l'intérêt commun. Cet inconvénient, trop souvent fatal aux États, avoit été prévenu par les sociétés ou fraternités d'armes, formées entre les enfans de la Chevalerie."

140. Ibid.; see third *Mémoire*, p. 659.

141. Ibid.; see third *Mémoire*, p. 648. On the similarities between Montesquieu and Sainte-Palaye, see Gossman, *Medievalism*, 92–93.

142. Sainte-Palaye, "Mémoires sur l'ancienne chevalerie," in *MAI*, 20:679; see fifth *Mémoire*.

143. Ibid.; see fifth *Mémoire*, p. 686.

144. Ibid.; see fifth *Mémoire*, p. 696.

145. On the idealizing aspect of Jean Froissart, see Peter Dembowski, "Chivalry, Ideal and Real, in the Narrative Poetry of Jean Froissart," in *Medievalia et Humanistica*, ed. Paul Maurice Clogan, n.s. 14 (Totowa, N.J.: Rowman and Littlefield, 1986), 1–15.

146. Anne Claude Philippe de Caylus, *De l'Ancienne Chevalerie et des Anciens Romans* (Paris: J. B. Sajou, 1813), 4; a detailed précis of this *Mémoire* can be found in *MAI*, 23:236–43. Volume 23 covers the activities of the Academy of Inscriptions for the years 1749, 1750, and 1751. The essay must have circulated in manuscript form, because, as we will see, Gaillard refers to it in his biography of Charlemagne.

147. Sainte-Palaye, "Mémoires sur l'ancienne chevalerie," in *MAI*, 20:613; see second *Mémoire*.

148. Caylus, *De l'Ancienne Chevalerie*, 11–12.

149. Ibid., 15–16.

150. *MAI*, 27:795.

151. "Prospectus," in *Bibliothèque universelle des romans, ouvrage périodique, dans lequel on donne l'analyse raisonnée des Romans anciens et modernes, François ou traduits dans notre langue; avec des Anecdotes et des Notices historiques et critiques concernant les Auteurs ou leur Ouvrages; ainsi que les moeurs, les usages du temps, les circonstances particulières et relatives, et les personnages connus, déguisés ou emblématiques* (*BUR*) 1 (July 1775): 3–4: "dirigée par la Philosophie & embrassant la généralité des fictions, [elle] devient l'étude la plus sûre & la plus suivie de l'Histoire la plus secrette & la plus fidelle. . . . La Roman a cet avantage sur l'Histoire, qu'il peint les mœurs en décrivant les fiats; qu'il développe & nuance les caractères; & qu'il représente toute une nation, dans le récit des aventures de quelques citoyens. Or, toutes les particularités répandues dan les Romans, forment le véritable corps del'Histoire."

152. See Henri Jacoubet, *Le Genre troubadour et les origines françaises du romantisme* (Paris: Belles Lettres, 1929), and *Le Comte de Tressan et les origines du genre troubadour* (Paris: Presses universitaires de France, 1923), as well as Gossman, *Me-*

dievalism, 257–58. On *Bibliothèque universelle*, see the studies by Roger Poirier, *La Bibliothèque universelle des romans: Rédacteurs, textes, public* (Geneva: Droz, 1976); and Angus Martin, *La Bibliothèque universelle des romans, 1775–1789*, "Studies on Voltaire and the Eighteenth Century, vol. 281 (Oxford: Voltaire Foundation, 1985). For the years we are looking at here, see also Léon Gautier, *Les Epopées françaises: Étude sur les origines et l'histoire de la littérature nationale*, 2:678–90, which contains an indignant criticism of *Bibliothèque* for the harm it did to "national literature."

153. See Martin, *Bibliothèque universelle*, 71–73.

154. *BUR* (February 1778): 9.

155. The French word *roman* stands for both the English words "romance" and "novel," and it is thus not easy to ascertain at what point "romances" became "historical novels" or even simply "novels." *Trans.*

156. *BUR* 1 (July 1775): 10.

157. *BUR* 1 (July 1775): 15–17; see p. 16; when writing about the historical romance, the editors note that only Xenophon's *Cyropedy* could be considered a precursor.

158. For the edition and manuscripts on which the editors of *BUR* based their translations, see the excellent analytical table compiled by Angus Martin in *Bibliothèque universelle*. They often worked with sixteenth-century editions.

159. *BUR* 1 (July 1777): 123, 131.

160. The translation was based on that of Robert Gaguin; see above, pp. 114–17.

161. *BUR* 1 (July 1777): 169–70; these are events told in the *Chanson des Saisnes*; the editors cite as their source "a romanesque poem on the *deeds of Charles the Great* found in a volume along with *Berthes au grand pied* [Big-footed Bertha]". The following volume adds some episodes from a manuscript provided in the meanwhile by Sainte-Palaye.

162. *BUR* 1 (July 1777): 170.

163. *BUR* (August 1777): 131.

164. *BUR* (August 1777): 141–42. See Dufresne, *Histoire des premières expéditions de Charlemagne, pendant sa jeunesse et avant son règne, composée pour l'instruction de Louis le Débonnaire; par Angilbert surnommé Homère (mis au jour et dédié au Roy de Prusse). Par Monsieur* —— [Dufresne de Francheville] (Amsterdam, n.d. [1741]); the description of Sigefroy's court is on pp. 100–114.

165. *BUR* (August 1777): 144.

166. *BUR* (August 1777): 146.

167. *BUR* (August 1777): 146–47.

168. *BUR* (August 1777): 155–56:

Des Orateurs éloquens & qui paroissoient animés d'un zèle patriotique osèrent, en présence de Charles même, faire un tableau flateur de l'Aristocratie, & une peinture odieuse du gouvernement Monarchique, qu'ils traitoient de despotisme. Le jeune Charles, sans montrer ni colère, ni humeur sur une question à laquelle il avoit, dans le fond, un si grand intérêt, parla, à son tour, aux États assemblés, & leur fit sentir que e système républicain avoit plus d'inconvéniens que le Monarchique. Quant au peuple, leur dit-il, il vaut mieux pour lui, trouver l'autorité réunie en un seul point & dans en seul homme, que de dépendre de tant de maîtres, dont les intérêts particuliers prédominent communément sur l'intérêt général.

In Dufresne's novel, this scene is more detailed, and, in addition to the aristocratic position, there is also talk of a sort of people's government: "The people, sectarian worshippers of novelty and always extreme in their judgments, had no sooner heard talk of this government than, interrupting the reading that the assembly was engaged in, they yelled out their approval" (250).

169. *BUR* (August 1777): 157.

170. *BUR* (August 1777): 168.

171. *BUR* (November 1777): 10.

172. *BUR* (December 1777): 214–15:

Quand on lui demandoit pourquoi
Les François étoient en campagne.
Il répondoit, de bonne foi,
C'est par l'ordre de Charlemagne:
Ses Ministres, ses Favoris,
Ont raisoné sur cette affaire;
Pour nous, battons ses ennemis,
C'est ce que nous avons à faire.
. . . .
Au paysan comme au bourgeois
Ne faisant jamais violence,
De la guerre exerçant les droits
Avec douceur & bienséance . . .

173. *BUR* (December 1777): 211.

174. Saint-Just, *Organt*, in *Œuvres complètes*, ed. Michel Duval (Paris: Éditions Gérard Lebovici, 1984), 82–83:

Devint brutal et fou de sens rassis;
Il a perdu son antique prudence:
Je ne veux plus que boire et que chanter.
. . . .
La soif de l'or le gosier lui sécha;
Pour en avoir, le peuple il écorcha.
Il eut de l'or, mais perdit, en échange,
Gloire et repos: le ciel ainsi nous venge.

175. Gabriel-Henri Gaillard, *Histoire de Charlemagne, précédée de Considérations sur la première Race, et suivie de Considérations sur la seconde*, vol. 3 (Paris: Moutard, 1782), 146.

176. Ibid., 202.

177. Ibid., 332–33.

178. Ibid., 461–62.

179. Ibid., 493, 495.

180. De Genlis, *Chevaliers du cygne*, 1:192–93.

181. Ibid., 192.

182. Ibid., xvi–xvii: "Un des grands avantages des romans historiques, . . . est de donner à la morale l'autorité si puissante de l'expérience et de l'exemple. Il est impossible qu'un personnage imaginaire produise autant d'impression qu'un héros dont la gloire a consacré le nom. . . . En peignant tout ce que l'héroïsme peut offrir de plus noble et de plus touchant je n'ai rien inventé, je n'ai été que l'historien de la vertu."

183. Stéphanie-Félicité, comtesse de Genlis, *Mémoires inédites de Madame la Comtesse de Genlis sur le XVIIIe siècle et la Révolution française depuis 1756 jusqu'à nos jours* (Paris: Ladvocat, 1825), 260–61.

184. On the issue of origins in relation to historical writing, see Michel de Certeau, *Ecriture de l'histoire*.

185. This is seen in a *History of National Assemblies in France* published in 1788 that draws a parallel between the Roman practice "[to gather] in a large field on the shore of the Tiber River" and that of the ancient French, who had "a place in the countryside designated [for people] to assemble from all their provinces and to decide on the interests of the nation." The author notes that in spite of the identical name and the resemblance of the practices, the French institution drew its name from the month of March rather than from the god of war (Antoine-François de Landine, *Des États Généraux ou Histoire des Assemblées Nationales en France, des Personnes qui les ont composées, de leur forme, de leur influence, et des objects qui y ont été particulièrement traités. Par M. de Landine, Avocat, Correspondant de l'Académie des Inscriptions, des Académies de Londres, Rouen, Nîmes, Dijon, Arras, Bourg-en-Bresse, Villefranche, et Bibliothécaire adjoint de celle de Lyon* [Paris: Cuchet, Librairie, 1788], 17).

186. Villette was a politician as well as a man of letters, who contributed to the *Chronique de Paris* and enjoyed some popularity. He was elected to the Convention but died the following year. This motion was first erroneously published as originating from the Jacobin Club (F.-A. Aulard, ed., *La Société des Jacobins: Receuil de documents pour l'histoire du Club des Jacobins de Paris*, vol. 1 [Paris: Librairie Léopold Cerf, Librairie Noblet, Maison Quantin, 1897], 153). Aulard corrected his error in volume 6, 684. It was taken up again by Augustin Challamel in *Les Clubs contre-révolutionnaires: Cercles, comités, sociétés, salons, réunions, cafés, restaurants et librairies* (Paris: L. Cerf, 1895), 420.

CHAPTER SEVEN. TO CONQUER AND TO SING PRAISES

1. The letter was signed "M. Tonso, président du collège électoral de l'arrondissement de Tortone" [M. Tonso, president of the electoral college of the *arrondissement* of Tortone], *Moniteur*, 19 Floréal of the year XIII (May 9, 1805), 959.

2. *Les Épopées françaises: Étude sur les origines et l'histoire de la littérature nationale*, 1st ed. (Paris: Victor Palmé, 1865), 43–44.

3. *Cours de philosophie: Leçons du cours de 1828, 10e leçon, 26 juin 1828* (Paris: Pichon et Didier, 1828), 4.

4. Paris, *Histoire poétique de Charlemagne*, 8.

5. See above, pp. 4–5.

6. On Stéphanie-Félicité de Genlis, see above, pp. 243–49.

7. Constant Victor Désiré Pierre, *Musique des fêtes et cérémonies de la Révolution française: Œuvres de Gossec, Cherubini, Leseur, Méhul, Catel, etc.* (Paris: Imprimerie nationale, 1899), 461–62; cited by Harry Redman, Jr., in *The Roland Legend in Nineteenth-Century French Literature* (Lexington: University of Kentucky Press, 1991), 30. Rouget de Lisle composed the song in May 1792.

8. I am quoting the refrain here. On Duval's "*chanson*," see Redman, Jr., *Roland Legend*, 34–35.

9. Alfred de Vigny, *Œuvres complètes*, ed. F. Baldensgerber (Paris: Conard, 1914), 1:126–27; Vigny wrote "Le Cor" in 1825; "La Neige," the poem preceding it in his *Poèmes modernes*, also evokes Charlemagne. On Vigny, see Paul Bénichou, *Les Mages romantiques* (Paris: Gallimard, 1988), 113–270.

10. See above, p. 242.

11. *Le Moniteur universel*, Wednesday, 29 Thermidor of the year XI (August 17, 1803), 1458.

12. *Le Moniteur universel*, Wednesday, 23 Ventôse of the year XII (March 14, 1804), 794.

13. *À au sujet des États-Généraux*, 12.

14. September 19, 1797, "Au Ministre des relations extérieures," in Napoléon, *Correspondance de Napoléon I* (Paris: Imprimerie impériale, 1859), 3:418.

15. *Gazette nationale ou le Moniteur universel*, 22 Nivôse of the year XII (January 13, 1804), 445–46.

16. *Le Moniteur universel*, Wednesday, 29 Thermidor of the year XI (August 17, 1803), 1458.

17. *Le Moniteur universel*, Saturday, January 4, 1806, 19.

18. *Le Moniteur universel*, Monday, January 6, 1806, 28.

19. The other three are now respectively: Louis-le-Grand, Henri IV, and Châtelet. These *lycées* were created in August and September of 1803; see Jean Tulard, *Dictionnaire Napoléon* (Paris: Fayard, 1987), 1102.

20. 10 Fructidor of the year XII (August 28, 1804); *Lettres de Talleyrand à Napoléon* (Paris: Jean Bonnot, 1967), 116.

21. Napoléon, *Correspondance*, 9:657–58.

22. Speech given during the public session of 6 Nivôse of the year XII and published in the *Moniteur universel* of 21 Nivôse (January 12, 1804), 443.

23. Letter to Directoire exécutif, Quartier général, Milano, 17 Vendémiaire of the year V (October 8, 1796), in Napoléon, *Correspondance*, 2:54.

24. *Gazette nationale ou le Moniteur universel*, no. 170, Sunday, 20 Ventôse of the year XII (March 11, 1804), 782.

25. See Danielle Gaborit-Chopin, *Regalia*; on the coronation, see H. Goubert, *Le Sacre de Napoleon I* (Paris: Flammarion, 1964); José Cabanis, *Le Sacre de Napoleon, 2 décembre 1804* (Paris: Gallimard, 1970); and Hervé Pinoteau, *Le Sacre de Napoleon* (Paris: Éditions du Palais Royal, 1969). Frédéric Masson discusses at

length Charlemagne's role in the way the coronation was conceived in his study *Le Sacre et le couronnement de Napoléon* (Paris: Jules Tallandier, 1978), 63–89, 126–34.

26. *Gazette nationale ou le Moniteur universel*, Tuesday, 27 Frimaire of the year XIII (December 18, 1804), 311–13 (see especially p. 311), and Saturday, 8 Nivôse of the year XIII (December 29, 1804), 356–57. The article was signed by Peuchet; the work was by Dietrich Hermann Hegewisch, *Geschichte der Regierung Kaiser Karls des Großen* (Hamburg: C. E. Bohn), and dates from 1791. The French translation, *Histoire de l'empereur Charlemagne* (Paris, year XII [1804]), is by Jean-François Bourgoing.

27. *Gazette nationale ou le Moniteur universel*, no. 87, Tuesday, 27 Frimaire of the year XIII (December 18, 1804), 312.

28. Ibid.

29. Letter dated January 6, 1806, in Napoléon, *Correspondance* (Paris, 1863), 11:643–44.

30. *Mémoires du Prince Talleyrand*, ed. duc de Broglie (Paris: Calmann Lévy, 1891), 2:100–101. (The English quotation used in the text and the one in the note are from *Memoirs of the Prince de Talleyrand*, ed. duc de Broglie, trans. R. L. de Beaufort [New York: G. P. Putnam's Sons, 1891], 76–77. *Trans.*) Of course, Talleyrand's account might not be entirely reliable, but the insistence with which he describes the scene leads me to believe it:

> Then the emperor left the Cardinal [Fesh] whom alone, up to then, he had taken to task. He generalized his anger, and on the word *obédience* [homage paid to the pope] in the oath, which he confounded with *obéissance* [submission], he became so heated as even to call the fathers a council of traitors . . . and he continued to talk for an hour with an incoherence, which would have left no recollection other than astonishment at his ignorance and his loquacity, if the phrase which follows and which he repeated every three or four minutes, had not revealed the depth of his thought. "Messieurs," he exclaimed, "you wish to treat me as if I were Louis le Débonnaire."

31. Cited by Marcel Dunan, *Napoléon et l'Allemagne: Le Système continental et les débuts du royaume de Bavière (1806–1810)* (Paris: Plon, 1942), 23–24. Dunan notes that "Dalberg had appended to his direct suggestions a work on Charlemagne's character, *Considérations sur le caractère de l'empereur Charlemagne* (Kayser, *Bücherlexikon*), translated at the same time into German with a preface by Nic. Vogt (Frankfurt, 1806), which inspired the officious Zapf from Augsburg to draw a parallel between the two emperors who equally merited the name of Great (*Baierns wiederhergestellte Königswürde*, preface, 75–77, 126–29)," in Dunan, *Napoléon et l'Allemagne*, 408–409 n. 40. Dunan cites Jean Gabriel Maurice Rocques, comte de Montgaillard, to illustrate the extent to which flatterers made a show of their enthusiasm for the idea of the revival of the empire, which, "after ten years of feudal wars," would have consecrated "the new political system of Europe" (Rocques, *Mémoires diplomatiques*, 206, cf. 236–38), in Dunan, *Napoléon et l'Allemagne*, 409; see also the entries by Roger Dufraisse on "Bavaria" and the "Holy Germanic Roman Empire," in Jean Tulard, *Dictionnaire Napoléon*, 172–77, 1503–6.

32. Jean François Léonor Mérimée, "À Monsieur le Secrétaire Général du Ministère de l'Intérieur," dated August 24, 1806, published by Henriette Bessis,

"Ingres et le portrait de l'Empereur," in *Archives de l'art français*, n.s. 24 (Paris: Nobèle, 1969), 90–91.

33. Charlemagne's globe is replaced in the painting of Napoleon by the hand of justice.

34. See the article by Jean-Baptiste Chaussard, "Salon de l'art 1806," *Journal de l'Empire*, October 4, 1806.

35. See the critique by Pierre Jean-Baptiste Chaussard, *Le Pausanias français ou Description du Salon de 1806* (Paris: F. Buisson, 1808), 177, 180; on the critiques of this painting, see Susan L. Siegfried, "The Politics of Criticism at the Salon of 1806: Ingres' *Napoleon Enthroned*," in *The Consortium on Revolutionary Europe Proceedings* (Athens, Ga.: Consortium on Revolutionary Europe, 1980), 2:69–81.

36. Louis Dubroca, *Les Quatre Fondateurs des Dynasties françaises ou Histoire de l'établissement de la Monarchie française, par Clovis; du renouvellement des Dynasties royales, par Pépin et Hughes Capet; de la fondation de l'Empire français par Napoléon-le-Grand* (Paris: Dubroca et Fantin, 1806). Dubroca wrote a fairly successful biography of Napoleon as well as an important treatise on women's education.

37. Ibid., 123.

38. Ibid., 123–24.

39. Ibid., 128.

40. Ibid., 130–31.

41. D'Arlincourt published passages from his poem in 1810 under the title *Une matinée de Charlemagne, fragmens tirés d'un poème épique qui ne tardera point à paraître* (Paris: Imprimerie de Chaignieau aîné, 1810), but he published the whole epic only in 1818: *Charlemagne ou la Caroléïde, poème épique en vingt-quatre chants* (Paris: Le Normant, 1818); there was another edition in 1818 and one in 1824 (revised and corrected by the author).

42. D'Arlincourt, preface to *Charlemagne ou la Caroléïde* (1818), viii.

43. Ibid., viii–ix.

44. D'Arlincourt, *Eloge de Charlemagne* (Paris: J. G. Dentu, 1818), 1.

45. D'Arlincourt, *Charlemagne ou la Caroléïde*, xi.

46. Ibid., xvi–xvii; the cited passage can be found in *De l'Allemagne*, ed. Jean de Pange, vol. 2 (Paris: Hachette, 1958–1960), part 2, chap. 11, p. 134: "The literature of the ancients as it is used by the moderns is a transplanted literature: romantic or chivalric literature is indigenous to us, and it is our religion and institutions that made it blossom."

47. I am using the 1819 edition here (Paris: Patris et Chaumerot). On the troubadour genre, see Fernand Baldensperger, "Le genre troubadour," in *Études d'histoire littéraire* (Paris: Hachette, 1907); Jacoubet, *Genre troubadour*; Herbert James Hunt, *The Epic in Nineteenth-Century France* (Oxford: Blackwell, 1941); and, more recently, *Moyen Âge et XIXe siècle: Le Mirage des origines*, special issue of *Littérales*, no. 6 (Paris: Presses universitaires de Nanterre, 1990).

48. Louis Antoine François de Marchangy, *La Gaule poétique* (Paris: C.-F. Patris, 1815–1817), 3:7 n. 1.

49. Ibid., 202.

50. Ibid., 202–203.

51. Ibid., 201, 203.

52. Ibid., 194.

53. It is within this context of the transmission and survival of values that we must understand the favoring of writing over the spoken word. The latter is reduced to "transitory noises," as Marchangy claims in his attack on Beranger's *written* songs: "Transitory noise carried away by the wind and of which soon nothing remains." Pierre Jean de Béranger, *Procès fait aux chansons de P. J. de Béranger*, published by P. J. de Béranger (Paris: Marchands de nouveautés, 1821), 17.

54. Marchangy, *Gaule poétique*, 3:205.

55. Ibid., 205.

56. Ibid., 197.

57. Ibid., 177.

58. Marcel Gauchet, "*Les Lettres sur l'histoire de France* d'Augustin Thierry: L'Alliance austère du patriotisme et de la science," in Pierre Nora, ed., *Les Lieux de mémoire*, 2:247–316. On the issue of liberal historiography and its relationship to literature, see in particular Stephan Bann, *The Clothing of Clio: A Study of the Representation of History in Nineteenth-Century Britain and France* (Cambridge: Cambridge University Press, 1984), chap. 1, "The Historian as Taxidermist: Ranke, Barante, Waterton," 8–31, and chap. 2, "A Cycle in Historical Discourse: Barante, Thierry, Michelet," 32–54; as well as Lionel Gossman, *Between History and Literature* (Cambridge, Mass.: Harvard University Press, 1990), chap. 4, "Augustin Thierry and Liberal Historiography," 83–151; and the classic study of Boris Reizov, *L'Historiographic romantique française (1815–1830)* (Moscow: Éditions en langue étrangères, 1962).

59. Gauchet, "Lettres sur l'histoire de France," 270.

60. Jean-Jacques Rousseau, *The Social Contract*, trans. Maurice Cranston (Harmondsworth, England: Penguin), 61.

61. Jules Michelet, *Histoire de France*, new ed., rev. and enl. (Paris: Marpon et Flammarion, 1879–1884), preface of 1869, 1; see also M. Gauchet, "Les Lettres sur l'histoire de France," 291–94.

62. Augustin Thierry, *Lettres sur l'histoire de France, pour servir d'introduction à l'étude de cette histoire*, 6th ed. (Paris: Just Tessier, Libraire éditeur, 1839).

63. Ibid., letter 11, 173:

> Peut-être, avant la grande et triste expérience que nous avons faite, il y a treize ans, et à l'aide des seules idées fournies par la vue de l'ancien régime, était-il impossible de discerner la véritable raison des mouvements politiques où fut entraînée la famille de Charlemagne. Le maintien de l'empire frank ne dépendait pas, comme tant d'historiens l'ont dit, en copiant Montesquieu, *de sage tempérament mis entre les ordres de l'état, de l'occupation donnée à la noblesse pour l'empêcher de former des desseins, et de la soumission filiale des enfants du prince.* Il ne s'agissait ni d'ordres de l'état, ni de noblesse, ni des autres classifications sociales de la monarchie moderne; il s'agissait de retenir sous une sujétion forcée plusieurs peuples étrangers l'un à l'autre, et dont la plupart surpassaient le peuple conquérant en civilisation et en habileté pour les affaires.

64. Ibid., letter 9, 151.

65. Ibid., letter 12, 199.

66. Ibid., letter 12, 211.

67. J. Michelet, *Histoire de France*, 1:370.

68. Ibid., 1:383.

69. Ibid., 1:387.

70. See Thomas W. Gaehtgens, *Versailles als Nationaldenkmal: Die Galerie des Batailles im Musée Historique von Louis-Philippe* (Berlin: Frölich and Kaufmann, 1985), 131–34.

71. His course on modern history includes "a general history of civilization in Europe from the fall of the Roman Empire to the French Revolution" and a "history of civilization in France from the fall of the Roman Empire until 1789" (Brussels: Méline, 1843), 8. These chapters are actually the courses Guizot taught between 1828 and 1830. Pierre Rosanvallon in his study *Le Moment Guizot* (Paris: Gallimard, 1985) notes that these two "histories" "are the two Guizot works that had the greatest circulation; they were constantly reprinted until the end of the nineteenth century" (384). Guizot writes at length on Charlemagne as "a great man" in his *Essais sur l'histoire de France pour servir de complément aux* Observations sur l'histoire de France *de Mably* (Paris: Ladrange, 1836), 263–84, 304–306.

72. Guizot, *Cours d'histoire moderne*, 298.

73. Ibid., 299.

74. Ibid., 300.

75. There are seven tables devoted to Charlemagne, whereas there were only two for the preceding period. Guizot's reflection on Charlemagne leads him to use the technique of tables more frequently.

76. Guizot, *Cours d'histoire moderne*, 298.

77. Ibid., 309–10.

78. Ibid., 304.

79. See Pierre Rosanvallon, *Le Moment Guizot*, and *Le Sacre du citoyen: Histoire du suffrage universel en France* (Paris: Gallimard, 1992), 230–42.

80. Guizot, *Cours d'histoire moderne*, 299.

81. Ibid., 310.

82. Ibid., 299.

83. Victor Hugo, preface to *Marion de Lorme*, ed. Anne Ubersfeld, in *Œuvres complètes: Théâtre I*, Bouquins (Paris: Robert Laffont, 1985), 685.

84. Victor Hugo, *Hernani*, in *Œuvres complètes: Théâtre I*, 626.

85. Ibid., 628.

86. Ibid., 642.

87. Ibid., 644.

88. Victor Hugo, *Le Rhin*, ed. Evelyn Blewer, in *Œuvres complètes: Voyages*, Bouquins (Paris: Robert Laffont, 1987).

89. Ibid., 406.

90. Ibid., 408.

91. Victor Hugo, *En marge du Rhin*, ed. Evelyn Blewer, in *Œuvres complètes: Voyages*, Bouquins 491.

92. Hugo, *Le Rhin*, 7.

93. Ibid.

94. Ibid., 61–63.

95. Ibid., 62: "Après quelques instants de contemplation, une majesté singulière se dégage de cet édifice extraordinaire, resté inachevé comme l'œuvre de Charlemagne lui-même, et composé d'architectures qui parlent tous les styles comme son empire était composé de nations qui parlaient toutes les langues."

96. Ibid., 68:

Ce sera une grande apparition pour quiconque osera hasarder son regard dans ce caveau, et chacun emportera de cette tombe une grande pensée. On y viendra des extrémités de la terre, et toutes les espèces de penseurs y viendront. Charles, fils de Pépin, est en effet un de ces êtres complets qui regardent l'humanité par quatre faces. Pour l'histoire, c'est un grand homme comme Auguste et Sésostris; pour la fable, c'est un paladin comme Roland, un magicien comme Merlin; pour l'église, c'est un saint comme Jérôme et Pierre; pour la philosophie, c'est la civilisation même qui se personnifie, qui se fait géant tous les mille ans pour traverser quelque profond abîme, les guerres civiles, la barbarie, les révolutions, et qui s'appelle alors tantôt César, tantôt Charlemagne, tantôt Napoléon.

97. Ibid., 70: "La ville elle-même, cette illustre et symbolique ville, s'est comme transfigurée dans mon esprit et sous mon regard. La première des deux masses noires que je distinguais encore, et que je distinguais seules, n'a plus été pour moi que la crèche d'un enfant; la seconde que l'enveloppe d'un mort; et par moments, dans la contemplation profonde où j'étais comme enseveli, il me semblait voir l'ombre de ce géant que nous nommons Charlemagne se lever lentement sur ce pâle horizon de nuit entre ce grande berceau et ce grande tombeau."

98. Ibid., 405.

99. "Aymerillot," in *La Légende des siècles*, ed. Jean Gaudon, in *Œuvres complètes: Poésies II*, Bouquins (Paris: Laffont, 1985), 620.

100. Ibid., 622.

101. Hugo found inspiration in an article by Achille Jubinal titled "Quelques romans chez nos aïeux" [Some of Our Ancestors' Romances], published in *Journal du Dimanche*, no. 6, November 1, 1846, 3–6.

102. The story of *Charlemagne* by Capefigue, an author who wrote on a number of different topics, brings out the parallels with Napoleon. Of particular interest among the novels is *L'Heritage de Charlemagne* by Charles Deslys, which was fairly successful and was illustrated by Édouard Zier in a deluxe edition published in 1864.

103. Claude-Charles Fauriel, *Chants populaires de la Grèce moderne recueillis et publiés avec une traduction française, des éclaircissements et des notes* (Paris: Didot, 1824), xxv.

104. Ibid., xxv.

105. Ibid., lxxx.

106. Ibid., lxxxix. Joseph Bédier rightfully shows the parallel between Fauriel's description and the one Wolf had made of the small poems he believed had been brought together to form the *Iliad* and the *Odyssey*; see *Les Legendes épiques: Recherches sur la formation des chansons de geste* (Paris: Champion, 1966; first edition, 1913), 3:205.

107. Fauriel, *Chants populaires*, xcvi.

108. Claude-Charles Fauriel, *Histoire de la Gaule méridionale sous la domination des conquérants germains* (Paris: Paulin, 1836), 1:543.

109. Ibid., 2:25–26.

110. See the pages Sainte-Beuve devotes to Fauriel in his *Portraits contemporains* (Paris: Didier, 1847), 2:482–592; see especially pp. 579–80.

111. *La Revue des Deux Mondes* 3 (1832): 543.

112. Ibid., 4:192.

113. Ibid.

114. Bédier uncovers in detail the fraud of the "Chants d'Altabiscar," of which Jubinal was supposed to have transcribed a section in his article in the *Journal du Dimanche*, where Victor Hugo found it and transformed it to suit the needs of his poem "Le mariage de Roland" (see above, this chapter, n. 101), in *Les Légendes épiques: Recherches sur la formation des chansons de geste* (Paris: Champion, 1908–1913), 3:232–36.

115. Jubinal, "Quelques romans," 3–6. Jubinal cites from Chateaubriand's *Études historiques*, in which Chateaubriand does indeed compare some of Notker's anecdotes with stories told by one of Napoleon's grenadiers (see *Études ou discours historiques sur la chute de l'Empire romain, la naissance et les progrès du christianisme et l'invasion des barbares, suivis d'une Analyse raisonnée de l'histoire de France* (Paris: Lefèvre, Ledentu, 1838; first edition, 1831), 548.

116. Jean-Jacques Ampère, *Histoire littéraire de la France avant le douzième siècle* (Paris: Hachette, 1839–1840).

117. Ibid., 3:20.

118. Ibid., 3:55. Ampère writes: "Alexander Hellenized the Orient, Charlemagne Latinized the West."

119. Ibid., 3:56.

120. Ibid., 3:55–56.

121. Pierre Larousse, "La Chanson de Roland ou de Roncevaux," in *Grand Dictionnaire universel* (Paris: Larousse et Boyer, 1867), 3:925, col. 3.

122. Ibid., 3:927–28.

123. See above, pp. 243–44.

124. Paris, *Histoire poétique de Charlemagne*, 30.

125. Ibid., 43–44.

126. Ibid., 48.

127. Ibid., 451.

128. However, Paris does preserve the unity of northern and southern France by speculating that there was a simultaneous production in the Midi that must have disappeared without a trace.

129. Among those who have argued the strongest for the Germanic origins of epic poetry in France are the Germans Friedrich von Schlegel and Ludwig Uhland, as well as Edgar Quinet and Charles D'Héricault in his *Essai sur l'origine de l'épopée française et sur son histoire Âge* (Paris: A. Franck, 1859); for an overall discussion of this issue see Bédier, *Légendes épiques*, 3:250–58.

130. Paris, *Histoire poétique de Charlemagne*, 33.

131. Ibid., 1.

132. Ibid., 4.

133. Ibid., 3: "L'épopée suppose chez un peuple une faculté poétique remarquable et le sentiment vif du concret, ce qui lui donne la puissance de personnifier, en les idéalisant, ses aspirations et ses passions; elle a besoin de s'appuyer sur une nationalité fortement enracinée."

134. Ibid., 15.

135. Ibid., 33: "La principale qualité qu'elle [l'histoire poétique] demande aux monuments qui l'occupent est la spontanéité; elle n'accorde qu'une attention distraite aux produits artificiels de la poésie lettrée; du moment qu'une œuvre est voulue et arbitrairement composée, l'histoire poétique lui refuse toute valeur comme document."

136. Ibid., 30.

137. Ibid.

138. Paul Meyer, "Recherches sur l'épopée française: Examen critique de *l'Histoire poétique de Charlemagne* de M. Gaston Paris" (Paris: A. Franck, 1867 [extract from *Bibliothèque de l'Ecole des Chartes*, 6th ser., 3:55]).

139. Léon Gautier, *Les Épopées françaises: Étude sur les origines et l'histoire de la littérature nationale*, 1st ed. (Paris: V. Palmé, 1865), 1:10, cited in Meyer, "Recherches sur l'épopée," 56.

140. Gautier, *Epopées françaises*, 1:43.

141. Ibid., 1:145–46: "Charlemagne a sauvé tout à la fois notre poésie nationale dans le passé et dans l'avenir. . . . Oui, Charlemagne a sauvé la future épopée française; il l'a sauvée volontairement et involontairement. Volontairement, en compliant le recueil de ces cantilènes, dont nos premières chansons de geste devaient un jour sortir si naturellement. Involontairement, par le spectacle magnifique de sa grandeur, de ses conquêtes, de sa gloire. Il n'a eu qu'à se montrer, et notre épopée fut."

In a second edition that was "completely reworked," published between 1878 and 1897, Gautier puts less emphasis on the Germanic nature of the *chansons de geste* and comes significantly closer to Gaston Paris's theses.

CHAPTER EIGHT. FINAL COMMENTS:
THE WANING POWER OF THE FIGURE OF CHARLEMAGNE

1. Charles Rochet, *Mon frère et la vérité sur la statue équestre de Charlemagne* (Paris: Imprimerie de la Veuve J. Juteau, 1878), 7.

2. Viollet-le-Duc's conclusions are cited at length in "Rapport préliminaire présenté par M. Lucien Lambeau au nom de la première sous-commission sur la statue de Charlemagne élevée dans le square du parvis de Notre-Dame," *Procès-verbaux, Commission du Vieux-Paris*, 1906, vol. 9 (Paris: Imprimerie municipale, 1907).

3. On this session and subsequent events, see the report by Lucien Lambeau, "Rapport préliminaire."

4. This time the proposal did not limit the length of time the statue could be exhibited. It was only in 1895 that the city of Paris bought the statue for thirty-five thousand francs, that is, for only the cost of the metal at the time.

5. Numa Denis Fustel de Coulanges, "Le Gouvernement de Charlemagne," *La Revue des Deux Mondes* 13, 3d series (Paris, 1876): 123–52; see p. 133. On Fustel de Coulanges, see Claude Digeon, *La Crise allemande et la pensée française (1870–1914)* (Paris: Presses universitaires de France, 1959).

6. Coulanges, "Le gouvernement de Charlemagne," 134.

7. Lucien Double, *Empereur Charlemagne* (Paris: G. Fischbacher, 1881), ix, xiii.

8. "La légende politique au XVIIIe siècle et son influence politique à l'époque de la Révolution française," *Mémoires de l'Académie des sciences, inscriptions et belles-lettres de Toulouse*, 7th ser. (Toulouse, 1878), 10:1–33; see p. 8.

9. "De l'origine des traditions nationales dans la politique extérieure avant la Révolution française," *Séances et travaux de l'Académie des sciences morales et politiques, Institut de France* (Paris: Alphonse Picard, 1882), 118:561–609; see p. 564.

10. Duméril, "Légende politique," 33.

11. A. Ammann and E. C. Coutant, *Notions sommaires d'histoire générale et révision d'histoire de France* (Paris, 1893), 183 (manual used in the training of elementary-school teachers in secondary schools); on the teaching of French history in secondary schools, see Christian Amalvi, *Les Héros de l'Histoire de France: Recherches iconographiques sur le panthéon scolaire de la Troisième République* (Paris: Phot'œil, 1979); *De l'art et la manière d'accommoder les héros de l'histoire de France* (Paris: Albin Michel, 1988); and Suzanne Citron, *Le Mythe national: L'Histoire de France en question* (Paris: Éditions ouvrières, 1987).

12. The French still remember France Gall's song, *Sacré Charlemagne*, which jokingly criticizes this founder of the French public school system.

13. On this collection, see Percy Ernst Schramm, *Kaiser, König und Päpste*, 342–44.

14. See, for instance, Krzysztof Pomian, *L'Europe et ses nations*, Le Débat (Paris: Gallimard, 1990), 26–30.

15. *Discours et messages; dans l'attente (février 1946–avril 1958)* (Paris: Plon, 1970), 350: "Je ne vois pas de raison, en effet, pour que, si le peuple allemand et le peuple français surmontent leurs griefs réciproques, et les intrigues extérieures, ils ne finissent pas par se conjuguer. En somme, ce seriat reprendre sur des bases modernes, c'est-à-dire économiques, sociales, stratégiques, culturelles, l'entreprise de Charlemagne."

INDEX

Einem, Herbert von, 303n3
Einhard, 10, 15, 307nn31–32, 307n34, 308n38, 311n6. *See also Vita Karoli Magni*
    on Charlemagne's tears, 37–38
Ellis, Harold A., 346n132, 346n134, 346nn137–38, 348n8
Empereur Charlemagne (Double), 297
empire
    Charlemagne the emperor separate from Charlemagne the king, 92
    Charles VII not wishing for, 106
    sixteenth-century attempts to detach Charlemagne from, 118
Empire of Charlemagne in 814, The (Lebas after Moreau), *Fig. 18*
Encyclopédie (Diderot), 189
epic
    fusion with knightly romance, 105
    power of the epic vision, 106
    role in compilations, 91
    theory and practice of, 172
epic of the north. *See* Saxons, war against
epic persona of Charlemagne, 8
    compared to heroes of Antiquity, 117, 119
    demythification
    —by Michelet, 271–72
    —by Pasquier, 131
    developed during his lifetime in "Karolus Magnus et Leo papa," 9
    in Einhard's *Vita Karoli*, 23
    in Notker, 35
    remythification in the eighteenth century, 207, 215
    in seventeenth century, 171–75
Epitome (Florus), 124
equestrian statue of Charlemagne (Rochet), 294–97, *Fig. 24*
Espagne conquise, par Charles le Grand, Roy de France, L' (Montreux), 137
Essai sur l'histoire universelle depuis Charlemagne (Voltaire), 204
Estates-General
    Hotman on, 133, 135
    pamphlets dealing with form of, 228
    tensions among the second estate, 133
Étude d'histoire (Condillac), 216–17, 238
    cited by Le Trosne, 221
Études historiques (Chateaubriand), 287
Europe, 9
    in *Chanson d'Aspremont*, 76

    Charlemagne as father of, in Lemaire de Belges, 110
    Charlemagne's empire as a first draft of, 10
    Portalis on ties between European identity and Christendom, 259
    reappropriation of Charlemagne by, 299–300
    term used by Notker, 31

Fauriel, Claude-Charles, 284–86, 288, 366nn102–6, 367nn107–9
Fénelon, François de Salignac de La Mothe-
    history of Charlemagne, 170
    Mémoire sur la cour de Rome, 170–71
Festugière, Paul, 340nn74–75
Fête de la Fédération, 248
feudal-vassalic ideology. *See also* chivalry
    in *Chanson de Roland*, 47
    as conflictual system in *Renaud de Montauban*, 77
    knightly morality and role of king as suzerain, 44
    and renewal of French monarchy starting with Louis VI, 43–44
Fierabras, 68–71
    in Aubert's *Croniques*, 100
    Mousket's use of, 86
    publications in seventeenth century, 164
    rewritten by Jean Bagnyon, 100
Flagellation session (1766), 223
Florence, Charlemagne and, 103–4
Florus, 124
Folz, Robert, 66, 304n8, 305n13, 305n15, 308n43, 311n12, 311n15, 313nn28–29, 316n59, 318n93, 319n13, 320n24, 321n27, 323n47, 326n3
Foncemagne, Étienne Lauréault de, 201–2, 349n36
Fontanes, Louis de, 256
Fossier, François, 354n111
France. *See also* French nation; French national identity
    Charlemagne and monarchical power in, 12
    emergence of modern France, 11
    identified with empire in *Chanson de Roland*, 49–50
    national origins, 10
    psychological characters of French people, 121

general assemblies, 9
    in *Annales Regni Francorum*, 15
    in Boulainvillers, 195
    in Hincmar, 39, 40
    referred to as parlements or estates-
        general in oratorical histories, 121
Genlis, Stéphanie-Félicité du Crest de
    Saint-Aubin, comtesse de, 230–31,
    234–35, 245–47, 265, 356nn128–29,
    360nn180–83
    on Charlemagne, 246, 252
    Gaillard's *Histoire de Charlemagne* as
        source, 243
German empire
    attempts to appropriate figure of
        Charlemagne, 83
    Charlemagne and monarchical power
        in, 12
    identification of Charlemagne with, 11
Germanist thesis
    supported by Abbé de Vertot, 200–201
    Voltaire on, 205
Gesta Dei per Francos, 67
Gesta Karoli Magni imperatoris (Notker the
    Stammerer), 14, 27–38
    excluded by Paris from *Histoire poétique
        de Charlemagne*, 45
    Primat's use of, 93, 94
    Vertot and, 201
geste, la, 14
    term used in *Chanson de Roland*, 46
Giesey, Ralph E., 331n63, 332nn64–68,
    351n57
gifts
    affirming power and greatness, 19, 22
    Charlemagne as great giver in Notker, 33
    potlatch logic, 19, 22, 33
    and spread of Charlemagne's power, 59
Gilbert, Gabriel, 168, 341nn85–86
Gille, 55
Gilles of Paris, 79–82
    critical of Philip Augustus, 81
    distancing himself from the *mithmi*, 79,
        81–82
    recentering the figure of Charlemagne,
        79–81
Gilson, Étienne, 308n47, 334n5
Girard of Vienna, 71–73
Girart d'Amiens, 320n22
God
    Charlemagne and, 50–51, 53–54, 62

—in *Annales*, 16
—in *Chanson de Roland*, 47, 49
—in *Pèlerinage*, 60
Charlemagne's gaze compared to that of
    the God of the Old Testament by
    Notker, 37
role in Pasquier's development of
    France, 129
weakening of the ties of the French
    monarchy to, 207
Godefroi de Viterbe, 114–15
Godefroy, Théodore, 154
Godman, Peter, 304n7
Gondeboeuf le Frison, 63
Gossman, Lionel, 356n132, 357n152,
    364n58
Goubert, H., 361n25
Goulart, Simon, 332n72
Grand Dictionnaire universel (Larousse),
    288
Grandes Chroniques de France (Primat), 14,
    51, 92–95
    on Carolingian race realized in Louis
        VIII, 79
    as "official" vision of the history of
        France, 92
    Pseudo-Turpin Chronicle included in, 51
Grand'Monarchie de France (Seyssel), 124
Grassaile, Charles de, 325n68
Gregory XI, pope, 104
Grell, Chantal, 333n1, 350n56
Grellet-Dumazeau, André, 346n138
Grétry, André, 253
Grimm brothers, 284
Grisward, Joël H., 61, 306n26, 314n43
Gros, Étienne, 342n89
Grossman, Lionel, 349n27
Grouzet, D., 333n82
Grundmann, Herbert, 319n13
Guenée, Bernard, 93, 316n60, 319n10,
    319nn15–16
Guibours Anselme de Sainte Marie, Pierre
    de, 346n133
Guillauche, Guillaume, 105–6
Guillaume le Conquérant (Duval), 253
Guillaume Tell, 253
Guizot, François Pierre Guillaume, 272–74,
    285, 295, 305n17, 306nn19–20, 306n22,
    308nn45–46, 309n48, 309n57,
    365nn71–78, 365nn80–82
    on *Gesta Karoli Magni*, 28

Louis XII, 125–26
  Charlemagne "patron" of, *Fig. 8*
Louis XIV
  Charlemagne at court of, 167–71
  compared to Charlemagne by Le Paige, 211
  ideological campaign of, 156–57
  represented as hero of antiquity, 146
Louis the German, 37
Louis the Pious, 8, 12, 37, 38
  elected by general assembly, 135
Löwe, Heinz, 307n34, 308n47, 310n59
Lugge, Margaret, 310n60
Lycurgus, 214

Mabillon, Jean, 338nn59–62
  describing Charlemagne's tomb, 200
  placing scholarship at center of monastic activities, 161–62
Mably, Gabriel Bonnot de, 211, 212–16, 255, 352nn69–86, 353n87
  cited by Genlis, 247
  Dubroca's use of, 263
  Gaillard and, 244
  influence on pamphlets about Estates-General, 228
  view of Charlemagne, 213–14
  —discussed by Moreau, 225–26
Machiavelli, Niccolò, 44
Madival, M. J., 356n127
Maines, Clark, 312n19, 318n8
Mairet, Jean de, 341n82
  Roland furieux, 167
Major, J. Russell, 329n32
Malesherbes, Chrétien Guillaume de Lamoignon de, 217
Mandach, André de, 305n15, 311n15, 312n17, 316n68
  on *Pseudo-Turpin Chronicle*, 51
Manzoni, Alessandro, 285
Marchangy, Louis Antoine François de, 241, 265–69, 291, 363nn48–50, 364nn51–57
  on Charlemagne, 266, 268
Marie de Medici, 153
Marin, Louis, 345n122
Marseillaise, 252
Martin, Angus, 357n152, 358n153
Martin, Henri-Jean, 340n70
Martini, Nicolaus, 337n48
Maskell, David, 344n106, 344n108

Masson, Frédéric, 361n25
Mauss, Marcel, 19, 306n27
Mazarin, Jules, 156
Méhul, Étienne, 253
Mémoires (Académie des Inscriptions), 200
Mémoires d'outre-tombe (Chateaubriand), 4–5, 251
Mémoires pour l'année 1661 (Louis XIV), 156
Mémoires sur l'ancienne chevalerie considérée comme un établissement politique et militaire (Sainte-Palaye), 232
Mémoire sur la cour de Rome (Fénelon), 170–71
Mémoire sur l'origine des maisons et duchés de Lorraine et de Boulle-le-Duc (Chantereau-Lefevre), 154
Ménager, Daniel, 332n75
Mencke, Johann Burckard, 324nn53–54
Mérimée, Jean François Léonor, 362n32
Mesnard, Paul, 341n87
Meyer, Paul, 368n138
Mézeray, François Eudes de, 334n11, 334n13, 334n17, 347n139, *Fig. 15*
  Histoire de France depuis Faramond jusqu'à maintenant, 149
  ignoring separation between history and myth, 150–51
  turning two dynasties into elective monarchies, 185
Michel, Christian, 333n1
Michel, Francisco, 63, 288
Michelet, Jules, 269, 271–72, 364n61, 365nn67–69
Middle Ages. See also chivalry; feudal-vassalic ideology
  as antiquity of modernity, 175, 189, 194, 232
  —Boulainvilliers and, 194
  basis of nobility's legitimacy, 187
  as direct source of the nation, 190
  according to Montesquieu, 209
  role of Charlemagne at the end of the Middle Ages, 85
  Sainte-Palaye's renewed vision of, 232
Mirabeau, Victor Riqueti, marquis de, 191, 347n2
Miroir historial (Vincent de Beauvais). See *Speculum historiale* (Vincent de Beauvais)
Mommsen, Theodor E., 326n4
Monfrin, Jacques, 305n15, 321n36, 323n50, 324nn51–52, 324n54

Moniteur, 257, 260, 262
Montaiglon, Anatole de, 324n65,
    342nn96–97
Montausier, Charles de Sainte Maride, duc
    de, 177
Montesquieu, Charles de Secondat, baron
    de la Brède et de, 190, 206–10,
    351nn59–62
  cited by Genlis, 247
  influence on pamphlets about Estates-
    General, 228
  rehabilitation of the Middle Ages, 209
  view of Charlemagne, 209–10
  —discussed by Moreau, 225, 226
Montesquiou-Fézensac, Blaise, comte de,
    320n25
Montreux, Nicolas de, 332n74
morality
  ancient heroes and, 146
  of Charlemagne
  —in Einhard, 25
  —in Notker, 29
  Le Moyne on morals of the king, 151
Moreau, Jacob-Nicolas, 224–27,
    354nn113–15, 355nn116–19
  assigned task of writing a royal history, 148
  collaboration with medievalists from the
    Academy of Inscriptions, 224
  pro-monarchist interpretation of the
    national past, 224
  and public repository of charters, 223
Moreau, Jean-Michel, dit le Jeune,
    353nn88–90, Fig. 18
Morgante Maggiore (Pulci), 104–5
  in the Bibliothèque universelle des romans,
    238
Mousket (Mouskès), Philippe, 51, 53, 86,
    304n9
  Aubert's approach similar to, 100
Mousnier, Roland, 346n132
Müller, H., Fig. 15
Mystères du peuple (Sue), 22–23
mythistory of Charlemagne. See also epic
    persona of Charlemagne
  invested with juridical value, 156
  rebirth in 1660s, 170

Naples, kingdom of, Charles VIII and, 102,
    103
Napoleon I, 250–65, 254–55, 361n14,
    361n21, 362n29

and Charlemagne
—blending of revolutionary and abso-
    lutist elements, 255
—proclaimed link to Charlemagne, 255,
    257, 261
—used as example and justification for a
    policy of rapprochement with the
    pope, 259
  insistence on being crowned by the pope,
    260
  linked to Charlemagne
—by Fontane, 256
—by Guizot, 272
  visiting the tomb of Charlemagne, 258,
    278
Napoleon on the Imperial Throne (Ingres), 262
Narbonne, Charlemagne's conquest of,
    282–83
negative portraits of Charlemagne, Gaillard
    on, 244
Néraudau, Jean-Pierre, 333nn1–2, 342n88
Neveu, Bruno, 347n3, 354n111
Neveu de Rameau, Le (Diderot), 189
Nichols, Stephen G., Jr., 305n15
Nicolai, Jean, 322n41
Nicolas de Senlis, 318n92
nineteenth century, 250–293
  Charlemagne
—Dubroca on, 263–64
—according to Hugo, 278, 280
—according to Michelet, 271
Nora, Pierre, 316n60, 364n58
Notker the Stammerer, 14, 27–38, 308n46,
    309n48, 309n52
Novalesa Chronicle, 7

Observations sur l'histoire de France (Mably),
    211, 212
  new edition by Guizot, 272
Odo (Eudes), 38
Oliver
  in Fierabras, 68–70
  in Galien li Restoré, 63, 64
  in Pèlerinage, 61, 62
oratorical history, 112, 118–22
Orcibal, Jean, 342nn93–95
Organt (Saint-Just), 242–43
Orlando furioso (Ariosto), 105, 107–8
  in the Bibliothèque universelle des romans, 238
  glorifying the Hapsburg emperor,
    139–40

view of Charlemagne, 204
—attacked by Moreau, 225
Vopiscus, Flavius (pseud.), 323n46
Voss, Jürgen, 327n11
*Vray Théâtre d'honneur et de chevalerie ou le
miroir héroique de la noblesse, Le*
(Vulson de la Colombière), 166
Vulson, Marc, sieur de la Colombière, 166
influence on Sainte-Palaye, 232–33

Walpole, Ronald N., 311n15, 312n21,
312n23, 313nn24–27, 313nn30–31,
314n32, 314nn34–35, 314n37, 317n80,
318n2, 318n4
warrior, Charlemagne as, 9
in *Annales Regni Francorum,* 18
in Einhard's *Vita Karoli Magni,* 24
in Gilles of Paris's *Karolus,* 80
in Notkers *Gesta Karoli Magni,* 35–36
and spread of power, 58
Wattenbach, Wilhelm, 307n34
Weinstein, Donald, 323nn47–48
Werner, Joseph, 333n2
Werner, Karl Ferdinand, 304 n7

White, Hayden, 306n18
Widukind, 55, 110, 131
William of Nangis, 94
William the Breton, 81, 83
Wolf, 284, 366n106
Works of Charlemagne, The (Pouzargues),
Fig. 22
Wright, Johnson Kent, 347n5, 352n69
writing, 22
Charlemagne's preoccupation with,
26–27
given word as written word under Philip
Augustus, 78
laws and, 26
royal archives created by Philip
Augustus, 78
used by Charlemagne against the
Felician heresy, 20

Yates, Frances A., 326n4

Zeller, Gaston, 96, 311n13, 318n93, 320n24,
323n47, 325n67, 328n23, 335n26,
336n36